Praise for *The Unconquerable World*

"A masterpiece for the new century . . . The book is not so much a prediction as a prescription—and a challenge—to today's leaders, and tomorrow's."
—Strobe Talbott

"Schell's book is timely. . . . It's not too late to debate the merits of a U.S. foreign policy that seeks to strike at nations before they strike at us."
—*San Francisco Chronicle*

"As he has before, the indispensable Jonathan Schell has written a book that will change thinking and prompt action on the most urgent question of all. The old dichotomies—idealism vs. realism, morality vs. politics, dream vs. possibility—are transformed by Schell's brilliant unity of purpose. A definitive reading of the last century, *The Unconquerable World* is sure to be one of the most important books of the century unfolding."
—James Carroll, author of
An American Requiem and *Constantine's Sword*

"Masterly . . . Schell's arguments are incontrovertible."
—*The Washington Post*

"Wise, passionate, eloquent, and infused with a historical vision rare in these dark times, Jonathan Schell's new book makes a powerful case for the realism of idealism in breaking the cycles of violence that threaten to destroy us all."
—John Dower, Elting E. Morison Professor of History at MIT
and Pulitzer Prize–winning author of *Embracing Defeat*

"Schell has offered—and not for the first time—what may be needed most: a hunch, a lever, a mental starting point for a long and difficult journey."
—*The New York Observer*

The Unconquerable World

The
Unconquerable
WORLD

POWER, NONVIOLENCE, AND
THE WILL OF THE PEOPLE

JONATHAN SCHELL

A METROPOLITAN / OWL BOOK
Henry Holt and Company | New York

Henry Holt and Company, LLC
Publishers since 1866
115 West 18th Street
New York, New York 10011

Henry Holt® is a registered trademark of
Henry Holt and Company, LLC.

Library of Congress Cataloging-in-Publication Data

Schell, Jonathan, 1943—
    The unconquerable world : power, nonviolence, and the will of the people /
Jonathan Schell.—1st ed.
        p.   cm.
    Includes bibliographical references and index.
    ISBN 0-8050-4457-4 (pbk.)
        1. Nonviolence.   2. War.   3. Social change.   I. Title.
HM1281.S34 2003
303.61—dc21   2002191235

First published in hardcover in 2003 by Metropolitan Books
First Owl Books Edition 2004

A Metropolitan / Owl Book

Designed by Kelly S. Too

Printed in the United States of America

1   3   5   7   9   10   8   6   4   2

*I dedicate this book
to the memory of my
mother, fighter for peace.*

Liberty, when men act in bodies, is power.

—EDMUND BURKE
Reflections on the Revolution in France

Contents

The Unconquerable World

The Towers and the Wall

December 17, 2002, New York City

"Of Arms, and the man I sing." So wrote Virgil, celebrator of the imperial Rome of his patron Caesar Augustus, in the opening lines of *The Aeneid*, as rendered in the seventeenth century by Dryden and memorized by generations of English schoolboys, who were soon sent out to rule an empire even more far-flung than Rome's. "The man": a patriot, bound to fight, and perhaps to die, for his country and all that it possessed and stood for. "Arms": the means whereby the man could vindicate his honor and defend his country or aggrandize its power and interests. The fighting man took life but also was ready to lay down his own, thereby bowing, in the mayhem of war, to a kind of rudimentary justice. Four centuries before Virgil, the Athenian statesman Pericles, much admired in both imperial Rome and imperial England, eulogized him in his funeral oration for the soldiers of Athens who had died at Marathon. "As for success or failure," Pericles said, "they left that in the doubtful hands of Hope, and when the reality of battle was before their faces, they put their trust in their own selves . . . and, in a small moment of time, the climax of their lives, a culmination of glory, not of fear, would be swept away from us." And so they would be accorded "praises that never grow old, the most splendid of sepulchres—not the sepulchre in which their bodies are laid, but where their glory remains eternal in men's minds, always there on the right occasion to stir others to speech or to action." On these foundations was reared a system—a system, at its best, of standing up for principle with force, right with might; at its worst, of plunder, exploitation, and massacre—that was to last from Pericles' time down to ours.

Yet alongside the martial tradition another, contrary one was born. At almost the very moment that Virgil was writing his lines, Jesus, the New Testament says, was speaking the even better-known words, "Put up thy sword. For they that live by the sword shall die by the sword." Following in the tradition of some of the Old Testament prophets, he sang of the man without arms. The sword in question was no symbolic weapon. It was the disciple Simon Peter's sword, and he had just cut off the ear of one Malchus, a servant of the high priest, who had been in the act of arresting Jesus in Jerusalem. It was in the heat and fury of this bloody altercation, not in the quiet of a philosopher's study, that Jesus gave his advice. And these words, too, took root somehow in people's hearts, and lasted down the centuries.

Since then, the two conflicting traditions—one worldly, sanctioning violence, the other spiritual, forbidding it—have coexisted. Each has seemed to express an ineradicable truth. Each has retained its power to inspire in spite of the other. Neither has been discarded in the name of the other. Western civilization has lived according to the rules laid down by Virgil's patron Augustus but has dated its calendar from the birth of Jesus. On the intellectual plane, many attempts to reconcile the two traditions have been made. The most notable was to declare, with St. Augustine—the great conjoiner of Roman and Christian thought of the early fifth century—that each principle applied to a distinct realm of existence. One was the City of God, a spiritual and personal realm, in which Jesus' law of non-violence and love should be followed, the other the fallen City of Man—the public, political realm, in which Caesar's law of force must, however regrettably, hold sway. Echoes of this distinction also sounded down the centuries: in Catholic just-war theory, in Machiavelli's distinction between what is good for one's soul and what is good for the republic, in Montesquieu's distinction between the virtue of the political man and the virtue of the Christian man. There is even a shadow of it in the modern separation of church and state. Certainly, Jesus' counsel was rejected for political affairs, except among a few people, regarded by almost everyone as dreamers or fools, blind to the iron laws that govern the political world.

And who with the slightest acquaintance with history, whether in the Western world or elsewhere, can deny the primal connection between politics and violence? Indeed, what may be the earliest historical document discovered so far, the so-called Scorpion Tableau, carved in stone some 5,250 years ago in Egypt and unearthed by archaeologists in 1995, seems to depict a scene of victory in battle. It shows a man with an upraised mace standing over a bound captive. The captor, the discoverers of the document believe, is one King Scorpion, the first unifier of ancient Egypt, and the captive is a king he has defeated and is leading to public execution.

Yet history has not left the character of violence unchanged. The bloody record of the twentieth century, which seemed to confirm as never before the strength of the tie between politics and violence, also showed that violence did not stay everlastingly the same. It was capable of fantastic mutation and expansion. If an evil god had turned human society into an infernal laboratory to explore the utmost extremes of violence, short only of human extinction, he could scarcely have improved upon the history of the twentieth century. Totalitarian rule and total war each in its own way carried violence to its limits—reaching what we can call total violence, as distinct from the technically restricted violence of earlier times. Violence was old, but total violence—violence that, as in nuclear conflict, can kill without limit, reaching no decision, no point of return—was new. Rule, when it resorted to total violence, turned out no longer to be rule, for rule is domination over living human beings, and the totalitarian regimes, in their most ferocious epochs, became factories of corpses. And war, when it laid hold of its ever more powerful instruments of destruction, was no longer war but annihilation, and annihilation was as unlike war as it was unlike peace. The means of annihilation paradoxically put their possessors in a predicament that was better described by the precepts of Jesus than by those of Augustus. Through the creation of the nuclear arsenals of the Cold War and their doctrinal accoutrement the strategy of nuclear deterrence, it became literally true that the users of the sword would die by the sword. (Nuclear rivals have been likened to scorpions in a bottle, creating the possibility that history's last document as well as its first will refer to the doings of scorpions.) The increase in available force, rooted in, among other things, fundamental scientific discoveries of the twentieth century, is not a change in attitude or beliefs but an irrevocable change in the world, at least as durable as any state or empire. It has called into question the age-old reliance of politics on violent means. The iron laws of the world have become different laws, and those who wish to live and act in the world as it really is must think and act differently.

The people of the twentieth century were, of course, dismayed by the unprecedented violence visited upon them and tried to find ways to escape it. Twice in the first half of the century the world went to war. Twice in the aftermath the victors attempted to uproot the system of war and replace it with a system of law—with the League of Nations in 1919 and the United Nations in 1945. And twice they failed. In the latter half of the century, a third global struggle was waged—not a hot war this time but the cold one—and on November 9, 1989, the day the Berlin Wall was breached by joyful East Berliners, it ended. In many respects, the opportunity to found an enduring peace appeared more favorable than ever before. No defeated power awaited the hour of vengeance, as defeated Germany had after its humiliation by the onerous terms of the Versailles treaty at the end the First World War. No ideological division threatened to divide the camp of the victors, as the antagonism between Soviet communism and liberal democracy had at the end of the Second World War. This time, however, no great effort was made to secure the peace. The victorious powers turned their minds to economic and other matters. A conviction seemed to settle in that the horrors of the twentieth century had ended of their own accord. Mere opportunity was mistaken for accomplishment, and nothing was done.

It is difficult to assign a cause to neglect, and perhaps it would be a mistake to spend much effort trying. Why, at the beginning of the twentieth century, did Europe blind itself to the approach of the First World War? Why, after that war, did the United States withdraw into isolation, condemning itself to fight again in the Second World War? The insouciance of the 1990s is equally hard to explain. Perhaps the victors of the Cold War wanted a vacation from its chronic apocalyptic anxieties, and so turned their attention to more agreeable matters—above all, to the getting and spending of the era of economic globalization. Perhaps they believed that the welcome reduction of the threat of nuclear war that the end of the Cold War brought had removed all nuclear peril. Or perhaps the United States, where a sort of complacent triumphalism developed, was simply too pleased with the status quo to imagine that it could be upset.

Whatever the reason, the spell was broken, of course, on September 11, 2001. The slumbering dragon of total violence had only twitched its tail; and yet with that one stroke the United States was brutally startled out of its sleep. This crime, in which, out of a clear blue sky one sparkling fall morning, the most imposing buildings in New York and Washington were attacked and struck down, leaving thousands dead, drove home a truth that the world should never have forgotten but did: that in our age of weapons of mass destruction all buildings, all cities, all nations, all people can likewise be reduced to ash in an instant.

And yet the awakening was selective. Even as the underlying dangers of the time were brought to shocking life, the equally remarkable and equally neglected opportunities to create a lasting peace that had appeared with the end of the Cold War were pushed into still deeper obscurity. The United States, facing the threat of further attack from a global, stateless terrorist network, launched its war on terrorism. Then it embarked on a full-scale revolution in its foreign policy that, while taking September 11 as its touch-stone, adopted goals and means that extended far beyond the war on terror. The policy's foundation was an assertion of absolute, enduring American military supremacy over all other countries in the world, and its announced methods were the overthrow of gov-ernments ("regime change") in preemptive, or preventive attacks. Almost immediately, other nations, as if taking their cue from the United States, also went to war or the brink of war. Palestinians stepped up their campaign of suicide bombings against Israel, and Israel responded with military incursions against the Palestinian Authority in the West Bank and Gaza. Russia intensified its war against "terrorism" in Chechnya. Nuclear-armed India embarked on its confrontation with nuclear-armed Pakistan after the parlia-ment in New Delhi was attacked by terrorists whom India linked to Pakistan, and the danger of nuclear war became a permanent feature of life in South Asia. The optimism and hope of the imme-diate post–Cold War years gave way to war fever and war. The burn-ing towers of 2001 eclipsed the broken wall of 1989.

What never occurred, as complacency gave way to sudden alarm, was a considered stocktaking of both the perils and the opportunities of the new era. In these pages, I will try to look past history's feints and tricks of timing and, in a view that encom-passes both the wall and the towers, pose afresh the issue of war and peace, of annihilation and survival. The terrible violence of the twentieth century, I will argue, holds a lesson for the twenty-first. It is that in a steadily and irreversibly widening sphere, violence, always a mark of human failure and a bringer of sorrow, has now also become dysfunctional as a political instrument. Increasingly, it destroys the ends for which it is employed, killing the user as well as his victim. It has become the path to hell on earth and the end of the earth. This is the lesson of the Somme and Verdun, of Auschwitz and Bergen-Belsen, of Vorkuta and Kolyma; and it is the lesson, beyond a shadow of a doubt, of Hiroshima and Nagasaki.

As the British scholar and political thinker Isaiah Berlin has rightly observed, no revolution in the twentieth century had a formative influence comparable to that of the French revolution on the nineteenth. It was not in fact a revolution but a war—the First World War—that played this decisive role, setting in motion a spiral of violence whose effects are still felt today. The century's first decade, like its last, was a period of economic growth, globalization, spreading liberalism, and peace. At a stroke, the First World War reversed all four tendencies, ushering in an era of depression, contraction of global trade, dictatorship, and war. In August 1914 there were two hundred divisions prepared to go to battle in Europe. When war broke out, "The submerged warrior society . . . sprung armed through the surface of the peaceful landscape," as the historian of war John Keegan has put it. In a sense, that warrior society never returned to its barracks. In defeated Germany and Russia, the suffering, humiliation, and incalculable social disorganization caused by the war created conditions that made possible the rise to power of mass totalitarian parties in the two countries. The seventy-five-year Bolshevik terror—which Solzhenitsyn called the Red Wheel—rolled out of the trenches of the First World War, as did its jagged counterpart the Nazi swastika, and the aggression and antagonism of these regimes led straight to the Second World War. For the next three decades, every effort to restore peace and sanity seemed doomed to failure in advance. In the words of the twentieth-century political thinker

Hannah Arendt, "Nothing which was being done, no matter how stupid, no matter how many people knew and foretold the consequences, could be undone or prevented. Every event had the finality of a last judgment, a judgment that was passed neither by God nor by the devil, but looked rather like the expression of some unredeemably stupid fatality."

As the new century begins, no question is more important than whether the world has now embarked on a similar cycle of violence, condemning the twenty-first century to repeat, or even outdo, the bloodshed of the twentieth. The elements of the danger are obvious. They are not, as before, the massed conventional armies and systematized hatreds of rival great powers. They are the persistence and steady spread of nuclear weapons and other weapons of mass destruction, the unappeased demons of national, ethnic, religious, and class fury, and, I believe, the danger that the world's greatest power, the United States, responding disproportionately and unwisely to these realities, will pursue the Augustan path of force and empire. These elements could, at some unforseeable point of intersection, bring an explosion, some nuclear 1914 or anthrax 1914, that would send history off the rails as irremediably as the guns of August did almost a hundred years ago. The use of just a few dozen of the world's thirty thousand or so nuclear weapons, let us recall, could kill more people in a single unthinkable afternoon than the two world wars put together. These dark prospects require that we step back from the emergencies of the moment and ask whether there is another path to follow.

I contend that, notwithstanding the shock of September 11 and the need to take forceful measures to meet the threat of global terrorism, such a path has opened up, and remains open. For in twentieth-century history another, complementary lesson, less conspicuous than the first but just as important, has been emerging. It is that forms of nonviolent action can serve effectively in the place of violence at every level of political affairs. This is the promise of Mohandas K. Gandhi's resistance to the British Empire in

India, of Martin Luther King, Jr.'s civil-rights movement in the United States, of the nonviolent movements in Eastern Europe and in Russia that brought down the Soviet Union, and of the global success of democracy in its long contest with the totalitarian challenge. It is even one of the unexpected lessons of the nuclear strategies of the Cold War. The century of total violence was, however discreetly, also a century of nonviolent action. Its success often surprised those who used it and always surprised those against whom it was used. Some of its forms, such as Gandhi's satyagraha and the social movements that pushed the Soviet Union into its grave, were radically new; others, such as the revival of liberal democracy in the century's last decades, were a fulfillment of developments whose roots went back hundreds, even thousands, of years.

The appearance of these forms did not herald the Second Coming. They did not float down from the City of God but were born in strife on the streets of the City of Man. They sprang up in revolution, in civil life, and even in the midst of war. They were as real and as consequential in history as the new forms of violence to which they were a response. They were mainly a product of action, as often stumbled upon as consciously invented, although political imagination of the highest order was also at work. In the mountainous slag heaps of twentieth-century history, they are the flecks of gold that the twenty-first century must sift out and put to use.

As I wrote these pages, I often paused to ask myself whether I had become a pacifist. Although my debt to pacifist thinkers and activists was large, I had to answer that I had not. As soon as I pictured myself a pacifist, my mind would teem with situations, both historical and imaginary, in which it was clear that I would support the use of force or myself use it. The difficulty with the creed for me was not the root of the word, *pax*, but its suffix, *ist*—suggesting that one rule was applicable to all imaginable situations. The emphasis of the word was at any rate wrong for this book. For it was not so much the horrors of twentieth-century violence, immense as they were, that I was seeking to describe as the birth, fostered by historical events, of an alternative—of what William James called "the moral equivalent of war." The path of relying on violence as the answer to violence lies open, and the world has seemed, in a wrong turn of epic proportions, to start down it, as it did in August of 1914. But there is another way.

Then shall the world, at long last, say its farewell to arms? That unrealized vision, I know, is as old as arms themselves. Is it necessary to add that today, too, the obstacles are mountainous; that the temptations of violence, including the longing for revenge, power, or loot—or, for that matter, visions of heaven on earth or of mere safety—still grip the imagination; that the quandaries facing the peacemakers confound the best minds; that as old forms of violence exit the historical scene new ones enter; that in many parts of the world growing scarcity and ecological ruin add new desperation to the ancient war of all against all; that one day's progress unravels the next day; that while in some places nonviolence advances, in others barbarism, including genocide, is unleashed with new vigor and ferocity; that both terror and counterterror are escalating; that the callousness of the rich incites the fury of the poor; that the dream of dominion has fresh allure in the counsels of the powerful; and that hardly a single step toward peace takes place without almost superhuman tenacity and sacrifice, including the supreme sacrifice, made by such heroes as Gandhi, King, Jan Palach, Anwar Sadat, and Yitzhak Rabin, to mention just a few? In downtown Grozny, the Congo jungles, Sierra Leone, Kashmir, Jenin, or Jerusalem, it is difficult to make out, even in the distance, the outlines of a world at peace. I shall contend, nevertheless, that quiet but deep changes, both in the world's grand architecture and in its molecular processes, have expanded the boundaries of the possible. Arms and man have both changed in ways that, even as they imperil the world as never before, have created a chance for peace that is greater than ever before. To describe those changes is the business of this book.

PART ONE

Violence

1

The Rise and Fall of
the War System

Some of the most important changes for the future of war have
come from within war itself. Those who have planned, equipped,
and fought wars have done more to alter the character of war than
those who have opposed it. In the modern age, war has in fact
undergone a metamorphosis so thorough that its existence has
been called into question. This metamorphosis has proceeded in
two distinct arenas: the traditional one of conventional war and
the new one of people's war. The transformation of conventional
war, propelled above all by the scientific revolution of modern
times, led finally to the invention of nuclear weapons and the
gruesome riddles of nuclear deterrence, whereby great-power
war was immobilized, and the immense arsenals were deployed,
according to the strategists, mostly to prevent their own use. At
the same time, the advent of people's war was paradoxically foreshadowing the forms of peaceful resistance that proved so successful against dictatorial regimes of both the right and the left in the
final decades of the twentieth century. At no stage in either journey did the warriors involved in either transformation cultivate

principles of nonviolence; on the contrary, they often were bent on using violence to the hilt. Nevertheless, nonviolence of a sort was the destination at which each journey wound up.

Clausewitz on War

In trying to understand the changes that have overtaken war in modern times, it's useful to begin with the eighteenth-century Prussian general and philosopher of war Carl von Clausewitz, who was born in 1780 and died in 1831. He lived and fought and wrote during one of the most important turning points in the history of war. For most of the eighteenth century, war had been largely the business of kings and aristocrats and whatever commoners they could hire or force into their service. Battles usually involved tens of thousands, not hundreds of thousands, of men on each side. The ends of war were often modest, and military strategy often consisted as much of maneuvers as of combat.

With the success of the French Revolution and the rise a decade later of Napoleon Bonaparte, a new force—the energy of an entire population fired with patriotic zeal—was poured onto the battlefield. As an officer in the Prussian service, Clausewitz experienced the effects of the change at first hand, and never more painfully than at the battle of Jena, in 1806, when Napoleon led his forces to a decisive victory over the numerically superior but antiquated and ill-led Prussian force. The French completed the conquest of Prussia in six weeks, and forced her to accept a 50 percent reduction of her territory in the Treaty of Tilsit, in 1807.

Clausewitz's experience turned him into one of the leaders of Prussian military reform. It also propelled him into a lifetime of reflection on the nature of war in general and the reasons for Napoleon's victories in particular. His magnum opus, *On War*, which many have called the greatest formal analysis of war ever made, was neither published nor even completed in his lifetime. His description of war does not fit war as we know it today. But precisely because he defined the war of his time and of times past more carefully and exactly than anyone had done before or has since, he provided us with a benchmark against which we can measure the revolutionary changes that it is the business of this inquiry to understand. It is exactly the dated aspects of his analysis that make it most interesting.

Three basic concepts define the structure of war as Clausewitz understood it. The first is his concept of "ideal war." By "ideal," Clausewitz did not mean ideally good, as when we speak of the ideal society; he meant what is perfect of its kind, as when we speak of an ideal specimen. He believed that war possesses a singular nature and, once the decision to draw the sword has been taken, develops according to a "logic" peculiar to itself. When this development is allowed to proceed unfettered, ideal war—war without constraint, fought to the death—is the result. If two armies are supplied with all their needs (munitions, logistics, manpower, a clear field of operation) but otherwise battle in a vacuum, like gladiators in a stadium, they will fight an ideal war.

Clausewitz recognized, however, that in actuality war is rarely supplied with all the materials it ideally needs and is never fought in a vacuum. Constraints are always present. For one thing, the plans and operations of armies are impeded by innumerable practical obstacles, all of which Clausewitz subsumes under the heading of "friction." Owing to friction, Clausewitz added to ideal war a second concept, that of "real war." Real war differs from ideal war in the way that a real vase, because it is chipped or slightly misshapen, differs from an ideal vase. A greater constraint than friction on ideal war is politics. Politics, in Clausewitz's view, is not something that unfortunately gets in the way of war; it is, or should be, in command of the entire operation. For war, Clausewitz believes, should be completely subordinate to the goals of the state that wages it. The supremacy of political goals over military goals is the third of his basic concepts. "War"—to give one variant of his most famous saying—"is a true political instrument, a

continuation of political intercourse, carried on with other means."
Clausewitz's writings sometimes seem to reflect a disappointment
that ideal war is spoiled by friction, but he does not regret that war
is held in check by politics. On the contrary, he regarded war that
has broken free of political guidance as "something pointless and
devoid of sense."

The Logic of War

The formulations that Clausewitz gave for the operations of ideal
war may at first seem obvious, but when he has placed them in the
wider context of politics, any appearance of self-evidence vanishes. On the first page of *On War,* Clausewitz wrote, "Countless
duels go to make up war, but a picture of it as a whole can be
formed by imagining a pair of wrestlers. Each tries through physical force to compel the other to do his will; his *immediate* aim is to
throw his opponent in order to make him incapable of further
resistance."

From this definition, a basic rule followed: Both sides must exert
themselves to the utmost: "War is an act of force, and there is no
logical limit to the application of that force. Each side, therefore,
compels its opponent to follow suit; a reciprocal action is started
which must lead, in theory, to extremes." There is nothing abstract
or metaphysical about this logic. It is the logic of any contest of
strength in which the last one standing is the winner: "The fact that
slaughter is a horrifying spectacle must make us take war more seriously, but not provide an excuse for gradually blunting our swords
in the name of humanity. Sooner or later someone will come along
with a sharp sword and hack off our arms." Attempts in principle
to avoid the extremes "always lead to logical absurdity."

The reciprocal action pressing the two sides to the extremes of
available force is the logic that drives war to assume its ideal
nature, which Clausewitz also calls "absolute war." Ideal war and

absolute war are the same. So are real war and limited war—except in those few cases in which the demands of politics and the absence of crippling friction permit war to run to its extremes. Then the real approaches the ideal and the absolute.

It's important to understand, however, that even though each side is driven to employ its strength to the limit, weakness is an indispensable element of war *as a system*. The importance of weakness for war is usually overlooked. Yet without it war could never decide anything, for no one could ever be rendered powerless. "All war," Clausewitz wrote, "presupposes human weakness and seeks to exploit it." Defeat—in which the strength of one side buckles and gives way—is the pivot of war. The victor only goes on doing what he had wanted to do and planned to do in the first place. It's on the losing side that the crisis, the reversal of fortune, the shattering of expectations, and the collapse of all plans, takes place. That is why "the loser's scale falls much further below the original line of equilibrium than the winner's side rises above it."

What Is Defeat?

The weakness, or "powerlessness," that precipitated defeat was not a simple thing. How could the victor know when defeat had occurred? Was it when the foe's armed forces fled the field of battle? When their capital was occupied? Clausewitz's definitions of war contain an ambiguity. In the metaphor of the wrestling match, the victor renders his opponent "incapable of further resistance." If we picture this—let's call it physical defeat—we see the opponent lying flat on the ground, incapacitated or dead. But Clausewitz calls this merely the immediate aim of war. The victor's larger—and crucially different—goal is to make the enemy "do his will." The distinction between the two becomes clearer in another passage: "The battle . . . is not merely reciprocal slaughter, and its effect is more a killing of the enemy's courage than of the enemy's soldiers," for "loss of moral force is the chief cause of the decision." Following Clausewitz's cue, let us call this moral defeat.

In physical defeat, scenes of which are familiar from heroic paintings, we see slain soldiers carpeting the battlefield, perhaps with the victorious general and a few of his aides surveying them on horseback. But in the second (less often painted) picture of moral defeat, we see the former enemies up and about, busily doing what the victor has commanded—for example, paying tribute, handing over a portion of the harvest, paying a tax, or even worshiping the victor's god. In this scene, the battle is long over. The victor or his proconsul has taken up residency in the capital of the defeated nation. He issues an order. Do the defeated people obey? Do they "do his will"? Perhaps he thought he had won the victory when the enemy forces dissolved; but now it turns out, according to Clausewitz, that the decision made by civilians far from the field of battle will determine whether he really was victorious after all. For the war "cannot be considered to have ended so long as the enemy's *will* has not been broken: in other words, so long as the enemy government and its allies have not been driven to ask for peace, or the population made to submit."

Even the early nineteenth century offered examples of generals who believed a foe had been defeated only to find that he went on fighting, and sometimes prevailed. Clausewitz cites Napoleon's invasion of Russia in 1812. Napoleon won every battle on his march to Moscow. The Russian forces retreated steadily, until he finally occupied the city, which then burned in a great fire. (It has never been determined whether it was started deliberately by the population or was accidental.) Weren't the Russians beaten? In fact, as all readers of Tolstoy's *War and Peace* know, the will of Russia was intact. It was Napoleon who was on his way to ruin.

The Great Democratic Revolution

The reciprocal action of the duel pushes it toward the extremes, toward absolute war. *Friction* clogs the gears, slows things down, perhaps brings them to a halt. Fear is a potent form of friction, as are exhaustion, faulty intelligence, and chance events so various that no category can easily encompass them. Weather is a good example of friction in war: "Rain can prevent a battalion from arriving, make another late by keeping it not three but eight hours on the march, ruin a cavalry charge by bogging horses down in the mud."

These are mundane matters, seemingly unsuitable for philosophical reflection, yet friction—this "resisting medium," in which war takes place—does have a grander aspect. Clausewitz is acutely conscious that different historical periods impose extremely different degrees of friction on war. He firmly believes that his picture of ideal war describes a potentiality that is timeless, but he is aware that it can be realized only in certain periods. In some periods, conditions are like molasses, in which war can scarcely get started and, if it does, remains a sorry, sluggish business.

When Clausewitz surveyed the history of war, he found his own period all but unique. Rarely, if ever, he believed, had war come so close to realizing its ideal form. The underlying reason was the French Revolution, which began in 1789, when Clausewitz was a boy. In 1793, when France sent immense conscripted armies into the field, he wrote, "a force appeared that beggared all imagination. Suddenly, war again became the business of the people—a people of thirty million, all of whom considered themselves to be citizens. . . . Nothing now impeded the vigor with which war could be waged." Not since the days of ancient Rome, he believed, had the ideal face of war shown itself more clearly. In the intervening centuries, war had for the most part been a crippled, faltering affair, dragging itself along "slowly, like a faint and starving man." In the preceding century, monarchical governments, cut off from popular support, had fought war in a formal, gentlemanly style. "Their means of waging war came to consist of the money in their coffers and of such idle vagabonds as they could lay their hands on." War thereby had been deprived of its "most dangerous" innate characteristic, the "tendency toward the extreme" dictated by its inner logic.

The larger force that swept aside these cobwebs of restraint was what the French political writer Alexis de Tocqueville, in 1835, called "the great democratic revolution" that "is going on amongst us." Because this democratic revolution touches the story of both war and nonviolence at every point, it requires discussion here. The revolution embraced not only the political upheavals that, beginning in the late eighteenth century, brought democratic governments to power, first in the United States and France and later in other parts of the world, but also the much deeper and broader democratization of the public world associated with a steady increase in the participation by masses of people in every phase of public life. This was the revolution that the early-nineteenth-century French novelist and political thinker Benjamin Constant envisioned as "mankind, emerging from an impenetrable cloud that obscures its birth, advancing toward equality over the debris of all sorts of institutions"; that the English historian Thomas Carlyle around the same time called "the new omnipotent Unknown of Democracy"; that in 1932 the Spanish philosopher Ortega y Gasset balefully assessed in *The Revolt of the Masses,* asserting that "one fact [of] the utmost importance in the public life in Europe" is "the accession of the masses to complete social power."

Those masses arrived by innumerable paths and in innumerable roles—as climbers in all the old hierarchies of privilege, as crowds on the barricades, as soldiers in conscripted armies, as guerrillas in jungles and deserts, as citizens in town meetings, as trade unionists on strike, as patriotic cheering sections for imperial conquests, as outraged native populations protesting those same conquests, as the ghostly bearers of "public opinion" in opinion polls, and, most recently, as women leaving the confines of the home, to take their places in the worlds of work and politics, or as homosexual men and women asserting their human dignity and demanding equality with heterosexuals. Everywhere these masses came, they brought a new, popular energy, a new power, destined to transform politics, war, and the relationship between the two.

What were the causes of this democratic revolution? Almost anything you cared to mention, according to its most profound expositor, Tocqueville. "The various occurrences of national existence have everywhere turned to the advantage of democracy," he wrote; "all men have aided it by their exertions: those who have intentionally labored in its cause and those who have served it unwittingly; those who have fought for it and those who have declared themselves its opponents, have all been driven along in the same track, have all labored to one end, some ignorantly and some unwillingly; all have been blind instruments in the hands of God." Even the achievements of democracy's enemies helped it, by "throwing into relief that natural greatness of man," which was perhaps the true source of the new energy. So deep-seated was the democratic principle of equality, Tocqueville thought, that its gradual development should be regarded as "a providential fact."

The French Revolution was the channel through which the stream of the democratic revolution first flowed onto the battlefields of Europe. In the words of the nineteenth-century French historian Adolphe Thiers, "The revolution, by setting the public mind in motion, prepared the epoch of great military achievements." In 1793, when the French Revolutionary Convention ordered the mass recruitment of citizens known to history as the *levée en masse*, its decree was the definitive announcement of society's unprecedented militarization. "From this moment on, until the enemies have been chased from the territory of the Republic," the convention ordained, "all Frenchmen are in permanent requisition for the service of the armies. The young men will go to combat; married men will forge weapons and transport food; women will make tents and uniforms and will serve in the hospitals; children will make bandages from old linen; old men will present themselves at public places to excite the courage of the warriors, to preach hatred of kings and the unity of the Republic." But it was Napoleon, the Corsican corporal who had himself been crowned emperor of France, who first made full use of the modern democratic army. It was under him that war, as Clausewitz put it, "took on an entirely different character, or rather closely approached its true character, its absolute perfection." Finally, "War, untrammeled by any conventional restraints, had broken loose in all its elemental fury."

War as the Final Arbiter

Friction, in Clausewitz's scheme, was an impediment to the logic of absolute war only *in fact*. The supremacy of politics over war was an impediment *in principle*. The first was an obstacle to war, like another foe in the field, the second a guiding rule that, in his view, must shape strategy from start to finish. Clausewitz has often been scolded as the intellectual founding father of absolute war, and has even been held responsible for the militarism in Germany that did so much to bring on the two world wars of the twentieth century. Nothing, as Clausewitz's biographer Peter Paret has pointed out, could be further from the truth. Having set forth his concept of ideal war, Clausewitz went on to argue with rigor and passion that the operations of war must be thoroughly subordinated to political ends. What is more, he fully understood that his two prescriptions for action—that, on the one hand, the logic of war required that it must be fought to the limit of one's strength and that, on the other, political considerations must limit and constrain war—were in conflict across the board. A lesser thinker might have expounded just one of these rules, but Clausewitz embraces both, and his attempt to reconcile them, though perhaps unavailing, forms one of the richest and most invaluable parts of his work. The following passage gives the context of his renowned saying, already quoted, concerning politics and war:

> It is, of course, well-known that the only source of war is politics—the intercourse of government and peoples; but it is apt to be assumed that war suspends that intercourse and replaces it by a wholly different condition, ruled by no law but its own.
>
> We maintain, on the contrary, that war is simply a continuation of political intercourse, with the addition of other means. . . . How could it be otherwise? Do political relations between peoples and between their governments stop when diplomatic notes are no longer exchanged?

In holding that war must be subordinate to politics, Clausewitz placed himself in the mainstream of the Western political tradition. Since Pericles praised the Athenian soldiers for their defense of their city and its way of life, war has been considered the ultima ratio—the final arbiter—in international affairs. In this tradition, war was seen not as an end in itself but as a servant of the polis—necessary for both its defense and its aggressive purposes. Whatever the costs of war or the wisdom or unwisdom of its goals, it was a political instrument of unquestionable worth. With war, empires were created, enlarged to the edges of the known world, or broken up; countries founded or extinguished; trade protected or cut off; plunder seized; tribute exacted; enemies punished; religions propagated or suppressed; balances of power preserved or upset. We shall never understand war until, even as we face its horror, we acknowledge, with Clausewitz and so many others, how great its usefulness and appeal as an arbiter has been. If we ask, "Arbiter of what?" the response is: Of those political disputes that could not be resolved peacefully. If we ask "Why final?" the tradition answers: Force should be introduced only after peaceful means have been exhausted. Arbitration by force is final, in the last analysis, because death is final, because the dead on the battlefield cannot pick themselves up to fight.

If the saying that war is the continuation of politics by other means assigned to war the last word in disputes, it also fixed limits on war by subordinating it to political goals. "Is war not just another expression of [a government's] thoughts?" Clausewitz asked. "Its grammar, indeed, may be its own, but not its logic." Yet this assertion apparently contradicted his claim that war did have a logic of its own—the logic that drove it to become absolute war. War thus appeared to be in the grip of two contending logics: one proceeding from war itself, the other from politics. If the politicians fixed upon "absolute" political ends (for example, the full conquest of an enemy's territory), then military and political policy might move smoothly in tandem. Clausewitz had lived through such a time—Napoleon's rise and fall. But in most periods, he knew, the logic of politics had worked against the absolutizing logic of war. Usually, the war aims fixed on by statesmen were not large enough to justify the extraordinary efforts and sacrifices required by absolute war. If in those circumstances the politicians let the logic of war take over, then "all proportion between action and political demands would be lost: means would cease to be commensurate with ends, and in most cases a policy of maximum exertion would fail because of domestic problems it would raise"— or, worse, the military tail would begin to wag the political dog. "Were [war] a complete, untrammeled, absolute manifestation of violence . . . war would of its own independent will usurp the place of policy the moment policy had brought it into being; it would then drive policy out of office and rule by the laws of its own nature." Clausewitz has been called a militarist, but rarely has a clearer warning against militarism been sounded by a military man.

The necessary remedy was to make certain that the restraining hand of policy overruled the logic of war, even though this might convert "the terrible battle-sword that a man needs both hands and his entire strength to wield, and with which he strikes home once and no more, into a light, handy rapier—sometimes just a foil for the exchange of thrusts, feints and parries." If we can hear a note of regret at this diminution of war, that only underscores the strength of Clausewitz's resolve to place politics in command.

Clausewitz was the first analyst to clearly identify the two logics that contended for the direction of war. The logic born out of war itself was not some Platonic form, floating above events; it was a dynamic principle, a compulsion, located in the activity of war itself. War was like the biblical mustard seed. You might choose not to plant that seed, but if you did, and nourished it properly, you should expect a mustard plant, not a lily. War had a life of its own, which, if not checked or limited (and the democratic revolution, by firing entire peoples with martial enthusiasm, removed limits previously in place), would dominate events. But since political logic, more often than not, defined aims that were less than absolute, it usually worked against the logic of war, reducing it to the level of modest, restrained real war—the thing encountered in most of history.

Clausewitz's account, however, contained an inconsistency. If politicians, unable to get the results they wanted by peaceful means, turned to soldiers to get them by force of arms, but then restrained those soldiers from running to the extremes at which decisions by arms occurred, how was war to be of any use to politics? Let us suppose, for example, that the politicians had in mind a limited military campaign to seize an island of only modest importance, and the enemy stalemated the attack with equal force. No extreme would have been reached, no one would have been rendered "powerless," no decision would have been rendered. What to do next? Give up? But then why make the attempt in the first place? Escalate? But then the vital "proportion" between the political goal and the military means that were used to attain it would be lost.

Napoleonic war, which extended the extremes at which the

decision by arms was reached, only made this conflict more acute. Clausewitz saw the problem plainly. The growing mismatch between political logic and military logic, he wrote, "poses an obvious problem for any theory of war that aims at being thoroughly scientific." By asserting the primacy of politics, he believed, the restraint needed to fight for small objectives could still be achieved. "The natural solution soon emerges," he explained: mastered by political calculation, "the art of war will shrivel into prudence, and its main concern will be to make sure the delicate balance is not suddenly upset in the enemy's favor, and the half-hearted war does not become a real war after all." Once this process is understood, "no conflict need arise any longer between political and military interests."

With the advantage of almost two centuries of hindsight, we can see that Clausewitz was mistaken. The gap between the two logics was in fact about to widen steadily. Indeed, what some historians are calling the "long nineteenth century" in Europe—lasting from Napoleon's defeat in 1815 to the outbreak of the First World War in 1914—can be seen as a protracted, ultimately unsuccessful effort to reconcile the two logics. With the outbreak of the First World War, the logic of war triumphed over the logic of politics, engulfing the world in a series of violent catastrophes that were to dominate the rest of the twentieth century.

Clausewitz's main misjudgment was to regard Napoleonic war as absolute war. The term "absolute," borrowed from philosophy and theology, clearly suggested a culmination, with no further developments to be expected. But we know now that Napoleonic war was in fact only an early stage of a lengthy development that would steadily expand the extremes of which war was capable. War should be a mere "instrument," Clausewitz had said. But the instrument was about to come alive in the hands of its user, and embark on a process of nonstop development that in the next century and a half would produce a revolution not only in war but in the relationship of war to its would-be employer and master, politics. It was not, indeed, until the invention of nuclear weapons that any true absolute—the unquestionable power of each side to annihilate the other—was reached. At that point, strange to say, war ceased, strictly speaking, to exist among the greatest powers. True absolute war, it turned out, was not war at all but some new thing, for which no one really had a good name.

The War System

The transformation of war that lay ahead took place in the context of the European conquest of most of the globe. When, as in Clausewitz's Europe, a number of armed states contend in a single geographical arena, sometimes making war, sometimes peace, sometimes making alliances, sometimes breaking or switching them, we can speak not merely of war but of a war system—or, when the arena is the whole world, of a global war system. In a war system, the logic of war is extended to the entire system, now pushing far-flung alliances toward the extremes at which decisions by arms are rendered. Military necessity then becomes such a powerful force that the formation of alliances may override all ideological or political considerations.

As in a game, the action in a war system may be complex, but the underlying strategies available to the players are simple and well known. All were discovered by the ancient Greek city-states. The most aggressive is the strategy of universal empire, and in the West ancient Rome was the first and last to succeed in it. The most common strategy historically has been the defensive one of seeking to maintain a balance of power, whereby one or more nations or an alliance of nations tries to hold any hegemonist at bay, as England did in Europe in the face of the rising power of France in the seventeenth, eighteenth, and nineteenth centuries. An alternative to both is collective security—rarely, if ever, successful—in which a league of nations agrees to keep peace among themselves by pooling their collective force to constrain any aggressor.

It would be wrong, however, if, by referring to a war system, we seemed to suggest that it was designed by somebody. It was not. Lack of a designer, however, does not mean lack of design. There are unintended systems as well as intended ones. The street grid of New York City and the constitutional system of the United States are intentional systems. Evolution and the market economy are unintended ones—systems that had no designer (though the market system soon had many powerful champions). In both, certain patterns and rules developed of their own accord, out of conditions that were provided largely or completely without planning.

The war system is such a system. When the curtain of recorded history goes up, a plurality of states are simply there, bristling with arms and ready to fight. To suggest that the war system was an intentional system would be to falsify and simplify the dilemma of war by seeming to suggest that it was the product of some "masters of war" to whom humanity could appeal to unmake their work.

Systems may also be either static—governed by rules that do not change—or dynamic, thus subject to development. The solar system is a static system. The planets will wheel around the sun without change until the system expires. Evolution and the market economy, by contrast, are dynamic systems. More specifically, they are dynamic systems of the adapt-or-die variety. An adapt-or-die system is one in which competitors can, by adapting themselves with particular skill to a changing environment, put themselves in a position to drive their rivals out of existence. The war system is a system of this kind. Adapt-or-die systems must be supplied with some reliable source of innovation—of new, advantageous possibilities *to which* the actors can strive to be the first to adapt. In the evolutionary system, one source of innovation is the random mutation of genes. In the market system, the chief source of change is technical innovation, which provides a ceaseless supply of new inventions that producers can exploit to make better or cheaper products.

For most of the history of war, few innovations were available. Combat was chiefly hand to hand, and the instruments of war—the sword, the spear, the bow and arrow, the chariot, the horse, the battering ram, the trireme, the fortification—were widely available and slow to evolve. Nations could rarely achieve a sudden, decisive advantage through an improvement in weapons or technique. (Briefly, the longbow conferred such an advantage.) In the modern period, however, the pace of innovation picked up abruptly, and the adapt-or-die character of the war system became all-important.

The Vortex of Power

It was an adaptive innovation—the mobilization of citizens by democratic revolutions—that prompted Clausewitz to announce prematurely that the era of absolute war had arrived. In the modern age, however, the democratic revolution was only one of four distinct great forces that poured newly created energy into the war system. The other three were the scientific revolution; the industrial revolution, whose mass-produced goods began to be incorporated into military armories in the mid-nineteenth century; and imperialism, which dragged the rest of the globe into the European war system. "The Great Powers were, as their name implies, organizations for power, that is, in the last resort for war," the historian A. J. P. Taylor has written. "They might have other objects—the welfare of their inhabitants or the grandeur of their rulers. But the basic tenet for them as Great Powers was their ability to wage war." Defining power this way was hardly new. What was new was the availability of the new forces of the modern age for military purposes. It was the dependence of military power on all four of its new sources of strength that turned the war system into a fast-paced, world-spanning, inescapable, adapt-or-die system, from whose ever-increasing pressure virtually no social enterprise—and certainly no nation—was exempt.

These forces did a great deal more than transform war. They were the constitutive elements in the rise of what some have called the modern world system and others have called the Western world system, as it led to Western domination of the globe. In the late nineteenth and early twentieth centuries, this system, implacable and merciless, compelled all "backward" nations to reform on pain of death—in short, to adapt to the modern Western system or die as independent countries. And which country was not, at some historical moment or other, "backward" and forced to play catch-up with some feared "advanced" nation? In the early modern age, only England—the first nation to avail itself of the modern financial, industrial, and scientific resources for war—escaped this role, with its burden of humiliation, *ressentiment*, and well-justified fear of subjugation. (Joseph Stalin, who explained many of his most ruthless measures as attempts to catch up with the capitalist West, said, "She [Russia] was beaten [in the First World War] because of her backwardness, because of her military, cultural, political, industrial, and agricultural backwardness. . . . Do you want our socialist fatherland to be beaten and to lose its independence? If you do not want that, then you must in the shortest possible time abolish its backwardness and develop a really Bolshevik pace in the establishment of its socialist economy.") Bolshevization, in the minds of its practitioners, was emergency modernization.

Military power, indeed, can be seen as a sort of clearinghouse in which the new forces of the modern age were assembled, brought into relation, and thrown into the contests in which the life or death of nations and empires was determined. We might say that in relation to this modern military exchange-market, each force brought forth both a benefit proper to it, analogous to what the economists call a "use-value," and a secondary, military benefit, analogous to what the economists call an "exchange-value." Use-value is the value a thing has directly for life. (The use-value of a glass of water is to slake a person's thirst, the use-value of a diamond is to be displayed.) Exchange-value is the price the thing will get when it is sold or bartered. So also in the modern world system, the fruits of democracy, science, industry, and imperialism had both a kind of direct use-value and a kind of exchange-value in the burgeoning market of military power. The democratic revolution brought the Rights of Man *and* millions of willing recruits for war; the scientific revolution offered pure knowledge *and* better artillery and explosives; the industrial revolutions created consumer goods *and* provided more matériel for larger and longer wars; imperial possession won trade and spoils *and* strategic global position.

Many writers have pointed out that through the process of "commodification" the free market possesses a remarkable capacity to draw ever-widening spheres of life into its orbit. The exchange market of modern military power had an even greater capacity to subordinate other realms of endeavor to its purposes, for, in that market, not just commodities but the democratic loyalty of citizens, the knowledge of scientists, the material wealth of industry, and the territories of empire were traded in for the common coin of military power—power that, in turn, could be used to gain more fervent loyalty, more material wealth, more territory, and so forth.

Pursuit of Knowledge, Pursuit of Power

The scientific revolution, as many observers have said, has changed the conditions of human life more radically than any other single, sustained force in history. The first round of the technical transformation of war of modern times—the gunpowder revolution—had already occurred by Clausewitz's time. Its effects had been felt in the entire organization of the modern state, having been no small factor in the rise of the absolute monarchs of continental

Europe. In the succinct formulation of the sociologist Charles Tilly, "War made the state and the state made war." A technical and economic rivalry among states was triggered, dictating, in an early demonstration of the modern adapt-or-die process, that the smaller states, like small firms in a cutthroat market, "must increase in size or go bankrupt." The cannon-bearing sailing ship, in its turn, laid the basis for the armed seafaring expeditions of the sixteenth and seventeenth centuries.

Fundamental characteristics of modern science—its grant of power, its irrevocability, its mobility, and its unpredictability—have been of immense importance for the development of war. In 1608, Francis Bacon, the first great philosopher of modern science, made the essential point regarding irrevocability. "The benefits of [scientific] discoveries may extend to the whole race of men, civil benefits only to a few particular places; the latter last not beyond a few ages, the former through all time." When analysts of the nuclear question rightly point out that nuclear weapons cannot be disinvented, they are describing a characteristic of all scientific invention. Scientific findings are mobile for the same reason that they are unrepealable—once made, they sooner or later can be repeated by any competent person in the world. Knowledge is by its nature ambulatory. And because science is a process of discovery, its findings—no less than its social applications—are unpredictable. A scientist's investigations are directed by hypotheses, which are in turn directed by theories, both of which enable scientists to make reasonable guesses regarding what they may find in any particular investigation. But they are in the dark when it comes to guessing what other scientists years in the future, guided by still undreamed-of hypotheses and theories, will discover. They are as unable to predict what science will bring to light fifty years ahead as Columbus was to predict what he would discover when he sailed west across the Atlantic.

These characteristics of science—each a positive feature in the context of science's own remarkable progress—are responsible in no small measure for the tyrannous, lethal pressure that the modern war system has placed on nations. They have left society quadruply helpless. Because science was power, nations felt unable to forgo the most destructive inventions; because science was irrevocable, they were unable to rid themselves of any invention once acquired; because science was unpredictable, they were helpless to know what inventions they would be handed next by scientists, and so to foresee the direction in which science was dragging them. On the bridge of the great ship of basic science, where, as Bacon put it, pure scientists were enjoying "contemplation of things as they are, without superstition or imposture, error or confusion," all was peaceful, calm, and orderly, but in the ship's mighty wake every other vessel, especially every military vessel, was buffeted by the currents or sucked under the waves.

The resemblances between the scientific and the democratic revolutions are striking. If ours has been an age of fantastic growth of human powers, then science and democracy have been the two deepest wellsprings of it. Both have been sleepless dynamos of historical change, spilling fresh energy decade after decade into the modern world. Both revolutions seemed to most observers in the eighteenth and nineteenth centuries to be agencies of continuous, cumulative human betterment. Both have been global and have tended to produce uniformity—eroding not only tradition but all local particularity. Both have proved, to use Tocqueville's word, "irresistible" and (so far, at least) irreversible. Both have transformed and continue to transform the world, including war, in ways unanticipated by the actors involved. Both have proffered gifts of previously undreamed-of human power yet have left nations unable to reject these gifts (new destructive inventions, new recruits for armies) if they so wished. Hasn't this powerlessness of humankind *not* to accept windfalls of unimagined power been a defining feature of the modern period?

From the Rights of Man to the Levée en Masse

In the nineteenth century, a pattern emerged in which the benefits proper to each of the new forces of the modern age yielded to exigencies of military need. The promise of both the American and the French revolutions was democracy itself—liberty, fraternity, equality, the Rights of Man. But the American revolutionaries found themselves instantly at war, and the French Revolution, as Clausewitz noted, was immediately militarized. No sooner had the Frenchman become a citizen than he rushed off to the front. The revolutionary zeal for war was memorably articulated by the leader of the dominant Gironde faction in the French Assembly, Jacques-Pierre Brissot, who proclaimed, "We cannot rest till Europe, and all Europe, is ablaze."

In one respect, as it turned out, the Girondins fatally miscalculated, for the emergency of war created ideal conditions for the rise of the Jacobin terror, in which many of them perished. But in another respect, the Girondins had prophesied truly, for after initial reverses the French revolutionary armies embarked on a series of smashing triumphs over neighboring monarchies that was not reversed until Waterloo, in 1815. "Here begins modern war," the nineteenth-century French historian Jules Michelet wrote. "Tacticians could never have invented such tactics. No calculation was involved."

Whereas the French had started with democracy and only then discovered the power of mass armies, the Prussians began with mass armies—French ones, invading their country—and only then discovered the need for popular reforms. Democracy always and everywhere involves the participation of the people; but whereas in France democracy initially meant the elevation of the French people over aristocrats and kings, in Germany it meant, from the start, recruitment of the people to fight other peoples, including, above all, the detested French conquerors (who were indeed defeated by the Germans in 1871). These effects of the democratic revolution deepened and were systematized throughout the nineteenth century, as states, in the wake of the French revolutionaries' *levée en masse,* mastered the techniques of conscription and mass propaganda. During the nineteenth century, Europe as a whole witnessed a slow evolution from "liberal nationalism," which pitted the common people ("the nation") of each country against its own monarchs and privileged classes, toward an increasingly militaristic, right-wing nationalism, which pitted all classes of the nation, plebeian and privileged alike, against other nations. Nationalism (a word that doesn't come into wide use until the end of the nineteenth century) was the militarization of democracy.

From Laissez-Faire to the Military Revolution

A parallel process of militarization occurred in the evolution of the industrial revolution. In Clausewitz's day, the effects of industrialization had yet to make themselves fully felt in war. The early champions of the free market, most of them British, had in fact looked to industry mainly to create the wealth of nations, as the title of Adam Smith's classic book had it, not the *power* of nations, which had been the preoccupation of their mercantilist predecessors. The advocates of laissez-faire declared the independence of economics from state power. (The eventual coining of the word "economics," identifying a distinct realm of human activity subject to its own laws, was one sign of their faith in that independence.) The market worked best, the worldly philosophers of the late eighteenth century believed, when the government kept its hands off it. Classical economics, in fact, "had no place for the nation, or any collectivity larger than the firm."

Smith's successors proceeded even further in this line of thinking. In the early nineteenth century, the most prominent champions of the market, including the British champions of laissez-faire Richard Cobden and John Bright, contended that free trade, by breaking down or ignoring national boundaries, naturally tended to foster world peace. The market, they ardently believed, was a solvent of national units and a pacifier of national conflicts. "I see in the Free Trade principle," Richard Cobden said in a speech in 1846, "that which shall act on the moral world as the principle of gravitation in the universe, drawing men together, thrusting aside the antagonism of race, and creed, and language, and uniting us in the bonds of eternal peace." In the United States, Ralph Waldo Emerson declared that "trade was the principle of Liberty; that trade planted America and destroyed Feudalism; that it makes peace and keeps peace; and it will abolish slavery." An unbroken thread of faith in free trade as an abettor of peace runs through the entire tradition of liberal internationalism, surviving many disappointments and continuing, if in attenuated form, to this day.

Yet soon a different relationship of markets to war emerged. Just as the nations of Europe could scarcely help noticing, in the wake of the French Revolution, that the mobilization of masses of people had hugely strengthened armies, so as the nineteenth century progressed they observed that the industrial revolution was doing the same. The military advantages of industrialism were put on convincing display in the American Civil War. Railroads and the mass manufacture of weapons played an important part in both its immense destructiveness and the ultimate victory of the North. In 1871, the Prussian victory over France drove the lesson home in Europe. If in the Napoleonic wars France had taught Prussia the value of patriotic masses, now Prussia's taught France—and all Europe—the value of industrialization and organizational skill. The Prussian victory was due in part to what came to be called the Prussian military revolution, in which the resources of industry, technology, and even education were exploited as never before for military purposes. This superiority of machine over man in war was sealed in the slaughter of the First World War, in which artillery and the machine gun—the emblems par excellence of the mechanization of war—laid waste to so many millions of young men. For the rest of the history of war, the strength of industrial economies and military power would be closely linked.

Imperialism's gift to the modern war system was access to nearly every inch of the earth for the military operations of the imperial powers. In the late nineteenth century, economic motives for empire steadily yielded to geopolitical ones. The importance of territory for war had always been recognized. It was not, however, until the forced opening of China and Japan in the mid-nineteenth century and the ensuing "scramble" for Africa and other imperial possessions that the whole earth became an indivisible military theater whose center was Europe. Between 1870 and 1900, European nations seized control of some ten million square miles of territory, on which a hundred and fifty million people lived. Only then was it possible to regard military initiatives in Siam, Natal, or Peking as moves on the chessboard of a truly global war system. The nineteenth-century English historian Frederic Seebohm famously commented that the British Empire was "acquired in a fit of absence of mind," but by the 1880s, absence of mind was at an end, replaced by jingoistic pride and ceaseless global military strategizing. In *Africa and the Victorians*, the scholars Ronald Robinson and John Gallagher have chronicled the change. The early Victorians, faithful to their laissez-faire principles, were content to let private interests take the lead in empire-building. The British government abjured direct rule, believing that the spread of commerce would itself lead "civilization with one hand, and peace with the other, to render mankind happier, wiser, better," in the words of Britain's foreign secretary, Lord Palmerston, in 1842. Even his gunboat diplomacy was aimed only at "opening" countries to trade, not ruling them. As late as 1890, the prime minister, Lord Salisbury, opposing direct British rule of Egypt, said, somewhat facetiously, "The only form of control we have is what is called moral influence, which in practice is a combination of nonsense, objurgation, and worry." He added, "In this, we are supreme."

However, events did not proceed as the liberal dabblers in

empire expected—neither in Asia nor in Africa nor in the Otto-man Empire. The economic arrangements forced upon those lands did not strengthen and liberalize their governments but under-mined them and drove them, one after another, toward collapse. The Egyptian government, for example, accepted loans from Europe, spent the funds on large but unproductive public projects, and, when these failed, sought to keep up payments on the loans by raising taxes on the poor, who grew discontented and rebel-lious. The imperial powers then were faced with what seemed a drastic choice: between withdrawing entirely and imposing direct rule. They chose direct rule.

By the turn of the century, most of the territories of the globe had been incorporated by imperialism into the European vortex. Any move anywhere—in the heart of Africa, in the Bay of Bengal, in the Strait of Tsushima—by any of the great powers now seemed to the others likely to upset a global balance of power and to require a countermove. The conservative British politician Lord Curzon spoke for his whole generation of statesmen when, after a long journey to the Middle East in 1890, he wrote, "Turkestan, Afghanistan, Transcaspia, Persia—to many these names breathe only a sense of utter remoteness or a memory of strange vicissi-tudes and of moribund romance. To me, I confess, they are the pieces on a chessboard upon which is being played out a game for the dominion of the world." Lord Haldane, describing his partici-pation in the unsuccessful Anglo-German negotiations on naval reductions of 1912, said, "I thought, from my study of the Ger-man General Staff, that once the German war party had got into the saddle, it would be war not merely for the overthrow of France or Russia but for the domination of the world." From that time on, fear that one power or another would take control of the planet became the nightmare of statesmen and peoples. It was a dread inherent in the logic of war once the war system had drawn all nations into its sphere.

The Triumph of the Logic of War

As the nineteenth century came to a close, the European war system, nourished by science, democracy, industry, and imperial conquest, was swollen with powers hardly dreamed of at the century's beginning. If, elaborating on Clausewitz, we liken war to a race that must be run to its finish before the prizes of victory and defeat can be handed out, then we might say that what had been a hundred-yard dash in Napoleon's time had become a potential marathon. Then, states might have had to sacrifice tens of thousands of men before the race was won; now the price would be the blood of millions. Then, Europe was chiefly involved; now the struggle would involve every continent. Then, soldiers marched to battle with muskets on their shoulders; now they would arrive by train with machine guns. The gap between the often modest political objectives of international diplomacy and the military means necessary to secure or defend them had widened into an abyss. And yet, because the war system was now global, tiny events in out-of-the-way places, in themselves without significance to the great powers, were vested with apocalyptic importance. Europe was at peace, but the logic of war had eclipsed the logic of politics.

Two diplomatic-military events—one in the colonial world, another in the heart of Europe—can illustrate the depth of the abyss with particular clarity. One is the Fashoda crisis of 1898, which brought France and England to the brink of war over minuscule claims in what is now southern Sudan. England, in full control of Egypt, did not yet rule its neighbor Sudan, which a few years earlier had been taken over by a radical Islamic movement, whose leader was called the Khalifah. The French, embittered by their exclusion from Egypt when England had occupied it in 1882, concocted a far-fetched scheme to turn the tables against England. An expedition of a hundred and fifty Senegalese and eleven Frenchmen under the leadership of Captain Jean-Baptiste

Marchand was dispatched on a thousand-mile overland expedition from West Africa to seize a small Sudanese town called Fashoda—a godforsaken place of "blazing heat, solvent humidity, elephant grass, and enveloping mud (when the rain began in May) and horizon-to-horizon mosquitoes."

Meanwhile, England dispatched an army of thirty thousand men under Lord Kitchener to destroy the Islamic forces in Sudan. For two years, he marched his army south along the Nile, accompanied by gunboats on the river, until, on August 31, 1898, he encountered the Khalifah and his forces at Omdurman and annihilated them. On September 19, he reached Fashoda. Marchand had arrived two months earlier with his small band of fellow explorers and claimed the town for France.

The two men met and had a cordial conversation. Yet for the next few weeks Britain and France stood at the edge of war over a fetid swampland, which neither country valued. The verdict of political logic regarding Fashoda was clear: it was worthless. But the logic of the military chessboard led to an opposite evaluation. Because Fashoda, like Egypt, supposedly sat astride England's "road to India," and since India was the heart of the British Empire, Fashoda must be defended at all costs. The disparity between the puniness of the prize and the immensity of the war being risked in Europe disturbed even the most pugnacious imperialists. Queen Victoria, ordinarily a hard-liner in imperial matters, remarked to Prime Minister Salisbury that "a war for so miserable and small an object is what I could hardly consent to." Yet at the height of the crisis war orders were sent to the English fleet in the Mediterranean. France, lacking comparable naval forces in the region, and holding a position at Fashoda that was, in Kitchener's words by telegraph to London, "as impossible as it is absurd," backed down. The crisis, which bore a close resemblance to others of the period—in Morocco, in Siam, in China—was one of many clear but unheeded warnings that confrontations in out-of-the-way places could push the world toward a pointless, global catastrophe.

The event in Europe that illustrated the same widening abyss between military and political logic was the negotiation, four years earlier, of the Franco-Russian alliance, forged to counter the growing power of Germany, which was allied with Austria and Italy. The treaty's aims, as the American diplomat and scholar George Kennan observes in his book *The Fateful Alliance*, were solely to win a war with Germany, and the treaty made no mention of any political object of the fighting. Instead, its provisions simply stated that if either power were attacked, no matter what the reason, the other would come to its aid by launching all-out war.

The framers of the treaty seem to have learned everything that Clausewitz had to say about the requirements of absolute war but nothing of what he said about the need to subordinate war to the goals of policy. In a state paper that laid the foundation for the treaty, Russian adjutant general Nikolai Obruchev observed, "Once we have been drawn into a war, we cannot conduct that war otherwise than with all our forces, and against all our neighbors. In the face of the readiness of entire peoples to go to war, no other sort of war can be envisaged than the most decisive sort." Not only must the war be total but it must be instantaneous. "The term 'mobilization' must now signify the inauguration of military operations themselves," Obruchev wrote. Therefore, once war had begun, "further diplomatic hesitation is impermissible." Would the diplomats and the statesmen at least have an opportunity to decide on political goals for the war *before* embarking on it? Not according to Obruchev. War against "all neighbors" meant that even partial mobilization by any member of the opposing alliance would have to be met with an immediate, full-scale attack on the entire alliance, for "it is hard to conceive that any war beginning on the continent could be limited to an isolated struggle between any two states."

The politicians undertaking the agreement apparently did not see a need to specify any war aims. The Russian foreign minister, Nikolai Giers, asked Czar Alexander III what the purpose of victory over Germany would be, and the Czar answered, "What we would gain would be that Germany, as such, would disappear." And when General Raoul Mouton de Boisdeffre, the principal architect of the treaty on the French side, was asked what France's intentions regarding Germany would be after a victory, he replied, "Let us begin by beating them; after that it will be easy." Regarding the war's aim, Kennan concluded, "There is no evidence, in fact, that it had ever been discussed between the two governments."

In the Fashoda crisis and the Franco-Russian treaty, we catch two glimpses of a world in which, though peace still reigned, military victory had become an end in itself. The logic of politics had not been merely challenged by the logic of war, it had been shut out completely. The war that now threatened had become the senseless thing that Clausewitz had once feared: "a complete, untrammeled, absolute manifestation of violence" that would "drive policy out of office and rule by the laws of its own nature."

The causes of war now arose not so much from political differences as from the structure of the war system itself—from each country's fear that, if war broke out, some small advantage won by a speedier or better-prepared rival would tip the scales of victory and defeat. When war did come in 1914, it fit this description exactly. It exhibited the grotesque disproportion foreshadowed by the Fashoda crisis and the Franco-Russian treaty. The immediate cause of war—the political fortunes of the small state of Serbia in southeastern Europe—was of negligible intrinsic importance to the great powers, but once the full machinery of the global system was mobilized for battle, the slaughter proved unstoppable until a true Clausewitzian victory had been won by the Allied forces. Nations that had no direct stake in the fortunes of Serbia— England, for example—suffered millions of casualties. As the war historian John Keegan has observed, "The war's political objects—difficult enough to define in the first place—were forgotten. . . . Politics played no part in the conduct of the First World War worth mentioning."

The statesmen of 1914 were notoriously unaware how bloody and protracted total war would be. Most believed that the fighting would last only a few months. One reason was that they saw at least three of the four great modern forces that had fed the war machine—science, democracy, and industry—chiefly as motors of human progress. They identified these forces with the advance of civilization, not its downfall. Even imperialism, in such bad repute later, was touted then as an advance guard of the "three Cs": civilization, Christianity, and commerce.

Among military men, however, the idea that war in Europe could only be total was widespread. In France, Marshal Foch, soon to command the French forces, was saying, "You must henceforth go to the limits to find the aim of war. Since the vanquished party now never yields before it has been deprived of all means of reply, what you have to aim at is the destruction of those very means of reply." From a Clausewitzian point of view, such a statement, which left political goals out of military calculations, was folly. But was it in fact baseless? The advocates of total war, who were ready to unleash war over a Fashoda and did so over Serbia, have often been blamed. Several generations of historians have accused them of losing a sense of proportion—"of forgetting that force should be used in amounts commensurate to the purpose at hand, no more, no less," in Kennan's words. Given the pressures of the adapt or die war system, however, was it realistic to expect nations to exercise restraint?

Attempts to reach disarmament agreements, such as the Anglo-German naval discussions of 1912, almost invariably failed; and unilateral restraints were as unthinkable for patriotic publics as they were for governments. Which country, in the name of preserving a peace that might shortly break down, dared to be the one to stop its armies short of a Fashoda or a Sarajevo and let the enemy plant his flag there first, or rest content with a smaller naval gun, or fix a slower timetable for mobilization, or reject an alliance with another power in the face of mortal peril from a third and fourth? And when war did come, was it possible *then*, in the midst of unprecedented slaughter, to *reintroduce* political calculations, and bring the fighting under control? Once the tremendous twentieth-century war machines had been assembled and hurled at one another, was it likely, or even conceivable, that they could be used in a refined, controlled manner—like Clausewitz's handy rapier—to adjudicate such modest, or even trifling, issues as the future of this or that African swamp or Balkan backwater? History famously discloses no alternatives, but the military history of the entire twentieth century strongly suggests that, whatever theorists might have recommended, the modern war machines, once built, had to be used to the full or left unused. Since 1870, no great powers have fought "limited" wars directly against one another (although many have fought small powers). They have fought total war or they have not fought at all.

The Collapse of Weakness

The First World War was a watershed not only for war but for the civilization that produced it. Europe, without quite knowing what it was doing, had for more than a century been pouring the awesome energies of modernity into the war system, and the result was the catastrophe of 1914. Now the influence between war and society started to run in the opposite direction, shaping the domestic life of nations, above all in ravaged Russia and Germany, which, in the wake of defeat and anarchy, soon gave birth to the Bolshevik and Nazi regimes. Meanwhile, the technology of war kept improving. By 1918, the democratic revolution—which had galvanized people, fueled the conscription of millions of young men into the armies, and propelled them to the front to die—had contributed all it had to offer to the war system. Mutinies in the French and Russian armies in the last years of the war had even suggested a limit to popular endurance for patriotic gore. The art of harnessing industry to war had been mastered. Imperialism likewise had reached its high tide. Science and industry, however, had much yet to give. The decades ahead would witness the development of tanks, more powerful explosives, and air forces, including long-range bombers, rockets, radar, and aircraft carriers, to name just a few of technology's new contributions to war. After the First World War, the biologist J. B. S. Haldane recollected his wartime experience with artillery and poison gas this way:

> Through a blur of dust and fumes there appear, quite suddenly, great black and yellow masses of smoke which seem to be tearing up the surface of the earth and disintegrating the works of man with an almost visible hatred. These form the chief parts of the picture, but somewhere in the middle distance one can see a few irrelevant-looking human figures, and soon there are fewer. It is hard to believe that these are the protagonists in the battle. One would rather choose those huge substantive oily black masses which are much more conspicuous, and suppose that the men are in reality their servants, and playing an inglorious, subordinate and fatal part in the combat. It is possible, after all, that this view is correct.

In *Weapons and Hope*, the physicist Freeman Dyson comments that observations such as this, which he absorbed as a child, led him and many of his friends in the interwar years to regard technology as "a malevolent monster broken loose from human control." Technology, however, had no will of its own, and to think that it did people had to hide from themselves the human wills that were in fact propelling it. We know who they were—the scientists who developed the technology and the statesmen and generals who ordered its use. And yet in a sense Haldane and Dyson were right, because these people lacked the discretion, except at terrible risk to their nations, to forgo the new inventions of war. They were as thoroughly trapped on the treadmill of the modern adapt-or-die war system as the soldiers in the trenches.

All the new inventions were used to the full in the Second World War, in which an estimated seventy million human beings were killed. But it was the last time. Even as the war was being fought, an instrument that would make such wars forever impossible was being prepared in the desert of New Mexico. Never has a single technical invention had a more sudden or profound effect on an entrenched human institution than nuclear weapons have had on war. For war was a paradoxical freak of evolution: a creature that depended for its survival on that unsung virtue of arms, their weakness—without which war's critical event, its gift to politics, defeat, could not occur. But human weakness, in the twentieth century, proved a dwindling asset. Like clean air, rain forests, stratospheric ozone, and passenger pigeons, it was being steadily depleted by technical progress. In July of 1945, it ran out. The logic of total war had carried its practitioners to the brink of a destination, the far side of human existence, to which the logic of politics could never follow. For politics was a human activity, and in the post-nuclear landscape there might be no human beings. The bomb revealed that total war was not an everlasting but a historical phenomenon. It had gone the way of the tyrannosaurus rex and the saber-toothed tiger, a casualty not of natural but scientific evolution, whose new powers, as always, the war system could not refuse. Its day was done.

2

"Nuclear War"

The atomic bomb that destroyed Hiroshima reverberated in every domain of human existence. It placed the human species at risk of extinction by its own hand. It signaled a reversal in the balance of power between humankind and nature, placing nature in jeopardy from human depradation. It threw into doubt the moral faith on which all civilization must be based—that the collective efforts of human beings will make life better than it otherwise would have been. But in our present context its most important consequence was that it rendered the global war system unworkable beyond any hope of repair. The new state of affairs was recognized by a succession of leaders of the nuclear powers. As early as 1952, President Harry Truman said, in his farewell broadcast to the nation, "Starting an atomic war is totally unthinkable for rational men." At the height of the Cuban missile crisis, the chairman of the Communist Party of the Soviet Union, Nikita S. Khrushchev, acknowledged in a letter to President John F. Kennedy that only "lunatics or suicides, who themselves want to perish and to destroy the whole world before they die," would start a nuclear war. The clearinghouse of the adapt-or-die war system, where the powers of the modern age were cashed in for the universal currency of military power, was abruptly closed for business at the global level. The vast set-piece battles that had long been history's favorite grand decision-making device sank into the past. (Where they did occur—between Iran and Iraq in the 1980s, or between Ethiopia and Eritrea in the nineties—they seemed anachronistic, as "backward" as the countries that were waging them.) Industrialists might still offer their products, scientists their inventions, and citizens their patriotic zeal, but now their contributions could only increase overkill—"strengthen our deterrent," or some such. The critical link between military power and political power, which Clausewitz had struggled to preserve, was severed at the highest level of international operations.

The most obvious solution to the new predicament was to abolish nuclear weapons, or even to liquidate the entire disabled war system. And in fact abolition was proposed by President Truman's representative to the United Nations, Bernard Baruch, in June of 1946. He asked the world to join with the United States in placing all nuclear facilities under international inspection and control and restricting their use to peaceful purposes. The Soviet Union rejected the proposal, and put forward one of its own, which the United States in turn rejected. Liquidation of the whole war system was attempted with the foundation of the United Nations. The U.N.'s central mechanism for peacekeeping was to be a system of collective security enforced by the powers that had just won the Second World War, all of whom were given permanent memberships on the Security Council and a right to veto its decisions. The operations of the council were soon spoiled for these purposes by the onset of the Cold War, which rendered collective decision making in the council impossible. In 1949, the Soviet Union detonated its first atomic bomb.

The great powers of the Cold War now had to decide how to conduct their business in a world that was *not* going to replace the rule of force with the rule of law but instead *was* going to equip itself with nuclear arsenals. Their dilemma was that they could neither use the most powerful instruments of force now at their disposal nor get rid of them. The bomb had ruined war by transforming it into mutual annihilation. Now the most important question was whether humankind would live or die; but the military paralysis of the great powers also raised the separate question of how, in war's absence, international conflicts would be resolved. What would be the final arbiter now?

Never had war "arbitrated" the destinies of nations more sweepingly than in the first half of the twentieth century. The First World War had undone the three imperial dynasties of continental Europe, swept a multitude of national governments from power, and sharpened the appetite for self-determination in colonies around the world. The Second World War had given Hitler the mastery of Europe, then taken it back; subjected the peoples of Asia to Japanese rule and then released them; drawn the Soviet Union deep into Europe; drained the power of England even in victory, giving the coup de grâce to its global empire; and raised up the United States to global preeminence. And now the question had become how, if global war could no longer be fought, conflict in the global order would proceed. People who wanted to make things happen would have to search for other means; but what were they to be? Through what riverbeds would the streams of historical change flow, now that this ancient one was blocked? What were to be the instruments of power?

For human strife had not dried up in deference to the energy released from the atom. On the contrary, a classic global confrontation between two blocs inspired by hostile ideologies was taking shape. At the same time, anticolonial movements were in full flood around the world, and often intersected with the Cold War struggle. Sometimes, regional antagonists dragged the superpowers into their conflicts, and sometimes the superpowers, thwarted by nuclear terror from pursuing their military ambitions directly, deflected them into proxy regional struggles, which, now vested with apocalyptic significance, often escalated back up the military ladder to "the brink," threatening nuclear war. Hanging over the scene was the old fear that one of two great powers, if left unchecked, would dominate the world.

Nuclear strategy had little if anything to offer to the resolution of the burning political issues of the time. At best, the leaders of the day increasingly realized, nuclear arsenals could freeze a global stalemate in place. Even this goal, however, was hard to achieve. Preserving the status quo, after all, is not a modest goal for statesmanship. For almost half a century, for example, it was the primary mission of the Concert of Europe, established following the Congress of Vienna in the wake of Napoleon's defeat, and it has generally been the broad goal of balance-of-power policies wherever these have been practiced. Under the dominant strategic doctrine of the new age, nuclear deterrence, force thus still did in a sense "arbitrate," and on a global scale. That arbitration, however, could deliver only one monotonous verdict: no one can move a muscle, everything must remain as it is.

The question that remained was how nuclear weapons could achieve even this limited goal when they could not be used. A solution was attempted by turning the war system into a system of pure nuclear terror, to which the name "balance of terror" was soon attached. Terror had been employed for political ends from the time of King Scorpion on, and never more lavishly than during the first half of the twentieth century—a period that witnessed the rise of totalitarianism, which used terror as a mainstay of rule, and also the rise of "strategic bombing," whose explicit aim was not to destroy military targets but to break civilian morale. The destruction of Hiroshima was in fact the culmination of a series of destructions of cities by firebombing, in both Germany and Japan.

The nuclear terror of the Cold War nevertheless was categorically different from all previous terror. As a tactic in war, terror is the use of force against some people to intimidate others. A classic example was the Nazi practice in occupied countries of announcing their intention to execute ten or more political prisoners in their jails for every German soldier killed by resistance fighters. Nuclear terror, by contrast, is the paradoxical attempt to produce terror on a mass scale without actually using force—an idea embodied in nuclear deterrence. Under this strategy, military force was handed a role—to prevent its own use—that it had never previously played in the same way before.

The doctrine, which took shape in the 1950s, became the declared policy of the United States in the 1960s, then won a partial, grudging acceptance by the Soviet Union, and went on to become the basis for the first nuclear-arms-control negotiations. According to its central tenet, each side would be stopped from attacking the other by the knowledge that it would be annihilated in return. Historically, military forces had been employed as often to deter war as to fight it. Military leaders had long been fond of the old Roman saying "If you seek peace, prepare for war." But that proposition had in fact been a mere corollary of another, which was too obvious for aphoristic expression: If you seek to fight and win wars, prepare for war. It was this second proposition that the bomb nullified. Seeking war made no sense when war to the finish meant annihilation for all involved. A new proposition, appropriate to the nuclear age, was articulated as early as 1946 by, among others, the American military analyst Bernard Brodie. He wrote, "Thus far the chief purpose of a military establishment has been to win wars. From now on its chief purpose must be to avert them. It can have no other useful purpose." The same argument was put forward by Winston Churchill, when he made his famed remark "It may be that we shall by a process of sublime irony have reached a stage in this story where safety will be the sturdy child of terror, and survival the twin brother of annihilation." Even though the system of nuclear terror was no longer a war system, it was still, let us stress, a system based on force; that is, force had not been exchanged for obedience to law, or for any form of willing cooperation. It was the way in which force was to be exploited that had changed.

If in the new system the *unleashed* force was no longer the final arbiter, we need to ask, then what, exactly, was? The answer was that there occurred a sweeping displacement of military conflicts from theaters of actual combat to a theater of appearances. The battles that *could not* be fought physically were to be fought out instead on psychological terrain. To borrow Clausewitz's concepts again, it was as if the policy makers wanted to achieve their opponents' moral defeat without passing through the stage of physical defeat. Clausewitz had written that "the destruction of the enemy's force underlies all military actions; all plans are ultimately based on it, resting on it like an arch on its abutment." He added, "The decision by arms is for all major and minor operations in war what cash payment is in commerce. Regardless how complex the relationship between the two parties, regardless how rarely settlements actually occur, they can never be entirely absent." But trying to preserve credit—or, in that much-used term of the nuclear age, "credibility"—without ever having to make the cash payment (engaging in nuclear war) was exactly the feat that the superpowers were attempting.

Nuclear credibility—the appearance of a readiness to use nuclear weapons when the chips were down—was a compound of several elements. One was obviously possession of a nuclear arsenal. A second was the readiness to use it. But these were entirely useless without an essential, if strangely intangible, third element, the *appearance* of having the first two. Creating this appearance was therefore *the* essential requirement of nuclear policy. Even with an arsenal in hand, however, creating the desired appearance was no simple matter, considering the suicidal consequences of performing the terrible deed; and a central—almost an obsessive—preoccupation of the Cold War leaders was with making people believe that they possessed the doubtful will to carry out their nuclear threats.

Such demonstrations were necessarily racked with contradictions, all of which were variations on a theme: under no circumstances could the act that gave the deterrent threat its effectiveness—namely, the actual launching of a nuclear attack—make any sense. The operational puzzle was what to do "if deterrence failed." It was a question without a reasonable answer, for it can never be in the interest of a country to perform an act (fighting a nuclear war) whose prevention is itself the goal of its policy. All of which is only a complicated way of saying that it could never make sense for the two rivals to blow themselves off the face of the earth.

In practice, the problem was solved by knowledge on all sides that, whether retaliation was rational or not, it was likely to happen. "The essence of the problem is the difficulty of attaching any rationality whatsoever to the initiation of a chain of events that could well end in the utter devastation of one's own society (even assuming indifference to the fate of the enemy society)," the historian of nuclear strategy Lawrence Freedman has written. "The resulting sense of an enormous bluff is, however, more likely to worry those relying on these threats . . . than those against whom they are directed." He concludes, "The Emperor Deterrence may have no clothes, but he is still Emperor." The mighty sword, curiously, had turned into a mere picture of a mighty sword. Freedman suggested that the Emperor Deterrence had no clothes, but considering the primacy of appearances in nuclear policy, it would perhaps be more appropriate to say that the clothes had no emperor. What this meant in practice can be illustrated by the most perilous episode of the Cold War—the Cuban missile crisis.

A Crisis of Appearances

By the time of the crisis, the peculiar new rules of the nuclear game were in full force, and the progress of the crisis reveals them in operation. On Sunday, October 13, 1962, American U-2 spy aircraft discovered Soviet nuclear-missile sites under construction in Cuba. On Monday, October 22, after a week of secret deliberations, President Kennedy made the fact known in a television address to the American people, and announced that he had imposed a naval quarantine on military goods being sent to Cuba, and was demanding the removal of the missiles. He made clear that the stakes in the crisis were total when he warned that any launch of nuclear weapons from Cuba would be met with "a full retaliatory response upon the Soviet Union," and, in a sentence that summed up the dilemma at the heart of policy in the nuclear age, stated, "We will not prematurely or unnecessarily risk the costs of worldwide nuclear war in which even the fruits of victory would be ashes in our mouth—but neither will we shrink from that risk at any time it must be faced."

Khrushchev's reasons for the deployment were unclear to Kennedy and his advisers. Secretary of Defense Robert McNamara flatly stated to the president that the missiles in Cuba would not materially alter the balance of strategic nuclear power. Most of Kennedy's other advisers agreed. What were Khrushchev's motives, then? Something like a consensus on this matter has subsequently emerged among historians. In the first place, Khrushchev saw the deployment as a means to protect Cuba against a repeat of the kind of attack that the United States had mounted at the Bay of Pigs to overthrow the socialist government of Fidel Castro in 1961, shortly after Kennedy had arrived in office. In the second place, he sought to redress a nuclear imbalance that favored the United States. In the late 1950s and early 1960s, the United States outmatched the Soviet Union in nuclear striking power. In 1960, for example, the United States possessed six thousand nuclear warheads, the Soviet Union three hundred. Of these, only a fraction were mounted on the Soviet Union's mere thirty-five missiles capable of reaching the United States. Khrushchev of course knew this, although during the presidential campaign of 1960 Senator Kennedy had erroneously claimed that it was the

United States that suffered from a "missile gap" with the Soviet Union. For a while the error suited the needs of Khrushchev, who was not only aware of his country's nuclear inferiority but afraid that the Americans would use it to advantage. He adopted a policy of bluster and bluff. In August of 1961, the head of the K.G.B., Aleksandr Shelepin, had proposed to an enthusiastic Khrushchev that the U.S.S.R. launch a campaign of disinformation to persuade the United States that its nuclear forces were more powerful than in fact they were. Khrushchev also threatened intermittently to shut off Western access to Berlin and, if the United States should oppose him, to annihilate its European allies. On one occasion, for example, he noted that six hydrogen bombs would be "quite enough" to destroy the British Isles, and nine would be enough for France. "Why should two hundred million people die for two million Berliners?" he asked.

Once in office, the Kennedy administration discovered, or feigned to discover, that there was no missile gap—or, rather, that there was one and it overwhelmingly favored the United States. In a speech delivered by Undersecretary of Defense Roswell Gilpatric in October of 1961, the administration set forth the facts. "The destructive power which the United States could bring to bear even after a Soviet surprise attack upon our forces," he stated, "would be as great as, perhaps greater than, the total undamaged force which the enemy can threaten to launch against the United States in a first strike." Now Khrushchev's bluff had been publicly called. One of his responses was to detonate the largest hydrogen bomb ever exploded on earth to date or since—a monster that unleashed fifty megatons of explosive power, equivalent to almost four thousand Hiroshima bombs. Another response may have been the decision to place nuclear-armed missiles in Cuba.

Kennedy's national security adviser, McGeorge Bundy, later noted that the administration he served did not believe that its immense nuclear superiority was a source of great political advantage. At the time of the missile crisis, American officials were more impressed, Bundy believed, by the tens of millions of casualties that the Soviet Union *could* cause than by the imbalance in the two countries' nuclear arsenals. Hence they were blind to the danger that Khrushchev, thinking the U.S.S.R. weak, might take reckless action to redress the inequality.

This persuasive account of the origins of the Cuban missile crisis illustrates the novel rules of the game in a nuclear-armed world. Only in the nuclear age could it be considered reckless for a great power to publicly expose the weakness of its adversary. For only in an age in which appearances in military matters take precedence over actualities would an inequality of forces *in fact* appear far more tolerable to the weaker side than an inequality of forces *in appearance.*

The resolution of the crisis teaches the same lesson. Khrushchev, perhaps without quite knowing it, had breached the rules of the game in a nuclear-armed world. He had taken a step that, in his adversary's eyes, threatened fatal damage to its own credibility. And yet reversal of that step would threaten *Soviet* credibility. The logic of credibility, once this situation had arisen, pointed toward war; but war in the nuclear age, as Kennedy and Khrushchev were aware, was senseless.

At the height of the crisis, Khrushchev wrote in his memoirs, he privately asked his generals if they could assure him "that holding fast would not result in the death of five hundred million human beings." He went on to report, "They looked at me as though I was out of my mind or, what was worse, a traitor. The biggest tragedy, as they saw it, was not that our country might be devastated and everything lost, but that the Chinese or the Albanians would accuse us of appeasement or weakness." He was led to wonder, "What good would it have done me in the last hour of my life to know that, though our great nation and the United States were in complete ruin, the national honor of the Soviet Union was intact?" Khrushchev's recollection of his fit of sanity in insane circumstances goes to the heart of the contradiction inherent in the nuclear policies of the Cold War era. On the one side of the nuclear ledger was the need to uphold "national honor," or credibility. This required shows of resolve, even military action. On the other side was the threat to the lives of hundreds of millions of human beings. This required restraint. The main aims that nuclear arsenals were meant to serve—preventing war and pursuing national interests—were now in collision, and one, it seemed, had to be given up.

In a parallel episode, Kennedy at a certain moment took his aide Pierre Salinger outside the room in which the Executive Committee dealing with the crisis was meeting, and asked him whether he thought the people inside realized that if he made a mistake there might be two hundred million dead. It's striking that both leaders felt so alone in their terrible knowledge that they were able to communicate it only in side conversations, or later in their memoirs. Perhaps Kennedy at that moment remembered some advice given him a few months earlier by former secretary of state Dean Acheson regarding the use of nuclear weapons in the Berlin crisis of 1961. Acheson counseled that "the president should himself give that question [whether to use nuclear weapons in a crisis in Europe] the most careful and private consideration, well before the time when the choice might present itself, that he should reach his own clear conclusion in advance as to what he would do, and that he should tell no one at all what that conclusion was." Bundy, who was present, drew the obvious conclusion: that Acheson, "The most ardent and eloquent advocate of energetic action to make nuclear risk credible to Khrushchev, a true believer in fighting hard with strong conventional forces for the freedom of West Berlin, nevertheless believed that at the moment of final choice, the course of 'wisdom and restraint' might be to accept local defeat without the use of nuclear weapons." What is notable about the story is that at the hour of truth the decision not to use nuclear weapons—certainly the most important that any president would ever make—had to be such a deep secret that even the man giving the recommendation to him in a private meeting dared not utter it in plain English. All *public* counsel, all statements of theory and policy, including, most especially, those made by the president, had to support the use of nuclear weapons. To do otherwise would be unilateral disarmament by verbal means. Only the president's private resolve, never to be spoken aloud—frail refuge of sanity, of safety for all humankind!—could counsel restraint. National leaders have often spoken of the loneliness of the decisions they must make. Surely, no decision could ever be lonelier than this.

Later, Kennedy formulated the quandary in which the Cuban missile crisis had placed him no less succinctly than Khrushchev had, and in almost identical terms. He and his advisers were well aware that the Cuban missiles did not change the strategic balance of power significantly. But, Kennedy explained, "it would have politically changed the balance of power. It would have appeared to, and appearances contribute to reality."

How, then, did Kennedy and Khrushchev escape war? The answer, in a word, was *secrecy.* If appearances—of soiled honor, of "weakness," of lost credibility, of lack of resolve, of humiliation in the eyes of Albanians, and so forth—were the problem, then what better solution than to hide the facts that might create those appearances? Khrushchev was the first to resort to this method. He sent two messages to Kennedy—one public, the other private. In the private message—a long, secret, personal letter expressing in vivid terms his horror of nuclear war and his determination to avoid it—he offered a deal in which the Soviet missiles in Cuba would be removed in exchange for a promise by the United States not to invade the island. This was highly acceptable to the United States. However, in his public stance, made known the next day, Khrushchev added a crucial condition—he demanded the removal of American missiles stationed near the Soviet Union in Turkey. While in private Khrushchev could afford to seem "weak," in public he had to appear "tough."

The administration had planned to remove the Turkish missiles soon in any case. Couldn't it simply go ahead with the plan as part of the settlement? The problem was credibility. The actual strategic position of the United States would not be harmed by the removal of the Turkish missiles. However, any public decision for removal under pressure of the Soviet deployment in Cuba would harm U.S. credibility, especially with its NATO allies.

Now it was the United States' turn to take refuge in secret assurances. The president resorted to the ploy of ignoring Khrushchev's tough, public stand while seeking to agree to the more moderate, private one. That was Kennedy's public position—a tough-seeming one, since it yielded no ground on the Turkish missiles. However, like Khrushchev, he also put forward a "weak" private position: he gave in on the Turkish missiles. But he did so only on condition that the concession remain forever secret. Keeping the missiles in Turkey, however useless militarily, had been declared American policy. Invading Cuba had not. Therefore, giving the no-invasion pledge would leave American credibility intact, while removing the missiles would undermine it.

This consideration illuminates an extraordinary action now taken by President Kennedy and a few officials of his administration. Without telling the whole Executive Committee what they were doing, they traded away the Turkish missiles in a back-channel deal. Then they took a vow of silence regarding the secret agreement, demanding and receiving assurances that the Soviets would do the same. We may suspect that the reason was domestic politics, especially when we recall that at a meeting of the Executive Committee McNamara said, "I'll be quite frank: I don't think there *is* a military problem here. . . . This is a domestic political problem." And unquestionably politics was on the minds of the president and his advisers, who feared Republican charges that they were "soft on Communism." But the dictates of high strategy seconded the requirements of domestic politics. In his speech to the nation on October 22, the president had confirmed the crucial geopolitical role of credibility in his thinking when he referred to the placement of the missiles in Cuba as an "unjustified change in the status quo which cannot be accepted by this country if our courage and our commitment are ever to be trusted again by either friend or foe." In a world in which appearances were not an afterthought of policy but its substance, the president and his advisers felt compelled to make their decisions on the basis not of the actual strategic balance but of what it looked like to the world at large.

From beginning to end of the crisis, the president and his advisers never deviated from this iron rule. When the Soviet ambassador, Anatoly Dobrynin, later gave Robert Kennedy a letter expressing his government's agreement to the Turkish missile deal in writing, Kennedy angrily handed it back, saying (according to Kennedy's notes of talking points for the conversation), "Take your letter—Reconsider it & if you feel it is necessary to write letters then we will also write one which you cannot enjoy. Also if you should publish any document indicating a deal then it is off & also if done afterward will further affect the relationship." The Soviets withdrew the letter, and the vow of secrecy was kept on both sides for years afterward.

The ingenuity, if not the propriety, of this bigovernmental conspiracy of silence against the rest of the world is remarkable. At first glance, it might appear that by agreeing to the American demand for secrecy Khrushchev was permitting the United States to preserve its credibility at the expense of his own—no small concession, given the central role that credibility played at all moments in the crisis on both sides. Certainly, Khrushchev was widely perceived by the general public as having backed down without having received much in return. In assessing this question, however, it is important to remember that credibility is an impression made by one party on another. Its value depends on the audience you wish to impress. In the case of the United States that audience included America's allies as well as congressional and public opinion. The record shows that the Kennedy men were

particularly worried about the response of NATO to a deal to surrender the Turkish missiles. Secrecy regarding the deal preserved
American credibility with its crucial audiences. Khrushchev, who
presided over a closed society, on the other hand, needed to maintain his credibility with a much smaller audience: high party
members, generals, and the leaders of a few independent-minded
communist parties. No congress or public would review his decisions. And no allied government other than the Chinese and
Albanian communist parties was in a position to second-guess
him. Only his immediate colleagues (who did in fact remove him
from power in 1964) were a danger. Khrushchev sent his first,
"weak" letter privately but drafted his second, "tough" one in
front of the Politburo. With this all-important audience, who
knew that Kennedy had yielded on the Turkish missiles, therefore,
Khrushchev's credibility might well be preserved. As for the world
at large, Khrushchev would have to make do with an American
pledge not to invade Cuba.

Two years later, Robert McNamara was asked at a congressional committee hearing, "Are you aware of any agreement, any
assurance, by yourself or anyone else in high government office,
to Khrushchev that if he would withdraw at the time under the
conditions that you showed us, the United States would thereby
commit itself to any particular course of action?" McNamara
answered, "I am not only unaware of any agreement, it is inconceivable to me that our President would enter in a discussion of
any such agreement. Moreover, there were absolutely no undis-
closed agreements associated with the withdrawal of the Soviet
missiles from Cuba." In calling the decision that the president had
actually taken "inconceivable," McNamara kept the administration's vow of secrecy, and gave powerful evidence of the primacy
of appearances in the strategies of the nuclear age.

Even if we are critical of this conspiracy of silence, *which included
the Soviet government while excluding the American people,* we
can still admire the dexterity with which both Khrushchev and

Kennedy extricated themselves from a logic that pushed both of them toward annihilation. Precisely because the most important moves had been made in secret, however, that logic remained unimpaired and in full force throughout the years of the Cold War, though without producing any further crises as severe as the Cuban missile crisis. It's a sobering commentary on the nuclear policy to which the two men were committed that their most statesmanlike decisions were those they had to hide most assiduously from the world.

The shift from the primacy of force to the primacy of appearances was momentous in the history of war. It signified a real, if equivocal, official recognition that the age-old war system had become an anachronism. The true targets of the missiles of the nuclear age have, in the more than half century since Nagasaki, been the minds, not the bodies, of opponents. The true instruments of this warfare have been not actual warheads flying across oceans but the images of those warheads conveyed in public statements and in the media. And the goal of policy, however shot through with contradiction and apocalyptic danger, was to head off war, not to fight it.

The gap between the political ends of foreign policy and the military logic of strategy that had been growing steadily since Clausewitz's time had widened to the point of no return. And if, possibly, the benefits of nuclear deterrence were real, in that a peace that otherwise might have broken down was preserved, so was its unremitting, intolerable cost: that, day by day, it risked the extinction of the human species and involved all the nuclear powers and their peoples in the complicity of actively planning for this supreme crime. But was there some other final arbiter—some method whereby freedom of action would be restored? To answer this question, we need to examine a military development that ran parallel to the nuclear revolution—the rise of people's war.

3

People's War

The ascending spiral of violence in which Clausewitzian war, driven by its own "logical" need to run to extremes, drew the newborn Promethean energies of the modern age, one after another, into its mighty orbit—leading, in a paradoxical culmination, to the terrorized calm of the nuclear stalemate—was one of the two major developments in the metamorphosis of war in the modern age. The second, concurrent development led in an opposite direction: away from the blackboards and computer screens in the superpowers' think tanks, scientific laboratories, and missile ranges, where they pursued ever-more-costly, technically elaborate methods of war, and down into poor, "underdeveloped" peasant villages and remote swamps and jungles, where scientifically unsophisticated people were incubating methods of warfare that, in their own way, were scarcely less "absolute" than the total war of the great powers and, in the long run, were to prove the more successful invention. These were the methods of people's war. If, to anticipate, nuclear weapons, by spoiling the old final arbiter, conventional war, posed the question of how disputes in the international sphere were *now* to be settled, then people's war, though not itself yet the answer the world needed, pointed the way to an answer. For while nuclear weapons were producing stalemate people's war was changing the political map of the earth.

The World Revolt

Like the invention of nuclear weapons, the rise of people's war has a wider context—the centuries-long movement of the peoples of the earth to achieve self-determination. Some rebellions were of colonies in revolt against a mother country, some were of nations with long histories of battling conquerors, and some were of indigenous populations oppressed by imperial overlords. The guiding principle of all of them, however, was to drive out a hated occupier and establish rule by local people—the "self" of the word "self-determination." The freedom to which a movement for self determination aspired was *sometimes* freedom of the individual; it was *always* freedom of the national, collective self from foreign rule. The period in question is roughly the same as that of the democratic revolution, of which the self-determination movement has been a part.

As its beginning we can plausibly name July 4, 1776, when the American Continental Congress declared to the world that the American people meant to "assume among the powers of the earth the separate and equal station to which the laws of nature and nature's God entitled them." It was also in the American Revolution that a form of people's war, the use of militias, made its first appearance in an anti-imperial cause of modern times. Some years later, one of the signers of the declaration, John Adams, looking toward what would prove a distant future, asked, "When will France, Spain, England and Holland renounce their selfish, contracted, exclusive systems of religion, government, and commerce?" And he answered with a prophecy: "They may depend upon it, their present systems of colonization cannot endure. Colonies universally, ardently breathe for independence. No man who has a soul will ever live in a colony under the present establishments one moment longer than necessity compels him."

Substantial fulfillment of Adams's prophecy came in August of 1991, when the president of Russia, Boris Yeltsin, and the presidents of two other republics of the Soviet Union declared the foundation of the Commonwealth of Independent States and the dissolution of the Soviet Union, the last of the European empires. Between 1776 and that date, all the empires that had existed, whether dynastic, colonial, or both, and all the territorial empires that subsequently arose, including those built on revolutionary foundations, were destroyed. In the former category were the Russian empire of the czars; the Austro-Hungarian Empire of the Hapsburgs; the German empire of the Hohenzollerns; the Ottoman Empire; and the colonial empires of Holland, England, France, Belgium, Spain, and Italy. In the latter category were the Napoleonic empire in the early nineteenth century, the Japanese "Co-Prosperity Sphere" in Asia in the 1930s and forties, Hitler's "thousand-year Reich," and the Soviet empire. (I leave until later the special case of the mainly nonterritorial empire of the United States that arose in the second half of the twentieth century.)

Broadly speaking, the peoples of the earth assumed their "rightful stations" in three waves. The first, which followed soon after the American War of Independence, commenced when the victims of Napoleon's imperial ambitions, including Clausewitz's Prussia, threw off the French yoke, giving birth, in the process, to a fullfledged conservative nationalism that would be replicated in various versions down to our time. It continued until the First World War, when the last of the great European monarchies fell. The example of the nation-states of Europe, in which peoples created states, or else the states created peoples, and in which both were wedded to a precisely defined, jealously defended national territory, became the model for the subsequent waves. Concurrently, the Spanish empire, an early victim of the anticolonial rebellion, was overthrown by the Latin American peoples.

In the second wave, which lasted roughly from 1905, when Japan defeated Russia, until the mid-1970s, when Portugal gave up its empire in Africa, the rest of the peoples of the European colonies and dependencies rose up, in what Leonard Woolf called a "world revolt," to liberate themselves from their Western (and Japanese) masters. Combining imitation with resistance, they adopted whatever they needed of European ideas and techniques to drive the Europeans out. In the nineteenth century, even as the nations of Europe were learning democracy at home, they had been practicing its opposite in the world at large. Their philosophy in the colonies was, on the whole, that of Lord Milner, the English proconsul in Egypt in the 1880s, who wrote in his *England in Egypt* that although, "As a true born Briton, I of course take off my hat to everything that calls itself Franchise, Parliament, Representation of the People, the Voice of the Majority, and all the rest of it," nevertheless, "as an observer of the actual condition of Egyptian society, I cannot shut my eyes to the fact that popular government, as we understand it, is for a longer time than anyone can foresee at present out of the question." Or, as Kipling, describing his vision of imperial rule, wrote approvingly of the English:

They terribly carpet the earth with dead,
    and before their cannons cool,
They walk unarmed by twos and threes,
    to call the living to school.

As this picture of massacre as a prelude to educational uplift suggests, the imperial policies of the European democracies were founded on a thoroughgoing contradiction. Claiming democracy and national independence, they denied it to the colonial peoples, who unsurprisingly resolved the contradiction in favor of independence.

In the third wave of self-determination, which occurred suddenly, as if the accumulated experience of the anti-imperial movements were now being applied in a hurry, the peoples of Eastern Europe and of the Soviet Union rose up against the Soviet empire, which, like a dynasty of old, departed the stage of history entirely.

The self-determination movement cut across all political dividing lines. No political system, feudal or modern, proved capable of resisting it. Neither monarchies (the Romanovs, the Hapsburgs, the Hohenzollerns, the Ottomans, Spain) nor liberal democracies (England, Holland, the United States) nor military dictatorships (France under Napoleon, Portugal under Salazar and Caetano) nor communist regimes (the Soviet Union; Vietnam, in its Cambodian venture) were able, in the long run, to perpetuate colonial rule. On the other hand, almost every political creed was adequate for winning independence. Liberal democracy (the United States in 1776, Eastern Europe in the 1980s and nineties), communism (China, Vietnam, Cambodia), racism (the Boers of South Africa), militarism (many South American states), theocracy (Iran and Afghanistan in the 1980s), and even monarchy (Germany in the first half of the nineteenth century), have all proved adequate foundations on which to base self-determination.

The methods of the movements were as diverse as their contents. Some resorted to military force (the United States, China, Vietnam, Algeria, to name only four); some were nonviolent (India, the nations of Eastern Europe, with the exceptions of Yugoslavia and Romania). Some arose from "below," after the pattern of the American and French revolutions, and some were led from "above," after the pattern of the foundation, under Bismarck, of modern Germany. Some won success overnight (the republics of the former Soviet Union), others so slowly that the process was almost imperceptible (Canada).

The independence of the countries of the world was not, on the whole, granted willingly but compelled. Even when independence was achieved by mutual agreement—as in India after the Second

World War—it was the result of decades of national struggle. The rulers of empires searched their tool kits of power in vain for the instruments that would bring rebellious colonial populations to heel—a lesson driven home once and for all by the failures of the United States in Vietnam and the Soviet Union in Afghanistan. The movement of resistance and reform in Eastern Europe and the Soviet Union, in the third wave, placed the power of popular resistance on even clearer display. Their victories posed in the sharpest possible form the question that the entire two-century-long movement for self-determination has put before the world: What power has enabled poorly armed or unarmed or entirely nonviolent popular movements to defeat the military forces of the most powerful empires of the past two centuries?

A Transformation of Politics

Although people's war was above all a phenomenon of the twentieth century, it first appeared in Europe during the peninsular war of 1807–14, in which the Spanish people mounted fierce resistance to Napoleonic conquest. (This is the war whose savagery is recorded in the work of Francisco Goya.) As it happens, Clausewitz devoted only one brief section of *On War* to people's war, but in those few pages he recognized the novelty and importance of the new kind of conflict. Guerrilla war per se (the Spanish rebellion gave the world this Spanish word) was not a new phenomenon. In the eighteenth century, it had been called *la petite guerre,* and before that, among other things, Parthian war, after the Parthians of antiquity, who were given to hit-and-run attacks on horseback. The unprecedented element in the early years of the nineteenth century was not guerrilla war but the sustained support given the guerrillas by the civilian population of the nation. Guerrilla bands took control of large areas of the Spanish countryside; waylaid French couriers, forcing them to travel with large armed guards; worked to deny the French supplies; harassed and attacked French troops; and spied on the French for the English. Just as important, they crippled the administration of Joseph Bonaparte by an organized refusal to pay taxes to his regime or otherwise cooperate with it. Soon, Joseph's administrators were going unpaid, his commands unfollowed. The French responded with draconian measures that would become all too familiar over the next two centuries: looting, rape, torture, burning of villages, wholesale executions and reprisals. The rebellion blazed most intensely in the city of Saragossa, where the population fought to "the last wall in the last house." "No supreme command had ordered the city to hold out; there was no supreme command. There was only the instinctive knowledge that a nation cannot keep its identity unless it is prepared to fight for it against all hope." Such was the new form of warfare that flared up in Spain—spontaneous, uncalculating, desperate, savage, unquenchable.

Clausewitz placed the new phenomenon in the wider context of the transformation of war that he was witnessing and analyzing. As examples of the "enormous contribution the heart and temper of a nation can make to the sum total of its politics, war potential, and fighting strength," he listed "the stubborn resistance of the Spaniards," which showed "what can be accomplished by arming a people"; the Russian campaign of 1812, which, by defeating Napoleon, showed that "eventual success does not always decrease in proportion to lost battles, captured capitals, and occupied provinces"; and the Prussian military recovery of 1813, which showed that a "militia can fight as well in foreign countries as at home." The recruitment of Napoleon's revolutionary armies had been Act I in the drama of the democratic revolution's influence on warfare, but now, with the Spanish guerrilla resistance to those armies, there was a second act. Clausewitz observed, "Clearly, the tremendous effects of the French Revolution abroad were caused not so much by new military methods and concepts as by radical changes in policies and administration, by the new character of government, altered conditions of the French people, and the like." He further explains:

> The military art on which the politicians relied was part of a world they thought was real—a branch of current statecraft, a familiar tool that had been in use for many years. But *that* form of war naturally shared in the errors of policy, and therefore could provide no corrective. It is true that war itself has undergone significant changes in character and methods, changes that had brought it closer to its absolute form. But these changes did not come about because the French government freed itself, so to speak, from the harness of policy; they were caused by the new political conditions which the French Revolution created.

In a word, "It follows that the transformation of the art of war resulted from the *transformation of politics.*"

There is no doubt that Clausewitz was right in seeing the French Revolution and the Spanish popular revolt as expressions of a single underlying phenomenon, the democratic revolution of his time. However, with the benefit of our century and a half of hindsight, it's clear that each was also the starting point for one of two long, diverging evolutionary transformations of war that led in different directions. The Prussian mobilization and reform, for example, aimed at raising vast armies of patriotic citizens in imitation of France, and so was a stage in the expansion of the conventional war system that led eventually to the nuclear stalemate of the Cold War. The commanders of conventional war had always wanted more men to fight with; now the "nation in arms" supplied men in unparalleled abundance. The commanders had always sought zealous, brave soldiers; now the recruits, fired by revolutionary and national enthusiasm, brought their inspiration with them.

The relationship of people's war, as practiced in Spain, to conventional war, on the other hand, was entirely different. Whereas the *levée en masse* of the patriotic citizens, like its later Prussian and other derivatives, nourished conventional war, people's war subverted it. In Spain, as in people's war of later times, the side with more men, more and better weapons, more logistical support was regularly bested by a militarily weaker opponent. Such results were completely contrary to the rules that were supposed to govern conventional war. The renowned military writer Henri Jomini, who fought in the French army in Spain, was one of the first to note the change. "No army, however disciplined," he wrote, "can contend successfully against such a system [people's war] applied by a great nation unless it be strong enough to hold all the essential points of the country, cover its communications and at the same time furnish an active force sufficient to defeat the enemy wherever he may present himself." The experience left Jomini with a feeling of awestruck horror: "The spectacle of a spontaneous uprising of a nation is rarely seen; and, though there be in it something grand and noble which commands our admiration the consequences are so terrible that, for the sake of humanity, we ought to hope never to see it." In later years, it would become a commonplace to say that to defeat guerrilla forces a conventional army needed a numerical advantage of ten to one, or even, some said, twenty to one. But how could that be? If superior force, supposedly the final arbiter, was no longer decisive, then what was? Was there, in people's war, an arbiter *beyond* the conventional final arbiter?

In an even more confusing departure from the rules governing conventional war, victory in battles over guerrilla forces did not advance victory in the war as a whole. Clausewitz had firmly stated the seemingly inarguable proposition (and several generations of German and other military leaders were to learn his advice by heart) that "All action is undertaken in the belief that if the ultimate test of arms should actually occur, the outcome would be *favorable*." Yet a French captain who accompanied Napoleon in

Russia, where his army, in addition to facing the Russian winter, was harassed by guerrilla bands, said, "Every victory is a loss to us"—a saying that the historian of guerrilla war Robert B. Asprey has called "a book of wisdom in a single sentence."

Inasmuch as neither possessing superior forces nor winning battles appeared to be the key to victory in people's war, the race to Clausewitz's "extremes"—to the massing and concentration of ever greater resources of violence characteristic of conventional war—did not take place. The Spanish guerrilla leader Mina, anticipating Mao Zedong by more than a century, said, "When the French pressure gets too hard, I retreat. . . . The French pursue me, and get tired, they leave people behind, and on these I jump." And a Prussian officer serving with the French later penned a lamentation of a kind that was on the lips of many a subsequent soldier sent to fight a guerrilla opponent. "Wherever we arrived, they disappeared," he complained, "whenever we left, they arrived—they were everywhere and nowhere, they had no tangible center which could be attacked." The pitched battle, which was the centerpiece of conventional war, was simply sidestepped in people's war. Rather than seeking to win battles, the people in arms sought mainly to endure. The superior importance in guerrilla campaigns of endurance was summed up by an American who had been in Vietnam, the foreign-service officer Norman B. Hannah, who said, "We ran out of time. This is the tragedy of Vietnam—we were fighting for time rather than space. And time ran out."

The Weapons of Civilization

The expansion of conventional war in the modern age was continuous and smooth. Once mass conscription, light artillery, or tanks were invented by one country, they were available for adoption by every country possessing the necessary technical abilities. The evolution of people's war, by contrast, was fitful. The experience and achievement of one generation often was unknown to the next. Books on people's war written in the nineteenth century went unread in the twentieth. Each imperial power, it seemed, tackled guerrilla resistance to its rule with refreshed ignorance.

During the balance of the nineteenth century, conventional war and the conventional thinking that went with it remained dominant. The center of Europe proved to be stony soil for people's war (although the French fought a rearguard partisan campaign after their defeat by Germany in 1871). By the turn of the century, the big army divisions appeared firmly in charge, and "the days of guerrilla wars seemed to be over," in the words of the historian Walter Laqueur. However, appearances misled. The twentieth century was to witness the fullest flowering of people's war. Colonial resistance to imperialism was its breeding ground.

The confrontation between the modern imperial West and the world's traditional societies presents one of the most extreme disparities in the power of civilizations that has ever existed—a disparity wider by far, for instance, than that between ancient Rome and the peoples she subjugated. When, in 1519, the Spaniard Cortés arrived in Mexico, dreaming of gold; when, in 1620, the first Puritan pilgrims landed in Massachusetts to practice their faith; when, in 1743, the Englishman Robert Clive arrived in India to make his fortune; when, in the early 1840s, English gunboats steamed up the rivers of China to enforce her acceptance of the opium trade; when, in 1853, Commodore Matthew Perry sailed an American fleet into Japanese waters to compel Japan to enter into trade and other relations with the rest of the world; when, throughout the nineteenth century, a swelling stream of merchants, adventurers, missionaries, outcasts, con men, criminals, philanthropists, soldiers, and explorers—in short, the whole gamut of imperial intruders—arrived in the villages of Africa, each of these Westerners was backed by instruments of modern power that most of the native populations were helpless to resist, or even to comprehend. (Incomprehension, at least, was mutual.)

The traditional civilizations of Asia, Africa, the Near East, and

South America were compelled, at gunpoint, to inaugurate full-scale revolutions not just in their politics but also, in most cases, in their economies, their cultures, and their social structures. In Leonard Woolf's words, "in no other period of the world's history has there been such a vast revolution as this conquest of Asia and Africa by Europe in less than 100 years." All felt compelled to Westernize, or modernize (two processes that were all but impossible to distinguish), almost every aspect of their collective lives. A generation of Chinese political reformers and intellectuals, for example, were forced to ask themselves what the sources of Western power were, and what China would have to do to create them. How much of traditional Chinese society and culture could be saved, how much should be thrown out? Could Western technical achievements be grafted onto Eastern social structures? Or were the roots of China's weakness, and of her humiliation at the hands of other powers, deeper still?

Such was the form that the implacable pressure of the adapt-or-die war system took in the colonial world. The pressure on the colonial peoples was of a piece with that felt not so long before by Prussia and Napoleon's other European victims. The difference was that whereas the latter, sharing the achievements of European civilization, were capable of catching up quite rapidly, the former, possessing civilizations largely unrelated to the European, needed more than a century to make their adjustments—if they have yet adjusted. Although the increasing power of the modern West had many roots, its cutting edge, in the East as elsewhere, was military force. Nowhere did A. J. P. Taylor's observation that for the great powers of the nineteenth century power meant the power to make war hold true more obviously than in the imperial theater, where the Great Game was played. And nowhere, in the adapt-or-die system that fastened its grip on the world at this time, was more of the dying going on than in the imperial colonies, in which nations by the dozen, and even whole peoples (for example, the native tribes in the Americas), were being propelled toward the evolutionary scrap heap designated for them in the social Darwinist theory fashionable at the time.

Although imperialism began as often as not with economic exploitation, almost all the confrontations between a traditional society and the West were resolved by a decisive test of arms, in which the power relations of the two sides were brutally clarified. For India, for example, it was the battle of Plassey of 1757; for China, the Opium Wars; for Japan, the mission of Commodore Perry. The sword of the West, honed and tempered in the fires of the modern scientific and social revolutions, sliced with terrifying ease through the Chinese "melon" (as it was called at the turn of the century), through the limbs of the Ottoman "sick man of Europe," through the grass houses of the defenseless villages of Kipling's "lower breeds without the law" in Africa and elsewhere. The story of colonial battles forms a monotonous record of one-sided slaughter, relieved only occasionally by the exceptions (the defeat of an English army by the Afghans in the early 1840s and of Italy by Ethiopia at Adowa in 1896).

The battle of Omdurman waged against the Sudanese forces of the Khalifah in 1898 by Lord Kitchener, on his way to his rendezvous with Marchand at Fashoda, can stand as a representative of all of these battles—the better for having been described firsthand by the talented young war correspondent Winston Churchill.

As Lord Kitchener's army moved up the Nile there stretched behind it those two prime symbols of power in the late nineteenth century, a new-built railroad and a telegraph wire. On the Nile, alongside Kitchener's line of march, proceeded two gunboats, transported, by way of the river, hundreds of miles into the desert. On the day of the battle, young Churchill took up a position on a hill overlooking the scene, and had lunch ("like a meal before the races"). Below him, the British forces had formed a square. Inside the square were Maxim guns; to one side a light-artillery regiment. The two gunboats on the Nile moved within range. The Khalifah's men massed behind a ridge. In midmorning, they appeared on its

crest, looking, from where Churchill stood like bushes. He describes
what happened next:

> Suddenly the whole black line . . . began to move. It was made of
> men, not bushes. Behind it other immense masses and lines of men
> appeared over the crest; and while we watched, amazed by the
> wonder of the sight, the whole face of the slope became black with
> swarming savages. Four miles from end to end, and as it seemed in
> five great divisions, the mighty army advanced swiftly. The whole
> side of the hill seemed to move. Between the masses horsemen gal-
> loped continually; before them many patrols dotted the plain;
> above them waved hundreds of banners, and the sun, glinting on
> many thousand hostile spear-points, spread a sparkling cloud.

Churchill confesses to a moment of anxiety. However, he had
confidence in "the weapons of science," which he also called "the
weapons of civilization." He knew what was waiting for the
onrushing Sudanese army: "The ranges were known. It was a matter of machinery." The weapons of civilization opened fire, and

> about twenty shells struck them in the first minute. Some burst
> high in the air, others exactly in their faces. Others, again, plunged
> into the sand and, exploding, dashed clouds of red dust, splinters,
> and bullets amid their ranks. The white banners toppled over in all
> directions.

For a moment, it seemed that the charging cavalry might reach the
English camel corps, but just in time one of the gunboats began to
fire its Maxim guns:

> The range was short; the effect tremendous. The terrible machine,
> floating gracefully on the waters—a beautiful white devil—
> wreathed itself in smoke. The river slopes of the Kerreri Hills,

crowded with the advancing thousands, sprang up into clouds of dust and splinters of rock.

And the English? Churchill describes a scene more like assembly-line production than war.

They fired steadily and stolidly, without hurry or excitement, for the enemy were far away and the officers careful. Besides, the soldiers were interested in the work and took great pains. But presently the mere physical act became tedious. The tiny figures seen over the slide of the back-sight seemed a little larger, but also fewer at each successive volley. The rifles grew hot—so hot that they had to be changed for those of the reserve companies. . . . Their empty cartridge-cases, tinkling to the ground, formed small but growing heaps beside each man. And all the time out on the plain on the other side bullets were shearing through flesh, smashing and splintering bone; blood spouted from terrible wounds; valiant men were struggling on through a hell of whistling metal, exploding shells, and spurting dust—suffering, despairing, dying.

When it was over, the tally of the dead was thirteen thousand Sudanese and forty-eight Englishmen. The youthful Churchill turned reflective. The Khalifah's military plan had been excellent, he thought. Its only flaw had been the "extraordinary miscalculation of the power of modern weapons." He rejected the thought that the Khalifah's forces were guilty of "mad fanaticism." He had been stirred by the courage of the Sudanese in the face of modern war. "For I hope," he wrote, "that if evil days should come upon our own country, and the last army which a collapsing Empire could interpose between London and the invader were dissolving in rout and ruin, that there would be some—even in these modern days—who would not care to accustom themselves to a new order of things and tamely survive the disaster." Thus did England's future prime minister, as he watched the Khalifah's army fall in the desert of Omdurman, anticipate the battle of Britain—a battle with a better result for the defenders. As he watched the British airmen in their silver planes hold the Nazis across the channel at bay, we may wonder, did he remember the sparkling cloud of the Khalifah's charge almost a half century before?

The lopsided casualty figures were typical of colonial battles. Cortés overthrew the civilization of the Aztecs with five hundred men, ten bronze cannons, and twelve muskets. In the battle of Blood River, in 1838, Boer forces slew three thousand Zulus while losing only three themselves. At the battle of Plassey, Clive, with a force of eight hundred Europeans and two thousand Indians, defeated an army of fifty thousand, with a loss of only twenty-two men. In 1865, in Tashkent, in just one of a series of such battles, a Tatar army of thirty thousand was defeated by a Russian army of two thousand. In 1897, "a Royal Niger Co. force composed of 32 Europeans and 507 African soldiers armed with cannons, Maxim guns, and Snider rifles defeated the 31,000-man army of the Nupe Emirate of Sokoto." In a "battle" that the English invader Young-husband waged against the Tibetans in 1903, six hundred Tibetans were killed without British losses, and then "The remnant simply turned and walked away with bowed heads."

People's war was a means to redress the shocking imbalance revealed by these battles, though not, it is true, the only means. In Japan, the solution was hell-bent imitation of the Western conventional model, including the highly self-conscious importation of the political and social organizations of the West. The Japanese race to adopt Western ways, which the writer Natsumei Soseki likened to an Olympics run by the insane, resulted in Japan's victory over Russia in 1905. Japan had accepted the military system whose rules had been fixed by the West, met a Western country on its own ground, and won. In India, the solution was Gandhi's satyagraha—the nonviolent path to independence from imperial rule, of which we will have more to say later. In China, in Vietnam, and in Algeria, among other places, the solution was people's war.

Politics in Command

Its first practitioners were the people of China. The Chinese revolutionary war of the 1920s through the 1940s was a war for independence (against the Japanese invaders) grafted onto a civil war (between the Communist Party and the Kuomintang government) associated with a worldwide revolutionary movement (the communist movement, presided over by the Soviet-run Comintern) fought within the overall context of a world war (the Second World War). Within this larger framework, however, the specific engine that propelled China toward communist rule was people's war. China was not as weak in relation to Japan as Sudan had been in relation to Lord Kitchener, yet battle after battle demonstrated China's inability to face Japan in conventional war. Mao Zedong, only recently confirmed as the undisputed leader of the Communist Party of China, acknowledged this humiliating fact with complete candor in June of 1938. He stated, "We are still a weak country, and, in striking contrast to the enemy, are inferior in military, economic and political-organizational power." Japan, by contrast, was "a powerful imperialist country which ranks first in military, economic and political-organizational power in the East and counts as one of the five or six outstanding imperialist countries in the world." Unable to compete on the conventional, Clausewitzian field of battle, China would, in a manner of speaking, open up a new field of battle—one on which, Mao believed, China's people themselves could appear in strength.

But how, exactly, could people's war enable a weak and backward people to defeat a modern nation-state equipped with the most technically advanced arms? What advantage did it possess? In a single chorus, the leaders of the Chinese revolution broadcast their answer to the world. It was the very word that Clausewitz had used to explain the surprising power of the Spanish guerrillas in their fight against Napoleon: "politics." Everything—tactics, strategy, recruitment, logistics, intelligence—must be subordinated to politics. Mao never tired of making the point:

> What is the relationship of guerrilla warfare to the people? Without a political goal, guerrilla warfare must fail, as it must if its political objectives do not coincide with the aspirations of the people and their sympathy, co-operation, and assistance cannot be gained.

And the most famous:

> Many people think it impossible for guerrillas to exist for long in the enemy's rear. Such a belief reveals lack of comprehension of the relationship that should exist between the people and the troops. The former may be likened to water and the latter to the fish who inhabit it. How may it be said that these two cannot exist together? It is only undisciplined troops who make the people their enemies and who, like the fish out of its native element, cannot live.

The politics in question were revolutionary politics, which meant winning the support of the population at large. Backed by the people, the communist forces could preserve the high morale of their forces, conceal themselves among the people when necessary, provision themselves in the countryside without incurring resentment, and enjoy an almost bottomless supply of fresh recruits. In the war years, China experienced a double political vacuum. In the first place, the ostensible government, the Kuomintang, had never fully succeeded in unifying the country after the fall of the Qing dynasty, in 1912. The power of the provincial warlords who had moved in to fill the political vacuum left by the dynasty's fall had never been completely broken. In the second place, by 1940 the Japanese invaders in the north of China and in selected areas in the south had pulled down such structures of central authority as existed and replaced them either with military rule or with a variety of puppet administrations. It was into this double vacuum that the Communists, who now enjoyed a secure base area among the peasants in the impoverished northwestern province of Yan'an, moved. In wide areas, and especially behind Japanese lines, "politics" therefore meant the creation from the ground up of civil administration.

In this, the Communist Party excelled. As early as the late 1920s, the Communists had governed "liberated" rural areas of China, and by the late 1930s had fully developed their techniques for educating and indoctrinating entire villages and enlisting them in a web of overlapping groups, associations, and governing units, all of which were finally answerable to the Party. The most enduring and important goal of these organizations was land reform, meaning the redistribution of land from the rich to the poor. In traditional rural China, where the gentry class had been supported largely by rents from its landholdings, the redistribution of farming land meant the destruction of one social class by another.

The Communists' guerrilla campaign against the Japanese, starting in 1937, was both an expression of the Party's political strength and a further source of it. It's no justification of Japanese atrocities, which were on a scale with those of the Nazis in Ukraine and Russia, to point out that when a whole population is enlisted in people's war, then the whole population is exposed to retaliation. The Japanese were the first—but unfortunately not the last—antiguerrilla force to whom it occurred that if the guerrillas were the fish and the people were the water, then one way to fight guerrillas was to drain the water. They engaged in a campaign of annihilation using the "Three-All Method"—"Burn all, kill all, destroy all"—in which the destruction of villages and crops and the massacre of all villagers and even animals was common procedure. It is estimated that in the region of greatest Communist strength, in north China, the population dropped in those years from an estimated forty-four million to twenty-five million. China scholars have debated whether the Communist Party's popular support was due more to their program of land reform or more to their resistance to the Japanese—whether more to revolution or more to nationalism. Whatever the answer, the salient point for the evolution of modern warfare is that in both revolution and national resistance "politics" was an essential source of military power.

The thoroughgoing politicization of war, which lent the Communists the strength that so surprised their Chinese and Japanese foes, was accompanied, however, by an equally thoroughgoing militarization of politics. For while it was true that "the better the political reform, the more enduring the War of Resistance," as Mao said, so also was it true that "the more enduring the War of Resistance, the better the political reform." While military "simpletons" had to be taught to place politics first, politicians had to learn to place war first, for "the whole party must pay attention to war, learn military science and be ready to fight." (In Mao's hands, militarized politics would soon come to mean totalitarian politics, whereby enemies were crushed, critics "reeducated," and citizens required to follow a political line determined by the government.)

It is illuminating to compare the formulas of Mao with those of Clausewitz, whose works Mao had studied. On one occasion, for example, Mao, quoting Clausewitz, said, "War is the continuation of politics; in this sense, war is politics and war itself is a political action, and there has not been a single war since ancient times that does not bear a political character." But even as he approves Clausewitz's dictum, he goes on to reverse it: "It can therefore be said that politics are bloodless war while war is the politics of bloodshed." In Clausewitz, the philosopher of conventional war, war seems to take over where politics leaves off. In Mao, the originator of full-scale people's war, war and politics are intermixed. This *fusion* of war and politics, so disturbing to the liberal conscience—torn between admiration for the political restraints placed on the communist soldiers, whose proper treatment of civilians and prisoners was legendary, and horror at the revolutionary brutalization of politics, including the lavish coercion and violence of the totalitarian regime to which people's war often gave birth—is the distinctive contribution that the Communist Party of China made to modern war.

Clausewitz and Mao

In the Western military tradition, it would have been considered absurd to introduce *political* activities onto the field of battle: whatever decisions they led to would instantly be overruled by arms. Wherever guns were doing the arguing, the last word was conceded to them. In the words of the Roman general, "Don't speak to me of laws; here the sword rules." Only when the fighting was over could the diplomats reach agreements, which, within certain limits of maneuver, would be ratifications of the new, military "facts on the ground."

In the world of Maoist thought and practice, however, it's obvious that no such priority can be given to force. For Mao, politics meant, above all, the activities and the interests, as he conceived them, of common people—and above all, as it turned out, the interests of the peasants. If anything, politics is the final arbiter, with force playing only an assisting role. All the special strengths of a people's army—its invisibility to the foe, its knowledge of enemy plans, its spirit, its indigenous sources of supply and recruitment—are likewise bound up with the local people and the local territory. It was political struggle that would enable "weak" China eventually to defeat "strong" Japan. Faced with superior political strength, superior military strength would over the long run (in "protracted war") slowly yield. Mao derided those who, as he said, proclaimed that "China's weapons are inferior and she will certainly be defeated in war." Rather, "Our view is opposite; we see not only weapons but also the power of man." In Mao's vision, political action without a military arm attached was at least thinkable, if unwise in the extreme, but military action without a political foundation was an absurdity.

However, the Chinese Communists' belief that political power was greater than military power was not unqualified. For all their hammering away at the folly of military action without political preparation, they still held on to the idea that the last stage of victory could be accomplished in a conventional battle. In the same essay in which Mao asserted the primacy of man over weapons he set forth a three-stage program for war: "mobile war," then "guerrilla war," and finally "positional"—that is, conventional—war. Mao rejected the idea that "the concept of guerrilla war is an end in itself and that guerrilla activities can be divorced from those of the regular forces."

And so it happened. Beginning in late 1948, the Communists, having mobilized more than two million peasants into their armies, embarked on a series of conventional campaigns against the Kuomintang (now backed by American money and arms), which carried them to victory, in 1949. Even in these final, conventional battles of the Chinese civil war, however, the dividends of political activity poured in, in the form of abundant support from the countryside and vast desertions by disillusioned Kuomintang soldiers. By the last months, it was hard to say which was occurring faster, the collapse of the government or the advance of the rebels.

The Forest of Political Defeat

The new relationship between political power and military power that had emerged in people's war was displayed to even more startling effect in the war in Vietnam. The world was slow to absorb the military lessons of people's war in China—just as, in the nineteenth century, it had been slow to absorb the lessons of people's war in Spain. The Second World War had been the greatest conventional war of all time, and guerrilla fighting—whether in China, Yugoslavia, Russia, or elsewhere—had been of secondary importance. When the Japanese occupation of China was cut short by the atomic bomb—an unparalleled display of brute firepower—it seemed clearer than ever that Churchill's "weapons of science," not Mao's irregular peasant armies, were to dominate military affairs.

There was in any case little inclination to reflect on the phenomenon of people's war. The defeated Japanese, living under American occupation, were scarcely in a position to launch a "Who lost China?" debate, which might have illuminated the nature of the Communist victory. That privilege was reserved for the United States, which had supported the Kuomintang until its defeat in 1949. But even then American officialdom, instead of studying the reasons for the Communist success, responded by hounding out of the foreign service as Communist sympathizers the few American firsthand observers who had made such a study. It was an act of willful blindness that, as many historians have noted, prepared the way for the American debacle in Vietnam. In retrospect, we can see, this self-inflicted wound, which occurred in the early 1950s, was part of a deeper policy mistake. Just at the moment when people's war was about to become the principle instrument of political change in the Third World, the United States turned its attention toward the sterile, changeless field of nuclear strategy, where the policy of "massive retaliation" became the order of the day.

It was in Vietnam—the hottest as well as the longest of the Cold War's limited wars—that the West's post–Second World War education in people's war got under way in earnest. After the Japanese were forced out of Vietnam, the French proceeded, with American help, to restore control over their former colony. The United States, which regarded the anticolonial struggle of the Vietnamese as the leading edge of "world communism," soon began to provide the French with supplies. Among all the Western powers, the French had had the most experience with people's war. Although Napoleon's experience in Spain was mostly forgotten, France had faced sporadic anticolonial opposition not only in Vietnam before the war but in its northern African colonies of Tunisia, Morocco, and, above all, Algeria.

The Vietnamese leaders, too, were veterans of people's war, having been steeped in Chinese revolutionary politics for two decades. Ho Chi Minh had lived in China in the twenties and thirties, and had even spent time in prison there. Many of the strategies the Vietnamese were to use against the French had already been battle-tested in China. They included concentration on the rural village as the essential unit of political organization; the foundation of multiple associations (the Peasant Association, the Women's Association, the Youth Association, and so forth) that drew everyone in the village into a tight network of participation and control; the fusion of communist revolution and nationalism; the targeted use of terror against the functionaries of the government; the appeal to popular sentiment together with the suppression of individual thought and opinion; a determined application of land reform; and, most important, an insistence, from start to finish, on the subordination of military action to political goals. The following quotations are a few among a superabundance that express this subordination. (In the first, the ritual bow to Clausewitz is worth noting.)

> Politics forms the actual strength of the revolution: politics is the root and war is the continuation of politics.—*Resolution of the Central Committee of the National Liberation Front.*

> Our political struggle is the manifestation of our absolute political superiority and of the enemy's basic weakness.—*Captured N.L.F. document, 1963.*

Douglas Pike, who served as an official of the U.S. Information Agency in Vietnam, agreed that the key to the N.L.F.'s strength was its political organization. In his book *Viet Cong*, which was written while the war was still in progress, he wrote:

> The purpose of this vast organizational effort was not simply population control but to restructure the social order of the village and train the villagers to control themselves. This was the N.L.F.'s one undeviating thrust from the start. Not the killing of A.R.V.N.'s [Army of the Republic of Vietnam's] soldiers, not the occupation of real estate, not the preparation for some great pitched battle at an Armageddon or a Dien Bien Phu but organization in depth of the rural population through the instrument of self-control—victory by means of the organizational weapon. The Communists in Vietnam developed a sociopolitical technique and carried it to heights beyond anything yet demonstrated by the West working with developing nations. The National Liberation Front was a Sputnik in the political sphere of the Cold War.

But it was French observers—among them the writers Jean Lacouture and Bernard Fall—who, among Westerners, were the first to come fully to terms with the nature and significance of people's war as it was being waged by the Vietnamese. Fall—an eyewitness to both the French and the American phases of the war—was in a position to compare the two. In *The Two Vietnams*, published in 1967, he stated boldly that North Vietnam's victory over the French lay "in the effective control of much of the countryside—*despite its occupation by a large Western army*—through the establishment of small but efficient administration units that duplicated the existing Franco-Vietnamese administration." This, of course, was precisely what the Chinese Communists had done behind Japanese lines in the 1940s. Fall called these Vietnamese administrative units *"hiérarchies parallèles,"* and said that it was they rather than "the existence of guerrilla battalions" that were "the source of France's defeat." So important was the point that Fall, a political writer immune to pseudoscience, went as far as to distill the essence of what he had learned into a formula. It was

$$RW = G + P$$

where RW is revolutionary war, G is guerrilla warfare, and P is political action. This formula called for violence, he noted, yet "the 'kill' aspect, the military aspect, definitely always remained the minor aspect: the political, administrative, ideological aspect is the primary aspect."

Of particular interest are Fall's applications of the lessons he learned in Vietnam to France's war in Algeria, where the Front de Libération Nationale had launched a guerrilla campaign to free its country from French colonial domination. The war had begun to heat up just as the French war in Vietnam was ending, in 1954. In the next several years, Fall noted, the French generals, by now steeped in the tactics of Mao Zedong that they had ignored in Vietnam, actually succeeded, to all intents and purposes, in militarily defeating the Algerian F.L.N., which, by 1958, had been reduced to a fraction of its former strength. Nevertheless, when Charles de Gaulle, the former leader of the Free French Force in the Second World War, returned to power as the president of the Republic, he understood that the native population of Algeria remained united in opposition to the French, and that as long as this remained the case French rule would be untenable. Fall comments pithily, "This is where the word 'grandeur' applies to President de Gaulle. He was capable of seeing through the trees of military victory to a forest of political defeat, and he chose to settle the Algerian insurgency by other means." Fall did not say so, but the Algerian story suggested a revision of his formula, for if revolutionary war could triumph even after the defeat of guerrilla operations, then political action alone might sometimes be enough for victory, and we would obtain

RW = P

in which force was missing altogether from the equation of revolution.

Notwithstanding the importance of revolutionary politics, the fall of the French in Vietnam, like the fall of the Kuomintang in China, came in a conventional engagement, the battle of Dien Bien Phu, in 1954, in which superior Vietnamese forces surrounded and decisively defeated the French. Once again, the underlying realities, though not themselves military in character, were given final expression in a set-piece battle, in accord with Mao's three-stage program. At the Geneva conference in 1954, the northern half of Vietnam was ceded to the revolutionary Viet Minh, and South Vietnam, destined soon to become a dependency of the United States, embarked on its brief, doomed existence.

A comment made by de Gaulle after he agreed to give Algeria its independence sheds further light on the contradictions explored by his countryman Fall. De Gaulle remarked that France could have prevailed in Algeria if she had been "a mastodon," and added that "only Russia, with its communist methods," could have won such a struggle. In fact, just two years earlier, in 1956, the Soviet Union had suppressed an uprising against it in Hungary. France, it seemed at the time, had suffered a failure, while the Soviet Union had enjoyed a success. However, de Gaulle's use of the word "mastodon," an extinct animal, proved accurate. He appears to have understood that the Soviet Union's reliance on terror as the method of rule, although a seeming strength, might be a fatal weakness in the end.

His comment is one of the few on record in that era hinting that the Soviet empire might collapse. But before that could happen, the United States intervened in Vietnam.

The Wills of Two Peoples

Much of the American experience on the ground in Vietnam consisted of bloodily learning the lessons that the French had already bloodily learned. Above all, the United States had to discover that the crucial war in Vietnam was not military but political. The immense American military buildup—a half million men at its peak, backed by a naval armada and the most powerful air force ever assembled for a single campaign—could not remedy the political failure but only mask it. In the words of Marine General Victor (Brute) Krulak, the big-unit battles with the National Liberation Front and the North Vietnamese "could move to another planet today, and we would still not have won the war," because "the Vietnamese people are the prize."

But if on the Vietnamese side the war remained the struggle for independence it had always been, the American war was quite different from the French. The United States saw it as just one of many theaters in its global struggle against communism—in the war that had to remain cold because hot war might mean the end of the world. As such, the Vietnam War for the first time brought face-to-face the two new kinds of power that stood at the end of the long, double transformation of war we have described. On the one side was the military power of the nuclear-armed—and nuclear-paralyzed—"superpower," seeking to create and maintain the elusive appearance of deliverable might summed up in the word "credibility." On the other side was the political power of a small nation waging a people's war.

In the broader picture of American strategic policy, the conceptual slot that Vietnam occupied was limited war, as distinct from "general war," which meant unfightable nuclear war. Limited war—as long as it did not get out of control, sending the antagonists back to the brink of nuclear war—*could* be fought, and in Vietnam it was. Limited war was thus the product of two, opposing strategic pressures. The first was the need to confine fighting to the nonnuclear level—meaning, probably, the "periphery." (On several occasions during the Vietnam War, military advisers to the president considered and recommended the use of nuclear weapons or the adoption of policies, such as attacking North Vietnam, that might have drawn Chinese troops into the war, and so precipitate nuclear war; but repeatedly the presidents, fearful of general war, refused.) The second, contrary pressure was the will to actively resist the communist foe—more particularly, to answer the challenge thrown down by Nikita Khrushchev when, in a speech in 1961, seeking to offset his nuclear weakness, he had vowed to support "wars of national liberation." In affirming this policy, which conformed to the long-standing Soviet opposition to Western colonialism, Khrushchev was aligning himself with one of the most durable and powerful movements of the twentieth century—the self-determination movement.

It was the misfortune of the United States that, by misnaming the national movements for independence in Vietnam and elsewhere as the advance guard of "world communism," it placed itself on the losing side of these struggles, and so, in Vietnam as elsewhere, found itself on the defensive. On the campaign trail in 1960, Kennedy had already identified Third World revolutions as Soviet emanations. "Their missile power," he had said of the Soviets, "will be the shield from behind which they will slowly but surely advance—through Sputnik diplomacy, limited brush-fire wars, indirect non-overt aggression, intimidation and subversion, internal revolution, increased prestige or influence, and the vicious blackmail of our allies. The periphery of the Free World will slowly be nibbled away. . . . Each such Soviet move will weaken the West; but none will seem sufficiently significant by itself to justify our initiating a nuclear war which might destroy us." On other occasions, invoking the two-century-old fear of global domination by a single power, he called this unconventional conflict a "twilight struggle"—blazing, high-noon war being inadvisable. (In an age when total war was ruled out, fear of indirect techniques, such as "subversion" and spying, became obsessive on both sides.)

The pressures that collided in America's Vietnam policy were more complex still. Although limited war had been conceived as an escape from the paralysis of nuclear deterrence, the Vietnam War in fact became tangled in it. In Vietnam, it turned out that limited war, just because it was supposed to be a surrogate for the unfightable all-out nuclear war at the center, became charged with an apocalyptic importance that it otherwise would have lacked. For if "indirect" fighting on the periphery was the only kind possible, then the country that mastered it might gradually win the Cold War, as the domino theory predicted. And if that were so, Vietnam was not a refuge from the Third World War, it *was* the Third World War.

Thus did Vietnam, a real war, acquire a symbolic importance in the war of appearances that now dominated nuclear strategy. In this thinking, collapse in Vietnam could lead to nuclear war, or to the collapse of the United States, or both—for all of this supposedly stood at the end point of a long row of collapsing dominos that would leave the United States at bay in a hostile, communized world. It would lead to "our ruin and almost certainly to a catastrophic war," in the words of Secretary of State Dean Rusk in June of 1965.

The consequence was that although the superpowers had gone to the periphery of their global struggle in order to liberate themselves from the futility of nuclear paralysis, they ended up importing that futility into the peripheral situations, to the high cost and sorrow of the resident peoples. In retrospect, it's easy to see that the two blocs were superimposing their struggle onto anticolonial struggles. The outcomes were sharp comeuppances for all concerned. The United States was not only defeated in Vietnam but suffered grievous domestic political harm. Yet it was the Soviets who were to experience the most bitterly ironic consequences. No doubt genuinely believing that they were supporting "international communism" in Vietnam (an illusion both superpowers shared), they were in fact supporting the final stages of a revolt against colonial rule. It apparently never occurred to the Soviet leaders that, in a world of triumphant national liberation, their own empire and union, which held half a dozen Eastern European nations in forcible subjection, and was itself composed of more than a dozen distinct major nationalities, might be a target for insurrection. They apparently thought they were to be the exception to the verdict history had rendered on all other empires of the modern age. They were wrong.

The differences between the geopolitical roles and strategies of France, a fading colonial power, and the United States, a global superpower, were reflected in the way each country fought its war in Vietnam. The most obvious difference was the incomparably greater firepower at the disposal of the United States. Vietnam was a limited war only in the sense that certain expansions of the war (for example, a ground invasion of North Vietnam) were ruled out. Within South Vietnam, the American military effort was unconstrained. By the end of 1966, the United States was pouring more explosive power day by day into that small territory than all the allies together had been using against Germany and Japan at the height of the Second World War. The B-52, an intercontinental bomber designed for a nuclear war with the Soviet Union, was retooled to drop a mile-long path of conventional bombs. Herbicides defoliated thousands of square miles of the country. Other large, populated areas were designated "free-fire zones," in which anything that moved was considered a target.

The immensity of the American military machine confronted the Vietnamese revolutionaries with a strategic problem that the French had never posed. In 1954, the French were defeated at Dien Bien Phu in a classic conventional siege and battle, but there was no hope of defeating American forces by these means. How—to give just one example—were the Vietnamese, who had no planes in the air in South Vietnam, even to touch the B-52s whose flights originated thousands of miles away, on the Pacific island of Guam, and loosed their payloads from an altitude of thirty thousand feet? No amount of political organizing in the Mekong Delta could have the slightest effect on these raids. In reserving the final act of people's war for a conventional victory on the battlefield, Mao, for all his insistence on the supremacy of political over military struggle, had kept one foot in the Clausewitzian world of conventional war, and Vo Nguyen Giap had done the same in his war against the French. Now Mao's blueprint for a three-stage war, culminating in a conventional victory, had to be thrown out. For the first time, the Vietnamese faced the question of how to eject a foreign power without a conventional finale.

The United States, on the other hand, was still unable even to begin to win the political victory without which all its battlefield successes were valueless. By about 1967, the war had reached a perfectly asymmetrical stalemate, from which no Dien Bien Phu could release the antagonists. Each side was supreme in its own sphere of activity—the Vietnamese communists in the sphere of politics, the United States in the sphere of force. Once the United States had committed ground troops in the hundreds of thousands, there was no chance that the Vietnamese could beat the Americans militarily. On the other hand, there was equally little possibility that the Americans and their client Vietnamese, who had all but destroyed the country they were supposedly saving, could win the political allegiance of the Vietnamese people. The two sides, each victorious in a different struggle, lacked, it appeared, any common playing field on which the match could be decided. Political victories won by the N.L.F. and the North Vietnamese in villages, which then were wiped off the face of the earth by American bombing, were as worthless as American military successes won without political support from Vietnamese villagers. In the meantime, everyone involved—the American soldiers, the South Vietnamese soldiers, the N.L.F., the North

Vietnamese Army, and, above all, the civilian population of Vietnam—was being killed in growing numbers.

The force that broke the stalemate came from without. It was a change of heart by yet another player in the game, the American public. The event that precipitated the change was the Tet offensive, in February of 1968. The Vietnamese revolutionaries, faced with unbeatable American military superiority, modified Mao's three-stage plan, with its conventional finale, and came up with a new idea—the general uprising. At Tet they sought to put it into practice. The concept was bold and original. The immediate target would be not United States forces but the South Vietnamese government. Military attacks at all points of the country would sweep aside this weak reed. Simultaneously, a general uprising among the urban population would demand the establishment of a new government. The Americans, though still undefeated militarily, would be left in a sea of visibly hostile Vietnamese, and would be forced to withdraw.

Measured by its own goals, the offensive failed disastrously. The military attacks did not spark a general uprising among the urban population, which remained, for the most part, passive. For once, the N.L.F. had made a huge political miscalculation. The South Vietnamese government did not fall, nor did its members defect to the N.L.F. Finally, in the absence of the uprising, the military attacks, although well coordinated and daring, were driven back by American forces, with high losses for the N.L.F. (In the process, the imperial capital of Hue was almost leveled, and parts of Saigon were bombed.) The attacks did not even pay political dividends in the Vietnamese countryside. A number of writers have shown that the N.L.F., badly weakened, lost organizational ground there.

And yet the offensive did bring the long American withdrawal, leading to the eventual victory of the Vietnamese. How, we need to ask, did this unequivocal battlefield defeat win a war? In the old Clausewitzian dispensation, in which force was the final arbiter, defeats in battles were the path to losing a war. But those rules were no longer in effect. In the new world of politically committed and active peoples, it was not force per se but the collective wills of those peoples that were decisive. And, in such a context, even a battlefield defeat could be a decisive victory for the losing side. So it was at Tet. When Richard Nixon was preparing to take office as president in 1968, he asked Rusk, "Where was the war lost?" Rusk answered, "In the editorial rooms of this country."

In March of 1968, President Johnson ducked defeat in the Democratic primaries by resigning his candidacy, stopping the bombing of North Vietnam, and opening peace talks. The Tet offensive had knocked an American president out of office. The war was to continue under Presidents Nixon and Ford for another seven years, yet the decision had been made. After Tet, in the regretful words of Henry Kissinger, Nixon's national security adviser and then secretary of state, "no matter how effective our actions, the prevalent strategy could no longer achieve its objectives within a period or with force levels politically acceptable to the American people." In 1958, President de Gaulle had seen through the trees of military victory to the forest of political defeat in Algeria, and had granted the country its independence. In the United States in 1968, it was not the head of state but the public at large that came to the same conclusion with regard to Vietnam.

However accidentally, the Vietnamese communists had added a new chapter to the annals of people's war: a war that is won not because the enemy is defeated in a conventional showdown but because the people on the other side, made to understand at last that the cause is ill-conceived and hopeless, *decides* to abandon the effort. Though relying on arms, such an outcome cannot be called a decision by arms. Mao had an inkling that political opinion in the country of the invading army might be decisive in people's war, and in 1938 predicted that revolution in Japan would eventually put an end to its invasion of China—a hope that, of course, was unrealized. It wasn't until the invader was a constitutional democracy that dissension on the home front could prove decisive. The United States lacked a de Gaulle, possessed of sufficient "grandeur" (a word impossible to apply to Richard Nixon), to write a quick finish to the tragedy, and the war staggered on to its humiliating conclusion; but the shift in opinion against the war was never reversed. Military force had played an important role on both sides, but in the last analysis it was the political will of the two peoples involved that was the *final* arbiter of the Vietnam War.

Beyond the Final Arbiter

In many respects, nuclear deterrence and people's war, each appearing at the end of the twofold metamorphosis of war that we have been tracing, were at opposite poles. One was a fruit of the scientific revolution, and depended on new technical instruments of unlimited destructive power; the other was mainly a fruit of the democratic revolution, and depended on the aroused will of peoples. One was a strategy of the powerful, the other a strategy of the wretched of the earth. One was geopolitical in scope, the other local. Yet in some respects the two strategies were interestingly akin. In both, a certain dematerialization of power occurred. In deterrence, it was the decline of actual war-fighting in favor of creating fearful appearances—credibility—that became the coin of military might in the nuclear age. In people's war, it was the eclipse of the power that flowed "from the barrel of a gun" by the political power that flowed from the hearts and minds of the people. In both shifts, violence became not so much an instrument for producing physical effects as a kind of bloody system of communication, through which the antagonists delivered messages to one another about will. In both, the intangible effect upon hearts and minds was paramount, and the tangible effect upon the opposing military forces was secondary. In both, we seem to see the human will detaching itself from physical fighting, as if getting ready to make a break and turn to other means, though without doing so.

In both, the capacity of force to decide political issues is thrown into doubt. In both, in short, the old final arbiter has lost its finality, and some new arbiter seems to be acting in the background. It is because of these developments, somehow occurring simultaneously at the apex and the base of the world's system of military power in the middle decades of the twentieth century, that it is more than a paradoxical phrase to speak of a kind of nonviolence, or at least a turn away from violence, that was occurring *within* war in this period.

The similarities between deterrence and people's war should not, however, unduly surprise us. Both were responses to the same broad, underlying historical development—the steady increase throughout the modern age of the violence at the disposal of military forces. Through people's war, non-Western peoples found a way to defend themselves against the awesome technical superiority of the superpowers. Through the strategy of nuclear deterrence, those superpowers themselves, finding that their weapons had become too destructive to be used against one another, tried as best they could to accomplish the old purposes with mere threats. The twentieth century had produced the most extreme violence that the human species had ever visited upon itself. It was natural—indeed, it was a necessity—that, in different ways, people would react against it, would seek ways to overcome it, to escape it, to go around it, to replace it. In earlier times, violence had been seen as the last resort when all else had failed. "Hallowed are those arms where no hope exists but in them," Livy had written. But in the twentieth century, a new problem forced itself on the human mind: What was the resort when that "last resort" had bankrupted itself? Nuclear deterrence and people's war were two groping, improvised, incomplete attempts to find answers to this question.

It is also true—to state what is perhaps more obvious—that nuclear deterrence and people's war marked two extremes of physical violence, two apogees of total war. Deterrence promised peace only at the price of threatening the world with annihilation.

People's war sought to assert the people's interests, but only by turning every section of the population, including women and children, into fighters and victims. Both strategies simultaneously evoke admiration and horror. Even as we are pleased with the peace that deterrence takes as its goal, we are revolted by the unlimited slaughter it menaces. Even as we are awed by the epic of human courage that people's war presents and the nobility of its goal of serving the interests of the least fortunate, we are disgusted by its frequent use of terror and by the totalitarian governments, with their various gulags and "reeducation camps," to which it has often given birth. Deterrence is only a stay of execution, not a reprieve. People's war immerses the people in the violence from which it seeks to deliver them. And yet, I suggest, in reaching each of these ambiguous extremes, we can, for the first time, catch a glimpse of a true rejection of the twentieth century's terrible legacy of violence, as when climbers, upon reaching a mountain-top, and able to climb no higher, first see the new land beyond, and turn their steps down the other side.

PART TWO

Nonviolence

4

Satyagraha

For most of history, military victory has been the royal road to political rule over a rival country, a sequence crystallized in the single word "conquest." The reason was no mystery. If, as Clausewitz said, an enemy was defeated only when he was ready to "do our will," then obviously military victory made rule possible by turning bold, angry enemies into frightened, obedient subjects. It was the genius of the inventors of people's war to challenge this deceptively self-evident proposition by discovering, in the very midst of battle, the power of politics. What if, the inventors of people's war asked, the people on the losing side declined to do the will of the conqueror and, taking a further step, organized itself politically to conduct its own business? In people's war, political organization did not stand on its own; it was interwoven with the military struggle into Mao's seamless fabric. Yet Mao and others placed politics first in the order of importance and military action only second, and this ranking at least suggested the question of whether, if the fabric were unraveled, political action alone might thwart an occupying power. Did revolutions have to be violent? Could nonviolent revolution—that is, *purely* nonviolent revolution—succeed?

The main schools of Western political theory in the modern age answered the question, with one voice, in the negative. Most thinkers, whether left, right, or center, agreed that revolution was in its nature violent. They believed, with Max Weber, that "politics operates with very special means, namely power backed up by *violence.*" For many, the resort to violence was the defining feature of the revolutionary act. Liberals no less than conservatives took it for granted that, as John Locke said, when the government uses "force without right upon a man's person," and "the remedy is denied by a manifest perverting of justice and a barefaced wresting of the laws to protect or indemnify the violence of injuries of some men," then people "are left to the only remedy in such cases—the appeal to heaven"—that is, to arms. For "in all states and conditions, the true remedy of force without authority is to oppose force to it." The upholders of absolutist monarchy had denied a right to revolt even in that case, but they certainly agreed that revolution was in its nature a bloody affair. Revolution, in the words of the eighteenth-century conservative parliamentarian and writer Edmund Burke, "becomes a case of war, and not of constitution. Laws are commanded to hold their tongues amongst arms; and tribunals fall to the ground with the peace they are no longer able to uphold."

The left-wing revolutionaries of the nineteenth and twentieth centuries more than agreed with the liberal contractarian thinkers who preceded them. "*Aux armes, citoyens!*" was the cry of the left from the time of the French Revolution down to the day of Mao and Ho. At the beginning of the nineteenth century, Napoleon, in exile on St. Helena, laid down the law in the following dictum: "General rule: No social revolution without terror. Every revolution is, by its nature, a revolt which success and the passage of time legitimize but in which terror is one of the inevitable phases." Karl Marx's famous formulation was "Violence is the midwife of every old society pregnant with a new one." (We must add that he didn't regard violence as the essence of revolution, which in his view was prepared above all by economic developments.) The leader of the Russian revolution of 1917, Vladimir Ilyich Lenin, asserted that "Not a single question pertaining to the class struggle has ever been settled except by violence." In a still broader generalization, he said, "Great problems in the life of nations are decided only by force."

Voices disagreeing with this wide consensus—the voices of a smattering of anarchists, some moderate Marxists and other socialists, and a few writers, including, above all, the Russian novelist and pacifist Leo Tolstoy—were rarely taken seriously by those who were in power, or even thinking about power. Lenin sneered at Tolstoy's "imbecile preaching about not resisting evil with force." And Max Weber, having declared that "the decisive means for politics is violence," added that "anyone who fails to see this is a political infant." It's hardly necessary to add to this list such right-wing enthusiasts of violence as Joseph de Maistre, who proclaimed, "All greatness, all power, all subordination rest on the executioner. He is the terror and the bond of human association." And when the right, turning revolutionary, produced fascism, it not only justified violence but reveled in it.

This consensus survived all but unshaken until recently, and undoubtedly played a role in the nearly universal failure to predict the downfall of the Soviet Union. The Soviet regime's monopoly on all the instruments of force seemed to render it invulnerable. If revolution had to be violent in order to succeed, then it seemed to have no chance against such a regime, which would thus have been well justified in its expectation (shared by so many of its awed detractors) that it would last, in effect, forever. The conviction that force was always the final arbiter was not in truth so much an intellectual conclusion as a tacit assumption on all sides—the product not of a question asked and answered but of one unasked. Only in the aftermath of the Soviet collapse have people been ready, perhaps, to open their minds to the idea that some power other than force can prevail in revolution and war. That was the utterly unexpected accomplishment of activists in Eastern Europe and the Soviet Union; but the man who first put the question fully to the historical test was Mohandas Karamchand Gandhi.

A Question of Life and Death

The inventors of people's war rewrote the rules governing the connection of politics to war. Gandhi, whose campaign to end Britsh rule in India was contemporaneous with Mao's revolution, was an even more radical tamperer with the relationships among basic human activities. He was a tireless workman in the shop in which new forms of human action and living are forged. He entered public life as the defender of a small, immigrant minority in a dusty corner of a global empire, but before he was done he had led a movement that, more than any other force, dissolved that empire, and in the process had proposed a way of life in which the constituent activities of existence—the personal, the economic, the social, the political, the spiritual—were brought into a new relationship.

Most important in our context was his fusion of politics and religion. Gandhi believed that to drive the gun out of politics he had to invite God in. It was an operation that, in his day of mostly secular politics, raised an array of new questions and problems even as it offered new solutions to old ones. But in order to better understand Gandhi's vision, in all its originality, strangeness, and greatness, we must first place it in its historical context.

As a youth, Gandhi, who was born in 1869 in the Indian city of Porbandar, on the Indian Ocean, exhibited no extraordinary talents of the testable kind. He takes his place on the long list of remarkable people who performed indifferently at school. His biographer Judith M. Brown titles her chapter on his young manhood "An Indian Nonentity." Sent by his family from India to London to study the law, he continued not to shine. He couldn't learn to dance; he couldn't master the violin; he failed his bar examinations on the first try, succeeding only on the second. Back in India, he couldn't get a law practice going. When he was finally given a case, in Bombay, he was struck dumb with shyness in the cross-examination and felt obliged to refund his client's fee. Proper employment did not come until 1893, when he accepted an invitation to handle a legal case for an Indian merchant in South Africa. In the new land, however, the mediocre student and failed barrister promptly demonstrated that he possessed at least one human quality to a superlative degree, and that was the capacity and the will to translate his beliefs into action.

Everyone forms opinions and beliefs, but most act on them only up to a certain point, beyond which fears, desires, doubts, prudence, laziness, and distractions of all kinds take over. Gandhi, as it turned out in South Africa, belonged to the small class of people, many of them religious or political zealots, who are able to act according to their beliefs almost without condition or reservation. On several occasions, he would read some advice in a book, or arrive at some new idea on his own, and put it into practice the next day. On a train from Durban to Pretoria, a white man had him thrown out of the first-class compartment for which he had paid, and when he protested the conductor dumped him onto the station platform. "I should try if possible," as he later wrote, "to root out the disease [of color prejudice in South Africa] and suffer hardships in the process." It was a decision, as things turned out, that would guide his actions for the next twenty-one years.

In 1894, having completed the legal business for which he had come, he had decided to leave South Africa, and a farewell dinner was held in his honor. That day, he had noticed an article in the *Natal Mercury* reporting that the British colony of Natal was about to pass a bill to disenfranchise Indians. His colleagues at dinner implored him to stay to fight the ordinance, and on the spur of the moment he decided he would. A decade later, he read

John Ruskin's *Unto This Last* during a twenty-four-hour train ride from Johannesburg to Durban. The book recommended a life of austerity, material simplicity, and self-control. "I arose with the dawn," he wrote later, "ready to reduce these principles to practice." The result was Phoenix Farm, the first of several experimental communities he was to found.

The political and racial issues in South Africa that Gandhi had committed himself to solving were many-layered. South African society was arranged in a four-tier, multinational, multiracial hierarchy. At the bottom was the completely unenfranchised and virtually rightless native black majority, outnumbering everyone else put together by about four to one. Next in the scale were Indians, who, by the turn of the century, were slightly more numerous than whites. Next were the local dominant whites, divided among Boers, who were the descendants of Dutch settlers, an English population, and a scattering of others. (In 1897 in Natal there were about four hundred thousand blacks, forty thousand Indians, and forty thousand whites.) At the top were the British imperial masters, trying to exercise ultimate control from London. In this hierarchy, the British, who would wage the Boer War at the turn of the century to prevent the Boers from seceding from the empire, were logical allies for the Indians, who suffered oppression at the hands of the local whites. South Africa was one of those complicated imperial situations in which a passion for self-rule by one group (the Boers, who by and large were more thoroughly racist than the British) meant even more severe repression for other groups.

Conflict arose when the Indians, imported to South Africa in the late nineteenth century under a system of indenture solely to serve as easily managed labor, began to acquire the aspirations of a normal human community: they began to buy and sell goods, to acquire land and farm it, to trade, to practice their religions, even to enter onto the fringes of political life. The local whites, Boer and English, were resentful and afraid of this new competition. Indian farming, they thought, would bring down the prices of agricultural goods by adding to the supply of food; Indian traders would take business from whites; Indian entry into politics would threaten white supremacy (though the modest Indians were far from having any such ambition).

Seized by a terror, which had no basis in fact, that millions of Indians would inundate South Africa, destroying the foundations of white rule, the whites took steps to suppress all the new signs of vigor and life in the Indian community. They passed bills that disenfranchised the few Indians who could vote; imposed exorbitant taxes on free Indians, to force them to re-indenture themselves; hampered and destroyed Indian traders by entangling them in a rigmarole of licensing and other restrictions; limited the areas in which freed Indians could live; restricted their travel; forbade them to use public facilities, including sidewalks; and even passed legislation to make non-Christian marriages illegal. In the background was the implicit threat that the Indian community would be driven out of South Africa altogether. "I clearly saw that this was a question of life and death for them," Gandhi wrote of his fellow Indians.

Lover of the British Empire

In theory, the ideals of the British Empire were liberal. In 1858, Queen Victoria had issued a proclamation declaring her wish that "our subjects, of whatever race or creed, be freely and impartially admitted to offices in our service." It was therefore not only to the local government but to London that the Indians of South Africa sent their numerous petitions and delegations for redress. A nascent black movement followed a similar strategy.

In 1903, we find the following characteristic peal of praise from Gandhi for the British Empire:

The Empire has been built up as it is on a foundation of justice and equity. It has earned a worldwide reputation for its anxiety and ability to protect the weak against the strong. It is the acts of peace and mercy, rather than those of war, that have made it what it is.

In 1905, on Empire Day, he is still eulogizing Queen Victoria:

> By her large heart and wide sympathy; by her abilities and queenly virtues; above all, by her personal goodness as a woman, she has forever enshrined herself in the hearts of every nation under the British flag.

At times, he seems a more eager imperialist than the British. On the eve of the Boer War, which aroused broad protest among liberals in England and was not popular with all South African Indians, either, Gandhi wrote to an English friend, "We are all fired with one spirit, viz., the imperial." Gandhi had made a decision to support the empire on the ground that although "justice is on the side of the Boers," the Indians, as citizens seeking to enjoy the rights promised by the empire, should "accord their support to acts of state." His enthusiasm was more for what he hoped the empire might become than for what he currently found it to be. His strategy was to shame the imperialists into living up to their professed ideals. He backed up his words by organizing an ambulance corps of Indians to support the British army in the war. In 1906, when war broke out with the Zulus, he repeated the performance.

Somehow coexisting with this enthusiasm for the British Empire, however, was a growing dislike for modern, technological civilization, of which England was obviously the chief global representative and disseminator. He called the "wonderful discoveries and the marvelous inventions of science, good as they undoubtedly are in themselves," an "empty boast," as they did nothing to advance the spiritual life. He denounced "the invention of the most terrible weapons of destruction, the awful growth of anarchism," and the "frightful disputes between capital and labor." His enthusiasm for the British Empire and his mounting dislike of the modern civilization that it embodied were obviously headed for a collision, and it was not long in coming.

Like many other Asian reformers of the late nineteenth and early twentieth centuries, Gandhi had begun by distinguishing between a strong, materialist West and a weak but spiritual East. He recognized that England's power did not depend on technology alone. It depended also, he firmly believed, on the individual courage, martial and civic, of its people. As a national characteristic, that courage was, he thought, a product in part of England's gradual democratic revolution. In 1906, we find him paying tribute to the sacrifices of heroes of England's struggle for religious toleration, parliamentary supremacy, and the rule of law. "The English honor only those who make such sacrifice," he wrote in *Indian Opinion*, a newspaper he founded and ran. "Their shining glory has spread just because great heroes have been and are still among them. Such were Wat Tyler, John Hampden, John Bunyan and others. They laid the foundations of England's supremacy. We shall continue to be in our abject condition till we follow their example." Cultivating a spirit of civic responsibility and courage was a kind of Westernization of which Gandhi approved.

Gandhi's list of English people to admire is pointedly selective. Missing are such names as Isaac Newton, founder of classical physics; James Watt, inventor of the steam engine; Richard Arkwright, inventor of the power-driven loom; the Duke of Wellington, who defeated Napoleon at Waterloo; or any of the other creators of nineteenth-century England's scientific, industrial, and military dominance. Gandhi wanted only one of the two great modern revolutions. He wanted democracy but not science. It's well known that Gandhi, champion of the spinning wheel, rejected Western technological civilization, but less often appreciated is that, even as a young man, he ardently admired the habits of civic virtue that he believed he saw in the West and associated with the democratic revolution. Those virtues were, in fact, more than anything else the foundation of his program and of his hopes for

South Africa and then India. Like the ancient Greeks, he regarded courage as the most important virtue, because it was the prerequisite for all the others.

In the first years of the twentieth century, he seems to be ransacking both history and the contemporary world for examples of courage to set before the Indian community of South Africa. He pens eulogies of, among others, George Washington, Giuseppe Mazzini, Socrates, Maxim Gorky, Abraham Lincoln ("the greatest man of the last century"), Tolstoy, and Thoreau. All were held up as models of the virtue he found wanting in his countrymen. In 1905, when Japan administered its defeat to Russia, Gandhi was overjoyed. "No one ever imagined that Japan was capable of such bravery," the budding pacifist wrote. "But in scouting and watchfulness, Japan surpassed all the others. Admiral Togo's spies were very accurate in their intelligence, and pounced upon the Russian fleet just when it was most vulnerable." As late as 1908 he could still write, "When Japan's brave heroes forced the Russians to bite the dust of the battle-field, the sun rose in the East. And it now shines on all the nations of Asia. The people of Asia will never, never again submit to insult from the insolent whites." Gandhi thought he knew the "secret" of the Japanese success. It was "unity, patriotism and the resolve to do or die," he said, in the tropes of late-Victorian nationalist fervor.

Yet even in these years Gandhi's interest in nonviolence was developing. In 1896 he had read Tolstoy's Christian pacifist manifesto *The Kingdom of God Is Within You* and was "overwhelmed" by it. A few years later, he entered into correspondence with Tolstoy, who celebrated Gandhi's work in *Letter to a Hindu*. As early as 1902, Gandhi gave a speech in Calcutta in which he said that although the "hatred" of the colonials against the Indians was great, what he proposed was "to conquer that hatred by love." His voracious consumption of the news of the day yielded useful examples of nonviolent action. He praised a Chinese boycott of American goods to protest anti-Chinese discrimination in the

United States. He saluted a Bengali boycott of British goods to protest the partition of Bengal by the English viceroy, Lord Curzon. He lauded the Irish movement against English rule.

The example that inspired him most, however, was the Russian revolution of 1905, whose first stages were largely nonviolent. For some years, he observed in *Indian Opinion*, the Russian revolutionaries had resorted to terrorist attacks. He admired the courage of the attackers, including "fearless girls, actuated by patriotism and a spirit of self-sacrifice, [who] take the lives of those whom they believe to be the enemies of the country, and themselves meet an agonizing death at the hands of officials." Nevertheless, their method was "a mistake." Now they had discovered a new method:

> This time they have found another remedy which, though very simple, is more powerful than rebellion and murder. The Russian workers and all the other servants declared a general strike and stopped all work. They left their jobs and informed the Czar that unless justice was done, they would not resume work. What was there even the Czar could do against this? It was quite impossible to exact work from people by force.

In these years, Gandhi's religious faith was deepening. He did not, however, connect spirituality with any one religion or civilization. In the late 1890s, Anglicized Indian that he was, he had become the South African representative of a group called the Esoteric Christian Union, which taught an eclectic faith.

Finding God in Political Action

In the first years of the twentieth century, the chief elements that made up Gandhi's outlook on the world hung together uneasily, if they hung together at all. Shortly, under the pressure of events, they were to rearrange themselves convulsively in his mind. The crisis, which spanned three years and amounted to a kind of full-scale revolution in the life of a single man, swept together his social program for his local community, his personal spirituality, his political activity on the South African stage, and his view of the British Empire and the world.

The revolution in Gandhi's local community came with the creation of Phoenix Farm, in November of 1904. Gandhi took nothing in this little community as given, but subjected everything, from the activities of daily life (how to brush your teeth, how to clean the latrine) to the most general and fundamental structures of politics and faith, to scrutiny and revision. Because this scrutiny took the form of experimentation, not obedience to any fixed scripture or dogma, the revision was endless. It included an aspect of his life that has baffled and often repelled many of his admirers—his lifelong tinkering with his austere diet and his Christian Science–like home cures, to both of which he directed great attention.

The turning point in Gandhi's personal life came in 1906, while he was leading his ambulance corps during the Zulu war. It struck him that only someone who was pledged to celibacy and poverty could lead a life of unfettered public service. He "could not live both after the flesh and the spirit," he decided. At the time, he wrote later, he had begun to ask himself some questions: "How was one to divest oneself of all possessions? . . . Was not the body possession enough? . . . Was I to destroy all the cupboards of books I had? Was I to give up all I had and follow Him?" Forthwith, he became celibate—renouncing sex even with his wife, though he remained married—and poor, and remained so for the rest of his life.

Vows of poverty and celibacy were, of course, no novelty. Priests and monks had been taking them throughout history. It was the use to which Gandhi put the life thus disciplined that was new. In the religious traditions of both East and West, holy vows have usually been accompanied by a withdrawal from the world and especially from politics. Gandhi proceeded in exactly the opposite direction. He took his ascetic vows in order to free himself for action.

Significantly, Gandhi likened the common British soldiers—the "Tommies"—he met in the Zulu war to Trappist monks. "Tommy was then altogether lovable," he wrote, and went on to compare them to Arjun, the hero of the Indian epic the Mahabarata. "Like Arjun, they went to the battlefield, because it was their duty. And how many proud, rude, savage spirits has it not broken into gentle creatures of God?" Gandhi's admiration for soldiers was lifelong. Like a monk, he would devote his life to God; but like a soldier he would fight for his beliefs in this world. Of his pursuit of God, he said, "If I could persuade myself that I should find Him in a Himalayan cave, I would proceed there immediately. But I know that I cannot find Him apart from humanity." The aim of his life would be to "see God," but that pursuit would lead him into politics. "For God," he said, reversing centuries of tradition in a short sentence, "appears to you only in action."

To the question of whether political power alone might win out over military power, Gandhi answered without equivocation that it could. His answer, however, raised another question that was of the first importance for the future of nonviolent action. If politics was to be free of violence, must it become religious? The objections to the wedding of secular and spiritual power are of course ancient, dating in the East as far back as Gautama Buddha and in the West as far back as Jesus, another religious activist who lived and taught in a backwater of an empire. Universal Christian love, expressed in the sayings "Love your enemy" and "Forgive those who trespass against you," is the spiritual underpinning of his advice of nonviolence to Simon Peter, "Put up thy sword." Certainly, faith in God and ethical responsibility toward others were inseparable for Jesus. On the other hand, although Jesus was caught up in the politics of his time and place, he conspicuously stopped short of rebellion, nonviolent or otherwise. He steered clear of any claim to political leadership (refusing to accept the title "King of the Jews," which his crucifiers affixed to his cross), and he advised payment of taxes to the Roman authorities, saying, "Render unto Caesar what is Caesar's." In other sayings, too, he seemed to place the realm of faith apart from the realm of politics. When Pilate asked him whether he claimed to be a king—a claim that would have been an offense to Caesar—Jesus answered that he was not "a king of this world." If he had been making a claim of temporal power, he went on, his disciples would have used violence to release him. That they did not showed that his kingship was otherworldly. His prophecy that the world would end soon and the kingdom of heaven come also drew a line of separation between Christian love and politics. What need was there to prescribe a rule for a political realm that was about to be destroyed? It was on the basis of these sayings that the disciple Paul and, much later, St. Augustine founded their far sharper separation of the City of God from the City of Man.

To these Christian ideas we may contrast a few of Gandhi's. As he began a nonviolent campaign in 1930, he declared of the Raj, "I am out to destroy this system of Government. . . . Sedition has become my religion." Gandhi admitted no distinction between the City of God and the City of Man. He installed a political conscience in religion and a religious conscience in politics, and called the two the same.

The objections to such a union have come over the years from both saints and politicians. Faith, saints have said, is a domain of purity that is in its nature unworldly, and will be corrupted and destroyed by association with politics, which is in its nature brutal. Rule, politicians have added, is a rough pursuit that will be enfeebled by any introduction of spiritual rules of conduct. (An object lesson—in the eyes of the eighteenth-century historian of ancient Rome Edward Gibbon—was the Christianization and fall of the Roman Empire.) Or else politics, which requires a spirit of tolerance if its natural, ineradicable violence is at least to be moderated, may, if inspired by faith, become fanatical, and even more brutal than it has to be.

To these objections, Gandhi proposed explicit or implicit answers. The most important was nonviolence itself, which he called ahimsa—literally, non-harm, or harmlessness—in Hindi. If the ardor of the spiritual, with its tendency toward absolute demands, was to be permitted to inspire political action, then it had to be purged of violence. The spirit must check its guns at the door, so to speak, before entering the saloon of politics. Otherwise, saints would prove more murderous than sinners. He required the intellect, meanwhile, to undergo a parallel renunciation. It had to rid itself of dogmatic certainty. Shedding dogma was the counterpart in the intellectual world of nonviolence in the physical world: it was mental disarmament. Only if the faithful were ready to open their minds to the worth and validity of other faiths were they likely to be able to hold to the vow of nonviolence. The test of the "absoluteness" of faith became not adherence to the exact prescriptions of any sacred text—what today we call fundamentalism—but the willingness to make sacrifices, including the sacrifice of one's life, for one's admittedly fallible beliefs. Sacrifice and suffering without violence ("self-suffering," as Gandhi put it), not doctrinal purity, was the evidence and "proof" of faith.

These were all ways to permit spiritual love to fuel politics; but they did not answer the question of whether politics, in order to be nonviolent, *required* a spiritual basis. The issue is important, because such a requirement would obviously restrict the appeal of nonviolence. It seems almost in the nature of things that only a small minority can ever take Gandhi as a model for their lives— just as only minorities have ever been drawn to the priestly or monastic life. In particular, Gandhi's asceticism—and especially his vow of celibacy even within marriage—which he regarded as essential to the practice of satyagraha, seems unlikely to serve as a model for very many. The question is what it is about religious faith that enables it to serve as a foundation for nonviolence and whether, outside religion, there may be other foundations.

Something Strange Happens

The transformation in Gandhi's political program in South Africa came just a few months after his vows of celibacy and poverty during the Zulu war. In August of 1906, the Transvaal Legislature announced a so-called Asiatic Law Amendment Ordinance. Its main provision required all Indians above the age of eight to be registered with ten fingerprints and to carry a residency permit thereafter, on pain of fine, prison, or deportation. In combination with other restrictions already in place, the act in effect reduced the Indian community to the status of criminals. Its acceptance, Gandhi believed, "would spell absolute ruin for the Indians in South Africa." In response, Gandhi led the South African Indian community to cross the line from petitioning or otherwise seeking redress within the law to nonviolent lawbreaking.

On September 11, 1906, some three thousand Indian men met at the Empire Theater, in Johannesburg. Gandhi writes, "I could read in every face the expectation of something strange to be done, or to happen." On the agenda was an item resolving that the members of the Indian community would go to jail rather than submit to the Ordinance. One man, Sheth Haji Habib, suggested that the meeting should not only vote for the resolution but publicly vow before God that they would abide by it. Gandhi supported the suggestion in a speech. Such a vow was far different from a mere resolution, he said. It could not be enforced by majority vote; each person had to decide for himself whether to take it and abide by it. But, having once taken the vow, each person was obligated thereafter to keep it, no matter what others did, for "a man who lightly pledges his word and then breaks it becomes a man of straw." All present rose and took the vow.

The "strange" thing had happened. Gandhi knew, he said later, "that some new principle had come into being." Before a year was out, several hundred Indians had gone to jail. This revolution in action, significantly, was born in action. "The foundation of the first civil resistance under the then-known name of passive resistance," he wrote later, "was laid by accident. . . . I had gone to the meeting with no preconceived resolution. It was born at the meeting. The creation is still expanding."

Gandhi was dissatisfied with the term "passive resistance" for what the Indians were doing, and as an alternative came up with the new coinage "satyagraha," which combined the Sanskrit word *sat,* meaning "that which is," or "being," or "truth," with *graha,* meaning "holding firm to" or "remaining steadfast in." It is usually translated as "truth force" or "soul force"—terms that, without further elucidation, are almost as mysterious to the English reader as "satyagraha." Concretely described, satyagraha is direct action without violence in support of the actor's beliefs—the "truth" in the person. The philosophy of satyagraha prescribes nonviolent action in which the actors refuse to cooperate with laws that they regard as unjust or otherwise offensive to their consciences, accompanied by a willingness to suffer the consequences. For the Indian community in Transvaal it meant deliberate violation of the Amendment Ordinance and a commitment to fill the local jails.

Sermon on the Sea

The final step in the revolution in Gandhi's life in these years—the reversal of his appraisal of the British Empire—came in 1909, after he had spent several months in England at the head of an Indian delegation fruitlessly pleading with the imperial government for relief from Boer repression in South Africa (which was now about to become the Union of South Africa). Gandhi had already led one delegation to London, right after the passage of the Ordinance, and on that occasion Lord Elgin, the colonial secretary, had played a trick on the Indians. He had informed them that the imperial government would disallow the legislation. Halfway home, they discovered to their joy that it had done so. When they arrived, however, they learned what Elgin had known all along—that the Transvaal would shortly be granted "responsible government," and would then be permitted to adopt the act at will, without imperial challenge, as it soon did.

The second visit was no more productive. The imperial government wished to uphold the appearance of liberalism without paying the price. From the Indian point of view, the problem was not autocratic or arbitrary use of the empire's strength but default and weakness. Notwithstanding the empire's victory in the Boer War, its power in South Africa was waning. Lord Morley, the secretary of state for India, told the Indians that the empire—which, he startlingly said, was "miscalled an imperial system"—could not "dictate to the colonies." The English strategy in South Africa was to shore up overarching imperial power by yielding increased grants of authority to the local whites. For the Cape of Good Hope, like Egypt and the Sudan, was one of those "roads to India" that had to be defended at all costs. Global power politics took precedence over the grievances of the local black majority and the Indian minority, which were hardly a speck on the great imperial horizon. "I have now got fed up," Gandhi wrote home in *Indian Opinion* toward the end of his 1909 visit. "I think the reader, too, must have grown tired of reading uncertain news." At the Empire Theater, Gandhi had broken with the Boers. Now his patience with the British was coming to an end.

The historical predicament faced by Gandhi and other Indian leaders, barred from influence and power in South Africa as well as their own country, was, in its broadest outline, similar to that facing the leadership of all the colonialized countries: how to oppose domination by a foreign state wielding the incomparably superior weapons of the modern West. India's "Omdurman" had been the battle of Plassey, fought in 1757 between English forces under Robert Clive, and those of Siraj-ud-daulah, the nawab of the Mogul Empire. Clive's victory was one of the earliest to show the extreme imbalance that would become such a regular feature of modern imperial war. The nineteenth-century British military historian Colonel Malleson was not exaggerating when he wrote, "The work of Clive was, all things considered, as great as that of Alexander." For after the battle of Plassey, with its loss to England of a handful of soldiers, the power of England over India was not to be seriously challenged again until Gandhi's time.

The power of imperialist Europe presented the Eastern countries with a dilemma that was cultural and psychological as well as military and political. Everywhere in Asia, nascent movements to resist Europe were national, just as, earlier in the century, the European resistance to Napoleon had been national. However much these movements battened on enthusiasm for their own cultures, the most obvious solution to the crisis in which Asia found herself was to abandon her ways and adopt those of the powerful, dangerous West—in short, to "modernize." Nor could this adoption be halfhearted or superficial. The foundations of traditional society, it seemed, had to be uprooted.

In China, the Ottoman Empire, Japan, India, and elsewhere, innumerable variations of this solution to the dilemma were tried out. Science, evidently, was a source of Western power. Why not, then, learn science, and graft it onto Eastern society, combining the strength of the "material" West with the wisdom of the "spiritual" East? Such was the thinking of early Chinese reformers, who, however, soon noted what Clausewitz had discovered—that democracy, too, was a source of Western military power. "Science and democracy" then became the rallying cry of an important school of reformers. Chen Duxiu, a moderate, wrote, "The basic task is to import the foundation of Western society, that is, the new belief in equality and human rights." These Chinese, goaded by their country's humiliation, were perhaps the first anywhere, East or West, to understand and clearly state that at the base of modern power were the scientific and democratic revolutions. But in the early twentieth century it became obvious to them that neither revolution could grow in a vacuum. Both had roots in the emancipation of the individual. In order to be strong, China would have to alter its culture, even its family structure—the very things that, according to earlier reformers, China had been seeking to protect by adopting science. The further one went in Westernizing in order to protect China, it turned out, the less of "China" there was to protect. Not far down this path lay the wholesale condemnation of Chinese tradition that would be expressed by the Chinese Communist Party. The Asian nations, in order to survive in the social Darwinist, adapt-or-die war system that Europe had imposed on the world, seemed to be faced with a choice between watching Europeans destroy their traditional societies or doing the job themselves. It was hard soil in which to grow what later came to be called "national identity."

On a steamer back to South Africa in November of 1909, Gandhi, writing in his native tongue of Gujarati, poured out the longest and most inflammatory political pamphlet he would ever write, *Hind Swaraj: Indian Home Rule*—also called *Sermon on the Sea*. It dealt head-on with the issue of Westernization. If violence is truly the midwife of revolution, as Marx said, then this pamphlet was the closest Gandhi ever came to preaching it. He portrayed the civilization of England and her empire as an unmitigated evil. Gone now was the praise for Queen Victoria, gone the praise for British justice, gone the vision of a harmonious union of "different sections of ONE mighty empire." The larger villain of the story, however, was not England herself but modern technical civilization, of which England was only one representative. He anathematized it with fundamentalist fury. "This civilization is irreligion," he declared. "According to the teachings of Mahomed this would be considered a Satanic Civilization. Hinduism calls it the Black Age. . . . It must be shunned." To imitate this civilization, as Japan had done and China was trying to do, would be madness. "The condition of England at present is pitiable. I pray to God that India may never be in that plight." He excoriated modern ways. Railways only enabled "bad men [to] fulfil their evil designs with greater rapidity," he said, with primitive logic. English prime ministers had "neither real honesty nor a living conscience." The English Parliament was "a prostitute." The civilization of modern Europe as a whole was a mere "nine-days' wonder" that shortly would destroy itself; one had only to wait.

Indian civilization, he now found, was the opposite of all this. "The tendency of the Indian civilization is to elevate the moral being," he claimed, "that of the Western civilization is to propagate immorality. The latter is godless, the former is based on a belief in God." The foundations of Indian civilization arose, he insisted, from religious roots, when her great religious men had established pilgrimages to holy places, such as the Ganges.

Gandhi's rejection of the West and embrace of his own land was more radical by far than that of other anti-Western leaders of the time. The idea that the East should protect her spiritual treasures by means of a judicious borrowing of Western material techniques had been the stock-in-trade not just of the Chinese and Japanese but of Indians as well. For instance, the religious leader Vivekananda, who in other ways foreshadows Gandhi, said, "It is . . . fitting that when the Oriental wants to learn about machine-making, he should sit at the feet of the Occidental and learn from him. When the Occident wants to learn about the Spirit, about God, about the Soul, about the meaning and the mystery of this universe, he must sit at the feet of the Orient." Gandhi, by contrast, turns his back entirely on Western material techniques, placing his faith in Eastern spirituality alone.

Gandhi's sweeping rejection of modern technology, let us note, was never put into practice in India, except by himself and a few of his followers. And even Gandhi, though remaining true to his belief, did not propose a wholesale program of deindustrialization, and at times confessed that certain industries might be necessary, as long as they were strictly devoted to the benefit of the people. It is in the arena of nonviolence that Gandhi's repudiation of technology has so far proved historically fruitful. By associating technical progress with violence and both with the West and, on the other hand, technical simplicity with nonviolence and both of these with India, Gandhi and his colleagues forged a nationalistic pride in nonviolence that was to endure from about 1920, when the Congress Party adopted Gandhi's program, until 1948, when India gained independence. Thus was nationalism, which usually feeds on self-aggrandizement and militarism, wedded in India to a principle of self-restraint. (Once independent, the Indian state promptly abandoned nonviolence and immediately went to war with the newly created state of Pakistan over the territory of Kashmir; and it now possesses a large military establishment and a nuclear arsenal.)

Gandhi's embrace of nonviolence provided an escape from the discouraging choice between imitation of the West and defeat by the West. Nonviolence was a method for fighting the West *without* imitating her. As Gandhi put it in *Hind Swaraj*, "My countrymen . . . believe that they should adopt modern civilization and modern methods of violence to drive out the English. *Hind Swaraj* has been written in order to show that they are following a suicidal policy, and that, if they would but revert to their own glorious civilization, either the English would adopt the latter and become Indianized or their occupation in India would be gone."

The idea that India possessed a priceless, spiritually superior civilization was a welcome salve to the injured pride of a people that had been taught for some two hundred years to regard everything English as superior. In the words of India's first prime minister, Jawaharlal Nehru, Gandhi wrought in the consciousness of India "a psychological change, almost as if some expert in psychoanalytic methods had probed deep into the patient's past, found out the origins of his complexes, exposed them to his view, and thus rid him of that burden." In Gandhi's Manichaean celebration in *Hind Swaraj* of one civilization and condemnation of another, there is a note of chauvinism of a kind he later avoided. (Although he never repudiated *Hind Swaraj*, he would declare, "East and West are no more than names . . . there is no people to whom the moral life is a special vocation.") Yet we note at the same time a new clarity and firmness of tone in the pamphlet. Anything of the Uncle Tom that may have clung to the frock-coated, silk-hatted Gandhi as he made the rounds of the ministries of the British Empire has been purged. Soon he would adopt the simplest Indian dress. The disparate elements that composed the worldview of this rootless, much-traveled, English-trained, Esoteric Christian, immigrant to Africa, had fused in a new unity. The verbal "violence" of *Hind Swaraj* was perhaps the violence needed to rend the emotional tie with the empire. Gandhi had discovered a way to serve as a true son of India—at one, he was sure, with the spirit of his forefathers.

The Power of Nonviolence

There was practical as well as moral calculation in Gandhi's satyagraha. The West possessed means of violence that India could not hope to match. Gandhi later said, "Suppose Indians wish to retain by force the fruits of victory won through satyagraha. Even a child can see that if the Indians resort to force they can be crushed in a minute." Sensibly, he did not want to play a losing hand. As he explained, "The Whites were fully armed. It was clear that if the Indians were to come into their own, they must forge a weapon which would be different from and infinitely superior to, the force which the white settlers commanded in such ample measure. It was then that I introduced congregational prayer in Phoenix and

Tolstoy Farm as a means for training in the use of the weapon of satyagraha or soul force." In 1909, contemplating the might of the British Empire, he wrote:

> You [British] have great military resources. Your naval power is matchless. If we wanted to fight with you on your own ground, we should be unable to do so, but if the above submissions be not acceptable to you, we cease to play the part of the ruled. You may, if you like, cut us to pieces. You may shatter us at the cannon's mouth. If you act contrary to our will, we shall not help you; and without our help, we know that you cannot move one step forward.

Gandhi's nonviolence, too, is a chapter in the story that began with Clausewitz's Prussia, which, faced with the superiority of the French revolutionary armies, had embarked on its policy of conscious imitation of the French innovations, and continued with the attempts of so many nations to "catch up" with more "modern" powers.

By the time Gandhi wrote *Hind Swaraj,* he had in effect nationalized the principle of nonviolence. He brought it down from the ether of universal beliefs and gave it a terrestrial home—India. Violence, meanwhile, seemed to have taken up residence in the modern West. But where, if anywhere, in Gandhi's newly moralized geography did his *prime* virtue, civil courage, now reside? Previously, he had found it mainly in England, and scolded his countrymen for lacking it. In *Hind Swaraj,* it seems to have been left geographically homeless. Inspiring his countrymen to take active responsibility for their own social and political lives was *the* Gandhian program, yet since India had been defined as the home of the spirit, courage in her case must not take a martial shape (brute force) but must be of a nonviolent kind (soul force). So just when Gandhi's diatribe against the satanic West reaches its highest pitch in *Hind Swaraj,* as if to justify and prepare the way for anti-

Western violence, the restraining hand of nonviolence seems to
reach in and turn the criticism and toward the passivity of his own
countrymen. Psychologically speaking, we can almost watch the
anger at the hated "other" being checked and directed back
toward the self, which is excoriated with double fury.

Whatever pleasures of national pride Gandhi may have offered
his countrymen when he called their ancient civilization the most
godly of all he now more than took back. He dashed the sweet cup
of national self-congratulation from the thirsting lips of the humil-
iated Indians. It is in the passages explaining England's domination
of India that *Hind Swaraj* began to chart new political territory.
Gandhi held Indians, not Englishmen, responsible for India's
colonial dependency. "The English have not taken India," he
wrote, "we have given it to them." He explained:

> They came to our country originally for purposes of trade. Recall
> the Company Bahadur. Who made it Bahadur? They had not the
> slightest intention at the time of establishing a kingdom. Who
> assisted the Company's officers? Who was tempted at the sight of
> their silver? Who bought their goods? History testifies that we all
> did this. In order to become rich all at once we welcomed the
> Company's officers with open arms. We assisted them.

Gandhi later elucidated his point:

> It is because the rulers, if they are bad, are so not necessarily or
> wholly by reason of birth, but largely because of their environ-
> ment, that I have hopes of their altering their course. It is perfectly
> true . . . that the rulers cannot alter their course themselves. If they
> are dominated by their environment, they do not surely deserve to
> be killed, but should be changed by a change of environment. But
> the environment are we—the people who make the rulers what
> they are. They are thus an exaggerated edition of what we are in the
> aggregate. If my argument is sound, any violence done to the rulers

would be violence done to ourselves. It would be suicide. And since I do not want to commit suicide, nor encourage my neighbors to do so, I become nonviolent myself and invite my neighbors to do likewise.

Liberal-minded people have often held that society's victims are corrupted by a bad "environment" created by their privileged masters. Gandhi was surely the first to suggest that the victims were creating a bad moral environment for their masters—and to preach reform to the *victims*. Even allowing for a certain raillery and sardonicism in these passages, there can be no doubt that Gandhi is in earnest. Here we touch bedrock in Gandhi's political thinking. All government, he steadily believed, depends for its existence on the cooperation of the governed. If that cooperation is withdrawn, the government will be helpless. Government is composed of civil servants, soldiers, and citizens. Each of these people has a will. If enough of them withdraw their support from the government, it will fall.

This idea had admittedly occurred to political thinkers in the past. For instance, the sixteenth-century French writer Étienne de La Boétie had observed of tyrants, "the more is given them, the more they are obeyed, so much the more do they fortify themselves," and therefore "if nothing be given them, if they be not obeyed, without fighting, without striking a blow, they remain naked, disarmed and are nothing." The philosopher of the English enlightenment David Hume likewise believed that all government, even tyranny, rested on a kind of support. "The soldan of Egypt or the emperor of Rome," he wrote, "might drive his harmless subjects like brute beasts against their sentiments and inclination. But he must, at least, have led his *mameluks* or *praetorian bands*, like men, by their opinion." And James Madison once wrote, "All governments rest on opinion."

Gandhi, however, was the first to found upon this belief a thoroughgoing program of action and a radically new understanding of the relationship of violence to politics. The central role of consent in all government meant that noncooperation—the withdrawal of consent—was something more than a morally satisfying activity; it was a powerful weapon in the real world. He stated and restated the belief in many ways throughout his life:

> I believe and everybody must grant that no Government can exist for a single moment without the cooperation of the people, willing or forced, and if people withdraw their cooperation in every detail, the Government will come to a standstill.

Gandhi's politics was not a politics of the moral gesture. It rested on an interpretation of political power and was an exercise of power. From his surprising premises Gandhi drew a conclusion more surprising still:

> The causes that gave them [the English] India enable them to retain it. Some Englishmen state that they took and they hold India by the sword. Both these statements are wrong. The sword is entirely useless for holding India. We alone keep them.

Gandhi does not merely say that English rule is made possible by Indian acquiescence; he goes a step further and charges that Indians "keep" the English, almost as if the English were struggling to get away and the Indians were pulling them back. Gandhi's claim flies in the face of the one conviction on which everyone else in the imperial scheme, whether ruler or ruled, agreed—that, in the words of the *London Times,* it was "by the sword that we conquered India, and it is by the sword that we hold it." (We cannot prove that Gandhi had read the *Times* editorial, but the similarity in wording of the passage above suggests that he had.) Some enthusiastically approved of this supremacy of the sword, some bowed to it, and some despised it, but only Gandhi denied that it was a fact. Not only was force, in Gandhi's thinking, not the "final arbiter," it was no arbiter at all. What arbitrated was consent, and the cooperation that flowed from it, and these were the foundation of dictatorship as well as of democratic government.

More Active Than Violence

Governments do not normally fall simply of their own weight. Action is required. The obligation to act, in Gandhi's view, took precedence over even the obligation to remain nonviolent. "Noncooperation is not a passive state," Gandhi said, "it is an intensely active state—more active than physical resistance or violence." Satyagraha was *soul* force, but equally it was soul *force.*

Asked to choose between violence and passivity, Gandhi always chose violence. "It is better to be violent, if there is violence in our breasts," he said, "than to put on the cloak of nonviolence to cover impotence. Violence is any day preferable to impotence. There is hope for a violent man to become nonviolent. There is no such hope for the impotent." "Activist" is a word that fits Gandhi through and through. "I am not built for academic writings," he said. "Action is my domain." Indeed, if he was a genius in any field, that field was action. "Never has anything been done on this earth without direct action."

In 1917, soon after he returned to India, he would say, "There is no love where there is no will. In India there is not only no love but hatred due to emasculation. There is the strongest desire to fight and kill side by side with utter helplessness. This desire must be satisfied by restoring the capacity for fighting. Then comes the choice." In 1918, he would shock his followers by enlisting as a recruiting sergeant for Indian troops to fight for the British in the First World War. How, his colleagues wondered, then and later, could the advocate of nonviolence recruit soldiers for this war—a mechanized slaughter of millions that surely had to rank as the prime exhibit in Gandhi's indictment of modern technical civilization for its "violence of the blackest sort"? His campaign, which proved almost fruitless, can be explained only by his belief that what India needed even more than nonviolence was the will and courage that would propel its people into action—even if this meant serving in war under the British.

Intuitively, nonviolence appears to have a restraining or crippling influence on action. To Gandhi, however, nonviolence appeared in exactly the opposite light. Nonviolent action had nothing to do with quietism or passivity. Noncooperation was, Gandhi believed, supremely energetic. "Another remedy [to injustice] there certainly is, and that is armed revolt," he acknowledged, but "Civil disobedience is a complete, effective and bloodless substitute." If Gandhi embraced nonviolence, it was not because, in the interest of an ideal, he accepted a competitive disadvantage. Satyagraha was not some pale sister of violence, embraced for her virtue alone. For Gandhi such acceptance would have constituted an unacceptable abdication of responsibility.

But how could someone who checked his energy be called more energetic and more powerful than someone who unleashed it without restraint? Weren't Gandhi's two dictates—that one must *act* directly, unhesitatingly, and fearlessly and that one must do so nonviolently—at war with one another? The kinship of action and violence, indeed, seems natural, and it's tempting to see Gandhi's nonviolence only as an attempted remedy for the danger. In this view, nonviolence would be seen as a reduction of freedom in which a certain passivity and loss of energy is the price paid for keeping the peace. And certainly Gandhi did see nonviolence as a cure for the danger inherent in mass action. He often said that in his time the rising tide of action would irresistibly occur whether leaders like him encouraged it or not, and that his job was to help guide it into peaceful channels. "A new order of things is replacing the old," he wrote as he embarked on a campaign of satyagraha on behalf of mill workers in his home city of Ahmedabad. "It can be established peacefully or it must be preceded by some painful disturbances. . . . I presumptuously believe that I can step into the breach and may succeed in stopping harmful disturbances during our passage to the new state of things.... I can only do so if I can show the people a better and more expeditious way of righting wrongs." He adamantly denied that the price of restraining violence entailed a reduction of energy and power. On the contrary, he claimed that satyagraha, far from being a restriction on action, was action at last unrestricted and unbound—action grown to the full height of its potential. "Nonviolence," he said, "is without exception superior to violence, i.e., the power at the disposal of a nonviolent person is always greater than he would have if he was violent."

Any action, Gandhi knew, called above all for willpower—for the sort of courage that was especially conspicuous in soldiers. But nonviolent action required even more courage of this sort. Gandhi was fond of a statue of Charles Gordon, a British general of imperial fame, which shows him carrying a mere riding crop instead of a weapon. Gandhi commented:

> The practice of *ahimsa* calls forth the greatest courage. It is the most soldierly of a soldier's virtues. General Gordon has been represented in a famous statue as bearing only a stick. This takes us far on the road to *ahimsa*. But a soldier who needs the protection of even a stick is to that extent so much the less a soldier. He is the true soldier who knows how to die and stand his ground in the midst of a hail of bullets.

Action, moreover, flourishes, Gandhi believed, in freedom; and nonviolent action, precisely because it requires the highest possible degree of courage, exhibits the largest freedom. Violence, although initiated in pursuit of political goals, can take on a life of its own, which distracts from the original goals, and may eventually compete with them or supplant them entirely. On the local scale, this leads to vendetta, which can outlast by generations any political or other purposes that gave rise to a quarrel. On a much wider scale, the logic of war can, as Clausewitz warned with such clarity, entirely supersede the political purposes that lend war whatever sense it may have. On each of these levels, the actors surrender their freedom of action to a process over which they have lost control.

The nonviolent actor exhibits the highest degree of freedom also because his action originates within himself, according to his own judgment, inclination, and conscience, not in helpless, automatic response to something done by someone else. He is thus a creator, not a mere responder. It is not digressive to recall a passage from a writer who might at first appear to be pretty much a polar opposite of Gandhi yet also associated nonviolence not with weakness but with a superabundance of energy and power. Friedrich Nietzsche, asking himself whether such a thing as a Christian turning of the other cheek was really possible, said that, if it were, it would be for only the strongest natures. He wrote:

> To be incapable of taking one's enemies, one's accidents, even one's misdeeds seriously for very long—that is the sign of strong, full natures in whom there is an excess of the power to form, to mold, to recuperate and to forget. . . . Such a man shakes off with a *single* shrug many vermin that eat deep into others; here alone genuine "love of one's enemies" is possible—supposing it to be possible at all on earth. How much reverence has a noble man for his enemies!—and such reverence is a bridge to love. . . . In contrast to this, picture "the enemy" as the man of *ressentiment* conceives him—and here precisely is his deed, his creation: he has conceived "the evil enemy," "THE EVIL ONE," and this in fact is his basic concept, from which he then evolves, as an afterthought and pendant, a "good one"—himself!

If such magnanimous characters—free alike of fear and lust for revenge, and braver than soldiers—had not found an appropriate arena for their kind of activity, they might have passed through history without leaving any mark but the admiration of a few people around them. Their arena could not, of course, be war. In fact, it was the arena of nonviolent action, soon to be strewn with the debris of the world's empires and some of its mightiest and most violent regimes.

Noncooperation in India

In 1915, Gandhi brought his battle-tested instrument of nonviolence from little Natal and Transvaal to great India. In South Africa, the forty thousand Indians had been a small minority, amounting to less than 10 percent of the total population. In India, they were a huge majority, of more than three hundred million, ruled over by a mere hundred thousand or so English. When forty thousand refused cooperation, it was a serious crisis for the imperial rulers; but if the three hundred million refused cooperation it was the end of the Raj, and probably of the British Empire as well. That, at least, was the view of Winston Churchill, who said in Parliament in 1931, "The loss of India would be final and fatal to us. It would not fail to be part of a process that would reduce us to the scale of a minor power." Gandhi agreed. "Through deliverance of India," he wrote, "I seek to deliver the so-called weaker races of the earth from the crushing heels of Western exploitation in which England is the greatest partner." History proved both men right.

Gandhi began modestly. Following the suggestion of his political mentor in India, the National Congress Party leader Gopal Krishna Gokhale, he maintained a public silence for a year, contenting himself with traveling throughout India in third-class railway compartments, in order to acquaint himself with the state of the country. Beginning in 1917, he engaged in a series of local satyagraha campaigns. One was in opposition to the exploitation of peasants cultivating indigo, out of which dye is made, in Bihar, in the Champaran district; a second was in support of decent wages for the mill workers in his native city of Ahmedabad; a third

1906. He called both "black acts," and resisted both with full-scale campaigns of noncooperation. He called the Rowlatt bills evidence of "a determined policy of repression," and announced that henceforth "civil disobedience seems to be a duty imposed on every lover of personal public liberty," declaring that he was ready to fight "the greatest battle of my life."

Noncooperation was to continue in India, on and off, for the next three decades. In February of 1919, Gandhi announced his first nationwide act of resistance—a *hartal,* or strike, against the Rowlatt legislation. The *hartal* was observed throughout the country. This was Gandhi's answer to Omdurman and the weapons of civilization—not India heaping the ground with English corpses but masses of Indians withdrawing cooperation from English rule. A few days after the *hartal,* however, the British arrested him, whereupon riots broke out in Ahmedabad, and Gandhi found himself facing a problem he had not faced in South Africa—violence by his own supporters. An English policeman and others were killed.

Gandhi's response was to launch "*satyagraha* against ourselves," by fasting for three days. "In the place I have made my abode I find utter lawlessness bordering almost on Bolshevism," he now wrote to the viceroy's private secretary. "Englishmen and women have found it necessary to leave their bungalows and to confine themselves to a few well-guarded houses. It is a matter of the deepest humiliation and regret to me. I see that I over-calculated the measure of permeation of satyagraha amongst the people. . . . My satyagraha . . . will, at the present moment, be directed against my own countrymen." In 1922, shortly after launching noncooperation on an even wider scale, he again suspended it, after mobs of protesters burned a police station in the city of Chauri Chaura, and hacked several policemen to pieces. "All of us should be in mourning," he said. "May God save the honor of India." He fasted for five days in penance and the protest never was resumed.

In a campaign of noncooperation against the salt tax in 1930—probably the most renowned of his actions—Gandhi marched with seventy-five or so followers to the sea to make salt, in defiance of an English monopoly on salt making, and then was jailed, after which his followers marched nonviolently upon the saltworks at Dharasana, suffering many dozens of casualties at the hands of police wielding clubs. The upshot was an invitation to meet the viceroy, Lord Reading. The two men agreed that Gandhi would represent India at a constitutional conference in London. The conference failed, and another decade of resistance and repression began. The final nationwide noncooperation campaign—the Quit India campaign—was launched in 1942, in the third year of the Second World War, and was quickly and violently repressed; India did not attain her independence until the war ended, when England's grip on all her imperial possessions was weakening.

It is not certain that it was satyagraha that broke England's grip on India. The great hoped-for day never came on which all India refused cooperation with the English rulers, who therefore, finding themselves barking orders at an indifferent population, had nothing left to do but pull up stakes and leave. The English weathered all the individual satyagraha campaigns. It's also true that many factors other than satyagraha conspired to drive the English out. English trade with India declined in importance. The depression and the two world wars weakened England, forcing her finally to yield her position of global preeminence to the United States.

On the other hand, satyagraha unquestionably succeeded in winning the battle for the hearts and minds of the people of India. When the Second World War ended, although the back of the Quit India campaign had been broken, the viceroy, Lord Wavell, was well aware that "while the British are still legally and morally responsible for what happens in India, we have lost nearly all power to control events; we are simply running on the momentum of our previous prestige." Just as de Gaulle came to understand in

Algeria that victories through repression and violence were in the long run as useless as conventional battlefield victories in a people's war, so now Wavell acknowledged that technical victories against nonviolent opponents would in the long run prove equally useless. All these imperial defeats pointed to a lesson, which was spelled out clearly in Gandhi's writings: in a struggle for independence in our democratic age, the decisive contest, whose essence is political and therefore nonviolent, is not for control of any piece of territory but for the loyalty and cooperation of the people. Violence, where it is present, plays only a supporting role. It was Gandhi's discovery that violence did not need to play any role at all.

The Shadow

That lesson, however, is in fact a secondary one. When Gandhi arrived back in India in 1915, he knew he faced not only the evil of British rule but also the mountainous social ills of India, most of which had predated the Raj and would outlast it. The most important tasks, he believed, were providing a decent life, including adequate food, shelter, and sanitation, for India's "dumb millions," establishing a system of active self-government in the country's seven hundred thousand villages, ending the Hindu system of untouchability, raising the status of women, and making and keeping peace among Hindus and Muslims. Although *swaraj*—"self-rule"—included ejecting the English, he always believed that addressing these ills was its deeper and more important task.

Noncooperation, taken by itself, was useless for this purpose. It could do nothing to feed the hungry, to relieve the oppressed, to make peace among India's quarreling ethnic and religious groups. For these purposes, positive action was required. Gandhi gave it the unostentatious name of "the constructive program." Noncooperation embodied the obligation to reject participation in oppression. The constructive program embodied the obligation to actively pursue social betterment—"truth." As such, it was closer than noncooperation to the central meaning of "satyagraha," which is "to hold fast to truth." The story of Gandhi's satyagraha has traditionally concentrated on the three great noncooperation campaigns; but his most persistent efforts were his unceasing work in support of the constructive program. It's notable, for instance, that all of his "fasts unto death" (from each of which he was released by progress in solving the issue about which he was fasting) were launched in the name of one plank or another of the constructive program—of bringing justice to the workers of Ahmedabad, of ending untouchability, of making peace between Hindus and Muslims. "Satyagraha," he said, "is not predominantly civil disobedience, but a quiet and irresistible pursuit of truth. On the rarest occasions it becomes civil disobedience."

A constructive program to address social ills may seem so elementary as scarcely to be an idea; yet few things caused more controversy in the Congress Party than Gandhi's dedication to it. In one of the lulls between noncooperation movements, Gandhi joked that in Congress "I stand thoroughly discredited as a religious maniac and predominantly a social worker." Most of the Congress leaders wanted to concentrate first on winning power and only then on addressing India's social ills. Gandhi reversed this order of business. He wanted Congress to address India's ills immediately and directly without regard to the English and their Raj. (The similarity between this program and the strategy of people's war is clear. In Gandhi's scheme, noncooperation was the nonviolent counterpart of guerrilla war while the constructive program was the counterpart of the Vietnamese *hiérarchies parallèles*.)

His thinking on the relationship of the constructive program to power was revealed in an answer to a letter from a reader of his journal *Indian Opinion* in 1931. The reader had written to protest that his constructive work was getting in the way of the attempt to take political power. "To me," the reader wrote, "political power is the substance, and all the other forms have to wait." Gandhi answered that "political power is not an end but only a means enabling people to better their condition in every department of life." Therefore, "Constructive effort is the substance of political power [while] actual taking over of the government machinery is but a shadow, an emblem." Five years later, at a time when he was devoting himself almost entirely to the constructive program, he wrote:

> One must forget the political goal in order to realize it. To think of the political goal at every step is to raise unnecessary dust. Why worry one's head over a thing that is inevitable? Why die before one's death? . . . That is why I can take the keenest interest in discussing vitamins and leafy vegetables and unpolished rice. That is why it has become a matter of absorbing interest to me to find out how best to clean our latrines.

If the goal was the renovation of India, why not proceed to it directly? Why not pick up a broom and sweep a latrine—as Gandhi in fact did at the first Congress meeting he attended, in 1915. If one concentrated too much on seizing the means of betterment, he feared, one might forget the goal. And in fact when India did achieve independence, this, in Gandhi's view, is exactly what happened. The Congress leaders took power but forgot what power was for. On October 2, 1947, when offered birthday congratulations, he answered, "Where do congratulations come in? It will be more appropriate to say condolences. There is nothing but anguish in my heart."

This is by no means to say, however, that Gandhi did not value political power, or did not believe in winning it or exercising it. He aimed at both throughout his life, though never as a government official. He did not say that the Congress Party should not take power; rather, he said that this was inevitable. Power might be only a "shadow"; on the other hand, there never was a thing that lacked its shadow.

He frequently suggested, indeed, that the constructive program was as effective a path to political power as noncooperation. Political power, he wrote, would in fact increase in "exact proportion" to success in the constructive effort. Whereas noncooperation drained power away from the oppressors, the constructive program generated it in the hands of the resisters. "When a body of men disown the state under which they have hitherto lived," he said in 1921, "they nearly establish their own government. I say nearly, for they do not go to the point of using force when they are resisted by the state."

Gandhi's view that winning state power, though necessary, should not be the supreme goal of India's political activity was also expressed in his arguments against adopting independence from England as the primary aim of Congress. As late as 1928, he opposed—successfully—a Congress independence resolution in response to the appointment by the English of a Statutory Commission for India. He had made his reasons clear as early as the publication of *Hind Swaraj*. Independence meant expelling the English and taking the reigns of government. But did India want "English rule without the Englishman"? Gandhi rejected this vision, as was not surprising for someone who at the time regarded the condition of modern England as "pitiable." He explained, "My patriotism does not teach me that I am to allow people to be crushed under the heel of Indian princes if only the English retire."

Independence meant dissociation—a merely negative goal. *Swaraj* meant building up something new. "Not only could *swaraj* not be 'given' to Indians," he said, "but rather it had to be created by them." Gandhi wanted action by Indians to better their own lives, not concessions or grants of authority from foreigners. *Swaraj*, as distinct from independence, must proceed from within each Indian. "Has independence suddenly become a goal in answer to something offensive that some Englishman has done?" he asked. And he went on, in simple words that seem to me to come close to the core of this arch-innovator's view of action and its proper place in the scheme of life, "Do men conceive their goals in order to oblige people or to resent their action? I submit that if it is a goal, it must be declared and pursued irrespective of the acts or threats of others." For Gandhi, ending untouchability, cleaning latrines, improving the diet of Indian villagers, improving the lot of Indian women, making peace between Muslims and Hindus—through all of which he believed he would find God—were such goals.

5

Nonviolent Revolution, Nonviolent Rule

Most of the formative revolutions of modern Western history were violent in one degree or another. They have been consigned—in political theory, if not in historical writing—to the anarchic state in which violence has always been assumed to be the final arbiter of events. The extreme violence of the French Revolution of 1789 and the Russian Revolution of 1917 is in fact probably the chief historical basis for the rarely doubted proposition that in revolution violence rules. We may inquire, though, in light of Gandhi's experience, to what extent the political theorists have been correct. In the chapters that follow, we will reflect upon a pivotal moment in four revolutions—the Glorious Revolution in England in 1689, the American Revolution, the French Revolution, and the Russian Revolution—and then we will turn to the recent Soviet collapse. Our purpose, needless to say, will not be to suggest that these revolutions were lacking in violence. It will be to ask what the roles of violent and nonviolent action were.

One point is clear at the outset: the possibility of nonviolent revolution is rooted in the democratic revolution of modern times.

Violence is a method by which the ruthless few can subdue the passive many. Nonviolence is a means by which the active many can overcome the ruthless few. In this respect, it is like people's war. If the people are not politically conscious—if they have not "risen to the height of political being," in the phrase of the German revolutionary Rosa Luxemburg—they can be neither a nourishing sea for the guerrilla fish nor a mighty army of non-cooperators. This is not to say that acts of civil disobedience by a few people, or even a single person, are unimportant. "I know this well," the American pioneer of civil disobedience Henry David Thoreau wrote in the 1840s: "If one thousand, if one hundred, if ten men whom I could name—if ten honest men only—ay, if one HONEST man, in this State of Massachusetts, ceasing to hold slaves, were actually to withdraw from this co-partnership, and be locked up in the county jail therefor, it would be the abolition of slavery in America." Yet in the long run the influence of such individuals will depend on the participation of the many. War cannot be waged without guns, tanks, and planes. Nonviolent resistance cannot be waged without active, steadfast, committed masses of unarmed people. The civil-rights movement led by Martin Luther King in the United States provides an illustration. The courageous campaign of a minority, mostly black, touched the conscience of an inactive majority, mostly white, who provided the political support necessary for the movement's historic judicial, legislative, and social victories.

It is also helpful to keep in mind the classic observation that revolutions pass through two distinct stages—overthrow of the ancien régime and foundation of a new one. Political theory as well as common sense suggests that overthrow, an act of destruction, should require violence. It seems equally obvious that the subsequent stage of foundation of the new regime, an act of creation, should be peaceful. However, the historical record shows that the reverse has much more often been the case. The overthrow has often been carried out with little or no bloodshed, while the foundation—and the revolutionary rule that follows it—has been bathed in blood.

The "Battle" of Salisbury Field

On Sunday, November 5, 1688, when the Dutch stadtholder, William of Orange, landed at the head of fifteen thousand troops at Brixham on Torbay, on the southern coast of England, there was every reason to suppose that the ensuing contest with King James II of England would be a bloody one. Still fresh in everyone's mind was the civil war of the 1640s, in which parliamentary armies had defeated the royal forces of Charles I, and in 1649 beheaded him. William, the head of the Dutch state, was James's nephew and son-in-law, and he had been invited to invade by powerful disaffected British nobles and clergy. The fundamental issues underlying the conflict—whether king or Parliament would be politically supreme and whether Protestantism would prevail in England—had first come to a head in the civil war.

James mustered his troops and sent them to Salisbury field, where they awaited William's army. The stage was set for a classic decision by arms. But no battle occurred, nor would one during the Glorious Revolution, also known as the Bloodless Revolution. Within a week, James, still in command of numerically superior forces, retreated from the field. A week later he ordered his commander in chief, Lord Feversham, to disband his force, but by then James's army was already dissolving as rapidly as if it had suffered decisive military defeat in classical Clausewitzian combat. James then ordered the destruction of the writs by which parliaments were summoned, threw the Great Seal—emblem of royal authority—into the river Thames, and fled.

What had happened? A contest not of arms but of defection and allegiance had taken place. The tide had run in one direction: the defection was almost all on the side of James, the allegiance on the side of William. The defectors included Colonel Cornbury, the son of Lord Clarendon, one of the king's principal advisers, John Churchill (the future Duke of Marlborough and ancestor of Winston Churchill), and, finally, King James's daughter, Princess Anne. Thomas Macaulay, the nineteenth-century historian and Member of Parliament, wrote in his seminal history of the revolution, "It was true that the direct loss to the crown and the direct gain to the invaders hardly amounted to two hundred men and as many horses. . . . But where could the King henceforth expect to find those sentiments in which consists the strength of states and armies?" He continues, "That prompt obedience without which an army is merely a rabble was necessarily at an end." For, "The material strength of the army were little diminished: but its moral strength had been destroyed." In the first epic battle for hearts and minds of the modern period, the decision had gone, bloodlessly, to the insurrectionary forces.

William did not frame a plan of nonviolent action; but he didn't quite stumble into his nonviolent victory, either. From the beginning, *waiting* had been his calculated strategy. He was an inveterate, zealous soldier—soon he would marshal a coalition of forces that would defeat the expansionist continental plans of Louis XIV, the Sun King of France—but in 1688 he calculated that combat with James would hurt his cause. Actual battle, he feared, would rouse the national spirit of the English against his mostly foreign troops. James, on the other hand, understood that the mere fact of battle would favor his cause. "The king was eager to fight," Macaulay explains, "and it was obviously in his interest to do so. Every hour took away something from his own strength, and added something to the strength of his enemies. It was important, too, that his troops should be blooded." Win or lose, James knew, a battle in which English soldiers were wounded and killed would stoke the patriotic ire of the English. Unfortunately for James, "All this William perfectly understood, and determined to avoid an action as long as possible."

Commanders in the field naturally weigh the strength of the

opposing forces. The two sovereigns who pondered battle at Salisbury, however, had a prior question to consider: *which* forces were the ones that would count, and *where* would the decisive struggle take place? Would it be on the field of combat, where soldiers wounded and killed each other, or would it be on that other, silent "battlefield," the hearts and minds of the people, where allegiance is won or lost? According to Macaulay, James and William somehow understood that the second field was the important one, and so combat played almost no role in the Glorious Revolution. "That great force," Macaulay writes of James's army, "had been absolutely of no account in the late change, had done nothing towards keeping William out, and had nothing towards bringing him in."

Much of what Macaulay—the great purveyor of liberal "Whig history"— wrote in the nineteenth century about the seventeenth has been challenged by historians in the twentieth, but his assessment of the role of violence in the revolution, on the whole, has not. In the 1930s, for example, G. M. Trevelyan wrote, "No encounter of the least military importance took place," and added, "the war was won and lost in the camp at Salisbury, and in the mind and heart of James." And the contemporary historian J. G. A. Pocock has described William's progress as follows: "William of Orange, a powerful European prince, landed in the west of England at the head of an army in campaign order, composed of regiments of long-service professionals in historic transition from the status of *condottieri* [mercenary commanders] to that of a national army. . . . The campaign of 1688 . . . had no military solution, only a political and revolutionary one; by 'revolution' would here be meant the dramatic collapse of a power structure and the overthrow of its head."

Pocock's words suggest that William found himself wrestling with the same distinction between military and political power that arose in people's wars in our century. If the Americans in Vietnam illustrated the negative proposition that military victory can be worthless without political victory, William illustrated the complementary proposition that political victory can be complete without military victory. That is why, whereas no amount of fighting could bring the Americans victory, no fighting at all was necessary to bring victory to William. In both cases, political victory was paramount. (What is perhaps most surprising to modern sensibilities about these pre-national or proto-national events is that William, a foreigner, was the popular, patriotic choice of the English, whereas the native James was spurned.)

William's popularity had not sprung out of nowhere. James's political support had ebbed among the people long before his armies melted away at Salisbury field. Two years earlier, James had sent his army to intimidate London, which was in a state of virtual rebellion against him. "The King . . . had greatly miscalculated," Macaulay tells us. "He had forgotten that vicinity operates in more ways than one. He had hoped that his army would overawe London: but the result of his policy was that the feelings and opinions of London took complete possession of his army." London was in fact the first of many modern capitals whose rebellious spirit was to infect and destroy the allegiance of an army of an ancien régime.

The outcome of this contagion had been prepared by what can aptly be called a protracted, nationwide movement of noncooperation. The principal issues in the civil struggle between the English Parliament and James II had been in contention throughout his reign: first, whether James, a Catholic, could impose his faith on the largely Protestant English and, second, whether the prerogatives of a king were to be subordinate to the rights and powers of Parliament in particular and of law in general, or whether James was to be an "absolute" monarch, like Louis XIV. The key events in the struggle against James were acts of nonviolent resistance by men ready to pay a high price for their disobedience. Their storied deeds included the refusal of Magdalen College at Oxford to accept the king's arbitrary attempt to impose a Catholic rector on that Protestant institution and the resistance of seven Anglican bishops to his demand that they read a declaration of indulgence, which was offensive to most Anglicans and other Protestants, in their churches. The bishops' resistance was followed by their trial and dramatic acquittal, all leading directly to the decision by the great lords, on the very day of the acquittal, to invite William to invade. When King James, attempting to create a submissive parliament, ordered his lords lieutenant to scour England for subservient electors, Lord Bath was forced to report back, "No one of note will accept." He went on, "Sir, if your Majesty should dismiss these gentlemen [then sitting in Parliament], their successors would give exactly the same answer."

When the king ordered the public reading by the rest of the Anglican clergy of his declaration of indulgence, the result was similar. Macaulay describes what happened in the king's own palace: "The minister who had officiated at the chapel in Saint James's Palace had been turned out of his situation, and a more obsequious divine appeared with the paper in his hand: but his agitation was so great that he could not articulate. In truth the feeling of the whole nation had now become such as none but the very best and noblest, or the very worst and basest, of mankind could without much discomposure encounter." Macaulay's enthusiastic summary is a portrait of the politically engaged portion of the country united in de facto nonviolent resistance to its ruler. "Actuated by these sentiments," Macaulay concludes, "our ancestors arrayed themselves against the government in one huge and compact mass. All ranks, all parties, all Protestant sects, made up that vast phalanx." Here was the victory that put William on the throne, though he was not to arrive in England until a year later. If Macaulay was right, then the face-off at Salisbury was the last act of a long nonviolent struggle that had been waged in civil society. What need was there for a battle if, with the mere passage of time, one side would throw down its arms?

Conquest or Consent?

It was one thing for William to defeat James, another to take the English crown. William's approach to foundation was entirely of a piece with his approach to overthrow. In both, he relied for success not on arms but on consent by those Englishmen who had the power to decide the matter. Macaulay explains:

> His only chance of obtaining the splendid prize [the British crown] was not to seize it rudely but to wait till, without any appearance of exertion or stratagem on his part, his secret wish should be accomplished by the force of circumstances, by the blunders of his opponents, and by the free choice of the Estates of the Realm.

William convened a Revolutionary Convention, composed of lords, representatives of the House of Commons, and city magistrates, to deliberate and decide the disposition of the crown and the constitutional shape of the future. The debates revolved around the question of how, in a political system in which most agreed that the throne was and should remain hereditary, an alteration in the line of succession could be justified.

Two factions, already known as Whigs and Tories, put forward their solutions. The Whigs, who had long favored parliamentary power and had led the resistance to James from the beginning, proposed a contract theory of governing, according to which the subject's oath of allegiance to the king must be reciprocated by a royal oath of service to the people and allegiance to the law of the land. A modest, deliberate breach in the succession (William being the son of James's sister), they alleged, would merely bring the underlying contractual character of kingship out into the open—a good thing, in their eyes, for their party and its predecessors had been agitating for a contractual basis for government for more than half a century. The Tories, who denied that there could be any contractual foundation for royal rule or *any* right of resistance to a king's commands by a subject, were in a quandary. They, too, had been driven into opposition to James—by his attack on Anglicanism, among other things. They had done in fact what they had disavowed in theory: they had resisted and then driven out their king. The question was how they could justify this. For some, William's joint investiture with his wife, Mary, James's elder daughter, and the nearest *Protestant* heir to the crown, provided some legitimacy to the deed. Others suggested that they were simply submitting to conquest; for, as Macaulay notes, "No jurist, no divine, had ever denied that a nation, overcome in war, might, without sin, submit to decisions of the God of battles." The advantage to the Tories of claiming that William had conquered England was that it delivered the country from any taint of the hated contract theory. What contract could there be when a people had submitted at swordpoint?

Unfortunately, the claim was clearly contrary to fact. True, armies had marched. True, they had arrayed themselves for battle. But they had never fought. In what sense, then, had the English been conquered? Everything William had won had been delivered to him by willing Englishmen, many of whom were Tories. In effect, the English had chosen a new king. William, ever the realist, declined the temptation to misinterpret his success as a conquest. "For call himself what he might," Macaulay comments, "all the world knew that he was not really a conqueror. It was notoriously a mere fiction to say that this great kingdom, with a mighty fleet on the sea, with a regular army of forty thousand men . . . without one siege or battle, had been reduced to the state of a province by fifteen thousand invaders. Such a fiction . . . could scarcely fail to gall the national pride . . ."

William chose the contractual solution. The choice was anything but arbitrary. More than half a century of struggle between Parliament and the king pointed in that direction. In his announcement of his invasion, he had sworn to defend "a free parliament." Now he would accept the crown only with the agreement of the Revolutionary Convention, on terms that it set forth.

They turned out to include a Declaration of Right, later formalized as the Bill of Rights. This decision by William, in turn, laid the foundation for government based on the supremacy of Parliament over the king and of law over both. Overthrow based on consent had made possible foundation based on consent, which in turn made possible government based on consent. Although no balloting had occurred, the English had chosen their political future freely, and they would continue, in greater and greater measure, to do so from then on. The basis for the creation of a government that was to become, after a long development, the liberal democratic rule we know today was, in fact, a nonviolent revolution.

It would be preposterous to present William of Orange—that great warrior-king—as any sort of pacifist. Nevertheless, the revolution he brought about rested not on fear but indeed on a kind of consent. William, who may have merely happened upon the power of nonviolence, was shrewd enough to seize the opportunity. But having seized it, he found himself subject to its laws. William was not a dreamer. His biographers describe him as "cold," "taciturn," "reserved," "gloomy." A Dutchman, he spoke English imperfectly and had little emotional attachment to England. "To him she was always a land of exile, visited with reluctance and quitted with delight." "What the king wanted was power," his recent biographer Stephen B. Baxter writes, "power enough to bring England into an alliance against Louis XIV and to keep her there." But the means to this end, he understood, was not to establish absolute rule in England, even supposing it were possible.

For most of the seventeenth century, William's Stuart predecessors had battled over the power of the purse with Parliament, which had responded at several key junctures by severely curtailing the king's resources for war on the continent. It was their strongest weapon in their fight with the king. William grasped that a free parliament might be willing to loosen its purse strings to an extent that a coerced, manipulated one would not. From his point of view, granting Parliament its freedom was a recipe for more, not less power in pursuit of his aim of fighting Louis on the continent. Thus for a second time William increased his power through an act of restraint. In deciding on both of these policies, he took his bearings from the same underlying fact: his support among the English public. And both policies were richly rewarded in exactly the coin he sought: power. What is more striking still, the system of government thus established proved a fountainhead of new power for the country that established it. England at that moment began the long rise to an international preeminence that lasted through the first several decades of the past century. It is true that England's power was based on other strengths as well, including its central bank and trading system, its technical genius, which placed it in the forefront of the industrial revolution, and its early development of the free-market system, but it may be doubted that any of these would have served England as they did if not reared on the foundation of the unique system of government created in 1689. In the words of Trevelyan, "The Revolution gave to England an ordered and legal freedom, and through that it gave her power."

The Glorious Revolution and Political Theory

The nonviolence of the Glorious Revolution, although plainly described and acknowledged in the dominant, Whig school of English history, failed to find reflection in English political theory, in which the conviction persisted that tyrannical rulers could be overthrown only by violence. Pocock has written an essay that bears on the neglect by Whig theorists of the nonviolence of 1689. John Locke's famed *Second Treatise on Government*, which appeared after the revolution, with a dedication to "our great restorer, King William" whose crown was rooted in "the consent of the people," was accepted over time as the classical statement of the principles of the revolution as well as a founding document of liberal thought. However, Pocock notes, the *Treatise* was written before the revolution—probably in the early 1680s. Locke defined conditions under which the "dissolution of government"—i.e., popular rebellion—was justified. The clear reference was to the extremely violent civil war between parliamentary and royal forces that had resulted in the overthrow and beheading of Charles I and the arrival in power of Oliver Cromwell in the 1640s. As Pocock points out, "There is no way of reading Locke's scenario of appeal to heaven [to battle], dissolution of government, and reversion of power to the people except as a scenario of civil war." And yet when revolution came, there was no civil war.

The failure of prophecy was hardly Locke's alone. It was as universal as the failure in our day to predict the nonviolent fall of the Soviet Union. For some, the consequences of the misjudgment were dire. Louis XIV, for one, was badly misled, and at a high cost. "For twenty years," the historian Lord Acton writes, "it had been his desire to neutralize England by internal broils, and he was glad to have the Dutch out of the way [in England] while he dealt a blow at the Emperor Leopold [of Austria]." But as Trevelyan, who quotes this passage, comments, Louis's hopes were "defeated by the unexpected rapidity, peacefulness and solidity of a new type of Revolution." Louis was calculating according to the Realpolitik of his day. How could he guess that a phoenix—the force of modern revolution based on the consent of the governed—would rise up from those obscure and peripheral English quarrels and, in violation of the political principles he and his "realist" advisers knew so well, thwart his continental ambitions? For as Trevelyan has said, "What happened was contrary to all precedent."

The failure of theory to come to grips with the nonviolence of 1689 left both the Whigs and the Tories without adequate terms to account for what had happened. The Whigs and a few moderate Tories, eager to claim the respectability of tradition for their actions, denied that any "dissolution" of the government had in fact occurred. According to them, everything had happened according to fully constitutional processes—in keeping with the "ancient constitution"—which supposedly had been in operation since the Magna Carta. This interpretation enlisted history on the side of contract theory but at the cost of denying that any revolution had occurred. "In 1689, both William's 'conquest' and James' 'treason' could have been read as dissolutions of government," Pocock notes, "but these were unacceptable interpretations, appealing to no more than a handful of radicals, and rejected unceremoniously by the Convention and the political nation at large." The claim that the continuity of royal governance was unbroken would prove especially appealing a hundred years later, when the French launched their bloody revolution, to which the peaceful English "restoration" could be smugly contrasted. As Macaulay boasted, "Because we had a restoration, we did not have to have a revolution."

Some Tories, engaging in an opposite sort of obfuscation, acknowledged that the dethronement of James and his replacement by William were indeed revolutionary but denied, for that very reason, that the events could have been "constitutional" or "bloodless." That is why they revived the idea, rejected by William himself, that the decision by force had in fact taken place. As the conservative Burke wrote later, "The Revolution of 1688 was obtained by a just war, in the only case in which war, and much more, a civil war, can be won." Calling the revolution an outcome of war, Burke could sidestep the detested conclusion that overthrowing kings was in any way provided for in the English constitution.

The idea of nonviolent revolution, although corresponding to the facts of 1689, would have to wait more than two hundred years, until the Indian community in South Africa took its oath in the Empire Theater in 1906. Looking back from the 1850s, Macaulay marveled at the apparent anomaly: "Never, within the memory of man, had there been so near an approach to entire concord among all intelligent Englishmen as at this conjuncture," he wrote, "and never had concord been more needed. Legitimate authority there was none."

was in opposition to a British-imposed tax that was ruining the peasants of the Kheda district. Each campaign was a grueling, self-contained, high-stakes drama, pitting the willingness of peasants and workers and of Gandhi himself to suffer for their cause against the will of powerful factory owners and state authorities. "A series of passive resistances is an agonizing effort," he wrote of these campaigns to a friend, Henry Polak. "It is an exalting agony. I suppose the agony of childbirth must be somewhat like it." His modus operandi in these and subsequent campaigns included, as his biographer Judith M. Brown has written, "the search for a peaceful solution at the outset, the sacred pledge as the heart of the struggle, strict discipline and self-improvement among the participants, careful publicity and the generation of an ambience of moral authority and pressure, and finally a compromise solution to save the face and honor of all concerned." In the Ahmedabad strike, he fasted in support of a cause for the first time since arriving in India. His aim was twofold—to bring the pressure of "self-suffering" to bear on his opponent and to purify himself spiritually. A few years later, he explained, "I can as well do without my eyes . . . as I can without fasts. What the eyes are for the outer world, fasts are for the inner." Gandhi's methods and style, which made the privileged, moderate leaders of the Congress Party deeply uncomfortable, appealed strongly to masses of ordinary Indians, and Gandhi became India's first truly national figure.

In 1917, in the most discouraging days of the First World War, England had announced a series of liberal reforms that would increase Indians' participation in the administration of their own country. Yet when the war ended, in November 1918, these hopes were thwarted by the passage of the repressive Anarchical and Revolution Crimes Act, known also as the Rowlatt Act, imposed after an investigation by the British authorities of the possibilities for terrorism and "sedition" in India. In Gandhi's eyes, the Rowlatt bills were for the India of 1918 what the Amendment Ordinance of the Asiatic Act had been for the South Africa of

"The appeal to heaven meant the drawing of the sword," Pocock aptly comments. "The only alternative for us to imagine is some Tolstoyan or Gandhian process whereby the people dissolve government and revert to natural society by means of purely passive disobedience, and this was not available in an England where subjects who possessed arms were expected to use them." But isn't the history of James II's reign, in which the English stood, as Macaulay says, "in one compact mass" against its king, replete with scenes from just such a process? And didn't this long movement of civil disobedience prepare the way for the defections from James to William at Salisbury? A theory of nonviolent revolution was missing but something close to the fact of it was present.

John Adams and the Jurors of Massachusetts

Like England's Glorious Revolution, the American Revolution laid the foundation for lasting constitutional government. There could, however, be no Salisbury field in the United States. The surprising turn of events by which the Glorious Revolution was peacefully accomplished—the dissolution of the army of one side—was not possible in America. When the English in 1688 switched their allegiance en masse from one prince to another, they in fact made the nation whole again under a new ruler and a changed system of government. "Treason" turned out to be the path to national unity. It was not likely, however, that the Americans would accomplish a similar miracle among the redcoats, who, in order to defect, would have had to switch national as well as party loyalties. In the United States, a radically new stake was on the table. Not just a new government but a new nation, separated from the old by thousands of miles of ocean and a hundred and fifty years of semiautonomous development, was being born.

Here, at least, battles would be fought; but what would be their role in deciding the outcome of the revolution? George Washington hinted at an answer when, en route to his victory over the English at Yorktown, in September of 1781, he stopped in Philadelphia to report to Congress. "I have been your faithful servant so far as it lay within me to be," he said. "I have endured." A seemingly modest claim—yet to endure had been the heart of Washington's strategy. As long as the army remained in the field, the will of the American people to prevail remained intact; as long as the will of the American people was intact, the British could not militarily defeat the United States; as long as the British could not militarily defeat the United States, the war would go on indefinitely—a burden that the British were not ready to shoulder. Eventually, they had to tire and leave. Washington defined what it meant to endure more precisely in a remark to a crowd of bystanders. "We may be beaten by the English . . . but *here* is an army they will never conquer," he said. Washington's fine but all-important distinction between an army that might be "beaten" and a people that could never be "conquered" expressed the essence of his strategy—a strategy that would have a long and rich history in the people's wars and nonviolent revolutions of the future.

To be sure, General Washington never deprecated victories and, even as he conducted a long series of retreats, won several, including the one at Trenton, New Jersey, following his renowned counterattack across the Delaware River. The war ended, of course, with the triumph at Yorktown, won with the assistance of the French navy. Yet Washington was always aware that his most important task was to insure the survival of his own forces—not strictly for military purposes but to personify the unconquerable will of the American people. The winter at Valley Forge—that epic of endurance, in which the enemy was not the British army but snow, cold, and short rations, and during which Washington invited his troops to read Tom Paine's *American Crisis,* praising these "winter soldiers"—has rightly gone down in American legend as a decisive event in the revolutionary war. Paine stated in clear terms what Washington, as leader of the revolutionary army, could only hint at—that British military victories might be useless to the

British cause. In one of the earliest and most succinct formulations of the strategy of nonviolent revolution, he said, " 'Tis not in numbers but in unity that our great strength lies; yet our present numbers are sufficient to repel the force of all the world." Therefore, "In the unlikely event that the British conquered the Americans militarily the victory would be utterly fictional." In Paine's view, his biographer John Keane comments, "Rulers can rule only insofar as they have the tacit or active support of the ruled. Without it, they become impotent in the face of citizens acting together in solidarity for the achievement of their own common goals." What is perhaps more surprising is to find the same point being made on the other side of the Atlantic by members of England's antiwar faction, led in Parliament by Edmund Burke. Burke was soon to enter into world-renowned debate with Paine over the nature of the French Revolution, but in the matter of the American Revolution the two men were in substantial agreement. Burke understood early that a policy of force in America was futile. As the British general Howe drove the Continental Army across New Jersey, Burke warned, in words that would be echoed for the next two hundred years by commanders seeking to quell people's war, "Our victories early on in the war can only complete our ruin."

In 1777, after the Americans defeated General Burgoyne at Saratoga, Burke introduced a Bill for Composing the Present Troubles in America. His argument for a quick settlement of the war on terms favorable to the colonies went to the heart of the distinction between power based on force and power based on popular consent, or "love"—a term Burke did not shy from using. The British government, he noted, wanted to obtain revenue from America through taxation. The terms of the tax legislation, however, could be guaranteed only by one of two possible means: "force" or "the honor, sincerity, and good inclination of the people." He argued, "If nothing but force could hold them, and they meant nothing but independency, as the Speech from the throne asserted, then the House was to consider how a standing army of 26,000 men, and 70 ships of war, could be constantly kept up in America. A people meaning independency, will not mean it the less, because they have, to avoid a present inconvenience, submitted to treaty."

There was more. The choice between force and consent was inseparable from the choice that England had made a century earlier for its own government, which, Burke said, was and must continue to be based not on fear but on "the love of the people." He wrote:

> Do you imagine . . . that it is the Land-Tax Act which raises your revenues? that it is the annual vote in the Committee of Supply which gives you your army? or that it is the Mutiny Bill which inspires it with bravery and discipline? No! Surely, no! It is the love of the people; it is their attachment to their government, from the sense of the deep stake they have in such a glorious institution, which gives you your army and your navy, and infuses into both that liberal obedience without which your army would be a base rabble and your navy nothing but rotten timber.

Before a Drop of Blood Was Shed

John Adams, who appointed the committee that wrote the Declaration of Independence, served as the first vice president and second president of the United States, and was called "the colossus of independence" by Thomas Jefferson, penned some reflections late in his life that form a perfect complement to those of Washington, Paine, and Burke. If these three had defined negatively what could *not* decide the outcome of the revolution—namely, force—Adams defined positively what it was that *did* decide it: the combination of noncooperation and a constructive program now familiar to us.

Adams, in his late seventies, lacked the time and strength, he said, to write a history of the revolution; and so he offered his reflections only in letters to friends. He was prompted to write by the news that one Major General Wilkinson was penning a "history of the revolution," which was to begin with the battle of Bunker Hill, in 1775. Wilkinson, Adams wrote, would "confine himself to military transactions, with a reference to very few of the civil."

Such an account, Adams protested, would falsify history. "A history of the war of the United States is a very different thing," he claimed, "from a history of the first American revolution." Not only was Wilkinson wrong to concentrate on military affairs; he had located the revolution in the wrong historical period. The revolution, Adams claimed, was over before the war began:

> General Wilkinson may have written the military history of the war that followed the Revolution; that was an effect of it, and was supported by the American citizens in defence of it against an invasion of it by the government of Great Britain and Ireland, and all her allies . . . but this will by no means be a history of the American Revolution. The revolution was in the minds of the people, and in the union of the colonies, both of which were accomplished before hostilities commenced.

To his correspondent, Thomas Jefferson, a former political antagonist, he made the point emphatically: "As to the history of the revolution, my ideas may be peculiar, perhaps singular. What do we mean by the revolution? The war? That was no part of the revolution; it was only an effect and consequence of it. The revolution was in the minds of the people, and this was effected from 1760 to 1775, in the course of fifteen years, before a drop of blood was shed at Lexington."

Adams described an event that for him was a true turning point in the revolution. The English crown had decided to pay the judges of the Massachusetts Supreme Court directly. The colonists were indignant, and, at the suggestion of John Adams, voted to impeach the judges in the Massachusetts House of Representatives. The crown ignored the impeachment. Then came the decisive step. Jurors unanimously refused to serve under the embattled judges.

Adams, who likes to use military metaphors to describe great deeds of peaceful noncooperation, remarks, "The cool, calm, sedate intrepidity with which these honest freeholders went through this fiery trial filled my eyes and my heart. *That* was the revolution—the decisive blow against England: In one word, the royal government was that moment laid prostrate in the dust, and has never since revived in substance, though a dark shadow of the hobgoblin haunts me at times to this day."

Adams's gallery of heroes are all civilians, his battles nonviolent ones. When he learns that Congress has appointed a national painter, he recommends paintings, to be executed in the grand style, of scenes of protest—a painting, for example, of Samuel Adams, his cousin and a sparkplug of the revolution, arguing with Lieutenant Governor Hutchinson against standing armies. "It will be as difficult," he remarks lightly, "to do justice as to paint an Apollo; and the transaction deserves to be painted as much as the surrender of Burgoyne. Whether any artist will ever attempt it, I know not."

Acts of noncooperation were one indispensable ingredient of what Adams calls "the real American revolution"; acts of association were another. At their center were the Committees of Correspondence, through which, beginning in the mid-1760s, the revolutionaries in the colonies mutually fostered and coordinated their activities. "What an engine!" Adams wrote of the Committees. "France imitated it, and produced a revolution. England and Scotland were upon the point of imitating it, in order to produce another revolution, and all Europe was inclined to imitate it for the same revolutionary purposes. The history of the world for the last thirty years is a sufficient commentary upon it. That history ought to convince all mankind that committees of secret correspondence are dangerous machines." Here, plainly, is another predecessor of the *hiérarchies parallèles*.

The decisive revolution, according to Adams, was thus the process by which ordinary people withdrew cooperation from the British government and then, well before even the Declaration of

Independence, set up their own governments in all the colonies. The war that followed was the *military defense* of these already-existing governments against an attack by what was now a foreign power seeking to force the new country back into its empire. In his view, indeed, independence was nothing that could be *won from* the British; it had to be *forged by* the Americans. "Let me ask you, Mr. Rush," he wrote to his friend Richard Rush in April of 1815, in phrases that startlingly resemble Gandhi's later denial that Indian independence could be "given" her by England, "Is the sovereignty of this nation a gift? a grant? a concession? a conveyance? or a release and acquittance from Great Britain? Pause here and think. No! The people, in 1774, by the right which nature and nature's God had given them, confiding in original right, assumed powers of sovereignty. In 1775, they assumed greater power. In July 4th, 1776, they assumed absolute unlimited sovereignty in relation to other nations, in all cases whatsoever; no longer acknowledging any authority over them but that of God almighty, and the laws of nature and of nations."

In a recent description of the process Adams described, the historian Gordon Wood has written, "The royal governors stood helpless as they watched para-governments grown up around them, a rapid piecing together from the bottom up of a hierarchy of committees and congresses that reached from the counties and towns through the provincial conventions of the Continental Congress." On May 15, 1776, Adams notes, the Continental Congress declared that "every kind of authority under the . . . Crown should be totally suppressed," and authorized the states to found "government sufficient to the exigencies of their affairs." "For if," Wood comments, "as Jefferson and others agreed, the formation of new governments was the whole object of the Revolution, then the May resolution authorizing the drafting of new constitutions was the most important act of the Continental Congress in its history. There in the May 15 resolution was the real declaration of independence, from which the measures of early July could be but derivations." James Duane, a delegate to the first congress, called this process "a Machine for the fabrication of Independence." Adams responded, "It was independence itself."

It is interesting to observe that another very notable authority on American political history also located the foundation of the Republic before July 4, 1776. "The Union is much older than the Constitution," Abraham Lincoln said in his First Inaugural. "It was formed in fact by the Articles of Association of 1774."

If we accept Adams's view, then both the overthrow of the old regime, laid in the dust (as Adams said) through a series of acts of noncooperation, and the foundation of the new one, accomplished the moment the Americans set up governments to govern themselves, were, like the overthrow and the foundation in 1688–89, nonviolent events, and the war that followed could be seen as a war of self-defense. In that war, Adams wrote to Rush, "Heaven decided in our favor; and Britain was forced not to give, grant, concede, or release our independence, but to acknowledge it, in terms as clear as our language afforded, and under seal and under oath."

6

The Mass Minority in Action: France and Russia

It might seem perverse to mention nonviolence in connection with the French Revolution, a notoriously blood-soaked event that produced, along with much else, the first instance of large-scale, organized revolutionary terror of the modern age. Let us nevertheless consider the best known of all the days of the revolution, July 14, 1789, commemorated in France as Bastille Day.

In June of that year, the Estates-General, an assembly representing the aristocracy, the clergy, and the bourgeoisie, had been summoned, as all French schoolchildren know, by the king to meet for the first time in one hundred and seventy-five years. Louis XVI hoped that if he granted the three "estates" an advisory voice in the country's affairs, their members would agree to raise the new taxes needed to reduce the royal government's perilously high debt, run up during the recent Seven Years' War. Upon meeting, however, the Estates-General immediately passed beyond the issues of taxes and budgets to launch a full-scale challenge to the absolute rule of the king. The representatives of the third estate, the bourgeoisie, declared themselves to be "the nation," and demanded that all three orders vote together, creating a body in which the third estate's large numbers would give it the decisive voice. The king, in alarm, locked the third estate out of its meeting hall, and the body proceeded to the famous tennis court, where it took the solemn Tennis Court Oath, declaring that henceforth they were a National Assembly. Within days, the other two estates yielded to this fait accompli and joined the third, whereupon the king also acceded.

On July 11, however, the king reversed course, firing his minister of finance, Jacques Necker, who was popular in the estates and among the people, and summoning royal troops from the frontier. The stage seemed set for a decision by arms, pitting the royal forces against the Parisian rebels. In fact, however, such a contest would no more occur than had a battle on Salisbury field. Mirabeau, the renowned orator and schemer of the early years of the revolution (and something of a student of the Glorious Revolution), predicted in one of his speeches to the Assembly the course that events actually took. "French soldiers are not just automata," he declared. "They will see in us, their relatives, their friends, and their families. . . . They will never believe it is their duty to strike without asking who are the victims." The French commander in Paris, the Baron de Besenval, apparently was aware of the uncertain loyalty of his troops, because instead of sending them forth to defeat the enemy, he confined them to their barracks. There, some took a secret oath not to act against the Assembly. The king's cavalry briefly got ready to attack a crowd in the Place Vendôme, but Besenval's Gardes Françaises appeared in the crowd's defense and the cavalry fled.

On the fourteenth came the celebrated "storming" by the rebellious Parisians of the infamous royal prison the Bastille. The nineteenth-century French historian of the revolution Jules Michelet describes, with almost a touch of embarrassment, what it actually consisted of: "The bastille was not taken; it surrendered. Troubled by a bad conscience it went mad and lost all presence of mind." After a confused negotiation and a brief skirmish, the governor of the fortress turned it over to the angry crowd. Michelet describes the mood of the prison's French defenders—called *invalides*—among whom were intermixed a few Swiss mercenaries:

> Shame for such cowardly warfare, and the horror of shedding French blood, which but little affected the Swiss, at length caused the *Invalides* to drop their arms.

The Parisian rebels had been ready for a violent showdown but it never materialized; nor did the mighty ancien régime, for all its "absolute" power, ever pull itself together to strike a serious military blow against the revolution. Itself a kind of *invalide,* it in effect dropped its arms without a battle. The nineteenth-century historian of the revolution Thomas Carlyle commented acutely on the reason.

> Good is grapeshot, Messeigneurs, on one condition: that the shooter also were made of metal! But unfortunately he is made of flesh; under his buffs and bandoleers, your hired shooter has instincts, feelings, even a kind of thought. It is his kindred, bone of his bone, the same *canaille* that shall be whiffed [fired upon with grapeshot]: he has brothers in it, a father and mother—living on meal husks and boiled grass.

It was with excellent reason that the Romantic poet Chateaubriand, in a comment that strongly resembles Adams's observations on the American Revolution, later remarked, "The French revolution was accomplished before it occurred." To the degree that a revolution in hearts and minds had taken place, his comments suggested, violence was unnecessary. Rifles were not fired but thrown down or turned over to the revolution. How can there be shooting if no soldiers will defend the old regime? Individual hearts and minds change; those who have changed become aware of one another; still others are emboldened, in a contagion of bold-ness; the "impossible" becomes possible; immediately it is done, surprising the actors almost as much as their opponents; and sud-denly, almost with the swiftness of thought—whose transforma-tion has in fact set the whole process in motion—the old regime, a moment ago so impressive, vanishes like a mirage.

Must we conclude, then, that all revolutions are over before they begin—or, at least, before they are seen to begin? If so, revolutions would all be nonviolent. In France, however, the revolution soon descended into carnage, signaled on the very day of the Bastille's fall by the beheading of two officials and public display of their heads on pikes. Still to come were the massacres in the prisons in September of 1792, the brutal war of repression in the Vendée, the wars against the other European dynastic powers, the execution of the king, the repeated intimidation of the new legislature by the Paris Commune, and, of course, the Jacobin terror. The revolution-aries would be more violent toward one another than they had been toward the old regime.

In the French Revolution, as in the English and the American, the stage of overthrow was nearly bloodless; but the stage of foun-dation was bloody—establishing a pattern that was to be repeated in more than one revolution thereafter, and never with more fear-ful consequences than in the Russian Revolution of 1917. (Let us here recall, too, that the foundation of the independent Indian state was violent. It precipitated the partition of India and Pak-istan, which cost almost a million lives.)

Nonviolent Revolution, Violent Rule

The Bolsheviks seized power in October 1917, through direct action in St. Petersburg, the capital of Russia. Their aim was to relieve the desperate poverty and humiliation of the workers and peasants of Russia by overthrowing the czarist regime and estab-lishing communism—all as a prelude to a wider revolution that would bring communism to the rest of Europe and, in the not-too-distant future, the world. Little, if any, blood was shed in the revolution, although the Bolsheviks were quite prepared to shed it. However, having seized state power without violence, they instantly began, like the French revolutionaries, to defend and consolidate it with extreme violence, directed against not only their adversaries from the overthrown Provisional Government and the former czarist regime but also their fellow socialists. The Jacobin regime of Maximilien Robespierre ruled by terror for a little more than a year, then was overthrown in the reaction of Thermidor, in 1794. The regime founded by Lenin in 1917 did not meet its Thermidor for seventy-four years.

The sequence in which an unexpectedly nonviolent overthrow of Russia's ancien régime produced an unexpectedly violent new regime has given rise to unending interpretive debates, which have been all the more difficult to sort out because the principal actors, including, above all, Lenin, stuck with political theory rather than the facts of the case in their interpretation of their deeds. The Bolsheviks doggedly insisted they had unleashed force to seize power, even sponsoring a movie, the Soviet director Sergei Eisenstein's film *October*, that showed the imaginary battles they believed theoretically necessary. And, to complete the confusion, they falsely denied that, once in power, they ruled by force—a far more sweeping lie.

The regime's legions of subsequent detractors strove to disprove the claim that Bolshevik rule was based on consent but tended, on the whole, to confirm the claim that the takeover had been violent. As happened after the revolution of 1689, historians plainly recorded that the revolution had succeeded almost without bloodshed but theorists insisted that battles had been decisive. Especially problematic has been the assertion, made by many of the Bolsheviks' opponents, that the revolution wasn't a revolution at all but a mere coup d'état—a procedure that by definition is characterized by violence. (According to Webster's, a coup d'état is "a sudden decisive exercise of force in politics; *esp:* the violent over-throw or alteration of an existing government by a small group.")

The issue does not admit of easy resolution. The Bolsheviks, an armed minority party, did indeed unilaterally seize power without seeking permission from anyone. When it was suggested to Lenin that he await the outcome of the forthcoming Russia-wide elections to a Constituent Assembly, his answer was, "No revolution waits for *that.*" The Bolsheviks were believers in violent revolution, even in flat opposition to the will of the majority. In July 1917, Lenin wrote, in words that scarcely could have been plainer, "In times of revolution, it is not enough to ascertain the 'will of the majority'—no, one must *be stronger* at the decisive moment in the decisive place and *win.* . . . We see countless instances of how the better-organized, more conscious, better-armed minority imposed its will on the majority and conquered it."

In February 1917, in the fourth year of the First World War, protests against shortages of bread in the capital city of Petersburg led to workers' strikes; the strikes led to demonstrations, and the demonstrations led to mass protest against both the war and the Romanov dynasty. For the second time since the new century began, the Russians were rebelling against the czar's rule. In 1905, after political concessions by the regime had failed to appease the protesters, the government put down an impending revolution by force. In 1917, however, the troops would not fight. They were receptive to the revolutionaries' socialist message of justice for the poor. Like many of James II's troops in 1688 and the Gardes Françaises in Paris in 1789, they went over to the side of the rebels. Once again, the revolutionary spirit of a capital city spread to troops, rendering them useless to the old regime. Once again, defections were pivotal, and Czar Nicholas II abdicated the throne, ending the dynasty.

Leon Trotsky, who had been a leader of the Petersburg soviet, or council, that had sprung up in 1905, had foreseen these defections and the reasons for them. In a speech he gave at his trial for his participation in the events of 1905, he proclaimed:

No matter how important weapons may be it is not in them, gentlemen the judges, that great power resides. No! Not the ability of the masses to kill others but their great readiness themselves to die—this secures in the last instance the victory of the popular rising.

For:

Only when the masses show readiness to die on the barricades can they win over the army on which the old regime relies. The barricade does not play in revolution the part which the fortress plays in regular warfare. It is mainly the physical and moral meeting ground between people and army.

These Gandhi-like predictions (let us recall that the revolution of 1905 inspired Gandhi as he forged satyagraha in South Africa just one year later) came true in the revolution of February 1917. The defection of the Petersburg garrison played a decisive role. In its wake, leaders of Russia's consultative congress, the Duma, and the military command joined in counseling the Czar's abdication. From start to finish, the February revolution took less than a week. In the words of the socialist Sukhanov, a firsthand observer of and actor in the revolution, it occurred with "a sort of fabulous ease." The description of these events by Aleksandr Kerensky, the second leader of the government that succeeded the Czar's, shows a remarkable resemblance to descriptions of the more recent collapse of the Soviet regime: "A whole world of national and political relationships sank to the bottom, and at once all existing political and tactical programs, however bold and well conceived, appeared hanging aimlessly and uselessly in space."

The Romanovs were succeeded by a system of "dual power," consisting of two ambiguously connected governing bodies: a Soviet, which was the successor to the Petersburg soviet of 1905, and a Provisional Government, composed chiefly of liberals and socialists, some of them leaders of the old Duma, which had melted away. The Soviet, though already exercising functions of government in the capital (to the extent that anybody did), was unwilling to claim full power, and invited the Provisional Government to share it. Broadly speaking, the Soviet directly represented workers, soldiers, and peasants, and the Provisional Government was the hope of the middle classes. In fact, both bodies were formally provisional, for both had agreed to yield to the Constituent Assembly, which was to be elected by all Russia in the fall and then was to establish a democratic, constitutional government for the nation.

The February revolution had revealed that the allegiance of the military—a largely peasant army, eleven million strong—was indispensable to victory. Other forces in society had, of course, played essential roles: members of the Duma eager to liquidate czarism, a radically disaffected intelligentsia, a peasantry eager and able to seize the land that it tilled, workers in the factories of Petersburg, Moscow, and other cities, and, of course, the radical political parties, including the Bolsheviks, Lenin's centralized "party of a new type." Yet "the decisive revolutionary agent," in the words of the historian Martin Malia, was "the peasant in uniform," for "it was his refusal to obey that neutralized the Imperial government."

The Overthrow

While Russia waited for the election of the Constituent Assembly, the country's politics swung between the extreme right and the extreme left. Although violence constantly threatened in this period, first from one side and then from the other, it never broke out to any great extent. The first and shortest swing was to the left. In late March, the Provisional Government sent its allies in the First World War a note that appeared to support imperialistic and annexationist war aims that were anathema to the left, which was dominant in the Petersburg Soviet, and demanded and obtained the resignation of Minister of War Aleksandr Guchkóv and Foreign Minister Pavel Milyukov. (In the politics of the time, pursuing the war was the position of the right and ending it was the position of the left.) In June, another attempt to revive the war effort was made by the new minister of war, Kerensky (later prime minister of the Provisional Government), who sought to rebuild the prestige of the new revolutionary government by launching an offensive against Austria and Germany. It failed catastrophically, creating conditions for the next swing to the left—the "July days," in which the Bolsheviks led armed demonstrations in the capital that, until the last moment, when the Bolsheviks backed off, gave every appearance of being an attempt to seize power. Now the pendulum swung back with equal force to the right. Lenin went into hiding, while much of the rest of the Bolshevik leadership, including Trotsky, was arrested. A right-wing czarist general, Lavr Kornilov, pursued tangled negotiations with the Provisional Government and then launched an insurrection against it. However, the forces he dispatched suffered a fate familiar to the student of revolutions: they melted away. In Trotsky's words, "After the February days the atmosphere of Petrograd becomes so red hot that every hostile military detachment arriving in that mighty forge, or even coming near to it, scorched by its breath, is transformed, loses confidence, becomes paralyzed, and throws itself upon the mercy of the victor without a struggle."

The way was open for the Bolshevik takeover, and the Party, whose most important leaders were now out of jail, began a debate on how to proceed. Lenin's recommendation was simple and clear. He championed an immediate "armed insurrection"—in other words, a straightforward coup d'état.

We can (if we do not "await" the Congress of Soviets) strike *suddenly* from three points: Petersburg, Moscow, and the Baltic Fleet . . . we have the technical capability to take power in

Moscow . . . we have *thousands* of armed workers and soldiers who can *at once* seize the Winter Palace.

However, Lenin encountered strong opposition, not only from other socialist parties when they got wind of his planned coup but also from other Bolshevik leaders, two of whom, Aleksandr Zinoviev and Lev Kamenev, resigned from the Party in protest. The Bolsheviks had "no right," the pair wrote publicly, "to stake the whole future of the present moment upon the card of armed insurrection." The Party, they observed, faced a basic choice between "the tactic of conspiracy and the tactic of faith in the motive forces of the Russian revolution." The latter path was peaceable; the former led to rule by force, for without a broad coalition, as the Central Committee member Nogin wrote, the regime would "eliminate the mass organizations of the proletariat from leadership in political life . . . and can be kept in power only by means of political terror." At one point, Lenin stood alone in the Central Committee in his championship of an immediate coup.

It was Trotsky who broke the impasse. More mindful of the importance of mass support than Lenin, he proposed an armed insurrection under the auspices of the upcoming second All-Russian Congress of Soviets, in which the political strength of the Bolsheviks was then on the rise. In other words, he proposed that the Provisional Government be overthrown by a Bolshevik armed insurrection legitimated by the Soviet assemblies. (Hence the legendary slogan "All power to the soviets.") But first Trotsky had to take over the Soviets. He promptly launched a successful effort to convene unilaterally an unauthorized, all-Russian Soviet that would be controlled by the Bolsheviks.

Events, however, played havoc with the expectations of all three factions of the Bolshevik Central Committee. Neither Lenin's naked armed coup, nor Kamenev and Zinoviev's peaceful, gradual acquisition of power, nor even Trotsky's subtler, Soviet-sanctioned coup came to pass. Instead, something unplanned by anyone occurred. With Lenin still in hiding, the chief improviser on the spot was Trotsky. In a meeting of the Petersburg Soviet on October 9, a worker affiliated with the Menshevik Party, Mark Broido, proposed the foundation of a Committee of Revolutionary Defense to prepare Petersburg against the advancing German army. The Bolsheviks opposed the plan until it occurred to Trotsky that the committee, which came to be known as the Milrevkom, would, if taken over by the Bolsheviks, be an ideal instrument for overthrowing the Provisional Government. The committee was then established. So important did Trotsky consider the foundation of the committee that he later claimed its creation was in fact a "dry" or "silent" revolution that won "three quarters, if not nine-tenths, of the victory." He meant that, without a shot being fired, the Bolsheviks now had in their hands a military instrument in the capital with which, as soon as they chose to employ it, they could seize full power.

What happened next lays bare with particular clarity the process by which revolutionaries can neutralize or win over the armed forces of the existing government. (Of the revolutions discussed here, only the American, as noted, had no chance of winning over the opposing army.) The pivotal event—second in importance only to the foundation of the Milrevkom—was a meeting with the regimental committees of the Petersburg garrison, at which a motion by Trotsky was passed assuring the Milrevkom of "full support in all its efforts to bring closer the front and rear in the interest of the Revolution." In the independent socialist Sukhanov's words, "On October 21, the Petersburg garrison *conclusively acknowledged the Soviet as sole power, and the military revolutionary committee as the immediate organ of authority.*"

In Sukhanov's opinion, this decision was more than the prelude to the takeover: "In actual fact, the overturn was accomplished the moment the Petersburg garrison acknowledged the Soviet as its supreme authority." He marveled at the blindness of others to what was happening. An "insurrectionary act" had occurred. The Provisional Government did not respond. It was "busy with something or other in the Winter Palace" (its headquarters) and took no notice. But even the Bolsheviks, Sukhanov thought, were not quite aware of what they had done. "War had been declared," Sukhanov, sounding like Lenin, notes, "but combat activities were not begun." At such a moment, the "correct tactics" in the revolutionary guidebooks were to "destroy, shatter, paralyze" the enemy command, which in this case was the general staff of the army, still following orders from the Provisional Government. A mere "three hundred volunteers" could have carried out the task "without the slightest difficulty," Sukhanov thought. Instead, he observed with a note of scorn, the Bolsheviks merely sent a delegation to the commander, Georgi Polkovnikov, demanding his obedience to the Milrevkom. Polkovnikov refused, but then entered into talks with the Soviet—talks that were still in progress four days later, when the events that have gone down in history as the October 25 Bolshevik takeover occurred.

Of the seeming passivity of the Bolsheviks, Sukhanov rightly comments, "This, to put it mildly, was hardly according to Marx." To that observation, we can add only that it was hardly according to Locke, Hobbes, Rousseau, or almost any other major thinker on revolution, either, since virtually all of them had taught that revolutions had to be decided by the use of force. The whole weight of this tradition bore down on the minds of the actors.

Sukhanov showed greater appreciation of Trotsky's tactics in his report on another important episode in the preparation for the takeover. On October 23, the commander of the Peter-Paul Fortress in the center of Petersburg announced his refusal to obey a commissar sent by the Soviet. Here, surely, a military confrontation was called for, and indeed the Bolshevik Vladimir Antonov-Ovseenko did recommend sending a loyal regiment to disarm their reluctant comrades in arms. Trotsky had another idea. "He, Trotsky," Sukhanov records, would "go to the Fortress, hold a meeting there, and capture not the body but the spirit of the garrison." And he did. He made a speech there that won over the soldiers. Such was the true nature of the "fighting" that occurred in Petersburg in the days leading up to the October revolution.

Trotsky vs. Trotsky

In his book *The Russian Revolution,* Trotsky took note of Sukhanov's bafflement regarding the Bolsheviks' failure to unleash force immediately. "The Committee," he explained, "is crowding out the government with the pressure of the masses, with the weight of the garrison. It is taking all that it can without a battle. It is advancing its positions without firing, integrating and reinforcing its army on the march. It is measuring with its own pressure the resisting power of the enemy, not taking its eyes off him for a second. . . . Who is to be the first to issue the call to arms will become known in the course of this offensive, this crowding out." Then, making an addition to our list of observers in various ages who commented that the revolution was over before it seemingly began, he added that the Soviet's "declaration of October 23 had meant the overthrow of the power before the government itself was overthrown."

It was because so much had been accomplished beforehand that the twenty-fifth itself came and went with little violence. Sukhanov reports that on that day Trotsky boasted, "We don't know of a single casualty," and added, "I don't know of any examples in history of a revolutionary movement in which such enormous masses participated and which took place so bloodlessly." Trotsky identified this bloodless activity as the main engine of the revolution. "The unique thing about the October revolution, a thing never before observed in so complete a form, was that, thanks to a happy combination of circumstances, the proletarian vanguard had won over the garrison of the capital before the moment of open insurrection." In point of fact, the garrisons had also been won over before the moment of insurrection in both the Glorious Revolution and the French Revolution. The difference was that Trotsky had deliberately engineered what had happened spontaneously in England and France. Although he didn't put it in so many words, Trotsky had grasped what Mao and Ho would later formulate more explicitly—that even when the readiness and capacity to act violently is present, political action is still the most important factor in a revolutionary struggle.

Quotations from Trotsky attesting to the decisive importance of strictly political action in the revolution could be multiplied many times over. However, he also made statements of exactly the opposite import, claiming that revolutions could succeed only through armed insurrection. For example, after claiming that the main task of the insurrection—winning over the troops—had been accomplished before the twenty-fifth, he went on to add, "This does not mean, however, that insurrection had become superfluous. . . . The last part of the task of the revolution, that which has gone into history under the name of the October insurrection, was therefore purely military in character. At this final stage, rifles, bayonets, machine guns, and perhaps cannon were to decide." Elsewhere, he wrote, "Only an armed insurrection could decide the question." And quotations of this kind, too, could be multiplied many times over. These assertions, however, are unsupported by evidence.

Why, we must ask, would Trotsky wish to contradict his own clearly drawn conclusions as well as the facts of history? One likely reason is that Trotsky wrote his history in the late 1920s, at the end of a decade-long, losing struggle with Stalin to become Lenin's heir, and it was Leninist dogma that the October revolution had been the armed insurrection that Lenin had beforehand asserted it must be. As such it had already gone down in myth and story, including *October*, in which a proper battle is shown. (Dur-

contradict his own plainly stated observations and conclusions, but there were other reasons as well. He had not shed blood in 1917, but by the time he wrote his history he had shed it abundantly—as commander and savage disciplinarian of the Red Army, as champion of "war communism," in which workers were subjected to military discipline, as a practitioner of and apologist for the "red terror" that was inaugurated in the first years of Bolshevik rule, and as the pitiless suppressor of the democratic Kronstadt rebellion against the Bolshevik dictatorship, in 1921. The day after the October 1917 overturn, the Bolsheviks carried out a wave of arrests and closed down all the opposition newspapers. The new rulers immediately made known their intention to monopolize power. It was on this occasion that Trotsky made an infamous threat to the non-Bolshevik socialist parties, who asked the Bolsheviks to share power with them. He said:

And now we are told: renounce your victory, make concessions, compromise. With whom? I ask: with whom ought we to compromise? With those wretched groups who have left us or who are making this proposal? . . . To those who have left and to those who tell us to do this we must say: you are miserable bankrupts, your role is played out; go where you ought to be: into the dustbin of history!

The Menshevik Party and others did in fact walk out of the meeting. Sukhanov, among those who left, later bitterly castigated himself for abandoning the field of the revolution to the Bolsheviks.

In short, while the Bolsheviks did not use violence to win power, they used it, instantly and lavishly, to keep power. Their insistence that they had needed violence to overthrow the Provisional Government provided cover of a sort for their unprovoked use of violence against their former revolutionary comrades who belonged to other parties. The repressive measures of the first days of Bolshevik rule were only the beginning of a wave of repression that almost immediately outdid czarist repression by an order of magnitude. If there was in fact a "coup," it was by the new revolutionary government against the other parties as well as opposition by ordinary citizens. The event was not so much a coup d'état as a *coup par l'état*—or a *coup de societé*—for it consisted not in the violent seizure *of* the state by military forces but in the destruction of society *by* the state once it had been taken over by the Bolshevik Party. Here, truly, were the origins of totalitarianism, to use Hannah Arendt's famous phrase.

The next step was taken in January, when the long-promised Constituent Assembly chosen in Russia's first nationwide election finally met and was promptly dispersed by Bolshevik troops. Eventually, the forcible takeover of society by the state proceeded from mere repression to Stalin's full-fledged totalitarian "war against the nation" (in the words of the Russian poet Osip Mandelstam).

But why would a party that had won power without bloodshed use it violently? The obvious answer is that the Bolsheviks' nonviolence was merely tactical. Indeed, it came as a surprise to them. Unforeseen in advance and forgotten later by Party theorists, the Bolsheviks' capture of the hearts and minds of the Czar's troops was an opportunity latent in events that the agile Trotsky had the wit to see and exploit. The nonviolence of October 25, you might say, belonged to the revolutionary situation, not to the ideology of the Bolsheviks, who believed in violence and used it unstintingly as soon as they deemed it necessary.

The curious record of the Bolsheviks' violence has a bearing on the question of whether October 25 was a mass revolution or merely a coup carried out by a small group of conspirators. Sukhanov, an anti-Bolshevik eyewitness, certainly believed that since the collapse of the Kornilov insurrection the workers of Petersburg had supported the Bolsheviks—"had been *their own people,* because they were always there, taking the lead in details as well as in the important affairs of the factory barracks." True, the Party had won its support because it had been "lavish with promises and sweet though simple fairy tales"; nevertheless, "the mass lived and breathed together with the Bolsheviks." Yet just a few years later the distinguished historian (and first president of Czechoslovakia) Tomáš Masaryk wrote in his work on the revolution, in direct contradiction of Sukhanov, "The October revolution was anything but a popular mass movement. That revolution was the act of leaders working from above and behind the scenes." And many historians have since followed Masaryk in his judgment.

In *The Russian Revolution*, Trotsky quoted and debated Masaryk. He claimed that the lack of street demonstrations and violent mass encounters was proof not of lack of mass support but of near-unanimity. Only because the Bolsheviks won every contest in the bloodless struggle for popular allegiance, he argued, could the takeover occur with so little commotion. All of this sounds very like John Adams describing the revolution in hearts and minds that preceded the Declaration of Independence. Trotsky likened the day of the twenty-fifth to an endgame in chess: "At the end of October the main part of the game was already in the past. And on the day of insurrection it remained to solve only a rather narrow problem: mate in two moves." He concluded, "As a matter of fact, it was the most popular mass-insurrection in all history."

In sorting out these contradictory claims, the most important data are probably the results of the national elections to the Constituent Assembly. They permit two conclusions: first, that in the country at large the Bolsheviks were a minority, commanding only 25 percent of the overall popular vote, and, second, that in Petersburg and Moscow—the two primary scenes of the revolution—they enjoyed a majority. (The Social Revolutionary Party, a rival revolutionary party with a large rural constituency, won 42 percent of the national vote, and the rest was divided among other parties. In the all-important Petersburg garrison, the Bolsheviks won 71 percent of the vote.) As a measure of public opinion, this election might be compared to a single photograph of a wrestling match taken with a flashbulb in a dark room, but its results are consistent with other evidence, such as elections to the Soviets in the period just before the takeover. There was factual support, in other words, both for Trotsky's and Sukhanov's claim that the masses supported the Bolsheviks and for Masaryk's claim that the Bolsheviks were in the minority. The Bolsheviks were, in fact, a *mass minority*. But that mass was concentrated where it most counted in 1917: in the revolutionary cities of Petersburg and Moscow, which were also the seats of government. (Much the same thing had happened in France, where the Parisian radicals assailed and dominated the National Assembly.) Thanks to the Bolsheviks, who evicted the Constituent Assembly at gunpoint, there are no other reliable election results to examine, but subsequent protests by factory and white-collar workers against the Bolsheviks strongly suggest that even urban support for them declined. Later, the leadership lost support among their own mass organizations, which they soon shut out of political life. What they did not lose—at least until late in the post–Cold War years— was the support of some hundreds of thousands or millions of Communist Party members and of the Red Army.

This pattern of minority mass support amid majority rejection or indifference, I suggest, is an important factor in explaining the paradox that a nonviolent revolutionary overthrow was followed by an act of revolutionary foundation that depended on violence beyond all historical precedent. If we fail to grant the Bolsheviks their measure of mass support, we cannot understand how they came to power in Petersburg *without* violence or why, once they were in power, they were able to impose their rule on almost the whole czarist empire *with* violence. In revolutions (as opposed to coups d'état), success in nonviolence depends on the extent of popular support—on the depth of what John Adams, Chateaubriand, and Trotsky (men so unlike in most respects) identified as the "revolution before the revolution," in hearts and minds.

The overthrow in Petersburg could be nonviolent, just as Trotsky said, because the Party enjoyed wide and deep mass support on that particular urban stage. The consolidation of the regime was violent because such support was absent in Russia at large, and therefore could be imposed only by force—force that the Bolsheviks could unleash because of the mass minority support that they *did* possess. In the first case, their support was strong enough that at the crucial moment effective opposition never arose in the locality of the takeover; in the second, it was strong enough to win the civil war and fuel the totalitarian engine of repression nationally—something that a small, isolated band of "conspirators" could not conceivably have done. For it is also true that terror is necessary for rule in the same proportion as support is limited—unless, of course, the party in charge is willing to yield its power to the majority. But this the Bolsheviks were never prepared to do.

Denial that the Bolsheviks enjoyed a degree of mass support may be born, in part, of an understandable wish to deny the last shred of legitimacy to their brutal rule, but this denial is won at the cost of historical accuracy. Their message of proletarian revolution in fact won support in the cities of Russia. Let me avoid any misunderstanding. Lenin and Trotsky were two of the most violent men of their supremely violent century. Together with Stalin, they were in fact the most important figures in the formation of totalitarian rule, which originates with them and only then proceeds, whether in imitation (Mussolini, Mao) or in reaction (Hitler), to spread around the world. Acknowledging all this, however, is no reason to deny the popular character of the revolution at the time it occurred in the particular cities in which it took place.

The Mass Minority in Power

By way of addendum, let us note that the story of Hitler's rise to power shows similar features. He first sought to win power in a violent coup—the Munich beer-hall putsch of 1923. When it failed, he turned, over time, to a "legal" strategy that carried him into the chancellorship in 1933. In certain respects, his strategy was one of building up *hiérarchies parallèles,* or even, in nightmarish reverse-image, a Gandhian constructive program. A comparison of these morally opposite characters of the twentieth century looks less outlandish if we recall that both Gandhi and Hitler were keen enthusiasts of direct action. Hitler, too, built up a sort of shadow government outside the existing regime. "We recognized," he explained in 1936, "that it is not enough to overthrow the old State, but that the new State must previously have been built up and be ready to one's hand. . . . In 1933, it was no longer a question of overthrowing a State by an act of violence; meanwhile the new State had been built up and all that remained to do was to destroy the last remnants of the old State—and that took a few hours." Grotesque as it might seem, Hitler even bragged about the nonviolence of his revolution. Sounding eerily like Trotsky on the day of his triumph, Hitler claimed that it had been "the least bloody revolution in history." Thereafter, his job was much easier than that of Lenin, who had to fight a civil war to consolidate his rule. Nevertheless, the procedures followed by the two men after arriving in power were of a kind: both mounted completely successful assaults by the state on the independent institutions of society, political and civil. Society, already partially enlisted in the mass movement, could not or simply did not resist.

Organizationally speaking, a disciplined, aggressive mass minority that had seized state power and was prepared to use any degree of violence to impose its will, in disregard of the will of the majority, was the dangerous new force. If by "democratic" we mean obedient to the will of the majority, then the Bolshevik mass minority was not democratic, and the Nazi movement may or may not have been (Hitler never won a majority in an election, but some historians believe that he gained majority support after coming to power); but if by "democratic" we mean propelled and sustained by the action of large masses of people, then both were democratic. Nevertheless, Trotsky's claim that the Russian Revolution was "the most popular mass-insurrection in all history" is certainly false. If he had been right, the Bolsheviks might well have achieved in all of Russia the bloodless triumph they achieved in Petersburg alone. (This larger miracle of nonviolence in fact had to await the *anti*-Bolshevik forces that in 1991 overthrew the regime Trotsky and Lenin had brought to power.) The English, the American, the French, the German, and the Indian revolutions all demonstrated the power of people to enervate and paralyze a regime by withdrawing support from it while at the same time building up parallel organizations. But unlike the English, the Americans, and the Indians, the French under Robespierre, the Russians under Lenin, and the Germans under Hitler disregarded or rejected the experience of nonviolence that their revolutions had accidentally brought to light, and turned instead—with a vengeance—to force as the method of their rule.

7

Living in Truth

The end of the regime founded by the Bolsheviks in 1917—the collapse, three-quarters of a century later, of the Soviet Union and its satellite regimes in Eastern Europe—presents the most sweeping demonstration so far of the power of "politics" without violence. The story combines many strands—economic, military, political. Among them, the failure of the Soviet economy, especially in comparison to Western economies, was of course especially important. Our subject, however, is chiefly the political processes involved. Two global developments already discussed were powerfully at work in the background. One was the nuclear paralysis of great-power war; the other was the global movement for self-determination. These two factors—one acting from "above," the other from "below," one rooted in the scientific revolution of modern times, the other in the democratic revolution—are basic to understanding the surprising manner in which the Soviet collapse unfolded.

The paralysis of great-power war imposed a stability on international relations that was new. A conviction, unknown perhaps since the days of the Roman Empire or certain dynasties of ancient China, took root that the current shape of things was likely to remain unchanged more or less forever. War itself became "cold." A moment of slightly reduced tension was a "thaw," when in a cooperative frame of mind the two powers aimed at "peaceful coexistence." In one of the acutest crises of the conflict, the Soviet Union's satellite government in East Germany built a wall around Berlin, and the United States acquiesced in the deed. "A wall is a hell of a lot better than a war," President Kennedy remarked to an adviser.

Nuclear strategy reinforced totalitarian strategy in important respects. In both nuclear deterrence and totalitarian rule, terror was used to paralyze. The men in power in Moscow, though putative revolutionaries, dreamed of stasis. In 1965, the Polish Party's first secretary, Wladyslaw Gomulka, asserted that once the Communists arrived in power in a country, they would never give it up. Even after Khrushchev's epochal secret speech denouncing Stalin's rule at the Soviet Party Congress in 1956, when the role of state terror was sharply reduced in the Soviet Union, political paralysis continued. Thereafter, the Soviet ruling class congealed into the privilege- and status-hungry *nomenklatura,* the "new class," or "Red bourgeoisie." The historian Adam Ulam has aptly called their philosophy *immobilisme,* and the state they ran a "bureaucrats' paradise." In 1968, the Soviet government formalized a principle of stasis in what came to be known, in honor of the chairman of the Communist Party of the U.S.S.R., as the Brezhnev Doctrine. On July 18, 1968, at the height of the movement for liberalization in Czechoslovakia called the Prague Spring, an open letter to the Central Committee of the Czechoslovakian Communist Party from a conclave of Communist Parties in Warsaw at which Brezhnev was present stated, "Never will we consent to allow imperialism, whether by peaceful or non-peaceful means, from within or without, to make a breach in the socialist system and change the balance of power in Europe in its favor."

However, it was Nadezhda Mandelstam, the widow of Osip Mandelstam, who penetrated to the heart of the matter. "There was a special form of the sickness—lethargy, plague, hypnotic trance or whatever one calls it," she wrote in the late sixties, in her memoir *Hope Against Hope*, "that affected all those who committed terrible deeds in the name of the 'New Era.' All the murderers, provocateurs, and informers had one feature in common: it never occurred to them that their victims might one day rise up again and speak. They also imagined that time had stopped—this, indeed, was the chief symptom of the sickness. We had, you see, been led to believe that in our country nothing would ever change again, and that it was now up to the rest of the world to follow our example and enter the 'New Era.'" George Orwell was another who worried that the new form of rule might be impervious to resistance. "The terrifying thing about the modern dictatorships is that they are something entirely unprecedented," he wrote. ". . . In the past every tyranny was sooner or later overthrown, or at least resisted, because of 'human nature,' which as a matter of course desired liberty. But we cannot be at all certain that 'human nature' is a constant. It may be just as possible to produce a breed of men who do not wish for liberty as to produce a breed of hornless cows."

As Orwell's shaken faith in freedom and loss of confidence in human nature show, the apparent success of totalitarianism in suppressing popular will in the name of that same will produced a crisis of faith in the liberal West. Had the will of the people, nemesis of aristocrats, kings, and emperors in the eighteenth and nineteenth centuries, been nullified in the twentieth by Gauleiters and commissars? Had the totalitarians discovered what had eluded the tyrants of every previous age, a foolproof antidote to human freedom? Had they, with the reinforcement of nuclear terror, wrestled Father Time himself to the ground? Cold indeed was the Cold War, whose dominant note, especially in its first decade, seemed to be this double obedience to terror. No global war, of course, broke out, yet force and the threat of force reigned over the world, all-pervading and ever-present. While the totalitarian leaders were hoping that, metaphorically, time had stopped, they and their Western antagonists were wheeling into place the nuclear machinery that could actually cut short historical time.

And yet the universal conviction proved wrong—stupendously wrong. Human freedom had not died under totalitarian rule. It was about to make a spectacular demonstration of its power. The Cold War, paralyzed at the summit of the world order, was moving along unnoticed, circuitous pathways toward its amazing denouement. Resistance, blocked in the time-tested arteries of military action, was forced into the world's unremarked-on capillary system, where, disregarded, it quietly advanced. And then it gushed forth in mass protest by entire societies. In retrospect, it's apparent that the long series of rebellions against the Soviet empire in Eastern Europe—in East Germany in 1953, in Poland and Hungary in 1956, and in Czechoslovakia in 1968—which at the time looked like exercises in noble futility, were actually stages on the way to the Soviet collapse. The actors were, among others, workers on factory floors, rebellious students, intellectuals talking to one another over kitchen tables or "writing for the drawer," dissidents who were promptly dispatched to concentration camps or psychiatric hospitals, disaffected technocrats, and even bureaucrats in the state apparatus. Every step they took was ventured without a chart or a clear destination. Yet the revolution they made was peaceful, democratic, and thorough.

The nonviolent popular resistance that brought down the Berlin Wall was as historically consequential—as final an arbiter—as either of the two world wars. It ended Soviet communism and its shadow, the specter of "international communism." It finished off an empire whose origins predated the communists. It initiated the creation of more than a dozen new countries. It was the equivalent of a third world war except in one particular—it was not a war.

A Better Today

It's often said, with good reason, that the Soviet collapse proceeded from the top down. It is no less correct to say that it traveled from the outside in—from the Eastern European periphery to the Soviet center. And in Eastern Europe it decidedly flowed from the bottom up. In the first stage of the collapse, the Solidarity movement of the early 1980s in Poland in effect dissolved the local communist system from within, demonstrating once and for all its previously unsuspected radical weakness of the entire structure of Soviet power. In Czechoslovakia and Hungary, quieter, more gradual movements were under way. It was not the first time that the occupied western territories of the empire proved to be its Achilles' heel. In 1945, in a cable from the American embassy in Moscow to the State Department, George Kennan noted that in the nineteenth century Russian repression had turned Poland into a "hotbed out of which there grew the greater part of the Russian Social Democratic Party which bore Lenin to power." Kennan was one of the few who understood that the Soviet Union's occupation of Eastern European nations after 1945 posed a lethal danger to Moscow. "Successful revolts on their part against Moscow authority," he wrote, "might shake the entire structure of Soviet power." Totalitarian rule, it was turning out, had not endowed the Soviet empire with immunity to the fever for self-determination and freedom that had by then overturned the Western colonial empires. It wasn't until the second stage of the collapse, when Mikhail Gorbachev came to power in Moscow and adopted his radical policies of perestroika and glasnost in the Soviet "center," that change from the top down led to the final dissolution.

Until the late 1970s, the idea that Soviet power might be challenged from within had been largely discarded, and the progress of the revolution from the edges of the empire to its heart caught almost everyone, observers and participators alike, by surprise. Until very late in the day, not even the activists who founded Solidarity imagined that they were inaugurating the collapse of their local, satellite governments, much less the downfall of the whole Soviet system. On the contrary, one of their most original achievements was to discover a way to act and fight for more modest, immediate goals *without* challenging the main structures of totalitarian power head on. Their ambition—itself widely condemned as utopian by Western observers—was merely to create zones of freedom, including free trade unions, within the Soviet framework. And yet once the disintegration at the edges of the empire began, it proved to have no stopping point. The contagion, which combined a longing for national self-determination with a longing for freedom, proceeded, in an unbroken progression from the Eastern European satellites to the peripheral republics of the union (in particular, Lithuania), and from there to Moscow itself, where, to the amazement of all, Russia joined the company of rebels against the Soviet Union, which, lacking now any territory to call its own, melted into thin air.

One of the puzzles of the Soviet downfall is how it happened that a peaceful revolution described by its authors as "self-limiting" (because it did not aim at state power) brought about this unlimited result. As guides to the Eastern European stage of the anti-Soviet revolution, we shall adopt three writer-activists—Adam Michnik, of Poland, Václav Havel, of Czechoslovakia, and Gyorgy Konrád, of Hungary. In the 1970s, the walls of the Kremlin fortress rose impregnable, as it seemed, before their eyes. Fresh in their minds was the succession of defeated rebellions against Soviet domination in East Germany (1953), Poland (1956), Hungary (1956), and Czechoslovakia (1968) From these routs the three writers drew a lesson that might have seemed a counsel of despair but in fact was the basis for a revival of hope and activity. They decided to accept the brute existence of the system as an unchangeable fact of life for the time being. "To believe in overthrowing the dictatorship of the party by revolution and to consciously organize actions in pursuit of this goal is both unrealistic and dangerous,"

Michnik wrote in 1976, in a pivotal essay called "A New Evolutionism." For "the Soviet military and political presence in Poland is the factor that determines the limits of possible evolution, and this is unlikely to change for some time."

In the mid-1980s, after a declaration of martial law in 1981 had temporarily suppressed Solidarity in Poland, Konrád was still writing, in his book *Anti-Politics,* "It is impossible to alter the . . . system from inside East Europe by means of dynamic, uncontrolled mass movements . . . because the limits of social change are fixed by the military balance, and by a Soviet power elite which labors to preserve the military status quo and has considerable means with which to do it—means that are political as well as military." The division of Europe that had been decided at the summit meeting at the Soviet Black Sea resort of Yalta at the end of the Second World War—an iconic event for Eastern Europeans, known to them simply as "Yalta"—symbolized, Konrád observed, the ancient idea that force has the last word in political affairs:

> The morality of Yalta is simple: those who have the bombs and tanks decide the social and political system. Since the United States and the Soviet Union had the most bombs and tanks, they were called to lead the world. Later—by the fearful light of Hiroshima— their calling was confirmed, for only these two giant nation-states had the resources to build arsenals of nuclear weapons.

Havel, commenting in a similar vein, wrote that what he called the "post-totalitarian" dictatorships of the Soviet empire were "totally controlled by the superpower center and totally subordinated to its interests." He, too, cited the nuclear standoff. "In the stalemated world of nuclear parity, of course," he wrote, "that circumstance endows the system with an unprecedented degree of external stability." Havel, it must be added, was considerably less impressed with the durability of the Soviet edifice than most of his colleagues in resistance. He was one of the very few who suggested that the worldwide self-determination movement, which the Soviets blindly believed to be working in their favor, might undermine the Soviet Union. In an essay in 1978, he took note of the rebellions that in one country after another had rocked the empire, and commented, "If we consider how impossible it is to guess what the future holds, given such opposing trends as, on the one hand, the increasingly profound integration of the [Communist] 'bloc' and the expansion of power within it, and on the other hand the prospects of the USSR disintegrating under pressure from awakening national consciousness in the non-Russian areas (in this regard the Soviet Union cannot expect to remain forever free of the worldwide struggle for national liberation), then we must see the hopelessness of trying to make long-range predictions."

Havel's agnosticism, however, led him to the same practical counsel that Konrád and Michnik were giving: it was a mistake to try to overthrow the system. Activism should be directed at achieving immediate changes in daily life. He proposed unshakable commitment to achieving modest, concrete goals on the local level. "Defending the aims of life, defending humanity," he asserted, "is not only a more realistic approach, since it can begin right now and is potentially more popular because it concerns people's everyday lives; at the same time (and perhaps precisely because of this) it is also an incomparably more consistent approach because it aims at the very essence of things." The three men in effect lowered their field glasses from the remote heights of state power and turned their gazes to the life immediately around them. Gandhi had faced neither totalitarian rule nor nuclear stalemate, yet he, too, had arrived at a decision to aim not at state power directly but at immediate local improvement of life, to be achieved through direct action in the form of the constructive program, which he, too, saw as the essence of things. When Eastern Europeans did this in their own way, a rich field of activity opened up to them, in what they soon began calling civil society.

Neither the term nor the fact of civil society was new. Tom Paine, who so greatly appreciated the power of nonviolent popular resistance during the American Revolution, was, according to his biographer John Keane, the first to fully elucidate the distinction between civil society and civil government. Until Paine, the terms had been used interchangeably. The key distinction had been the much older one between the wild, contractless, stateless state of nature and the orderly civil state, which was the fruit of the "original contract" among the people. Paine now asserted the existence of two contracts—the original contract, by which the people quit the state of nature and entered *society,* and a second one, by which people in civil society created a *government.* The consequence was the addition of a third state, a purely social state (hence civil "society"), between the traditional state of nature and the civil state. In language that foreshadows the distinctions the Eastern Europeans would draw, Paine praised society at the expense of government:

> Society is produced by our wants, and government by our wickedness; the former promotes our happiness *positively* by uniting our affections, the latter *negatively* by restraining our rule. The one encourages intercourse, the other creates distinctions.

For Paine, the foundation of civil society was an almost entirely benign first step, the foundation of government a regrettably necessary second step.

In the hands of the Eastern European activists, the idea of civil society underwent further development. It was turned into a rival—almost an alternative—to government. Their new rule of thumb was to act not *against* the government but *for* society—and then to defend the accomplishments. In 1976, in "A New Evolutionism," Michnik asserted that the suppression of the Prague Spring and of a Polish student-protest movement in March of 1968 had spelled the end of any hope of reforming the state from within. The new generation must learn to act in a new way: "I

believe that what sets today's opposition apart from the propo-
nents of those ideas [of reform in the past] is the belief that a
program for evolution ought to be addressed to an independent
public, not to totalitarian power. Such a program should give
directives to the people on how to behave, not to the powers on
how to reform themselves." Michnik later set forth what he called
a "philosophy of political activity in a post-totalitarian system."
"Why post-totalitarian?" he asked. "Because power is still totalitarian, whereas society isn't any more; it is already anti-totalitarian,
it rebels and sets up its own independent institutions, which lead
to something we could call civil society, in Tocqueville's sense.
That is what we tried to build: civil society."

Michnik's words of 1976 fell on fertile ground. They anticipated (and helped to produce) a blossoming of civic and cultural
activity in Poland. An early example was the Worker's Defense
Committee. Its purpose was to give concrete assistance to workers
in trouble with the authorities—assistance that the organization
referred to as "social work." Help was provided to the families of
workers jailed by the government. Independent underground
publications multiplied. A "flying university," which offered
uncensored courses in people's apartments and other informal
locations, was founded. Organizations devoted to social aims of
all kinds—environmental, educational, artistic, legal—sprouted.
In both form and content, these groups were precursors to the
ten-million-strong Solidarity movement that arose in 1980.

The Explosive Power of Living in Truth

What Michnik called a new evolutionism or building civil society
Havel called "living in truth"—the title of an essay he published in
1978. Living in truth stood in opposition to "living in the lie,"
which meant living in obedience to the repressive regime. Havel
wrote:

We introduced a new model of behavior: don't get involved in diffuse general ideological polemics with the center, to whom numerous concrete causes are always being sacrificed; fight "only" for those concrete causes, and fight for them unswervingly to the end.

Why was this living in truth? Havel's explanation constitutes one of the few attempts of this period—or any other—to address the peculiarly ineffable question of what the inspiration of positive, constructive nonviolent action is. By living within the lie—that is, conforming to the system's demands—Havel says, "individuals confirm the system, fulfill the system, make the system, *are* the system." A "line of conflict" is then drawn through each person, who is invited in the countless decisions of daily life to choose between living in truth and living in the lie. Living in truth—directly doing in your immediate surroundings what you think needs doing, saying what you think is true and needs saying, acting the way you think people should act—is a form of protest, Havel admits, against living in the lie, and so those who try to live in truth are indeed an opposition. But that is neither all they are nor the main thing they are. Before living in truth is a protest, it is an affirmation. Havel, who sometimes makes use of philosophical language, explains as follows:

> Individuals can be alienated from themselves only because there is *something* in them to alienate. The terrain of this violation is their essential existence.

That is to say, if the state's commands are a violation deserving of protest, the deepest reason is that they disrupt this *something*—some elemental good thing, here called a person's "essential existence"—that people wish to be or do for its own sake, whether or not it is opposed or favored by the state or anyone else.

This is the point, it seems to me, that John Adams was getting at when he said that the American Revolution was completed before the war, and that Gandhi was making when he suggested that, if independence is a goal, then "it must be declared and pursued irrespective of the acts or threats of others." Like them (and like Nietzsche), Havel rebels against the idea that a negative, merely responding impulse is at the root of his actions. He rejects the labels "opposition" and "dissident" for himself and his fellow activists. Something in *him* craves manifestation.

Of those labels he writes:

> People who so define themselves do so in relation to a prior "position." In other words, they relate themselves specifically to the power that rules society and through it, define themselves, deriving their own "position" from the position of the regime. For people who have simply decided to live within the truth, to say aloud what they think, to express their solidarity with their fellow citizens, to create as they want and simply to live in harmony with their better "self," it is naturally disagreeable to feel required to define their own, original and positive "position" negatively, in terms of something else, and to think of themselves primarily as people who *are* against something, not simply as people who are what they are.

For Havel, this understanding that action properly begins with a predisposition to truth—often considered a merely private or personal endowment—has practical consequences that are basic to an understanding of political power:

> Under the orderly surface of the life of lies, therefore, there slumbers the hidden sphere of life in its real aims, of its hidden openness to truth. The singular, explosive, incalculable political power of living within the truth resides in the fact that living openly within the truth has an ally, invisible to be sure, but omnipresent: this hidden sphere.

Havel is describing, in words that anticipated the fall of the Soviet Union before that event had occurred, a secular variant of what Gandhi had called "truth force." If Michnik's words anticipated the sudden rise of Solidarity, Havel's bore fruit in the rise of the resistance movement in Czechoslovakia called Charter 77 and in the "velvet revolution" that put an end to communist power in Czechoslovakia.

Konrád offered what might be called a Hungarian version of living in the truth. Having witnessed the slow but surprisingly broad liberalization of the Hungarian system in the 1970s and eighties, he hoped that the changes under way in society would infect the communist functionaries, who would come to see "that their interests were better served by forms of government other than dictatorship." Konrád, who in such passages obliquely debated his Polish and Czech contemporaries on how change might occur, urged "confidence in this growing complexity—in the fact that a society can gradually slough off dictatorship, and that the prime mover in that process is a growing middle class." In his scheme, this liberalization, called "goulash Communism" by some, would gradually turn into goulash decommunization. Konrád wanted society to "absorb" the regime in a "ripening social transformation." He wanted the "iceberg of power . . . melted from within." He cited the historical precedent of the surrender of the dictatorial, right-wing regime of Francisco Franco in Spain to democratic forces in the 1970s. "Proletarian revolution didn't break out in any country of southern Europe," he commented. "If it had, the military dictatorships would only have hardened."

In all three of the Eastern European movements, the strategy was to bypass the government and tackle social problems directly, as Gandhi had done with his constructive program. But whereas "social work" presented no challenge to the Raj, it did challenge the Soviet regime. Within the class of repressive regimes, the Raj was an authoritarian regime, and left vast areas of Indian life untouched. The Raj had no difficulties with Gandhi's constructive program, to which it offered no rival; it was compelled to react only when he practiced noncooperation with the state. To the totalitarian Soviet regime, which sought to control almost every aspect of life, very much including the social, on the other hand, any independent activity looked like the beginnings of a rival governing power. Gandhi had said that once people disown the state under which they live they have "nearly" established their own government. On rare occasions, leaders of totalitarian regimes have also shown that they also understood the danger. In his memoirs, Khrushchev described his fear of the thaw he had started by his secret de-Stalinization speech of 1956. "We were scared—really scared," he wrote. "We were afraid the thaw might unleash a flood, which we wouldn't be able to control and which could drown us. It could have overflowed the banks of the Soviet riverbed and formed a tidal wave which would have washed [away] all the barriers and retaining walls of our society."

We have noted the central role in revolutions of defections among the troops of the old regime. Under a totalitarian regime, which seeks to mobilize the entire population in support of its ideological cause, the people become a sort of army on whose obedience the regime relies. But the very immensity of this army presents a target of opportunity for the opposition. If the essence of totalitarianism is its attempted penetration of the innermost recesses of life, then resistance can begin in those same recesses— in a private conversation, in a letter, in disobedience of a regulation at work, even in the invisible realm of a person's thoughts. Havel gives the example of a brewer he knew who, putting aside official specifications for making beer, set about making the best beer he could. Such was a brewer's living in truth.

Once the unraveling of the single, indivisible fabric of totalitarianism began, the rapidity of the disintegration could be startling. In Havel's prophetic words, "Everything suddenly appears in another light, and the whole crust seems then to be made of a tissue on the point of tearing and disintegrating uncontrollably."

Totalitarian rule made constructive work and noncooperation difficult and costly but at the same time was especially vulnerable to those tactics. The pessimistic stock observation that Gandhi could never have succeeded against a totalitarian regime had an optimistic corollary. If such a movement could ever get going, as it did in the Soviet empire, the unraveling would be sudden and irresistible. The "Salisbury field" of a totalitarian regime was its entire society.

The radical potential of constructive work was implicit in a famous saying of Jacek Kuron, an intellectual adviser to Solidarity, who in the late 1970s counseled angry workers, "Don't burn down Party Committee Headquarters, found your own." And that is what they did, in August of 1980, when a spontaneous strike by workers in the Baltic shipyards spread like wildfire through Poland. Soon something like a general strike was under way, and the regime was forced to come to terms by granting, among other concessions, the right to form an independent trade union. The regime would not collapse for another nine years, but its death throes had already begun.

Even before the rise of Solidarity, Havel had reflected on the potential for developing power by founding new associations and organizations. The natural next step for an individual already trying to live in truth in his individual life, he advised in 1978, was to work with others to found what the writer Václav Benda called "parallel structures." These could be expected to arise first, Havel writes, in the realm of culture, where a "second culture," in the phrase he borrows from the rock musician Ivan Jirous, might develop. The step beyond that would be the creation of a "parallel polis" (another phrase of Benda's). This was the Czech version of Kuron's advice to the Polish workers to build their own headquarters.

In 1980, when Solidarity sprang into existence, it preferred on the whole to soft-pedal these radical possibilities, which, its leaders believed, might well provoke the Soviet Union to intervene, as it had in the past in Eastern Europe. They proposed instead a novel division of functions. "Society" would run itself democratically, but "power," which is to say the central government (and especially that part of it in charge of foreign affairs), would be left in the hands of the Communist Party dictatorship, whose survival would serve as a guarantee to the Soviet Union that its security interests would not be challenged. Long debates within the Solidarity movement were devoted to negotiating and fixing the boundaries of such a compromise. The debates came to an end only with the impostion of martial law, in December of 1981.

The similarities between the Eastern European movements and Gandhi's movement in India are obvious. If there were evidence that Havel had pored over Gandhi's works, we might suppose that his phrase "living in truth" was an inspired translation of "satyagraha"—a term so difficult to render into other languages. In both movements, we find a conviction that the prime human obligation is to act fearlessly and publicly in accord with one's beliefs; that one should withdraw cooperation from destructive institutions; that this should be done without violence (Gandhi endorses nonviolence without qualifications; each of the Eastern European writers enters some qualifications); that means are more important than ends; that crimes shouldn't be committed today for the sake of a better world tomorrow; that violence brutalizes the user as well as his victim; that the value of action lies in the direct benefit it brings society; that action is usually best aimed first at one's immediate surroundings, and only later at more distant goals; that winning state power, if necessary at all, is a secondary goal; that freedom "begins with myself," as Michnik said, is oriented to love of truth, and only then discovers what it hates and must oppose; and that state power not only should but actually does depend on the consent of the governed.

The differences are also obvious. The Eastern Europeans demonstrated that revolution without violence did not have to depend on religious faith or an abstemious life. Whereas Gandhi's movement was spiritual in inspiration, the Eastern European movements were largely secular (although the Catholic Church played an important role in Poland). Whereas Gandhi called for a strict renunciation of selfish desires in favor of civic obligation, the Eastern Europeans sought to separate the private and other realms of life from political intrusions, of which they were heartily sick after decades of totalitarian rule. (The last thing they would have wanted was a single standard, whether imposed by God, "truth," or anything else, to which people had to subordinate every realm of their existence.) Whereas Gandhi was radically antimaterialistic, the Eastern Europeans were, variously, either only moderately so or hugely interested in material abundance for society. (There can be no such thing as goulash satyagraha.) Whereas Gandhi was an ascetic, the Eastern European leaders tended, in their personal lives, to be *hommes moyens sensuels.* Whereas Gandhi dreamed of a village-based cooperative society unlike any ever seen, then or since, the Eastern Europeans wanted to adopt the kind of parliamentary democracies and free-market economies already functioning in much of the world.

Although nonviolence was not an article of dogma for the Eastern Europeans, it was an essential element of their chosen form of action. "The struggle for state power," Michnik wrote, "must lead to the use of force; yet . . . according to the resolution passed at the memorable Solidarity Congress in Gdansk, the use of force must be renounced." One reason for the choice of nonviolence was pragmatic. The totalitarian state's monopoly on the instruments of violence required a search for some other means. "Why did Solidarity renounce violence?" Michnik asked while in prison after the imposition of martial law. He answered, "People who claim that the use of force in the struggle for freedom is necessary must first prove that, in a given situation, it will be effective, and that force, when it is used, will not transform the idea of liberty into its opposite. No one in Poland is able to prove today that violence will help us to dislodge Soviet troops from Poland and to remove the Communists from power. The USSR has such enormous power that confrontation is simply unthinkable. In other words: we have no guns." But in a comment that adds to our collection of remarks from various times and places claiming that the real revolution has occurred before the fighting (if any) breaks out, Michnik wrote, "Before the violence of rulers clashes with the violence of their subjects, values and systems of ethics clash inside human minds. Only when the old ideas of the rulers lose their moral duel will the subjects reach for force—sometimes."

Also like Gandhi, the Eastern Europeans shunned violence for moral reasons: they did not wish to become like the enemies they despised. The point was not to change rulers; it was to change the system of rule, and the system they opposed had been based on violence. Michnik again: "My reflections on violence and revolution were sparked by my puzzlement about the origins of totalitarianism. I searched for clues in the writings of George Orwell, Hannah Arendt, Osip Mandelstam, and Albert Camus, and I came to the conclusion that the genesis of the totalitarianism system is traceable to the use of revolutionary violence."

Havel concurred. He and his colleagues had "a profound belief that a future secured by violence might actually be worse than what exists now; in other words, the future would be fatally stigmatized by the very means used to secure it." In *Anti-Politics*, Konrád expressed full agreement, and drew an important conclusion. His mention of an active search for an alternative to the traditional ultima ratio is especially noteworthy:

The political leadership elites of our world don't all subscribe equally to the philosophy of a nuclear *ultima ratio,* but they have no conceptual alternative to it. They have none because they are professionals of power. Why should they choose values that are in direct opposition to physical force? Is there, can there be, a political philosophy—a set of proposals for winning and holding power—that renounces *a priori* any physical guarantees of power? Only antipolitics offers a radical alternative to the philosophy of a nuclear *ultima ratio*. . . . Antipolitics means refusing to consider nuclear war a satisfactory answer in any way. Antipolitics regards it as impossible in principle that any historical misfortune could be worse than the death of one to two billion people.

Violence, the Eastern Europeans found, was to be shunned for another reason: it was useless—more or less beside the point—for the sort of action they had resolved to pursue. Someone once remarked to Napoleon that you can't mine coal with bayonets. Neither are bayonets helpful for writing a book, cleaning a room, designing a microchip, or dressing a wound. Violence might or might not be useful for overthrowing a state, but Solidarity had renounced this ambition.

What Is and What Ought to Be

The comments of Michnik, Havel, and Konrád bring into the open a question never far from the surface when people choose nonviolent over violent action. Should nonviolence be chosen more for moral and spiritual reasons or more for practical ones? The issue is important because the believer in nonviolent action seems, to an unusual degree, to be ready to suffer defeat rather than abandon his chosen means. For Gandhi, nonviolence was foremost a moral and spiritual requirement. No mere circumstance—least of all the approach of defeat—could justify abandoning it. That is what he meant when he said that nonviolence was for him a creed, not a policy. For Michnik, by contrast, nonviolence was more a policy. He said he wanted the Russians to know that if they used force to put down the Polish movement, they would find themselves "spitting up blood." These are words that Gandhi could never have spoken. On the other hand, as we've seen, Gandhi's nonviolence was founded in part upon the recognition that in a violent fight with the English, the Indians would be "crushed in a minute." In other words, as Michnik said of the Poles, the Indians had no guns. And Gandhi had used language close to Michnik's when he declared that the Indians therefore must create a weapon "which would be different from and infinitely superior to the force which the white settler commanded." In these words, too, there is a kind of ambiguity. Gandhi sought spiritual victory above all else, yet he wanted to win in this world as well.

With Gandhi, we might say, the moral motive is primary, the pragmatic secondary, while with the Eastern Europeans the reverse is true. Either way, it seems to be in the very nature of principled nonviolent action that it tends to combine moral and practical calculation—just as it seems to be in the nature of violent action that, justifying means by ends, it tends to separate the two. That nonviolent action won more and more impressive successes even in the violent twentieth century has, I suggest, a meaning. Isn't it entirely fitting that, in a time when violence has increased its range and power to the point at which the human substance is threatened with annihilation, the most inventive and courageous people would cast about for something better to use? But the wonder of it is not that they have sought but that they have found. Michnik and his colleagues told themselves that they and others had discovered the political equivalent of the "atomic bomb," and they were right—except that their invention in fact accomplished what no actual atomic bomb could accomplish, the defeat of the Soviet Union. When they began their agitation, the iron law of the world dictated that revolution must be violent because violence was the foundation of power, and only power enables you to storm that citadel of violence and power, the state, and so to *take power*. When they were finished, and state after repressive state had been dissolved with little or no use of violence, a new law of the world had been written, and it read: Nonviolent action can be a source of revolutionary power, which erodes the ancien régime from within (even if its practitioners don't aim at this) and lays the foundation for a new state. If totalitarianism is a perversion of the democratic revolution, then the rise of nonviolent revolution is totalitarianism's antidote and cure, pointing the way to a recovery of democracy and, perhaps, to a deeper and truer understanding of democracy's nature, which is bound up with the principle of nonviolence.

Hanging over these political issues are questions of a more philosophical character, having to do with whether or not people are to suppose that the conduct they require of themselves is patterned upon, or takes its cue from, some underlying order of things, natural or divine, or whether, on the contrary, human beings live in an alien, inhuman universe. The tendency of philosophers at least since Nietzsche has been to take this latter view. Neither Gandhi nor Havel considered himself a philosopher, but both plainly thought otherwise. It is striking, for instance, that both chose the word "truth"—perhaps the key word for philosophy— as the touchstone for their actions. Each had very concrete, even mundane, things in mind—for example, the good beer the Czech brewer wanted to brew or the sanitary conditions in India's villages that absorbed Gandhi so much. But each also occasionally touched on metaphysical issues. Describing the illness and death after a jail term in South Africa of a *satyagrahi* called Valliama, Gandhi said, "The world rests upon the bedrock of *satya* or truth. *Asatya,* meaning untruth, also means non-existent, and *satya* or truth also means that which *is.* If untruth does not so much as exist, its victory is out of the question. And truth being that which is can never be destroyed. This is the doctrine of *satyagraha* in a nutshell." For Gandhi, this "truth" was God. In the essay "Politics and Conscience" Havel, a secular man, wrote in terms that were quite different yet conveyed a similar meaning:

At the basis of this world are values which are simply there, perennially, before we ever speak of them, before we reflect upon them and inquire about them. It owes its internal coherence to some-

thing like a "pre-speculative" assumption that the world functions
and is generally possible at all only because there is something
beyond its horizon, something beyond or above it that might
escape our understanding and our grasp but, for just that reason,
firmly grounds this world, bestows upon it its order and measure,
and is the hidden source of all the rules, customs, commandments,
prohibitions.... Any attempt to spurn it, master it, or replace it
with something else, appears, within the framework of the natural
world, as an expression of *hubris* for which humans must pay a
heavy price.

To live in accord with this "something" was to live in truth. A similar confidence was expressed in the saying that, in the Western
tradition, must be considered the foundation stone of any philosophy of nonviolence, namely Jesus' "They that live by the sword
shall die by the sword." The advice does more than prescribe conduct; it makes a claim about the nature of the human world. We
cannot suppose Jesus means that everyone who kills will be killed.
But we can suppose he means that violence harms the doer as well
as his victims; that violence generates counterviolence; and that the
choice of violence starts a chain of events likely to bring general
ruin. What Gandhi, Havel, and most of the others who have won
nonviolent victories in our time believed and made the starting
point of their activity was a conviction—or, to be exact, a faith—
that if they acted in obedience to certain demanding principles,
which for all of them included in one way or another the principle
of nonviolence, there was, somewhere in the order of creation, a
fundament, or truth, that would give an answering and sustaining
reply.

Revolution from the Side

The rise of Solidarity, in which millions of Poles actively and naturally opposed a Soviet-sponsored communist regime, foreshadowed

the collapse of the Soviet Union a decade later. Solidarity laid bare the previously invisible weakness of Soviet rule. The trance of totalitarian power of which Nadezhda Mandelstam had spoken was broken. And yet the collapse of the Soviet Union itself—"the center," as it was called—proceeded along a different path. Moscow was two steps behind Poland in 1980. The formative events for Soviet liberals had been the Prague Spring of 1968, which aroused their hopes that communism could acquire a "human face," and the intense disappointment, bordering on despair, they felt when Soviet tanks rolled into Czechoslovakia. The leaders of the Czech Party, who were trying to liberalize the Party from within, had spoken the language of "reform communism," which Soviet officialdom understood, whereas the Poles in the 1980s already spoke the language of a post-communist era, which not even Soviet dissidents could yet imagine. Moscow had not experienced even Czech-style reformism, much less anything like Michnik's new evolutionism or Havel's living in truth. Khrushchev's reformist de-Stalinization of 1956 had been the limit of their experience of liberalization, and Khrushchev had been deposed by hard-liners. Such heroic oppositional figures as the novelist and author of *The Gulag Archipelago* Aleksandr Solzhenitsyn, the father of the Soviet H-bomb and leader of the human-rights movement Andrei Sakharov, his wife Yelena Bonner, and the dissident scientist Yuri Orlov had served as moral tuning forks for many who shared their beliefs, if not their almost superhuman courage; but in the face of repression they had not been able to spark a mass political movement. The recovery of civil society in the Soviet Union began only in the late 1980s, after Gorbachev's reforms had been under way for a few years. Nevertheless, the two processes had something in common. The nonviolence of the mass movement at the bottom permitted a largely nonviolent, reformist response. If Solidarity and Charter 77 had been violent, the nonviolent Gorbachev reforms would have been unthinkable.

The specific events in the Soviet Union that led directly to its collapse thus started with drastic reform at the top, not with a mass movement at the bottom of society. Revolution from the top, which dates from Peter the Great's attempts at Westernization, has a long history in Russia. In his memoirs, Gorbachev explained his thinking. "By the mid-1980s," he said, "our society resembled a steam boiler. There was only one alternative—either the Party itself would lead a process of change that would gradually embrace other strata of society, or it would preserve and protect the former system. In that case an explosion of colossal force would be inevitable." To head off the explosion, he made sure—for much too long, his critics assert—that he remained the leader of the Communist Party, the better to keep it under control. At the same time, he embarked on his programs of glasnost and perestroika—of introducing market reforms, decentralizing the state, liberalizing the press, and gradually democratizing the political process.

In order to understand the importance of the movements in Eastern Europe for the collapse of the Soviet Union, we must recall that the union, like the czarist regime before it, was not only an empire but an empire that ruled an empire. (The Soviet Union proper, that is, was an empire long before it acquired its Eastern European satellites, which were held in subjection by Moscow but never incorporated into the union.) Under the czars, Russia had never experienced a national revolution of the kind that had occurred throughout Western Europe in the late eighteenth and nineteenth centuries. One reason had been precisely that Russia, as an empire, ruled over many nationalities. "For the tsars," the historian Richard Pipes writes, "the imperial principle meant that loyalty to the dynasty, and to the Orthodox faith, took priority over Russian nationalism in the hierarchy of values." Had Russian nationalism become the basis for the state in 1917, it might have caused the breakup of the empire, just as Turkish nationalism under Kemal Ataturk spelled the end of the Ottoman Empire only a few years after the Bolshevik revolution. In 1917, the empire did briefly break up into several independent nations. Its restoration under the Bolsheviks—Stalin's job, accomplished in the civil war and in the years immediately following—was an act of imperial reconquest carried out in the name of revolution. The high tide of this effort was reached in the unsuccessful Bolshevik war against Poland in 1920, which Trotsky, showing a lingering respect for the idea of popular will, opposed, on the ground that revolution cannot be imposed "at the point of a bayonet." Not until the Second World War, when Stalin wished to stir Russian—as distinct from Soviet—patriotism against the German invaders, did the Party explicitly play the national card in Russia, the largest of the union's republics. Even then, it refused to provide Russia with its own "national" communist party.

It would be a mistake, however, to regard the Soviet Union as simply an instrument of Russian domination over imperial colonies—a domination similar, say, to Britain's over its empire. Even though Russians had a preeminent role in governing the union, Russia was to a certain extent one more nation oppressed by a multinational central government, which was at the same time oppressing Ukraine, Armenia, Georgia, and so on. (Stalin, let us recall, was a Georgian.) After the Second World War, when Eastern Europe was incorporated into the socialist "bloc," Russians were often resentful that Russia was subsidizing the Eastern European satellites, many of which did in fact enjoy living standards higher than those in Russia.

Owing to this unique history, there was no clear dividing line in the Soviet Union between "domestic" rule and external conquest, and the methods used in both were extremely similar, if not identical. In *Revolution from Abroad*, the historian Jan Gross observes that the techniques the Soviets used to subjugate Polish society when they invaded Poland in 1939 were the ones they had employed to subjugate their own society in the "war against the nation" in the thirties. The repression that the totalitarian state imposed abroad was a domestic export. The resulting consistency of rule at home and in the satellites meant that a crack in any part of the edifice was more likely to rend the whole. The indivisibility of Soviet rule underlay the indivisibility, from rim to rim of the great empire, of the Soviet collapse.

Nonviolence from the Top Down

When Mikhail Gorbachev came to power in 1985, he embarked on his epic attempt to reform Soviet communism through perestroika and glasnost. He soon realized that reform at home could not succeed if at the same time he was trying to crack down in Eastern Europe. He therefore made a radical decision that few had foreseen, and that even today stands out as remarkable. In a rare act of what we might call nonviolence from the top down, he withdrew the threat of Soviet military invasion that, throughout the Cold War, had been the final guarantee of the survival of the Eastern European communist regimes. In December of 1988, in a speech at the United Nations, he said, "Necessity of the principle of freedom of choice is clear. Denying that right of peoples, no matter what the pretext for doing so, no matter what words are used to conceal it, means infringing even that unstable balance that it has been possible to achieve. Freedom of choice is a universal principle, and there should be no exceptions." His decision marked an acceptance of the new political reality that had been created by Solidarity, Charter 77, and other protest movements in Eastern Europe. (A history of unforced surrender of imperial possessions would make a slender volume. De Gaulle's relinquishment of Algeria even after the military defeat of the F.L.N. would be another of its few chapters.) Military crackdowns in the new conditions might or might not have eventually succeeded. What is certain is that they would have been savage and bloody, and it is for avoiding this that Gorbachev is justly admired. What Gorbachev did not foresee was that by withdrawing the invasion threat, he was pulling the plug on the communist regimes and that their collapse would pull the plug on the Soviet Union itself. Exactly a year after the U.N. speech, the first partially free elections were held in Poland, and the results amounted to a death warrant for communism. Not a single communist running for a contested seat won office. Poland was on its way to full independence and freedom—and after Poland came, in rapid succession, Czechoslovakia, Hungary, East Germany, Bulgaria, and Romania.

Why did the unraveling not stop there? When Britain lost its empire, its domestic system did not collapse. Neither did that of France in the wake of the liquidation of the French empire—although after de Gaulle had announced his readiness to grant Algeria independence he did face a coup attempt by military forces stationed in Algeria. Had the Soviet Union been a nation-state, founded, like England and France, upon the consent of its people, it, too, might well have survived. Soviet rule "at home," however, was too much of a piece with Soviet rule "abroad," and the corrosion in the outer empire jumped over into the inner empire. Armenia, Azerbaijan, and Georgia all stirred, but the portal through which the Eastern European sickness (or cure, as we might prefer) entered the union was the Baltic lands, of which the first to rebel was Lithuania.

Having enjoyed semiautonomous status under the czars, the Lithuanians were given their independence after the First World War. In 1939, owing to the Molotov-Ribbentrop pact, in which the U.S.S.R. and Nazi Germany agreed to partition Poland, the Lithuanians were forced to join the Soviet Union. Though living under direct Soviet rule, their memory of an independent national existence was recent and strong. In 1990, they demanded independence. Now the Soviet Union itself was threatened. If the Lithuanian independence movement were crushed, it was unlikely that perestroika could be saved in Russia: the use of the repressive apparatus "abroad" would very likely strengthen it decisively at home. On the other hand, if Lithuania were let go, its release would be a precedent that any or all of the other republics might follow. Now the indivisibility of the choice facing the entire union and empire—a choice, at bottom, between government based on force and government based on consent—became obvious to all. No less clear at that moment was what consent meant: the dissolution of the union. Gorbachev's reforms had activated forces that, if not violently suppressed, were bound to sweep simultaneously from the periphery of the empire into its center and from the bottom of society to the top.

An appeal launched at this hour shed a clear light on the significance of the Lithuanian events for the future. It came from Boris Yeltsin, then president of the Russian Parliament, and it amounted to a call for Russian forces to refuse to participate in a Lithuanian coup. Speaking from the territory of Lithuania's neighbor Estonia, Yeltsin addressed his appeal to the "soldiers, sergeants, and officers of the Soviet Union." He declared, "Today . . . you may be given the order to act against legally created state bodies, against the peaceful civilian population that is defending its democratic achievements. Before you undertake the storming of civilian installations in the Baltic lands, remember your own homes, the present and the future of your own republic, and your own people. Violence against the people of the Baltics will bring new serious crisis phenomena in Russia itself." What gave Yeltsin's words weight was the popular support he had been given in Russia after he had been drummed out of the Party leadership in 1988 and then had quit the Party, paving the way for his election as Russia's president. The last act of the collapse was, naturally, the Russian act.

As the movement spread from the edges into the center, it did not gain in popular intensity and strength. Resistance to Soviet rule was never as strong in the Soviet lands as it was in Eastern Europe. In Poland, there was an explosion; in Russia there was an implosion. Yeltsin, a careful student of the structure of the Soviet Union, had taken note of Stalin's fear of Russia and his refusal to establish a Russian communist party. "God forbid it should rise up and be a counterweight," Yeltsin said in a 1990 interview in the magazine *Soyuz,* elucidating Stalin's thinking. "Understandably, a small republic could not affect the entire Union," he said. "But with giant Russia, if it were to assume its real position, it would be difficult to fight it, or, rather, impossible." Politically, Yeltsin noted, Stalin had made "a precise calculation." Yeltsin made a precise calculation, too. He would use Russia to destroy the Soviet Union. He did not conceal his intention. "It was clear to me," he said, "that the vertical bureaucratic pivot on which the country rested had to be destroyed, and we had to begin a transition to horizontal ties with greater independence of the republic-states. The mood of the people, the democratization of society and the growth of that people's national self-awareness led directly to this."

Yeltsin's opponents, including his rival Gorbachev, have taken him to task for using his support in Russia to break up the union. He used his presidency of Russia, they charge, as a mere instrument for opposing Gorbachev, the union president. And yet the rebellion of Russia against the union—perhaps the least-predicted event in the entire chain of unpredicted events—was of a piece with the story from start to finish. For the last act in Russia, like the first in Poland and most of those in between, was at once democratic, national, and nonviolent. In truth, Russia's self-assertion, putting an end to the Soviet empire, was the final act in the much longer drama of the two-century-long world revolt of nations against the immense empires that ruled over them.

The end came with the failed coup against both Gorbachev and Yeltsin by conservative communist forces, in 1991. While Gorbachev was held captive by the plotters in his summer retreat in the Crimea, it was left to Yeltsin to win the necessary battle for hearts and minds in Moscow. He had already consolidated his position as the first elected president of Russia in its history. When Gorbachev had sought to bar the election in which he was chosen, tens of thousands of demonstrators had assembled in Moscow in support of Yeltsin, and Gorbachev had backed down. Now, with Gorbachev in captivity and many of his own ministers and aides launching a coup against him, the question was whether the people would obey orders given by the self-appointed coup leadership or those given by Yeltsin. They chose Yeltsin. The decisive factors, it appears, were the crowd that assembled at the risk of its lives in support of democracy in front of the parliament building and the refusal of soldiers and security forces to attack them. As in so many revolutions, including the one in Russia in 1917, the changed mood of the population had spread to the troops, who then went over to the opposition.

When Russia rebelled, "the center" was left suspended in air. Center of what? Where was it? Was it in the Kremlin—a sort of "Kremlinistan"? Or in outer space, where the Soviet Union's manned space station was still orbiting the globe? In Soviet times, Russia, lacking a communist party to call its own, had been called a "ghost state" in the union. Now it was the Soviet Union that would prove the ghost. A few months later, it was gone.

8

Cooperative Power

The professionals of power, in or out of government, were consistently caught off guard by the failures of superior force and the successes of nonviolence. In 1930, when Gandhi was in negotiations with the Raj, Winston Churchill announced that he found it "nauseating and humiliating" that Gandhi, "formerly a Middle Temple lawyer, now posing as a fakir of a type well-known in the East," was to be seen "striding half-naked up the steps of the Viceroy's palace to confer with the representative of the King-Emperor." (Upon hearing of the comment Gandhi wrote, "Dear Prime Minister, You are reported to have the desire to crush the 'naked fakir,' as you are said to have described me. I have been long trying to be a fakir and that naked—a more difficult task. I, therefore, regard the expression as a compliment, though unintended. I approach you, then, as such, and ask you to trust and use me for the sake of your people and mine, and through them those of the world. Your sincere friend, M. K. Gandhi.") Several American administrations were unable to fathom the political power that, in conjunction with inferior instruments of force, was overmatching their military superiority in Vietnam. Soviet leaders soon had a similar experience in Afghanistan. Later, Soviet hard-liners watched in astonishment as state power slipped out of their hands and their empire crumbled with scarcely a shot being fired, and even the nonviolent rebels who brought about this result were startled by their own accomplishment. Most contemporary political theory, wedded to the ageless idea that force was the final arbiter in politics and war, was equally barren of tools for understanding these events, which it could neither foresee nor explain after the fact.

One thinker who did shed light on the new phenomena was Hannah Arendt, whose description and analysis of revolution anticipated the antitotalitarian movements in Eastern Europe with remarkable precision. (Her writing also had a modest influence upon several of the more intellectual-minded Eastern European activists.) Arendt did not oppose violence on principle, and in her book *Eichmann in Jerusalem* she supported the death penalty for Adolf Eichmann, the Nazi bureaucrat who ran the transportation system for Hitler's program to exterminate the Jews of Europe. Nor was she given to underestimating the role of violence in politics. Born in 1906 into a secular Jewish family in Hanover, Germany, she spent a week in a German prison in 1933 for involvement in a Zionist organization, and shortly fled the country for Prague. She remained stateless for the next eighteen years. In her pioneering work *The Origins of Totalitarianism,* which she wrote in this period, she became one of the first to describe and analyze the full dimensions of the role of terror in totalitarian rule. Nevertheless, in the years that followed she broke decisively with the tradition of political thought that held that the foundation of power is the sword.

Violence vs. Power

In approaching the question of power, Arendt followed a procedure characteristic of her thought. Her frequent method was to boldly take sides in debates on the meanings of certain words. Her advocacy of a given meaning might be seen as a bid to push the word in question in one direction or another. The operation proceeded toward both a clarified understanding of the meaning of the word and a new interpretation of historical events. Such was the method she followed when, in the teeth of a tradition as long as history, she asserted that violence, far from being the essence of power, was in fact antithetical to it. It was not enough, she wrote in *On Violence* (1969), to say that "violence and power are not the same." Rather, "Power and violence are opposites; where the one rules absolutely, the other is absent." Therefore, "to speak of nonviolent power is actually redundant." To appreciate just how unorthodox, even shocking, this claim was, we only have to recall A. J. P. Taylor's definition of the great powers of the nineteenth century as "organizations for power, that is, in the last resort, for war." His assumption that an organization for power is "for war" was, of course, perfectly in keeping with the conventional wisdom of his time and ours. Or we can recall the assertion by Max Weber, quoted by Arendt, that the state can be defined as "the rule of men over men based on the means of legitimate, that is allegedly legitimate, violence."

By contrast, Arendt held that power is created not when some people coerce others but when they willingly take action together in support of common purposes. "Power," she wrote, "corresponds to the human ability not just to act but to act in concert." Such action requires "the making and keeping of promises, which in politics may be the highest human faculty." The human endowment Arendt was pointing to was not something mysterious or rare. One of her favorite examples was the Mayflower Compact, in which a small company of people on the high seas swore to "solemnly and mutually in the Presence of God and one another, covenant and combine ourselves together into a civil Body Politic." The idea that power is born out of action in concert had not gone unnoticed in political thought. Burke summed it up in a ing the filming, several people were accidentally killed, leading one wit to remark that more people died in the filming of the storming of the Winter Palace than in the actual event.)

A comical episode on the day of the takeover suggests that Lenin, who resumed command of the Party only the day before, never did understand the nature of Trotsky's accomplishment. On the twenty-fourth of October, Bolshevik forces began to move through the capital, taking control of key points, such as the central telephone office. They encountered no resistance, leading one observer to liken the takeover to a mere "changing of the guard." Could this be the "armed insurrection" that revolutionary doctrine called for? Lenin thought not. Where was the gunfire? Where were the bodies in the streets? In his history, Trotsky notes how different from expectation events turned out to be. "The final act of the revolution seems, after all this, too brief, too dry, too businesslike—somehow out of correspondence with the historic scope of the events. . . . Where is the insurrection? . . . There is nothing of all that which imagination brought up upon the facts of history associates with the idea of insurrection."

Although Trotsky doesn't say so, one imagination brought up on these "facts of history" was Lenin's. Emerging from his hiding place in disguise, he could make out nothing that looked to him like the battles he had insisted upon. In despair at what he misjudged to be the irresolution of his colleagues, he harangued them to act. "We are confronting questions that are not solved by consultations, not by congresses (even by congresses of Soviets)," he railed, "but exclusively by the people, by the masses, by the struggle of the armed masses." Failing to see in Trotsky's having captured the spirit rather than the body of the garrison the victory that had been won, he cried out, on the day that the revolution was being accomplished without violence, for the violent revolution he had always believed in.

Trotsky's lip service to Lenin's afactual dogma would have been reason enough, in the late 1920s in the Soviet Union, for him to sentence when he said, "Liberty, when men act in bodies, is power." Tocqueville said much the same in his analysis of the vibrant civil society he witnessed in the United States in the 1830s. "There is no end which the human will despairs of attaining," he asserted, "through the combined power of individuals united into a society." Referring to the "power of meeting," he remarked, "Democracy does not confer the most skillful kind of government upon the people, but it produces that which the most skillful governments are frequently unable to awaken, namely an all-pervading and restless activity, a superabundant force, and an energy which is inseparable from it, and which may, under favorable circumstances, beget the most amazing benefits." We have already noted that Adams's characterization of the peaceful, rebellious civil activity before the revolutionary war—especially in his beloved Committees of Correspondence—is a portrait of the power generated by peaceful association. Gandhi's claim that through acts of noncooperation *satyagrahis* "nearly establish their own government" obviously refers to the same phenomenon, as does his view that political power, though not necessarily a goal of constructive social action, was its inevitable by-product. Havel's "living in truth" and Benda's creation of a "parallel polis" were incarnations of cooperative power. Examples given by Arendt were the "revolutionary councils" that arose, repeatedly and spontaneously, at the beginning of almost all the modern revolutions, including the popular societies of the districts of Paris in the French Revolution, the soviets in the Russian Revolution (in her view, the soviets were promising and positive institutions that were manipulated, abused, and eventually liquidated by the Bolsheviks to win and keep dictatorial power), and the German *Räte* that briefly came into existence in the socialist rebellion of 1918–19. The Interfactory Strike Committees, which coordinated the protests in factories in Poland in 1980 to create the powerful national Solidarity movement, were the very model of the power of concerted action, though Arendt did not live to witness them.

Arendt's conception of power was different in important respects from the liberal conception. The liberal thinkers generally located power in government, and went on to ask what its foundation should be. Some answered with Weber that at bottom it was and had to be fear, inspired by the ever-present threat of violence, while others answered that it should be popular consent. Arendt, by contrast, located power not in government but in societies, whose people generated it by their action in concert, and then might go on to vest it, for a while, in a particular government. Like freedom, which was its foundation, power was not to be found in all societies. It existed only latently, until activated by deeds such as the Mayflower Compact and the activities of the revolutionary councils. If citizens became passive, power would evaporate. For, "Where power is not actualized, it passes away, and history is full of examples that the greatest material riches cannot compensate for this loss." When a government was based on the concerted action of its citizens, its power, on the other hand, would be at its maximum. For this to happen, the council system, by which society would organize itself into spontaneous deliberative local bodies, would have to become the foundation of a system of government—something that, to Arendt's regret, had never been accomplished. (An example she cited was Thomas Jefferson's proposal after the American Revolution to divide the counties into town meeting–like "wards.")

In this view, power did not reside, as is usually said, in officials who issue commands but in citizens who follow them. A long tradition had identified the officials as the powerful ones. Arendt quoted her contemporary, the political thinker Bertrand de Jouvenal: "To command and to be obeyed: without that, there is no Power—with it no other attribute is needed for it to be." Or as Weber put it, "Power means every chance within a social relationship to assert one's will even against opposition." Arendt answered, with Hume, Burke, Gandhi, and Havel, that in a deeper sense power is in the hands of those who obey the commands, which is to say with society. Power is indeed "never the property of an individual," she writes; "it belongs to a group and remains in existence only so long as the group keeps together." If society withdrew its obedience, the commander's rule was at an end. Even Clausewitz, let us recall, was of this opinion, for he understood that military victories were useless unless the population of the vanquished army then obeyed the will of the victor. The resolute society that dislikes its ruler can find another ruler; but where would a ruler who had lost the obedience of his society find another society?

If power was the force that is created by action in common and sustained by mutual promises, then it followed that violence, which is the action of one person against another, was in fact destructive of it, inasmuch as violence breaks up the relationships of trust on which power is based. A violent state or group, Arendt well knew, could defeat a more "powerful" rebellion of people acting together peacefully, at least in the short run: "In a head-on clash between violence and power, the outcome was hardly in doubt." What violence could never do was create power: "While violence can destroy power, it can never become a substitute for it. From this results the by no means infrequent political combination of force and powerlessness, an array of impotent forces that spend themselves often spectacularly and vehemently but in utter futility."

Surprisingly, perhaps, Arendt's principal example of the powerlessness of violence was the totalitarianism she had studied so deeply. Precisely its unprecedented dependence on violence, she asserted, deprived it of what she defined as power. "Nowhere is the self-defeating factor in the victory of violence over power more evident," she wrote, "than in the use of terror to maintain domination, about whose weird successes and eventual failures we know perhaps more than any generation before us." Terror, even as it keeps its practitioners in office for a time, destroys the foundation of their power. "The climax of terror is reached when yesterday's executioner becomes today's victim," she observes. "And this is also the moment when power disappears entirely."

Such were the insights that underlay her prophetic comments regarding the long-term fate of Soviet totalitarianism. They permitted her, for example, to perceive that each time the Soviet Union used its tanks to crush a rebellion in Eastern Europe, it was diminishing its power, not increasing it, as most observers thought. In *The Origins of Totalitarianism,* she had taken the full measure of the totalitarian evil, yet she was one of the few writers of the Cold War years to perceive the Soviet Union's underlying weaknesses. It's one thing to grasp in hindsight that the succession of rebellions against Soviet rule in Eastern Europe were shocks portending the fall; it was another to write in 1969, just after the suppression of the Prague Spring, that "the head-on clash between Russian tanks and the entirely nonviolent resistance of the Czechoslovak people is a textbook case of a confrontation between violence and power," and to comment, "To substitute violence for power can bring victory, but the price is very high; for it is not only paid by the vanquished, it is also paid by the victor in terms of his own power." For even as this use of violence restored rule, it destroyed the last reserves of support—even if these amounted only to a minimal, grudging acquiescence or tolerance—that the regime required. The ground was prepared for the later rebellions in Eastern Europe, in which millions of ordinary people, acting together for what they believed in and so creating genuine power in Arendt's sense, precipitated the final convulsion of the Soviet system. Arendt indeed foresaw a more general "reversal in the relationship between power and violence, forshadowing another reversal in the future relationship between small and great powers."

In a passage that both portrayed the collapses of the anciens régimes that she knew from history and dramatically anticipated the Soviet collapse, she described what happens when, behind the unchanging, impressive facade of violence, the reserves of power run too low. Then, "the situation changes abruptly. Not only is the rebellion not put down but the arms themselves change hands—sometimes, as in the Hungarian revolution, within a few hours. . . . The dramatic sudden breakdown of power that ushers in revolution reveals in a flash how civil obedience—to laws, to rulers, to institutions—is but the outward manifestation of support and consent."

The commonalities between Arendt and Gandhi are obviously many. Her observation that the power of a government depends wholly on civil obedience and evaporates if this is withdrawn is virtually identical to Gandhi's many observations on the subject. Like Gandhi, Arendt also believed not only that revolution can be nonviolent but, among other things, that any politics worth its salt must be rooted in direct action; that the obligation to act is therefore a paramount requirement, after which the mode of action can be considered; that at the heart of action lies freedom, which both inspires action and lends it meaning, and, in fact, lends life meaning; that courage is the sine qua non of freedom and action; that action must proceed by agreement among equals, not through suppression by violence of one party by another; that rule based on violence is in its nature not only destructive but in the long run self-destructive; and that authentic, enduring power must be based on nonviolent action—that, in Arendt's memorable words, "Power is actualized only where word and deed have not parted company, where words are not empty and deeds not brutal, where words are not used to veil intentions but to disclose realities, and deeds are not used to violate and destroy but to establish relations and create new realities."

This closely connected complex of ideas not only is shared by Arendt and Gandhi but is shared, as far as I'm aware, by them alone among twentieth-century analysts of political power. (The nearest exceptions, perhaps, are the Eastern European writers I have cited.) And yet Arendt mentions Gandhi even less often than the Eastern Europeans did. In all of her work, there are only a handful of references to him, and she never quotes him. (All of the mentions, it is true, are admiring. For example, she refers to "Gandhi's enormously powerful and successful strategy of nonviolent resistance"—although she joins those who surmise that it would have failed against a Stalin or a Hitler. Elsewhere, without mentioning Gandhi, she nevertheless seems to refer to him. "Popular revolt against materially strong rulers ... may engender an almost irresistible power," she writes, "even if it forgoes the use of violence in the face of materially vastly superior forces. To call this 'passive resistance' is certainly an ironic idea; it is one of the most active and efficient ways of action ever devised, because it cannot be countered by fighting, where there may be defeat or victory, but only by mass slaughter in which even the victor is defeated, cheated of his prize, since nobody can rule over dead men.")

On at least one fundamental point, however, Arendt couldn't have differed from Gandhi more sharply. Whereas he turned to spiritual love as the source and inspiration of nonviolent action, Arendt was among those who argued strenuously against introducing such love into the political sphere. Her objections were not those of the realist school, which holds that love is too weak a force to be effective in politics, which is and must be governed by force. Rather, she regarded love as extraordinarily powerful, and expressed intense admiration for those who, like Jesus, she believed were capable of it. It is in part for this reason, she urges, that the wall of separation between the City of God and the City of Man must be left intact.

Politics wrecks love, in her version of the venerable argument, because love's proper domain is the hidden world of the spirit and the heart, and publicity, which is necessary for politics, will coarsen and corrupt it by turning it into a public display, a show. Love wrecks politics also because the demands of the spirit and the heart are peremptory, and cannot endure the legal restraints that must prevail in a sound political order. She cites Robespierre's "terror of virtue" and its Bolshevik epigones. Robespierre's virtue counts for her as "love" because its inspiring motive was "pity" for the suffering of the poor, which she saw as a kind of love. Such pity may be admirable in itself but, if "taken as the spring of virtue, has proved to possess a greater capacity for cruelty than cruelty itself."

Gandhi, the uniter of religion and politics, asserted, "A *satyagrahi* has no other stay but God, and he who has any other stay or depends on any other help cannot offer *satyagraha*." He admitted that a nonbeliever could still be "a passive resister" or a "noncooperator," but "not a true *satyagrahi*." Echoing the liturgy of many faiths over many centuries, he added, "Only in His strength are we strong." The political secularist, however, will answer with Arendt that there is something forbidding, even tyrannical, in the fact of subordinating every sphere of life to the demands of religion. The secularist will be more at home with her careful separation of these spheres and her search within each for virtues proper to each. "Moderation is best in all things," the secularist will say with Montesquieu, "even virtue."

Although Arendt was not as thoroughgoing an opponent of violence as Gandhi, her views were in one respect even more radically subversive than his of any political justification for violence. Gandhi mounted an attack upon violence, so to speak, from outside politics, demanding that politics live up to divine law. Accepting that violence might indeed be a source and instrument of power, he rejected it on moral and spiritual grounds. Arendt, on the other hand, finds all she needs for rescuing politics from violence in politics itself. She calls for no rescue by God. On the contrary, she merely lets the political man know that if he relies on violence he may score successes but in the long run will lose what he most wants, namely power.

Arendt, however, leaves many questions raised by Gandhi unaddressed. Gandhi, we recall, proposed to answer the objections to the spiritualization of politics by placing his *satyagrahis* under two severe restraints as they entered public life: the renunciation, on the physical plane, of violence and, on the intellectual plane, of any claim to absolute truth. Gandhi showed he was in earnest about these restraints by ending satyagraha whenever his followers violated them. Might these two renunciations make "love" safe for political expression? Arendt left us without her reflections on the subject, citing only instances in which the politicization of spiritual love bred fanaticism and violence. What she did leave was her daring bid to redefine politics and, with it, a deeply thought-through approach to nonviolent action that is distinctly un-Gandhian. To the question what the usefulness of violence was and was not, Arendt answered that violence, even when used in the service of goodness, lies outside politics and is destructive of it. And to the question what the role of nonviolent action in politics is, her answer was: politics *is* nonviolent action.

What Do We Love?

Even as Arendt's distinction between power and violence illumines not only the sudden Soviet collapse but aspects of all the revolutions we have discussed, it creates a conceptual problem. It seems to leave dictatorship dangling, linguistically speaking, in midair, without any political properties to call its own. "Tyranny prevents the development of power, not only in a particular segment of the public realm but in its entirety," Arendt wrote. Yet if tyrants—including the totalitarian variety—were not "powerful," what were they? The Bolsheviks' loss of power did not catch up with their dependence on violence for seventy-four long years. What word was appropriate for the sway they exercised in that period?

Gandhi was a more thoroughgoing advocate of nonviolence than Arendt, yet he spoke, as we've seen, of the existence of two kinds of power. "One is obtained by the fear of punishment," he said, "and the other by acts of love." His power based on love closely resembled in practice what Arendt simply called "power." Its methods were noncooperation and constructive action, both of course nonviolent. His power based on fear—what he called *dura-*

graha (bodily, or coercive, force)—corresponded to what she called violence. But Gandhi's distinction has the advantage over Arendt's of acknowledging the existence of a kind of power based on support without outraging common usage by denying, as Arendt does, the title of "power" to rule by force and fear.

I suggest that the power that is based on support might be called cooperative power and that the power based on force might be called coercive power. Power is cooperative when it springs from action in concert of people who willingly agree with one another and is coercive when it springs from the threat or use of force. Both kinds of power are real. Both make things happen. Both are present, though in radically different proportions, in all political situations. Yet the two are antithetical. To the extent that the one exists, the other is ruled out. To the degree that a people is forced, it is not free. And so when cooperative power declines, coercive power often steps in to fill the vacuum, and vice versa. Society's need for power of one kind or another is so great that in the absense of popular government people will often accept dictatorship, creating a sort of desperate "consent" that is quite different from the "liberal obedience" (in Burke's phase) that is the bedrock of a system of cooperative power. Likewise, when coercive power weakens, cooperative power may suddenly appear, as it did in the latter days of the Soviet empire.

In this distinction between two kinds of power, love and fear are functional equivalents (both are sentiments, and both produce obedience, on which, all schools agree, government depends). In a coercive system, fear, of course, is the product of force. But of what, in a cooperative system, is love the product? What summons up the love that produces the consent, the support, the willing agreement on which cooperative power depends?

The answer to this question, obviously of fundamental importance to any politics based on cooperation rather than coercion, is curiously elusive. The things that inspire fear—death, threat of injury—as well as the behavior it prompts have a monotonous uniformity, like the bending of blades of grass in a wind, which is the oldest of metaphors for obedience to oppressive power. But if we ask ourselves what inspires love in the public realm the possible specific answers seem unlimited. For if no one forces us to do his bidding, we are simply free to desire and do anything we may get it into our heads to desire or do, for any reason whatsoever, trivial or grave, wicked or virtuous: build a school, take a bribe, eat an apple, kill a neighbor, save a neighbor's life at the cost of our own. We are left not with a particular goal but with the latitude to choose any goal. In other words, we are left with freedom. According to Tocqueville, a passionate believer in political freedom, it was indeed unworthy of the ideal to identify any particular good as freedom's aim. In his words, "What has made so many men, since untold ages, stake their all on freedom is its intrinsic glamour, a fascination it has in itself, apart from all 'practical' considerations. For only in countries where it reigns can a man speak, live, and breathe freely, owing obedience to no authority save God and the laws of the land. The man who asks of freedom anything other than itself is born to be a slave."

Gandhi, of course, gave a clear and unequivocal answer to the question. The love that should guide political action, he believed, was the love of God, or truth, which for him were the same. "If God who is indefinable can be at all defined," he wrote, "then I should say that God is TRUTH. It is impossible to reach HIM, that is TRUTH, except through LOVE." Havel, too, resorted to the word "truth," but in a secular definition, though now and then he ventured metaphysical explanations. Many other political figures have, without resorting to religion or metaphysics, also drawn a distinction between love, always associated with freedom, and fear. John Adams was drawing it in 1776, when he wrote that in an independent American republic "love and not fear will become the spring of their [the people's] obedience." And Montesquieu stated that "government is like everything else: to preserve it, we must love it." The love he had in mind was "love of the laws and of our country"—a love, he added, "peculiar to democracies." None other than the arch-realist Machiavelli also linked love and freedom. In a passage in *The Prince*, he commented, "Men love at their own free will but fear at the will of the prince." (He therefore recommended *fear* as the basis of government, for "a wise prince must rely on what is in his power and not on what is in the power of others.") Hard as it is to fix any bounds on what people may spontaneously admire, we know how to identify a free person. We call that person free who, in disregard of force and fear, acts in accord with what his soul prompts him to love.

Opinion

One political thinker who reflected on the dual character of political power was the liberal English thinker par excellence of the nineteenth century, John Stuart Mill. In *Representative Government* he put the question, "What is meant by power?" He answered, "Politically speaking, a great part of all power consists in will." "Will" here obviously refers to the capacity for spontaneous, willing allegiance and action that is at the root of cooperative power. Because will was politically important, "opinion," which guides the will, was also important. "Opinion is itself one of the greatest active social forces," he observed, and those who, by teaching or example, could offer people something they admire or believe in therefore may be the most powerful figures on the social landscape. For "They who can succeed in creating a general persuasion that a certain form of government, or social fact of any kind, deserves to be preferred, have made nearly the most important step which can possibly be taken towards ranging the powers of society on its side." He gave two examples. One was the first Christian martyr, St. Stephen, who was "stoned to death in Jerusalem while he who was to be Apostle to the Gentiles [St. Paul] stood by 'consenting unto his death.'" "Would anyone," Mill asked of these first Christians, "have supposed that the party of that stoned man were then and there the strongest power in society? And has not the event proved that they were so? Because theirs was the most *powerful* of then existing beliefs." The other example was Martin Luther at the Diet of Worms, who, because he founded a faith that the people freely chose, was "a more powerful social force than the Emperor Charles the Fifth, and all the princes there assembled."

If, as Mill pointed out, opinion guided the will, and the will moved people to give political support, and political support was the foundation of power, then the most powerful people seemed to be those who, whether in government or out, had the capacity to create or do something that inspired the respect, admiration, loyalty, faith—all of which, again, is to say the love—of others. Power, according to this conception, which dovetails closely with Arendt's, begins with the capacity to create or discover something (including, for example, a republic) that other people cannot help but love—a definition about as far as one can get from A. J. P. Taylor's "organizations for war" or Jouvenel's "to command and be obeyed."

Yet in speaking of someone as more "powerful" than those stoning him to death, or than the princes of his day, because later generations were persuaded by his teaching and example, don't we reach the boundaries of what can be understood by the word "power"? Don't we begin to speak in mere conundrums? If this is the measure of power, then is anyone who catches the attention of the world in one way or another politically "powerful"? The inspiring example of a human being stoned to death is only one ingredient even of cooperative power, which depends on the responding active support of many, and to call such a person powerful is admittedly to flirt with paradox. Why insist on *this* word to describe the phenomenon? Wouldn't it be better to reserve the word, as is so often done, for those who occupy high positions in government or command tank divisions, and leave it at that?

The events of our time, however, rule out this reversion. For in our day the dual aspect of power lies not only in the uses of the word but in the new phenomena it must describe. The power that flows upward from the consent, support, and nonviolent activity of the people is not the same as the power that flows downward from the state by virtue of its command of the instruments of force, and yet the two kinds of power contend in the same world for the upper hand, and the seemingly weaker one can, it turns out, defeat the seemingly stronger, as the downfall of the British Raj and the Soviet Union showed. Therefore, although it may lead to paradox and linguistic tangles to speak of martyrs as being more "powerful" than the authorities who put them to death, the exercise is inescapable. For it is indeed a frequent mistake of the powers that be to imagine that they can accomplish or prevent by force what a Luther, a Gandhi, a Martin Luther King, or a Havel can inspire by example. The prosperous and mighty of our day still live at a dizzying height above the wretched of the earth, yet the latter have made their will felt in ways that have already changed history, and can change it more.

PART THREE

The Civil State

9

The Liberal Democratic Revival

Everything we have discussed so far—conventional war, nuclear war, people's war, and revolution—falls under the heading of what the contract theorists of the seventeenth century called the state of nature: their term for conditions, domestic or international, that lie outside the protection of states and their laws. For most of these thinkers, the state of nature was indistinguishable, or scarcely distinguishable, from a state of war, and was the last place they would have gone searching, as we have done, for an escape from political violence. The unexpected appearance in these normally chaotic, blood-spattered precincts of new and historically potent forms of nonviolent action is one measure of the radical difference between their time and ours. Now in the same quest we turn, more conventionally, to the ordered realm of the civil state, and its underpinning, law, to which not only theorists but ordinary people have long looked to give relief from anarchy and violence—to pacify the warring tribes, to prevent the attack of neighbor upon neighbor, to fix the boundaries of states and regulate weights and measures, to mete out justice and provide for the common good.

Most visions of world peace, indeed, have traditionally been based on some notion of extending the structures of civil rule to the international realm. The idea that the foundation of a universal state—world government—would put an end to war has been a perennial dream.

One development in the civil sphere that holds promise as a foundation for peace is the liberal democratic revival of the late twentieth century. This revival, however, has been so tightly entangled with contrary forces, including the traditional imperial proclivities of many democratic states, that its potential contributions to peace may be foreclosed before even being offered.

If satyagraha, living in truth, and the spontaneous foundation of institutions of civil society are the forms that cooperative power takes in the state of nature, then liberal democracy is the chief form it takes in the civil state. We have already noted the association of nonviolent revolution and democracy. No less striking is the tendency, noted by recent scholars, of liberal democracies to refrain from war among themselves. This disposition found one of its first articulations in Immanuel Kant's essays "Perpetual Peace" (1795) and "Idea for a Universal History" (1784), in which he called for "a universal civic society," and named the goal "the highest problem Nature assigns to the human race." He advocated a "civic union" of republics that would establish universal and perpetual peace in the world. However, the liberal revival must have a central place in any discussion of nonviolence for a deeper reason: the goal of taming violence is written into liberalism's genetic code.

According to the contract theorists (whose thinking stands behind the rise of liberal government), the choice between force and consent is perennial, because of the ineradicable fact of human existence that human beings are many but inhabit together a world that is one. It was hardly necessary, of course, to postulate an "original" state of nature (which even in Locke's time was proposed more as a thought-experiment than as a description of historical reality) or to travel to a war zone to confirm the truth of this commonsense observation. A visit to any playground, family living room, office, or street corner—not to speak of any company boardroom, university department, or legislature—would do. "The latent causes of faction," James Madison wrote, "are . . . sown in the nature of man." Or, in the words of Thomas Hobbes, who, though no liberal, must be classed among the contractarians, "If any two men desire the same thing, which nevertheless they cannot both enjoy, they become enemies; and . . . endeavor to destroy, or subdue one another." Thus arose his "war of all against all."

Broadly speaking, the contractarians identified two possible solutions to the dilemma. The first was that one party imposed its will on the others by force; the second was that the parties found their way to agreement. The first saved the freedom of one party at the expense of the others'; the second saved the freedom of all parties, because all had given their approval—had, though perhaps surrendering a portion of their ambitions, given their consent to the final result. The first was an institutionalization of what we have called coercive power and the foundation of authoritarianism, the second—the liberal program—an institutionalization of cooperative power and the foundation of civil freedom.

Any constitution based on freedom must of course be complex, yet its essential requirements have been defined with remarkable consistency over the more than two thousand years of the democratic tradition. They were summarized in the riposte that, according to Greece's first great historian, Herodotus, the Spartan Demaratus gave to the Persian king Xerxes, who challenged him to explain how Greece, which endowed its citizens with freedom, could produce obedient, steadfast soldiers. "They are free—yes—but not entirely free," Demaratus answered, "for they have a master, and that master is Law, which they fear much more than their subjects fear you." Cicero described the citizen of a free Rome in similar terms. "He obeys the laws not, of course, because of fear," he wrote; "he complies with them and respects them because he judges that such a course is extremely advantageous. He says nothing, does nothing, thinks of nothing except in a free and voluntary manner. All of his plans and all of his acts proceed from himself, and he himself is also the judge of them."

The connection between nonviolence and freedom in a liberal democratic constitution, a moment's thought will show, lies in the nature of both. Freedom is twofold. In the first place, it is a power inherent in the human being to decide to do things and to do them. Shall I eat a pear or a peach? Shall I vote for this candidate or that? Shall I start a school? Yet, having made my decision and embarked on a course of action, I may encounter some obstacle—perhaps prison walls, or a police barricade. If the obstacle is removed, then I am "free" to proceed. And so in the second place freedom is the lack of an external obstacle to my action once I have embarked on it. "Liberty, or freedom," Hobbes wrote, defining this second aspect of freedom, "signifieth, properly, the absence of opposition; by opposition, I mean external impediments of motion."

In the political sphere, the innate human power of doing things is displayed in what has been called positive freedom, which is the capacity to participate in political life, by such acts as voting, demonstrating, even rebelling against the government. Its exercise satisfies the human desire to be an active agent of one's own fate, not just the passive object of the wills of others. The second aspect of freedom—Hobbes's absence of external impediment—has been called negative freedom, which is the citizen's freedom from coercion by the state, typically codified in bills of rights and the like.

The two aspects of freedom are tightly connected in the liberal democratic scheme of government. Negative freedoms such as bills of rights and other legal protections of citizens do not come into existence by themselves; they are creations of those same citizens as exercisers of positive freedom, who either make the laws or choose those who will do so. Negative freedoms represent a collective decision by the citizenry not to use the state's monopoly to coerce themselves as individuals. In a word, negative freedoms are institutional acts of restraint, which is to say acts of nonviolence. By participating in politics, citizens exercise their positive freedom; by institutionally restraining their collective violence, they show respect for the positive freedom of other citizens. But at the same time such restraints on the state's coercive power are precisely what we mean by negative freedom. On the side of the receiver, negative freedom is what Hobbes said it was, absence of impediment. On the side of the bestower, negative freedom is nonviolence.

The nonviolent revolutionary exercises the same restraint, and for the same reason, although in an utterly different context. By declining to coerce his opponent, he grants him a kind of raw negative freedom. Of course, in the midst of a revolutionary contest for power, this freedom cannot take the form of legal guarantees but merely that of leaving the opponent safe from violent harm at one's own hands. Yet nonviolent revolution and liberal government both restrain violence in the name of freedom—the freedom, that is, of *others,* including opponents. Those who "live in truth," and so refrain from violence, even against their oppressors, for fear of reproducing tyranny, are receiving ideal training for office (including the office of citizen) in the liberal state, which must refrain from any violence against the political opposition.

Although Gandhi emphasized love more than freedom—just as he emphasized social service more than politics—he, too, believed that freedom was essential to any healthy political order. "No society can possibly be built on a denial of individual freedom," he said. "It is contrary to the very nature of man. Just as man will not grow horns or a tail so he will not exist as man if he has no mind of his own." The beauty of satyagraha is that it saved the freedom of both the doer and the done to. It is a system of respect for individual freedom without benefit of the civil state. In both satyagraha and liberal democracy, nonviolence reconciles the individual's freedom with his exercise of power. Herein lies the inextricable—indeed the definitional—connection of freedom and nonviolence. These two are inseparable and their union is rooted in the very nature of action and of every scheme so far invented, whether within the civil state or outside it, that seeks to reconcile the exercise of positive freedom with enjoyment of its negative partner.

To the degree that the ideal is realized, a country's constitution and its laws in fact become a hugely ramified road map for the peaceful settlement of disputes, large and small. For if it is true, as the Romans said, that *inter arma silent leges* (when arms speak, the laws fall silent), it is equally true that when the laws speak arms fall silent. Otherwise, who would bother with laws? Every peaceable transfer of power in accord with the decision of an electorate is a coup d'état avoided. Every court case—however acrimonious the lawyers—is a possible vendetta or bloodbath averted. And so the spread of democracy, if it rests on a solid foundation, is an expansion of the zone in which the business of politics is conducted along mainly nonviolent lines. In this basic respect, the long march of liberal democracy is a "peace movement"—possibly the most important and successful of them all.

It is not, of course, liberal government alone that seeks to give society relief from its violent tendencies. Every form of government accepts this responsibility, at least in theory. However, the liberal commitment to nonviolence is deeper than the authoritarian promise to end the war of all against all. Whereas the authoritarian promises only to deliver society from its own "natural" violence, the liberal wants to protect it also from the violence of the state. Beginning by saving human beings from their mutual violence through the establishment of government, it then tries to save them from the savior, by guaranteeing the negative freedoms of the citizen. Why, Locke asked, would men fear violence from one another but not fear the violence of Leviathan? To imagine that, he said, would be to think men are "so foolish that they take care to avoid what mischiefs may be done them by polecats or foxes, but are content, nay, think it safety, to be devoured by lions."

Authoritarian rule is in fact not so much an escape from violence as a rearrangement of it, in which the violence at the disposal of each person is pooled in the hands of the state. Locke took the critical next step. By insisting that government be rooted in the willing support of the people, he sought to change their relationship to it to one of consent—or love, if Montesquieu and Burke speak truly. The fundamental change occurs in what Montesquieu described as "the spirit" of the laws, and what others have called hearts and minds. It is the spirit of consent—this willing disposition of the people, Burke's "liberal obedience"—that is, wherever it exists, the true foundation of the liberal democratic state, just as it is the true foundation of nonviolent direct action. The inner moral change in hearts and minds from fear to consent is the specific genius of liberal democracy, permitting its citizens to remain free even as they obey the commands of the law.

In the teeth of this venerable tradition, many observers have, of course, continued to insist that the foundation of all state power is force. Pointing out that governments claim the power to enforce the laws, they conclude that political power always and everywhere rests on a foundation of violence. Their mistake is to confuse police power with political power—or, in Arendt's terms, violence with power. These two are in fact the same only in a police state. In newly democratic South Africa, for example, the police are called on to enforce the law. Indispensable as enforcement is, its existence doesn't mean that the authority of Parliament, the ministers, and the courts rest on a foundation of police power. On the contrary, their political power obviously depends on the willing support and obedience of the great majority of the public, expressed in free elections. By comparison, the power of the police is a marginal affair. Much less does the domestic power of the government rest on the military, whose abstention from politics is essential to the democratic contract. The instant that the majority of citizens withdrew their support from the system of government, the South African state would cease to be democratic, and revolution or dictatorship would ensue.

An American Reformation

In reality, of course, liberal governments live up to their ideals only to a limited extent. Gross, long-lasting, injustices commonly exist alongside real freedoms. The United States—to give one illustration—has been a genuine republic for more than two hundred years, but for its first eighty years it was also a slave power and for a century after that systematically denied fundamental human and democratic rights to its black minority. In the segregated South, blacks were held in subjection by an interlocking system involving the states, local government, and economic and social repression. Protest was met with economic sanctions, petty humiliation, beatings, imprisonment, lynching, and other forms of abuse. Not until the civil-rights movement of the 1950s and sixties were legal remedies enacted, and even then social and economic discrimination remained facts of American life. That movement—the most successful expansion of freedom during the past hundred years in the United States (only the labor movement and the women's movement are in the same class)—was nonviolent. It illumines in practice the kinship of democratic government and nonviolent direct action.

In certain respects, the position of blacks in the American constitutional order was like the position of the Indians of South Africa in the English imperial order. Both groups appealed to the highest constituted authority—the federal government of the United States in the first case, the imperial government in London in the second—for relief from local oppression. Both restricted themselves to nonviolence. Neither had any hope of securing its rights through the establishment of an independent nation. (Gandhi's movement in India, on the other hand, aimed at and achieved independence.) The black minority in the United States had suffered far more at the hands of the dominant white majority than that majority had ever suffered at the hands of the English in the years leading up to independence, impelling the Americans "to separation," as the Declaration of Independence says. The Muslim black nationalist Malcolm X, who believed that "there can be no revolution without bloodshed," was certainly correct when he pointed out that the founders of the United States had not hesitated to resort to violence under far milder provocation.

Yet however justified by white precedent, the plan of separation and violence was impractical for the black American minority, if only because it amounted to no more than 15 percent of the population. What Gandhi came to understand in South Africa and Michnik came to understand in Poland—that violence would be self-defeating—was even more obviously true for the black minority in the United States. As Lawrence Guyot of the Student Nonviolent Coordinating Committee put it, "They'll shoot us quicker if we're armed." In these demanding, confining circumstances, an accommodation with the white majority was the only route to equal rights. If blacks could not *separate,* as the white American colonists had done in their revolution, then they must *integrate.*

The strategy of the movement was direct nonviolent action by masses of people in defiance of the Jim Crow laws of the South. The response of the white-run state and local governments and of allied white vigilante groups such as the Ku Klux Klan was ferocious repression. Movement activists asserting their legal rights were hosed, jailed, beaten, bombed, tortured, and murdered. A civil-rights protester in the South of the democratic United States in the early 1960s was almost certainly in more danger of physical violence than an activist in totalitarian Eastern Europe in the 1970s or 1980s. (On the other hand, jail terms were more common and much longer in Eastern Europe, and other basic freedoms, such as freedom of speech, were absent.)

"Unearned suffering is redemptive," said the movement's pre-eminent leader, Dr. Martin Luther King, Jr. Those to be redeemed by this suffering were, in the first place, the black protesters them-selves. One who acts nonviolently in support of justice "lives in the kingdom NOW, and not in some distant day," King declared. And the Birmingham civil-rights leader the Reverend Fred Shut-tlesworth asserted that the black preacher was "the freest man on earth." "They can't enjoin us from being free," he pointed out. Those to be redeemed were, in the second place, the white major-ity, who were challenged to live up to their professed ideals. By bringing the unearned suffering imposed by the system into the light of day, the civil-rights movement forced the white majority to make the choices that it had ducked for a century—either to embrace and fully institutionalize repression or to lift it. Not until public opinion had thus been changed did the national politicians act. It would be wrong, however, to deprive them of credit. On several occasions, they rose above political expediency, and took risks for what they had come to believe in. For example, on June 9, 1963, in the midst of the desegregation crisis in Birmingham, Alabama, President Kennedy decided spontaneously to appear on national television to support an omnibus civil-rights bill. Resist-ing dismayed advisers who pointed out that he had no carefully prepared text, Kennedy delivered what the *New York Times* called "one of the most emotional speeches yet delivered by a president who has often been criticized as too 'cool and intellectual.'" Kennedy's words "rose from the twin moorings that anchored King's oratory at the junction of religious and democratic sources," Taylor Branch, a chronicler of King and his movement, has writ-ten. "We are confronted primarily with a moral issue," Kennedy said. "It is as old as the Scriptures and is as clear as the American Constitution." And President Johnson, whose support for desegregation was stronger than Kennedy's, fought to pass the decisive Civil Rights Act of 1964 in the face of distinct warnings that the political price could be immense for the Democratic Party. "I think we just gave the South to the Republicans," he said prophetically after signing the civil-rights bill.

The civil-rights movement took its stand at the crossroads of democracy and nonviolence. Nonviolence acts upon totalitarianism from without, as a corrosive agent. Under totalitarian rule, the radical suppression of the freedom, or "truth," inhering in each person renders nonviolent action not only exceptionally costly to practice, but, once under way, exceptionally powerful. Precisely because totalitarian control is so thoroughly based on coercive power, nonviolence possesses the capacity, once it appears, to unravel an entire system with breathtaking suddenness. The influence of nonviolent action on democracy is different. Because both are based on cooperative power, nonviolent action can, if successful, strengthen democracy. Under a totalitarian system, nonviolence is revolutionary; under a democratic system it is an agent of reform. For the one it is lethal, for the other curative, as it was for the United States in the time of the civil-rights movement.

King and his colleagues understood the inner unity of democracy and nonviolence more deeply, perhaps, than any earlier leaders of a social movement. They were virtuosos in the art of summoning the American republic to live up to its declared principles. In that sense, they were American conservatives. But because the deepest principles of the American polity—that all men are created equal, that all should live in freedom—are, if taken seriously, radical, the civil-rights leaders were also radicals.

The movement's strategy was to break the law in the name of the law—to practice civil disobedience of the repressive laws of the Southern states in the name of constitutional law. In King's words in his "Letter from a Birmingham Jail," "I submit that an individual who breaks a law that conscience tells him is unjust and who willingly accepts the penalty of imprisonment in order to arouse the conscience of the community over its injustice, is in reality expressing the highest respect for law."

Nonviolence had little to do with moderation. The civil-rights protesters were fearlessly militant. "We mean to kill segregation or be killed by it," said Shuttlesworth. "You know my friends, there comes a time when people get tired of being trampled over by the iron feet of oppression," King told his audience in his first major speech in support of the famed bus boycott against segregation in Montgomery, Alabama. But when the crowd thundered its approval, he immediately went on, "Now let us say that we are not here advocating violence. We have overcome that." And, "There will be no crosses burned at any bus stops in Montgomery. There will be no white persons pulled out of their homes and taken out on some distant road and murdered. There will be nobody among us who stand up and defy the Constitution of this nation." For "If we are wrong—the Supreme Court of this nation is wrong. If we are wrong—God Almighty is wrong! . . . We are determined here in Montgomery—to work and fight until justice runs down like water, and righteousness like a mighty stream!"

King's nonviolence, of course, had foundations deeper than mere legal strategy. It was rooted in the Christian faith of the black churches of the South, which were both a point of origin and a mainstay of the movement, as were Gandhian political methods, which King and a number of other leaders of the movement, including James Lawson, James Bevel, Robert Moses, Bayard Rustin, and Diane Nash, had carefully studied. Gandhi's example was especially important for the youthful Student Nonviolent Coordinating Committee, which was the source of many of the movement's most successful specific techniques of direct action, such as sit-ins and voter-registration drives. King liked to say that Jesus gave him "the message," and Gandhi gave him "the method." King did not distinguish between a City of God and a City of Man any more than Gandhi had, and he moved back and forth between the two realms with singular dexterity. Like Gandhi, he based his political action squarely on love, the polestar of both his faith and his politics. "Standing beside love," he said at twenty-six, "is always justice."

However, the message of Gandhi—a man as little known to the black minority in the United States as to the white majority—was overshadowed by the message of faith, which offered a bond between the two races. Just as King the legal activist called on America to live up to its Constitution, King the preacher called on it to live up to its Christian and Jewish faiths. (The importance of the Old Testament, and especially of the book of Exodus, to the black community created a tie of particular warmth between the civil-rights movement and the American Jewish community.) In any case, King, a Baptist minister, found all that he needed to say about love in the Bible. When his house was bombed during the boycott in Montgomery, and an angry crowd of black supporters assembled, he counseled, "Don't get panicky. Don't get your weapons. If you have weapons, take them home. He who lives by the sword will perish by the sword. Remember that is what Jesus said. We are not advocating violence. We want to love our enemies. I want you to love your enemies. Be good to them. This is what we must live by. We must meet hate with love." Later he said, "Somebody must have sense enough and morality enough to cut off the chain of hate and the chain of evil in the universe. And you do that by love." When an officer who had just called Shuttlesworth a "monkey," then kicked him in the shin and was taking him off to jail, asked him—perhaps in disappointment—"Why don't you hit me?" Shuttlesworth replied, "Because I love you," and smiled.

Democratic Revival

The kinship of nonviolence and democracy—and of both with peace among nations—was put on more extensive display in the parade of democratic revolutions of the last quarter of the twentieth century. The threads of liberal development that had been snapped by the global descent into violence in 1914 were picked up in the century's final years. Time after time—as in England in 1689—the power of nonviolent action showed itself, and time after time it led to democratic government. Like the self-determination movement, the liberal revival included defeat of dictatorial governments of every political shape and form—right as well as left, totalitarian as well as authoritarian—and on every continent. Its centerpiece was the democratization of Eastern Europe and, we can still hope, Russia; but it began in southern Europe in the 1970s. In 1974, a junta of Greek colonels, who had overthrown the democratic government of Constantine Karamanlis in a coup in 1967, yielded power to civilians, after the military intervention in Cyprus in support of the Greek community. Next came the overthrow in Portugal of the autocratic regime of Marcello Caetano, successor to the dictator Salazar, by pro-democratic Portuguese military officers abetted by a powerful civil movement. It's a suggestive historical detail that this second in the series of liberal democratic revolutions brought the downfall of the last of the Western European colonial empires in Africa. It might appear a paradox that the feeble, backward, superannuated regime founded by Salazar was able to hold on to its empire longer than the other, more impressive colonial powers. Portugal was hardly mightier than France or England, or more adept at the imperial arts. Rather, its advantage was precisely its backwardness. Its repressive rule abroad was fully consistent with its repressive rule at home. The regime, wedded equally to both, lost both at once. It was a story not to be repeated until the Soviet empire and the Soviet state collapsed in a single cloud of dust. In both Portugal and the Soviet Union, the home population rebelled in the aftermath of colonial revolt as if its country had been just one more colony of the empire.

After Portugal came its neighbor, Spain. In 1975, following Franco's death, the regime, increasingly deserted by important elements in the Catholic Church and by the king, Juan Carlos, yielded without violence to democratic government. Although the liberal revival so far was largely a southern European affair, the fall of Franco foreshadowed the Soviet collapse in certain respects. Among many right-wing dictatorial regimes founded in Europe in the 1930s, only Spain's and Portugal's had survived into the postwar period. Spared the destruction visited by the Allies on Nazi Germany and Fascist Italy in the Second World War, they, like the Soviet Union, were permitted to live out (so to speak) their natural lives. In Spain, the Francoist Cortes, or parliament, helpfully smoothed the path to its own extinction by providing for a free election in which most of its members were defeated. It was not surprising that as the Soviet empire headed toward history's dustbin the Portuguese and Spanish events attracted the attention of Eastern European observers. All three of these violent regimes defied expectation by giving up the ghost with a minimum of violence, or even struggle. By the end of the century, all Europe was under democratic government—the culmination of a remarkable transition on the continent that had given birth to both the right-wing and left-wing versions of totalitarianism and as recently as the late 1930s had been ruled mostly by dictatorships.

Similar events unfolded in Latin America. In 1982, the draconian regime of Argentina's generals surrendered power after suffering defeat by Great Britain in the war over the Falkland Islands, and a year later a civilian president, Raul Alfonsín, came to power in an election. In 1985, a military regime was removed in neighboring Brazil. In 1989, the military dictator of Chile, Augusto Pinochet, also yielded power to an elected government (a successor government later considered prosecuting him). In the same years and in the years following, a profusion of more or less democratic governments replaced outright military dictatorships in most of the other countries of Latin America.

Meanwhile, in Asia several authoritarian governments were giving way to democracies. The dictatorship of Ferdinand Marcos in the Philippines yielded in 1986 to a vigorous, peaceful, popular resistance, led by the Catholic Church and a rebellious faction in the military. Pressure from allies, including the United States, which had previously supported Marcos, played a role. Two years later in South Korea, the autocratic Chun Doo Hwan agreed to an election that led to his replacement by his rival Roh Tae Woo. In Taiwan, the first multiparty legislative and local elections were held in 1989, after four decades of one-party rule by the Nationalist Party that had once governed mainland China.

In the late 1990s, the autocratic regime of General Suharto fell in Indonesia; free elections were held in Nigeria in 1999; and in Iran a strong opposition challenged the autocratic rule of Islamic mullahs who had installed themselves in power in the revolution of 1978–79, against the regime of Shah Mohammad Reza Pahlavi. In 2001, seventy-one years of unbroken rule by the People's Revolutionary Party in Mexico was ended in a free election won by the presidential candidate of the National Action Party, Vicente Fox. In October of that year, the murderous regime of Slobodan Milosevic in Serbia was overthrown by a nonviolent, democratic movement. In this revolution, the affinity of nonviolence and democracy was demonstrated with particular clarity, for the movement arose in support of election results that had given victory to the democratic forces but had then been falsified by the Milosevic regime. In all previous nonviolent revolutions, the revolt had preceded the elections; in Serbia, the procedure was reversed.

Of all the peaceful transfers of power from tyranny to democracy of the late twentieth century, however, perhaps the most remarkable was the one in South Africa. There, almost every kind of major strife of the twentieth century seemed to be tangled in a single inextricable knot. The conflict was racial: a white minority ran an all-white government along democratic lines but ruled and oppressed a black and "colored" majority under the system of apartheid. (In 1958, Prime Minister Hendrik Verwoerd had announced, "Our motto is to maintain white supremacy for all time to come over our own people and our own country, by force if necessary.")

It was national: most whites and more than one group of blacks considered themselves a nation. It was colonial: the whites had installed themselves in Africa in several waves of imperial invasion. It was ideological: the dominant, white government believed in capitalism, but the dominant black organization, the African National Congress (A.N.C.), was socialist, and many of its leaders were communists. As if all this were not enough, the white regime introduced nuclear arms into the picture. In the mid-seventies, South Africa became Africa's sole possessor of nuclear weapons, and this complication, too, required resolution. (Among the deadly poisons of the era, only religious hatred was largely missing.)

The leader of the African National Congress, Nelson Mandela, was not a believer in Gandhian nonviolence; in the early 1950s, in fact, he explicitly rejected it. In 1951, the A.N.C. had declared a defiance campaign that called for nonviolent disobedience of racial laws; in the face of government repression, it faltered, and the A.N.C. embarked on a reappraisal of its tactics. Gandhi's influence was strong, especially among the A.N.C.'s Indian members; the organization's black president, Albert Luthuli, a Christian, was a Gandhi admirer. "The urge and yearning for freedom springs from a sense of DIVINE DISCONTENT," Luthuli wrote, "and so, having a divine origin, can never be permanently humanly gagged." He argued for a continuation of peaceful resistance. But Mandela argued for armed insurrection, and prevailed. He then went underground to create the Umkhonto we Sizwe, Spear of the Nation. "The attacks of the wild beast," he said, quoting an African proverb, "cannot be averted with only bare hands." Later, he explained, "I saw nonviolence on the Gandhian model not as an inviolable principle but as a tactic to be used as the situation demanded."

In South Africa, however, violent rebellion somehow never developed into full-scale people's war. The government was easily able to withstand Umkhonto we Sizwe's attacks, which were few and far between. Mandela was arrested with other leaders of the

A.N.C. in July of 1963, sentenced to prison for life, and sent to a jail on Robben Island. The protest of the fifties was followed by what came to be known as "the silent sixties." (South Africa appears to have been one of the few countries on earth that was quiet in that noisy decade.) "Luthuli, Mandela and [the A.N.C. leader Walter] Sisulu were perceived dimly, as if they belonged to another time, long past and long lost," the *Washington Post* writer Jim Hoagland wrote at the time.

Political protest against South Africa's apartheid system revived in the 1970s, and this time it developed, without any particular reference to Gandhi, into something resembling the mass-based civic action that would break out in Eastern Europe a few years later. It engaged mainly in local boycotts and protests in support of concrete causes, such as rent abatement and better sanitation, or in protest against concrete injustices, such as the government's attempt to force all South Africans to learn the white Afrikaners' language, Afrikaans. In 1982, a few years after Havel and Michnik had first argued for resolute activism for limited social objectives, the Soweto Civic Association leader Popo Molefe was urging boycotts and other actions for local objectives that were "essential, real and vital." These, he said, would give people "the confidence that through their united mass action they can intervene and change their lives on no matter how small a scale." Only then could they "start to build progressively more political forms of organization—a process which would culminate in the development of a national democratic struggle." In 1983, this new wave of protest led to the foundation of the United Democratic Front, an umbrella group of more than five hundred civic organizations.

Meanwhile the imprisoned Mandela's influence was growing. By sheer force of courageous and restrained personal example, he established a kind of ascendancy over both his fellow prisoners and his prison guards. He and the other prisoners held marathon political discussions, read literature (Shakespeare was their favorite), and studied for correspondence degrees. While the Polish activists were establishing a flying university, the A.N.C. prisoners on Robben Island were establishing a captive one. Here the new generation of activists of the seventies and eighties, many of whom knew little of the A.N.C., received an unexpected education from their elders. Mandela's reputation spread and grew. Seemingly powerless in jail, he was on his way to becoming the fulcrum and pivot of South African history.

Behind the myth of the great man—the A.N.C. propaganda, the hero worship—there was in fact a great man. The government, under pressure from spreading disturbances, and from a growing international movement to impose economic sanctions on the apartheid regime, began to meet with their prisoner Mandela, probably hoping to divide the movement by entering into separate agreements with him. Those hopes foundered on Mandela's unswerving commitment to full majority rule. Nevertheless, Mandela's oppressors found reassurance in the qualities of the person. Instead of finding a broken, pliable man, they encountered the giant who, in spite of them, had grown in stature in their prisons. The first to meet with Mandela, Hendrik Coetsee, the minister of justice, recorded his impressions. "It was quite incredible," he said. "He acted as if we had known one another for years, and this was the umpteenth time we had met. . . . He was like the host." Coetsee continued, "He came across as a man of Old World values. I have studied Latin and Roman culture, and I remember thinking that this is a man to whom I could apply it, an old Roman citizen with *dignitas, gravitas, honestas, simplicitas.*" Most surprising was Mandela's lack of bitterness and his capacity for forgiving those who had caused him so much suffering— a capacity that not only was to be writ large in the final settlement of the conflict but perhaps was to make it possible. "Mandela had become famous above all as the man who forgave the enemies who had jailed him," his biographer Anthony Sampson writes. But he goes on to add, "It was not an obvious role for him to play."

The ability to forgive is a spiritual quality, but in Mandela it was not rooted in religion. He was a stoic, as Coetsee's comments suggest, but not an ascetic. "Gandhi took off his clothes," Mandela's friend Fatima Meet has commented. "Nelson *loves* his clothes." Regarding religion, there is no reason to doubt Mandela's assessment of himself—"I'm just a sinner who keeps on trying. I am not particularly religious or spiritual. I am just an ordinary person trying to make sense of the mysteries of life."—or to doubt the assessment of the Nigerian poet Wole Soyinka, who commented that Mandela's character was "the unselfconscious manifestation of uncluttered humanity."

The refusal of bitterness was a matter of both prudence and conviction. "When one is faced with such situations [of provocation and brutality]," Mandela has remarked, "you want to think clearly, and obviously you think more clearly if you are cool, you are steady, you are not rattled. Once you become rattled you can make serious mistakes." He also said, "Bitterness would be in conflict with the whole policy to which I dedicated my life." Of his forgiveness, he once commented, "Courageous people do not fear forgiving, for the sake of peace." Commenting on this stance, Anthony Sampson observes, rightly and factually, "Forgiveness was an aspect of power."

Few countries seemed to have less in common in the late 1980s than South Africa and the Soviet Union, yet the paths to democracy the two of them took have a surprising resemblance, as if the world, at certain moments, were indeed guided by a secret Zeitgeist, just as Hegel said. In both countries, the leader of the ruling establishment—in the Soviet Union, Gorbachev; in South Africa, President Frederik de Klerk—made an astonishingly bold commitment to change that led, against his expectation, to the dissolution of the regime he headed. Both leaders, it appears, stayed faithful to *principles*, even when it turned out that in the name of them they had to surrender cherished *goals*—in the case of Gorbachev, it was a humanistic communist Soviet Union, and in the case of de Klerk, who wound up becoming vice president under

President Mandela, it was a regime of power sharing that would have preserved a white veto over legislation. Of de Klerk after Mandela's release, Allister Sparks, a chronicler of the A.N.C.-government negotiations, commented, "His own process of change kept pace with events, which is what has saved him—and South Africa. And so he remains on the scene, although in a lesser role." De Klerk's acceptance of the outcome of the process he unleashed, even more than the original decision to end apartheid, is, as Sparks wrote, "the real measure of the man's reflective intelligence."

In both countries, violence on the grand scale was averted—although in South Africa over the four years of negotiation between the A.N.C. and the regime several thousand people were killed, most by the government or its agents. In both, the opposition discovered the virtues of restraint and "self-limiting revolution." In both, "truth and reconciliation" won out over revenge. People have often spoken of a "South African miracle." The government negotiator Albie Sachs has protested the use of the phrase. The settlement, he accurately claims, was "the most predicted and consciously and rationally worked-for happening one could ever have imagined, and certainly the most unmiraculous." But that of course was precisely the miracle.

The Western Settlement

The Washington think tank Freedom House keeps a record of countries it considers to be democracies. In 1971, it counted thirty; in 2001, after a quarter century of the liberal revival, it counted one hundred and twenty-one. The question is what such a development portends for peace. Gigantic claims have been made, the most grandiose of which was probably the assertion in 1989 by the American political scientist Francis Fukuyama that the liberal democratic revival heralded the "end of history." He did not mean, naturally, that no new events were to be expected. He was only suggesting that the widespread adoption of liberal democracy constituted humanity's final judgment that, among all the forms of government, this one had shown itself to be the best.

A more modest and defensible claim—itself sufficiently sweeping—is that the revival constituted a grand settlement along liberal lines of what might be called the Western civil war of the twentieth century. This civil war began in 1914, with the outbreak of the First World War; paused for two decades after 1918; and resumed with the Second World War, followed of course by the Cold War. At issue was which of the three dominant models of government of the period—fascism (and its various offshoots, such as Japanese militarism and Spanish Falangism), communism, or liberal democracy—would prevail. The first stage of the settlement came when, following their defeat, Germany and Japan enthusiastically took to the democratic systems imposed upon them by the victorious Allies. By making democracy their own, they robbed fascism of almost all of its glamour and appeal for the rest of the century. (What country, upon overthrowing a regime and establishing a new one, has announced that it will model itself on Hitler's Germany or Mussolini's Italy?) The second stage was the overthrow from within of the Soviet Union by the peoples over whom it had ruled, which left liberal democracy standing alone in the Western ring.

In the light of twentieth-century history, the potential importance of this settlement for world peace appears great, even if liberal democracy does not continue to spread, and even if it turns out that its existing spread has in many places been superficial and reversible. Since it was the Western world, after all, that, thanks to its creation of the global adapt-or-die war system and imperialism, twice turned its local wars into world wars, settlement of the Western civil war at least removes the prime specific cause of the world's most violent wars of the last century. Whatever the cause of war in the future, it is unlikely to be a conflict between Germany and France. The emergence of a political consensus in the West on *any* form of government would have reduced the likelihood of intra-Western war; but a consensus on liberal democracy was especially promising. It laid the basis in Europe for the now–burgeoning European Union, which institutionalizes liberal democratic principles on the regional level.

However, if in the wake of September 11, pacification of the West turns out to set the stage for conflict with an Islamic "East," or a bid for American military hegemony over the entire world, there may be no net gain. The Western settlement also leaves open the question of its relations with the generally poorer, weaker countries of the rest of the world. Once called the Third World, these countries are now more often called the South, while the West, in another shift in quadrant of the world's political compass, has been renamed the North. By the end of the twentieth century, the South had driven back and destroyed the territorial empires that the North had forced upon them. Didn't this reversal deliver the West a blow that undercut its global preeminence? As it turned out, just the opposite has been the case. It is true that the global influence of several European nations—most notably England and France—was reduced (while that of the United States grew). But if we consider the Western world as a whole, it responded to the loss of its territorial empires as if throwing off a burden.

For one thing, territorial imperialism, even as it advanced the market system, had been a source of wars that had impeded that system's smooth spread and weakened democracy at home. (World trade, which had reached a historical high point in the first decade of the twentieth century, steeply declined in the twenties and thirties.) For another, no sooner did the South drive out its imperial oppressors than it found itself reincorporated into the Northern market system, now more pervasive and less escapable than ever. Imperialism had always been economic as well as military. Whether trade was following the flag or vice versa (and the history of imperialism offers abundant examples of both), the two had marched together almost everywhere.

The liquidation of the colonial regimes by no means meant liquidation of economic influence. On the contrary, a united West—a North—was in certain respects more formidably powerful in the Third World than the old, divided West, whose powers were often played off against one another by the countries they ruled. Nor did those countries manage to confront this united, liberal West with any rival political or economic model that held wide appeal, even to one another, much less to the world. After the Soviet collapse, socialism lost ground almost everywhere. The most prominent new political model, the theocracy of Islamic fundamentalism, first embodied in revolutionary form in the Iranian regime of the Ayatollah Khomeini, could by its nature appeal only to Islamic countries. Even in these it proved more attractive as an inspiration for rebellion than as an actual form of government. (Today, a majority of Iranians regularly vote for moderate candidates who seek to soften the repressive rule of the mullahs.) Of course unliberal governments of all types are still to be found in the Third World, but none of them have been widely imitated. Now that "there is no alternative," as people like to say, the original elements of the West's predominance—its science, its arms, its capitalism, and to some extent its liberal democracy—have become harder than ever to reject.

Precisely because the post–Cold War market system—sometimes called "the Washington consensus," sometimes simply globalization—has become so pervasive, it exerts the sort of irresistible, impersonal, adapt-or-die pressure that the war system exerted in its heyday. The international currency speculators who pulled the rug out from under the Mexican and Argentinean pesos, the Thai baht, the Indonesian rupiah, and the Russian ruble had no interest in humiliating or weakening Mexico, Argentina, Thailand, Indonesia, or Russia; they were seeking only to fatten their bottom lines. The *New York Times* columnist Thomas Friedman has called this system "the golden straitjacket." Golden it may or may not be (Russians, Mexicans, Indonesians, Thailanders, Argentineans, and most Africans, among others, have excellent reasons for finding it less than golden); a straitjacket it certainly is. The paradox of the global market system is that while it offers a wide choice of goods to many consumers within the system, it closes off choice among systems. Countries going shopping for economic systems will find only one product on the shelf. This theoretical enemy of monopoly has itself become a global monopoly. If in the birth canals of the future, some other, better system is getting ready to be born, it is in acute danger of being aborted by the monopolistic pressure of the existing system.

Totalitarianism, in the view of some of its most penetrating analysts, was a monster created from the rib of the predominantly liberal European civilization of the nineteenth century. "If it is true," Hannah Arendt wrote in *The Origins of Totalitarianism*, "that the elements of totalitarianism can be found by retracing the history and analyzing the political implications of what we usually call the crisis of our century, then the conclusion is unavoidable that this crisis is no mere threat from the outside, no mere result of some aggressive foreign policy of either Germany or Russia, and that it will no more disappear with the death of Stalin than it disappeared with the fall of Nazi Germany. It may even be that the true predicaments of our time will assume their authentic form—though not necessarily the cruelest—only when totalitarianism has become a thing of the past."

That day has come. Imperialism, whose tradition is as long in the West as the tradition of democracy, was one of the points of origin of totalitarianism that Arendt identified. Imperialism began not with conquest but with trade, and with corporations licensed by royalty to exploit faraway lands. Economic globalization has so far widened the global gap between rich and poor. "Our British colonizers stepped onto our shores a few centuries ago disguised as traders," the Indian writer Arundhati Roy notes. "Is globalization about 'eradication of world poverty,' or is it a mutant variety of colonialism, remote-controlled and digitally operated?" she asks. On the answers the prosperous countries give to such questions will depend in considerable measure the ability of the liberal nations of the North to make a contribution to the peace of the world.

The Imperial Temptation

It would be tempting to suppose that imperialism is an alien product imposed upon the liberal democratic political system by the global market system. And it is certainly true that in many places the market system distorts and threatens to overwhelm democracy, which has proved highly vulnerable to the inroads of corporate power. The record suggests, however, that republican political systems have by no means been perverted only by economic pressures. The tendency of republics to engage in imperialism existed before the modern age and the rise of capitalism. Periclean Athens, the birthplace of democracy, was both democratic and energetically imperial. The Roman republic was the only power that has ever conquered almost the whole known Western world. Holland of the seventeenth century had both quasi-republican institutions and a global empire. Not long after France became a republic, Napoleon sent its armies out to conquer Europe. England was both the "mother of parliaments" and the ruler of the most extensive empire the world had ever known. The United States is a republic that now styles itself the "world's only superpower" and increasingly claims the mantle of global hegemony.

There is something in republicanism itself, it appears, that is prone to imperialism. It is equally true, however, that imperialism has been a menace to republican government, destroying the institutions out of which it arose. The conflicts have been persistent and deep. They were described by the historian of the Peloponnesian wars Thucydides, who attributed democratic Athens' downfall to its imperial overreaching, which culminated in its disastrous, unsuccessful invasion of the city of Syracuse. The Roman republic fell victim to the Roman Empire—an event symbolized forever by Julius Caesar's decision to send his imperial army across the Rubicon to intervene in the domestic affairs of Rome. The intellectual founders of modern democracy were fully conscious of the lesson. In Jean-Jacques Rousseau's words, "Whoever wants to deprive others of their freedom almost always ends by losing his own; this is true even of kings, and very much more true of peoples." According to Montesquieu, who wrote a book analyzing the downfall of the Roman republic, "If a democratical republic subdues a nation in order to govern them as subjects, it exposes its own liberty, because it entrusts too great a power to its magistrates sent into the conquered provinces." Both opponents and supporters of the European empires also reflected deeply on the contradiction. For example, in his classic *Imperialism* (1902), which had a strong influence on Lenin, J. A. Hobson wrote, "Imperialism and popular government have nothing in common: they differ in spirit, in policy, in method."

As long as colonial peoples remained politically passive, the contradiction could be ignored. But when they began to demand their freedom, a decision was forced. In the 1920s, Leonard Woolf, who had served in the British colonial service in Ceylon, described what this clash of principles led to in practice. "European civilization, with its ideas of economic competition, energy, practical efficiency, exploitation, patriotism, power, and nationalism, descended upon Asia and Africa," he wrote. "But with [nationalism] is also carried, involuntarily perhaps, another set of ideas which it had inherited from the French Revolution and the eighteenth-century forerunners of the French Revolution." These—he meant the ideas of liberty, equality, and fraternity—embodied the principles of democracy. He concluded, "The question imperialism posed was whether or not these [democratic] ideas were really universal. If not, they were discredited at home. If so, imperialism was discredited abroad."

An unusually interesting pro-imperial analyst of the problem, the Frenchman Jules Harmand, who served as the commissioner general in Tonkin (later North Vietnam) in 1884, and in 1910 published *Domination and Colonization,* came to similar conclusions. Imperial conquest, he frankly declared, was based on coercion. "The two ideas of true empire and of force, or at least of constraint," he wrote, "are correlative or complementary. According to the time, circumstance, and procedures, force can be more or less strong or weak, open or hidden, but it can never disappear. On the day when constraint is no longer required, empire will no longer exist. . . . What was taken by force," he went on, "had to be held by force"—indeed, by the "uninterrupted use of force." On the other hand, democracy at home, he well knew, was based on "political liberty" and "equality" of all. Accordingly, imperial conquest was necessarily "disturbing to the conscience of democracies."

Harmand had defined the choices that, over the long run, faced the citizenry of a republic bent on imperialism. They must either reconcile themselves to the uninterrupted use of force, in which case their republic, like that of the Romans, might be lost, or they must "stay at home." Few champions of imperialism have had the frankness to acknowledge this choice. Most have preferred to bridge the gulf between their principles and their actions with what Hobson called "a sea of vague, shifty, well-sounding phrases, which are seldom tested by close contact with fact," while hoping vainly that some respectable and dignified middle course would present itself.

In the internal politics of dozens of liberal democratic countries, governments really do regularly succeed one another without intervention by armies or secret police; decisions *are* made by elected representatives, freedom of speech and assembly *are* realities, the news media *do* operate with some independence, and most disputes *are* settled by legal means. However, in their foreign dealings many of those same countries have backed dictatorships, supported or sponsored massacres and terrorism, and engaged in imperialism. To the extent that democratic procedure is simply corrupted or overridden by military ambition or economic interest—and no one can doubt that this frequently happens—there is no paradox. However, to the extent that the contradiction emerges from the political system itself, then the question becomes why republics so often generate imperial policies that are destructive of their own domestic institutions. The country that today faces the choice between republic and empire is the United States, of which we will have more to say later.

Democracy and Militarism

The military historian Victor Hanson has recently argued, in a series of books, that the association of democracy and military aggression predates the modern age. Democratic Athens, he has shown, invented the savage set-piece battles between disciplined infantries that we have come to call conventional war. (Previously, war had been a more disorganized affair, consisting of a series of opportunistic sallies and retreats by cavalry and mounted bowmen, often with little bloodshed.) "Shock battle," as Hanson calls it, gave Western arms a superiority they have never lost. It was not only in modern times that Western armies won lopsided victories. The epochal naval battle at Salamis, at which the Persians lost some forty thousand men, mostly by drowning, and the Greeks probably only a few thousand, revealed a pattern that would often be in evidence from then on.

The decisive advantage, Hanson suggests, was freedom. Because the soldiers of a free state were also citizens and fought for their own freedom as well as that of their city, their morale was high. Because they were leagued with their fellow citizens, they fought with discipline and were ashamed to flee the battlefield. ("Infantrymen of the *polis* think it is a disgraceful thing to run away, and they choose death over safety through flight," Aristotle wrote. "On the other hand, professional soldiers, who rely from the outset on superior strength, flee as soon as they find out they are outnumbered, fearing death more than dishonor.") Because they and their fellow citizens enjoyed free speech, their military campaigns could be discussed and harshly criticized in their assemblies, and so they could learn from their mistakes. Because they could write freely, they could record their own histories. Until recent times, Hanson notes, military history was close to being "an exclusive Western monopoly." (At Omdurman, for example, there was no Sudanese equivalent of Churchill, whose recording eye and hand may have been as important an element of Britain's long-term military superiority as Kitchener's gunboats.) Because their political constitutions were strong, they were able to preserve their communal will and quickly replenish their forces. When the Greek historian Polybius sought the cause of Rome's rise to "universal dominion" in the fifty-two years between 220 B.C. and 167 B.C., he found it in Rome's constitution.

A recurring tragedy of republics has been that freedom, far from enervating the state, as authoritarians have claimed, in fact generates power, which then can be converted into force, which, as in classical tragedies, not only creates nightmares for other nations but recoils upon its possessors, extinguishing the freedom from which it arose. Arendt's precept that violence is inimical to power comes into play, and the empire destroys the republic. James Madison, who was acutely aware of the danger, put it well in a comment on the destruction of the Roman republic that seems pertinent to the United States today: "The veteran legions of Rome were an overmatch for the undisciplined valor of all other nations, and rendered her mistress of the world. Not the less true is it that the liberties of Rome proved the final victim to her military triumphs; and that the liberties of Europe, as far as they ever existed, have, with few exceptions, been the price of her military establishments." The danger, now as in other times, is that democracy's basic nonviolent principles, so promising for the peace of the world, can be undermined by the very power the system generates, bringing itself as well as its neighbors to ruin.

10

Liberal Internationalism

When Caesar crossed the Rubicon, he resolved the contradiction between empire and republic in favor of empire. Others have tried to resolve it the other way around: instead of sending soldiers across the Rubicon into the republic, they have sought, so to speak, to send jurists and citizens from the republic across the Rubicon to tame the savage international arena. The martial tendency of democracy to evolve into empire has its mirror image in the pacific dream that all the world can be turned into a republic. This has been the program of the liberal internationalists. If imperialism and war are lethal to liberalism, they have asked themselves, does not liberalism contain within it a principle that, if extended to international affairs, could be lethal to imperialism and war? For the plan of the liberal democratic state is based on a formula that seems to beg for application in the international sphere. Might not nations enter into a social contract just as individuals supposedly once did? Why should domestic governments alone be founded on nonviolent principles? Why stop at national borders? Shouldn't a system of cooperative power, the key to resolving disputes without violence, be extended to the limits of the earth? Thought glides smoothly and easily to this conclusion. The mechanism is known, its procedures proven within many national states. Liberalism, moreover, lays claim, as science and religion do, to universal principles (that "all men are created equal," that all must enjoy the "rights of man") and feels itself confined and incomplete on a merely national stage. Having asserted the dignity of man against the arrogance of aristocrats and kings, it looks in vain in its stock of principles for any good reason to confine this benefit to just *one* people. (Conservatism, by contrast, looks only to a particular place and circumstance, and proclaims not the rights of man but, with Burke, the "inherited . . . rights of Englishmen.")

Wherever liberalism has flourished domestically, it has been accompanied by visions of liberal internationalism. With few exceptions, the thinkers and statesmen of the liberal tradition have dreamed such dreams or sought to make them a reality. As early as the late seventeenth century, William of Orange was already "busy with a scheme remarkably like the ideal which the League of Nations [attempted] to achieve," in the words of his biographer G. J. Renier. William envisioned a system of collective security that would keep the France of Louis XIV in check. Disputes would be arbitrated by an impartial court, and "recusants would be brought to reason by force of arms."

In the age of revolution, scarcely any of the contract theorists failed to champion some liberal scheme for international harmony. In May 1776, Tom Paine proposed a "European Republic," to be guided by a "General Council," to which nations would submit disputes for arbitration. In *Common Sense,* published in the same year, he recommended, as everyone knows, a union of states to the American colonies—with more telling effect. In his work we find, perhaps for the first time, the belief that republics will be more peaceful abroad than monarchies. But it was in England in the nineteenth century that liberal internationalism took root most deeply. When Jeremy Bentham, the founder of utilitarianism, wrote *The Principles of International Law* (thereby introducing the word "international" into common usage), he included a "Plan for a Universal and Perpetual Peace." To the liberal English mind of the nineteenth century, civil liberties at home, enlargement of the franchise, championship of national movements for independence, like those of Greece, Italy, and the Balkan states, and support for the arbitration of international disputes belonged together, because all were expressions of the fundamental liberal faith in popular self-government under the rule of law. Indeed, a conviction that it is possible to base all policy, foreign and domestic, on the same basic principles, and therefore on a single moral standard, has been one of the enticements of liberal thought since its birth. (This conviction has also been from the beginning a butt of criticism from conservatives, who have regarded it as foolishly idealistic or utopian.)

The statesman with whose name liberal internationalism was most closely associated in the nineteenth century was the Liberal prime minister William Gladstone, who, together with his Tory rival Benjamin Disraeli, dominated British politics in the century's latter half. Gladstone's opposition to Disraeli's policies of imperial expansion and Realpolitik in European affairs had its origins in his belief in the self-determination of nations, which he associated with England's own independence and freedom. His desire for a single standard for judging all conduct was evident in his reaction to news that a British general was carrying out executions of Afghans who resisted British rule. Wasn't it "monstrous," he asked, to "place ourselves in such a position that when the Afghan discharges the first duty of a patriot—namely, to endeavor to bring his countrymen to resist the foreign invader—that is to be treated as a sin?" Each person's right—and patriotic duty—to seek self-government was also the keynote of his epic, unsuccessful campaign to pass a home-rule bill for Ireland. Laws passed in England for Ireland might, he conceded, sometimes be "good laws," but that was beside the point. For "the passing of good laws is not enough in cases where the strong permanent instincts of the people, their distinctive marks of character, the situation and history of their country, require not only that these laws should be good but that they should proceed from a congenial and native source and besides being good laws should be their own laws."

On the moral foundation of self-determination Gladstone built a strategic vision. It emerged most clearly in his response to the crisis in the Balkans in the late 1870s. The strategic problem for Britain in the area was the expansion southward of Russia, which the English regarded as a potential threat to their rule in India. (The Balkans were seen as another of the "roads to India.") At the same time, several Balkan peoples, whose populations were largely Christian, stepped up their resistance to the Ottoman imperial master. The Turks responded with massacres. Russia intervened militarily and, after initial failure, prevailed over the Turks.

Britain's traditional policy, based on keeping the Russians' Balkan road to India shut, had been support for Turkey, a policy that became morally awkward once Turkey, a Muslim power, began butchering Christians. Gladstone's archrival Disraeli nonetheless favored support for Turkey in order to defend the empire. To the intense indignation of Gladstone, he belittled accurate reports of the massacres as "coffee-house babble." "What our duty is at this critical moment," Disraeli said, "is to maintain the Empire of England."

In his election campaign of 1880, Gladstone wove all the strands of liberal internationalism into an appeal that, more than anything else, carried him into office. On the ground of con-science alone, the massacres had to be condemned: "There is not a criminal in a European jail; there is not a cannibal in the South Sea Islands whose indignation would not arise and overboil at the recital of that which has been done." His policy was also strategic. A string of independent Balkan states, Gladstone believed, would form a stronger barrier against Russian expansion than the faltering Ottoman Empire. "Give those people freedom and the benefits of freedom," he said; "that is the way to make a barrier against despotism." Giving voice in familiar terms to the bedrock faith of liberalism that the will of peoples will prevail over tyranny and force, he added, "Fortresses may be levelled to the ground; treaties may be trodden under foot—the true barrier against despotism is in the human heart and the human mind."

At the same time, he championed an extension of the principle of law to the world at large. He proposed a strengthened Concert of Europe, which would be empowered to adjudicate "disturbances, aggrandizements, and selfish schemes." In 1880, he wrote, "Certain it is, that a new law of nations is gradually taking hold of the mind, and coming to sway the practice of the world; a law which aims at permanent authority . . . the general judgment of civilized mankind."

Gladstone's liberal internationalism proved easier to preach than to practice. He had excoriated Disraeli's imperialism as "dangerous, ambiguous, impracticable, and impossible." In particular, he called for an "Egypt for the Egyptians." And yet two years later he found himself, to his dismay, ordering military intervention in Egypt (which set the stage for the farce at Fashoda nearly two decades later). He would have been happy to let the Egyptians have Egypt if he had believed that Egypt was the only stake on the table; but Egypt, too, was seen as a station on Britain's road to India—a country to which even Gladstone was unwilling to apply the cherished principle of self-determination. Without dropping out of the Great Game altogether (that is, giving up India), he discovered, he could not indulge his liberalism in Egypt. Whatever its other merits, liberal internationalism made a poor adjunct to the Realpolitik of imperial strategy. Either Egypt was a hitching post on the road to India, or it was a nation, with a right to determine its own affairs. It could not be both.

Not for the first or the last time, the two expansionary tendencies of liberalism—imperialism and liberal internationalism—were in collision. Imperialism extended power by coercive means; liberal internationalism did so by cooperative means. Not for the first or last time, either, empire prevailed.

The Wilsonian Apogee

The fullest expression of liberal internationalism, however, came not in Britain but in the United States, in the statesmanship of President Woodrow Wilson. The political climate of the United States was even more promising than England's for the growth of liberal internationalism. Whereas the English constitution had evolved over hundreds of years, the American constitution had been written at a single convention. Whereas England possessed a global territorial empire, in the 1910s the United States was still mainly a regional power. It was easier for Americans, lacking experience with other countries, to imagine that their constitutional miracle could be repeated on a global scale. The lines of connection between Gladstone's liberalism and Wilson's are nevertheless clear and direct. In September 1915, one year after the outbreak of the First World War, the British foreign secretary, Lord Grey, dispatched a telegram to Wilson. In words that might have been taken directly from Gladstone's speeches in 1880 regarding the Concert of Europe, he inquired, "Would the President propose that there should be a League of Nations binding themselves to side against any Power which broke a treaty . . . or which refused, in case of dispute, to adopt some other method of settlement than that of war?"

The President would. He began a process of reflection that led to his proposal for the League of Nations, which would embody the liberal international program in full. He argued for nothing less than a sudden, complete, systemic change in the international order, which would do for nations in the current anarchic international state of nature what the social contract, according to liberal theory, had done for particular peoples in the primeval state of nature. Wilson intended to revolutionize the international system—to "do away with an old order and to establish a new one," as he said in London as the war was ending. "The question upon which the whole future peace and policy of the world depends," he had declared in January of 1917, "is this: Is the present war a struggle for a just and secure peace, or only for a new balance of power? . . . There must be not a balance of power but a community of power; not organized rivalries, but an organized common peace." The next year, he called for "the destruction of every arbitrary power anywhere that can separately, secretly and of its single choice disturb the peace of the world; or, if it cannot be presently destroyed, at the least its reduction to virtual impotence. . . ." "Trustees of peace," he said not very convincingly, would shoulder this task. In short, Wilson proposed a wholesale liquidation of the war system and its replacement by a structure of cooperative power framed, like the Constitution of the United States, on liberal democratic principles.

The All-or-Nothing Choice

The watchwords of Wilson's vision were democracy, freedom, self-determination, the rule of law, and peace—principles that still command assent. Yet Wilson of course failed utterly. He failed in his own country, whose Senate rejected the League of Nations, on the ground that Article 10 of its charter, requiring collective action to prevent aggression, would abrogate Congress's constitutional power to declare war. And Wilson failed in the world, which proceeded, as he had warned it would, to a second, even more destructive bout of global war. His scheme foundered upon the huge, interlocking structures of violence—imperialism, totalitarianism, and the war system itself—that were to produce the carnage of the twentieth century. His principle of self-determination would have required dismantling not only the European empires but also the United States' imperial acquisitions of the turn of the century—

the Philippines, Hawaii, and Guam. "All the great wrongs of the world," he said, "have their root in the seizure of territory or the control of the political independence of other people." The second of his renowned Four Principles, announced on January 29, 1917, as a basis for settling the war, was "that people and provinces are not to be bartered about from sovereignty to sovereignty as if they were mere chattels and pawns in a game, even the great game, now forever discredited, of the balance of power." Rather, in the words of his fourth principle, "all well-defined national aspirations shall be accorded the utmost satisfaction."

America's allies, England and France, however, had no intention of relinquishing their empires. Neither, for that matter, did the United States propose to give up its new colonies. The victorious powers' chief interest was in parceling out Germany's few colonies among themselves. Western imperialism was at its zenith. The English were still rulers of an empire on which the sun never set. During the war, England, France, and Italy had been secretly and shamelessly bartering peoples from sovereignty to sovereignty. England and France, for example, had signed the secret Sykes-Picot agreement, in which they divided up large chunks of the Middle East between them without consulting either the peoples of the region or their leaders. Japan demanded and received promises of fresh colonial acquisitions in China's Shandong Peninsula in payment for its contributions to the Allied war effort—an outrage that spurred a protest movement in China that turned out to be the precursor to the rise to power of the Communist Party. Italy presented a similar bill for services in the war, in the form of a demand for the Balkan territories of Trieste and Dalmatia. Near the end of the peace conference at Versailles, after Wilson had surrendered ground to his allies on many colonial issues while publicly holding fast to his general principles, the English prime minister, David Lloyd George, remarked with a chuckle to an aide, "He has saved his precious principles, but we got our colonies."

Well might Lloyd George chuckle. Neither Wilson nor the

League of Nations that he championed would put the smallest dent in the European colonial empires. The empire that *had* already collapsed in 1918 was the Austro-Hungarian one, in the heart of Europe, and it was here that the Allies could all agree to apply the newly trumpeted principle of self-determination. Unfortunately, this was a part of the world in which such a principle faced immediate, insuperable obstacles. Self-determination calls for each people, or nation, to take sovereign power over the territory in which it lives, but in the lands of the former Austro-Hungarian Empire national populations were mixed. No matter how the boundaries might be drawn, they divided some people from their national brothers, while intermixing nationalities that did not wish to share a common state. If, in one of these territories, one people claimed national sovereignty, others necessarily were deprived of their rights.

If imperialism was a mature, well-developed structure of violence, totalitarianism, born in and of the late war, was just coming to life. The liberal ideology that had seemed so securely rooted at the turn of the century was about to suffer its worst reversal since the late eighteenth century. Since then, liberal principles had steadily gained ground. In countries with popular suffrage, the franchise was slowly widened and extended, and civil liberties were consolidated. Even in places, including Germany and Russia, in which dynasties remained in power, popular participation in government had steadily increased. The First World War gave birth to an opposite trend. Never had the damage of war to liberalism been more catastrophic. In Russia and Germany, the combination of unprecedented casualties with destruction or defeat created social conditions essential for the rise of totalitarianism. Even in the democracies, the war produced a general disillusionment and bitterness that put democratic institutions on the defensive. In a word, the blow that the war system had already landed on liberalism turned out to have been incomparably more powerful than a staggering liberalism's answering blow. Wilson was in this respect like a man who proposes the construction of additional floors of a building at exactly the moment that the floor he's standing on is collapsing under his feet.

The most intractable of the structures of violence that Wilson faced, however, was the one he had targeted directly, the war system. It was in its prime. The nation in arms, the industrialization of war, and heavy artillery, the tank, the modern battleship, the submarine, the machine gun were already in existence. The full panoply of air war, including the aircraft carrier and strategic bombing, was already under preparation.

Wilson spoke for many in his time when he identified the causes of the First World War as systemic. The origins of the war lay not so much in the ambitions of one actor or another as in the precariousness of an international system that could tip the world into catastrophe if the slightest imbalance of power appeared. In 1898, the imbalance had been at Fashoda, but war had somehow been averted. In 1914, the imbalance had been in the Balkans, and war had come. As Wilson put it, "War had lain at the very heart of every arrangement of Europe—of every arrangement of the world—that preceded the war." But now "Restive peoples . . . knew that no old policy meant anything else but force, force— always force. . . . They knew that it was intolerable."

Sometimes, a revolution can be accomplished in stages. That was not possible with Wilsonism. A fatally flawed global system required a full systemic substitute—a new "constitution for the whole world produced in eight days," as the French Prime Minister Georges Clemenceau, who opposed the plan, described it mockingly. The choice was all or nothing. In the words of the diplomat Harold Nicolson, who attended the Versailles conference as a member of the British delegation and at first was an ardent supporter of Wilson, "Instinctively, and rightly, did we feel that if Wilsonism was to form the charter of the New Europe it must be applied universally, integrally, forcefully, scientifically." If the Wilsonian palace were to be built, the edifice of the war system had to be torn down.

If the war system were to survive, it could not be adulterated with Wilsonism. In the Wilsonian system, the sovereignty of nations had to be abandoned, but in the war system sovereignty was inviolable except by force. In the Wilsonian system, the safety of nations required disarmament, but under the war system safety required arms. Wilsonism called for a league of all nations in a system of cooperative security; the balance of power called for specific alliances against specific enemies. Wilsonism hearkened to considerations of equity and justice; the war system attended only to calculations of force.

The best illustration of the stark character of the choice forced upon the conferees at Versailles was the potential threat to victorious but exhausted France from prostrate Germany, whose population and industrial capacity were nevertheless still the greatest in Europe. France wanted guarantees that these strengths would not be brought to bear against it one day in another war. There were two possible solutions to the problem—Wilson's League and a continuation of the balance-of-power policy that belonged to the war system. Each precluded the other. Wilson's plan called for generous treatment of Germany and reconciliation with it. A balance of power required harsh measures—a permanent, enforced second-class status for Germany and ironclad defense guarantees for France by England and the United States. The exorbitant and unrealistic demand for reparations from an impoverished Germany in the Versailles treaty and France's occupation of the German Ruhr in 1923 were elements of such a policy. Ineffective as they were, they nonetheless created a two-tier system of nations based on force, which ruled out Wilson's solution of a concert of equal nations, including Germany, based on a shared conception of international justice. Likewise, the balance-of-power solution would have been ruined by Wilsonian measures—disarmament and conciliation with Germany were hardly compatible with Germany's enduring subjugation.

Wilson's insistence upon a systemic solution may have been

hopeless, but it was not gratuitous. He had located the source of the problem at its true depth, and outlined a solution on the scale necessary to solve it. That the cure was beyond the will or capacity of the world of his day does not impeach the accuracy of the diagnosis. Wilson has often been taken to task for the naïveté of his solution, but his analysis of the problem was more realistic—and more prophetic—than that of his detractors. Unfortunately, the flaws in Wilson's system did not mean that the alternative, realist system—the system that had already brought on the First World War and the death of millions—had suddenly become a formula for peace and stability. Clemenceau spoke in Parliament of "an old system which appears to be discredited today, but to which I am not afraid of saying I am still faithful." But his faith, too, was tragically misplaced. The balance of power was never righted. The world was not rescued from another world war by its rejection of Wilsonism.

There is, as George Kennan has remarked, a naïveté of realism as well as a naïveté of idealism. Clemenceau's realist successors fell victim to it. It could, of course, be no comfort to idealists that realism was as unrealistic as their idealism. The interwar period, it appears, was one of those unfortunate times when each school is shrewd in its critique of its rival's plan but credulous regarding its own. There is such a thing as a disease that cannot be cured, and in the first half of the twentieth century the growing cancer of the war system may have been one of them.

In fairness to both the realists and the idealists of the time, however, it must be admitted that neither of their medicines was administered in a full dose. France neither received the real security guarantees that might conceivably have prevented the revival of the German threat nor was given the protection of any genuine system of collective security. What actually happened was that England and the United States offered rhetorical assurances of collective security to France while the League of Nations dissolved. In the 1930s, halfhearted realism vied with quarter-hearted idealism, and the curative effects of neither, even if they were available, were experienced.

In any case, when the participants of Versailles came to understand that Wilson's vision, of which they were already skeptical, might not be backed by the United States, they retreated with alacrity to the known and familiar. "The defensive value of armaments, strategic frontiers, alliances, and neutralization," in Harold Nicolson's words, "could be computed with approximate accuracy: the defensive value of 'virtue all round' could not be thus computed. If in fact Wilsonism could be integrally and universally applied, and if in fact Europe could rely upon America for its execution and enforcement, then indeed an alternative was offered infinitely preferable to the dangerous and provocative balances of the European system."

The puzzle was how, without writing a constitution for the world in eight days, to tackle the war system that had brought disaster. Even Nicolson was impaled on the dilemma. The political credo he offered in *Peacemaking 1919* remained a summation of the liberal internationalist faith.

> In spite of bitter disillusionment, I believe [in the principles of Wilson] today. I believed, with him, that the standard of political and international conduct should be as high, as sensitive, as the standard of personal conduct. I believed, and I still believe, that the only true patriotism is an active desire that one's own tribe or country should in every particular minister to that idea. I shared with him a hatred of violence in any form, and a loathing of despotism in any form. I conceived, as he conceived, that this hatred was common to the great mass of humanity, and that in the new world this dumb force of popular sentiment could be rendered the controlling power in human destiny. "The new things in the world," proclaimed President Wilson on June 5, 1914, "are the things that are divorced from force. They are the moral compulsions of the human conscience."

Yet having delivered himself of this anathema against force and in favor of the human conscience, Nicolson declared in almost the next breath that force must be the linchpin of the system he had wanted Wilson to build. Asking himself how he had placed his faith in Wilson at the beginning of the conference, he answered unequivocally that it was not the originality of Wilson's ideas, for Wilson "had not . . . discovered any doctrine which had not been dreamed of, and appreciated, for many hundred years." Rather, "The one thing which rendered Wilsonism so passionately interesting at the moment was in fact that this centennial dream was suddenly backed by the overwhelming resources of the strongest Power in the world." For "Here was a man who represented the greatest physical force which had ever existed and who had pledged himself openly to the most ambitious moral theory which any statesman had ever pronounced." Therefore, he possessed "the unquestioned opportunity to enforce these ideas upon the whole world."

Here was a contradiction to contend with. Force was to be expunged from world affairs by the greatest force that had ever been known. Yet if enough force was assembled to overpower the most powerful aggressors, then the question naturally arose what else might be done with that force. The "war to end war" would have to do its job, it seemed, with as much war as it ended. Liberalism called domestically for a limitation on the force in the hands of the state, but here would be force without limit. In reality, the League of Nations never came remotely near to posing such a threat, yet the central quandary had been posed.

On the one hand, there was the likelihood that the League's powers of enforcement would not be strong enough to prevent aggression. On the other hand, there was the danger that if the League did become strong enough, it would have to become something like a world government. Yet a world government based on force would be a global Leviathan. No halfway house, no mere reformist program could resolve this quandary. And given a choice between international anarchy, no matter how bloody, and global Leviathan, how could anyone who loved liberty—that is, how could any *liberal*—choose Leviathan?

The liberal tradition, which had broken the state's reliance on the sword in domestic affairs, seemed full of promise for peace in the world, but Wilsonism was unable to deliver on it. In order to have any part of the Wilsonian program, you had to have all of it, but all of it was too much. This was the unsolved riddle that the liberal internationalist project placed before the world in 1919.

11

Sovereignty

The objections to Wilson's international liberalism had a name, in which the mountainous impediments to its enactment were summed up: national sovereignty. The conflict between Wilsonism and sovereignty was fundamental. No international organization could preserve peace in the world without a grant of immense power, but the principle of sovereignty reserved ultimate power to the national authorities. The American senators who kept the United States out of the League of Nations accordingly asserted that membership in the League would abridge America's sovereign right to decide when to go to war. Would the League or Congress, they demanded to know, make this life-and-death decision? In vain did Wilson argue that the decisions of the League's council would be merely advisory and had to be unanimous in any case, so that the United States could by itself prevent any unwanted outcome. The opposing senators countered that if the United States did not mean to keep its pledge to enforce world peace it should not make it in the first place. "Guarantees must be fulfilled," Senator Henry Cabot Lodge explained. "They are sacred promises—it has been said only morally binding. Why, that is all there is to a treaty between great nations."

The events of the twentieth century that require a rethinking of the sources of political power also require a rethinking of the nature of sovereignty. To this end, we need to return to the intellectual roots of sovereignty, in sixteenth-century Europe. Both the fact and the idea of sovereignty have undergone deep changes. In essence we will see that the idea that power is indivisible, which is at the core of the concept of sovereignty, and has been the greatest of the obstacles to liberal internationalism, turns out to belong to coercive power alone. In the 1920s, the historian E. H. Carr said, "All power is indivisible." He should have said, "All coercive power is indivisible." For cooperative power, the story of democracy shows, can be divided. And this possibility, together with the radical changes in the war system that we have already described, opens up large new possibilities for cooperative action in international politics.

The Sovereignty of Kings

When the idea of sovereignty arose, it did not create a new political reality; rather, at a particular moment in history it legitimatized a preexisting conception of the state that proved to have remarkable appeal and endurance, not least because the stewards of the state found it to their liking. From the beginning, sovereignty faced in two directions—inward, toward the domestic arena, in which the monarchs of continental Europe were beginning to assert their absolute power, and outward, toward the foreign arena, where, around the time of the Treaty of Westphalia, in 1648, the war system assumed the form of the "Westphalian system" of sovereign states. Since then, sovereignty has, until recently, undergone remarkably little evolution in the foreign sphere; but in the domestic sphere of many countries it has changed a great deal.

The widely acknowledged intellectual father of the concept of sovereignty is Jean Bodin, a French political thinker of the late sixteenth century whose work provided a theoretical basis for the absolute rule of the French monarchs, then in its formative stage. He asserted with unblushing frankness that state power has only one basis: force. "In matters of state the master of brute force," he wrote, "is the master of men, of the laws, and of the entire commonwealth." And so, "An absolute sovereign is one who, under God, holds by the sword alone." In short, according to Bodin, sovereign power was a name given to what we have called coercive power. He knew well that such a thing as cooperative power, based on consent, existed, but he deliberately denied it any role in the state. If cooperation by anyone else were solicited, Bodin asserted, then sovereignty was lost, for if the sovereign "holds of another, he is not sovereign."

What logically followed was the second chief characteristic of sovereignty—that the power of the state must be "indivisible," and must therefore be held entirely in the hands of a single authority, which meant the king. Bodin deduced this aspect of sovereignty from the nature of politics and government, without appealing to any higher authority or sanction. In the words of the scholar Julian H. Franklin, he presented the indivisibility of sovereignty not as an ideal or goal but as "an analytic truth." The indivisibility of sovereignty ruled out consent because consent requires a division of power—between the ruler and those upon whose consent he relies. And so "the principle mark of absolute sovereign majesty, absolute power," is "the right to impose laws regardless of their consent." For, "If the prince can only make law with the consent of a superior he is a subject; if of an equal he shares his sovereignty; if of an inferior, whether it be a council of magnates or the people, it is not he who is sovereign."

Bodin believed his rule was valid for all forms of government, not just monarchy. The sovereign might be a king, a body of aristocrats, or even the people, but it had to be *one* of these. Bodin argued with particular vehemence against the ancient Greek and

Roman concept of "mixed" government, in which power was divided among a people, an aristocracy, and a king. In a mixed system Bodin saw only a recipe for civil war. (The civil strife between aristocrats and kings in the France of his time provided a vivid example.) Conflicts between the parties, he wrote, "could only be resolved by an appeal to arms, until by this means it was decided whether final authority remained in the prince, or a ruling class, or in the people." He added a telling analogy: "Just as God, the great Sovereign, cannot make a God equal to Himself because He is infinite and by logical necessity two infinities cannot exist, so we can say that the prince, whom we have taken as the image of God, cannot make a subject equal to himself without annihilation of his power."

The logic at work was simply the logic of force. Every violent conflict must run to extremes, at which point one side wins and the other loses, creating an extreme—an absolute—inequality between the two parties. Here indeed is the root of the all-or-nothing choice imposed by the idea of sovereignty. "All": whatever command I give, the others must obey—or be killed. "Nothing": whatever command I am given, I must obey—or die. In such relationships, there can be no question of consent or of mixed, divided, or balanced powers. It's no surprise, then, that in Bodin's view "Reason and common sense alike point to the conclusion that the origin and foundation of commonwealths was in force and violence."

Having placed all power in a single pair of hands, Bodin went on to identify a single function of government as the heart of sovereignty: the legislative power. The law, he observed, does not appear out of thin air; it requires a lawgiver. But someone who makes the law obviously cannot, like others, be under that same law. Ipso facto, there must be someone who is above the law, and that someone is the sovereign. Bodin's vision of an indivisible monarchical power came to life in seventeenth-century Europe in the growth of absolute rule, based on newly founded standing armies, centralized bureaucracies, and marginalization of the other estates of the realm, including the aristocracy. The absolute monarchs of the age also asserted a new independence from religion—a position captured in the comment by the chief minister of the French state, Cardinal Richelieu: "Man's salvation occurs ultimately in the next world, but States have no being after this world. Their salvation is either in the present or nonexistent."

The Sovereignty of Legislatures

Considering that Bodin's system rested without equivocation on force, it may seem surprising that his central concept of sovereignty would be adopted by the social-contract theorists, whose system was based on consent. Certainly, no self-respecting liberal could embrace the principle that government should rule "by the sword alone." The concept of sovereignty nevertheless survived in liberal thought. For example, Rousseau, who named the people as the new sovereign, placed them as high above the law as Bodin had placed kings, and this understanding of the matter was enshrined in the French Constitution of 1791, which declared that "Sovereignty is one, indivisible, unalienable and imprescriptible; it belongs to the Nation; no group can attribute sovereignty to itself nor can an individual arrogate it to himself." Even the English contractarians, who had defeated absolutism in 1689 and established exactly the sort of mixed, or "balanced," government Bodin had mocked, held fast to the idea of sovereignty, so obviously favorable to the centralized rule that they hated. Locke, for example, called for "one people, one body politic, under one supreme government," and Blackstone, the eminent exegete of English law of the eighteenth century, declared that "an absolute despotic power must reside somewhere." He located it in Parliament. "The power and jurisdiction of Parliament," he wrote, "... is so transcendent and absolute that it cannot be confined, either for causes or persons, within any bounds. . . . It hath sovereign and uncontrollable authority. It can change and create afresh even the constitution of the kingdom and of parliaments themselves. . . . True it is that what the parliament doth no authority upon earth can undo." Could Louis XIV have asked for more?

It is *not* surprising, however, that English liberal thinkers, having once decided that they needed an indivisible—even a "despotic"—sovereign in their system, identified it as Parliament, for they, in agreement with Bodin, believed that the essential power of government was the legislative. Here, too, there is unexpected continuity between the absolutists and the liberals. The French revolutionaries were of like mind. "What is a nation?" the French revolutionary constitutional theorist Emmanuel-Joseph Sieyès asked, and answered, "A body of associates living under one common law and represented by the same legislature." The foundation of the legislative power inspired even the normally reserved Locke to raptures. The legislature, he wrote, "is the soul that gives form, life, and unity to the commonwealth," for "from hence the several members have their mutual influence, sympathy, and connection, and, therefore, when the legislative is broken or dissolved dissolution and death follows."

The Sovereignty of Peoples

In the light of the agreement among absolutists and liberals that the legislative power is the core of sovereignty, we can ask with greater precision why it is that sovereignty is conceived as supreme and indivisible. The question becomes what it is about the legislative power that, in the opinion of so many thinkers of so many different persuasions, renders it impervious to division. One way to approach the question is by addressing the closely related question of minority rights. According to classical liberal doctrine, the rights of minorities are guaranteed by the protection of individual rights. The members of minority groups can, the liberal argues, fully satisfy their aspirations through the exercise of the same rights of free speech, assembly, and political participation that the majority enjoys. It would therefore in this view be a mistake to offer minorities "collective rights" in addition. Collective rights are ones that, to be realized, must be offered not to an individual but to a group—the right, for example, of an ethnic minority to choose what language will be spoken in the schools its children attend, or of the people of a particular ethnicity or religion to elect a certain proportion of Members of Parliament from their number. Collective rights, the liberal argues, are special privileges that, once granted to a group, will soon lead to a bidding war among all groups for special privileges that has no logical limit and can have no fair or just resolution. In other words, while every individual must have rights, groups must not. In fact, there is only one group that can enjoy rights collectively, and that is the sovereign people.

This solution has left many unsatisfied. One of the earliest and most lucid expositions of its weaknesses was made in 1934 by C. A. Macartney, who was secretary to the Minorities Committee of the League of Nations. In his book *National States and National Minorities,* he described and analyzed the failure of the Minorities Treaties established by the Treaty of Versailles to protect minorities in the states that, thanks to the treaty's sweeping application of the principle of self-determination, were born in Central Europe after the First World War. As he noted, no matter how small one chopped the pieces of the crumbled Hapsburg and Ottoman empires, the resulting units included unhappy national minorities. Macartney quotes Acton: "By making the State and the Nation commensurate with each other in theory, it reduces practically to a subject condition all other nationalities that may be within the boundary."

Strife arises if a minority, seeking more than individual rights, "aspires to political expression," as Macartney put it, or if the dominant nationality tries to make the state "the exclusive instrument of their own national self-expression," in which case "the rule of the majority, exercised, most often, under the title of democracy, is a true tyranny." Such tensions, moreover, had a dangerous tendency to spill across borders and trigger international war of the conventional kind, for the minority in one country "is usually nationally identical with the majority in another, which is often its neighbor." Therein lay the chief concern of the League—charged, above all, with maintaining the peace. It failed in fact either to protect the minorities *or* to prevent war. The ill-treatment of minorities continued and became an important factor in the outbreak of the Second World War.

The roots of the problem lay in the very concept of "self-determination." The "self" in question was, again, a collective self—the particular population that, distinguishing itself from the rest of mankind, announced itself as one of the world's peoples, possessing the right to form a government and so assume the "rightful station" among the peoples of the earth that had been promised so long ago in the American Declaration of Independence. It is this collective self—the nation—that international law endowed with sovereign rights. The formula could not fail to create conflict in those places, such as Central Europe between the world wars and since, in which individual selves in the same locality wished to belong to different collective selves. In our day, for example, when the Bosnian Serbs of the city of Banja Luka "determined" in the early 1990s that their city was to become part of the new collective self of the Republic of Srpska, they proceeded to "ethnically cleanse" their city of those who wished to be part of the collective self of the Bosnian state.

Such clashes are a symptom of a political dilemma of a fundamental character that bedevils sovereignty. It is a basic, structural fact of politics that humankind is divided into a multitude of peoples. The dilemma is how they should be formed. We can call it the separation question. Exactly how should the population of the earth be carved up into political units? First comes the issue of membership. Who shall belong to a given nation? Who's in? Who's out? Who decides? If a nation is to be democratic, the people must decide what their form of government shall be; yet in order to make that decision, they must first choose one another. Before there can be a constitution of the United States, there must be an American people corresponding to the "we the people" that, in the Constitution's preamble, "ordain and establish" the Constitution. What *is* a people, anyway? How can you—or they—tell when a collection of individuals is one? Is it a population that defines itself by preexisting, extrapolitical characteristics, such as race, language, or religion, and then goes on to found a state to protect those characteristics, sometimes called its "identity"? Is it simply any group that decides that it *is* a nation, no matter what the reason? Or is the nation perhaps defined by the state, so that anyone who agrees to the terms of citizenship may belong? But, in that case, what criteria should the state use to choose the population (for instance, when it comes to immigration)? For until the day comes that all humankind lives in a single body politic, every act of foundation—of self-determination—must at the same time be an act of separation, a kind of secession, or perhaps we should say "self-separation." And in this act of separation, dividing Us from the Other, often lie the seeds of murderous hatred and war. For inasmuch as the lines of separation divide one nation from another, the nature and method of this act is obviously of elemental importance for the character and tone of the relations among nations, which thereby become "inter-national" affairs.

In addition to choosing its members, a nation must decide what territory it claims. For just as each body politic lays claim to only a portion of humankind, so those people will occupy only a portion of the earth's surface. Having decided who is a Russian, the Russians must determine where Russians shall live. Where are the borders? Is Chechnya to be part of Russia? Don't the Chechnyans have the same right of self-determination that Russians have? But, if so, then why not any group, of any size or description, living anywhere in Russia?

The final basic issue to be resolved in answering the separation question is how peoples and the territory should match up with states. The preferred solution in modern times has been simple and clear: the people, the territory, and the state should be coextensive. *One* state should possess exclusive authority over *one* people residing in *one* territory. This is the formula for national sovereignty. For self-determination is nothing but sovereignty under conditions of democracy. "National sovereignty" means that the people, through the agency of their state, justifiably reject any interference in their affairs or on their territory. What the state may do to its own people—or what the majority of its people may do to some minority among them—is solely their own business and no one else's. The solution perfectly fits—and not by accident—the demands of military planning. Only well-consolidated nations living in well-defined territories can have clear, defensible borders. The system so constituted can accept no halfway houses, no dispersed populations, no divided or joint jurisdictions. Under this formula, there cannot be two states with jurisdiction over one territory, or one territory comprising two peoples, or one people on two territories. Under the name of national sovereignty, the absolutism of kings became the absolutism of peoples.

Such was the depth of the issues that Macartney faced when he tackled the minorities question in Central Europe between the wars. The liberal leaders of the victorious powers in the First World War were "guided by their own experience," he wrote. Schooled in "the traditional idealism of Western liberal and humanitarian thought," they naturally turned for models to the efforts of their own countries to provide "full civil and political rights" to Catholics and Jews, among others. Those rights—"liberty, equality, toleration"—were all that these minorities wanted. For example, Jews in the United States requested no special legislation (not to speak of a legislature) to manage Jewish affairs. Nor did Catholics in England demand any "collective rights." Full enjoyment of the individual rights possessed by everyone was all that either group asked for.

It was quite different with minorities in Eastern Europe, who (then and since) found themselves suddenly cut off from a majority of their group in a neighboring country and oppressed by an alien majority in the land and state to which they were assigned. They were not, could not be, satisfied with individual rights. They wanted, at the very least, some collective rights. But collective rights are, in fact, powers—the powers of a group to make decisions about itself. More precisely, they are legislative powers, for a legislative power is nothing but a decision taken by a group and binding upon all its members. A division of legislative powers, however, was exactly the thing that the entire European tradition of national sovereignty, including its liberal branch, ruled out as an abridgment of sovereignty. Liberal theory of the day left the minorities of Central Europe without recourse. They had to either accept repression or seek indivisible legislative rights of their own, which meant that they had to found a nation of their own, through partition, with all its customary bloodshed and horror.

Were these minorities greedy and overambitious? Shouldn't they have contented themselves with individual rights, themselves hard to come by in Central Europe in the 1930s? Weren't "universal" rights enough for them? The problem was that the things they wanted could not be obtained by an exercise of such rights. The right to get an education in a certain language cannot be secured by an individual; a legislature must decide it by majority vote, if the state in question is a democracy. The dilemma of the minorities was that in the states in which they found themselves they could never realistically hope to become a majority, and so could always be outvoted.

The liberals who argued that the minorities of Central Europe should be content with individual rights were in a false position. They had never been prevented from using their own languages or practicing their own customs. For they, *without quite being aware of it,* enjoyed full collective rights—that is to say, full legislative powers. They participated in nation-states in which they were either in the majority or could reasonably expect one day to be in the majority. For what is the democratic state itself but the full—indeed, the *sovereign*—expression of collective rights, in the form of national legislative rights? In other words, they were in full possession of immense powers a mere fraction of which the Central European minorities aspired to enjoy.

The bad faith of the liberal citizen who unconsciously enjoys full sovereign legislative powers but thinks that minorities are seeking special favors when they demand a fragment of these privileges leads into the heart of the whole complex of elemental issues raised by the idea of the indivisibility of sovereign legislative power. For to join a body politic is not merely to acquire rights but to join a body of co-legislators. The right of self-determination begins with the right to decide who those co-legislators, those co-sovereigns, will be. Liberal doctrine specifies that "the people" are to choose their form of government and their governors, but is silent on the matter of who is to choose the choosers, and by what procedure they are to do it. In territories of mixed populations seeking self-determination, people have generally found brutal answers: repression, expulsion, ethnic cleansing, genocide.

Stated theoretically, the idea of collective rights may at first sound either recondite or abstract. In practice, it is neither. It was to get these rights that former Yugoslavs drove each other out of their homes, locked each other up in concentration camps, and cut each other's throats. It was to get these rights, too, that the American colonies, the Irish, and the Indians, among others, battled for independence from the English.

In the nineteenth century, Ireland was represented in the English Parliament (as Northern Ireland still is). In that respect, the Irish enjoyed the rights of the citizens of a democracy. But it was not enough. They wanted also to enjoy the right of choosing their fellow nationals, their co-sovereigns. Americans had the same desire in 1776. They opposed, as every American schoolchild once knew, "taxation without representation." But that slogan did not in fact go to the heart of the matter. In the debates leading up to the Declaration of Independence, the question arose of whether, if the colonies were given due representation in the British Parliament, they might accept the taxation and stay within the British Empire. The answer was no. The Virginia Resolves, authored by Patrick Henry, after stating the principle that "no taxes be imposed" on the people "but with their own consent," added, "the people of these colonies are not, and from their local circumstances cannot be, represented in the House of Commons in Great Britain." To the famous slogan we should therefore add a second one: "And no taxation *with* representation, either"—at least, not if the representation was in England. For it was not merely the issue of representation that was decisive; it was the composition of the population that would send the representatives to the legislature. The critical phrase in Henry's Resolve was the unassuming "from their local circumstances." In that phrase was quietly contained the demand not just for universal "rights and liberties" but for a *nation*—a new body of citizens, on a new territory, assuming the full legislative power themselves. To be ruled by a foreign tyrant was one evil. But to be ruled by a foreign representative government—even *with* representation of one's own—was, in the colonists' opinion, another evil. They rejected both. They wanted "collective rights." They wanted full legislative power. They wanted self-determination. They wanted sovereignty.

As it happened, after independence an instance soon arose—trivial in itself but important for what it revealed—of a claim of a right to separate that the Americans chose *not* to honor. Certain towns in western Connecticut and Massachusetts took the position that each town, regardless of its size, should have one representative in its state legislature. In these towns, which were in a state of virtual insurrection in the years just before and after independence, "it was as if all the imaginings of political philosophers for centuries were being lived out in a matter of years," as the historian Gordon Wood has written. The objective was modest, but the reasoning behind it radical. "Every town government," one William Gordon wrote at the time, "is an entire body politic"—in effect, a nation. Weren't the towns "in the same situation with reference to the state that America is to Britain?" he wanted to know.

Some towns in New Hampshire made similar claims, in language that spelled out the underlying issues with exceptional clarity. The Declaration of Independence, they said, had "nullified all governmental authority." Therefore, their town incorporations were "miniature constitutions that made every one of the towns 'a state by itself,' able to justify binding its minority by the majority." But these claims, too, were rejected. What was a nation? Which bodies of people have the right to separate themselves from all others and lay claim to the sovereign power? No one could say. But somehow almost everyone knew that the United States of America might become a nation while the towns of western Connecticut, Massachusetts, and New Hampshire definitely could not.

National sovereignty can mean many things—the right to speak in one's own tongue, to worship one's own God, to decide to wage war, to be ruled by a native tyrant rather than a foreign one, to invade and occupy a neighbor, to participate in politics as an equal with one's fellow citizens. But in the framework of liberal thought the New Hampshire towns were right: sovereignty was the power to select, and separate from humanity at large, a population among whom a majority binds any minority, thereby exercising the legislative power.

Once we have clearly grasped that this is what sovereignty meant in a democratic context, we can better understand why the doctrine of sovereignty, which seems to trail so much illiberal, absolutist baggage in its wake, was nevertheless so firmly embraced by liberals in the eighteenth century. For in liberal no less than in absolutist doctrine, sovereignty is the foundation of the legislative power that performs the first and greatest of all political miracles. It lifts unprotected, aggressive, perpetually warring human beings out of the anarchic state of nature and places them under the shelter and protection of the civil state, which is meant, above all else, to provide peace. The virtue of the legislature is that it is the source of law, and the virtue of law is that *all* must obey it, submitting their disputes to its dictates, and so quelling the war of all against all that might otherwise break out. In Locke's words, the "union of the society consisting in having *one will*, the legislative, when once established by the majority, has the declaring and, as it were, keeping of that will." (Emphasis added.) This much Locke and Bodin had in common. If the legislative power is what we essentially mean by sovereignty, then to tamper with sovereignty would be to abort this miracle: to endanger the civil state, destroy the protection it affords the citizen, and consign society to anarchy—a prospect that horrifies the liberal as much as it does the conservative.

To divide the contract was to destroy the contract. To have two judges on earth, Bodin and Locke agreed, was to have no judge. Two judges meant war. One judge—and one alone—meant peace.

The reason neither the minorities of Eastern Europe nor the New Hampshire townships could be permitted to form a body politic within the nation, the reason nations have not been able to find a way to live peacefully together on a single territory in the Balkans, the Middle East, or elsewhere, and the reason neither the League of Nations nor the United Nations could form a supranational body politic was, at least as far as theory goes, the same: sovereignty could not be divided without courting disaster.

Sovereignty and Consent

One of the first events to open a breach in this remarkably broad embrace of sovereignty was the foundation of the United States of America. During the revolution, however, the American revolutionary leaders joined the consensus. For example, John Adams stated, in words that could have been penned by Bodin, that England and America were debating "the greatest question ever yet agitated," namely the question of sovereignty, which in his opinion dictated that in "all civil states it is necessary there should somewhere be lodged a supreme power over the whole." In the words of Gordon Wood, on whose account of the sovereignty question in the revolution and in the constitutional settlement I draw here, "The doctrine of sovereignty almost by itself compelled the imperial debate to be conducted in the most theoretical terms of political science." Blackstone's conception of the absolute sovereign power of the English Parliament obviously precluded any sharing of the legislative power with an American legislature or American legislatures. And when, in the course of the debate that led to independence, some suggested that America, while forming its own legislative bodies, could still remain in the empire through loyalty to the crown, thus creating a sort of dual, or joint, legislative sovereignty, it turned out that most Americans agreed with their English antagonists that sovereignty was indivisible, and the idea was rejected. All that was left was the all-or-nothing choice between full imperial rule and full independence, which the idea of sovereignty always imposes on international relations. As the republican John Adams wrote, in words that again echoed the absolutist Bodin, two legislatures could not coexist in one body politic "any more than two supreme beings in one universe."

The Latin phrase that referred to the supposed impossibility of dual sovereignty was *"imperium in imperio"*—or "sovereignty within sovereignty"—which was described by Adams as "the height of political absurdity." Benjamin Franklin—who had once sought colonial representation in Parliament—had now drawn the inevitable conclusion when he said that "no middle doctrine can well be maintained" between the proposition "that Parliament has a right to make *all laws* for us, or that it has a power to make *none* for us." (His "no middle" position crystallized in microcosm the dilemma faced by Wilson more than a hundred years later when he faced the decision between the war system and his new constitution for the whole world.) At the beginning of the debate, Americans claimed, with perfect sincerity, that all they demanded was their full "rights as Englishmen." But because those rights included exercise of sovereign legislative power, it turned out that they could enjoy the full rights of Englishmen only by becoming Americans.

One of the few significant voices to dissent from this grand transatlantic consensus among otherwise irreconcilable antagonists was Edmund Burke, champion of reconciliation with the colonies. Just as Burke, lover of the gradual and the organic, would later condemn the doctrine of the rights of man for its abstractness, so now he opposed the abstract character of the doctrine of sovereignty, which in the hands of the English ministers compelled England to make war on the colonies. In 1774, he advised England to keep its mind on concrete colonial issues, and "leave the rest to schools." Assertion of indivisible British sovereignty might provoke the rebellion in the United States that it was meant to suppress. "If, intemperately, unwisely, fatally, you sophisticate and poison the very source of government by urging subtle deductions and consequences odious to those you govern, from the unlimited and illimitable nature of supreme sovereignty," he warned, "you will teach them by these means to call that sovereignty in question." Many observers on both sides of the Atlantic opposed the war between England and America, but Burke was the only important voice, as far as I'm aware, to so much as whisper a word of criticism of the underlying doctrine of sovereignty that forced the two lands toward their irreparable division. Rarely asked—then as now—is whether there could have been another, more flexible conception of state power that would have permitted the American states to govern their own local affairs while remaining conjoined in a voluntary, multinational union.

It was not until the late 1780s, when the Americans turned from their act of separation to their act of consolidation, the framing of the Constitution, that the logic of sovereignty came under serious challenge. The old Latin axioms that had made separation from England seem necessary seemed to make the union of the states impossible. Invocation by the Constitution's opponents of the indivisibility of rule drove the Federalists into genuine political terra incognita. They were now proposing two distinct challenges to the traditional understanding of sovereignty. One was federalism, which divided power between the states and a federal government, and the other was the doctrine of the separation of the federal government's own powers. How, Federalist supporters of the Constitution had to ask themselves, could "sovereign" states combine to form a federal government if sovereignty could not be divided? Wasn't it logically necessary for the national legislature, for example, to make *all* laws or to make *none*? The Anti-Federalists certainly thought so, and did not fail to confront the Federalists with all the familiar arguments. For example, Samuel Adams, an Anti-Federalist, called the Constitution a plan for the absurd "*Imperia in Imperio,* justly deemed a solecism in politics."

James Madison now found his way to the middle ground that theory had so long forbidden as "absurd." He asserted, with uncharacteristic vagueness, that under the Constitution the government would be "not completely consolidated, nor . . . entirely federal." It would be "of a mixed nature," being made up of "many co-equal sovereignties." Alexander Hamilton called a federation "an assemblage of societies." Was there a "sovereign" in the United States? The Constitution remains silent on the point. The word nowhere appears in the document. Strangely, it was not the militant movement for independence of the 1770s but the supposedly "conservative" movement to found the national government in the 1780s that carried the United States into these chartless waters. The Declaration of Independence is the United States' most fiery document but the Constitution is its most radical.

The Dissolution of Domestic Sovereignty

The American formulation marked the beginning of a new chapter in the saga of sovereignty. Sovereignty had proved a pilgrim.

Invented for the use of kings, it migrated, in the hands of the English Whigs, to Parliament. Then, in American and French keeping, it descended to the people. In France, at first, sovereignty—*une et indivisible*—remained undividable. In the United States, events took a different turn. Just how, in "the crisis years" between the Declaration of Independence and the ratification of the Constitution, popular sovereignty came to be defined is a marvelous tale of action and thought told in Gordon Wood's *The Creation of the American Republic*. The important point for our purposes is that the Federalists clinched the argument in favor of their cause when they asserted that sovereignty in a republic resided not in the states or in the federal government—or, for that matter, in any governmental body—but in the people, who were therefore entirely free to add to existing political structures (such as the states) any other structures (such as the federal government) that they might desire. If sovereignty belonged to neither the federal government nor the states, then neither had to possess indivisible power, and a middle ground could be found between them. The institutional innovation that permitted this solution was the state constitutional convention, which, bypassing the state governments, enabled the citizens of each state to ratify or reject the federal constitution directly, in an unmediated exercise of their sovereign power. The constitutional conventions in each state did not so much override the state governments as simply circumvent them through a fresh, direct recourse to the power of the people.

Sovereignty was not like some precious heirloom that could pass unchanged from one pair of hands to another. It was transformed as it made its way from its royal pinnacle to the people. As it descended, it fragmented. The English had resorted to the ungainly phrase "King-in-Parliament" in order to go on imagining that their system, described by themselves as "mixed," nevertheless contained a single, indivisible sovereign. By the time sovereignty was in the people's hands, it had in fact lost its indivisibility.

If Bodin had proved that sovereign power—which for him was the same as coercive power—was indivisible, the American Federalists, founders of a national government based on consent, proved that cooperative power was divisible. Far from endowing any single authority with the power to make all decisions, the framers of the Constitution required the concurrence of many authorities in order to make almost any decision. They created a veritable maze through which power had to travel in order to achieve its appointed ends.

But perhaps, someone might argue, the power of the new sovereign, the people, was in fact indivisible. If that were so, however, it was hard to explain why, as Madison commented in *The Federalist Papers,* the "true distinction" of the American Constitution, "lies in the total exclusion of the people in their collective capacity from any share" in the government. It was a fact that the people, using their powers to amend the Constitution, could, both legally and peacefully, pull down the whole edifice, including their own amending power, and in that sense were supreme. Yet it was no less true that in the ordinary business of government the people were barred from directly making almost any decision. (The exceptions are referenda in certain states.) They could dynamite the whole building but were powerless to so much as change the curtains in any of the rooms. For instance, if the public dislikes a Supreme Court decision, it can try to elect three or four presidents in a row who might appoint a majority of justices who might reverse the decision (as the opponents of abortion have tried to do in recent years), or else the people can convene a constitutional convention and change the document to undo the court's work. But short of these cumbersome or drastic recourses, the people are powerless.

The American Constitution deliberately shuns the establishment of any single, indivisible organ of power. The whole document, one might say, is a device for heading off such a development.

Liberal thinkers adopted the doctrine of sovereignty from their absolutist forebears because it embodied what was *the* central requirement of the liberal civil state—namely, procedures for the peaceful arbitration of the disputes that are endemic in human existence. It's evident that the American Constitution provides such procedures. Laws *are* passed; they *are* obeyed; disputes among citizens *are* settled and do *not* lead to the war of all against all. Yet all this happens without concentration of indivisible power anywhere in the system.

Should the word "sovereignty," then, still be applied to name anything in the American system, or were the drafters of the Constitution right to shun the term? Wasn't the doctrine of the indivisibility of sovereignty disproven by the American experience? Hadn't the time come to search for new words? I suggest that the change has been so profound that the word should be dropped. In the United States, sovereignty—if we accept the definition of the word employed for hundreds of years—did not merely change its location or character but disappeared.

This is a linguistic point. The substantive point is that the claim that the power of the well-ordered state must be indivisible was a deeply entrenched theoretical mistake. The division of sovereignty, in the United States and other liberal democracies all over the world, does not belong merely to the rather large class of events that mainstream theory failed to predict; it belongs to the more select class that mainstream theory had ruled out as impossible but that then happened. The nonviolent collapse of the Soviet Union also belongs to this class. In both cases, an overestimation of the role of force in politics was involved. In fairness to the theorists, though, it has to be admitted that the successful division of state power was a possibility that not even the statesmen accomplishing the feat believed possible. They were almost as surprised by what they had wrought as anyone else.

The Persistence of International Sovereignty

The eclipse of sovereign, coercive power and the rise in our time of divided, cooperative power in the domestic affairs of dozens of governments suggest that a similar eclipse in the international sphere is possible. Isn't it conceivable that states no longer insisting on indivisible, centralized power at home could sooner or later stop insisting on it in their relationships abroad? In that case, might not the international sphere experience growth of the same variety of mixed and federalistic forms of power that the domestic sphere has witnessed in so many countries?

If sovereignty in international affairs were a mere concept, its decline would be a merely intellectual event. In reality it has been much more than that. Above all, it has been an intellectual and juridical crystallization of conduct imposed upon states by the tyranny of the war system. Its first principle—that power was based on force—was the first rule of life under the war system. Its second principle—that power was indivisible—was simply an obvious corollary. As long as the war system remained intact, the new forms of divided power were condemned to remain bottled up within national borders. There was no room in this framework, as Wilson was forced to recognize, for interesting federalistic experiments, or Madisonian "mixed sovereignty." There was room only for the wholesale, go-for-broke replacement of the war system with something like the League of Nations. But in actual practice, of course, it turned out that there was no room for this, either.

The war system, however, has now been revolutionized by the metamorphosis we have chronicled. The age of total wars and world-spanning territorial empires has ended. The implacable pressures of the adapt-or-die system that undid the league and have disabled the U.N. have been lifted. The question arises whether in this new world the new forms of power at home may not be extended to the world at large. There are already promising signs that they might be. The place where the most interesting experiments in divided power are occurring is not, however, the United States but the birthplace of modern sovereignty, Europe, where a quiet but powerful incremental movement is afoot to join the formerly warring lands of that continent into a body politic whose outlines are as unclear as they are unprecedented. But before turning to this matter, we need to discuss the fresh perils, which may prove no less implacable than the old, that have accompanied the new opportunities of our day.

PART FOUR

The Shapes of Things to Come

12

Niagara

Black and hideous to me is the tragedy that gathers, and I'm sick beyond cure to have lived on to see it. You and I . . . should have been spared this wreck of our belief that through the long years we had seen civilization grow and the worst become impossible. The tide that bore us along was then all the while moving to *this* as its grand Niagara—yet what a blessing we didn't know it. It seems to me to *undo* everything, everything that was ours, in the most horrible retroactive way—but I avert my face from the monstrous scene!—

HENRY JAMES, LETTER TO RHODA BROUGHTON, AUGUST 10, 1914

In these pages so far I have sought to trace, alongside the awful history of modern violence, a less-noticed, parallel history of non-violent power. The chronicle has been a hopeful one of violence disrupted or in retreat—of great-power war immobilized by the nuclear stalemate, of brutal empires defeated by local peoples fighting for their self-determination, of revolutions succeeding without violence, of democracy supplanting authoritarian or totalitarian repression, of national sovereignty yielding to systems of mixed and balanced powers. These developments, I shall argue, have provided the world with the strongest new foundations for the creation of a durable peace that have ever existed. But first we must turn to the more familiar task of assessing the new violent dangers of our time—most of them present before September 11—that have the potential to make the twenty-first century even bloodier than the twentieth. Many of them are in fact connected with the new opportunities. Even as the self-determination movement was toppling the world's territorial empires, it was fueling a multitude of wars, some of them genocidal, among the successor states and peoples. Even as the Western liberal settlement ended the inter-Western wars that had disrupted the peace of the world for so long, the most prosperous nations were confronting the poorer ones with a new concentration of economic and military power that threatened to create a new line of conflict along a North-South axis. Even as liberal democracy was spreading, the most powerful of the liberal democracies, the United States, was, like ancient Rome, in danger of transforming itself from a republic into a fearsome empire. And, to say what is obvious but too often overlooked, even as nuclear terror paralyzed the old danger of total war, it created a new danger of annihilation—a danger, moreover, that was evolving, for in the post–Cold War period nuclear technology and other technology of mass destruction were rapidly spreading.

Wars of Self-Determination

In the post–Cold War period, the world boiled, as it always has, with local and regional wars, but in at least one respect their general character was different from those of the recent past. They were occurring almost entirely within nations rather than between them. In 2001, according to the Stockholm International Peace Research Institute, twenty-four wars were in progress, of which twenty-one were mainly within nations. Taken by itself, the decline of classic, conventional wars among full-fledged nation-states marks a profound, welcome change. Its causes include the dampening influence of nuclear arsenals; the collapse of the territorial empires, which historically have been a prolific cause of wars; and the absence of any worldwide ideological struggle among states in the post–Cold War world. (The American war on terrorism is so far the nearest thing to a new ideological cause.)

Some of the wars within national borders are turf battles among local warlords, some are civil wars, some are class wars, some are religious wars, some are ethnic wars, and most are a combination of several of the above. One category, however, stands out as prevalent. It is what we can call war of self-determination, in which the issue is the definition, ethnic composition, or birth of a nation. There are several kinds. One is the war of foundation. Historical examples include the three wars that the Prussian Chancellor Otto von Bismarck waged in the 1860s and seventies in order to found the German Reich and the wars waged by Slovenia, Croatia, Bosnia, and Kosovo in the 1990s to extricate themselves from the Yugoslavian federation and establish their independence. The war between Israel and the Palestinians has been a double war of national foundation: first, Zionists fought to found the state of Israel in Palestine; now Palestinians fight to found a Palestinian state in the lands conquered by Israel in 1967. Both parties are, in their own opinion, fighting for their national existence. Another kind is the war of secession—such as the American Civil War or the war of partition that accompanied the withdrawal of Pakistan from India in 1948—in which one part of a nation breaks away from the whole, either to join another or to establish its independence. Still another kind is the territorial war, in which two countries each lay claim to one piece of land that lies between them, as India and Pakistan do with respect to Kashmir. (In Kashmir, there is also an independence movement, adding a third dimension of self-determination to the conflict.)

Because the formula for self-determination—the exact congruity of people, state, and territory—is, in our democratic age, also the formula for national sovereignty, it would be equally appropriate to call wars of self-determination wars of national sovereignty.

The global self-determination movement, which has contributed so much to peace by ridding the world of its colonial empires, has in the postimperial world become a disturber of the peace. Expelling the imperial master turned out to be only the first step in self-determination. The liberated peoples then had to carve up the imperial territories among themselves. In short, imperial withdrawal confronted them with the separation question. In the eighteenth century, when the democratic revolutions occurred in the United States and Europe, many of the peoples involved had the good fortune already to belong to fairly well-defined national populations living within well-defined national borders. The revolutionaries who took to the streets in Paris in 1789 did not have to ask who qualified as a French person or what territory should be their homeland. Those questions had been largely answered by several centuries of dynastic war. The extent of the United Kingdom likewise was quite clear by the middle of the eighteenth century. (The remaining contested zone was Ireland.)

It was different in the lands evacuated in our time by the European empires, where, as in the Balkans, national populations were often mixed in one territory or dispersed among many territories. Most, as Macartney observed, were unable to find any means but warfare to create nation-states according to the approved formula for self-determination and sovereignty. *People's* wars (wars of the people against imperial overlords), you might say, gave way to *peoples'* wars (wars among newly liberated peoples). The latter have been as sanguinary as the former and certainly less tractable. In people's war against an imperial power, a clean resolution is at least possible. The occupier, once he has decided to leave, can pull up stakes almost overnight. A local people can hardly do the same. People's war ends when the conquerors have had enough and go home. Peoples' wars tend to go on indefinitely, because everyone already is at home.

The end of the British Empire alone touched off a multitude of wars of self-determination. The fall of the Raj led directly to the violent partition of Pakistan and India and set the stage for the three succeeding wars between the two countries. Britain's incomplete withdrawal from Ireland in 1922, which left six mainly Protestant northern counties under British control, created the conditions for the Catholic-Protestant violence that erupted in the late 1960s. Britain's surrender of its mandate over Palestine in 1948 left a political vacuum that was soon filled by Arab-Israeli strife. The British withdrawal from Cyprus prepared the ground, in time, for conflict between its Greek and Turkish communities (backed respectively by Greece and Turkey) and finally the enforced partition of the island. The fall of the Soviet empire also touched off several territorial wars—between Georgia and Abkhazia, between Armenia and Azerbaijan, and between Russia and Chechnya. The disintegration of Yugoslavia led to the multiple, interlocking wars of the 1990s on that territory. The Treaty of Sèvres of 1920, marking the end of the Ottoman Empire, promised the Kurdish people a state of their own but in actuality left them partitioned among and repressed by Iraq, Turkey, Iran, and Syria. Many of the wars now afflicting Africa also have postimperial aspects. Borders established by the imperial powers in the nineteenth century often reflected the outcome of inter-imperial jockeying more than local realities. The imperialists divided tribes by means of "national" boundaries, forced peoples hostile to each other together, and often ran roughshod over distinctions of language, religion, and culture. Often, the movements that won independence had little in common but their hatred for the imperial overlords, and began to fall apart soon after taking power, or even before. Sometimes, the imperial rulers deliberately set one tribe or ethnic group against another, dividing to conquer, and then left the locals to fight it out after they had withdrawn. For example, the Belgian rulers of Rwanda and Burundi fostered divisions between the Hutu and Tutsi tribes that led to the genocidal campaign waged by the Hutu against the Tutsi in Rwanda in 1994.

The anarchy that has often broken out in lands of what some have called "failed states," such as Somalia and Sierra Leone, may be regarded as misbegotten wars of national foundation. In those places of Hobbesian nightmare, no group—be it tribe, clan, religious sect, or political party—generates enough power, whether cooperative or coercive, to found a state, and the country is carved up by chieftains and warlords or simply preyed upon by armed bands or mafias with no clear political loyalties. The people may have had too little in common or too feeble a political will to found a nation. Not abuse of power but default of power is the problem. Whatever may be wrong with the nation-state per se, these cases remind us, its existence is nothing to be taken for granted. Where it does exist, it is an achievement, not a gift.

Inasmuch as the age of the territorial empires has ended, it is possible that the supply of wars of self-determination that often follow in their wake is slowly running out—that these are not the first stage of a new wave of anarchy about to engulf the world, as some have suggested, but rather the last stage of a long wave that will gradually recede. This hope, however, is small comfort for the near future, since wars of self-determination are among the most durable conflicts on record. For example, the conflicts between India and Pakistan and between Israel and the Palestinians, both of which broke out in earnest in the late 1940s, are still continuing a half-century later. And the conflict created by English colonization and domination of Ireland, which may finally be ending, has lasted for almost four hundred years—some would say longer. Shortly after the First World War, Winston Churchill marveled at its durability. "The integrity of their quarrel is one of the few institutions," he quipped, "that has been unaltered in the cataclysm that has swept the world."

Nations that have solved the separation problem by accomplishing the approved triple overlap of nation, state, and territory have been called "achieved" nations, while those that have fallen short in one way or another have been labeled "unachieved." When we witness the catastrophes that the wars of self-determination have brought to mixed populations, we can well appreciate the value of an achieved nation, such as France or England. Yet this solution to the separation problem has also come with a high price attached. For the homogeneity of peoples that has brought peace *within* state borders has encouraged jingoistic passions that support war *across* state borders. The mutual hatreds removed from the domestic sphere have again and again assumed the familiar form of chauvinistic resentment and hatred of another country, fueling straightforward, old-fashioned conventional war. This is what happened, for example, in South Asia, which has the unfortunate distinction of having run almost the entire gamut of possible forms of violence. Under the Raj, Hindus and Muslims frequently engaged in "communal" violence in their villages; then came "ethnic cleansing" during partition; then the series of conventional wars between the nation-states of Pakistan and India; and now the nuclear buildup and the nuclear confrontation.

It would in truth be hard to decide which was worse in the twentieth century—the killing at close quarters in the postimperial wars within unachieved nations or the wars fought across national borders by the achieved nations. Either way, the formula that required identity of state, people, and territory has brought catastrophe. The achieved nations of Germany and France, for instance, fell on one another with the utmost savagery in the world wars, bringing to bear all the concentrated violence that technical progress had put in their hands. The riddle is how to avoid both sorts of war, for both are forms of a single dilemma: How can the nation determine its collective self without cultivating murderous hostility toward others? This problem is the unsquared circle of international politics, and, though the frequency of interstate wars has now waned, the internecine variety are rife as the twenty-first century begins.

The Second Nuclear Age and the Last Man

The seeds of wars of self-determination are local or regional. The same is true of most revolutions, coups, and ethnic and religious strife, most terrorism and the quarrels of mafias and warlords out for power or lucre. These conflicts need no global war system to keep them going. Their persistent, smoldering flames burn in or under home soil, like peat fires, and can survive the rise and fall of international systems.

Nuclear arsenals, by contrast, are by nature global in their influence and, since the bomb's advent, have continuously been a prime factor shaping the structure of the international political and military systems of the era. It was of course the bomb's arrival that disabled the global war system at its upper levels and replaced it for the duration of the Cold War with the new system of nuclear deterrence. That system, we can see in retrospect, was a strategic adjustment to two dominant historical realities, one political, the other technical. The political reality was the division of the world into two ideologically hostile camps. The technical reality was the restriction of the newborn capacity to build nuclear weapons to just a few nations. (The eventual legal expression of this nuclear oligopoly was the Nuclear Nonproliferation Treaty, which created two classes of powers. One consisted of the five nuclear-weapon states—the United States, the Soviet Union, China, England, and France—who were permitted to retain their nuclear arsenals, on condition that they made good-faith efforts to reduce and then eliminate them, and the other consisted of all the other signatories, who agreed to forgo nuclear arsenals.)

Now both of these realities have been washed away. The world's bipolarity ended with the collapse of the Soviet Union, and the nuclear oligopoly has been steadily yielding to nuclear proliferation. In the late 1980s, Iraq came within perhaps a year of attaining nuclear weapons, but in the aftermath of its defeat in the Gulf War was required to dismantle its bomb-making facilities under the supervision of U.N. inspectors. In 1998, the inspectors were forced out. After September 11, 2001, the United States began to brandish its threats to overthrow the Iraqi government, and the inspectors were readmitted. In May of 1998, India had conducted five nuclear tests, and Pakistan responded with seven, and both nations pronounced themselves nuclear powers, creating the first nuclear confrontation entirely unrelated to the Cold War; in the spring of 2002, after terrorist attacks on the Indian Parliament that India blamed on Pakistan, the two countries went to the brink of nuclear war. North Korea and Iran both have nuclear programs, and in October 2002, North Korea announced that it possessed nuclear weapons. In our day, nuclear danger has been supplemented by the spread of biological and chemical weapons, not only to states but to terrorist groups. If bipolarity shaped the strategy of the first nuclear age, then proliferation, if it is not reversed, is destined to define that of the second.

In assessing nuclear proliferation, it is important to distinguish between the capacity to construct a nuclear arsenal and the deed of actually constructing one. By the count of the State Department, forty-four nations have the capacity, which is to say there are forty-four nations that, if they choose to build nuclear weapons, can be reasonably certain of success. Whereas developing nuclear weapons requires a political decision, acquiring the capacity happens almost of itself. Switzerland, for instance, has never made a decision to acquire the capacity, yet no one can doubt that Switzerland has it. Being a modern, technically competent nation is enough.

This excess of capacity over possession points to the fundamental fact of the nuclear age, known from the beginning to all who have worked on the weapons, that the basic building block of nuclear arms, which is the knowledge required to build them, was destined to spread. In 1945, for example, the physicist Leo Szilard, one of the discoverers of nuclear fission, predicted the terrorist threat that now so deeply worries the United States and other countries. "The position of the United States in the world may be adversely affected by [nuclear weapons'] existence," he wrote. "Clearly if such bombs are available, it will not be necessary to bomb our cities from the air in order to destroy them. All that is necessary is to place a comparatively small number in major cities and detonate them at some later time. . . . The long coastline, the structure of our society, and the heterogeneity of our population may make effective controls of such 'traffic' virtually impossible." In the long run, there can be no "secret" of the bomb. A historical period that, like the nuclear age, is defined by a technology has a natural life cycle. At its birth, the technology may be held by a single pair of hands—in this case, the United States'. In its youth, the technology may be confined to a few nations, as during the Cold War. But in its maturity, which comes with the mere passage of time, it is destined to be available to all. The reason is the innate mobility of scientific knowledge. An era of information and free trade is an especially difficult one in which to keep technical secrets. Like a battery that is slowly charging, the proliferation of nuclear capacity creates a growing potential—a potential that may or may not end in sudden, violent discharge but, as the years go by, *can* be released by an ever-increasing number of states or groups in an ever-increasing number of ways.

The Cold War may have retarded proliferation, but even its continuation probably could not have stopped it. (Would India and Pakistan have been *less* likely to nuclearize their conflict if the Cold War had continued?) The Cold War was in fact a sort of two-power disguise temporarily assumed by the nuclear predicament. This form of the dilemma depended on certain historical conditions that looked highly durable but turned out to be temporary. Its new form will be based on the universal availability of nuclear know-how that is written into the predicament's makeup. To para-phrase Clausewitz, the Cold War was a restricted, "real" form of the nuclear predicament, and now we are on our way to facing it in its unlimited, hydra-headed, "ideal" form. "Ideal," in this context, means that the threat is not only all-embracing but also originates at all points of the compass. And this underlying change will occur irrespective of any military and political decisions. I do not mean that all nations will inevitably build nuclear weapons. I mean that all will be *able* to do so and, in that restricted yet fundamental sense, emanate nuclear danger. The question is to what extent nations will turn capacity into hardware—into nuclear bombs.

Chemical and biological weapons, which are easier to acquire than nuclear weapons, are equally unconfinable. Both are banned by international conventions, although these so far lack adequate provisions for inspection and enforcement. In late September and early October of 2001, three letters containing spores of the lethal virus anthrax were sent to three addresses in the United States, including the office of Senate Majority Leader Tom Daschle. It was the first use in history—however limited—of an acknowl-edged weapon of mass destruction on American soil. Five people died, Senate buildings were shut down, and the postal service was disrupted for several months. If sophisticated delivery sys-tems had been used, tens of thousands could have died. If the pathogen released had been smallpox, which is contagious, rather than anthrax, which is not, millions of people, experts say, might have died.

During the Cold War, the capacities for violence of the great powers were in effect compressed into a single integrated explo-sive device, to which a warning sign was affixed that said, "You have the power to set off this device, but if you do, you, too, and perhaps all humankind, are doomed." The doom was real enough, but the compression could not last. As the Cold War ended, and the compression began to weaken, the contents of the device began to seep into the world. During the Cold War, a variety of "thresholds," enforced by strong taboos, confined the danger to a certain extent. One was the clear distinction between the nuclear powers, few in number, and the many nonnuclear powers. Another was the threshold between conventional and nuclear war. Still another was "the brink" between the two superpowers. Today, all these boundaries have been breached or blurred. The line between conventional and nuclear war is being blurred by many developments—by the increasing power of conventional weapons, such as the fifteen-ton American "daisy-cutter" bomb, and by the miniaturization and refinement of American nuclear weapons, including the proposed so-called bunker buster, designed for use against caves deep underground, and by the rise of the chemical and biological threats. The single nuclear abyss on whose dizzying edge the nuclear-armed superpowers stood (and still stand) has, in effect, branched out to form innumerable smaller abysses. They run through Wall Street, where the September 11 attacks occurred; through Kashmir, dividing nuclear-armed India from nuclear-armed Pakistan; through Pyongyang and Beijing; through Peshawar, Manila, and Mindanao, or wherever Al Qaeda or its like may be preparing weapons of mass destruction for use against the United States or others; and through New Jersey suburbs and Washington post offices and wherever else the anthrax-laden letters may arrive.

Proliferation has still another dimension. Some scientists fear that new, even more deadly and more easily concocted instruments of mass destruction, based on the newly developed techniques of genetic engineering and nanotechnology, may be discovered before long. Bill Joy, a cofounder of Sun Microsystems, has noted that the production of nuclear, and even of today's biological and chemical, weapons of mass destruction requires the resources of states—or, at least, of large teams of scientists. However, the technologies of the future may well lie within the reach of far smaller teams, or even solitary individuals. In Joy's words:

As this enormous computing power is combined with the manipulative advances of the physical sciences and the new, deep understandings in genetics, enormous transformative power is being unleashed. These combinations open up the opportunity to completely redesign the world, for better or worse: The replicating and evolving processes that have been confined to the natural world are about to become realms of human endeavor. I think it is no exaggeration to say we are on the cusp of the further perfection of extreme evil, an evil whose possibility spreads well beyond that which weapons of mass destruction bequeathed to the nation-states, on to a surprising and terrible empowerment of extreme individuals.

Joy's fears, though fortunately still speculative, help to understand the novel character of the forces that are defining what we may call the second nuclear age. At the beginning of history, the homicidal "first man," to borrow a term from Nietzsche, confronted his enemy with only his bare hands. Then, at one of history's turning points, or possibly its origin, he availed himself of his first destructive instrument, perhaps a stick or a rock. From that time on, the curve of humanity's technical capacity for violence rose steadily until, in 1945, it invented a device with which it could exterminate itself as a species. Yet that moment, for all its seeming finality, was not the end of the story. Nuclear weapons were hard to make and remained in just a few hands. Since then, the line to watch has been the ascending curve of distribution, which places this apocalyptic power as well as new ones in ever more hands. Its logical end point would be the person—let us borrow another term of Nietzsche's and call him the "last man"—who could concoct and release an unstoppable, contagious bacterium that could end human life.

Nuclear weapons, as all believers in deterrence know, are instruments of *terror*. We should not be surprised to find that they are of particular interest to *terrorists*. Osama bin Laden has sought to acquire nuclear weapons and, soon after the September 11 attack, he announced that he possessed them—but only (shades of the Cold War) for purposes of "deterrence." It's likely that both parts of the statement were false, yet no one can rule out the possibility that Al Qaeda or another group will obtain nuclear weapons. Science is delivering the mass over to the whim of the individual. The bewildering dilemma that the last man—the terrorist with an instrument of annihilation in his or her (as we must add after the suicide bombings by young Palestinian women) hands—presents to the world is the ever-increasing likelihood that a small band of criminals, or even a single evildoer, even today can conceivably cause the death of millions and in a conceivable future could cause the death of all.

"Liberal" Threats to the Peace

Many observers in the prosperous democracies like to imagine that the post–Cold War world's disorder and violence arise only in poor, misgoverned, anarchic lands. Historically, of course, it has been otherwise: the West has been the world's most active military volcano, bringing destruction upon itself through war and on the rest of the world through imperial conquest and exploitation. (The cost of imperialism in human lives rivaled strictly inter-European slaughter. For example, it has been estimated that in the Congo Free State alone, the death toll under the colonial administrations of King Leopold of Belgium and his successors was between ten and twenty million.) Although the Western civil war has been stilled by the liberal settlement, and old-style Western colonial rule has been ended by the world revolt, economic exploitation is alive, active, and rapidly developing new forms, which could prove as destructive—to the natural environment of the earth as well as to its poorer inhabitants—as the old.

The issue of imperial exploitation now arises in the context of economic globalization. According to some, the end of the territorial empires meant the end of imperialism. In Francis Fukuyama's view, for example, imperialism is an anachronism—"an atavism, a holdover from an earlier stage in human social evolution." Others contend that globalization is in fact imperialism in a new guise—"neo-imperialism." An increasingly powerful popular movement has arisen to oppose it. Its members observe that in the era of globalization the gap between the rich and the poor has increased, along with the power of wealthy countries to dictate economic policies to poor ones, that international economic decisions increasingly escape democratic control, and degradation of the environment is proceeding at a gallop. Among the instruments of economic control are the International Monetary Fund, the World Bank, and the World Trade Organization, all of whose decisions are dominated by wealthy countries; but even more powerful pressure is brought to bear by the global market system itself. States that structure their economies along approved lines do so not because they fear that otherwise their capitals will be bombarded and their lands occupied, as in the days of gunboat diplomacy, but because they know that if they do not, international loans and investments will dry up, their currencies will crash, and the living standards of most of their people will nose-dive. A balance sheet of gains and losses to the poorer countries is difficult to draw up, but it's possible that these new strictures, imposing what some call "structural violence" on the poor, may in fact bring more suffering to ordinary people than overt imperial violence once did.

The prosperous nations themselves are, it is true, also subject to market pressures—although generally to a lesser extent, since the system's rules have been written in good measure to advance their interests. The overall health of the global market system depends, as the war system's once did, on a precarious balance that the great powers must exert themselves mightily to preserve. Whereas in 1914 the ministers of foreign affairs flew into a panic when the balance of military power began to tip one way or another, now the ministers of finance scurry to take action when the economic order is threatened by a plunge in the currency in Jakarta, Buenos Aires, or Phnom Penh. These are the Fashodas and Sarajevos of the global market system, which, like the war system, is placed at risk of collapse by local crises that have the potential to start a broader unraveling of the system.

The World's Only Superpower

Whether economic globalization will benefit the world or become a new kind of imperialism—a sort of global rule by the rich over the poor—is a question that will be decided by many countries. Whether overt force, as distinct from economic pressure, will be used to renew imperial domination will depend above all on a single country, the United States—the sole power that has military resources on the scale necessary to harbor such an ambition.

In the early years of the Cold War, the United States, born in rebellion against the British Empire, styled itself, as it had for most of its history, an opponent of the European sort of imperialism. But soon in the name of anticommunism the United States was supporting many colonial regimes, including, with notably disastrous results, that of the French in Vietnam. Before long, the United States became the supporter and often the installer of murderous right-wing dictatorships on every continent—a pattern of conduct that, in its brutality and indifference to the will of local peoples, strongly resembled the supposedly rejected European precedent. A short list of such regimes would include those of Shah Reza Pahlavi in Iran, the dictator Saddam Hussein in Iraq (until he invaded Kuwait), the House of Saud in Saudi Arabia, Mobutu Sese Seko in the Congo, Fulgencio Batista in Cuba, Park Chung Hee in South Korea, a succession of civilian and military dictators in South Vietnam, Lon Nol in Cambodia, Suharto in Indonesia, Marcos in the Philippines, the colonels' junta in Greece, Franco in Spain, and a long list of military dictators in Argentina,

Chile, Brazil, Uruguay, Guatemala, El Salvador, Nicaragua, and Pakistan. In supporting such governments, the United States was acting in pursuit of both Cold War geopolitical aims and economic advantage: the regimes in question were in general both anticommunist and friendly to American interests.

When the Cold War ended, the United States began to support the revival of democracy, and many of the repressive regimes it had backed, as we've seen, fell from power. At the same time, however, the unexpected collapse of the Soviet Union left the United States standing alone in the world as a military superpower. In economic strength, the United States had peers and near-peers— the European Union, Japan, China—but in military might it was in a class by itself. American military spending equaled that of the next dozen or so countries put together. In the 1990s, as the United States implemented a "revolution in military affairs," which applied information technology to warfare, its lead only increased. Never in history had any single power possessed such military advantage, qualitative as well as quantitative, over any or all other nations, and never had the likelihood of another nation catching up seemed more remote.

The emergence of this freakish imbalance, which came as quickly and unexpectedly as the Soviet collapse that was its proximate cause, posed a fundamental question for both the international order and the United States. The founders of the country had detested "standing armies"—an innovation of the despised absolutist monarchs of Europe. The founders feared that a large army with nothing to do would look for wars to fight. They also feared executive control of the military. In the words of John Jay in the *The Federalist Papers*, "absolute monarchs will often make war when their nations are to get nothing by it, but for purposes and objects merely personal, such as a thirst for military glory, revenge for personal affronts, ambition, or private compacts to aggrandize or support their particular families or partisans. These and a variety of other motives, which affect only the mind of the sovereign, often lead him to engage in wars not sanctified by justice or the voice or interests of his people." That is why the constitution they wrote declares, in one of its shortest and least equivocal statements, "The Congress shall have power to declare war."

The United States had often assembled great military forces, but always for a specific war, and had disbanded them when the war was over, as it did, for example, after the First World War. Even after the Second World War, American forces were reduced. (It's also true, however, that the effect of the reduction was more than offset by the creation of a growing arsenal of nuclear weapons—then an American monopoly.) With the end of the Cold War, the situation most feared by the founders came into existence. The nation was, for the first time in its history, in possession of a gigantic military force with no particular enemy to fight. Meanwhile, Congress had in practice yielded its power to declare war to the president.

In the 1990s, the question arose: Would the United States, having lost its global competitor, demobilize (as it had after the two world wars), or would it find some new mission for its military machine. If so, what would that mission be? These questions were especially acute in regard to the nation's thousands of nuclear weapons, whose deployment had been geared almost exclusively to Cold War purposes. Some in power asked (as Secretary of State Madeleine Albright, frustrated by American inaction in the Balkans, once did of Chairman of the Joint Chiefs of Staff Colin Powell), "What's the point of having this superb military that you're always talking about if we can't use it?" Others—distant from power—asked why, if there was little use for such military forces, the United States had to have them.

In the last decade of the twentieth century, the United States arrived at no clear answer: it neither dismantled its military machine nor found a mission for it. Overall military spending briefly dipped, and then resumed an upward curve. In the 1990s, the lone superpower was also a reluctant one. With regard to the two sources of most acute danger—local wars, including wars of self-determination, and weapons of mass destruction—the United States pursued vacillating policies. The American nuclear arsenal, literally deprived of its raison d'être by the disappearance of the Soviet target, fell into a sort of political vacuum. The policies of the United States in regard to nuclear proliferation were equally uncertain. An early decision to preserve the American nuclear arsenal indefinitely and a long hiatus in the START negotiations with Russia (owing in good measure to the decision to expand NATO to include Poland, the Czech Republic, and Hungary) helped prompt other, anxious or ambitious countries to seek or acquire their own arsenals. When the Soviet Union collapsed, the Clinton administration did succeed in brokering the denuclearization of Ukraine, Belorussia, and Kazakhstan, leaving Russia alone as the legatee of the Soviet Union's nuclear arsenal, but the exchange of nuclear tests by India and Pakistan in 1998, in disregard of weak American sanctions, left subsequent American nonproliferation policy in tatters.

A string of local and regional wars provoked American responses with no clear theme. President George H. Bush appeared to adopt a strongly interventionist stance when, in the name of a "new world order," he successfully reversed Iraq's annexation of Kuwait; but when violence of near-genocidal proportions broke out in Yugoslavia Secretary of State James Baker declared, "We have no dog in that fight," and the United States stayed out. The lesson seemed to be that the United States intervened only when its interests were at stake. As a presidential candidate, Bill Clinton castigated Bush for his inaction in the Balkans, but as president he, too, was at first inactive there. Only after Serbian forces had laid a long siege to Sarajevo did the United States conduct a bombing campaign under the aegis of NATO to protect the city. In 1999, Clinton ordered American forces to bomb Serbia to obtain its withdrawal from Kosovo. Meanwhile, in 1993, when American soldiers in a force that the United States had sent to stop a famine in Somalia were killed in a battle with a local warlord, Clinton promptly withdrew those troops, creating a strong impression that the United States would use its forces only when it could be sure they would not suffer casualties.

"Humanitarian intervention" was the official description of each of these interventions. Yet the Clinton administration did nothing to stop the worst atrocity of the era, the genocide in Rwanda. Nor did Clinton's Republican opposition—torn between its hawkish wing and its isolationist wing—offer a clear or consistent alternative policy. The reaction of the rest of the world to the uncertain superpower's use of its power was likewise equivocal. On the one hand, many nations—especially European nations—supported the use of American might in the crises in the Gulf, Somalia, and the former Yugoslavia; on the other hand, many nations (including some of the same nations) made clear their alarm that the use of such immense power, even if for ends defined as humanitarian, set a precedent that could soon be abused and was dangerous to the international order.

Then came the attack of September 11. Like the starting gun of a race that no one knew he was to run, this explosion set the pack of nations off in a single direction—toward the trenches. Although the attack was unaccompanied by any claim of authorship or statement of political goals, the evidence almost immediately pointed to Al Qaeda, the radical Islamist, terrorist network, which, though stateless, was headquartered in Afghanistan and enjoyed the protection of its fundamentalist Islamic government. In a tape that was soon shown around the world, the group's leader, Osama bin Laden, was seen at dinner with his confederates in Afghanistan, rejoicing in the slaughter. Historically, nations have responded to terrorist threats and attacks with a combination of police action and political negotiation, while military action has played only a minor role. Voices were raised in the United States calling for a global cooperative effort of this kind to combat Al Qaeda. President Bush opted instead for a policy that the United States alone among nations could have conceivably undertaken: global military action not only against Al Qaeda but against any regime in the world that supported international terrorism. The president announced to Congress that he would "make no distinction between the terrorists who commit these acts and those who harbor them." By calling the campaign a "war," the administration summoned into action the immense, technically revolutionized, post–Cold War American military machine, which had lacked any clear enemy for over a decade. And by identifying the target as generic "terrorism," rather than as Al Qaeda or any other group or list of groups, the administration licensed military operations anywhere in the world.

In the ensuing months, the Bush administration continued to expand the aims and means of the war. The overthrow of governments—"regime change"—was established as a means for advancing the new policies. The president divided regimes into two categories—those "with us" and those "against us." Vice President Cheney estimated that Al Qaeda was active in sixty countries. The first regime to be targeted was of course Al Qaeda's host, the government of Afghanistan, which was overthrown in a remarkably swift military operation conducted almost entirely from the air and without American casualties.

Next, the administration proclaimed an additional war goal—preventing the proliferation of weapons of mass destruction. In his State of the Union speech in January 2002, the president announced that "the United States of America will not permit the world's most dangerous regimes to threaten us with the world's most destructive weapons." He went on to name as an "axis of evil" Iraq, Iran, and North Korea—three regimes seeking to build or already possessing weapons of mass destruction. To stop them, he stated, the Cold War policy of deterrence would not be enough—"preemptive" military action would be required, and preemption, the administration soon specified, could include the use of nuclear weapons. Beginning in the summer of 2002, the government intensified its preparations for a war to overthrow the regime of Saddam Hussein in Iraq, and in the fall, the president demanded and received a resolution from the Security Council of the United Nations requiring Iraq to accept the return of U.N. inspectors to search for weapons of mass destruction or facilities for building them. Lists of other candidates for "regime change" began to surface in the press.

In this way, the war on terror grew to encompass the most important geopolitical issue facing the world: the disposition of nuclear weapons in the second nuclear age. The Clinton administration had already answered the question regarding American possession of nuclear weapons: even in the absence of the Soviet Union, the United States planned to hold on to its nuclear arsenal indefinitely. In 2002, the Bush administration gave an answer to the question regarding nonproliferation, which throughout the nuclear age had been dealt with exclusively by diplomacy and negotiation, or, on occasion, economic sanctions.

The new answer was force. Nuclear disarmament was to be achieved by war and threats of war, starting with Iraq. One complementary element of the new policy, embraced long before September 11, was the decision to build a national missile defense system to protect the United States against nuclear attack by "rogue nations." But the fundamental element was a policy of preemptive war, or "offensive deterrence." This momentous shift in nuclear policy called, in addition, for programs to build new nuclear weapons and new delivery vehicles; confirmed new missions for nuclear weapons—retaliation for chemical or biological attacks, attacking hardened bunkers unreachable by other weapons—in the post–Cold War world; and listed seven countries (Russia, China, North Korea, Iraq, Iran, Libya, and Syria) for which contingency plans for nuclear attack should be considered. To achieve all these aims, nuclear and conventional, the president asked for an increase in military spending of forty-eight billion dollars—a sum greater than the total military spending of any other nation.

The sharp turn toward force as the mainstay of the policies of the United States was accompanied by a turn away from treaties and other forms of cooperation. Even before September 11, the trend had been clear. Now it accelerated. The Bush administration either refused to ratify or withdrew from most of the principal new international treaties of the post–Cold War era. In the nuclear arena alone, the administration refused to submit to the Senate for ratification the Comprehensive Test Ban Treaty, which would have added a ban on underground tests to the existing bans on testing in the air; withdrew from the A.B.M. Treaty, which had severely limited Russian and American deployment of antinuclear defensive systems; and jettisoned the START negotiations as the framework for nuclear reductions with Russia—replacing them with the Strategic Offensive Reduction Agreement, a three-page document requring two-thirds of the strategic weapons of both sides to be removed from their delivery vehicles, but then stored rather than dismantled. In addition, the Bush administration withdrew from the Kyoto Protocol of the United Nations Framework Convention on Climate Change, which had become the world's principal forum for making decisions about reducing emissions that cause global warming; refused to ratify the Rome treaty establishing an international criminal court; and declined to agree to an important protocol for inspection and enforcement of a U.N. convention banning biological weapons.

The consequences of this revolution in American policy rippled through the world, where it found ready imitators. On December 12, the Indian Parliament was attacked by terrorists whom India linked to Pakistan. Promptly, nuclear-armed India, citing the American policy of attacking not only terrorists but any state that harbored them, moved half a million men to the border of nuclear-armed Pakistan, which responded in kind, producing the first full-scale nuclear crisis of the twenty-first century. In South Asia, nuclearization did not produce the cautionary effects that the theorists of deterrence expected. High Indian officials openly threatened Pakistan with annihilation. Rajnath Singh, the minister for the state of Uttar Pradesh, declared, "If Pakistan doesn't change its ways, there will be no sign of Pakistan left," and when India's army chief, General S. Padmanabhan, was asked how India would respond if attacked with a nuclear weapon, he answered that "the perpetrator of that particular outrage shall be punished so severely that their continuation thereafter in any form of fray will be doubtful." In Pakistan, the dictator General Pervez Musharraf stated that, in the event of an Indian conventional invasion of Pakistan, "as a last resort, the atom bomb is also possible." In March 2002, Israel, citing the same American precedent and calling for U.S. support for its policy on this basis, responded to Palestinian suicide bombings by launching its own "war on terrorism"—a full-scale attack on the Palestinian Authority on the West Bank.

The revolution in American policy had been precipitated by September 11, but went far beyond any war on terror. It remained to give the policy comprehensive doctrinal expression, which came in an official document, "The National Security Strategy of the United States of America," issued in September 2002. In the world, it stated, only one economic and political system remained "viable": the American one of liberal democracy and free enterprise. The United States would henceforth promote and defend this system by the unilateral use of force—preemptively, if necessary. The United States, the president said, "has, and intends to keep, military strengths beyond challenge, thereby making the destabilizing arms races of other eras pointless, and limiting rivalries to trade and other pursuits of peace." In other words, the United States reserved the entire field of military force to itself, restricting other nations to humbler pursuits. In the words of the "National Security Strategy," "Our forces will be strong enough to dissuade potential adversaries from pursing a military build-up in hopes of surpassing, or equaling, the power of the United States." If the United States was displeased with a regime, it reserved the right to overthrow it—to carry out "regime change." "In the world we have entered," President Bush has said, "the only path to safety is the path of action. And this nation will act."

Niagara

A policy of unchallengeable military domination over the earth, accompanied by a unilateral right to overthrow other governments by military force, is an imperial, an Augustan policy. It marks a decisive choice of force and coercion over cooperation and consent as the mainstay of the American response to the disorders of the time. If wars of self-determination and other kinds of local and regional mayhem multiply and run out of control; if the wealthy and powerful use globalization to systematize and exacerbate exploitation of the poor and powerless; if the poor and the powerless react with terrorism and other forms of violence; if the nuclear powers insist on holding on to and threatening to use their chosen weapons of mass destruction; if more nations then develop nuclear or biological or chemical arsenals in response and threaten to use them; if these weapons one day fall, as seems likely, into the hands of terrorists; and if the United States continues to pursue an Augustan policy, then the stage will be set for catastrophe. Each of these possibilities represents a path of least resistance. Local and regional conflicts have been the way of the world since history began. The spread of nuclear- as well as biological- and chemical-weapon know-how is an automatic function of technical progress, and the spread of nuclear arsenals is a self-feeding process of action and reaction. Continued possession of nuclear weapons by those who already have them is the path of inertia, of deep sleep. The imperial temptation for the United States is the path of arrogance and ignorance.

At the intersection of these tendencies is a Niagara higher and more violent than the one that a heartbroken Henry James lived to witness in 1914. It is of course impossible to predict how and where history might again go over the precipice. It could be nuclear war in South Asia, bringing the deaths of tens of millions of people. It could be the annihilation of one or several cities in the United States in a nuclear terrorist attack, or the loss of millions in a smallpox attack. It could be a war spinning out of control in the Middle East, leading by that route to the use of weapons of mass destruction in the Middle East. It could be war in Korea, or between the United States and China over Taiwan. It could even be—hard as it is to imagine now—intentional or semi-intentional nuclear war between Russia and the United States in some future crisis that we cannot foresee but cannot rule out, either. Or it could be—is even likely to be—some chain of events we are at present incapable of imagining.

After September 11, people rightly said that the world had changed forever. Before that event, who could have predicted the galloping transformation of the politics of the United States and the world, the escalating regional crises, the vistas of perpetual war? Yet the use of just one nuclear weapon could exceed the damage of September 11 ten-thousandfold. Would the global economy plunge into outright depression? Would the people of the world flee their menaced cities? Would anyone know who the attacker was? Would someone retaliate—perhaps on a greater scale? Would the staggering shock bring the world to its senses? Would the world at that moment of unparalleled panic and horror react more wisely and constructively than it has been able to do in a time of peace, in comparative calm, or would it fall victim to an incalculable cycle of fear, confusion, hatred, hostility, and violence, both between nations and within them, as it did after 1914—but this time, in all likelihood, far more swiftly and with incomparably direr consequences? In the face of these questions, predictive powers dim. But attempts at prophecy are in any case the wrong response. Decisions are required.

13

The Logic of Peace

The escalation of violence around the world has been so rapid since September 11, 2001, that this day may appear already to have been the August 1914 of the twenty-first century. The parallels are striking. In 2001 as in 1914 a period of political liberalization, economic globalization, and peace (at least in the privileged zones of the planet) was summarily ended by a violent explosion. The fundamental decision now, as it was then, is between force and peaceful means as the path to safety, and the world has seemed to make a decision for force. Again, observers have been compelled, as Henry James was in 1914, to recognize that the immediate past has been a time of illusion—a time when the world was heading toward a precipice but did not know it, or did not care to know it. Again, an unpredictable chain of violent events has been set in motion—some today have even said that a "third world war" is upon us.

And yet, since history does not repeat itself, the analogy between 1914 and 2001, like all measurements of the present with yardsticks from the past, is useful only for querying events, not for predicting them. There are equally important differences between the two moments, some of them obvious, others less so. In 1914, the great powers' preparations for war were complete. The arms were piled high, the troops massed, the war plans mapped out in detail, the mobilization schedules fixed, the treaties of alliance signed and sealed. Even before the first shot was fired, the whole of the long war to come lay waiting in the file cabinets of the chanceries of Europe, needing only the right incident to spring to life. And when that incident came and the armies were hurled across the borders, no power on earth, including the governments involved, could call them back until the war had run its full bloody course. Our moment, by contrast, is one of exceptional unpredictability and fluidity. No inexorable timetables or web of alliances among great powers threaten to drag everyone together into a new abyss. The unexpected—new crises, abrupt developments, sudden opportunities—is the order of the day. The strength of the forces that attacked on September 11 is unclear, and appears likely to wax or wane in response to events. The Bush administration has announced a series of wars that it may decide to fight, but there will be points of decision at every step along the way. Developments in the field can quickly alter political opinion at home. The proliferation of weapons of mass destruction can inhibit as well as provoke war. Elections can bring new people to power. Other countries are watching and waiting, uncertain where and how to bring the weight of their influence to bear. The effect of a series of wars, if such occur, on global economic integration is unknown, and huge uncertainties shadow the economic scene.

As shocking as September 11 was, it was not a decisive catastrophe, but rather a warning. No irrevocable decision has in fact been made. The scope for choice remains unusually large, and the new cycle of violence can still be broken or reversed, and new policies adopted. Seen narrowly, September 11 posed the specific question of how the United States and the civilized world should deal with a global terrorist network ready to commit any crime within its power. That question requires all the urgent attention and action that it is receiving. A the same time, I submit, we should be asking what the larger and more fundamental decisions for policy may be. If we take this broader approach, the profound changes that have occurred in the character of violence, politics, and power over the last century will command our attention. In 1918 and 1945, a decision in favor of coercive power clearly meant in practice choosing the old war system, and a decision in favor of cooperative power meant choosing to create ex nihilo a Wilsonian system of global collective security based on international law. Today, neither of these alternatives is open to us. Others are on the table. Let us consider each of the two paths, beginning with the choice of coercive power, then turning to the choice of cooperative power.

Violence as the Solution to Violence: The End of Balance

Now as in 1918 and 1945, organized violence plays a double role in the decision, for violence is both the problem to be solved and one of the solutions on offer—a solution to itself. This remedy is of course as old as history. When, as we have noted, Clemenceau rejected Wilson's vision in favor of an old system in which he still had "faith," he was referring to definite plans for defending his country within the framework of the global war system. And when the diplomat Harold Nicolson began to lose confidence in Wilsonism and repaired to that old system because the value of "armaments, strategic frontiers, alliances" was already proven, he was reverting to the same faith. Both held to the idea, codified in the realist school of political thought, of creating a balance of power, which had always been the main hope for peace of those who planned to deploy the instruments of violence to prevent violence. When nuclear weapons were invented, war among the great powers became unworkable, yet the idea of balance survived, in the new form of the balance of terror. Some have continued to call the balance of terror a balance of power, but a better term might be a balance of powerlessness, inasmuch as its stability rests on the willingness of the parties to enlist in a community of total jeopardy.

The balance of powerlessness may have been more effective than the balance of power exactly because the penalty for failure, nuclear annihilation, was so much greater. It cannot, of course, be demonstrated conclusively that nuclear terror prevented a third world war. Too many ifs of history are involved to make a firm judgment. (Since we cannot in the present predict what history *will* do, what makes us think that we can say what history *would have done* if such and such an imaginary event had occurred?) For example, we would have to determine that a third world war had been straining to occur—only to be checked by fear of the bomb. We would also have to show that the presence of nuclear weapons did more to prevent world war than to cause it. After all, the most acute crisis of the Cold War, the Cuban missile crisis, was brought about by the deployment of nuclear weapons. If nuclear strategic thinking had anything to do with resolving that crisis (something that is in itself difficult to demonstrate), it was only after causing the crisis in the first place.

Nevertheless, it is as possible as it is necessary, even without resolving these unanswerable questions, to acknowledge that the presence of the bomb weighed heavily in the calculations of the statesmen of the Cold War, inclining them against major war each time a crisis occurred. Their increasing recognition that, as President Ronald Reagan put it, "nuclear war cannot be won and must never be fought" was a central fact, in theory and in practice, of the Cold War.

With these developments, nuclear strategy acquired a Wilsonian dimension. It had evolved into a war stopper. The importance of the role of the balance of terror as a peacekeeper becomes clearer if we consider the varying fates of the century's two major organizations for peacekeeping, the League of Nations and the

United Nations. The League was discredited by a series of aggressions and conflicts it was unable to prevent or halt, then swept aside by the Second World War. The Cold War played a similar role in sidelining the United Nations.

President Franklin Roosevelt and Winston Churchill, who first called for such an organization in the Atlantic Charter in 1941, had sought to draw lessons from the fate of the League. Instead of assigning the peacekeeping function to a large council, as the League did, they vested it in an alliance of the prospective victors of the Second World War—the United States, the Soviet Union, China, England, and France—each of whom was given a permanent seat on the Security Council and a veto over its decisions. The hope was that this small, tight-knit group of great powers could guarantee the peace more effectively than the multitude of nations charged with that responsibility under the provisions of the League. But almost immediately after the organization's foundation in 1946, this arrangement was for all intents and purposes nullified by the advent of the Cold War. In 1950, the Korean War, sanctioned by the Security Council after the Soviet Union walked out of its proceedings, confirmed that the breakdown in relations between the United States and the Soviet Union was irreparable.

If this geopolitical split had been the only reason for the U.N.'s failure to perform its central role, the story would be a familiar one, well-known to analysts of the League's collapse: collective security fails to get off the ground because the powers that are supposed to enforce it fall out with one another. The designated peacemakers become the peace-breakers, and no one else is strong enough to bring them into line. In fact, however, the U.N.'s marginalization occurred for another reason as well—the onset of the nuclear age. By an accident of historical timing, the bomb was first tested and dropped in the hiatus between the designing of the United Nations and its founding.

In April of 1945, in San Francisco, the Conference on International Organization formally agreed on the outlines of the U.N.

Charter. On October 24, the U.N. came into existence. On August 6, however, the destruction of Hiroshima radically transformed the nature of the main problem, great-power war, that the new organization had been fashioned to solve. Conceived in one age, the U.N. was born in another. Having been designed to cope with a world dominated by the global war system, it came into existence after that system's death knell had been sounded. The central purpose of the U.N. was to prevent a third world war—to, in the words of the Preamble to its Charter, "save succeeding generations from the scourge of war, which twice in our lifetime has brought untold sorrow to mankind." But as the years passed it was not to the U.N., disabled by the Cold War, that the great powers turned to save them from a third world war but to nuclear arsenals. Even as the Cold War was wrecking the U.N. as an instrument for keeping the peace, nuclear deterrence was coopting it. Thus the U.N. was not swept away, as the League had been by approaching world war; it was permitted to live on to perform important, if secondary services—supplying humanitarian relief in disasters of every description, sending peacekeeping forces to calm local conflicts, providing a forum for the expression of international opinion.

With the end of the bipolar Cold War order, and the acceleration of nuclear proliferation, however, the new, nuclearized form the balance is crumbling. For reasons both political and technical, nuclear terror is rapidly shedding its "Wilsonian" role as a preserver of stability and peace.

Some, it is true, have argued to the contrary that the balance of nuclear terror can actually be extended and strengthened by proliferation. Just as nuclear weapons stopped the two superpowers of the Cold War from fighting a hot war, so, it is suggested, they can immobilize ten or twenty or thirty nuclear powers, in a grand peace based on universal terror. The political scientist Kenneth Waltz, for example, has suggested that "the gradual spread of nuclear weapons is more to be welcomed than feared." He hopes that the Soviet-American stalemate enforced by deterrence during the Cold War might be enlarged to include many more nations. What has not been explained, however, is how a steadily growing number of nuclear powers, each capable of annihilating some or all of the others, can balance their forces in a way that would leave any of them feeling safe. Mutual assured destruction is a policy whose logic fits a bipolar relationship. It defies adjustment to a multi-nuclear-power world.

Proliferation, indeed, undermines stability in every sense of that word. In the first place, it destroys strategic stability. Strategic balance during the Cold War was supposed to depend on the attempt to maintain a rough equality between the forces of the two sides; but in a world of many nuclear powers this goal would be unreachable. If Country A and Country B were to painstakingly craft a stable nuclear balance (something, incidentally, that the Soviet Union and the United States failed to do for as long as the Cold War continued), it could be overthrown instantly by any nuclear-armed Country C that suddenly allied itself with one or the other. The necessary changes in targeting could be accomplished in just a few hours or days. Even in today's world of eight nuclear powers (or perhaps nine, if North Korea's claim to possess nuclear weapons is true), some of the imbalances inherent in nuclear multipolarity are evident. There is little hope of balance, for example, in the quadrilateral relationship of the United States, China, India, and Pakistan. India has stated that it became a nuclear power to balance nuclear-armed China, by whom it was defeated in a conventional border war in 1962. Pakistan became a nuclear power to balance India. If India seeks again to balance China, however, will Pakistan seek to keep up? China, moreover, has supplied nuclear technology to Pakistan. And Pakistan has supplied some to North Korea, receiving missile technology in return. Will India therefore feel compelled to build a nuclear arsenal that equals both China's and Pakistan's? The United States meanwhile has decided to build national missile defenses, which, if they turn out to work, will erode or nullify China's capacity to strike the United States. China has already said that it will respond by building up its still modest nuclear forces. That will put additional pressure on India. Nor can we forget that Russia may, at any point, step into the picture with its still-huge arsenal. The spread of ballistic- and cruise-missile technology, whose proliferation is as predictable as that of nuclear technology, compounds the problem geometrically.

In the second place, proliferation is bound to undermine the foundations of technical stability. During the Cold War, the United States and the Soviet Union sought a kind of safety in the policy of mutual assured destruction. In practice, however, they found that their nuclear command-and-control systems were so vulnerable to a first strike that the retaliation required by the doctrine could not in fact be assured. To cure the problem, the two governments resorted to policies of "launch on warning"—that is, each planned to launch its retaliatory strike after receiving a warning that the other side had launched its first strike but before the missiles had arrived. This system placed severe time pressure on any decision to launch in retaliation, increasing the risks of accidental war. The presidents of the two nations were—and still are—required to make these decisions within five minutes of receiving warning of an incoming strike. The pressures on Russia, which now faces a technically superior American force, have grown especially severe.

If the United States and Russia, with all their resources and an ocean between them, cannot guarantee the survival of their command-and-control systems, is it reasonable to expect that smaller, poorer nations, facing many potential adversaries, with little or no warning time, will accomplish this? The warning time between India and Pakistan, for instance, is effectively zero. For them, not even launch on warning is possible. The requirements for nuclear stability under the doctrine of deterrence are thus altogether lacking.

In the third place, what the experts call arms-control stability—meaning conditions favorable to negotiated limits on or reductions of nuclear arsenals—would be destroyed. During the Cold War, the United States and the Soviet Union, unable to agree on numerical offensive limits, built up their collective arsenals to the preposterous collective level of some seventy-five thousand nuclear warheads. In a multipolar nuclear world, arms-control agreements would become exponentially harder to achieve. How could twenty or thirty nations, few of whom trusted the others or were sure what they were doing, be able to adjust the scores of nuclear balances among them? Containing proliferation (if someone should wish to return to that policy somewhere down the road) would be a pipe dream. How would, say, the twentieth nuclear power persuade the twenty-first that building nuclear weapons is a bad idea?

In the fourth place, multiplying nuclear arsenals would increase the danger of nuclear terrorism. A world of proliferation would be a world awash in nuclear materials. Terrorists who acquired them would be indifferent to nuclear threats from others. The balance of terror depends on fear of retaliatory annihilation, but many terrorists have no country of whose annihilation they are afraid. They are unafraid to lose even their own lives, and blow themselves up with the bombs they aim at others. The terrorist bent on self-immolation with a weapon of mass destruction is the nemesis of balance. Deterrence has no purchase on the dead.

Violence as the Solution to Violence: Empire

If the balance of power and the balance of terror are no longer available, does the storehouse of systems of coercive power still offer any resource for keeping peace in the world? One option remains to be considered: universal empire, substantially achieved only once in the history of the Western world, by the Romans. (Even they were unable to conquer certain outlying territories.) The nation now aspiring to a global imperial role is, of course, the United States. Its military dominance is one more reason that a

balance of power has become impracticable. Obviously, there can
be no balance when one power is mightier than all the others put
together. Not a balance of power but a monopoly of power—or, at
any rate, of force—is the present American ambition. The new state
of affairs is sometimes referred to as "unipolarity," but the term is
an oxymoron within a single word, for by definition "polarity"
requires two poles. (The Bush administration's official statement of
its global policy, the "National Security Strategy," falls into a similar confusion when it speaks of a "balance of power in favor of
freedom." A balance that is "in favor of" one side is again by definition not a balance.)

Although both the balance-of-power system and the balance of
terror were primarily based on coercion, both contained significant admixtures of cooperation. Both depended on a sort of brute
equity among two or more powers. If the balance was to be maintained, neither could claim a right to attack the other: they must
coexist. Under the balance of terror, the element of cooperation
was even stronger. The two sides were bonded in the common
project of avoiding the war that would annihilate both. They were
paradoxical partners in survival. A global hegemonic peace, on the
other hand, would mark the triumph of coercion. Its foundation
would be not equality of any kind but the absolute and unchallengeable superiority of one power and the vassalage of others—
not mutual nonaggression but preemption, not coexistence but the
right of one, and only one, to execute "regime change."

The idea of American global hegemony thus carries the rule of
force to an extreme. And yet, fantastic and unreal as the ambition
may be, there is a logic underlying it. Means, this logic runs, must
be adequate to ends. Since proliferation is in its nature global so
must American domination. The United States will employ its
overwhelming military superiority to stop proliferation all around
the world. It applies to the world the reasoning that Bodin applied
to the state four hundred years ago: the world is now a community; a community needs order; to provide order there must be

a sovereign; the sovereign can be none other than the master of the sword; the United States alone can lay a claim to mastering the sword; therefore the United States must be the global sovereign. And so on behalf of its own and the world's safety, the United States will fight a series of what can be called disarmament wars. Under this plan the United States would, indeed, become a "disarmament empire," dedicated to preserving the world from nuclear destruction. (Of course, all empires are in a sense disarmament empires: they rule by defeating—by destroying or disarming—every foe and rival.) It is not going too far to say that *if* the solutions to the danger of nuclear proliferation were restricted to coercive systems, then some form of imperial domination would be the form it would have to take.

To acknowledge the existence of this logic, which lends the American bid for hegemony whatever legitimacy it has, is not to overlook the more mundane and sordid aspects of American imperial ambition. Every empire in history has concealed coarse self-interest behind a veil of noble ideals, and there is no reason to believe that American imperialism would be an exception. The most obvious and the rawest of these motivations is the wish to take control of the oil reserves of Central Asia, the Middle East, and elsewhere. Far more sweeping is the assertion in the "National Security Strategy" that in all the world there is now "a single sustainable model for national success": the American one of "freedom, democracy, and free enterprise." It is a formulation that, when wedded to the assertion of unchallengeable American military superiority and the right to intervene militarily anywhere on earth, plainly sets the stage for attempts to impose America's will on nations in almost any area of their collective existence.

A plan for global hegemony, however, has not suddenly become feasible simply because the balance of power and the balance of terror no longer work. Even if we supposed that the United States were to complete the transition from republic to empire, there are powerful reasons to believe that it would fail to realize its global ambitions, whether idealistic or self-interested. Any imperial plan in the twenty-first century tilts against what have so far proved to be the two most powerful forces of the modern age: the spread of scientific knowledge and the resolve of peoples to reject foreign rule and take charge of their own destinies. If the history of the past two centuries is a guide, neither can be bombed out of existence.

The most persuasive rationale for empire is its promise of deliverance from the threat of weapons of mass destruction. The views of most countries on this subject, however, are far different from those of the United States. The Bush administration looks out upon the world and sees "evildoers" trying to procure terrible weapons; the world looks back and sees a hypocritical power seeking to deny to others what it possesses in abundance and even plans to use preemptively. Most countries fear those who already have nuclear weapons at least as much as they fear those who are merely trying to get them. In their view, stopping proliferation deals at best with a secondary aspect of the nuclear problem. They still see what has perhaps become invisible to American eyes—that the United States and Russia have thousands of nuclear weapons pointed at one another and at others and have refused to surrender these arsenals. They also see that the club of possessors has grown to include South Asia, where the danger of nuclear war has become acute, and they note that no plan is on the drawing board to denuclearize these powers, either. On the contrary, nuclearization has been a ticket into the good graces of the United States for both countries. Finally, they observe that the Nuclear Nonproliferation Treaty, under which a hundred and eighty-two countries have agreed to forgo nuclear arms, is in jeopardy of breaking down because the five nations that possess nuclear arsenals under the terms of the treaty show no sign of fulfilling their pledge under its Article 6 to eliminate them. (Three other nuclear powers—India, Pakistan, and Israel—are nonmembers of the treaty, and the fourth, North Korea, has announced its intention of withdrawing.) It was in defiance of this nuclear double standard that India set off its nuclear tests in 1998, prompting Pakistan's responding tests. Was "regime change" an option in these cases? Is it in North Korea? Will it be if Iran, Egypt, Syria, or, for that matter, Japan or Germany builds a nuclear arsenal? Does the United States propose to overthrow the government of every country that, rebelling against the attempt to institutionalize the double standard, seeks to acquire weapons of mass destruction? The attempt indeed appears more likely to provoke than prevent proliferation, as has already happened in North Korea. Nations threatened with that nightmare of the ages, a great power seeking global domination, will go to desperate lengths to redress the balance. Weapons of mass destruction are an obvious means.

What is true for proliferation of nuclear weapons is also likely to be true for their use. Force, history teaches, summons counter-force. What goes around comes around. The United States is the only nation on earth that has used these weapons of mass destruction. An American attempt to dominate world affairs is a recipe for provoking their use again, very possibly on American soil.

It's unlikely that the passion for self-determination will be any easier to suppress than the spread of destructive technology. Empire, the supreme embodiment of force, is the antithesis of self-determination. It violates equity on a global scale. No lover of freedom can give it support. It is especially contrary to the founding principles of the United States, whose domestic institutions are incompatible with the maintenance of empire. Historically, imperial rule has rested on three kinds of supremacy—military, economic, and political. The United States enjoys unequivocal superiority in only one of these domains—the military, and here only in the conventional sphere. (Any attempt at regime change in a country equipped with even a modest deliverable nuclear arsenal is out of the question even for the United States.) American economic power is impressive, yet in this domain it has several equals or near equals, including the European Union and Japan, who are not likely to bend easily to American will. In the political arena the United States is weak. "Covenants, without the sword, are but words," Hobbes said in the late seventeenth century. Since then, the world has learned that swords without covenants are but empty bloodshed. In the political arena, the lesson of the world revolt—that winning military victories may sometimes be easy but building political institutions in foreign lands is hard, often impossible—still obtains. The nation so keenly interested in regime change has small interest in nation-building and less capacity to carry it out. The United States, indeed, is especially mistrusted, often hated, around the world. If it embarks on a plan of imperial supremacy, it will be hated still more. Can cruise missiles build nations? Does power still flow from the barrel of a gun—or from a Predator Drone? Can the world in the twenty-first century really be ruled from thirty-five thousand feet? Modern peoples have the will to resist and the means to do so. Imperialism without politics is a naive imperialism. In our time, force can win a battle or two, but politics is destiny.

Can a nation that began its life in rebellion against the most powerful empire of its time end by trying to become a still more powerful empire? It perhaps can, but not if it wishes to remain a republic. Secretary of State John Quincy Adams defined the choice with precision in 1821. After giving his country the well-known advice that the United States should not go abroad "in search of monsters to destroy" but be "the well-wisher to the freedom and independence of all ... the champion and vindicator only of her own," he added that if the United States embarked on the path of dominating others, the "fundamental maxims of her policy would insensibly change from liberty to force. . . . She might become the dictatress of the world. She would no longer be the ruler of her own spirit."

A country's violence, Hannah Arendt said, can destroy its power. The United States is moving quickly down this path. Do American leaders imagine that the people of the world, having overthrown the territorial empires of the nineteenth and twentieth centuries, are ready to bend the knee to an American overlord in the twenty-first? Do they imagine that allies are willing to become subordinates? Have they forgotten that people hate to be dominated by force? History is packed with surprises. The leaders of the totalitarian Soviet empire miraculously had the good sense to yield up their power without unleashing the tremendous violence that was at their fingertips. Could it be the destiny of the American republic, unable to resist the allure of an imperial delusion, to flare out in a blaze of pointless mass destruction?

The Cooperative Path

In sum, the days when humanity can hope to save itself from force with force are over. None of the structures of violence—not the balance of power, not the balance of terror, not empire—can any longer rescue the world from the use of violence, now grown apocalyptic. Force can lead only to more force, not to peace. Only a turn to structures of cooperative power can offer hope. To choose that path, the United States would, as a first order of business, have to choose the American republic over the American empire, and then, on the basis of the principles that underlie the republic, join with other nations to build cooperative structures as a basis for peace.

For Americans, the choice is at once between two Americas, and between two futures for the international order. In an imperial America, power would be concentrated in the hands of the president, and checks and balances would be at an end; civil liberties would be weakened or lost; military spending would crowd out social spending; the gap between rich and poor would be likely to increase; electoral politics, to the extent that they still mattered, would be increasingly dominated by money, above all corporate money, whose influence would trump the people's interests; the social, economic, and ecological agenda of the country and the world would be increasingly neglected. On the other hand, in a republican America dedicated to the creation of a cooperative world, the immense concentration of power in the executive would be broken up; power would be divided again among the three branches, which would resume their responsibility of checking and balancing one another as the Constitution provides; civil liberties would remain intact or be strengthened; money would be driven out of politics, and the will of the people would be heard again; politics, and with it the power of the people, would revive; the social, economic, and ecological agendas of the country and the world would become the chief concern of the government.

Which path the United States will choose is likely to be decided in a protracted, arduous political struggle in the years ahead. Its outcome cannot be predicted. For the time being, the United States has chosen the coercive, imperial path, but that decision can be reversed. Of course, no American decision alone can secure peace in the world. It is the essence of the task that many nations must cooperate in it. If they do, however, they will find that twentieth-century history has presented them, together with all its violence, an abundance of materials to work with. There are grounds for optimism in the restricted but real sense that if the will to turn away from force and toward cooperation were to develop, history has provided more extensive and solid foundations for accomplishment than have ever existed before. For the anatomy of cooperative power has been transformed by the events of the past century as fully as that of coercive power.

Much that Woodrow Wilson hoped for has in fact come to pass. He wanted a world of popular self-determination. His vision is our reality (to a fault, as the tangled wars of self-determination of recent years demonstrate). He dreamed that the world would be made safe for democracy. We can begin to imagine, in the wake of the liberal democratic revival and the Western liberal settlement, that spreading democracy will help to make the world safe. He hated the territorial empires of his time. Today, they are on history's scrap heap.

Hopeful developments that Wilson could not have foreseen have also occurred. The Wilsonian peace was destroyed in good measure by the rise of totalitarianism. Now totalitarianism, too, lies in the dust. In Wilson's day, revolution was widely thought to be in its nature violent. We have witnessed the power of nonviolent revolution, which was responsible for the downfall of the greatest empires of the previous two centuries, the British and the Soviet. In his day, the global adapt-or-die war system was at the apex of its power. In ours, it is disabled. Each of the aforementioned developments indeed curtailed that system in a different way. The military power deployed at the top of the system ran into the buzz saw of even greater power based on popular will at the bottom. As in Alice in Wonderland's croquet game, in which the mallets were flamingos and the balls were hedgehogs, the pawns in the imperial game, mistaken for inanimate objects by the imperialists, came alive in their hands and began, universally and unstoppably, to pursue their own plans and ambitions. In this new dispensation, which can guarantee against global domination far more reliably than the balance of power ever could, the wills of innumerable local peoples play the role previously played by the resolve of major powers to go to war to stop a global conqueror.

While the self-determination movement was encasing the giant's feet in cement, nuclear weapons were immobilizing his head and limbs. What need was there to obey the dictates of the war system's global logic of force when at the end of every military path was neither victory nor defeat but a common annihilation? Coexistence had always been a wise policy; now it became a necessity. It remains so—American conventional military superiority notwithstanding—for all nuclear-capable powers. Even tiny, impoverished North Korea can deter the United States and all its might if it possesses half a dozen nuclear weapons and the means to deliver them. Of course, it is still quite possible to stumble across the dread threshold, committing genocide and suicide in a single act, but the option is hardly tempting.

Even as self-determination movements and nuclear arsenals were, in their different ways, paralyzing force as the final arbiter in global affairs, nonviolent revolution in the Soviet bloc and elsewhere was proving the existence of a force that now *could* arbitrate. Gyorgy Konrád was right, far-fetched as it may have seemed at the time, to suggest that his "antipolitics" pointed a way out of the Cold War and the nuclear stalemate, and so was Adam Michnik when he said that he and his colleagues had discovered a political equivalent of the atomic bomb. Has the effectiveness of what William James called the moral equivalent of war ever been more effectually demonstrated?

At the same time, the revival of liberal democracy was creating a growing, informal bloc of nations whose members enjoyed peaceful relations not because they bristled with arms or had established a cumbersome structure of collective security but merely because they lacked any reason or inclination for war and possessed cooperative means for resolving such disagreements as did arise.

The success of the self-determination movement, the rise of nuclear capacity, the success of nonviolent revolutions, and the liberal democratic revival are deep-rooted historical realities. Even as (with the exception of nonviolent revolution) they have created new dangers, they have laid down new foundations for a world that can move away from violence as the principle arbiter of its political affairs.

Shall we, then, return to the fray with a third round of Wilsonism? Shall we attempt once more to write a constitution for the whole world? We must answer in the negative. It would not make sense to apply twice-failed solution to problems that no longer exist. The entrenched war system defeated Wilson, and it is perhaps the most important of our inestimable advantages that we do not face this monster. Its fall has opened up new avenues for action. No longer is it necessary, as it was in his time, to put in place a global system of law as a *precondition* for dismantling the structures of force. The two tasks can proceed along separate tracks, each at its own pace. No longer do we face the impossible task of uprooting the war system in its entirety or leaving it in place. The all-or-nothing dilemma has dissolved. Seeing, just as Wilson did, that by continuing to rely on systems of violence we condemn ourselves to catastrophe and horror, we can adopt his radical goal of creating a peaceful world while remaining at liberty to carry it out step by step. We can borrow a leaf from the Eastern Europeans. Rejecting a choice between accommodation and violent, all-or-nothing revolution, they decided upon the incremental pursuit of revolutionary ends by peaceful, reformist means. Acting on the basis of common principles yet without any blueprint—"in cooperation without unification," in the phrase of the French sociologist Pierre Bourdieu—they pooled the variegated forces of society to achieve a radical renewal of their lives that in the end accomplished everything that was necessary. A revolution against violence in the world at large today would, in imitation of this process, not be the realization of any single plan drawn up by any one person or council but would develop, like open software, as the common creation of any and all comers, acting at every political level, within as well as outside government, on the basis of common principles.

One day, humankind may organize itself into a true body politic. Perhaps this will be some remote variation on the United Nations, whose hand now lies so lightly on the world; perhaps it will be some new organizational form. That day had not come in Wilson's time. It has not come in ours. Even as an ideal, the structure of a global body politic remains uninvented. Such a novel object is unlikely to take a familiar form. The need for global political structures to deal with the globalized economy and the swiftly deteriorating global environment is manifest. Yet it would be premature, for instance, to suppose that they should constitute a "world government" or a "world state." The words "state" and "government" carry too much unwanted baggage from the past. Why should an organization whose purpose and surrounding context would be so different from those of national governments repeat their structures? (The federal tradition is the most promising one perhaps, but no existing federation provides a model.) Nation-states, for example, have been in a condition of unceasing rivalry and conflict with one another and this condition has shaped basic elements of their anatomies. A global body politic, by contrast, would exist alone on earth—a circumstance that must have the profoundest consequences for its character, if only because of the blood-chilling possibility that, if it were endowed with anything like the powers to which existing states are accustomed, it might become repressive, leaving no corner of the earth free. There is a raw freedom in the plurality of states that the world should not surrender easily, or without the firmest confidence that a more civilized freedom can be defended and maintained.

In our new circumstances, the starting point of a world politics based in cooperative power would be not a blueprint for an ideal system of law but the reality that has already emerged on the ground. It is a reality for which there is as yet no adequate name. The word, when it appears, will refer to the power of action without violence, whether in revolution, the civil state, or the international order. I have followed convention in referring to this thing as nonviolence, but the word is highly imperfect for its purpose. "Nonviolence" is a word of negative construction, as if the most important thing that could be said about nonviolent action was that it was *not* something else. Yet that which it negates—violence—is already negative, a subtractor from life. A double negative, in mathematics, gives a positive result. And in fact the thing itself—nonviolence—is entirely positive, as Gandhi said. Yet in English there is no positive word for it. It's as if we were obliged to refer to action as "non-inaction," to hope as "non-hopelessness," or to faith as "non-unbelief." It was in search of a solution to this problem that Gandhi coined his untranslatable "satyagraha." Havel spoke, only somewhat less mysteriously, of "living in truth." Arendt sought to wrest the word "power" from its normal usage and turn it to this end. John Adams and Thomas Jefferson— who differed about many things—spoke of the power of citizens that flowed from the disposition of their hearts and minds, and recognized that such action was the foundation of all systems of political freedom. I have resorted in these pages to the plain phrase "cooperative power," as distinct from "coercive power."

The agenda of a program to build a cooperative world would be to choose and foster cooperative means at every level of political life. At the street level, this would mean choosing satyagraha over violent insurrection—the sit-down or general strike or "social work" over the suicide bombing or the attack on the local broadcasting station. At the level of the state it would mean choosing democracy over authoritarianism or totalitarianism (although some, such as Jefferson, Arendt, and Gandhi, have hoped for the invention of a political system that would provide more participation for citizens than representative democracy does); at the level of international affairs, it would mean choosing negotiation, treaties, and other agreements and institutions over war and, in general, choosing a cooperative, multilateral international system over an imperial one; at the level of biological survival, it would mean choosing nuclear disarmament over the balance of nuclear terror and proliferation. There is no reason to restrict the idea of cooperative power to individuals acting together. We can, to paraphrase Burke, just as well say, "freedom, when nations act in concert, is power." The choice at each level is never merely the rejection of violence; it is always at the same time the embrace of its cooperative equivalent.

Such a program of action, though lacking the explicit, technical coherence of a blueprint, would possess the inherent moral and practical coherence of any set of actions taken on the basis of common principles. History shows that violence incites more violence, without respect for national borders or the boundaries that supposedly divide foreign from domestic affairs. All forms of terror, from the suicide bombing in the pizza parlor to the torture in the basement to the globe-spanning balance of terror, foster one another. Nonviolence is likewise synergistic and contagious. For just as there is a logic of force, there is a logic of peace—a "cycle of nonviolence." Just as violent revolution creates the conditions for dictatorship, nonviolent revolution paves the way for democracy. Just as dictatorships incline toward war, democracies, if they can resist imperial temptations, incline toward peace with one another. Just as war is the natural environment for repression and dominance by the privileged few, peace is the natural environment for human rights and justice for the poor. Consider, for example, the ramifications of the peaceful rebellion against Soviet rule. It was met, as a violent revolution surely would not have been, with Gorbachev's nonviolent, reformist response, which led, however unintentionally, to the end of the Soviet regime, which in turn created the conditions for peace between the Cold War powers. And recall, by contrast, the outbreak of the First World War. It led to the rise of totalitarianism, which led to the Second World War, which led in turn to the advent of the Cold War and the species-threatening nuclear balance of terror. No one planned or could have foreseen these chains of consequences but they were as sure and real as anything anyone did plan.

A revolution against violence—loosely coordinated, multiform, flexible, based on common principles and a common goal rather than on a common blueprint—would encompass a multitude of specific plans, including ones for disarmament, conventional as well as nuclear; democratization and human rights; advancement of international law; reform of the United Nations; local and regional peacekeeping and peacemaking; and social and ecological programs that form the indispensable content of a program of nonviolent change. To neglect the last of these would be to neglect the lesson that campaigns of noncooperation are empty without constructive programs. Justice for the poor (victims of "structural violence") and rescue of the abused environment of the earth (victim of human violence done to other living creatures) are indispensable goals. They are already served by a rich new array of nongovernmental organizations and movements, constituting the beginnings of an international civil society. They range from local protest and rebellion by the poor against their exploitation, through movements of protest in rich countries against undemocratic and anti-environmental trade agreements, through nongovernmental organizations, and philanthropic organizations, both secular and religious, dedicated to human rights, the alleviation of poverty, and other causes, to former statesmen still eager to be of public service in the cause of peace (the former Soviet president Mikhail Gorbachev, the former American president Jimmy Carter, and the former president of Costa Rica, Oscar Arias, are notable examples).

Of equal or greater importance is the feminist revolution, itself a part of the much broader democratic revolution of modern times. The public world has hitherto been run by males, and it is clear that, whatever their virtues and vices, their way of doing things has reached an impasse. Experts can dispute whether the unmistakable male proclivity for war is innate or learned, the product of nature or nurture, but one thing we cannot doubt is that historically organized violence has been bound up with the male way of being human—with men's needs, men's desires, and men's interests. It is no less clear that historically the pursuits of women have been more peaceful. Could it be that nature in her wisdom created two genders in order to have a "second sex" in reserve, so to speak, for just such an emergency as the one we now face? There may be a less violent way of doing things that is rooted in female tradition and now will move to the fore, together with the gender that created it.

Peace begins, someone has said, when the hungry are fed. It is equally true that feeding the hungry begins when peace comes. Global warming cannot be stopped by B-52s any more than nuclear proliferation can; only cooperation in the form of binding treaties can accomplish either task. Peace, social justice, and defense of the environment are a cooperative triad to pit against the coercive, imperial triad of war, economic exploitation, and environmental degradation. Lovers of freedom, lovers of social justice, disarmers, peacekeepers, civil disobeyers, democrats, civil-rights activists, and defenders of the environment are legions in a single multiform cause, and they will gain strength by knowing it, taking encouragement from it, and, when appropriate and opportune, pooling their efforts.

Among the innumerable possible specific plans that such a program could entail, I have picked four to discuss here—not because they are in any way comprehensive, or even, in every case, necessarily the most important ones that can be imagined, but because they all bear directly on the choice between cooperation and coercion, and seem to me to be timely, realistic, and illustrative of the unity in diversity that a broad choice in favor of cooperation would manifest. They are a worldwide treaty to abolish nuclear arms and other weapons of mass destruction; a program of international intervention to ameliorate, contain, or end wars of self-determination on the basis of a reformed conception of national sovereignty; enforcement of a prohibition against crimes against humanity; and the foundation of a democratic league to lend support to democracy worldwide as an underpinning of peace and to restrain existing democracies from betraying their principles in their foreign policies.

A Decision to Exist

In Wilson's day, rejecting violence meant rejecting war—above all, world war. In our time, we must secure not only peace but survival. The menace of annihilation—of cities, of nations, of the species—arguably suppressed the menace of world war, and now we must suppress the menace of annihilation. A decision for non-violence, in our time, is a decision to exist.

An agreement to abolish nuclear arms and all other weapons of mass destruction is the sine qua non of any sane or workable international system in the twenty-first century. Any other attempted settlement of the issue of weapons of mass destruction will clash with other efforts to bring peace, with common sense, and with elementary decency. No tolerable policy can be founded upon the permanent institutionalization of a capacity and intention to kill millions of innocent people. No humane international order can depend upon a threat to extinguish humanity. Abolition alone provides a sound basis for the continued deepening and spread of liberal democracy, whose founding principles are violated and affronted by the maintenance of nuclear terror: "a democracy based on terror" is, in the long run, a contradiction in terms. And abolition alone can, by ending the nuclear double standard, stop proliferation and make effective the existing bans on other weapons of mass destruction. The logic of abolition is the real alternative to the logic of empire.

In practice, abolition means that the eight or nine nations that now possess nuclear weapons must join the hundred and eighty-two that have renounced them under the terms of the Nuclear Nonproliferation Treaty. (The four nations—Israel, India, Pakistan, and Cuba—that have declined to join the treaty must do so.) The signatories may also wish to convert the treaty into a Nuclear Weapons Convention, which would take its place alongside the existing conventions banning biological weapons and chemical weapons. At that point, the signatories might wish to merge these three conventions into one, banning all weapons of mass destruction, including any that might be invented in the future. The step would be logical and practical, inasmuch as the means of inspection and enforcement would overlap considerably and would gain strength through coordination.

But won't the abolition of nuclear weapons undo one of the very building blocks of peace that I have named? If the ever-present danger of nuclear annihilation has paralyzed great-power war, won't great-power war spring to life once nuclear weapons are removed from the picture? The answer to the question lies at the root of the nuclear predicament. It is a profound misunderstanding of the nuclear age to suppose that its basic features emanate from nuclear hardware. They do not. They emanate, as we have seen, from the knowledge that underlies the hardware. The number of nuclear warheads in the world can fall and the number of fingers on the nuclear button can decrease, even to zero, without subtracting a single digit from the physical equations on which the bomb is based.

It is the spread of this knowledge throughout the world that guarantees that the war system can never operate on a global basis as it did before. The persistence of the knowledge—the inherent capacity to rebuild nuclear arsenals, or to produce other weapons of mass destruction—will stand in the way. Let us imagine that nuclear weapons have been abolished by treaty, and that a nation then violates it by, secretly or openly, building a nuclear arsenal and threatening to use it to bully the world. As soon as the threat has been made, scores of other nations, all nuclear-capable, would be free to build and threaten to use their own nuclear arsenals in response, in effect deterring the violator. Not global hot war but a reflation of cold war would be the result. A crude system of mutual assured destruction would be reestablished, and wider war would be deterred, just as it is in our world of large nuclear arsenals. The important point, as always in matters of deterrence, is not that this would necessarily be done (although the scenario has a credibility that many existing ones lack) but that any government would know in advance that such a response was available, and would have every reason to desist from reckless schemes in the first place. The threat would not constitute nuclear deterrence in the classic sense of threatening instant nuclear retaliation; yet it would still be a kind of deterrence.

Abolition, when seen in this cold light, cannot mean a return to the pre-nuclear age, whether one might wish for such a development or not, nor can it rule out once and for all a resurgence of nuclear armaments in some future dark age, whose coming no one can preclude. It does, however, mean that a return to the global adapt-or-die war system is impossible. Abolition, in view of these circumstances, which as far as we know are unchangeable, would be nothing more—or less—than an indispensable though insufficient recognition by the human species of the terrible, mortal predicament it has got itself into, and a concrete expression of its resolve to find a solution. Abolition should not be undersold but it should not be oversold either.

There is thus more continuity between a policy of nuclear abolition and nuclear deterrence than at first meets the eye. It is as if we were saying, Let us take the deterrence theorists at their word that the goal of deterrence has been to prevent war. Unfortunately, we have to note an obvious fact: if you seek to avoid doing something by threatening to do that same thing, you have, at least to some extent, undermined your own purpose. So let us begin to move to a policy in which the "not using"—called by some "the tradition of nonuse"—gradually predominates, and the "threatening to use" fades away. Abolition then would fulfill the promise that deterrence now makes but cannot keep.

If this happened, the deterrence policy of the Cold War years might appear in history in a more favorable light than is now likely. It might then be seen as a system that in effect *extracted* the violence of the war system of the twentieth century, compacted it into a single world-destroying device, and *shelved* it—declaring to all: "If you want to use violence, then you must use *all* of it, so be wise and use none of it. And, just to make sure that you take us seriously, we are actually going to build and deploy tens of thousands of thermonuclear warheads and place them on rockets on hair-trigger alert." If followed by abolition, this act of extraction and consolidation would be revealed in retrospect as having been a halfway house to the full transformation of the war system into a peace system.

In this sequence, nuclear deterrence replaces the war system with a threat-of-annihilation system; abolition then replaces the threat-of-annihilation system with a peace system—or, at least, with the necessary foundation for a peace system. For abolition would not in itself constitute anything like a full peace system; it would only mark the world's commitment to creating one. The alternative is that Cold War deterrence will prove to have been the training ground for the full nuclearization of international affairs—that is, for nuclear anarchy.

Even after abolition, a critical decision remains to be made: whether or not to continue to rely as a matter of policy on nuclear rearmament in the event that the abolition treaty is violated. The nuts and bolts of any abolition agreement would be highly detailed arrangements for suppressing certain technologies—all, of course, inspected to the hilt. The agreement would specify exactly which nuclear-bomb materials are permitted, in what quantities, and where. There will assuredly be an enforcement provision in any such treaty, specifying what it is that the menaced nations of the world are entitled or obliged to do in the event of the treaty's violation. If nuclear rearmament is specified as a response, and technical arrangements suitable for it are provided, then, to an extent, the world would still be relying on nuclear terror to counter nuclear terror. Such provisions would embody what I have called "weaponless deterrence" and the scholar Michael Mazarr has called "virtual nuclear arsenals." If, on the other hand, the treaty bans nuclear arms absolutely, and forbids nuclear rearmament even in the face of its violation, whose remedy is to be sought by other means, then the world would formally and finally have renounced all dependence on nuclear terror for its safety.

The distinction between abolition, which is achievable, and a return to the pre-nuclear age, which is not, is necessary at the very least in order to understand and appreciate the radical difference between Wilsonism, which proposed to replace war with law, and abolition, which more modestly proposes merely to ratify the abolition of great-power war already imposed by the nuclear age, and to improve on this situation by retiring nuclear terror, which never can be utterly purged from human life, as deep into the background as is humanly possible. In practice, it may well be that if abolition of the hardware takes place, this will be such a momentous event morally, politically, and legally that, once some time has passed, and the world has gained confidence in its new arrangement, the deeper renunciation of nuclear terror will not be a difficult step. It would be deceptive, however, to suggest that a world without nuclear arms would be a world without danger, or even without nuclear danger. The risks, including the risk of nuclear rearmament, would be real. It is, rather, by comparison with the nuclear anarchy or the vain attempts at imperial domination that will otherwise probably be our future that the goal is attractive.

The dangers of abolition stem from potential violators of an abolition agreement. Two concerns have been uppermost—that the agreement could not be adequately inspected and that it could not be adequately enforced. I will confine myself here to a comment on each.

If historical experience is the test, possession of a nuclear monopoly (which a nation would have if it violated an abolition agreement) is much less valuable than nuclear theory predicts. At first glance, it appears that a country possessing a nuclear monopoly would possess an insuperable advantage over any adversary; nuclear-deterrence theory, which teaches that nuclear arsenals can be offset only by other nuclear arsenals, takes this for granted. The matter has already been put to the test several times in the history of the nuclear age, however, and in no case has possession of a nuclear monopoly translated into the foreseen military or political advantage—or, for that matter, into any detectable advantage at all. Nuclear powers have repeatedly fought, and even lost, conventional wars against small, nonnuclear forces, without being able to extract any benefit from their "ultimate" weapons. In the Suez crisis of 1956, nuclear-armed Britain, allied with France and Israel, failed to attain any of its aims against nonnuclear Egypt. France likewise found no utility in its nuclear monopoly in its war against the independence movement in Algeria. Neither did the Americans in Vietnam, or the Soviet Union in its war in Afghanistan, or Israel in its wars in Lebanon and in the West Bank, or China in the border war it fought and lost with Vietnam in 1979. If the only examples were the English, French, American, and Israeli ones, we might wonder whether democracies are constrained from using nuclear bombs by scruples absent in totalitarian regimes. The presence of the Soviet Union and China on the list, however, suggests that other factors are at work. (It's also worth recalling in this connection that the only country ever to use nuclear weapons was a democracy, the United States.)

The question of just why none of these powers used nuclear weapons in these losing wars is not easy to answer. Nevertheless, I would like to suggest a possible reason. Isn't it conceivable that heads of state are reluctant to use nuclear weapons simply because they don't want to kill millions of innocent people in cold blood at a single stroke? This "self-deterrence" may be a more powerful force than theorists have allowed. The moments in which the use of nuclear arms has in fact been seriously threatened have mostly been times when, as in the Cuban missile crisis, two nuclear-armed adversaries were in collision. One-sided threats of use—after the actual use on Hiroshima and Nagasaki—are conspicuous by their rarity. If these reflections have any foundation, then theory has libeled history, and the one clean secret of the nuclear age may be a hidden minimal sanity or humanity in the heads of state who have presided over nuclear arsenals.

However that may be, the relevance to the abolition question of this history is that if six powers, both democratic and totalitarian, in possession of nuclear monopolies, lost six conventional or guerrilla wars against small forces without nuclear arms, then we can hardly suppose that the entire family of nations, having recently staked its security on a nuclear abolition treaty, would stand helpless before a single miscreant regime that, having manufactured a concealed arsenal, stepped forward to give orders to the world. Since a prospective cheater would know that other nations would be fully capable of nuclear rearmament, violation of an abolition agreement could never be a rational plan. Indeed, a policy of one nation bellowing nuclear destruction to the whole world would be plain insanity. To this we can add that if it were done anyway, the world would possess more than adequate means to respond. It is unimaginable that a cowering world would knuckle under to the demands of the cheater. Far more likely, it would react with determination to quell the threat or, at the least, quickly reestablish a balance of terror.

The effectiveness of enforcement is linked to the effectiveness of verification. Verification would include the right of peremptory, unannounced inspection of all suspect facilities. One widely accepted conclusion among experts is that although the discovery of secret facilities for the construction of new nuclear arsenals, which are necessarily extensive, would be comparatively easy under a maximal regime of inspection, the discovery of caches of weapons hidden away before the agreement came into effect—of "bombs in the basement"—would be difficult. Some experts have even suggested that this problem is the fatal flaw in any plan of nuclear abolition. A nontechnical consideration, however, offers reassurance. Any nuclear arsenal, even a hidden one, must not only be maintained and guarded by a large cadre but also supervised by a military and political chain of command leading from the lowest technician up to the head of state. The United States' expenditure of four and a half billion dollars a year on "stockpile stewardship" shows that maintenance of a nuclear arsenal is highly complicated, requiring many hands and minds. There must also be delivery vehicles, plans for mating the warheads to the delivery vehicles, strategies, military and political, for using the weapons, and strategists to draw up the plans. Moreover, changes of regime, whether by violent or peaceful means, will multiply at a stroke the numbers of people privy to the secret. Many of those leaving office, often unwillingly, may be ill-disposed toward those replacing them and inclined to tell what they know; or else the newcomers may disagree with their predecessors' secret treaty violation and fear the wrath of the world. Few undertakings have ever been more secret than the Manhattan Project, yet some of its most highly classified information leaked in profusion to Stalin's spies.

In sum, it is in the nature of things that, over time, a growing body of people will share the secret of a hidden arsenal, and any one of them can reveal its existence to the world. With every year that passes, this body will grow. As in proliferation, the irresistible tendency of knowledge to spread shows itself—in this case to the advantage of disarmament. Time is the friend of inspection and thus of an abolition agreement. In the long run, the secret of a hidden arsenal would be as hard to keep as the secret of the bomb itself.

Like a nuclear monopoly, the bomb in the basement looks much more dangerous in theory than in the context of politics and history. In both circumstances, the natural repugnance that human beings have for nuclear weapons may have real-world consequences unforeseen in the denatured calculations of nuclear strategists—in the first case, inspiring among statesmen who wield monopolies an unexpected reluctance even to consider using their supposed advantage, in the second inspiring whistle-blowers to reveal activities that, under the terms of an abolition agreement, would be named and understood by all to be crimes against humanity.

All-or-Nothing Again?

Haven't I, though, simply reintroduced the fatal, all-or-nothing Wilsonian dilemma by insisting on the abolition of nuclear weapons rather than, say, their reduction to lower levels, or their reconfiguration in a more stable mode? Could it be that, by demanding abolition, we would be condemning ourselves to the same collapse of an overambitious plan that Wilson suffered? Admittedly, the proposal is ambitious. Yet nuclear abolitionism differs from Wilsonism in critical respects. The war system of Wilson's time was a workable and working machine, tightly integrated into the decision making of global politics, and so able to serve as the "pursuit of politics by other means." This cannot be said of the system of nuclear deterrence that supplanted it. After Nagasaki, no one has figured out how to gain political advantage from using, or even from possessing, nuclear weapons. The nuclear system is far more dangerous and far less useful than the war system was. As such, it should be much easier to clear out of the way.

Another difference is that nuclear arsenals, unlike the old war system, can be eliminated step by step. The first steps have in fact already been taken through arms control agreements. It is the unequivocal commitment to the goal, accompanied by unmistakable steps to achieve it, and not the rapidity of its achievement, that is most important. To be more precise, the period of implementation must be short enough to persuade potential nuclear proliferators that to build a new arsenal would be a worthless and dangerous expense, while being long enough to inspire confidence among the nuclear powers that inspection and enforcement are adequate.

Notwithstanding the absolutist ring of the word, abolition is not "all," even in the context of the nuclear predicament. Thanks to the indelible character of nuclear scientific know-how, the "all" in this matter, however ardently we might desire it, has been moved beyond our reach forever. All we can do in the circumstance is set ourselves against the evil day with the full force of our concerted political will.

It's in the context of a cooperative approach to nuclear nonproliferation that the logic of a cooperative approach to terrorism, nuclear or otherwise, is best understood. Like war, terrorism must now be divided into two categories. Just as we distinguish between conventional war and unconventional war (meaning war with weapons of mass destruction), so we must distinguish between conventional terrorism, using ordinary explosives, and unconventional terrorism, using weapons of mass destruction. Unconventional terrorism—the problem of the small group that wields immense destructive power because it has got hold of one of these weapons—can be addressed only by gaining control over the technology involved. After all, not even the most successful war on terrorism imaginable can reduce the population of terrorists to zero. The rigorous global inspection system of an abolition agreement would be the ideal instrument to choke at its source the danger that terrorists will acquire weapons of mass destruction. Even if such a system were in place, it must be admitted, the problem would not be completely solved. It might still be possible for a group to clandestinely create the needed technology. But the problem might be 98 percent solved, which is perhaps the most that can be hoped for. At each step along the path, the danger of diversion or construction of weapons of mass destruction would decline.

The hope of combating stateless global terrorism of the kind represented by the Al Qaeda network (which must be distinguished from the innumerable local varieties of terrorism around the world) likewise appears destined for disappointment without the creation of cooperative international structures involving the great majority of nations. A global threat requires a global response, and a global response will be possible only if governments work together rather than against one another. Historically, the greatest successes in reducing terrorism have been accomplished by a combination of police action and political attention to underlying causes. There is no reason to suppose that a global version of these largely national efforts would be different.

It is difficult to imagine the United States, acting alone or together with just a few nations, will be able to coerce or overthrow every regime that "supports" terrorism or, for that matter, defeat or destroy every proliferator of weapons of mass destruction. The cooperation of governments, not their antagonism, is the indispensable precondition for a successful policy of opposing and reducing global terrorism of any kind. A cooperative policy alone likewise avoids the danger, posed by the imperial approach, that hostile action, in the Middle East or elsewhere, will widen the pool of recruits for terrorist groups. At the same time, it is the likeliest basis for the political efforts that, over the long run, are the only lasting solution to terrorist threats.

Delaminating Sovereignty

Sovereignty, the conceptual crystallization of the all-or-nothing trap, is, as its first intellectual exegete Jean Bodin knew so well, a bundle of powers forced together under the pressure of military necessity or ambition. That was why at the birth of the concept of sovereignty its two inseparable defining principles were complete reliance upon the sword and indivisibility. That, too, was why, in the later, popular incarnations of sovereignty, the people, their territory, and the land had to be congruent, excluding all overlaps, mixed national populations, collective rights, or divided authorities. Yet long experience with popular government, in the United States and elsewhere, has revealed that when power is cooperative rather than coercive—based on action willingly concerted rather than compelled—then, in the domestic sphere, at least, it does not have to be indivisible. It can be federated; it can be divided among branches of government and localities; it can be delaminated.

It was not clear, on the other hand, whether such division could occur in the international sphere. Certainly, division was out of the question as long as the global adapt-or-die war machine subjected nations to its crushing pressure. However, now that that machine has been paralyzed and the pressure lifted, we can ask the question again. And in fact there are already signs of change. In regions in which coercive power, sovereign and indivisible, has yielded, structures of cooperative power, limited and divisible, have flourished. The most striking example is the European Union. Let us recall that sovereignty was first asserted in Europe by absolutist kings as a scythe to cut down the tangled thickets of medieval political institutions, with their dense, overlapping webs of ecclesiastical as well as secular rights, privileges, and duties. Although sovereignty is now defended as the guarantor of the plurality of states, originally it was diversity's enemy. It was the instrument of a radical simplification of politics, reducing the array of political actors to subjects on the one side and a sovereign on the other. The development of the European Union, however, shows that democratic states at peace with one another are now free to create a rich variety of hybrid arrangements, most of them unimaginable under the terms of the choice between a Wilsonian global constitution and the old war system. The E.U., as the former chancellor of Germany Helmut Schmidt has commented, "marks the first time in the history of mankind that nation-states that differ so much from each other nevertheless . . . have *voluntarily* decided to throw in their lot together." The result has not been a simplification of politics. The union's economic and political institutions, which inch forward year by year, are already characterized by a complexity not far from the medieval. They defy analysis on the basis of such simple, clear principles of the recent past as sovereignty, whether of the people, the state, or anyone else.

Formulas for shared or limited sovereignty are also a necessary part of any solution to most wars of national self-determination, in so many of which the requirement of one state for one people on one territory has proved to be a recipe for nightmare. The most ingenious and promising solution is the on-and-off Good Friday accord of 1998, which may one day lead to a resolution of the conflict in Northern Ireland. In the European Union, the absence of conflict made structures of divided power possible; in Ireland, divided structures of power are being used to try to end a conflict—a more difficult challenge.

The Irish conflict, although possessing many singular local and historical features, nevertheless arose out of a dilemma of a kind shared by many other wars of national self-determination. Two neighboring peoples (in this case, the Irish and the English) have a long history of conflict (in this case going back at least four centuries). Between them is a disputed territory, on which their peoples are intermixed. (Northern Ireland, which remained under British rule after Irish independence in 1922, contains a narrow Protestant majority dedicated to preserving the union with Britian and a large Catholic minority of "nationalists" eager to join the Irish Free State.) Similar elements can be found in lands as diverse as Sri Lanka, Kashmir, Crete, Rwanda, several of the former Soviet republics, almost all the former Yugoslavian nations, and Palestine.

The two communities in Northern Ireland appeal to common principles—the right of self-determination and majority rule. The problem is that each has drawn the boundaries of the "self" that is to be "determined" differently. The Protestant unionists draw a line that encompasses Great Britain, then crosses the Irish Sea and runs around the borders of Northern Ireland. Within that circle, which describes an existing institutional reality, the majority is British and Protestant. The Catholic nationalists wish to draw a line that simply circumscribes the Irish island (including, of course, Northern Ireland). Within that circle, representing the dream of a unified Ireland, the majority would be Irish and Catholic. The two circles overlap in Northern Ireland. If the first circle is accepted as "the nation," then majority rule for now dictates that Northern

Ireland will remain part of Great Britain; if the second circle is accepted, then Northern Ireland would join Ireland. The problem is the one that lies at the heart of the separation question: Which groups have the right to form themselves into a body politic, in which a vote of the majority binds the minority? This is the question to which liberal democratic thought, from the time of the American Revolution down to our day, has been unable to offer any answer. Indeed, two of its elementary principles, self-determination and majority rule, seem to be part of the problem. An answer can be found only by dividing the supposedly indivisible—by disaggregating the powers fused in national sovereignty. That is what the Good Friday accord does.

The immediate problem was the savage internecine warfare that broke out between nationalist and unionist extremists in Northern Ireland. The path to a solution could not be found in Northern Ireland alone. It lay, as John Hume, the leader of the nationalist Social Democratic and Labour Party, came to understand, also in London, Dublin, Brussels (home of the European Parliament), and even in Washington, where President Bill Clinton played a mediating role. First, the two outside state parties, the United Kingdom and the Irish Republic, had to surrender any claim to a right of sovereignty over Northern Ireland. The Irish Republic did so by amending its constitution, which had claimed sovereignty over the whole island. Great Britain, to which Northern Ireland now belonged, renounced any "selfish, economic" interest in the territory. That is, if Northern Ireland itself wanted to leave the United Kingdom, Great Britain would let it.

The remaining question was how, if the two outside claimants were ready to surrender their claim, the future national status of Northern Ireland was to be determined. The accord's answer was "the principle of consent": the people of Northern Ireland would decide their own future by democratic procedures. In the language of the accord, "It is hereby declared that Northern Ireland in its entirety remains part of the United Kingdom," unless, "voting in a poll," it decides to "form part of a united Ireland."

These provisions ended the tug-of-war between the United Kingdom and the Republic of Ireland for control over Northern Ireland but left intact the tug-of-war—the sanguinary terrorist conflict—between extremists in the two local communities, each longing for union with a different country. The Protestants, still in the majority (though a dwindling one, as the Catholic population is growing faster than the Protestant), would opt for continued union with the United Kingdom, and also might continue to use their majority power to abuse and repress the Catholic minority. Inasmuch as such repression had been a primary cause of the conflict in the first place, it could hardly be taken lightly.

The accord addressed that problem with several further provisions, among them a plan to include a due proportion of nationalists in the Northern Ireland police force and a plan for political power sharing between the two communities. One important feature of the latter was an agreement to apportion ministers of the government of Northern Ireland in accord with party strength in the assembly, rather than adopting a winner-take-all arrangement. This provision was a dramatic grant of exactly the sort of collective minority rights that classical liberal democratic theory was unable to approve. It ordained something that has always been a bête noire of classical liberalism—"concurrent majorities," in which overlapping communities each vote separately for their representatives, who then must share power. In the first government under the accord, half of the ministries went to the minority nationalists.

Still another provision established a North/South Ministerial Council to make decisions on matters of mutual concern, such as agriculture, inland waterways, trade, and tourism. Created by legislation passed both in the British Parliament and in the Irish Republic's Oireachtas, the council includes the Irish Taoiseach and First Minister of Northern Ireland as well as other ministers, and is to arrive at decisions "by agreement of the two sides." A Council of the Isles was also created to deal with matters involving all of Ireland and Britain.

The parties to the Good Friday accord did not set out to dismantle sovereignty, yet that is what the accord does. We will look in vain in this agreement for power that can be called sovereign. The people of Northern Ireland remain citizens of the United Kingdom, yet they have been granted a constitutional right that the citizens of few, if any, other nation-states enjoy—the right to remove themselves and their land and goods to another country upon a majority vote. (It is a right that the Muslims of Kashmir, the Tamils of Sri Lanka, and the Tibetans in China, to give three of many possible examples, would love to acquire.) They have a clear *right* to remain British but no *obligation* to do so. Such a right is, indeed, perhaps the most elementary collective right a people can possess, the right of self-determination, which is the essence of national sovereignty. And yet in Northern Ireland this right, which is in truth a power, is obviously conditioned and limited. It was created by decisions in the United Kingdom, and can be suspended by the United Kingdom, which can restore direct rule over Northern Ireland, as it has done several times in the past three decades. (However, if the people of Northern Ireland once were to exercise their right to join the Irish Republic, England's power to suspend the government would be at an end.) And although it permits the people of Ulster to define themselves politically by a vote, their options are limited. They are not permitted, for example, to establish themselves as an independent state.

As for the Irish Republic, it explicitly renounced its demand for sovereignty over Northern Ireland, yet thereby gained, through the Ministerial Council, more actual influence over the North than ever before. This arrangement has left traditional notions of sovereignty in the dust, clearing the path, as the peoples involved may decide, for all kinds of incremental, mixed institutions and arrangements for shared power that would be far richer and more nuanced than the bare choice between union with Great Britain and union with the Irish Republic. All the while, the Irish Republic can expect a day when Northern Ireland may of its own volition switch allegiance from the United Kingdom to Ireland by a mere majority vote.

At the same time that the United Kingdom was entering into this agreement, it was devolving new powers upon Scotland and Wales, in the most radical constitutional reforms in Britain of the twentieth century. When we consider that both innovations were occurring within the context of the steadily evolving constitutional arrangements of the European Union, we arrive at a picture of fundamental political transformation at every level of European politics, and grasp that national sovereignty is now in the process of giving way to new forms in the very Europe in which the concept was born.

The influence of the Good Friday accord, if it succeeds, may extend far beyond Europe. It would be the first peaceful settlement since the end of the Cold War of a war of national self-determination—the first squaring of the circle. The Irish protagonists admittedly enjoy advantages that the parties in other wars of national self-determination lack. Probably the most important is that all the governments involved—the Irish Republic's, the British, and Northern Ireland's—operate according to democratic principles. Alternatives to the gun—elections, parliamentary debates, free discussion—have always been available for use and have been used. For example, a gradual shift of the Irish Republican Army from violent struggle to electoral struggle has been one of the keys to progress brought by the agreement. In addition, the two governments in the dispute were willing to renounce their claims in favor of a decision by the people of the territory.

Such a combination of advantages is unavailable in almost any of the world's other many wars of national self-determination, in most of which either one or both of the warring parties is authoritarian or is unyielding in its territorial claim. (For example, India, though a democracy, has never been willing to let the people of Kashmir decide their future in a vote.) Nor would a success in Ireland have much value as a model in the lands of failed states, where the problems are more likely to be extreme poverty, lack of civil institutions, and underdevelopment than to be the excessive, murderous strength of political factions. There are parts of the world where neither violent nor nonviolent solutions offer ready answers, where patience is the better part of wisdom, and amelioration of the worst evils, such as famines, or merely heading off further catastrophic deterioration of a situation, may be the best that outside intervention can provide for the calculable future.

Nevertheless, the value of a successful Good Friday accord as a precedent for resolving wars of self-determination could be real, and the idea of delaminating sovereignty has already been proposed as a component of the settlement of other conflicts. In Sri Lanka, any solution to the conflict between the Tamil Tigers, who have been seeking an independent state in the north of the island, and the government that represents the Sinhalese majority will undoubtedly require some kind of power sharing. Some analysts have proposed that if the Israelis and the Palestinians ever return to a peace process, they may want to provide for dual sovereignty over the holy sites of Jerusalem, where not only national populations but religious buildings of high symbolic importance to several faiths are under contention. The Wailing Wall forms one side of a hill on which the Temple, the Jews' most holy site, once stood but on which the Al Aksa mosque, Islam's second-most holy site, now stands. One might suspect that a mischievous God, by permitting this interpenetration of holy objects, had decided to create, in the medium of architecture, a tangible symbol of the riddle of wars of national self-determination. The question He thus put before us was: How, when you cannot physically separate peoples (or their sacred buildings), can you organize the political world so that each people can be true to its deepest beliefs while living in peace with others? The tangible quandary of the holy sites poses an intangible riddle, which, in the words of the Israeli writer Avishai Margolit, is "How does one divide a symbol?" Precisely because a clash of faiths is involved in Jerusalem, which is a holy land for three religions, a settlement there one day would transcend the Good Friday accord in symbolic meaning.

Delaminating Self-Determination

The possibility of addressing wars of self-determination by delaminating sovereignty could open wider horizons of international reform. The scholar of international law Gidon Gottlieb, for example, has outlined a provocative legal program of surgery upon sovereignty. It would be foolish, he recognizes, to suppose that theoretical breakthroughs can solve real conflicts with long histories. "How 'relevant' are mere ideas and concepts," Gottlieb asks, "when much blood has been shed and where enemies are locked in mortal combat? . . . The setting for peacemaking in ethnic wars is both grim and discouraging. Political efforts are invariably situated in the context of long and complex local histories of strife, of grievances, and of crimes well remembered. Layers upon layers of promises ignored, broken pledges, and treaties violated form the usual background to new promises, new pledges, and new treaties offered."

Yet new ideas have a role to play when they are based on new realities in the situations in question. Gottlieb proposes that the two basic components of sovereignty, the nation and the state, might in some circumstances be separated. The problem of mixed populations, he has suggested, might be easier to solve if the international community created, alongside states but separate from them, a juridical status for nations. The individual person would then have available two internationally recognized statuses—one as a citizen of a state, the other as a member of a nation. In this "deconstruction" of sovereignty, the old unity of state, people, and territory would be dissolved. Each of the two statuses would confer rights and privileges but not the same ones. State rights, for instance, might include all the classical rights of individual liberty, while national rights might include such collective rights as the right to speak one's own language, to control local schools, or to practice one's faith. Special passports to travel between the states that are hosts to one nation might be granted. One nation then could overlap many states, and vice versa.

Among other examples, Gottlieb cites the dilemma of the Kurdish people, now living under the sovereignty of Turkey, Iraq, Iran, and Syria, in all of which they are more or less embattled. The classic solution to the dilemma, establishment of a sovereign Kurdish state according to the traditional rules of self-determination, would solve the problem for the Kurds but at the certain cost of bloody upheaval in four states and the possible creation of the reverse problem of repression of Turks, Iraqis, Iranians, and Syrians within newly drawn Kurdish borders. Instead of heading down this road, something that seems exceedingly unlikely to happen in any case, Gottlieb proposes conferring his formal national status upon the Kurds, guaranteeing them certain cultural and other rights and privileges within the framework of each of the four states. He proposes similar solutions for the struggles of national self-determination in Cyprus, in Canada (over the status of Quebec), and in Armenia and Azerbaijan (over the contested Nagorno-Karabak and Nakhichevan enclaves).

Delaminating sovereignty entails delaminating self-determination, at least as this has traditionally been conceived. Self-determination, one might say, must yield to self-*determinations* and *selves*-determination—that is, to permission for more than one nation to find expression within the border of a single state and to permission for individuals and groups to claim multiple identities—for example, Kurdish and Turkish. As the story of American independence demonstrates, the connection between the concepts of sovereignty and self-determination, otherwise called independence, has been close. Reasoning about the nature of sovereignty compelled the colonists to conclude that the choice they faced belonged in the all-or-nothing category—either full independence or full subordination to Britain. It could not be otherwise in an age when sovereignty was regarded as the prime attribute of a body politic.

Yet even during the age of the colonial empires, some of the best minds cast sidelong glances at middle courses between empire and independence. We have already mentioned the plan that called for replacement of the British Empire by "an association of states endowed with British liberties, and owing allegiance directly to the sovereign head." Similar in character was the "Galloway plan," for a "colonial union under British Authority which included a legislative council made up of representatives from the colonial assemblies and a president general to be appointed by the king." For such plans to have succeeded, either the empire would have had to transform itself into a body based on consent, which is to say into a true federation, or the colony would have had to bow to force. Burke, one of the few Englishmen of his time ready to apply English principles of liberty and consent to the empire as a whole, was also one of the first to glimpse the full difficulty of the task, even in purely intellectual terms. "There is not a more difficult subject for the understanding of men," he commented in words that have held true down to this day, "than to govern a large Empire upon a plan of Freedom."

The difficult subject would arise many more times in the history of modern empires. The French-Algerian crisis of the 1960s inspired the novelist and thinker Albert Camus to tackle another incarnation of it. France had settled a large colony of its citizens—the *pieds-noirs*—in Algeria, whose native population began, in the 1950s, to agitate for independence. Camus, himself a *pied-noir,* devised a confederal plan, in which the fundamental character of the French state would change to incorporate Algeria. An Algerian regional assembly representing Algerian citizens and dealing with Algerian problems would be established under a unicameral federal Senate, which would preside over a Commonwealth consisting of France and Algeria, and elect a confederal government. It would mean, Camus explained, the end of the single nation-state born in 1789, and "the birth of a French federal structure" that would create a "true French Commonwealth." Camus understood, as Burke did, what a profound reconception of the state, called *une et indivisible* in the French Declaration of the Rights of Man and the Citizen, would be entailed in such a plan for a multinational state. "Contrary above all to the deep-rooted prejudices of the French Revolution, we should thus have sanctioned within the Republic two equal but distinct categories of citizens," Camus wrote. "From one point of view, this would mark a sort of revolution against the regime of centralization and abstract individualism resulting from 1789, which, in so many ways, now deserves to be called the *Ancien Régime*." Of particular note in our context is Camus's hope that the new structure might show the way for "the European institutions of the future."

As Jeffrey C. Isaac, a scholar of Camus and of Hannah Arendt, has pointed out, Arendt had been prompted to think along similar lines in the late 1940s in regard to the establishment of Israel. The problem, once again, was two nations—Palestinian and Jewish—on one soil. She, too, believed that the only peaceful solution to dilemmas of this kind was a confederal one. The alternative was imposition of Israeli rule on Arabs and Arab territory by force. "The 'victorious' Jews," she wrote, "would live surrounded by an entirely Arab population, secluded inside ever-threatened borders, absorbed with physical defense to a degree that would submerge all other interests and activities." The accuracy of this prediction does not mean that Arendt's solutions were feasible. (The fact that one solution fails doesn't mean the alternative would have worked.)

What is certain is that the hour of the consensual multinational state had no more come in the Middle East in the late 1940s than it had come in England in the 1770s or France in the 1960s. Indivisible national sovereignty remained the rule, and force remained its guiding principle. Not until our day has that hopeful hour perhaps arrived for one or two regions of the world.

Enforcement

In a program whose overall object is to wean politics from its reliance on force, the question of *enforcement* is obviously vexatious. It's clear, however, that if the international community should ever embark on such a program, enforcement will be a necessary element. The question is what its scope, provenance, and limitations should be. At one extreme is the American imperial plan, which is almost all enforcement—the unilateral right of a single power to attack and overthrow other governments at will. At the other extreme is no enforcement. Somewhere in between is a vision of an international community that fundamentally relies on consent and the cooperative power consent creates, but nevertheless reserves the right to resort to force in certain well-defined, limited circumstances. A nuclear-abolition agreement, for example, would require enforcement in the event of a violation, as would a coordinated international effort to combat global terrorism. Ideally, force would play the restricted policing role it does in a democratic state. I say "ideally," because if an international police force is to be legitimate there must exist an international order whose legitimacy is generally recognized, and this is just what is largely missing in the world today.

In these circumstances—which not even the implementation of every proposal in this book would fundamentally alter, since they do not envision a world state, legitimate or otherwise—there could hardly be a police force acting in the name of such a body to enforce its laws. Yet, as we tackle this question, the advantage of our circumstances over Wilson's are again evident. Because of the war system's demise, we are not in any way required to establish an overwhelming international military force that could impose its will on all miscreants. For excellent reasons, this idea no longer even crosses most people's minds; the only plan remotely like it is the current fantasy of hegemony that tempts American policy makers. And so we are free in the area of enforcement, too, to proceed incrementally. To whatever extent the international community decides to exist—and no further—it can seek to enforce a few selected internationally agreed-upon principles. Such an approach, it is true, would not end war at one stroke, as the League of Nations was supposed to do, but it would close the all-too-familiar demoralizing gap between grandiose rhetoric and trifling deeds—a perennial consequence of the bad faith of good intentions that was the curse of attempts at international peacemaking in the twentieth century.

The immediate need is for a principle defining a task that is achievable, or may soon be achievable, by the international community. One such principle has already been identified: the obligation to prevent and punish crimes against humanity. The concept of crimes against humanity first gained currency at the trials at Nuremberg in 1945, in which the victors of the Second World War held Nazi leaders accountable for the atrocities of their regime. Recently, it has been applied again in legal proceedings in special international tribunals against the former president of Yugoslavia Slobodan Milosevic and against the perpetrators of genocide against the Tutsis in Rwanda. The newly constituted International Criminal Court (I.C.C.), making use of the language of the Nuremberg Charter, has defined crimes against humanity as acts, including murder, torture, rape, forced disappearance, and persecution, when committed "as part of a widespread or systematic attack directed against any civilian population . . ." The key distinction therefore is between abuses of individuals, which are not crimes against humanity per se, and abuses that occur as part of an assault against a defined group, whether ethnic, religious, racial, or national.

The most historically important of the crimes against humanity—specifically outlawed by the Convention on the Prevention and Punishment of the Crime of Genocide, of 1948—is genocide, which may be roughly defined as an assault upon the life of one of the earth's peoples. There has been debate over whether the definition should include only ethnic, national, and racial groups or social classes and political groups, too. If the more expansive definition is accepted, then the definition of genocide will be hard to distinguish from the I.C.C.'s definition of crimes against humanity, and the two concepts would merge.

Why groups, however? Why should the international community concern itself especially with collectivities rather than individuals as such? An obvious pragmatic reason is that if the international community accepted responsibility for enforcing individual human rights, it would in effect have to constitute itself as a world state. The justifications for collective international intervention would be unlimited, since there is no country on earth in which some human-rights abuses do not occur. There is also a legal reason. All positive law is the law of a community. Whereas each national community is a community of individuals, the international community has, so far, been mainly a community of states, whose sovereignty has been guaranteed by international law (including the U.N. Charter). It therefore makes sense that international law would be especially concerned with states and peoples. When one person kills another, the order of the national community is violated. When a state kills a people, the order of the international community is violated.

Laws mandating international action to set aside sovereignty in the name of stopping crimes against humanity would revise this understanding without throwing it out. The *state* would still be recognized as the prime international actor, but it would no longer necessarily be recognized in every case as the *nation's* legitimate representative. The international community (although not any single power) would assert a sharply limited and exceptional right to judge the fitness of a state to represent its people. Such a recognition would form a natural complement to the revisions of sovereignty needed to settle the wars of national self-determination. In most cases the claims of states, even of repressive states, to represent a nation would be recognized. But when a state perpetrated crimes against humanity upon its own population, it would forfeit its claim to represent them and open itself to international intervention. The right of states to rule in their own territories would cease to be absolute; rather, it would be like a license, valid in almost all circumstances but revocable in limited and extreme cases, to be defined by stringent and well-known principles.

In this shift, the rights of states would not be eliminated in favor of the rights of individuals, thereby opening the floodgates of unlimited intervention; rather, the rights of states would partially yield to the rights of nations—that is, of peoples—whose right of self-determination would remain untouched, and might at times be supported by intervention from without. When Slobodan Milosevic sought to forestall intervention against his genocidal campaign in Kosovo, he invoked sovereignty. In response, the international community could only argue circuitously that his crimes within his own borders were a "threat to peace." A simpler and stronger answer would have been, "In what sense can you call yourself the sovereign representative of a people that you are seeking to destroy? Your genocide nullifies your sovereignty."

Stopping crimes against humanity would be a new vocation for the international community, which has generally looked the other way when such crimes have occurred. Not until very recent times has the concept of collective rights made headway. An enforced prohibition of genocide, based on the conviction that the international community can no more tolerate the murder of one of its peoples than national communities can tolerate the murder of a person, would meet this welcome trend coming the other way. It would be a sheet anchor for the collective rights of peoples. (It is obvious, however, that enforcement even of this limited principle faces large obstacles. It is one thing, for example, to bring the former leader of a small, weak state, such as Serbia, to book for his crimes. It would be quite another to do the same to the leader of a large powerful state, such as Russia or the United States.)

Once established, collective rights might, over the long run, take their place as elements of a grand bargain, a new settlement of the rights, powers, and obligations of the individual, states, nations, and the international community. In such a settlement, the rights of peoples would be increasingly protected by a coherent body of law. Most important, peoples would possess the negative right not to be extinguished. They would possess in addition the positive right to self-determination. This right, while recognized in law, would be guaranteed chiefly by each people's own powers of resistance—powers whose effectiveness were put on such stunning display in the anti-imperial independence movements of the twentieth century—and only secondarily by limited collective assistance from the international community. The right would be understood as belonging, in the last analysis, to nations rather than to their governments. On the other hand, even when thus properly located, it would not be absolute—not be, that is, sovereign.

A commitment to stop crimes against humanity is a natural corollary to a program that demands nuclear abolition, fosters democracy, and delaminates sovereignty. The required shift in principle would look beyond states to peoples, in whom the roots of political legitimacy would be acknowledged. The principle would also apply to the nuclear threat, whereby not only every people but the human species as a whole has been placed at risk of extinction. The doctrine of deterrence, which "assures" the safety of one people from nuclear attack at the hands of another by menacing both with annihilation, is—described without hyperbole—a policy of retaliatory genocide. Adoption of this policy was the destination to which the great powers, once they had failed to agree on the abolition of nuclear weapons in 1946, were to a certain extent helplessly driven by the logic of the war system in which they were entangled. Nevertheless, it is inescapable that carrying out genocide in the event of nuclear attack is the heart of the policy. One of the deepest and most important consequences of a prohibition of genocide would be a prohibition of the policy of nuclear deterrence.

A Democratic League

Even as the main structures of coercive power are gradually being retired from use, structures of cooperative power must gradually be built up. One of these would be the foundation of a democratic league, designed to foster and build upon the peaceful proclivities already found in the core of the democratic process. It is true that the power of democratic states to promote democracy outside their own borders is, by the nature of democracy, limited. States cannot create democracies; only peoples can, through their actions and consent. (On the other hand, states are perfectly capable of creating dictatorships, which rule by force over unconsenting peoples.) Nevertheless, democratic states can give assistance to one another or to peoples already seeking to found or preserve democracy. Such assistance would be strengthened by the foundation of an alliance made up of the democratic countries of the world.

The idea first appears in history in the fourth century B.C., when the Athenian statesman Arata, facing a threat to Greece from Philip of Macedon, who was making common cause with autocratic Greek city-states, founded an alliance of the democratic city-states. Whereas Arata's ultimate objective was to win a war, the purpose today would be to preserve and strengthen democracy where it exists, to give it support where it is struggling to come into existence, and, most important, to jointly curb and correct the warlike and imperial tendencies that historically have accompanied the rise of this form of government and forestalled its potential contributions to peace. Such was precisely the purpose of Kant's proposal of a "peaceful union" of republics, which would "gradually spread further and further by a series of alliances."

The main alliances in which the democracies now are involved present an anomalous picture. They are founded on every possible principle but democracy itself. The Clinton administration participated in the establishment of a Community of Democracies devoted to some of these purposes, but, though it now counts 110 nations among its members, it has yet to become a major forum for foreign policy decisions or international policy. NATO is an alliance made up entirely of democracies, but its purpose is strictly military. The central obligation of the treaty—to come to the defense of any member who is attacked—depends in no way on the character of the regimes involved. In the absence of the Soviet Union, whose advance into the center of Europe at the end of the Second World War prompted the alliance's creation, the need even for this pledge of mutual assistance is unclear. The only war in NATO's history—the campaign to drive Serbian forces out of Kosovo—did not involve an attack on a member.

The European Union is another alliance made up of democracies. (It was not until 2001 that the Organization of American States adopted a "democratic charter.") Founded originally to foreclose a military danger—recurrence of war among the nations of Europe—it has evolved over the decades into an organization in which economic concerns predominate. Recently, the European nations have been asking themselves what political and military functions the union might also assume. Although the union has led to many remarkable and hopeful political innovations, including the European Parliament, the European Commission, and the European Court of Human Rights, its boldest initiatives, culminating in the launch of the euro, have so far been commercial. In consequence, when the time came for the West to embrace the newborn democracies in Eastern Europe in the wake of the Soviet collapse, the chief consideration was not the strength of their commitment to democracy but the weakness of their economies. Blocked by this economic hurdle from "joining Europe"—a phrase often used in the broad sense of joining the now-democratic system of the West through joining the E.U.—Poland, Hungary, and the Czech Republic took the easier step of joining NATO. Had a democratic league existed at the time, it would have provided all the Eastern European countries with a way to "join Europe" that was appropriate to the new situation (the end of Soviet rule and the foundation of democracy); that was possible (no economic hurdle would have stood in the way); and that was inoffensive to Russia. Not until 2002 was the decision to invite these countries into the E.U. finally made. A democratic league would also serve to bind the Atlantic community by a tie that really should continue to bind it; namely, a commitment to freedom. The military glue that binds NATO is weakening in the absence of an enemy; and the economic glue of the E.U., although strong, tends in many areas to divide the Europeans from other democracies in the world. A democratic league, on the other hand, would possess a clear, positive, common purpose that NATO lacks—adherence, irrespective of wealth or geographic boundaries, to democracy.

The qualifications for joining the league would of course be observance of exacting standards of democratic governance and human rights. No state that failed to meet the standards could join; any state that departed from them would be subject to sanctions or expulsion. The league's requirements would give expression to the strong interest that every democratic country has in the preservation of democracy elsewhere in the world. The democratic character of all the states involved would also make supranational institutions among them far easier to establish than they are at the United Nations, where dictatorships have equal voice with democracies in votes on human rights. Juridical and legislative institutions of restricted scope could be added to executive ones. The European Convention on Human Rights, which established the European Court of Human Rights, and gives that court jurisdiction over human-rights violations within member states, could be a model— as could the European Parliament, whose members are directly elected, giving limited expression to an all-European public opinion.

The simplest and most obvious direct contribution that such a league could make to international peace would be to pledge to resolve disputes among its members without recourse to war, thus formalizing the historically demonstrated inclination of democracies to remain at peace among themselves. A vow by democratic Finland not to attack democratic India and vice versa would perhaps not be the end of history, yet the creation of a large body of nations in all parts of the earth that, both formally and actually, had renounced war in their mutual relations would provide a powerful example and, over time, perhaps a direction for the world as a whole.

Natural corollaries would be a commitment by the league to support the elimination of weapons of mass destruction, to steadily reduce the sale of conventional arms to other countries, and to devote its resources to restraining or ending wars of self-determination wherever it could.

Far more important and difficult would be a commitment to checking the aggressive tendencies that, in modern as in ancient times, have constituted the brutal, exploitive side of many democracies' relations with the rest of the world. The most serious and lasting contribution of a democratic league would be to choose democracy over imperialism once and for all. In order to be worthy of the name, a democratic league must be an anti-imperial league. Member nations would jointly resolve not to create or support repressive regimes, not to use armed force merely to advance commercial or other national interests, and in general to address international problems on a cooperative basis. A democratic league that sought to keep the peace among its own members even as it fostered aggressive ambitions in the world would destroy its own purpose.

Merely to state such goals, however, is once again to throw into distressing relief the policies of the one democracy in the world that today threatens to make the fearful transition from republic to empire, the United States. It is hard to know which is the greater tragedy—that, as the twenty-first century begins, the United States approaches the world with a drawn imperial sword, or that it discredits and disables its rich and in many ways unique republican traditions, which, especially in their treatment of sovereignty, offer many useful starting points for the new forms of international cooperation, peacemaking, and peacekeeping that the world so badly needs.

The Unconquerable World

Fifty-eight years after Hiroshima, the world has to decide whether to continue on the path of cataclysmic violence charted in the twentieth century and now resumed in the twenty-first or whether to embark on a new, cooperative political path. It is a decision composed of innumerable smaller decisions guided by a common theme, which is weaning politics off violence. Some of the needful decisions are already clear; others will present themselves along the way. The steps just outlined are among the most obvious.

I have chosen them not merely because their enactment would be desirable. They represent an attempt to respond to the perils and dangers of this era as it really is, by building on foundations that already exist. For even as nuclear arms and the other weapons of mass destruction have already produced the bankruptcy of violence in its own house, political events both earthshaking and minute have revealed the existence of a force that can substitute for violence throughout the political realm. The cooperative power of nonviolent action is new, yet its roots go deep into history, and it is now tightly woven, as I hope I have shown in these pages, into the life of the world. It has already altered basic realities that everyone must work with, including the nature of sovereignty, force, and political power. In the century ahead it can be our bulwark and shield against the still unmastered peril of total violence.

In our age of sustained democratic revolution, the power that governments inspire through fear remains under constant challenge by the power that flows from people's freedom to act in behalf of their interests and beliefs. Whether one calls this power cooperative power or something else, it has, with the steady widening and deepening of the democratic spirit, over and over bent great powers to its will. Its point of origin is the heart and mind of each ordinary person. It can flare up suddenly and mightily but gutter out with equal speed, unless it is channeled and controlled by acts of restraint. It is generated by social work as well as political activity. In the absence of popular participation, it simply disappears. Its chief instrument is direct action, both noncooperative and constructive, but it is also the wellspring of the people's will in democratic nations. It is not an all-purpose "means" with which any "end" can be pursued. It cannot be "projected," for its strength declines in proportion to its distance from its source; it is a local plant, rooted in home soil. It is therefore mighty on the defensive, feeble on the offensive, and toxic to territorial empires, all of which, in our time, have died. It stands in the way of any future imperial scheme, American or other. This power can be spiritual in inspiration but doesn't have to be. Its watchwords are love and freedom, yet it is not just an ideal but a real force in the world. In revolution it is decisive. Allied with violence, it may accomplish immense things but then overthrow itself; tempered by restraint it can burn indefinitely, like a lamp whose wick is trimmed, with a steady flame. Under the name of the will of the people it has dissolved the foundations first of monarchy and aristocracy and then of totalitarianism; as opinion, it has stood in judgment over democratically elected governments; as rebellious hearts and minds, it has broken the strength of powers engaged in a superannuated imperialism; as love of country, it has fueled the universally successful movement for self-determination but, gone awry, has fueled ethnic and national war and totalitarian rule, which soon suffocate it, though only temporarily. It now must be brought to bear on the choice between survival and annihilation. It is powerful because it sets people in motion, and fixes before their eyes what they are ready to live and die for. It is dangerous for the same reason. Whether combined with violence, as in people's war, sustained by a constitution, as in democracy, or standing alone, as in satyagraha or living in truth, it is becoming the final arbiter of the public affairs of our time and the political bedrock of our unconquerable world.

Notes

PAGE   INTRODUCTION: THE TOWERS AND THE WALL

1 *"As for success or":* Thucydides, *The History of the Peloponnesian War,* trans. Rex Warner (New York: Penguin, 1954), p. 116.

7 *"The submerged warrior":* John Keegan, *A History of Warfare* (New York: Knopf, 1993), p. 22.

8 *"Nothing which was being":* Hannah Arendt, *Imperialism* (New York: Harcourt, Brace & World, 1968), p. 147.

1. THE RISE AND FALL OF THE WAR SYSTEM

15 *"War is a true":* Carl von Clausewitz, *On War,* eds. Michael Howard and Peter Paret (Princeton, N.J.: Princeton University Press, 1976), p. 87.

16 *"something pointless and":* Ibid., p. 605.
    "War is an act": Ibid., p. 77.
    "The fact that slaughter": Ibid., p. 260.

17 *"the loser's scale falls":* Clausewitz, *On War,* p. 604.

18 *"loss of moral force":* J. F. C. Fuller, *The Conduct of War* (New York: Da Capo Press, 1982), p. 246.

"cannot be considered to": Clausewitz, *On War*, p. 90.

19 *"Rain can prevent a"*: Ibid., p. 120.

"a force appeared that": Ibid., p. 591.

"slowly, like a faint": Ibid., p. 589.

20 *"tendency toward the extreme"*: Ibid., p. 589.

"the great democratic revolution": Alexis de Tocqueville, *Democracy in America*, ed. and trans. Henry Reeve (New York: Schocken Books, 1961), p. lxviii.

"one fact [of] the": José Ortega y Gasset, *The Revolt of the Masses* (New York: W. W. Norton, 1932), p. 11.

21 *"The various occurrences of"*: Tocqueville, *Democracy in America*, p. lxxi.

"From this moment on": Simon Schama, *Citizens* (New York: Knopf, 1989), p. 762.

22 *"War, untrammeled by"*: Clausewitz, *On War*, p. 592.

Clausewitz has often been: For example, the British military historian B. H. Liddell Hart charged in 1931 that Clausewitz "had proclaimed the sovereign virtues of the will to conquer, the unique value of the offensive school carried out with unlimited violence by a nation in arms and the power of military action to override everything."

23 *"It is, of course"*: Clausewitz, *On War*, p. 605.

24 *"Is war not just"*: Ibid., p. 605.

"all proportion between": Ibid., p. 585.

"Were [war] a complete": Ibid., p. 87.

"the terrible battle-sword": Ibid., p. 606.

26 *"The natural solution soon"*: Ibid., p. 604.

"no conflict need arise": Ibid., p. 607.

29 *"The Great Powers were"*: A. J. P. Taylor, *The Struggle for the Mastery of Europe* (New York: Oxford University Press, 1954), p. xxiv.

30 *"She [Russia] was beaten"*: Bruce D. Porter, *War and the Rise of the State* (New York: Free Press, 1994), p. 227.

32 Charles Tilly, *"War made"*: Ibid., p. xix.

"must increase in size": Ibid., p. 59.

"The benefits of [scientific]": Francis Bacon, *Novum Organum* (New York: Modern Library, 1930), p. 85.

33   *On the bridge of:* Lewis Mumford, *The Pentagon of Power* (New York: Harcourt, Brace, Jovanovich, 1964), p. 119.

Tocqueville's word, "irresistible": Tocqueville's claim that the democratic revolution is "the most permanent tendency to be found in history" closely parallels Bacon's claim that scientific findings benefit "the whole race of men . . . through all time." When Tocqueville called the democratic revolution a "providential" fact, he was not making a theological point. He was reaching for the strongest possible metaphor to express the inexorability of the social phenomena he wished to describe. (His advice was that since you couldn't stop democracy, the wisest course was to guide and direct it as well as you could.)

34   *Brissot, who proclaimed:* Albert Mathiez, *The French Revolution* (New York: Knopf, 1928), p. 285.

"Tacticians could never": Jules Michelet, *The French Revolution,* trans. Charles Cooks (Chicago: University of Chicago Press, 1967), p. 328.

35   *"had no place for":* E. J. Hobsbawm, *Nations and Nationalism since 1780* (Cambridge: Cambridge University Press, 1990), p. 26.

36   *"I see in the":* Richard Cobden, *The Liberal Tradition,* eds. Alan Bullock and Maurice Shock (New York: Oxford University Press, 1956), p. 53.

Emerson declared that "trade": Liah Greenfeld, *Nationalism* (Cambridge, Mass.: Harvard University Press, 1992), p. 448.

37   *Between 1870 and 1900:* Walter La Feber, *The American Search for Opportunity 1865–1913* (Cambridge: Cambridge University Press, 1993), p. 85.

As late as 1890: Ronald Robinson and John Gallagher, *Africa and the Victorians* (New York: Anchor, 1968), p. 78.

38   *Lord Curzon spoke for:* Kenneth Rose, *Superior Person* (New York: Weybright & Talley, 1969), p. 229.

Lord Haldane, describing his: Barbara Tuchman, *The Guns of August* (New York: Dell, 1963), p. 72.

39   *An expedition of:* David Levering Lewis, *The Race to Fashoda* (New York: Weidenfeld & Nicolson, 1987), p. 3.

40   *Queen Victoria, ordinarily:* Thomas Pakenham, *The Scramble for Africa* (New York: Avon, 1991), p. 552.

France, lacking comparable naval: Ibid., p. 549.

41 *In a state paper:* George F. Kennan, *The Fateful Alliance* (New York: Pantheon, 1984), p. 268.

Therefore, once war had: Ibid., p. 264.

War against "all neighbors": Ibid., p. 265.

42 *The Russian foreign minister:* Ibid., p. 105.

And when General: Ibid., p. 95.

The war that now: Ibid., p. 253.

43 *"The war's political objects":* John Keegan, *A History of Warfare* (New York: Knopf, 1993), p. 21.

"of forgetting that force": Kennan, *Fateful Alliance,* p. 254.

45 *"Through a blur of":* J. B. S. Haldane, as quoted in Freeman Dyson, *Weapons and Hope* (New York: Harper & Row, 1984), p. 122.

2. "NUCLEAR WAR"

47 *As early as 1952:* McGeorge Bundy, *Danger and Survival* (New York: Random House, 1988), p. 235.

At the height of: Michael Beschloss, *The Crisis Years* (New York: HarperCollins, 1991), p. 87.

51 *He wrote, "Thus far":* Jonathan Schell, *The Abolition* (New York: Knopf, 1984), p. 42.

52 *"The decision by arms":* Carl von Clausewitz, *On War,* eds. Michael Howard and Peter Paret (Princeton, N.J.: Princeton University Press, 1976), p. 97.

53 *"The essence of the":* Lawrence Freedman, *The Evolution of Nuclear Strategy* (London: Macmillan, 1981), pp. 397–99.

54 *stated, "We will not":* Aleksandr Fursenko and Timothy Naftali, *One Hell of a Gamble* (New York: W. W. Norton, 1997), p. 246.

In 1960, for example: Beschloss, *Crisis Years,* p. 65.

55 *In August of 1961:* Fursenko and Naftali, *Hell of a Gamble,* p. 138.

On one occasion: Beschloss, *Crisis Years,* p. 244.

In a speech delivered: Ibid., p. 330.

56 *He was led to:* Ibid., p. 523.

57 *Acheson counseled that:* Bundy, *Danger and Survival,* p. 375.

"The most ardent and": Ibid., p. 376.

58 *But, Kennedy explained:* Ibid., p. 452.

59 *We may suspect that:* Beschloss, *Crisis Years,* p. 446.

60 *When the Soviet ambassador:* Ibid., p. 547.

61 *McNamara answered, "I am":* Bundy, *Danger and Survival,* p. 448.

3. People's War

66 *Their philosophy in the:* John A. Hobson, *Imperialism* (Ann Arbor: University of Michigan Press, Ann Arbor Paperbacks, 1971), p. 123.

Or, as Kipling: Richard Koebner and Helmut Dan Schmidt, *Imperialism* (Cambridge and London: Cambridge University Press, 1964), p. 216.

69 *The rebellion blazed most:* J. Christopher Herold, *The Age of Napoleon* (Boston: Houghton Mifflin, 1963), p. 217.

"No supreme command had": Ibid., p. 218.

"Clearly, the tremendous": Carl von Clausewitz, *On War,* eds. Michael Howard and Peter Paret (Princeton, N.J.: Princeton University Press, 1976), p. 609.

70 *"The military art on":* Ibid., p. 610.

"It follows that the": Ibid.

71 *The renowned military writer:* Walter Laqueur, *Guerrilla* (New York: Little, Brown, 1976), p. 109.

The experience left Jomini: Ibid., p. 109.

"All action is undertaken": Clausewitz, *On War,* p. 97.

Yet a French captain: Robert B. Asprey, *War in the Shadows* (New York: William Morrow, 1994), p. 97.

72 *"a book of wisdom":* Ibid., p. 87.

The Spanish guerrilla leader: Laqueur, *Guerrilla,* p. 40.

And a Prussian officer: Ibid., p. 40.

The superior importance: Harry B. Summers, *On Strategy* (San Francisco, Calif.: Presidio Press, 1982), p. 89.

73 *"the days of guerrilla wars":* Laqueur, *Guerrilla,* p. 98.

74 *"in no other period":* Leonard Woolf, *Imperialism and Civilization* (New York: Garland Publishing, 1971), p. 12.

76 *"Suddenly the whole black":* Winston Churchill, *The River War* (London: New English Library, 1973), pp. 249–50.

"about twenty shells": Ibid., p. 263.

"The range was short": Ibid., p. 268.

77 *"They fired steadily and":* Ibid., p. 264.

When it was over: Karl de Schweinitz, Jr., *The Rise and Fall of British India* (London: Methuen, 1983), p. 242.

"extraordinary miscalculation of": Churchill, *The River War,* p. 264.

"For I hope": Winston S. Churchill, *The River War: An Historical Account of the Reconquest of Soudan* (London: Longmans, Green & Co., 1899), p. 162.

78 *In the battle of:* C. E. Carrington, *The British Overseas* (Cambridge: Cambridge University Press, 1968), p. 319.

At the battle: Ibid., p. 165.

In 1865, in Tashkent: V. G. Kiernan, *From Conquest to Collapse* (New York: Pantheon, 1982), p. 63.

"a Royal Niger Co.": Daniel R. Headrick, *The Tools of Empire* (Oxford: Oxford University Press, 1981), p. 8.

"The remnant simply turned": Kiernan, *Conquest to Collapse,* p. 71.

79 *"We are still":* Mao Zedong, *Selected Works,* 2 vols. (London: Lawrence & Wishart, 1954), 2: 168.

"a powerful imperialist country": Ibid., 2: 167.

80 *Mao never tired of:* Asprey, *War in the Shadows,* p. 255.

And the most famous: Ibid.

82 *"the more enduring the":* Mao, *Selected Works,* 2: 177.

"the whole party must": Ibid., 2: 270.

"It can therefore": Ibid., 2: 20.

83 *"China's weapons are":* Ibid., 2: 159.

84 *Mao rejected the idea:* Asprey, *War in the Shadows,* p. 254.

86 *"Politics forms the":* quoted in Jonathan Schell, *The Real War* (New York: Pantheon, 1988), p. 16.

"Our political struggle": quoted in Douglas Pike, *Viet Cong* (Cambridge, Mass.: M.I.T. Press, 1966), p. 106.

87 *"The purpose of this":* Pike, *Viet Cong,* p. 111.

"in the effective control": Bernard Fall, *The Two Vietnams* (New York: Praeger, 1967), p. 133.

"the existence of guerrilla": Ibid.

88 *"the 'kill' aspect":* Bernard Fall, *Last Reflections on a War* (New York: Doubleday, 1967), p. 210.

"This is where": Ibid., p. 221.

89 *De Gaulle remarked that:* Laqueur, *Guerrilla,* p. 294.

90 *In the words of:* Neil Sheehan, *A Bright and Shining Lie* (New York: Random House, 1988), p. 631.

91 *"Their missile power":* quoted in Lawrence Freedman, *The Evolution of Nuclear Strategy* (London: Macmillan, 1981), p. 230.

92 *It would lead to:* A. J. Langguth, *Our Vietnam* (New York: Simon & Schuster, 2000), p. 371.

96 *When Richard Nixon:* Ibid., p. 514.

After Tet, in the: Schell, *The Real War,* p. 30.

4. SATYAGRAHA

104 *They believed, with Max:* Gene Sharp, *Gandhi as a Political Strategist* (Boston: Porter-Sargeant Publishers, Extending Horizons Books, 1979), p. 240.

"force without right": John Locke, *The Second Treatise on Government* (New York: Macmillan, 1952), p. 13.

"in all states and": Ibid., p. 88.

"becomes a case of": Edmund Burke, *Reflections on the Revolution in France* (New York: Anchor, 1973), p. 42.

At the beginning of: J. Christopher Herold, *The Age of Napoleon* (Boston: Houghton Mifflin, 1963), p. 37.

"Violence is the midwife": Karl Marx, *Capital* (New York: Modern Library, 1959), p. 824.

105 *The leader of the:* Merle Fainsod, *How Russia Is Ruled* (Cambridge, Mass.: Harvard University Press, 1963), p. 135.

In a still broader: Adam Ulam, *The Bolsheviks* (New York: Macmillan, 1992), p. 455.

Lenin sneered at: Martin Green, *The Challenge of the Mahatmas* (New York: Basic Books, 1978), p. 85.

And Max Weber: Bruce D. Porter, *War and the Rise of the State* (New York: Free Press, 1994), p. 303.

"All greatness, all power": quoted in Isaiah Berlin, *The Crooked Timber of Humanity* (New York: Knopf, 1991), p. 117.

107 *On a train from:* Stanley Wolpert, *Gandhi's Passion* (New York: Oxford University Press, 2001), p. 35.

His colleagues at dinner: Mohandas K. Gandhi, *Essential Writings,* ed. V. V. Ramana Murti (New Delhi: Gandhi Peace Foundation, 1970), p. 39.

108 *"I arose with the":* quoted in Joan Bondurant, *The Conquest of Violence* (Princeton, N.J.: Princeton University Press, 1958), p. 155.

109 *"I clearly saw that":* Mohandas K. Gandhi, *The Selected Works of Mahatma Gandhi,* ed. Shriman Narayan, 6 vols. (Ahmedabad, India: Navajivan Publishing House, 1968), 3: 135.

In 1858, Queen Victoria: Mohandas K. Gandhi, *The Moral and Political Writings of Mahatma Gandhi,* ed. Raghavan Iyer, 3 vols. (Oxford: Clarendon Press, 1986–87), 3: 278.

"The Empire has been": Mohandas Karamchand Gandhi, *The Collected Works of Mahatma Gandhi,* 100 vols. (New Delhi: Publications Division, Ministry of Information and Broadcasting. Government of India, 1999), 4: 302. The edition of the Collected Works cited here may also be found on the CD "Mahatma Gandhi" produced by the Publications Division, Patiala House, Tilak Marg, New Delhi.

110 *"By her large heart":* Ibid., 4: 293.

"We are all fired": Ibid., 2: 325.

an "empty boast": Gandhi, *Moral and Political Writings,* 1: 291.

He denounced "the invention": Ibid., 1: 288.

111 *"The English honor only":* Gandhi, *Collected Works,* 5: 384.

112 *"No one ever imagined":* Ibid., 4: 312.

"When Japan's brave": Ibid., 8: 405.

"unity, patriotism and": Ibid., 4: 313.

"overwhelmed" by it: Gandhi, *Essential Writings,* p. 55.

"to conquer that hatred": Gandhi, *Collected Works,* 2: 433.

113 *"fearless girls, actuated":* Ibid., 5: 327.

"This time they have": Ibid., 5: 8.

114 *"could not live both":* Ibid., 44: 326.

"How was one to": Ibid., 44: 287.

115 *"Like Arjun, they":* Ibid.

Of his pursuit of: Judith M. Brown, *Gandhi* (New Haven: Yale University Press, 1989), p. 83.

"For God appears": Erik H. Erikson, *Dimensions of a New Identity* (New York: Norton, 1974), p. 44.

116 *As he began a:* Sharp, *Gandhi as a Political Strategist,* p. 49.

118 *"would spell absolute ruin":* Gandhi, *Selected Works,* 3: 135.
"I could read in": Ibid., 3: 140.
"a man who lightly": Ibid., 3: 144.

119 *"that some new principle":* Gandhi, *Collected Works,* 1: xi.
"The foundation of the": Gandhi, *Essential Writings,* p. 440.

120 *"dictate to the colonies":* quoted in Gandhi, *Collected Works,* 4: 208.
"I have now got": Gandhi, *Collected Works,* 10: 184.

121 *The nineteenth-century British:* J. F. C. Fuller, *Military History of the Western World,* 3 vols. (New York: Da Capo Press, 1955), 2: 240.
Chen Duxiu, a moderate: Jonathan Spence, *The Search for Modern China* (New York: W. W. Norton, 1990), p. 315.

122 *"different sections of ONE":* Gandhi, *Collected Works,* 4: 313.
"This civilization is": Gandhi, *Moral and Political Writings,* 1: 214.

123 *"The condition of England":* Ibid., 1: 209.
"bad men [to] fulfil": Ibid., 1: 220.
"neither real honesty nor": Ibid., 1: 211.
was "a prostitute": Gandhi, *Collected Works,* 10: 256.
"nine-days' wonder": Ibid., 10: 58.
"The tendency of the": Gandhi, *Moral and Political Writings,* 1: 233.
"It is . . . fitting that": Vivekananda, *The Yogas and Other Works,* ed. Swami Nikhilananda (New York: Ramakrishna-Vivekananda Center, 1953), p. 698.

124 *"My countrymen . . . believe":* Gandhi, *Essential Writings,* p. 440.
In the words of: Erik H. Erikson, *Gandhi's Truth* (New York: W. W. Norton, 1969), p. 265.

125 *"East and West are":* Gandhi, *Collected Works,* 8: 211.
"Suppose Indians wish": Gandhi, *Essential Writings,* p. 8.
"The Whites were fully": Ibid., p. 49.

126 *"You [British] have great":* Mahatma Gandhi, *Hind Swaraj and Other Writings,* ed. Anthony Parel (Cambridge: Cambridge University Press, 1997), p. 114.

127   *"They came to our"*: Gandhi, *Collected Works*, 10: 256.

    "It is because the": Gandhi, *Essential Writings*, p. 179.

128   *For instance, the:* Peter Duvall Ackerman, *A Force More Powerful* (New York: St. Martin's Press, 2000), p. 11.

    "The sultan of Egypt": quoted in Maurizio Passerin d'Entreves, *The Notion of the State* (Oxford: Clarendon Press, 1967), p. 196.

    "All governments rest": James Madison, Alexander Hamilton, and John Jay, *The Federalist Papers*, No. 49 (London: Penguin Classics, 1987), p. 314.

129   *"I believe and everybody"*: quoted in Sharp, *Gandhi as a Political Strategist*, p. 11.

    "The causes that gave": Gandhi, *Moral and Political Writings*, 1: 216.

    it was "by the": Philip Curtin, *Imperialism* (New York: Harper & Row, 1971), p. 293.

130   *"it is an intensely"*: Gandhi, *Essential Writings*, p. 99.

    "It is better to": quoted in Bondurant, *Conquest of Violence*, p. 28.

    "I am not built": Raghavan Iyer, *The Moral and Political Thought of Mahatma Gandhi* (New York: Oxford University Press, 1973), p. 10.

    "Never has anything": Mohandas K. Gandhi, *Non-violent Resistance* (New York: Schocken, 1951), p. 110.

    "There is no love": quoted in Ved Mehta, *Gandhi and His Disciples* (New York: Viking Press, 1976), p. 183.

131   *"Another remedy [to injustice]"*: Gandhi, *Essential Writings*, p. 99.

    "A new order of": quoted in Erikson, *Gandhi's Truth*, p. 338.

132   *"Nonviolence is without"*: Gandhi, *Essential Writings*, p. 136.

    "The practice of ahimsa": Ibid., p. 137.

133   *"To be incapable of"*: Friedrich Nietzsche, *On the Genealogy of Morals,* trans. Walter Kaufmann and R. J. Hollinsdale (New York: Vintage, 1967), p. 39.

134   *That, at least, was:* Martin Green, *The Origins of Nonviolence* (State College, Penn.: Pennsylvania State University Press, 1976), p. 35.

    "Through deliverance of India": Gandhi, *Essential Writings*, p. 226.

135   *"A series of passive"*: quoted in Wolpert, *Gandhi's Passion*, p. 96.

"the search for a": Brown, *Gandhi*, p. 121.

"I can as well": quoted in Brown, *Gandhi*, p. 122.

136 *"the greatest battle of"*: quoted in Wolpert, *Gandhi's Passion*, p. 99.

"In the place I": quoted in Brown, *Gandhi*, p. 132.

"All of us should": quoted in Wolpert, *Gandhi's Passion*, p. 114.

137 *In a campaign of*: Wolpert, *Gandhi's Passion*, p. 151.

On the other hand: Brown, *Gandhi*, p. 359.

139 *"Satyagraha is not"*: quoted in Bondurant, *Conquest of Violence*, p. v.

"To me," the reader: Gandhi, *Essential Writings*, p. 259.

140 *"Constructive effort is the"*: Ibid.

"One must forget the": Ibid., p. 274.

"Where do congratulations come": quoted in Green, *Challenge of the Mahatma*, p. 29.

141 *"exact proportion" to success*: Iyer, *Moral and Political Writings*, 1: 306.

"When a body of": Gandhi, *Essential Writings*, p. 33.

"English rule without": Gandhi, *Hind Swaraj*, p. 205.

England as "pitiable": Ibid., p. 237.

"Not only could swaraj": quoted in Brown, *Gandhi*, p. 67.

"Do men conceive": Gandhi, *Essential Writings*, p. 254.

5. NONVIOLENT REVOLUTION, NONVIOLENT RULE

144 *"If one thousand"*: Henry David Thoreau, *The Annotated Walden; Or Life in the Woods*, ed. Philip Van Dorenstern (New York: Clarkson N. Potter, 1970), p. 465.

146 *"It was true that"*: Thomas Babington Macaulay, *The History of England* (London: Penguin Classics, 1986), p. 272.

"That prompt obedience": Ibid.

"The material strength of": Thomas Babington Macaulay, *The History of England*, 2 vols. (New York: Dutton, 1966), 2: 267.

Unfortunately for James: Ibid., 2: 263.

147 *"That great force"*: Ibid., 2: 384.

"No encounter of the": George Macaulay Trevelyan, *The English Revolution, 1688–89* (New York: Oxford University Press, 1938), p. 117.

"William of Orange": J. G. A. Pocock, "The Revolution of 1688–89: Changing Perspectives," in *The Varieties of British Political Thought*, ed. Lois G. Showerer (Cambridge: Cambridge University Press, 1993), p. 55.

148 *"The King . . . had greatly":* Macaulay, *History of England*, 1: 578.

149 *"Sir, if your Majesty":* Ibid., 1: 126.
      "The minister who had": Ibid., 1: 209.
      "Actuated by these": Ibid., 1: 238.

150 *"His only chance of":* Ibid., 2: 284.

151 *"No jurist, no divine":* Ibid., 2: 319.
      "For call himself what": Ibid., 2: 320.

152 *"To him she was":* Ibid., 2: 16.
      "power enough to bring": Stephen B. Baxter, *William III, and the Defense of European Liberty* (New York: Harcourt, Brace, 1966), p. 234.

153 *"The Revolution gave":* Trevelyan, *The English Revolution*, p. 240.

154 *"There is no way":* Pocock, "The Revolution of 1688–89," p. 61.
      "For twenty years": quoted in Trevelyan, *The English Revolution*, p. 105.
      "What happened was": Trevelyan, *The English Revolution*, p. 106.

155 *"In 1689, both":* Pocock, "The Revolution of 1688–89," p. 202.
      As the conservative Burke: Ibid.
      "Never, within the memory": Macaulay, *History of England*, p. 279.

156 *"The appeal to heaven":* Pocock, "The Revolution of 1688–89," p. 61.
      George Washington hinted at: Page Smith, *A New Age Now Begins*, 2 vols. (New York: McGraw Hill, 1976), 2: 1,664.

157 *"We may be beaten":* quoted in ibid., 2: 1,826.

158 *" 'Tis not in numbers":* quoted in John Keane, *Tom Paine* (Boston: Little, Brown, 1995), p. 121.
      "In the unlikely": Ibid., p. 146.
      "Rulers can rule": Ibid., p. 121.
      As the British general: Conor Cruise O'Brien, *The Great Melody* (Chicago: University of Chicago Press, 1992), p. 155.

"If nothing but force": quoted in ibid., p. 159.

159 *"Do you imagine":* Edmund Burke, *Selected Writings* (New York: Random House, 1960), p. 175.

160 *"confine himself to military":* John Adams, *The Works of John Adams,* vol. 10 (Boston: Little, Brown, 1956), p. 85.
"A history of the": Ibid., p. 180.
"General Wilkinson may": Ibid.
"As to the history": Ibid., p. 172.

161 *"The cool, calm":* Ibid., p. 197.
"It will be": Ibid., p. 253.
"the real American revolution": Ibid., p. 283.
"What an engine!": Ibid., p. 197.

162 *"Let me ask you":* Ibid., p. 159.
"The royal governors stood": Gordon S. Wood, *The Creation of the American Republic* (New York: W. W. Norton, 1972), p. 314.
"For if, as Jefferson": Ibid., p. 132.

163 *"The Union is much":* quoted in Mario M. Cuomo, *Lincoln on Democracy* (New York: HarperCollins, 1990), p. 204.
"Heaven decided in our": Adams, *Works,* p. 159.

6. THE MASS MINORITY IN ACTION: FRANCE AND RUSSIA

165 *"French soldiers are not":* quoted in Simon Schama, *Citizens* (New York: Vintage, 1990), p. 371.
The King's cavalry: Ibid., p. 380.
"The bastille was not": Jules Michelet, *The French Revolution* (Chicago: University of Chicago Press, 1967), p. 176.

166 *"Shame for such cowardly":* Ibid., p. 177.
"Good is grapeshot": Thomas Carlyle, *The French Revolution* (New York: Oxford University Press, 1989), p. 179.
"The French revolution": quoted in Carl Becker, *The Declaration of Independence* (New York: Vintage, 1942), p. 30.

169 *When it was suggested:* Richard Pipes, *The Russian Revolution* (New York: Vintage, 1991), p. 472.
"In times of revolution": quoted in ibid., p. 358.

170 *"No matter how important":* quoted in Isaac Deutscher, *The Prophet Armed* (New York: Oxford University Press, 1954), p. 156.

"a sort of fabulous": N. N. Sukhanov, *The Russian Revolution, 1917* (New York: Oxford University Press, 1955), p. 74.

"A whole world of": quoted in Pipes, *Russian Revolution*, p. 336.

171 *"the decisive revolutionary"*: Martin Malia, *The Soviet Tragedy* (New York: Free Press, 1994), p. 90.

172 *"After the February"*: Leon Trotsky, *The History of the Russian Revolution* (Ann Arbor, Mich.: University of Michigan Press, 1957), p. 131.

"We can (if we": quoted in Pipes, *Russian Revolution*, p. 472.

173 *The Bolsheviks had "no"*: Trotsky, *Russian Revolution*, p. 154.

The Party, they observed: Ibid., p. 159.

"eliminate the mass": quoted in Deutscher, *The Prophet Armed*, p. 334.

174 *So important did Trotsky:* Pipes, *Russian Revolution*, p. 479.

"full support in all": Ibid., p. 487.

"On October 21": Sukhanov, *Russian Revolution*, p. 583.

175 *"War had been declared"*: Ibid., p. 592.

"three hundred volunteers": Ibid., p. 589.

"This, to put it": Ibid., p. 592.

176 *"He, Trotsky," would:* Ibid., p. 596.

"declaration of October 23": Trotsky, *Russian Revolution*, p. 118.

"We don't know of": Sukhanov, *Russian Revolution*, p. 627.

"The unique thing about": Trotsky, *Russian Revolution*, pp. 181–82.

177 *"This does not mean"*: Ibid., p. 181.

"Only an armed": Ibid., p. 87.

178 *"The final act of"*: Ibid., p. 232.

In despair at what: Pipes, *Russian Revolution*, p. 490.

179 *"And now we are"*: quoted in Sukhanov, *Russian Revolution*, p. 639.

180 *"had been their own"*: Sukhanov, *Russian Revolution*, p. 529.

181 *"lavish with promises"*: Ibid.

"The October revolution": quoted in Trotsky, *Russian Revolution*, p. 232.

"At the end of": Trotsky, *Russian Revolution*, p. 294.

"As a matter of": Ibid., p. 232.

The Social Revolutionary Party: Pipes, *Russian Revolution,* p. 543.

184   *"the least bloody revolution":* quoted in Joachim Fest, *Hitler* (New York: Harcourt, Brace & Jovanovich, 1973), p. 447.

7. Living in Truth

187   *"A wall is a":* quoted in Michael Beschloss, *The Crisis Years* (New York: HarperCollins, 1991), p. 278.

    "Never will we consent": Adam B. Ulam, *The Communists* (New York: Scribners, 1992), p. 309.

188   *"There was a special":* Nadezhda Mandelstam, *Hope Against Hope* (New York: Athenaeum, 1970), p. 48.

    "The terrifying thing": quoted in Jeffrey C. Isaac, *Arendt, Camus, and Modern Rebellion* (New Haven, Conn.: Yale University Press, 1992), p. 43.

190   *"hotbed out of which":* George Kennan, *Memoirs* (New York: Pantheon, 1967), p. 534.

    "Successful revolts on": Ibid., p. 533.

191   *"To believe in":* Adam Michnik, *Letters from Prison* (Berkeley: University of California Press, 1985), p. 142.

192   *"the Soviet military":* Ibid., p. 14.

    "It is impossible to": George Konrád, *Anti-Politics* (New York: Harcourt Brace Jovanovich, 1984), p. 70.

    "The morality of Yalta": Ibid., p. 2.

    "In the stalemated world": Václav Havel, *Living in Truth,* ed. Jan Vladislav (London: Faber & Faber, 1986), p. 37.

193   *"If we consider how":* Ibid., p. 111.

    "Defending the aims": Ibid., p. 89.

194   *"Society is produced by":* Thomas Paine, *Common Sense* (New York: Peter Eckler, 1998), p. 1.

    "I believe that what": Michnik, *Letters from Prison,* p. 144.

195   *"Why post-totalitarian?":* Adam Michnik, *Letters from Freedom* (Berkeley: University of California Press, 1998), p. 59.

196   *"We introduced a new":* Václav Havel, *Disturbing the Peace* (New York: Knopf, 1990), p. 83.

    Havel says, "individuals": Timothy Garton Ash, *The Uses of Adversity* (New York: Random House, 1989), p. 192.

"Individuals can be": Havel, *Living in Truth,* p. 57.

197 *"it must be declared":* Mohandas K. Gandhi, *Essential Writings,*
ed. V. V. Ramana Murti (New Delhi: Gandhi Peace Foundation,
1970), p. 225.
"People who so define": Havel, *Living in Truth,* p. 76.
"Under the orderly": Ibid., p. 57.

198 *In his scheme:* Konrád, *Anti-Politics,* p. 73.
"iceberg of power": Ibid., p. 145.
"Proletarian revolution didn't": Ibid., p. 73.

199 *"We were scared":* quoted in Ulam, *The Communists,* p. 104.
"Everything suddenly appears": Havel, *Living in Truth,* p. 59.

200 *The step beyond that:* Ash, *Uses of Adversity,* p. 195.

202 *"The struggle for state":* Michnik, *Letters from Prison,* p. 89.
"People who claim": Ibid., p. 86.

203 *"Before the violence":* Ibid., p. 87.
"My reflections on violence": Ibid., p. 106.
"a profound belief that": Havel, *Living in Truth,* p. 93.
"The political leadership": Konrád, *Anti-Politics,* p. 91.

205 *"which would be different":* Gandhi, *Essential Writings,* p. 49.

206 *"The world rests upon":* Mohandas K. Gandhi, *The Selected
Works of Mahatma Gandhi,* ed. Shriman Narayan, 6 vols. (Ahmed-
abad, India: Navajivan Publishing House, 1968), 2: 389.
"At the basis of": Havel, *Living in Truth,* pp. 137–38.

209 *"By the mid-1980s":* Mikhail Gorbachev, *Memoirs* (New York:
Doubleday, 1996), p. 349.

211 *"Necessity of the principle":* quoted in Archie Brown, *The Gorbachev Factor* (New York: Oxford University Press, 1996), p. 225.

213 *He declared, "Today":* John Morrison, *Boris Yeltsin, from Bolshevik to Democrat* (New York: Dutton, 1991), p. 222.

214 *"It was clear":* quoted in ibid., p. 143.

8. Cooperative Power

216 *"nauseating and humiliating":* Martin Green, *Challenge of the
Mahatmas* (New York: Basic Books, 1978), p. 122.
Upon hearing of the: Ibid.

218 *"violence and power are":* Hannah Arendt, *Violence* (New York:
Harcourt Brace Jovanovic), p. 56.

"Power and violence are": Ibid.

"the rule of men": quoted in ibid., p. 35.

"Power corresponds to": Ibid., p. 44.

"solemnly and mutually": Ibid., p. 172.

219 *"Democracy does not":* Alexis de Tocqueville, *Democracy in America* (New York: Schocken, 1961), p. 295.

220 *"Where power is not":* Hannah Arendt, *The Human Condition* (Chicago: University of Chicago Press, 1958), p. 200.

"To command and": Hannah Arendt, *On Violence* (New York: Harvest, 1970), p. 37.

"Power means every": Max Weber.

221 *"never the property of":* Arendt, *On Violence,* p. 44.

"In a head-on": Ibid., p. 37.

"While violence can": Arendt, *The Human Condition,* p. 202.

"Nowhere is the": Arendt, *On Violence,* pp. 54–55.

222 *"The climax of terror":* Ibid., p. 55.

"the head-on clash": Ibid., p. 53.

general "reversal in the": Ibid., p. 11.

223 *"the situation changes":* Ibid., pp. 48–49.

"Power is actualized": Arendt, *The Human Condition,* p. 200.

224 *"Gandhi's enormously powerful":* Arendt, *On Violence,* p. 53.

"Popular revolt against": Arendt, *The Human Condition,* p. 200.

225 *"taken as the spring":* Arendt, *On Revolution,* p. 89.

"Only in His strength": Mohandas Karamchand Gandhi, *Nonviolent Resistance,* ed. Bharatan Kumarappa (New York: Schocken, 1951), p. 364.

226 *"One is obtained by":* Raghavan N. Iyer, *The Moral and Political Thought of Mahatma Gandhi* (New York: Oxford University Press, 1986), p. 53.

228 *"What has made so":* Alexis de Tocqueville, *The Old Regime and the French Revolution* (New York: Anchor, 1969), p. 168.

"If God who is": quoted in Judith M. Brown, *Gandhi* (New Haven, Conn.: Yale University Press, 1989), p. 199.

"love and not fear": quoted in Gordon S. Wood, *The Creation of the American Republic* (New York: W. W. Norton, 1972), p. 67.

"love of the laws": Montesquieu, *The Spirit of the Laws* (Berkeley and Los Angeles: University of California Press, 1977), p. 130.

229 *"Men love at their":* Niccolò Machiavelli, *The Prince* (New York: Random House, Modern Library, 1950), p. 63.

"What is meant": John Stuart Mill, "Considerations on Representative Government," in *Utilitarianism,* ed. H. B. Acton (London: J. M. Dent & Sons, 1972), pp. 196–97.

230 *"a more powerful social":* Ibid., p. 197.

Power, according to: A more recent exposition of the power of opinion is the concept of "soft power," introduced by Joseph Nye, Dean of the Kennedy School of Government at Harvard. According to Nye, a nation's soft power, which he distinguishes from its "hard power" (which corresponds to coercive power), is the attractive pull of its best qualities—its culture, its ideology, its prosperity. "This aspect of power—getting others to want what you want—I call soft power," he writes. "It co-opts people rather than coerces them" (from Joseph Nye, *The Paradox of American Power* [New York: Oxford, 2002], p. 9). A difference between soft power and cooperative power is that whereas the first is generated by a single actor (whether a saint or a country) and belongs to that actor, the second, being a product of action in concert, in its nature can belong only to a group. However, the two are related. Cooperation depends on agreement, and agreement depends on the discovery of common ground. For example, the admiration that one country inspires in another—or that both feel for a common goal or principle—is the sine qua non of common ground. Thus does the "soft power" that countries exert upon one another lay a basis for action in concert, which is the foundation of cooperative power. It follows that it is just as important—though less remarked on—for the United States to find things to admire in other countries as for other countries to admire the United States. Mutual respect creates the opportunity for joint action—for cooperative power.

9. THE LIBERAL DEMOCRATIC REVIVAL

236 *He advocated a "civic":* Immanuel Kant, *On History,* ed. Lewis White Beck (Indianapolis, Ind.: Bobbs-Merrill, 1963), pp. 16–17.

237 *"The latent causes of":* James Madison, Alexander Hamilton, and

John Jay, *The Federalist Papers* (New York: Penguin, 1987), p. 124.

"If any two men": Thomas Hobbes, *Leviathan* (Cambridge: Cambridge University Press, 1996), p. 87.

"They are free": quoted in Orlando Patterson, *Freedom*, vol. 1 (New York: Basic Books, 1991), p. 93.

"He obeys the laws": Cicero, *On the Commonwealth*, trans. George Holland Sabine and Stanley Barney Smith (Columbus, Ohio: Bobbs-Merrill, Library of Liberal Arts, 1960), p. 55.

238   *"Liberty, or freedom":* Hobbes, *Leviathan*, p. 145.

239   *"No society can":* Raghavan N. Iyer, *The Moral and Political Thought of Mahatma Gandhi*, (New York: Oxford University Press, 1986) p. 351.

240   *"so foolish that they":* John Locke, *The Second Treatise on Government* (Indianapolis, Ind.: Hackett Publishing, 1980), p. 53.

243   *"They'll shoot us":* quoted in Taylor Branch, *Pillar of Fire* (New York: Simon & Schuster, 1999), p. 331.

244   *"Unearned suffering is":* quoted in Diane McWhorter, *Carry Me Home* (New York: Simon & Schuster, 2001), p. 154.

"the freest man on": quoted in ibid., p. 61.

"They can't enjoin": Ibid., p. 109.

245   *"I think we just":* quoted in Branch, *Pillar of Fire*, p. 94.

But because the deepest: King's radicalism emerged clearly in his opposition to the Vietnam War. Not content to rest on his laurels as an elder statesman of the highly successful civil-rights movement, he felt compelled in the late 1960s to apply his nonviolence in this new area against the very president—Lyndon B. Johnson—who had brought the civil-rights movement to legislative fruition.

246   *"We mean to kill":* quoted in McWhorter, *Carry Me Home*, p. 22.

"You know my friends": quoted in Taylor Branch, *Parting the Waters* (New York: Simon & Schuster, 1998), p. 140.

"If we are wrong": quoted in ibid.

247   *"Standing beside love":* Ibid.

Later he said: Ibid., p. 166.

When an officer: McWhorter, *Carry Me Home*, p. 228.

250   *In 1958, Prime Minister:* Bruce Ackerman and Jack Duvall, *A Force More Powerful* (New York: Palgrave, 2000), p. 357.

251   *the organization's black:* Anthony Sampson, *Mandela* (New York: Vintage, 1999), p. 89.
       "The attacks of the": quoted in ibid., p. 149.
       "I saw nonviolence": Ibid., p. 68.

252   *"Luthuli, Mandela and":* Ibid., p. 259.
       These, he said, would: Ackerman and Duvall, *Force More Powerful,* p. 345.
       Only then could they: Ibid., p. 347.

253   *The first to meet with:* Allister Sparks, *Tomorrow Is Another Country* (Chicago: University of Chicago Press, 1995), p. 24.
       "Mandela had become": Sampson, *Mandela,* p. 512.

254   *Mandela's friend Fatima:* Ibid., p. 68.
       "I'm just a sinner": quoted in ibid., p. 415.
       "the unselfconscious manifestation": Ibid., p. 546.
       "When one is faced": Ibid., p. 242.
       "Bitterness would be": Ibid., p. 406.
       "Courageous people do not": Ibid., p. 515.

255   *"the most predicted":* Ibid., p. 484.

259   *"If it is true":* Hannah Arendt, *The Origins of Totalitarianism* (New York: Harvest/Harcourt Brace Jovanovic, 1973), p. 460.
       "Our British colonizers": Arundhati Roy, *The Nation,* February 18, 2002.

261   *"Whoever wants to deprive":* Jean-Jacques Rousseau, *Political Writings* (Madison, Wisc.: Wisconsin University Press, 1986), p. 242.
       "If a democratical": Montesquieu, *The Spirit of the Laws* (Berkeley and Los Angeles: University of California Press, 1977), p. 193.
       "Imperialism and popular": John A. Hobson, *Imperialism* (Ann Arbor: University of Michigan Press, Ann Arbor Paperbacks, 1965), p. 150.
       "European civilization, with": Leonard Woolf, *Imperialism and Civilization* (New York: Garland Publishing, 1971), p. 34.

262   *"The two ideas of":* quoted in Philip D. Curtin, *Imperialism* (New York: Walker, 1971), p. 292.
       "a sea of vague": Hobson, *Imperialism,* p. 206.

263   *The decisive advantage:* Victor Davis Hanson, *Carnage and Culture* (New York: Doubleday, 2001), p. 48.

264   *"an exclusive Western monopoly":* Ibid., p. 252.
       rise to "universal dominion": Polybius, *The Rise of the Roman Empire,* ed. F. W. Walbank (London: Penguin, 1979), p. 42.
       "The veteran legions of": Madison, Hamilton, and Jay, *The Federalist Papers,* Article 1, Section 8, Clause 12, p. 268.

10. LIBERAL INTERNATIONALISM

266   *"busy with a scheme":* G. J. Renier, *William of Orange* (New York: D. Appleton, 1933), p. 84.

267   *When Jeremy Bentham:* Carlton J. Hayes, *The Historical Evolution of Modern Nationalism* (New York: Richard R. Smith, 1931), p. 131.
       Wasn't it "monstrous": Alan Bullock and Maurice Shock, *The Liberal Tradition* (Oxford: Oxford University Press, 1956), p. 158.

268   *"the passing of good":* quoted in ibid., pp. 177–76.
       To the intense indignation: Philip Magnus, *Gladstone* (New York: E. P. Dutton, 1964), p. 240.
       "What our duty is": quoted in ibid., p. 241.
       "There is not": Ibid., p. 242.

269   *"Fortresses may be":* quoted in Bullock and Shock, *Liberal Tradition,* p. xxxix.
       He proposed a strengthened: Ibid., p. 163.
       "Certain it is": quoted in Henry Kissinger, *Diplomacy* (New York: Simon & Schuster, 1994), p. 161.

270   *"Would the President propose":* Ibid., p. 223.

271   *Wilson intended to:* August Heckscher, *Woodrow Wilson* (New York: Macmillan, 1991), p. 508.
       "The question upon which": quoted in Kissinger, *Diplomacy,* p. 51.
       "the destruction of every": Ibid., p. 52.

272   *"All the great wrongs":* quoted in Robert Tucker, *The New Republic,* February 24, 1992, p. 30.
       The second of his: Arthur Walworth, *Woodrow Wilson, World Prophet,* vol. 2 (New York: Longmans & Green, 1958), p. 156.

"*He has saved his*": quoted in Ferdinand Czernin, *Versailles, 1919* (New York: G. P. Putnam & Sons, 1964), p. 430.

274   "*War had lain at*": Ibid., p. 398.

"*constitution for the whole*": quoted in Heckscher, *Woodrow Wilson*, p. 520.

"*Instinctively, and rightly*": Harold Nicolson, *Peacemaking, 1919* (New York: Harcourt, Brace & World, 1965), p. 70.

276   *Clemenceau spoke in:* Heckscher, *Woodrow Wilson*, p. 510.

277   "*The defensive value of*": Nicolson, *Peacemaking, 1919*, p. 192.

"*In spite of bitter*": Ibid., p. 36.

278   "*the unquestioned opportunity*": Ibid., p. 191.

11. Sovereignty

280   "*Guarantees must be fulfilled*": quoted in Ferdinand Czernin, *Versailles, 1919* (New York: G. P. Putnam & Sons, 1964), p. 112.

282   "*In matters of state*": Jean Bodin, *On Sovereignty*, ed. Julian H. Franklin (Cambridge: Cambridge University Press, 1992), p. 108.

"*An absolute sovereign*": Jean Bodin, *Six Books of the Commonwealth*, trans. M. J. Tooly (Oxford: Basil Blackwell, 1967), p. 36.

"*holds of another*": Ibid.

"*an analytic truth*": Julian H. Franklin, *Jean Bodin, and the Rise of Absolutist Theory* (Cambridge: Cambridge University Press, 1973), p. 23.

"*the principle mark of*": Bodin, *Six Books*, p. 32.

"*If the prince can*": Ibid., p. 43.

283   "*Just as God*": Bodin, *On Sovereignty*, p. 50.

"*Reason and common sense*": Bodin, *Six Books*, p. 19.

284   "*Man's salvation occurs*": quoted in Liah Greenfeld, *Nationalism* (Cambridge, Mass.: Harvard University Press, 1992), p. 115.

"*Sovereignty is one*": www.Britannica.com.

"*one people, one body*": John Locke, *The Second Treatise on Government* (Indianapolis, Ind.: Hackett Publishing, 1980), pp. 47–48.

"*an absolute despotic power*": quoted in Hannah Arendt, *On Revolution* (New York: Compass, 1967), p. 160.

"*The power and jurisdiction*": quoted in R. R. Palmer, *The Age of*

Democratic Revolution, vol. 1 (Princeton, N.J.: Princeton University Press, 1959), p. 142.

285 *"What is a nation?":* C. A. Macartney, *National States and National Minorities* (London: Oxford University Press, 1934), p. 46.

"is the soul that": Locke, *The Second Treatise,* p. 108.

286 *Macartney quotes Acton:* Macartney, *National States and National Minorities,* p. 17.

"aspires to political expression": Ibid., p. 16.

287 *"is usually nationally identical":* Ibid., p. 18.

292 *The Virginia Resolves, authored:* Frank Friedel, Richard N. Current, and T. Harry Williams, *A History of the United States,* vol. 1 (New York: Knopf, 1961), p. 120.

"it was as if": Gordon S. Wood, *The Creation of the American Republic* (New York: W. W. Norton, 1972), p. 285.

293 *"Every town government":* quoted in ibid., pp. 186–87.

"miniature constitutions that": Wood, *American Republic,* p. 288.

294 *"union of the society":* Locke, *The Second Treatise,* p. 119.

"the greatest question ever": quoted in ibid., p. 345.

295 *"The doctrine of sovereignty":* Wood, *American Republic,* p. 345.

some suggested that America: John Keane, *Tom Paine* (Boston: Little, Brown, 1995), p. 100. Cartright's famous letters in favor of American independence were called *American Independence, the Interest and Glory of Great Britain.* They demanded, Keane writes, "the replacement of the British Empire by a free association of states endowed with British liberties and all of them recognizing the king as their sovereign head."

was "imperium in imperio": Wood, *American Republic,* p. 351.

described by Adams as: Ibid.

Benjamin Franklin—who had: Ibid.

296 *"If, intemperately, unwisely":* quoted in Conor Cruise O'Brien, *The Great Melody* (Chicago: University of Chicago Press, 1992), p. 143.

297 *For example, Samuel Adams:* Wood, *American Republic,* p. 528.

James Madison now found: Ibid., p. 559.

"an assemblage of societies": James Madison, Alexander Hamilton,

and John Jay, *The Federalist Papers* (London: Penguin, 1987), p. 122.

299 *The "true distinction" of:* Alexander Hamilton, James Madison, and John Jay, *Federalist Papers,* ed. Clinton Rossiter (New York: Penguin, 1961), p. 355.

12. NIAGARA

305 *"Black and hideous to":* Henry James and Leon Edel, eds., *Henry James Letters* (Cambridge, Mass.: Harvard University Press, 1984), p. 713.

314 *"The position of the":* Leo Szilard and Nina Byers, "Physicists and the Decision to Drop the Bomb," *CERN Courier,* November 2002, p. 270.

317 *"As this enormous":* Bill Joy, "Why the Future Doesn't Need Us," *Wired,* April 2000.
Its logical end point: Francis Fukuyama made use of these terms of Nietzsche's in his book *The End of History and the Last Man.* With all respect to Fukuyama and Nietzsche, my use of the terms seems to me more fitting than theirs. Their first man was an energetic savage, and I follow them in this. Their last man, however, was an enervated, hypercivilized person, who, all savage energy spent, was incapable of almost any feat. It's hard to see how he would be the "last" of anything, unless he expired out of sheer boredom. My last man, on the other hand, would literally and truly be the last, since he would destroy everybody, himself included. It has always struck me likewise that *The End of History* was a perverse term to use in the nuclear age to refer to anything but human extinction by nuclear arms.

319 *"an atavism, a holdover":* Francis Fukuyama, *The End of History and the Last Man* (New York: The Free Press, 1992), p. 265.

321 *"absolute monarchs will often":* *The Federalist Papers,* p. 14.

322 *"What's the point":* Bill Keller, "The World According to Powell," *New York Times,* November 25, 2001.

328 *"If Pakistan doesn't change":* quoted in Rajiv Chandrasekaran, "Terrorism Casts Shadow Over India's Campaign," *Washington Post,* January 27, 2002.

"the perpetrator of that": quoted in Celia Dugger, "Indian General Talks Bluntly of War and a Nuclear Threat," *New York Times*, January 12, 2002.

"as a last resort": quoted in Rory McCarthy and John Hooper, "Musharraf Ready to Use Bomb," *The Guardian*, April 6, 2002.

13. THE LOGIC OF PEACE

336   *"the gradual spread of"*: Scott Sagan and Kenneth Waltz, *The Spread of Nuclear Weapons* (New York: W. W. Norton, 1997), p. 44.

344   *"fundamental maxims of her"*: quoted in James Chace, "Imperial America," *World Policy Journal* (spring 2002).

358   *For abolition would not:* This understanding of abolition as shifting the source of deterrence from hardware to software leaves open an important question. If deterrence survives beyond abolition, aren't we still snared in the riddles and corruption of threatening annihilation to avoid annihilation? Formally speaking, the objection is valid. Abolition so conceived does not purge the "sin" mentioned by Robert Oppenheimer, the scientific leader of the Manhattan Project, in his remark, "In some irredeemable way, the physicists have known sin." What it does do is to back the world across a critical symbolic threshold in the moral and psychological realm (psychology being the whole essence of deterrence in the first place).

359   *The dangers of abolition:* For a fuller treatment of my views on these matters, see my books *The Abolition* (New York: Knopf, 1984) and *The Gift of Time* (New York: Metropolitan Books, 1998).

367   *If the first circle:* This state of affairs may be changing, for a surprising reason. To the great dismay of the Ulster Protestants, the people of Britain, according to recent polls, are not eager to hold on to the Ulster counties, and would not mind seeing them join the Irish Republic.

373   *"How 'relevant' are mere"*: Gidon Gottlieb, *Nation Against State* (New York: Council on Foreign Relations, 1993), p. 50.

375   *"There is not a"*: quoted in Conor Cruise O'Brien, *The Great Melody* (Chicago: University of Chicago Press, 1992), p. 113.

376 *"The 'victorious' Jews":* quoted in Jeffrey C. Isaac, *Arendt, Camus, and Modern Rebellion* (New Haven, Conn.: Yale University Press, 1992), p. 214.

383 *"gradually spread further":* Immanuel Kant, "Perpetual Peace," in *Political Writings,* ed. Hans Reiss (Cambridge: Cambridge University Press, 1970), p. 105.

Acknowledgments

This book was long in the making, and the list of those to whom I am indebted is long. I want to thank the John D. and Katharine T. MacArthur Foundation's Program on Global Security and Sustainability, the John Simon Guggenheim Foundation, the W. Alton Jones Foundation, and the Samuel Rubin Foundation for their support. The welcome stipend from the Lannan Literary Award for Nonfiction in 1999 was extremely helpful.

Since 1998, I have been the Harold Willens Peace Fellow at the Nation Institute, my indispensable professional home. I want especially to thank Hamilton Fish, the president of the Institute, who has been ingeniously and tirelessly resourceful in making it possible to work on the book and other projects having to do with nuclear disarmament, and Taya Grobow, who with infallible good cheer has kept my working life functional in this period. Elizabeth Macklin's editorial assistance was indispensable. I also wish to thank Matthew Maddy, Kabir Dandona, Jenny Stepp, and Marisa Katz for their long hours of careful research and fact-checking.

I am grateful to Strobe Talbott for holding a seminar at the Brookings Institution, which provided invaluable commentary on the manuscript, and to Paul Kahn who both read the manuscript and organized an equally helpful study session on it at the Yale Law School. I also wish to thank the Joan Shorenstein Center for the Press, Politics, and Public Policy and its wonderful staff, at the John F. Kennedy School of Government at Harvard University, where I was a fellow in the fall of 2002. A number of seminars, at the Center and elsewhere at the University, were sources of very helpful reactions and advice.

With superabundant generosity my friend Wallace Shawn provided detailed comments that became a turning point in the evolution of the book. Robert Del Tredici made wise and useful observations on a late draft. Jerome Kohn and Fred Leventhal made helpful suggestions regarding individual chapters. In the early years of writing the book, my conversations with Niccolo Tucci were an inspiration, and his memory shines as a model of what the writing life should be.

My agent, Lynn Nesbit, guided the book expertly through innumerable tangles over many years. Sara Bershtel, of Metropolitan Books, has been steadfast in her support, in the face of unmerciful delays. Shara Kay skillfully and tactfully saw me and the book through the ins and outs of the publishing process.

My editor Tom Englehardt has become that rarest of treasures for a writer, a person whose opinions and reactions are as necessary as—going far beyond the call of duty—they are available.

I owe more than I can express to my wife, Elspeth, and my children, Matthew, Phoebe, and Thomas.

Index

About the Author

The author of several works, including *The Time of Illusion, The Fate of the Earth,* and *The Village of Ben Suc,* Jonathan Schell has been a contributor to *The Nation, The New Yorker, Harper's, The Atlantic,* and *Foreign Affairs,* and has taught at Wesleyan, Princeton, and Emory, among other universities. Currently a visiting professor at Yale and the Harold Willens Peace Fellow at the Nation Institute, he lives in New York City.

ROOTED IN THE LAND

ESSAYS ON COMMUNITY AND PLACE

EDITED BY William Vitek and Wes Jackson

YALE UNIVERSITY PRESS   NEW HAVEN AND LONDON

To Clark and Nancy Decker, and the entire Decker family—
three generations making good their promise to the land.
They first introduced me to this valley landscape
and then taught me to care for it.

W.V.

To Bob Swann and Susan Witt.
They have carried on the legacy of those who
have thought these thoughts down
through the ages, and have added
important insights of their own.

W.J.

contents

preface

IN an age of information overload and growing concern about the environmental impact of a consumptive society, one ought to have good reason to create another book—or to buy one. Perhaps Wes Jackson's and my justification for creating this book will help with your decision about whether to purchase it or use it in a course.

Two trends in America are currently receiving increased attention in the media, in universities, and in our public discourse. The first is that aspect of the environmental movement focused on preserving landscapes and species. Numerous laws and policies seek to protect America's wild places and to preserve ecosystems and their inhabitants. Fine work is being done in this area, but much of the debate assumes that nature is best left alone and that wild landscapes are those in which humans are only visitors. The second trend is the renewed interest in social communities. The demise of rural America is chronicled and lamented, and urban social issues are cast in terms of the lack of community structure and commitment. Generally missing in this discussion is any mention of the places where we live as biological communities or the importance of human communities rooted in a storied landscape.

This book is a collection of new and previously published essays that take as their central theme the importance of "placed" human communities. Not all landscapes should be inhabited by human beings, but each of us is enriched to the extent that we can belong to, and participate in, a well-ordered human community integrated into the natural landscape of a particular place. A long tradition of philosophers and social activists describes human beings as communal by nature and advocates a life of civic virtue. And it was Aldo Leopold in *A Sand County Almanac* who clearly articulated the inclusive notion of citizenship, a relation to land founded on awareness, respect, and restraint. *Rooted in the Land* offers the philosophical perspectives and personal commitments of life lived with others and in place.

We believe that this book stands out in another way. Our contributors represent a rich cross-section of academic disciplines and social activism. Some authors engage in theoretical distinctions, but always with a certain sense of their practical applications. Many use personal narratives and experiences to describe or validate theories of community or ecology. There are spirited defenses of community life, theoretical discussions of the nature of community, and practical suggestions for becoming connected to others and native to a place. The book is divided by themes, not by disciplines, and our contributors were asked to write for a general audience of reflective readers with a wide variety of educational experiences. Our book is itself a community of writers and activists, speaking from widely different perspectives but sharing similar goals and commitments.

We hope that our readers too reflect a diversity of interests, professions, and avocations and will find enrichment here. From an academic perspective, this volume offers many variations and possibilities. It has a place as a primary or secondary text in college and university courses in, for example, rural sociology; in environmental literature and nature writing; in environmental ethics, politics, and science; and in agriculture. But the book would also be useful in community and economic development offices, for city and county planners, for citizens active in their communities, and for anyone interested in challenging or enriching their ideas about community and place.

The idea for *Rooted in the Land* originated in 1991 as the two of us were driving in northern New York, somewhere between Potsdam and Syracuse. I had invited Wes to Clarkson University to talk about his work at the Land Institute and at Matfield Green. On the return trip to the airport we started talking about community. At one point Wes turned to me and said "You know, we ought to do a book on community and place some day." These are not words an assistant professor takes lightly, so I pestered Wes about the project for a year. We finally decided that while we would work together on the book's conceptual slant and in identifying possible contributors, I would contact authors, do the editing, seek permissions, and write the introductory material. Our roles have been very different, but equally necessary. My sincere thanks to Wes for his vision and inspiration, the clarity of his ideas, and his sound advice along the way.

I am grateful also to my colleagues at Clarkson: to Jan Wojcik for introducing me to Aldo Leopold; to John Serio, consummate and award-winning editor; and to Steve Doheny-Farina, fellow communitarian. Owen Brady and Jerry Gravander, in their capacities as dean, provided me with release time and financial support during crucial moments in the project. Numerous authors in the collection offered their insights, suggestions, and moral support; it has been a pleasure and honor to work with all of them. My special gratitude goes to David Ehrenfeld. Jean Thomson Black at Yale University Press has been an expert guide through the publication gauntlet. Like a skillful coach, she knew when to push and when to praise. Thanks also to Vivian Wheeler for her skillful and diligent copyediting. The significant comments of two anonymous reviewers improved the collection. Jack Shumaker's straightforward advice was always welcome and appreciated. And I am indebted to Bruce Omundson for his insightful reading of my contributions to this volume.

The energy and stamina required for this book would not have been possible without a number of important influences. The writings of Wendell Berry and Gary Snyder have had a profound influence on my thinking about community issues; these two individuals have been my mentors at large. Greg Cooper, Frank Kalinowski, and I had many memorable evening discussions of Aldo Leopold's work. I have also been sustained by friends and neighbors: the Deckers, of course, and Walt Cook, Don Doig, Doug Jones, David Katz, Phil Neisser, Alex MacKinnon, Robin McClellan, Dick Mooers, Jon Montan, Don and Colette Purcell,

Dave and Erton Sipher, Paul Stevenson, and George and Daryl Thompson. They are natives to this place.

Walking is my primary mode of transportation in the village of Potsdam, where I live and work. Seven years of traversing well-worn paths have not exhausted what I can learn about this landscape. The Racquette River is a constant reminder of permanence and change. Stone Valley, Ives Park, and Bayside Cemetery are special places on its banks. The abundant wild flora and fauna attracted to this watershed make it difficult to forget that I am part of a larger community. There is, even at thirty-five below, the constancy of chickadees, and in spring the sweet harvest of sugar maples. The St. Lawrence Valley's expansive skies have given me much pleasure. It is no exaggeration to say that I have been reshaped by living with and among this community.

A final and most important acknowledgment goes to my family. My parents, Jane and Edward, continue to cheer me on with words and gestures of support. My children, Ian, Carolyn, Elizabeth, and Andrew, are wonderful companions. They live fully in the moment, with plenty of laughter, and have no shortage of insights and kind words. Their mother, my wife, Maria, has helped with many details of this book; her tough editing always improves my writing. More important, she is living the practiced life prescribed by many of the authors in this collection. She has done much more than consciously choose to remain at home; she has *made* a home. She is at the center of my life and of our family.

W. V.

rediscovering the landscape

WILLIAM VITEK

PLACE WHERE FOLKS LIVE IS THEM FOLKS.

—John Steinbeck, *The Grapes of Wrath,* 1939

THE American landscape is broad in dimension and rich in diversity. The contiguous states alone contain eleven major bioregions, from Palouse Prairie to Eastern Deciduous Forest. The fertile soils of this landscape feed us, and we are renewed and inspired by its rivers and mountain peaks. Americans love their state and national parks, and flock to them annually.

But it is a young love that we bring to the land, fleeting and uninformed. We are perpetually on the move—every three to five years, from place to place, and no place in particular. We crowd the scenic vistas while ignoring the local streams, the indigenous flora and fauna, and the glacial moraines and drumlins of our home territory. We count with pride our bushels of corn, but neglect to consider the soil lost to the wind. And our young welcome spring in raucous rituals on sun-drenched beaches, but rarely hear the more ancient sounds of geese on the wing.

The first European Americans were newcomers to this landscape, and they brought to it a cultural heritage of domination and ownership that could only alienate them and their descendants from the land's deeper significance. These European settlers came to America with a worldview inspired by Baconian science and Lockean philosophy. Francis Bacon's scientific method is rooted in the belief that God gave nature to man as a puzzle to solve. The solution requires a "diligent dissection and anatomy of the world." John Locke's labor theory of property suggests that the land becomes valuable only after humans transform and improve it. Locke too provided the intellectual framework and justification for the individualism and materialism that are the bulwark of American society today. With such views guiding their decisions, it should not be surprising that early Europeans set forth with vigor to acquire and technologically control the American landscape while seeking individual and monetary self-interest. Three centuries later, the land is still more likely to be owned than known, controlled without being fully understood, and loved only for its instrumental value. Many of us remain visitors in a landscape we call home, and are estranged from the people who, in another time, would be rightly called our neighbors.

Rediscovering the landscape and our place in it requires new ways of thinking about the relationship between humans and the natural world, and offers new challenges as well. Slowing down, staying put, opening our senses, practicing humility and restraint, knowing and caring for those around us, and finding our natural place in the natural world are simple yet significant steps in the rediscovery of place and the sense of community it holds.

Such change will not be easy. In a culture best identified by its uncompromising commitment to individual rights, enlightened self-interest, and the icon of the self-made person, any discussion of a life lived in place and in common with others will seem quaint, romantic, idealistic, and thoroughly backward looking. But we forget, or never knew, that there is an alternative view of human nature that sees membership in a community as the central feature of a successful and prosperous life. The intellectual traditions of civic humanism and communitarianism are kept alive in the writings of Aristotle, Machiavelli, Harrington, Montesquieu, Tocqueville, Michael Oakeshott, Charles Taylor, Robert Putnam, Amitai Etzioní, and J. G. A. Pocock, to name a few. The United States Constitution was born out of debate over how to develop "public virtues in democratic citizens" (Bellah et al. 1985, 254). Social movements, including populism, progressivism, socialism, and the trade union movement, as well as numerous federal social programs in the last half of this century, have attempted to blunt the sharp edges of industrial capitalism and create pockets of community and common interest. Moreover, a myriad of small communities in the United States have dedicated themselves to staying put, working together, and living well.

Many of the contributors to *Rooted in the Land* have been part of or have been informed by the contemporary literature on place and community. Others have demonstrated with their commitments and actions that community life is not merely romantic vision. This volume's central theme is that human communities live and function within larger natural ecosystems. The health and integrity of both ecosystem and community depend on the recognition of and respect for this interrelationship. John Livingston captures this insight well in his contribution to this collection: "A sense of community is most simply put as an awareness of simultaneous *belonging* to both a society and a place."

The phrase "rooted in the land" is inspired by Aldo Leopold, but the notion that human communities must actively participate in a known landscape has ancient origins and is shared by all of the contributors to this volume. The notion of being rooted invokes images of dark, damp, subterranean pathways. But it is a strong notion too, unapologetic about the sorts of structures necessary both to hold something in place and to nourish it. There are uncanny resemblances between subsoil root structures, leafless trees on a winter landscape, and the neural pathways of the human brain. To the naturalist these are reminders of nature's economy and of our interconnectedness. How can we divide the root from the sap, the syrup from the sustenance, the neural impulse from the thought? Human communities too must be rooted in a place and fully connected to the natural world that surrounds us and that is us.

The editors of *Rooted in the Land* invited writers from across the intellectual and ideological spectrum to contribute clear, nontechnical essays that explore the authors' reflections on, commitments to, and insights into community and place. Their writings are interpretive rather than academic, lacking footnotes, empirical data, and analyses of such data. The collection celebrates community life in meditative, provocative, and exploratory essays that describe, defend, and advo-

cate our living together and sharing. Its authors write about where they live, and
they live what they write. Their prose, lucid and to the point, is put to the task of
doing useful work.

Nearly a quarter of the essays in this book are devoted to agricultural, ranching, and rural issues. Historically, agriculture and rural life have strongly influenced
both the theory and practice of community life, from Xenophon to Varo to Jefferson and Crèvecoeur. Many of the contributors, for example, share Jefferson's
assumptions about agriculture, civic virtue, and the need for decentralized, interdependent community landscapes. In addition, much of the contemporary resurgence in community thinking has originated in the practice of agriculture, by
those who have a working relationship with the land.

The connection between human communities and place is not unique to rural
areas, but here one can be certain that the land is not mere scenery and hiking trail,
or resources in need of extraction. Here the land becomes part of people's lives,
intermingled with buying and selling, working and playing, living and dying. It is
both history and future. In rural communities is an opportunity for the land's
rhythms to become part of everyday life, an immediate linkage between
the land's fertility and the community's prosperity. Those who work directly on the
land know it in ways that are simply unavailable to those who wish to keep their
hands clean and their preconceptions unchallenged. In rural communities one
learns that it is possible to love the forest one cuts; to honor the bull calf on his
way to the slaughterhouse; and to respect the land one clears, plants, and harvests.
To the farmer and rancher these are not logical contradictions to be avoided for
the sake of some artificial consistency, but immediate and natural paradoxes one
accepts up front and lives by. Here the wisdom of limitations accrues incrementally but forcefully in daily routines and practices informed by communal labor
and natural rhythms. Rural living creates full-bodied understanding. "The word
understand means to possess physical knowledge; it means to have a corporeal grasp,
a surety that the body owns. A purely cerebral construct is *not understanding.* And
—going back the other way—something that one has truly understood is so personal and visceral that it's almost impossible to express in words" (Kappel-Smith
1994, 51). Perhaps this explains why farmers and ranchers are stereotypically short
on words, but often long on good sense.

At their best, working agricultural and rural landscapes provide insight into
the types of communities, practices, virtues, and values that will facilitate the transition to an environmental ethos. We have already seen agricultural and rural areas at their worst: well water unfit to drink, soil washed of its fertility, extractive
monocultures and clear cuts, two farms where there were twenty, and large numbers of people disconnected, dispirited, and unemployed. We may be decades away
from fully understanding all the parts and cogs that constitute vital social communities engaged in sustainable and healthy work with the land. However, some
of the ideas and efforts necessary to revitalize our communities and landscapes are
represented in this collection.

In choosing the contributors to *Rooted in the Land,* we focused on the authors' prominence in their field, their interests in—and advocacy of—community, and their ability to address a general audience. Seventeen of the essays are new, while the remaining pieces are contemporary classics. Space constraints required that choices be made. It is reasonable to assume that we neglected some important work. There is, for example, no discussion or analysis of utopian communities and the communitarian efforts of the 1960s and 1970s in the United States. The history of such communities, and history generally, is not a primary subject here. And while there is a strong and growing community resurgence in many of our nation's urban areas that includes the formation of new social groups, architectural innovation, and ecologically sensitive urban planning, our collection does not contain any essays that speak either to these developments or to the cohousing movement.

Finally, this volume contains very little concentrated effort to define the community concept. Some contributors speak in broad terms about what they mean by "community," others simply present their experiences as evidence thereof. Writing about community—like living in a community—resembles a process and a narrative rather than a series of definitions and axioms, however valuable the latter turn out to be for theoreticians and citizens alike. Readers who are ecologists by training or who are aware of the literature in this scientific field know that the community concept in ecology is neither unambiguous nor universally accepted. The relevant scientific debate is likely to continue unabated for some time, though our collection is not intended as a contribution to it. In the meantime it is reasonable, and indeed fruitful, to continue to speak of social and ecological communities both in terms of metaphors and as living, functioning entities. Human communities must make critical decisions about their ecosystems, and the efficacy of these decisions often depends on the current state of scientific knowledge, however incomplete. In addition, the contemporary discussion of community—both metaphorical and scientific—thoughtfully informs the discourse concerning human communities and their interdependence with place.

A book this large is improved by an imposed structure, however artificial and arbitrary. For the reader who is interested in specific authors and essays, the contents should suffice. But the book is also organized thematically. Part One is titled Standing Firm. Divided into three sections (Rootlessness, Perspectives Local and Global, and Valuing Community) it consists of writings that demonstrate the ways in which contemporary life erodes our interest in, and even our capacity to engage in, communities rooted in a place; that offer examples of living and prospering communities; and that highlight the values and virtues of community life.

Part Two, Community Foundations, is more theoretical in nature. It too is divided into three sections: Place, The Ecological Connection, and Community Criteria. This section has as its central theme questions having to do with the origins, coherence, and structure of communities. What, for example, is a community, and what are its boundaries? Both Aristotle and Plato believed that the ideal community consists in a specific number of people. Jefferson argued that commerce and the migration to cities would destroy the moral values inherent in small rural communities. Is there an ideal size for a community? Essays in this section address the concept of place in the Hebrew scriptures, awareness and community living among plants and animals, various theoretical approaches to community, criteria to measure the well-being of a community, the use of ecological accounting in community rebuilding, and such community concepts as territory, necessity, memory, foodsheds, dwelling, and inhabitation. While this section may seem esoteric to some, thinking about community at the level of theory and concept is a preliminary step in bringing the community concept to the forefront of our personal commitments, our intellectual debates, and our social policies.

The final theme in Part Three—Becoming Native—addresses the practical concerns of building a community, putting down roots, and becoming native to a place. In two sections—Conceptual Development and Community Development—contributors offer advice and warn of the challenges that come with putting the community concept to work in our personal lives. This section highlights land trusts, community-supported agriculture, alternative farming systems, the building of social capital, rural education, the renewal of civic virtue, and community farming. Whether we want to rebuild a community, design educational programs, farm sustainably, or simply put down roots in a landscape that we have decided to call home, those who have preceded us can serve as role models and teachers.

Despite the ambitious array of essays and themes gathered here, *Rooted in the Land* is a hearty contribution to only one side of the debate about community living and the need to become rooted in a place. It is not balanced between pro and con; there are no essays that reject or are even marginally critical—in the usual sense—of the communitarian perspective. But the essays are critical in another sense. The word "critic" does not imply negativity, but rather a social perception, a keen discernment, of what is being observed. The authors in this collection are certainly critical in this respect. They recognize that there are limitations to a life lived in one place and in one community. Small communities can become provincial and stagnant, community structures can become oppressive, and life in one place can become boring. America is a nation of restless, rootless, largely unattached individuals in part because our European ancestors rejected their traditional, well-ordered, and placed communities. A price has been paid for this wholesale rejection, though it is difficult to measure. But we cannot go back, and no contributor to this collection thinks we *should* return to the past. We can, however, begin to measure what has been lost, and consider a life committed to a community and to a place, that preserves a central core of the freedoms and dignities we have come to expect in a democratic society dedicated to preserving and promoting individual self-interest. Identifying the central elements of this core will continue to be a source of debate; but this collection, and others like it, insist that such a debate take place in our homes, across fences, in our town halls, at our universities, and in the halls of government.

Communities are also set into political, social, ecological, and economic contexts and these directly affect a given community's health and well-being. There may no longer be land enough for the world's population to live in small, self-sufficient communities. Small-scale community life may prove an impossibility to those directly affected by wars, droughts, and overpopulation, not to mention the increasingly large number of global citizens and governments who have set their sights on a modern, materialistic, and individuated American lifestyle.

The authors in this volume understand these contexts and limitations. Each is realistic though hopeful, but not naive. Some of them speak directly to the challenges of rediscovering community in an industrial age. All of them believe that social communities placed in a landscape are both necessary and possible, despite the challenges and drawbacks, seen and unseen. This book—and the position it represents—is a small but lively counterweight to the promises and pronouncements of contemporary culture.

The collection's greatest drawback, however, lies in the limitations of the spoken word. Books are not shovels, arguments are not commitments, and collections of essays are not communities. We should not measure our success by the number of books published every year devoted to community or by the number of copies sold. Some of us have found a calling in thinking and writing for a living, and no doubt the resurgence of community—if it is to occur—requires words devoted to it. But books must not become our crutch, our excuse, to postpone the more difficult task of community building. We can always read another book; it is a device familiar to many writers and academics. Yet at some point, and soon, we must all begin or continue the challenging tasks of getting to know our neighbors, picking stones, saying no to upward mobility, complicating our scientific models or our academic specialties, planting a garden, and saying yes to a place. If this collection gets you—as Wendell Berry has phrased it—off of your horse and out of your car, all the better. If *Rooted in the Land* sends you to yet another book, then its success is only partial.

Perhaps we ought not to be too hard on ourselves. The most enduring lesson of *Rooted in the Land,* and other collections like it, is that we are more likely to fail than to succeed at building communities. History, the belief in progress, and cultural forces are all against us. Such failures, however, when borne well and with unflagging optimism and humor, both prepare us for the commitments ahead and unite us in a common experience. Farmers and ranchers know only too well the lessons of failure: hail, drought, temperamental animals and machinery, and uncooperative bankers. All the same, many remain committed to their work, united in their communities, and remarkably lighthearted.

Similar failures are not unknown to the oldest of our literary characters. A tired warrior spends nineteen years of mostly failure trying to get home to a

woman who, against all odds, waits for him. The first couple is expelled from paradise. Even our own earliest memories must contain the failure of displacement, as
we are pushed out and separated from what we know best. But infants do not despair. Their first act out of the womb is inherently communal, reuniting mother
and child. John Steinbeck uses this image in the conclusion of a modern epic, *The
Grapes of Wrath,* to express the hope that can arise from despair.

Success, too, can arise from failure if we are diligent, tenacious, and mindful
of our homefulness. *Rooted in the Land* is dedicated to the search—both conceptual and real—for a community life rooted in a place that is known, loved, and
honored. Such places already exist and their numbers and members are growing.
Neither the commitment nor the hopefulness expressed in this book are unwar-
ranted. Its authors speak about the experiences, people, plants, animals, and places
they know, and what they know is inherently good.

part one   STANDING FIRM

WHAT IS NO GOOD FOR THE HIVE IS NO GOOD FOR THE BEE.

—Marcus Aurelius, *Meditations*

leave if you can

HARRY W. PAIGE

THERE is a town in the southwestern desert that exists only in my imagination. It could be in west Texas, New Mexico, Arizona, or southern California. It is a composite of all the hot, dusty, blowing, and rusting places I have ever seen and loved. It is a setting for fiction, fantasy, and nostalgia, yet in a vital sense it is real— as a dreamscape can be real or a vision. For my town I have borrowed the name Sal Si Puedes (Leave If You Can), from a hand-printed, weathered sign I once saw on the Baja Peninsula. Somehow it is a better name for the town than Rimrock, Loco, or Sundown. Most of the people who live there are Mexican-Americans and for them there is a hurting irony in that Spanish phrase.

Baked by the sun and raked by the constant winds, Sal Si Puedes sits brooding between distant horizons. A dark snake of a superslab slices the town for a mile, less than a minute in time, and then is gone on its way to El Paso, Las Cruces, Tucson, and Bakersfield. Tumbleweed and clouds of dust come and go on the vagrant winds. A pink adobe gas station, and next to it a blue cafe, are both dirtying from the years. A pale adobe church patiently waits for Sunday behind shadow-skirts of yucca. All protective coloring against lonesome! From a distance the town is seen as a random splashing of pastels on an empty brown canvas.

Because it is *my* place, peopled with my characters, I can ask questions with impunity.

"Why do you stay, Esteban?"

The old man with the brown stubs of teeth and the creased, leathery skin smiles and shrugs. "Why? Because it is home," he says simply and then adds, "*Sal si puedes.*"

"Why, Rosita, why? You are only twenty. Your whole life . . ."

She smiles shyly, nervously, not answering. Then she too shrugs, talking without words. She has her reasons, reasons she does not wish to share with a stranger. *Sal si puedes.*

"And you, Stefano?"

"Me? I am a prisoner here," he says mysteriously, bitterly, sadly. "In this prison without walls. *Sal si puedes.*" His words are flung on the wind like a dare.

Even in our mobile and transient times many people still have a sense of place—a place where roots can be put down. And even though the place may be forbidding to others, it is still considered home. It may be a barren, brown, and blowing place. Or a snow-draped, frozen land, sculptured into shrouded time. But it is home.

Some people are trapped in a place as surely as if the roof had caved in on them. Trapped in the rubble and debris of poverty. They stay because they cannot leave: they cannot make a new life because the old one still has them by the throat.

Some are trapped by steel webs of duty and responsibility. They cannot bring themselves to leave the young, the old, or the dependent. To do so would be to be haunted by living ghosts—a face at a window or a cry from the dark. To leave would be to desert someone or something. "Better to desert your own dreams!" a voice says to them.

Some are trapped by a way of life—a position, an opportunity, a store, a ranch—the quicksands if not of success then of survival. Some by inertia, following like a desert trickle the path of least resistance. Others are trapped by fear. The fear of uprooting. The fear of a leap in the dark. The fear of the unknown. And so they stay on, listening to the hollow chorus within, mocking them: *Sal si puedes!* Leave if you can!

Home may be the streets of a city. A walkup flat in a faded brownstone, a piece of rock set in anonymity where neon pulses through swollen veins, transfusing only some of the lonely nights. Where the manswarm flows like a rush of insects from a nest. To some it is a cold and heartless place, this city of foul breath and days too gray for laughter. Others call it home and are tuned to its excitement, its frantic rhythms.

And roots will burrow out the nourishment in almost anything if given time. In rock or sand or even concrete. A flower will usually find the crack in the sidewalk.

The word "home" would be certain to appear on any list of the ten most beautiful words in the English language. More than one unearthed hut of prairie sod has been found to be ringed by the bones of its defenders. And the gray, pitted, slanting headstones behind old New England homes have marked the resting of those for whom a lifetime was too brief a stay.

In steaming savannas natives mark their home with myth, setting present boundaries with grinning skulls. Under the volcano the people listen to the steaming breath and molten gurgling that has spoken to them for centuries. The burning mountain has long since lost its god-voice: it murmurs a distant and secular warning now. But the people have lived in its shadow, waiting, their eyes drawn to the hissing crater and the wisps of smoke that warn of the river of fire that has sometimes crusted the valley. There are those who straddle geologic faults, waiting for the earth rumbles and the great trembling, their seismic instruments poised to catch the first tremors. Los Angeles holds such a people. San Francisco too.

There are those whose island homes have been washed into the sea and will be again. But the people remain. They go on with their lives as though the seawall could never fail. They remain under the restless volcano. Above the earth tremors. On the barren rock pounded by an angry sea.

Perhaps they stay because home is not a place only, but a condition of the heart. Barren, frozen, burning, trembling, or sinking—it is a house of breath. A living place, ghosted with histories and fused with the bones of our fathers. Loved or hated, home is a part of us, a living cell slowly dividing into memory. An ache or a warmth; a sound or an echo; a dream or a nightmare.

The territorial imperative is not reserved for lower animals alone. Man also shares in the need to stake out a claim, and he has paid dearly for it in agony and blood. Sometimes in ecstasy, seeing again after many years the hills of home. Maps are man's invention, whether drawn in sand or printed in books. But boundaries and borders are the signs of other things as well, whether they walk, swim, crawl, or fly. In one way or another they express the idea, this is our place! Yet, tragically, man is the only one who knows it cannot finally be, that it can never be his any more than the winds can be his or the clouds that dissolve before his very eyes. And he knows the agony as well as the comfort that illusions of permanence bring.

How many treaties with the Native Americans ceded Indian lands to them for "as long as the grass shall grow and the rivers flow"? Then the poetry melted in a few short springs and uncovered a winter truth. The sacred Black Hills of the Lakota still harbor ancient ghosts, but they are fewer now and the summer swarms of tourists come between the dreamers and their dreams. How many abandoned farms were once a sacred legacy? A stake in a future that never came? So it is with empires, their sands sifted by scholars for the broken pillars that will make the temples rise again—but only in memory, in imagination. The gods have gone.

Yet man continues to act as though he has at least one foot in eternity. His maps, charts, and treaties continue to divide up places as though his drawings make it so. As though the map is the territory itself. Borders are not to be violated. Seas have their offshore limits; airspace is not to be crossed. This place is ours! The electronic pulses of the night probe in all directions to find the intruders.

The Mohawk Indians of northern New York and Canada have a saying that no Indian has been buried in Brooklyn. Many of these same Indians have done high steel construction work on the skeletal towers of Manhattan and some have died on the job, falling like broken eagles into an alien valley. But in the end they have come home, boxed for the earth, to lie finally in ancestral grounds. This is our place! *Sal si puedes!*

There are people, products of modern times, with little or no sense of place. There are the rootless ones. There are the people of the suburbs, those places of interchangeable parts strung like beads on a commuter line. One such place is much like another, and sometimes the only way you can tell your home from your neighbor's is by the color of the front door. Such people move from place to place as their careers or their wishes dictate. Usually they end up in their retirement years in a place in the sun—Florida, Arizona, or the packaged communities of the Southwest. Life is easier perhaps, but these are not always places to call home. They are places for the nomad heart. The people there will tell you that they are glad to have come in out of the cold, the crowds, or the rat race. Between rounds of shuffleboard, golf, or sunbathing they will sing the praises of the carefree life, but secretly they are nagged by the memory of a distant grandchild or the snow-breasted hills of Vermont. Deep within, they suffer the malaise of the fugitive heart.

Even the rootless, perhaps *especially* the rootless, must look to the ending. So they make out their wills and testaments and with all the authority of print and seal designate their final resting places. These are seldom places of sea and sun, seldom places where the tourists swarm. The heart's compass may spin in all directions but it finally comes to rest on home.

Places, like people, may die through accident, disaster, and neglect. Or from an exodus of hope. I have wandered through the ghost towns of the American West. I have heard the gossip of ghosts, the lonely door slam with no one to answer. I have seen the leaves of catalogs and Bibles turning in the wind. Seen the stickballs of tumbleweed travel house to house and finally come to rest in the corners of things.

Cities too die under bombs or are toppled by earthquakes. But the sense of place often remains, even in the ruins. The rubble is still London, San Francisco, Dresden, Hiroshima. People still pray in the cathedrals of the mind even as they walk through the wasted aftermath.

Ultimately a few square miles is all we know of earth. And though our umbilicals now stretch to other worlds, this earth is still our home. The music of the spheres is often lost on a prairie wind. Henry Thoreau once remarked that he had traveled a great deal in Concord, preferring, as he did, inner space. He knew that every place is a microcosm, a world in miniature. He knew that Walden Pond contained all the seas, that the world was in a clod of earth. He knew that man is finally a prisoner of place, if only the few cubic centimeters within his skull.

Sal si puedes! Leave if you can!

the rootless professors

ERIC ZENCEY

SHORTLY after I moved to Vermont to teach, I was gassing up at a general store—one of those eclectic commercial institutions for which Vermont is justly renowned—and overheard a conversation that I marked as peculiar. One young man was admiring another's car, allowing that he had once owned one like it.

"So," the car owner said, "you from around here?"

"No," came the reply. "I'm from North Montpelier."

I found this strange, because the place where we stood was only two short miles from the village of North Montpelier.

At the time I thought I had overheard a classic instance of the parochialism of rural life. I certainly wouldn't have answered the question that way; having moved to Vermont from graduate school thousands of miles away, I tended to think of myself as being near home if I was anywhere within twenty miles of my newly rented house. But with time and thought that exchange came to strike me as something else: a manifestation of a different geographical sensibility, with its different notions of territory, home range, and locale. In some ways that sensibility is superior to the cosmopolitanism that I was trained to as a college professor.

As citizens of the *cosmo polis,* the mythical "world city," professors are expected to owe no allegiance to geographical territory; we're supposed to belong to the boundless world of books and ideas and eternal truths, not the infinitely particular world of watersheds, growing seasons, and ecological niches. Most professors get their jobs through national searches, and while we may have our preferences for specific regions of the country, most of us are living wherever we could find work. The ethos of rootlessness is so strong in academe that I suspect the experience of an acquaintance of mine is exceptional only for the bluntness with which the message was conveyed: having gotten his degrees from the university in the state where he was born, and having worked at that institution for a few years as a lecturer on a semester-by-semester appointment, he was told flatly (though unofficially) by the chair of his department that he was "too much a native" ever to become a permanent faculty member.

Though the majority of American college students attend institutions in their home states, they are taught by and large by cosmopoles, by this class of transient exotics. It would be surprising if the rootlessness of the professorial class didn't have some effect on their charges, the students who go on to become the best-informed and most educated portion of the American public. Unrooted teachers tend to mistake "disconnected from locale" for "educated." They tend to think of education as little more than an organized assault on the parochial point of view, the view of the rooted "I." Education can be that; education certainly ought to broaden one's horizons; but it can and ought to do more. And however we define that "more," one thing seems clear: because professors tend to be rootless, they are systematically ignorant of a key aspect of an integrated life, the life that is, after all, a primary goal of a good liberal arts education. They are woefully ignorant of the values of connectedness to place.

The most obvious consequence of this trained rootlessness is our ignorant and exploitative relationship to nature. An unrooted class is likely to see nature as so much visual furniture—a barely differentiated backdrop to life's important activities, the land you drive through or fly over to get where you're going. How many college professors (excluding hydrologists and geographers, who may be assumed to have a professional interest) can describe the watershed in which they live? The absolute necessity of water to life is well known; ninety-some percent of the body is water; yet most academics have no idea whence theirs comes or where it goes when its incorporative service is done. From the vantage of cosmopolitan transcendence, even something as large as a watershed can seem a parochial detail. This learned ignorance, felt as a *worthy* ignorance, is a significant root of our culture's ongoing environmental crisis. For decades our best and brightest planners and policymakers have behaved as if nature were no more than inert, scarcely differentiated, infinitely manipulable "stuff." They could hardly have learned otherwise in school, for their teachers, rootless, knew no better themselves.

Another, less obvious consequence of academic rootlessness is its effect on the political psyche of the nation. I think it contributes, through a connection that is subtle but undeniable, to the shallow and emotional nationalism that is too much in evidence on our campuses. In encouraging young people to abjure their citizenship in the political, biotic, and familial communities of their nativity and to embrace citizenship in the world city of ideas and culture, our rootless professors encourage them to give up real and immediate connections to things concretely observable in favor of a less immanent connection to abstraction. The lesson is learned, and is applied politically: the nation, a more general and abstract polity than the neighborhood, town, or watershed, is the correct, enlightened locus of citizen loyalty. The world of books and ideas and culture, a world that encourages transcendence of this identification according to narrow political boundaries, is a bit too abstract for some of our youth; their emotional need to belong is not satisfied by membership in a world that is neither corporally nor temporally present, a world in which they are likely to be only spectators, never full participants, a world that has no mechanism by which to acknowledge their membership (or even their simple presence). These are shortcomings the nation-state is careful to avoid. With its flags and heroes and simple villains, with its nondiscriminatory acceptance of all who embrace it, with its rituals, its reductive, Manichaean morality, and its call to the easy sacrifices of an altruism based on self-interest, the nation-state will always be more effectively and compellingly symbolized than the world of cosmopolitan culture. I believe this is why college students as a group are dismayingly ready to accept jingoistic slogans and patriotic appeals in lieu of moral or even practical argument. Membership in the nation offers immediate emotional satisfactions that life as a cosmopole offers only after much training of the sensibilities. It isn't surprising that once students have been disconnected from locale they choose the nation-state over the larger abstraction of "culture." They want the gratification of belonging, and the nation-state has a thousand seducers. Membership is easy, satisfying, expected, rewarded.

Nationalism is but one symptom of the etherealization of modern culture, that process by which the elements of culture are made progressively more distant, abstract, general, and ultimately less than fully satisfying. Our educational system and especially the professoriate as a rootless class are implicated in that process. Why drag eighteen-year-olds to an appreciation of cultural works by long-dead, distant Europeans? This cosmopolitan project has been criticized by champions of the marginalized cultures it excludes; I think it time to criticize it from the vantage of a rooted education. From that perspective, multicultural inclusiveness doesn't necessarily solve the problem: multiculturalism tends to perpetuate a politics of placeless identity rather than a politics of rootedness in place. Meanwhile, likely as not, beyond the campus walls lie the last vestiges of an indigenous regional culture struggling to maintain its identity in the face of the forces of cultural homogenization, a culture that represents a unique adaptation of people and tradition to place. Yes, the classic works of our (or any) culture have something to teach us about being human, for they transcend the limits of historical and geographical origin in their beauty, insight, meaning—but how can a student appreciate this quality without being able to appreciate how those works are, at the same time, rooted in the particularness of the place and time of their creation? How can students appreciate the latter quality if they have no knowledge of how they themselves are tied to locale and time? Experience of regional culture, of the systems of meaning that people have created that do not aspire to a kind of placeless universality, would provide a needed complement, a necessary rooting. Such an experience would bring universality into focus through contrast rather than by default. A rootless, cosmopolitan professoriate is both disinclined and incompetent to give students such experience.

Of course there are virtues in cosmopolitanism. It guarantees that teaching will not be captive to local concerns and perspectives, or overly subject to the tyranny of state legislatures, or overly restricted in its presentation of ideas, beliefs, and exemplars of life choices and orientations. The national market for professors has helped us avoid prejudice and pettiness and narrowness of thinking in academe, has helped to spread alternative and unconventional schools of thought. But along with the modern communication and transportation systems that have made it possible, that market has also contributed to the homogenization of culture in our nation. Each part of our country is now less different from every other part than it was even twenty years ago, and that is not an unmixed blessing. Loss of diversity—even if the differences have sometimes manifested themselves in benighted and oppressive practices—can never be wholly beneficial.

But the problem traces back farther than market forces. At issue ultimately is a cardinal point in the Western tradition, manifest most clearly in the theories of knowledge we employ. We in the Western world have traditionally valued the universal over the particular, the general statement over the local exception, the grand, capital-T Truth over the particular details of the specific cases from which that truth was induced. The truths that our professorial class carries with it are supposed to be the truths that transcend time and place. How could that carriage not be a good thing?

Here is an example, by way of analogy. Sometime in the year after the accident at Three Mile Island nuclear plant, a majority of Americans polled in a survey agreed with the proposition that nuclear power is a necessary component of the nation's energy system. A majority also agreed, however, with the proposition that nuclear power is inherently unsafe, and said they would not want a nuclear plant built near their home. In the Western, rootless tradition our tendency has been to credit the wishes of the majority responding to the first question and to discount or dismiss the wishes of the majority responding to the second. The first question, tradition would have it, deals with the issue in its "purest," most general form, divorced from any consideration of circumstance or context; the responses to the second are infected, apparently, with narrow self-interest or (to use a phrase I have heard Marxists use) "local particularism."

But why? To reason this way is to give preference to the voice of the abstract at the expense of the voice of the particular. This we can only do if we dismiss out of hand the possibility that because moral questions come to us not in the abstract but as concrete, particular problems, solutions to moral questions will necessarily be particular and specific. In epistemology and in morals, a plea for a diversity of approaches would have us defend the possibility that particularism has something to offer, and it is just this possibility that tends to be denied by an educational system that relies on rootless professionals for its personnel.

What is to be done?

Unfortunately, the underlying causes of the rootless professorial class are not amenable to dramatic alteration. The philosophical tradition that values the general over the particular is being reconstructed, but it seems unlikely that the national market for academic services will ever disappear—not as long as transportation is cheap, not as long as that market is so tight that candidates consider themselves lucky to get a job at all, let alone one in a region they could conceivably call home. We are very far from the days when students attended the local college and the most gifted among them were recruited to serve on the faculty after graduation. If we cannot get rid of the causes of the problem, we can at least alleviate the symptoms. And, as it turns out, this may be the better course, for it gives us the opportunity to keep what is good in both cosmopolitanism and provincialism.

First, the academy has to overcome its prejudice against the local and provincial, so that its hiring committees do not include nonnative status as an implicit qualification for employment. The acquaintance I mentioned sought a job for which he was qualified in a region whose species, seasons, and landforms he knew; that knowledge, it seems, counted against him. It shouldn't have. The diversity with which we presume to challenge students should include that rarest of all academics, the learned professor at home in a place.

Second, professors should take the trouble to include local content in their courses. Not abstract theories about distant peoples, but concrete realizations about observable communities; not airy generalizations that transcend student experience and lie beyond their powers of criticism, but specific conclusions whose skeptical testing they can perform themselves; not social-science hearsay taken on faith, but evidence weighed critically, firsthand: these are the substance of a rooted education. If education involves making the student's world by turns problematic and comprehensible, puzzling then scrutable, local content will also increase teaching effectiveness. Transforming the world immediately outside the classroom into a laboratory will tend to erase the artificial boundary between the roles of student and citizen, thereby encouraging in the latter the habits of the former. A citizenry that is curious, skeptical, and reasonable, one that takes little on faith and is accustomed to carrying careful inquiry into the world, is a citizenry that more nearly fits the mold that democracy requires.

Third, professors should take more seriously the regional branches of the professional organizations in the various disciplines, rather than seeing them as proving grounds for bright graduate students and low-level professors. If they were to serve as forums for the development of curricula rooted in locale, the work there could have real meaning and importance, rather than being a political alternative to or a pale reflection of the agenda of the national organizations.

Finally, academics in all disciplines ought to work to acquire a kind of dual citizenship—in the world of ideas and scholarship, yes, but also in the very real world of watersheds and growing seasons and migratory pathways and food chains and dependency webs. What is needed is a class of cosmopolitan educators willing to live where they work and to work where they live, a class of educators willing to take root, willing to cultivate a sense of place. These educators could then exemplify in their teaching and in their lives their own manner of accommodation to the fruitful tension between local and universal, particular and general, concrete and abstract. In an age when humanity's relationship to nature is so in need of careful, farsighted attention, this much is clear: academics do a disservice to their students, and to the future of human culture on the planet, if they do anything less.

pseudocommunities

DAVID EHRENFELD

TO begin with a little anecdote. There is a classroom, an ugly, badly shaped, windowless room in a modern university building designed with students not in mind. In this room is a small class, my class. We have rearranged tables and chairs in a semicircle around my place to defy the terrible ambience and to allow all twenty-five students to see and hear one another and me. I am talking. Two students sitting together in the front row—a thirty-year-old man with a pager on his belt and a twenty-year-old woman—are speaking to each other and laughing quietly; they see that I am looking at them and they continue to laugh, not furtively or offensively but openly and engagingly, as if I weren't there. I don't know what they are laughing about. Both of these students will eventually receive an A in the course for exceptionally fine work.

As I speak to the class, part of my mind is thinking about these students and wondering why they are laughing. Is there chalk on my face or a hole in my pants? Have I repeated myself or unconsciously misused a word or inverted a phrase? Then I remember something Bruce Wilshire wrote and the paranoia fades. The laughter has nothing to do with me. Bruce, a philosopher who works in a nearby building on campus, described the same attitude in his own classes in his book *The Moral Collapse of the University.* This passive and casual rudeness, a fairly new phenomenon, has a simple cause, he said: "I sometimes see students looking at me as if they thought I could not see them, as if I were just somebody on their screen." When my students were laughing, they had no idea that I would be bothered. At that moment they were treating me as if I were a face on television.

That's what it is; I'm sure of it. The students (at least most of them) and I inhabit different worlds, even when we sit in the same room. In my world, the people I speak with are real: if I offend them they are hurt or angry *with me,* if I give them pleasure they smile *at me,* if I bore them they find an excuse to move away *from me.* We are alive to one another. The world of my students is far more complex, a hybrid world, a world in transition. For them, some of the old world survives but it is confusingly intermingled with the artificial world of electronic communication. Up to now, this has been mostly one-way communication; the recipients are physically and mentally passive. The faces on the television screen speak—my students have been watching and listening in some cases for five hours a day or more, starting at age two or three. I cannot compete. Three hours of class a week for fourteen weeks is no time at all compared with the television they have seen. Their authority figures are two dimensional and cannot hear. They neither take offense nor do they rebuke; their brief utterances are well suited to the wandering, superficial mentality fostered by the ever-flickering tube.

The world of television, by inducing passivity and unresponsiveness, has cut many of the human threads and connections that once bound people together into working communities. Lewis Mumford compared life in front of the television screen to life in a space capsule, frightening in its absolute isolation. Passivity and alienation are not communal virtues.

To the extent that television has weakened American communal life, it has weakened communal power, the only effective power that can limit consumption, pollution, and the degradation of nature. We would appear to be locked into a hopeless spiral of decline, for television promotes these very evils while weakening the communal ability to resist them.

If this were all the threat that electronic communication has to offer, we might conceivably find ways to cope with the challenge, formidable as it is. We might, for example, take advantage of the fact that television, which has helped to ruin communities, has not eliminated the desire of each person to be part of a community. A lonely consumer, however passive, is a dissatisfied consumer—unstable, even rebellious. Could we use this instability to fashion a revolt against television, even against the mind-numbing menace of video games? Not any more, I'm afraid. There is more electronic trouble in the offing.

Perhaps unconsciously, the developers of electronic communication have come up with the perfect counterstrategy to prevent us from using the loneliness of people caught in the television culture to wean them away from the tube and back into the community. This counterstrategy is the creation of *pseudocommunities,* my word for assemblages of electronically linked people. Pseudocommunities are arising as substitutes for the real ones that are gone. Pseudocommunities will make everyone feel good again, will replace enervating passivity with a semblance of activity, creativity, and choice, and, sad to say, will keep the reality of true communal responsibility and judgment as far away as it is now. Interactive and other sophisticated electronic communication systems have arrived on the scene.

One of the most familiar, albeit relatively primitive, systems, a precursor of the pseudocommunity, is commonly referred to as voice mail. Few people are left in the United States and Canada who have not had their blood pressure raised five or ten points by a patronizing recorded voice saying, "If you want information about schedules, press 1 now; if you want the office of the director, press 2 now; if . . ." Making fun of voice mail is like shooting a sitting duck—I leave it to those who earn a living as nightclub comedians or humor columnists. But a few words will not be amiss. Voice mail is a threat to communities, a precursor of pseudocommunities, in that it accustoms us to dealing with facsimiles of people in our daily lives. Whether people or facsimiles do a better job is irrelevant—there is more to life than maximizing the efficiency of daily transactions (although voice mail rarely does that).

Lately, when the wonders of the age of information and communication have got me down, I have revived my spirits by rereading two exceptional books, Jane Austen's *Emma* and Elizabeth Gaskell's *Wives and Daughters.* Both, set in the days before railroads started us on our present perilous path, take place almost entirely within a few miles of the houses of the central characters, and both describe the incredible subtlety and wealth of interactions, for good and for evil, that one experiences in a true community.

I would love to quote from these books to illustrate my point, but no brief extract of a few lines could convey the diversity of the human existence within the communities that these authors knew and portrayed. Suffice it to say that in the sort of communities described by Austen and Gaskell, the passions and activities of love, hatred, sexuality, compassion, selfishness, and intellectual intercourse, modulated by and expressed through the life of the community, take on a complexity and richness that is not found in an electronically facilitated pseudocommunity.

It seems that almost every advance of our technology brings more social disintegration. Consider the videophone. To the voice in the receiver has been added the face on the screen, and this changes everything. The feature that has kept the conventional telephone from destroying communities is the *lack* of visual information that accompanies the voice. The disembodied voice is a constant reminder of what the telephone really brings about: communication between people who are actually, demonstrably, perhaps distressingly, distant from one another. Like a letter, a phone call is received in private from someone who is elsewhere. Add a picture and the privacy and sense of distance are disturbed, replaced by an illusion of proximity, a mockery of context. This is a huge step on the road to pseudo-community.

Knowing the danger of videophones can help us understand the more insidious challenge to communities that is called E-mail, electronic mail. Here I fly in the face of conventional opinion. E-mail is supposed to be a liberating force in society. Using electronic mail, one can send a message to any person in the world who is in the network, or direct it to large groups of people simultaneously. What better way to promote the free, democratic exchange of ideas, to create a "global community"?

The grave problem with E-mail is that it creates the sensation of being part of a community of people working, creating, and playing together for the common good. But the sensation is only that, for at the end of the day when you in Vermont and your E-mail correspondent in western Texas go to sleep, your climates will still be different, your soils will still be different, your landscapes will still be different, your local environmental problems will still be different, and—most important—your neighbors will still be different, and while you have been creating the global community with each other, you will have been neglecting them.

The speed and simplicity of communicating by E-mail can be alluring and addictive, at least at first. Unlike letter writing, anything that comes to mind can be conveyed instantly and can receive an instantaneous response. Tens of thousands of streams of consciousness are flowing through the cables. But this is not an advantage; it is a problem. In a proper relationship many thoughts, after care-

ful reflection, should be left unsaid. And careful reflection takes time and sometimes privacy, assets that we have stupidly wished away. There is no easy, glamorous
way to be part of a community. The pseudocommunity of E-mail detracts from
the real work of community building which, although deeply gratifying, requires
a painstaking, persistent effort and a perpetual learning that last as long as one keeps
on breathing.

Communication is worthwhile and necessary, but not at the expense of communal integrity, which requires a balancing measure of isolation of one community from another, and, at times, of one individual from another. Electronic communication systems lack this balance, this subtle regulation of communal function.
In the pseudocommunity of E-mail it is becoming harder and harder to maintain
the kind of personal boundaries that add strength and diversity to real communities and keep them from flying apart. One example: it is possible for the sender to
find out whether the addressee has read one's E-mail message, and at what time.
How can any relationship survive this kind of intrusiveness?

Soon there will be new products and systems of electronic communication
on the market. It does not take much imagination to envision the various combinations of videophones, mobile miniature cameras, holographic display software, and E-mail that are likely to be devised. Some already exist as prototypes at
Bell Laboratories and elsewhere. Reality is being replaced with virtual reality.
Where will this end? For it *will* end in the not too far-off future. It will end because the global pseudocommunity is and will increasingly become economically
unstable. For the great majority of users, electronic communication does not help
to create wealth. The human and natural resources devoted to these systems do
not result in any socially acceptable outpouring of material goods and necessary
services. Instead, production, local economic stability, and communal security are
sacrificed to transient efficiencies and the quick profits of distant entrepreneurs.

Although it does not create wealth, the new communication enables it to be
shifted rapidly from place to place. Now, with global trade (especially free trade),
instantaneous global finance, instantaneous global exchange or theft of wealth-
producing ideas, and facilitated global exploitation of distant resources, it is becoming impossible for most real communities—and people—to continue the
slow accumulation or even maintenance of assets that is a condition of survival.
When our real communities are mostly bankrupt, the wealth and social order that
support Bell Labs, the costly electronic hardware, the fiber-optic cables, and the
whole network will disappear.

And the new systems of communication will be rejected for social reasons. In
addition to being exploitative and expensive, consumers of wealth rather than
generators of wealth, pseudocommunities are also thin and above all unsatisfying.
Although it is fun to play bridge simultaneously with five hundred partners in ten
countries, mere fun does not sustain any but the shallowest of existences. Moreover, the loss of privacy and independence, the breakdown of human boundaries
of self and community, will not, I think, be tolerated by most of us for very long.

I remember a photograph of a baby monkey in a psychological experiment; it was being raised in isolation with a surrogate "mother" made of wire covered with terrycloth. The monkey was clinging to the device but looked profoundly sad and anxious. Most people using videophones or E-mail do not look sad or anxious. Electronic communication is still new and exiting. Indeed, for some who are infirm or handicapped, it can provide a new source of human contact. But for most of us, in the end, as the dust gathers and the glamour fades, our pseudo-communities of silicon and plastic and liquid crystal will prove no more comforting and no more nurturing than a surrogate mother of wire and terrycloth.

from monoculture to polyculture

PAUL CUSTODIO BUBE

DRIVING across Kansas is often stereotyped as a boring experience, presumably because of its flatlands geography. I first experienced this stereotype when I moved to Kansas, but soon found that it is not a very accurate depiction of a state that has as much attractive rolling hill country as it has flatlands.

Why the stereotype? I suspect it derives from the fact that most Kansas farmland is cultivated with a single crop—wheat. In late spring a drive through almost any part of the state is a trek through endless miles of wheat fields punctuated by freeway exits and grain elevators. In other words, most Kansas farmland is planted with "monocultures," fields of all one crop. Monocultures are often impressive in their uniformity; but they are extremely vulnerable to disease and pests, they significantly deplete the soil's nutrients, and—true to the stereotype—they are rather boring.

Wes Jackson argues that monocultures are not intrinsic to the way the Kansas prairie originally evolved. Rather, native prairie is "polycultural," inhabited with innumerable varieties of plants and animals. Jackson's Land Institute has been experimenting with sustainable farming practices that mimic this polycultural state, because crop diversity minimizes the need for the fertilization and pest control that threaten the survival of monocultures. And though I do not know to what extent this aspect motivates the Land Institute's experimentation, polycultures are aesthetically more interesting than monocultures.

I think the metaphors of monoculture and polyculture help us to appreciate one of the great American culture wars of this century: the clash between positivism and fundamentalism. Although these worldviews initially emerged as intellectual movements in philosophy and religion respectively, they have moved beyond the classroom and the pew into the center of the American cultural landscape, filling editorial pages of newspapers, sometimes battling each other in courtrooms, and increasingly appearing in political races ranging from school board elections to presidential campaigns.

As much as these two movements seem to each other and to most observers to be polar opposites I suggest they are essentially similar in their monoculturalism. To recognize this underlying similarity helps us to see them as surprisingly allied in their implications for living in community. Like the wheat monocultures growing in Kansas, fundamentalism and positivism initially appear strongly rooted, impressive in their respective uniformities and sense of certitude. Yet fundamentalism and positivism, like agricultural monocultures, are not well adapted to the American environment. At best they provide a precarious sense of rootedness for their adherents, and may at worst deplete America of its rich inheritance. This essay explores how they are similar in their monoculturalism and their implications for the American scene, and suggests an alternative polycultural world-view that is better adapted to America's environment.

During the first half of the twentieth century, much of American philosophy became enamored with scientific method and rejected earlier philosophies as speculative and nonempirical. Philosophical positivism found in scientific materialism a new foundation. It argued that "attempts to claim knowledge outside the natural sciences are to be measured against the procedures used within them, and that philosophy [that is, positivism] has recently become scientific and rigorous" (Rorty 1982, 213). Positivist philosophy is guided by the principle of verification: meaningful statements are those verifiable by scientific method or follow analytically from the structure of language (see Ayer 1952). The problem is that much of what previous philosophy thought of as meaningful, including aesthetics, ethics, and religion, falls outside these limits. Religious statements, in particular, are singled out as neither scientifically verifiable nor analytic. At best they are confused attempts to express ill-defined emotive states of the speaker; at worst they are mere nonsense.

Positivism's cultural influence is disseminated throughout American universities. Not only has it dominated philosophy departments since the 1940s but its ideal of a rigorous, scientific approach to scholarship has strongly influenced scholars in most fields of the humanities and social sciences. Philosophical rigor in other humanities disciplines such as literature and ethics requires reduction of traditional concepts such as beauty and goodness to descriptions of feeling states, sociological dynamics, or other phenomena that can be studied scientifically. Indeed, some traditionally humanistic disciplines such as history and anthropology now position themselves as social sciences, aspiring to the model of scientific rigor. As a consequence of positivism's hegemony in the sciences, social sciences, and humanities, it remains well entrenched among America's educated elite.

Interestingly, fundamentalism began to emerge as a self-conscious movement in American Protestantism at about the time positivism was gaining ascendancy in this country's universities. As a formal movement, fundamentalism took its name from a series of essays published between 1910 and 1915 called *The Fundamentals.* By 1919 the World Christian Fundamentals Association was formed to oppose liberalism and modernism across denominational lines (Ammerman 1991, 2, 23–24; Packer 1958, 28–29). Early on, fundamentalists saw themselves pitted against what they saw as a capitulation of mainstream Christianity to secularism, especially scientific materialism. Fundamentalists interpreted secularism as, in large part, an outgrowth of the rise of the scientific spirit, particularly embodied in Darwin's theory of evolution.

The central "fundamental" is the view that the Bible is the inspired, literal, inerrant word of God. The notion of inerrancy is the belief that the Bible contains no errors about faith, morality, and the nature of the physical world. This doctrine was developed most fully by Scottish Common Sense Realism, a movement among Princeton theologians, which argued that since God's purpose was perfect, God's medium for communicating that purpose must also be perfectly comprehensible—in other words, literally true. If the Bible is not literally true, then God's revelation is not perfect, thus God is not perfect—which is self-evidently false. In short, the Bible is viewed as a repository of facts that form the trustworthy basis of all knowledge: theological, ethical, and scientific. Any statement found to contradict the Bible is false and to be rejected.

Like positivism, fundamentalism's cultural impact has been significant. The success in the 1980s of the now-disbanded Moral Majority, and the growing prominence of its baby-boomer offspring, the Christian Coalition, has placed fundamentalism firmly in contention with mainline Christianity for religious and political loyalty among the American middle class. Ammerman (1991, 2) cites a 1982 Gallup poll indicating that 39 percent of all Americans have a fundamentalist understanding of the Bible, and 44 percent call themselves creationists. Even in the area of science education, fundamentalists have been successful in propagating the study of so-called creation science, which is eroding and sometimes eliminating discussion of evolutionary theory in elementary and high school text books. Thus, while positivism has remained strong in American universities, fundamentalism has been staging something of a takeover of America's elementary and high school boards. Put differently, fundamentalism is quickly gaining hegemony over "low" culture, while positivism remains entrenched among the guardians of "high" culture.

In summary, both positivism and fundamentalism are contemporaneous responses to the success of scientific thought at the turn of the century. One might characterize positivism as having embraced science as the sole measure of experience, whereas fundamentalism rejected science as a threat to the experience that counts most to people of faith. Nonetheless, they tend to share as much as they differ: both define the nature of the world and experience in relatively narrow terms; both are exclusivist in their self-conception as the only true way of understanding the world; both see meaningful language, whether philosophical or biblical, as literal and univocal (notice the similarities between the principle of verification and the principle of biblical literalism); hence both are reductionistic in explaining the world, whether in terms of scientific or biblical laws. Interestingly, the similarity between fundamentalism and positivism was recognized by an early fundamentalist preacher, A. T. Pierson, who said, "I like Biblical theology that . . . does not begin with an hypothesis, and then warp the facts and the philosophy to fit the crook of our dogma, but [is] a *Baconian* system, which first gathers the teachings of the word of God, and then seeks to deduce some general law upon which the facts can be arranged" (Ammerman 1991, 9; italics added).

These shared characteristics constitute what I refer to as their monoculturalism. Each denies the validity of the other, reducing the other to its opposite: fundamentalism tends to reduce science to a pseudofaith; whereas positivism attempts to reduce faith to a primitive attempt at scientific explanation. In either case, one part of our cultural landscape—scientific or spiritual—is sacrificed in order to safe-guard the other. In either case, the loss is profound. However, mutual rejection is not the only consequence of their monoculturalism. The more profound impli-cations can be seen by looking briefly at a representative from each worldview.

E. D. Hirsch, Jr., a professor of English at the University of Virginia, has raised a storm of controversy in American education with his publication of *Cultural Literacy: What Every American Needs to Know* (1987) and *The Dictionary of Cultural Literacy* (with Joseph F. Kett and James Trefil, 1988). Prior to these books, Hirsch was known in university circles for his theory of interpretation (Hirsch 1967). His claim that a text has objective, verifiable meaning, that is, what was intended by the author, reflects the positivist temperament that meaning is univocal and can be discovered only by rigorous analysis.

Hirsch's positivism carries over to his view of cultural literacy. He argues that a basic definable content of cultural information is "needed [by all Americans] to thrive in the modern world" (Hirsch 1987, xiii). The cultural inheritance of eth-nic groups such as African-Americans, Latinos, Asian-Americans, and others, is largely peripheral to cultural literacy because it is not "mainstream." Elements of these ethnic cultures may make their way into cultural literacy, as did the ethnic word "pizza," and the art form "jazz," only when they become important to main-stream culture (1987, 28). Hirsch's designation of what is ethnic makes it clear that he considers mainstream culture to be *Anglo* culture. Thus, cultural literacy is in-herently monocultural rather than multicultural or polycultural.

Hirsch is quick to reject criticisms that he is insensitive toward America's di-verse ethnic cultures, devoting all of his fourth chapter to the issue of diversity. The gist of his position is that it is to the advantage of non-Anglo ethnic groups to become assimilated into mainstream culture (1987, 24). Hirsch argues that a common stock of cultural knowledge promotes the shared framework for com-munication necessary for democracy and efficiency in an industrialized nation. Cultural literacy provides an "impersonal, context-free" basis for communicating that empowers culturally divergent groups to have their views potentially heard within mainstream culture (1987, 72–74).

However, what Hirsch proposes as a common cultural inheritance is hardly "impersonal" or "context free." His list of "What Literate Americans Know" is essentially a digest of Anglo-Eurocentric (and androcentric) cultural knowledge (1987, 146-215). The best way to illustrate this is to list some of the terms Hirsch deems essential next to names absent from his digest, which represent American cultures that are not Anglo-Eurocentric.

Hirsch's List	Absent Polycultural Possibilities
Norman Mailer	James Baldwin
Jerry Falwell	Dalai Lama
A Streetcar Named Desire	*A Raisin in the Sun*
Adolf Eichmann	Simon Wiesenthal

Beatles	Temptations
Mein Kampf	*Diary of Ann Frank*
KKK	SCLC (Southern Christian Leadership Conference)

Hirsch's proposal that a "rigorous traditional education" in cultural literacy would allow non-Anglo cultures to find mainstream acceptance of their heritages seems well intentioned (see 1987, 23). He also acknowledges value in learning about nondominant cultures: "In the best of worlds, all Americans would be multiliterate. But surely the first step in that direction must be for all of us to become literate in *our own* national language and culture" (1987, 93; italics added). Yet he begs the question of what our own language and culture is. We are not only a white, middle-class culture. Moreover, he fails to see that his "first step" is a subtle, eroding process of conformism that often saps non-Anglos of the rich cultures they have to offer. Middle-class Anglos, except by way of personal choice, rarely need to familiarize themselves with the other cultures with which they share this country.

The fact is that American culture, like its native prairies, is actually made up of numerous—and growing numbers of—cultures. To find a single cultural core shared by all cultures seems a chimera; and to promote one culture at the expense of others is simply chauvinistic. Would it not be more faithful to social reality to acknowledge our polyculture and construct education around at least some awareness of the various cultures?

Peter Wagner is a professor of evangelism at Fuller Theological Seminary, the largest nondenominational seminary in the country. Although Wagner would probably prefer the designation "evangelical" over "fundamentalist," his "strong belief in the authority and infallibility of the Bible as the Word of God" fits the historical meaning of fundamentalism (Wagner 1979, 3). In *Our Kind of People: The Ethical Dimensions of Church Growth in America* Wagner proposes a "homogeneous church model" as a basis for promoting church growth. This model advises pastors of churches in ethnically mixed neighborhoods to give up trying to maintain one integrated congregation. Instead, pastors should set up separate, ethnically homogeneous congregations that meet at different times, though under the same roof. Wagner argues that these monocultural congregations grow more rapidly than a single polycultural congregation because of the social scientific "fact" that people prefer to be with people who are like themselves.

Recognizing that his church growth model is controversial, Wagner argues it is moral because it is biblical. Jesus' commandment, "Go therefore and make disciples of all nations" (Matt. 28:19), justifies using the homogeneous growth model as a means of bringing people to Christianity (4). Wagner concedes that Jesus' commandment does not justify the use of *any* means of converting people, and adds a qualification: "If Jesus and Paul did not carry out their ministries in accord with this theory [of homogeneous growth], it would not be worthy of further investigation" (109). That is, he feels that a literal interpretation of Jesus and Paul vindicates the homogeneous growth model.

Wagner asserts, first, that the Bible depicts Jesus as calling his first disciples from among only one ethnic group, the Galileans (117). Second, early on, the church was confronted with a conflict between Hebrew and Hellenistic Jewish Christians (Acts 6) that emerged because two homogeneous ethnic groups were in such close contact that they became "fissionable material" (120). The conflict was resolved by the church's division along parallel, monocultural tracks that allowed for growth unhindered by ethnic rivalry (121). Third, the eventual emergence of Gentile Christianity under Paul's leadership occurred because Paul worked separately from Hellenistic Jewish Christianity (124 ff.).

Wagner's "literalism" is both strained and idiosyncratic. When he says that Jesus' inner circle was made up entirely of Galileans, he ignores the differences in class, education, and skin color among that group. When he points out the conflict between Hebrew and Hellenistic Jewish Christians, he fails to note that the Bible nowhere says that the ethnic groups separated; rather, Hellenistic Jewish Christians were invited to share leadership with Hebrew Christians. Finally, even if we accept the controversial claim that Gentile Christianity only began to grow when it separated from Hellenistic Jewish Christianity, Wagner ignores the incredibly polycultural makeup of Gentiles in the first-century Roman Empire. In short, Wagner's literalism seems to assume what it aims to prove.

In spite of Wagner's monocultural model, he acknowledges, rather like Hirsch, that polycultural community is a worthy ideal—one even desired by God. Unlike Hirsch, Wagner wants to avoid an assimilationist position that robs ethnic groups of their unique cultural identities (143). He believes that after persons come into a homogeneous church where they feel comfortable, they will eventually come to appreciate God's plan for a polycultural world and develop the appropriate attitudes of acceptance and respect for differences (142). However, it is not obvious how people who do not concretely experience differences in church will come to see acceptance and respect for differences as part of God's polycultural ideal. Indeed, if one is taught that the Bible directs people to come to God without needing to encounter the differences of their neighbors, it is not clear why one would ever be motivated to encounter the differences of neighbors, or even to recognize those who are different as neighbors. Hence, Wagner's avoidance of assimilationist monoculturalism comes at the expense of a separatism that merely fragments monocultural Christian communities along ethnic lines.

Wagner's perspective on monocultural communities seems well intentioned. Nonetheless, it is mind-boggling to imagine the effect his method of church growth would have had on race relations had it been widely accepted in the 1960s. Even if Wagner is not racist in intent, his views offer seductive support for racist ideology, as illustrated by an anonymous comment on the back cover of his book: "*Our Kind of People* attacks the Christian guilt complex arising from the civil rights movement and puts it to rest with a skillful mixture of scriptural precedent and human psychology. In doing so, Wagner transforms the statement that '11 a.m. on Sunday is the most segregated hour in America' from a millstone around Christian necks into a dynamic tool for assuring Christian growth." What sort of growth comes from a dynamic tool of segregation?

Although Hirsch and Wagner come from very different backgrounds and are speaking to very different audiences, their views tend toward a remarkably similar monocultural understanding of community. Both are trying to achieve laudable goals: Hirsch wants education to prepare citizens to communicate effectively so as to enhance the democratic process; Wagner wants to equip the Christian church with tools that will allow it to attract and serve people more effectively. Both are aware that they can be charged with bigotry and insensitivity, but both think that their brand of monoculturalism can somehow provide a path beyond bigotry. Both fail to offer a convincing description of how this is possible. Where they differ is that Hirsch's monoculturalism is assimilationist, Wagner's separatist.

Neither approach is in the long run adequate for our actual diverse social situation. Which culture could persuade the others that it is the norm to which the others should assimilate? How can we survive as one nation (or church) if each ethnic group lives in separatist isolation? If I am correct that positivism and fundamentalism are monocultural views of human community that are inadequate to our social situation, then it would seem that we need to explore an alternative worldview that would allow for a polycultural concept of community more suited to the American landscape.

Research by sustainable agriculturalists in planting polycultures demonstrates how crop diversity enhances the viability of the separate plants: what one plant's roots take from the soil, another's roots are putting in; one plant's resistance to pestilence decreases another plant's vulnerability; the postseason decay of one plant is fertilizer for others. In short, polycultures offer a potential for mutual benefit that is missing in monocultures. I suggest the potential is just as real for human polycultures.

It is not enough to say, however, that all that is needed is a polycultural worldview, and then simply to choose from several possible candidates. Although many so-called postmodern worldviews—ranging from various Continental alternatives such as poststructuralism to more American offerings such as neopragmatism and process thought—break free from the monocultural mindset that seems endemic to the modernist movements of positivism and fundamentalism, we need to give greater consideration to a worldview that can respond to the profounder impulses that initially motivated adherence to positivism and fundamentalism.

In the case of positivism, the success of the model of scientific reasoning was, and continues to be, a powerful lure. However, science itself, particularly physics and biology, has advanced beyond the positivist model (Barbour 1991, ch. 2). In the case of fundamentalism, the attraction of a spiritual dimension to experience relates one to a transcendent source and goal in life and is accessible to all, not just biblical scholars. Yet even literalist theology abounds in esoteric issues—such as the number and duration of "dispensations" in salvation history—just as inaccessible to the average Christian.

A survey of postmodern options is not possible here, but a word can be said about why I would be reluctant to turn to either Continental postmodern movements or neopragmatism. In general, Continental options are not likely to have widespread appeal because they do not have deep roots in the American landscape. Neopragmatism, particularly as promoted by Richard Rorty, has maintained the positivist indifference toward religious experience. Process thought has neither of these liabilities: it emerged within the same American context as did pragmatism and has generally affirmed the validity and value of religious experience. Moreover, process thought finds itself in full agreement with the empirical ideal of later twentieth-century science, expanding the notion of empirical experience to include the ethical, aesthetic, and religious (Barbour 1991).

Process thought grows out of the philosophy of Alfred North Whitehead, whose work in mathematics and theoretical physics led him to articulate a metaphysical description of the world consistent with the emerging insights of modern physics and with commonsense human experience (Whitehead 1978). Whitehead was no less impressed with the achievements of modern science than was positivism, but he understood science as one "adventure in ideas" that was historically conditioned. He also appreciated the validity of religious experience as a historical and personal force that had to be accounted for by any adequate philosophy.

Whitehead's metaphysics affirms, on the one hand, the evolutionary development of the cosmos from the inorganic to the organic, from simple organisms to complex human beings; and, on the other, the necessity of a single entity, God, who is the ground of novel, complex order in the evolving universe and who experiences all that is experienced by other beings. As Whitehead puts it, God is "the fellow-sufferer who understands." God's aim in the evolving universe is to create novel possibilities that can "lure" or "persuade," rather than coerce, all beings to achieve richer, more intense, more complex, and more harmonious levels of experience.

Henry James Young, in his *Hope in Process: A Theology of Social Pluralism* (1990), explicitly ties process thought to a polycultural view of community. For Young the process view of God as the ground or source of novel possibilities for experience confirms the value of polycultural community (92). The diversity of polycultural communities makes them inherently more capable of being responsive to God as the source of novelty for individual and communal fulfillment, whereas monocultures resist the possibilities for novelty provided by God, thereby eventually leading toward social stagnation. Moreover, in the process view of God as the one who experiences all that is experienced by other beings, Young finds further support for cultural diversity. God feels the sufferings and joys of the rich and poor, male and female, white, black, and brown, and even the oppressed and the oppressor. Yet God's feelings of the world are integrated into a new divine vision of liberated existence capable of luring the present diversities toward harmonious community. Finally, the divine ideal of polycultural community not only allows for new, richer possibilities of social existence that can enrich its members, but it can also enrich the experience of God. As Young suggests, polycultural community is the means by which God's kingdom can be realized within history (132).

Of course enormous risks are associated with the ideal of polycultural community. As Whitehead notes, the greater the possibilities for good, the greater the risks for evil. The two most obvious risks are the increased possibilities for conflict, on the one hand, and the potential of devolving into fragmented, individualistic coexistence, on the other. Wagner was particularly concerned with the former, and Hirsch with the latter.

As noted, Wagner suggests that bringing different ethnic groups together can be explosive. One could point to the dissolution of the former Yugoslavia as empirical support for this claim. Here, one might say, polycultural diversity brought about violence and war, destroying both the larger community and the ethnic groups that constituted it. However, this sort of criticism fails to understand the real causes of Yugoslavia's violent conflict, which resulted from a revival of ethnic nationalism, particularly on the part of the Serbs, and seeks to preserve an imagined ideal of monoculturalism. Serbian separatism is a result of never having embraced the possibilities of polyculture. Thus, far from being an example of the danger of polyculturalism, the demise of Yugoslavia is indicative of the inherent implications of monoculturalism. Of course, polyculturalists need to take into account a cautionary note from this situation. The unity of Yugoslavia prior to the demise of communism was externally imposed. On the surface the country did appear to be a polycultural community. However, the unity attained by the communist state was achieved not through a rich interchange among cultures, but by suppressing and replacing these polycultures with a substitute monocultural ideology, namely, Soviet-style communism.

The second danger, more descriptive of America's current situation, lies behind Hirsch's call for cultural literacy. Hirsch feels difference breeds indifference. Diversity brings confusion about cultural identity and undermines national unity. He argues that monocultural literacy can provide a common identity that overcomes differences and creates the basis for national unity. Though a seductive argument, it holds implications that are ultimately more dangerous than individualism and social fragmentation. Hirsch's version of cultural literacy would impose one group's culture on the others. This assimilationist project, it seems to me, was in effect in the former Yugoslavia. The imposition of monoculture at best provides only a superficial, fragile unity, and at worst breeds potentially explosive underlying resentments. Given the alternatives, I would prefer the risk of individualism and social fragmentation to a coercively imposed unity that has, all too often in history, ended up in some form of "ethnic cleansing."

I suggest the best way that individualism and social fragmentation can be avoided in polycultural community is by remembering the richness that comes from encountering differences at all levels of experience, and by recognizing the transcendent value such richness has even for God. More than forty years ago, Ralph Ellison made a similar point:

> Whence all this passion toward conformity anyway?—diversity is the word. Let man keep his many parts and you'll have no tyrant states. Why, if they follow this conformity business they'll end up by forcing me, an invisible man, to become white, which is not a color but the lack of one. Must I strive toward colorlessness? But seriously, and without snobbery, think of what the world would lose if that should happen. America is woven of many strands; I would recognize them and let it so remain. . . . Our fate is to become one, and yet many—This is not prophecy, but description. (1953, 499)

This is not only a description of the American landscape, it is America's historical roots. Polyculturalism is as necessary to sustaining a healthy American community as Wes Jackson would argue that polycultural agriculture is to sustaining farming in Kansas. Today, when I travel around Kansas and observe the grandiose efforts of agribusinesses to turn the land into a monoculture, I think a lot about the poverty of the monocultural ideal. And when I notice how the prairie persistently encroaches on the wheat fields, I am reminded that "diversity is the word" for both nonhuman and human community. Indeed, the challenge of polyculturalism to become a more inclusive community points one step further to affirm that the richest possibilities for community will only be attained when we achieve a diversity that extends beyond all forms of anthropocentrism as well as ethnocentrism. The ultimate ideal is to include all forms of human and nonhuman community in a greater polyculture that would be our true community and God's fullest realization.

an amish perspective

DAVID KLINE

I want to talk about our farm. It is on the 120 acres of rolling Ohio land that the county courthouse records show belongs to my wife and me and our family. It is here that I can do great harm to nature or where I can live, or at least try to live, in peaceful coexistence with the land. Here on our farm I can exploit nature or nurture it. Here is where nature giveth and nature taketh away.

But first we need to look at the past. We of northern European stock were not the first humans on the land that is now our farm. There is ample evidence otherwise.

Last fall as I was harrowing the last round in the field that was to be sown to wheat, something on the ground caught my eye. Stopping the team, I reached down and picked up what looked like a piece of chert. It was a small arrowhead, perfect except for a small chip broken from its tip. While the horses rested, I turned and sat on the harrow to admire my find.

Less than an inch in length, the triangular piece of flint was obviously crafted by a human. As I turned it over in my hand and wiped it clean of soil, I pondered on how much the previous owner of the arrowhead had depended on flint—cryptocrystalline quartz—for survival. It occurred to me that I too depend on a tiny speck of quartz, not to slay a deer, but to tell me when it is time to unhitch.

Let's suppose that in early October of 1492 a small band of Erie hunters from the Cat nation left their village along the shore of the lake now bearing their name and traveled south to gather provisions for the coming winter months. (Early historians wrote that all kinds of game, wild fruits, and succulent roots abounded in this part of Ohio.) One of the hunters may have waited in ambush for a black bear or a white-tailed deer to leave the cover of the marshland below and travel to the ridge to feed on acorns from the white oaks and nuts from the beeches. As the animal passed the hunter's little coign of vantage, the Erie's bowstring snapped and the arrow streaked toward its target. But en route the arrow nicked a twig, deflecting it enough that it missed the animal and disappeared into the leaf litter of the autumn woods.

This Erie hunter, from the time called the Woodland Indian period, was not the first Native American to visit our land. I have found blades and spear points from the Archaic period, but until a few years ago I had never found any evidence from the Paleo-Indian period while working the fields. Then one spring our youngest son, Michael, and I were crossing Salt Creek with the horse and hack, on our way to repair fence along the bottom pasture, when we bounced across some rocks. We stopped and looked over the dashboard at the boulders below. My astonished eyes saw, an inch behind the horse's foot, the most beautifully knapped spear point I had ever been fortunate enough to find. The blade of black flint had not a nick on it and surely had been washed away from the creek bank only recently by high water. I am told it is from the late Paleo-Indian period. So there is evidence that the land we call our farm has been inhabited by humans, at least periodically, for many centuries.

For over three hundred years the small dart I held in my hand had lain undisturbed and, covered by an annual fall of leaves, had sunk deeper into the humus. Sheltered by the great oaks whose roots knitted the soil together and whose leaves added fertility, the arrowhead was not aware of the changes to come.

Nor was the Erie hunter to know that his own people, the powerful Cat nation, would be annihilated by the Iroquois, the Five Nation Confederacy, in 1656. For more than fifty years after the demise of the Eries, no Indians hunted on this land.

Then sometime in the early 1700s the Iroquois, now the Six Nations, gave this part of Ohio to the Delaware Indians, who were being pushed out of the east by European settlers. But even with the increased human activity, the flora and fauna of the land changed little. Occasionally centuries-old oaks died or were blown down by storms. The openings in the forests soon flourished with new seedlings, new trees that now number more than 250 growth rings.

Following the war of 1812 this land was visited by fewer and fewer Native Americans until by the early 1820s none at all came. The Indians who did not die from disease epidemics (which were arrogantly interpreted by some Europeans as God's way of clearing the land for His Elect) were forced to move west.

In 1824 our farm was settled and in 1825 a deed, signed by President Monroe, was given to that pioneer family. A deed, as Robert Frost wrote, that followed many deeds of war. Now the family had the right to pay taxes and to post "No Trespassing" signs. Other settlers came. Our farm was joined on the north by the Pomerene family. West were the Walters, east the Rosses, and to the northeast were the French Catholic settlers of the soon-to-be-prosperous community of Calmoutier.

I can only speculate what happened in the next fifty to seventy-five years. Quite obviously a struggle to control nature took place. From the sketchy history available, most of the vast forests—white and red oaks, chestnuts, hickories, beeches, and other hardwoods—were felled into windrows, left to dry for a year or two, and then burned. For many weeks of the year in the early to mid-1800s the skies over this part of Ohio were hazy from burning hardwoods, millions of board feet of the finest oaks on earth. As the trees went, so did much of the wildlife. Around 1850 the state legislature passed a law forbidding the burning of timber to open the land.

My small arrowhead escaped from being in a windrow of torched trees. The intense heat would have fractured the flint. With the opening of the land, the pioneer family began plowing between the stumps and sowing and planting crops of wheat, rye, oats, and corn.

For the first fifty years after being deeded, the farm, with the high fertility of its woodlands soils (Wooster silt loam), produced enough wealth for the family to prosper. Then starting around 1875 things began to go awry. The health of the soil deteriorated. The marriage between the steward and the land was in trouble. After being mined for too long, the fiddler's pay came due. And payment was taken in the reduced yields of the crops.

Soon after 1900 not enough income was generated from the farm to pay for the taxes. So the county sheriff ordered the "farmed-out" land and the buildings to be sold at public auction to the highest bidder. It was the old truism: "shirtsleeves to shirtsleeves in three generations." One could say that nature won the battle for the farm. But in reality, both humans and nature lost. Both were poorer for the experience.

What caused the farm to fail?

From a number of possible reasons let me suggest just a few. First, the depression of the 1890s did not help matters, I am sure. A second reason was the lack of legumes growing on the farm. When my uncle moved here in 1918 the primary plants growing were Canada thistles and timothy. Legumes play a vital part in the health of a sustainable farm, since the rhizobium bacteria in legumes have the ability to convert atmospheric nitrogen into plant food. The conversion nourishes the leguminous plants as well as companion plants of other species. For instance, bluegrass and white clover in a pasture field are the perfect pair.

As bluegrass and white clover are to each other, so should be our connectedness with nature, a connection of life that is difficult to put into words. I like the way the eighteenth-century Mennonite clover farmer David Mellinger framed it. He lived in the Palantinate, the section of southwestern Germany squeezed between the Rhine River and the French region of Alsace and Lorraine. This area is where the Mennonites and the Amish learned how important clover is, if you farm, in getting along with nature. Menninger said: "I should have already given princes and other great lords a description of my operation and how I achieved it, but I cannot tell it so easily . . . one thing leads to another. It is like a clockwork, where one wheel grabs hold of another, and then the work continues without my even being able to know or describe how I brought the machine into gear." Maybe this wheel of life is one of the mysteries of God.

The Apostle Paul wrote that we should serve faithfully as stewards of the mysteries of God. Perhaps the inference is that the stewards are the ministers of the Word. But if we lift our eyes not away from the earth, the mysteries of God can also be His creation. We should be stewards or caretakers of creation.

Science, I think, has attempted to gather these mysteries and set them in concrete. This is something of which religion also may be guilty. Once we rely too much on human cleverness, nature suffers and we become alienated from it. Johann Goethe thought the worst thing that can happen to man is alienation from nature.

As dressers and keepers of the earth, I believe we need some unconcreted mysteries. We need the delight of the unknown and the unexplainable in nature, what

Rachel Carson called the sense of wonder. How can the bobolinks find their way back to the farm after spending our winter in the austral summer of Argentina? When in late April the first returning male bobolink's bubbling, cheerful flight song drifts across the hayfield, my faith in the mysteries of God is renewed. And who can fail to feel a sense of wonder in the presence of a spectacular display of northern lights, as were seen here in early November last year?

To restore a depleted farm takes time. Especially a hill farm where extensive soil erosion took place. What took years to harm takes years to heal. It is estimated that it takes nature several hundred years to build an inch of top soil (150 tons per acre). With poor farming practices that amount can be lost to erosion in ten years.

I can still remember as a boy in the 1950s when the last gully disappeared beneath a thick cover of sod. Now the water leaving the farm during a hard rain is clear and clean.

Quite often the most overlooked and perhaps the most abused part of nature is the life in the soil. The healing process beings there. A gram of good soil may hold as many as four billion microbiotic organisms. These can be nurtured with the growing of legumes alongside grasses, the use of animal manures mixed with straw or fodder grown on the farm, and annual crop rotations.

The rotations we use date back to the Palatinate farmers of the eighteenth century. The field that is hay this year will be planted to corn next year. Following the corn will be oats, and then wheat which will be seeded to hay, and the cycle will be complete.

The health of a farm and nature is not brought about by some "heroic feat of technology, but rather by thousands of small acts and restraints handed down by generations of experience," to quote Wendell Berry. These are acts my family and I often perform as the teams are resting while plowing and planting. Maybe it is only carrying a rock off the field, or moving a piece of sod to some low spot to check possible erosion, or moving a killdeer's or horned lark's nest out of harm's way. These small acts of stewardship, multiplied a thousand times, do add up. Confucius said, "The best fertilizer on any farm is the footsteps of the owner."

To earn one's livelihood from a farm while at the same time caring for and preserving nature is sometimes difficult particularly in growing seasons as abnormal as the past four years have been. What might appear to be a conflict between exploiter and nurturer could be more accurately described as farmer and land involved in a sort of dance. It is an attempt to achieve a balance between give and take, without too much stepping on each other's toes.

Wendell Berry writes: "An exploiter wishes to earn as much as possible by as little work as possible. The nurturer expects to have a decent living from his land but his characteristic wish is to work as well as possible."

A great deal depends on whether we look at the farm as a food factory where nature suffers at the expense of profit, or we look at the farm as a place to live, where—to quote Aldo Leopold—"there is a harmonious balance between plants, animals, and people; between the domestic and the wild; between utility and beauty" (Leopold 1991, 326).

This balance of utility and beauty that I strive for on the farm, my wife achieves so well in the garden, a delightful blend of the domestic and the wild. She has several gardens, but the one I want to mention is practically on our doorstop and its primary food function is as a provider of fresh salad makings—lettuces, broccoli, cauliflower, radishes, onions, a few cucumber plants, and several early tomatoes—that end up on the table only minutes after leaving the garden. After all, doesn't the quality of life begin on the dinner plate? However, only about half of the garden space—the domestic—is for our culinary benefit. The rest tends toward the wild—plantings for birds and butterflies and beauty. Annuals and perennials.

While most of the perennials are native to this part of the country (the wild rose, butterfly weed, black-eyed susan, bergamot, and New England aster), a few are not; the coreopsis and purple coneflower are transplanted prairie natives. The annual flowers include a row of mixed zinnias, impatiens, petunias, and salvias.

The blending of domestic and wild works so well. An American goldfinch may be feeding on the stickum-like seeds of the coneflowers, while a chipping sparrow searches for cabbage loopers on the broccoli. A ruby-throated hummingbird hovers near the delicate impatiens blossoms, sipping their nectar, while swallowtail butterflies prefer the nectar of the bergamot and the zinnias.

Maybe the main reason I love this part-domestic, part-wild garden so much is that it is located between the house and the barn. Whenever I enter or leave the house, I linger for several minutes in the garden. Perhaps I eat a radish or a tender green onion, but more often I just pause to watch the life of the garden. What is going on may determine my day's work. If it is morning and there is hay to be made, I watch the wild things. If the bees and the birds are exceptionally active and the maple leaves show their undersides in a slight breeze, I figure rain is on the way and change my plans from hay mowing to corn cultivating (or maybe fishing).

Aldo Leopold once said that a good farm must be one where the wild flora and fauna have lost ground without losing their existence. Even though much has been lost here since that 1825 deed, we need to cherish what remains. And a farm is a good place to do this cherishing. Where else can one be so much a part of nature and the mysteries of God, the unfolding of the seasons, the coming and going of the birds, the pleasures of planting and the joys of harvest, the cycle of life and death? Where else can one still touch hands with an earlier people through their flint work? Sure, there are periods of hard work. But it is labor with dignity, working together with family, neighbors, and friends. Here on our 120 acres I must be a steward of the mysteries of God.

the common life

SCOTT RUSSELL SANDERS

ONE delicious afternoon while my daughter, Eva, was home from college for spring vacation, she invited two neighbor girls to help her make bread. The girls are sisters, five-year-old Alexandra and ten-year-old Rachel—both frolicky, with eager dark eyes and shining faces. They live just down the street from us here in Bloomington, Indiana, and whenever they see me pass by, on bicycle or on foot, they ask about Eva, whom they adore.

I was in the yard that afternoon mulching flower beds with compost, and I could hear the girls chattering as Eva led them up the sidewalk to our door. I had plenty of other chores to do in the yard, where every living thing was urgent with April. But how could I stay outside, when so much beauty and laughter and spunk were gathered in the kitchen?

I kept looking in on the cooks, until Eva finally asked, "Daddy, you wouldn't like to knead some dough, would you?"

"I'd love to," I said, "You sure there's room for me?"

"There's room," Eva replied, "but you'll have to wash in the basement."

Hands washed, I took my place at the counter beside Rachel and Alexandra, who perched on a stool I had made for Eva when she was a toddler. Eva had still needed that stool when she learned to make bread on this counter; and my son, now six feet tall, had balanced there as well for his own first lessons in cooking. I never needed the stool, but I needed the same teacher—my wife, Ruth, a woman with eloquent fingers.

Our kitchen is small; Ruth and I shared that cramped space by moving in a kind of dance we have been practicing for years. When we bump each other, it is usually for the pleasure of bumping. But Eva and the girls and I jostled like birds too numerous for a nest. We spattered flour everywhere. We told stories. We joked. All the while I bobbed on a current of bliss, delighting in the feel of live dough beneath my fingers, the smell of yeast, the piping of child-voices so much like the birdsong cascading through our open windows, the prospect of whole-wheat loaves hot from the oven.

An artist might paint this kitchen scene in pastels for a poster, with a tender motto below, as evidence that all is right with the world. All is manifestly *not* right with the world. The world, most of us would agree, is a mess: rife with murder and mayhem, abuse of land, extinction of species, lying and theft and greed. There are days when I can see nothing but a spectacle of cruelty and waste, and the weight of dismay pins me to my chair. On such days I need a boost merely to get up, un-curl my fists, and go about my work. The needed strength may come from family, from neighbors, from a friend's greeting in the mail, from the forked leaves of larkspur breaking ground, from rainstorms and music and wind, from the lines of a handmade table or the lines in a well-worn book, from the taste of an apple or the brash trill of finches in our backyard trees. Strength also comes from memories of times when I have felt a deep and complex joy, a sense of being exactly where I should be and doing exactly what I should do—as I felt on that bread-making afternoon.

I wish to reflect on the sources of that joy, that sense of being utterly in place, because I suspect they are the origins of all that I find authentic in my life. So much in life seems to me unauthentic, I cannot afford to let the genuine passages slip by without considering what makes them ring true. It is as though I spend my days wandering about, chasing false scents, lost; then occasionally, for a few ticks of the heart, I stumble onto the path. Making bread with my daughter and her two young friends, I was on the path. So I recall that time now as a way of keeping company with Eva, who has gone back to college, but also as a way of discovering in our common life a reservoir of power and hope.

What is so powerful, so encouraging, in that kitchen scene? To begin with, I love my three fellow cooks; I relish every tilt of their heads and turn of their voices. In their presence I feel more alive and alert, as if the rust had been knocked off my nerves. The armor of self dissolves, ego relaxes its grip, and I am simply there, on the breeze of the moment.

Rachel and Alexandra belong to the Abed family, with whom we often share food and talk and festivities. We turn to the Abeds for advice, for starts of plants, for cheer—and they likewise turn to us. Not long ago they received troubling news that may force them to move away, and we have been sharing in their distress. So the Abed girls brought into our kitchen a history of neighborliness, a history all the more valuable because it might soon come to an end.

The girls also brought a readiness to learn what Eva had to teach. Eva, as I mentioned, had learned from Ruth how to make bread, and Ruth had learned from a Canadian friend, and our friend had learned from her grandmother. As Rachel and Alexandra shoved their hands into the dough, I could imagine the rope of knowledge stretching back and back through generations, to folks who ground their grain with stones and did their baking in wood stoves or fireplaces or pits of glowing coals.

If you have made yeast bread, you know how at first the dough clings to your fingers, and then gradually, as you knead in more flour, it begins to pull away and take on a life of its own, becoming at last as resilient as a plump belly. If you have not made yeast bread, no amount of hearing or reading about it will give you that knowledge. You have to learn through your body, through fingers and wrists and aching forearms, through shoulders and back.

Much of what we know comes to us that way, passed on from person to person, age after age, surviving in muscle and bone. I learned from my mother how to transplant a seedling, how to sew on a button; I learned from my father how to saw a board square, how to curry a horse, how to change the oil in a car. The pleasure I take in sawing or currying, in planting or sewing, even in changing oil—like my pleasure in making bread—is bound up with the affection I feel for my teachers and the respect I feel for the long, slow accumulation of knowledge that informs our simplest acts.

Those simple acts come down to us because they serve real needs. You plant a tree or sweep a floor or rock a baby without asking the point of your labor. You patch the roof to stop a leak, patch a sweater to keep from having to throw it out. You plug a banjo because it tickles your ears and rouses Grandpa to dance. None of us can live entirely by such meaningful acts; our jobs, if nothing else, often push us through empty motions. Unless at least some of what we do has a transparent purpose, answering not merely to duty or fashion but to actual need, then the heart has gone out of our work. What art could be more plainly valuable than cooking? The reason for baking bread is as palpable as your tongue. After our loaves were finished, Eva and I delivered two of them to the Abeds, who showed in their faces a perfect understanding of the good of bread.

When I compare the dough to a plump belly, I hear the sexual overtones, of course. By making the comparison, I do not wish to say with Freud that every sensual act is a surrogate for sex; on the contrary, I believe that sex comes closer to being a stand-in, rather brazen and obvious, like a ham actor pretending to be the whole show, when it is only one player in the drama of our sensual life. That life flows through us constantly, as long as we do not shut ourselves off. The sound of birds and the smell of April dirt and the brush of wind through the open door were all ingredients in the bread we baked.

Before baking, the yeast was alive, dozing in the refrigerator. Scooped out of its jar, stirred into warm water, fed on sugar, it soon bubbled out gas to leaven the loaves. You have to make sure the water for the yeast, like milk for a baby, is neither too hot nor too cold, and so, as for a baby's bottle, I test the temperature on my wrist. The flour, too, had been alive not long before, as wheat thriving in sun and rain. Our nourishment is borrowed life. You need not be a Christian to feel, in a bite of bread, a sense of communion with the energy that courses through all things. The lump in your mouth is a chunk of earth; there is nothing else to eat. In our house we say grace before meals, to remind ourselves of that gift and that dependence.

The elements of my kitchen scene—loving company, neighborliness, inherited knowledge and good work, shared purpose, sensual delight, and union with the creation—sum up for me what is vital in community. Here is the spring of hope I have been led to by my trail of bread. In our common life we may find the strength not merely to carry on in face of the world's bad news, but to resist cruelty and waste. I speak of our life as common because it is ordinary, because we make it together, because it binds us through time to the rest of humanity and through our bodies to the rest of nature. By honoring this common life, nurturing it, carrying it steadily in mind, we might renew our households and neighborhoods and cities, and in doing so might redeem ourselves from the bleakness of private lives spent in frenzied pursuit of sensation and wealth.

In valuing community, I do not mean to approve of any and every association of people. Humans are drawn together by a variety of motives, some of them worthy, some ugly. Anyone who has spent recess on a playground knows the terror of mob rule. Anyone who has lived through a war knows that mobs may pretend to speak for an entire nation. I recently saw, for the first time in a long while, a bumper sticker that recalled for me the angriest days of the Vietnam War: AMERICA—LOVE IT OR LEAVE IT. What loving America seemed to mean, for those who brandished that slogan back around 1970, was approval of everything the government said or the army did in our name. "All those who seek to destroy the liberty of a democratic nation ought to know," Alexis de Tocqueville observed in *Democracy in America,* "that war is the surest and the shortest means to accomplish it." As a conscientious objector, with a sister who studied near my home in Ohio on a campus where National Guardsmen killed several protesters, I felt the force of despotism in that slogan.

Rather than give in to despotism, some of my friends went to jail and others into exile. My wife and I considered staying in England, where we had been studying for several years and where I had been offered a job. Instead we chose to come home, here to the Midwest where we had grown up, to work for change. In our idealism we might have rephrased that bumper sticker to read: AMERICA—LOVE IT AND REDEEM IT. For us, loving America had little to do with politicians and even less with soldiers, but much to do with what I have been calling the common life: useful work, ordinary sights, family, neighbors, ancestors, our fellow creatures, and the rivers and woods and fields that make up our mutual home.

During the more than twenty years since our return to America, I have had some of the idealism knocked out of me. But I still believe that loving your country or city or neighborhood may require you to resist, to call for change, to speak on behalf of what you believe in, especially if what you believe in has been neglected.

What we have too often neglected, in our revulsion against tyranny and our worship of the individual, is the common good. The results of that neglect are visible in the decay of our cities, the despoiling of our land, the fouling of our rivers and air, the haphazard commercial sprawl along our highways, the gluttonous feeding at the public trough, and the mortgaging of our children's and grandchildren's future through our refusal to pay for current consumption. Only a people addicted to private pleasure would allow themselves to be defined as consumers—rather than conservers or restorers—of the earth's abundance.

In spite of the comforting assurances, from Adam Smith on, that the unfettered pursuit of private wealth should result in unlimited public good, we all know that to be mostly a lie. If we need reminders of how great that lie is, we can look at the savings and loan industry, where billions of dollars are stolen from small investors by rich managers who yearn to be richer; we can look at the Pentagon, where contracts are routinely encrusted with graft, or at Wall Street, where millionaires finagle to become billionaires through insider trading; we can look at our national forests, where logging companies buy timber for less than the cost to taxpayers of harvesting it; or we can look at our suburbs, where palaces multiply, while downtown more and more people are sleeping in cardboard boxes. Wealth does not precipitate like dew from the air; it comes out of the earth and from the labor of many hands. When a few hands hold onto great wealth, using it only for personal ease and display, that is a betrayal of the common life, the sole source of riches.

Fortunately, while our tradition is heavily tilted in favor of private life, we also inherit a tradition of caring for the community. Although Tocqueville found much to fear and quite a bit to despise in this raw democracy, he praised Americans for having "carried to the highest perfection the art of pursuing in common the object of their common desires." Writing of what he had seen in the 1830s, Tocqueville judged Americans to be avaricious, self-serving, and aggressive; but he was also amazed by our eagerness to form clubs, to raise barns or town halls, to join together in one cause or another. "In no country in the world, do the citizens make such exertions for the common weal. I know of no people who have established schools so numerous and efficacious, places of public worship better suited to the wants of the inhabitants, or roads kept in better repair."

Today we might revise his estimate of our schools or roads, but we can still see all around us the fruits of that concern for the common weal—the libraries, museums, courthouses, hospitals, orphanages, universities, parks, on and on. Born as most of us are into places where such amenities already exist, we may take them for granted; but they would not be there for us to use had our forebears not cooperated in building them. No matter where we live, our home places have also benefited from the granges and unions, the volunteer fire brigades, the art guilds and garden clubs, the charities, food kitchens, homeless shelters, soccer and baseball teams, the Scouts and 4-H, the Girls and Boys Clubs, the Lions and Elks and Rotarians, the countless gatherings of people who saw a need and responded to it.

This history of local care hardly ever makes it into our literature, for it is less glamorous than rebellion; yet it is a crucial part of our heritage. Any of us could cite examples of people who dug in and joined with others to make our home places better places. Women and men who invest themselves in their communities, fighting for good schools or green spaces, paying attention to where they are, seem to me as worthy of celebration as those adventurous loners who keep drifting on, prospecting for pleasure.

A few days after our breadmaking, Eva and I went to a concert in Bloomington's newly opened arts center. The old limestone building had once been the town hall, then a fire station and jail, then for several years an abandoned shell. Volunteers bought the building from the city for a dollar and renovated it with materials, labor, and money donated by local people. Now we have a handsome facility that is in constant use for pottery classes, theater productions, puppet shows, art exhibits, poetry readings, and every manner of musical event.

The music Eva and I heard was *Hymnody of Earth,* for hammer dulcimer, percussion, and children's choir. Composed by our next-door neighbor Malcolm Dalglish, and featuring lyrics by our Ohio Valley neighbor Wendell Berry, it was performed that night by Malcolm, percussionist Glen Velez, and the Bloomington Youth Chorus. As I sat there with Eva in a sellout crowd—about a third of whom I knew by name, another third by face—I listened to music that had been elaborated within earshot of my house. I heard my friend play his instrument, I watched those children's faces shining with the colors of the human spectrum, and I felt the restored building clasping us all like the cupped hands of our community. I knew once more that I was in the right place, a place created and filled by our lives together.

A woman who recently moved from Los Angeles to Bloomington told me that she would not be able to stay here long, because she was already beginning to recognize people in the grocery stores, on the sidewalks, in the library. Being surrounded by familiar faces made her nervous after years in a city where she could range about anonymously. Every traveler knows the sense of liberation that comes from journeying to a place where nobody expects anything of you. Everyone who has gone off to college knows the exhilaration of slipping away from the watchful eyes of Mom and Dad. We all need seasons of withdrawal from responsibility. But if we make a career of being unaccountable, we have lost something essential to our humanity, and we may well become a burden or a threat to those around us. A community can support a number of people who are just passing through, or who care about no one's needs but their own; the greater the proportion of such people, however, the more vulnerable the community, until eventually it breaks down. This is true on any scale, from a household to a planet.

The words "community," "communion," and "communicate" all derive from "common," and the two syllables of "common" grow from separate roots, the first meaning together or next to, the second having to do with barter or exchange. Embodied in that word is a sense of our shared life as one of giving and receiving—music, touch, ideas, recipes, stories, medicine, tools, the whole range of artifacts and talents. After twenty-five years with Ruth, that is how I have come to understand marriage, as a constant exchange of labor and love. We do not calculate who gives how much; if we had to do that, the marriage would be in trouble. Looking outward from this community of two, I see my life embedded in ever-larger exchanges—those of family and friendship, neighborhood and city, countryside and country—and on every scale there is giving and receiving, calling and answering.

Many people shy away from community out of fear that it may become suffocating, confining, even vicious; and of course it may, if it grows rigid or exclusive. A healthy community is dynamic, stirred up by the energies of those who already belong, open to new members and fresh influences, kept in motion by the constant bartering of gifts. It is fashionable just now to speak of this open quality as "tolerance," but that word sounds too grudging to me—as though, to avoid strife, we must grit our teeth and ignore whatever is strange to us. The community I desire is not grudging; it is exuberant, joyful, grounded in affection, pleasure, and mutual aid. Such a community arises not from duty or money but from the free interchange of people who share a place, share work and food, sorrows and hope. Taking part in the common life means dwelling in a web of relationships, the many threads tugging at you while also holding you upright.

I have told elsewhere the story of a man who lived in the Ohio township where I grew up, a builder who refused to join the volunteer fire department. Why should he join, when his house was brick, properly wired, fitted out with new appliances? Well, one day that house caught fire. His wife dialed the emergency number, the siren wailed, and pretty soon the volunteer firemen, my father among them, showed up with the pumper truck. But they held back on the hoses, asking the builder if he still saw no reason to join. The builder said he could see a pretty good reason to join right there and then, and the volunteers let the water loose.

I have also told before the story of a family from that township whose house burned down. The fire had been started accidentally by the father, who came home drunk and fell asleep smoking on the couch. While the place was still ablaze, the man took off, abandoning his wife and several young children. The local people sheltered the family, then built them a new house. This was a poor township. Yet nobody thought to call in the government or apply to a foundation. These were neighbors in a fix, and so you helped them, just as you would harvest corn for an ailing farmer or pull a flailing child from the creek or put your arm around a weeping friend.

I am not harking back to some idyllic past, like the one embalmed in the *Saturday Evening Post* covers by Norman Rockwell or the prints of Currier and Ives. The past was never golden. As a people, we still need to unlearn some of the bad habits formed during the long period of settlement. One habit we might reclaim, however, is that of looking after those who live nearby. For much of our history, neighbors have kept one another going, kept one another sane. Still today, in town and country, in apartment buildings and barrios, even in suburban estates, you are certain to lead a narrower life without the steady presence of neighbors. It is neither quaint nor sentimental to advocate neighborliness; it is far more sentimental to suggest that we can do without such mutual aid.

Even Emerson, preaching self-reliance, knew the necessity of neighbors. He lived in a village, gave and received help, and delivered his essays as lectures for fellow citizens whom he hoped to sway. He could have left his ideas in his journals, where they first took shape, but he knew those ideas would only have effect when they were shared. If you visit Emerson's house in Concord, you will find leather buckets hanging near the door, for he belonged to the village fire brigade, and even in the seclusion of his study, in the depths of thought, he kept his ears open for the alarm bell.

We should not have to wait until our houses are burning before we see the wisdom of facing our local needs by joining in common work. We should not have to wait until gunfire breaks out in our schools, rashes break out on our skin, dead fish float in our streams, or beggars sleep on our streets before we act on behalf of the community. On a crowded planet we had better learn how to live well together, or we will live miserably apart.

In cultural politics these days there is much talk of diversity and difference. This is all to the good, insofar as it encourages us to welcome the many distinctive traditions and visions that have flowed into America from around the world. But if, while respecting how we differ, we do not also recognize how much we have in common, we will have climbed out of the melting pot into the fire. It is also dangerous to separate a concern for human diversity from a concern for natural diversity. Since Europeans arrived in America, we have been drawing recklessly on beaver and bison, trees and topsoil, petroleum, coal, iron and copper ore, clean air and water. Many of the achievements on which we pride ourselves are the result not of our supposed virtues but of this plundered bounty. There is no contradiction between caring for human beings and caring for the rest of nature; on the contrary, only by attending to the health of the land can we measure our true needs or secure a lasting home.

Just before Eva was to leave again for college, she and I went for a hike in a nature preserve along Clear Creek, near Bloomington, to look at the hepatica and bloodroot and listen to the spring-high water. At the edge of the preserve, a sign declared that the riding of horses was prohibited. The trail had been freshly gouged by horseshoes and was eroding badly. Trash snagged in the roots of sycamores along the stream. Much of the soil and its cover of wildflowers had washed from the slopes where people scrambled up to picnic on the bluff. Some of the cans they had left behind glinted among white stars of trillium.

I wondered what it would take to persuade the riders to get down off their horses and go on foot. What would it take to discourage people from dumping their worn-out washing machines in ditches? What would convince farmers to quit spraying poisons on their fields, suburbanites to quit spraying poisons on their lawns? What power could stop loggers from seeing every tree as lumber, stop developers from seeing every acre of land as real estate, stop oil-company executives from seeing our last few scraps of wilderness as pay dirt waiting to be drilled? What would it take to persuade all of us to eat what we need, rather than what we can hold; to buy what we need, rather than what we can afford; to draw our pleasure from inexhaustible springs?

Signs will not work that change of mind, for in a battle of signs the billboards always win. Police cannot enforce it. Tongue lashings and sermons and earnest essays will not do it, nor will laws alone bring it about. The framers of the Constitution may have assumed that we did not need a Bill of Responsibilities because religion and reason and the benign impulses of our nature would lead us to care for one another and for our home. At the end of a bloody century, on the eve of a new millennium that threatens to be still bloodier, few of us now feel much confidence in those redeeming influences. Only a powerful ethic might restrain us, retrain us, restore us. Our survival is at stake, yet worrying about our survival alone is too selfish a motive to carry us as far as we need to go. Nothing short of reimagining where we are and what we are will be radical enough to transform how we live.

Aldo Leopold gave us the beginnings of this new ethic nearly half a century ago, in *A Sand County Almanac,* where he described the land itself as a community made up of rock, water, soil, plants, and animals—including *Homo sapiens,* the only species clever enough to ignore for a short while the conditions of membership. "We abuse land because we see it as a commodity belonging to us," Leopold wrote. "When we see land as a community to which we belong, we may begin to use it with love and respect." To use our places with love and respect demands from us the same generosity and restraint that we show in our dealings with a wife or husband, a child or parent, a neighbor, a stranger in trouble.

Once again this spring, the seventy-seventh of her life, my mother put out lint from her clothes dryer for the birds to use in building their nests. "I know how hard it is to make a home from scratch," she says, "I've done it often enough myself." That is not anthropomorphism; it is fellow feeling, the root of all kindness.

Doctors the world over study the same physiology, for we are one species, woven together by strands of DNA that stretch back to the beginnings of life. There is, in fact, only one life—one pulse animating the dust. Sycamores and snakes, grasshoppers and grass, hawks and humans all spring from the same source and all return to it. We need to make of this common life not merely a metaphor, although we live by metaphors, and not merely a story, although we live by stories; we need to make the common life a fact of the heart. That awareness, that concern, that love needs to go as deep in us as the feeling we have when a child dashes into the street and we hear a squeal of brakes, or when a piece of our home ground goes under concrete, or when a cat purrs against our palms or rain sends shivers through our bones or a smile floats back to us from another face.

With our own population booming, with frogs singing in the April ponds, with mushrooms cracking the pavement, life may seem the most ordinary of forces, like hunger or gravity; it may seem cheap, since we see it wasted every day. But in truth life is expensive, life is extraordinary, having required five billion years of struggle and luck on one stony, watery planet to reach its present precarious state. And so far as we have been able to discover, from peering out into the great black spaces, the life that is common to all creatures here on earth is exceedingly uncommon, perhaps unique, in the universe. How, grasping that, can we remain unchanged?

It may be that we will not change, that nothing can restrain us, that we are incapable of reimagining our relations to one another or our place in creation. So many alarm bells are ringing, we may be tempted to stuff our ears with cotton. Better that we should keep ears and eyes open, take courage as well as joy from our common life, and work for what we love.

What I love is curled about a loaf of bread, a family, a musical neighbor, a building salvaged for art, a town of familiar faces, a creek and a limestone bluff and a sky full of birds. Those may seem like frail threads to hold anyone in place while history heaves us about, and yet, when they are braided together, I find them to be amazingly strong.

living with the land

HELENA NORBERG-HODGE

THE rough, winding road from Srinagar climbs through the moss-green pine forests of Kashmir to the Zoji-la Pass, a dramatic boundary between two worlds. Ahead, in the parched rainshadow of the Himalayas, the earth is bare. In every direction are mountains, a vast plateau of crests in warm and varied tones from rust to pale green. Above, snowy peaks reach toward a still, blue sky; below, sheer walls of wine-red scree fall to stark lunar valleys.

This is Ladakh, one of the harshest environments on earth. Each step you take sends up a cloud of sand and dust. Rain is so rare that it is easy to forget its very existence. In the summer, an unrelenting sun scorches the earth; in the winter, the ground is frozen solid for eight months and temperatures can plummet to minus forty. How, you wonder, can life be sustained in this wilderness?

But soon, brilliant green oases come into view, set like emeralds in a vast elephant-skin desert. You come upon fields of barley, fringed with wild flowers and herbs and the clear waters of glacial streams. Above the fields you see a cluster of houses, gleaming white, three stories high, and hung with finely carved balconies; brightly colored prayer flags flutter on the rooftops. Higher still, perched on the mountainside, a monastery watches over the village.

As you wander through the fields, or follow the narrow paths that wind between the houses, smiling faces greet you. It seems impossible that people could thrive in such desolation, yet all the signs are that they do. Everything has been done with care: fields carved out of the mountainside are layered in immaculate terraces, one above the other; the crops are thick and strong and form such patterns that an artist might have sown their seeds. Around each house, fruit trees and vegetable and flower gardens are protected from the goats by a stone wall on which cakes of dung, to be used as fuel for the kitchen stove, lie baking in the sun. On the flat roof, animal fodder—alfalfa and hay, together with leaves of the wild iris— has been stacked in neat bundles for winter. Apricots left to dry on yak-hair blankets and potted marigolds give a blaze of brilliant orange.

Here in a barren Himalayan desert, the Ladakhis have coevolved with their environment. And they have prospered.

The vast majority of Ladakhis are self-supporting farmers, living in small settlements scattered in the desert, at altitudes ranging from ten thousand to fourteen thousand feet. The size of each village depends on the availability of water, which comes from the melted snow and ice of the mountains. Over the centuries, stone-lined channels have been built that bring the meltwater from the high valleys above to the fields below. The water is often channeled for several miles.

Life in Ladakh is dictated by the seasons. The agricultural cycle begins sometime between February and June, depending on the altitude. Sowing is a time of lyrical beauty. The sun's arc is higher now, and the valley alive once more. On an eastern exposure high above the village, a large pile of stones in the form of an obelisk (*nyitho*) acts as an agricultural calendar. The point on which its shadow falls determines when various activities should start. Sowing, irrigating, harvesting may all be represented by specific landmarks. When the sun reaches the right place for sowing, the astrologer is consulted. He studies his charts to ensure that work begins on an auspicious day; he attempts to match the elements of earth and water. Someone whose signs he deems favorable is chosen to sow the first seed.

Next, the spirits of the earth and water—the *sadak* and the *lhu*—must be pacified: the worms of the soil, the fish of the streams, the soul of the land. They can easily be angered; the turning of a spade, the braking of stones, even walking on the ground above them can upset their peace. Before the sowing, a feast is prepared in their honor. For an entire day a group of monks recites prayers; no one eats meat or drinks *chang* (the local barley beer). In a cluster of trees at the edge of the village, where a small mound of clay bricks has been built for the spirits, milk is offered. As the sun sets, other offerings are thrown into the stream.

Some weeks earlier, manure has been brought on the backs of donkeys and placed in heaps beside the fields. Now, at dawn, the women quickly spread it in the furrow. As the sun appears, the whole family gathers. Two men carry the wooden plow; ahead a pair of massive *dzo* (a cross between the local cow and a yak) dwarf the children who lead them. Work and festivity are one. People drink chang from silver-lined cups, and the air hums with the sounds of celebration. A monk in robes of deep maroon chants a sacred text; laughter and song drift from field to field. The ravages of winter are over.

The dzo are yoked. Docile beasts, but proud, they will not be hurried. Casually almost, they pull the plow. Behind, the sower throws the seeds and sings:

Manjushri, the embodiment of wisdom, Hark!
The gods, the Lhu, and owner spirits of the Mother Earth, hark!
May a hundred plants grow from one seed!
May a thousand grow from two seeds!
May all the grains be twins!
Please give enough that we may worship the Buddhas and Bodhisattvas,
That we may support the Sangha and give to the poor!

Once the sowing has been completed, the crop does not need much care—only watering, which is usually done on a rotational basis, sometimes established by dice. In most villages irrigation is regulated by a *churpon,* who is appointed or elected from within the village. He operates the flow of water, blocking and opening the canals as required. Householders are allotted a certain period of time every week when they can divert the main channel into their own fields. Watching a mother and her two daughters watering, I saw them open small channels and, when the ground was saturated, block them with a spadeful of earth. They managed to spread the water remarkably evenly, knowing just where it would flow easily and where it would need encouragement: a spadeful dug out here, put back there; a rock shifted just enough to open a channel—all this with the most delicate sense of timing. From time to time they would lean on their spades and chat with their neighbors, keeping one eye on the water's progress.

Harvesttime is particularly festive. A line of reapers, old and young, men and women, sing as they cut the crop low to the ground with sickles. In the evening people gather to sing, drink, and dance. A butter-lamp is lit in the kitchen, and garlands of wheat, barley, and peas are wrapped around the wooden pillars. The crop is piled in sheaves, then carried off in backloads to be threshed. A large circle of packed earth about thirty feet in diameter forms the threshing floor. A number of animals, attached in a line to a central pole, trample the crop, bending down to feast on the grain as they walk. Dzo are best for this purpose; not only are they vast and heavy, but once stirred they can contentedly trudge around and around for hours. Often there will be a combination of animals, as many as twelve or so; the dzo will be on the inside, with only a short distance to cover, while horses and donkeys run along on the outside, scampering to keep up. Behind them, the thresher—sometimes a child—shouts words of encouragement and exhorts them in song: "*Ha-lo baldur, ha-lo baldur . . .*" To prevent animal dung from soiling the grain, the thresher carries a wicker basket, catching the dung with dextrous ease before it lands on the ground. A reserve dzo stands nearby waiting its turn, while the other animals that have been brought down from the summer pastures munch on the stubble of the fields. Winnowing is extraordinarily graceful. In perfect, easy rhythm, the crop is scooped up into the air; the chaff blows away on the wind, and the grain falls to the ground. Two people work together, facing each other with wooden forks. They whistle as they work, inviting the wind.

In one of my first years in Ladakh, Sonam, a friend from the remote village of Hemis Shukpachan, invited me home for Skangsol, the harvest festival. I woke to the fragrant smell of *shukpa,* or juniper. Sonam's Uncle Phuntsog was walking from room to room carrying an incense burner, the scent wafting into every corner. This daily ceremony ensures a spiritual cleansing and is performed in all Buddhist houses.

I walked out onto the balcony. Whole families—grandfathers, parents, children—were working in the fields, some cutting, some stacking, others winnowing. Each activity had its own particular song. The harvest lay in golden stacks, hundreds to a field, hardly allowing the bare earth to show through. A clear light bathed the valley with an intense brilliance. No ugly geometry had been imposed on this land, no repetitive lines. Everything was easy to the eye, calming to the soul. Farther down the valley, a man sang to his animals as they plowed his fields:

> Oh, you two great bulls, sons of the wild yak!
> Your mother may be a cow, but you are like the tiger and the lion!
> You are like the eagle, the king of birds!
> Aren't you the dancers of the high peaks?

Aren't you the ones who take the mountains on your lap?
Aren't you the ones who drink the ocean in one gulp?
Oh, you two great bulls, pull! pull!

Above me on the roof the deep, rumbling sound of the *zangstung,* eight-foot-long copper horns, signaled that the ceremony was about to begin. Like all religious occasions, this was a social event too, and several guests had already arrived. Men and women were being entertained in separate rooms. They were sitting at low tables intricately carved with dragons and lotus flowers; on the walls were frescoes many generations old. The men wore long homespun robes (*gonchas*), some a natural beige color, some dyed the deep maroon of the hills. Many wore a large turquoise earring with the traditional hairstyle—a plait at the back, with the front of the head shaved. The women were dressed in fuller robes, topped with a waistcoat of brocade. They wore magnificent jewelry—bracelets, rings, necklaces—and dazzling *peraks,* headdresses studded with dozens of turquoises and corals. An older man waved me over to sit down next to him. "This is my new daughter-in-law," he said, introducing me to the others. His eyes sparkled mischievously as they all laughed.

Some of my best memories of living in Ladakh come from experiences at the high pastures, or *phu.* One summer I spent several weeks with Ladakhi friends at Nyimaling, "the meadow of the sun." Sheep, goats, cows, yaks, and dzo all spend their summer at Nyimaling. The sheep and goats are taken to the hillsides above the valley, every day to a different area so as to avoid overgrazing. Meanwhile the cows wander along the floor of the valley. The dzo and yak, always independent, forage up high near the glaciers, climbing the steep mountain walls with ease. These majestic animals forage over vast distances, providing another example of how the Ladakhis make the most of the scant resources of the region. As the animals graze, they gather together energy from hundreds of square miles—energy that, in addition to fuel from their dung, is used by people in the form of food, clothing, and labor. In the summer a lot of time is devoted to tracking down the dzo, as they have a habit of wandering off many miles, sometimes two or three days' walk over high mountain passes. Often they will turn up unexpectedly at the village, having found their way down from the pasturelands. To protect the crops, they are immediately escorted back to the phu. From a distance, my eye saw them as nothing more than black dots against the purple scree. But my friend Deskit's ten-year-old son, Angchuk, could not only tell they were dzo, as opposed to yaks or cows, but could distinguish his own animals from the others.

Nyimaling: a twenty-one-thousand-foot peak towering above the bowl of the valley; patches of green, carpets of wild flowers; marmots whistling to one another; the air ringing with the sounds of flutes and young shepherds' songs. For those few days at the phu, I glimpsed what life must have been like for thousands of years. The closeness between the people and the land and the animals they depended on was deeply touching—something that had never been part of my life, yet something that felt familiar.

We lived in one of the stone huts that serve as summer dwellings, modest in comparison with the houses of the village. Beyond the low entrance a small, dark kitchen led to a storage area, where we kept the sacks of flour we had brought. Dry stone walls and five-foot-high ceilings created a cavelike atmosphere. Yet in the evenings the cramped and smoky room, with a wick-lamp giving off just enough light to distinguish faces, was filled with warmth and vitality. We sang, the little ones danced, and there were always stories.

One night there was a crash outside, and we heard Uncle Norbu shouting *"Shangku! Shangku!"* We all ran outside, and at the other side of the pen I saw a dark shadow disappear into the night. A wolf! Norbu got the lamp from inside and took it over to a young calf. All the other animals were at the opposite side of the pen. The calf would not live long; a huge slice had been carved from its rump as if by a razor. I found myself shaking with horror, yet wondering how teeth could make such a clean cut.

The Ladakhis were calm. Norbu led the calf away to a pen where it could live its last hours in peace. Back in the kitchen, he explained how he had suddenly seen the wolf just outside the stone walls of the pen where he was leading the goats. He had thrown a stone and missed, and the wolf had stayed there, ripping at the calf. Only when he leaped over the wall and started beating the wolf with a stick did it give up its prey and head off into the mountains.

Village houses in Ladakh are large structures two or three floors high, with a floor area of four thousand square feet or more. Whitened walls slope gently inward toward a flat roof, giving the house grace despite its massive, fortresslike proportions. A new house is never built without concern for the *sadak,* the spirits of the earth. First of all, a high lama comes to bless the land. He uses a brass mirror to reflect all the surroundings, thus capturing the sadak in order to protect them from harm during construction. The mirror is carefully placed in a box, where it remains until the house is finished. At that time the lama opens the box in a final ceremony and sets the spirits free.

Although stone is often used for the first floor, the main building material is mud. Together the whole family prepares the bricks; even small children join in putting mud into the wooden molds. The bricks are left to dry in the sun and are ready for use after a couple of weeks. Walls are often three feet thick, plastered with a fine clay called *markala* (literally, butter-mud) and then whitewashed with limestone. Poplar beams, with willow branches placed in a herringbone pattern across them, form the flat roof. (Trees in Ladakh are extremely scarce and are reserved for these purposes; they are never burned for fuel.) *Yagdzas,* a shrub rather like heather, which is said to last for a hundred years, lies on top of the wood and is packed with mud and earth. Since there is so little precipitation, any snow is simply brushed off, and it rarely rains enough to cause leakage.

The house is more than just functional; time is spent on details that are purely aesthetic. Windows and doors receive special attention. Some have ornately carved lintels (the work of the village carpenter); the most popular design is the lotus. A jet-black border, about ten inches wide and made from a mixture of soot and clay, contrasts with the white walls. Small balconies, again finely worked, adorn the upper floors.

The entrance to the house faces east, for this is considered auspicious. A stone stairway takes you straight up to the first floor, the ground floor serving as a stable for the animals. Beyond the entranceway stretches the kitchen, which, together with the attached storage rooms, takes up most of the first story; above, light beams in from a large courtyard on the second floor.

The kitchen is the heart of the house; here the family spends most of its time. Kitchens are usually so large that it can be difficult to talk to someone on the opposite side of the room. Other than a few low tables and mats, there is little furniture; two-thirds of the floor area is left completely uncluttered. Along one wall a row of ornate wooden shelves is filled with a dazzling array of pots of every size. A large, shiny black stove is the focal point of every kitchen. Although it looks like wrought iron, it is in fact made of clay. Its sides are decorated with good-luck symbols and other Buddhist motifs, often studded with turquoise and coral. The fire is fed with dried dung and kept alight with goatskin bellows.

Much of the house is given over to storage, as for more than half the year nothing grows outside. Off the kitchen is the main storeroom, its thick walls ensuring that it stays icy cool in the heat of summer. It is filled with large wooden barrels for chang, clay pots for milk and yogurt, and vast bins brimming with barley and wheat flour. The roof is stacked with alfalfa grass for the animals and shrubs and dung for the kitchen stove. In the summer yak-hair blankets are always spread on the roof, with vegetables, apricots, and sometimes cheese drying in the sun.

On the top floor, surrounding the courtyard, are usually two or three rooms—typically the guest room, a summer bedroom, and the family "chapel," the most elaborate and expensive part of the house. The guest room, which is where more formal entertaining goes on, is lavishly decorated and carpeted throughout with Tibetan rugs. The chapel is filled with religious texts and other treasures that have been passed down for generations. The strong smell of apricot oil pervades this dark and silent room. Worn *thankas* (religious paintings on cloth) cover the walls, and a large drum hangs from the ceiling. An intricately carved and painted altar is lined with silver bowls and butter-lamps. On special days of the Buddhist calendar, monks gather here to perform religious ceremonies, and each morning and evening one of the family makes offerings, lighting the oil-filled lamps, filling the bowls with water, and chanting mantras and prayers.

Ladakhis have only the most basic tools. The only artifact besides the plow and the loom that we might label "technology" is the water mill, an ingeniously simple design complete with a friction-operated grain-release mechanism that obviates the need for supervision. Otherwise, only implements such as spades, saws, sickles, and hammers are used. Nothing more sophisticated is necessary. For many tasks in which we would employ large machinery, Ladakhis have animals and teamwork instead, each task accompanied by song.

Whole caravans of yak, dzo, horses, and donkeys carry most provisions. Bricks and stones are often transported by long lines of people who pass them along one by one; for something like a large tree trunk, groups of men will form a team.

With only simple tools at their disposal, Ladakhis spend a long while accomplishing each task. Producing wool for clothes involves the time-consuming work of looking after the sheep while they graze, shearing them with hand tools, and working the wool from beginning to end—cleaning, spinning, and finally weaving it. In the same way, producing food, from sowing the seed until the food is served on the table, is labor intensive. Yet I found that the Ladakhis have an abundance of time. They work at a gentle pace and have a surprising amount of leisure.

Time is measured loosely; there is never a need to count minutes. "I'll come to see you toward midday, toward evening," they will say, giving themselves several hours' leeway. Ladakhi has many lovely words to depict time, all broad and generous. *Gongrot* means from after dark till bedtime; *nyitse* means literally sun on the mountain peaks; and *chipe-chirrit,* bird song, describes that time of the morning, before the sun has risen, when the birds sing.

Even during the harvest season, when the work lasts long hours, it is done at a relaxed pace that allows an eighty-year-old as well as a young child to join in and help. People work hard, but at their own rate, accompanied by laughter and song. The distinction between work and play is not rigid.

Remarkably, Ladakhis only work, really work, for four months of the year. In the eight winter months, they must cook, feed the animals, and carry water, but work is minimal. Most of the winter is spent at festivals and parties. Even during summer, hardly a week passes without a major festival or celebration of one sort or another, while in winter the celebration is almost nonstop.

Winter is also the time for telling stories. In fact, there is a saying in Ladakh, "As long as the earth is green, no tale should be told." This prohibition on storytelling in the summer must arise from the need to concentrate on agriculture in those few short months. People sit around the fire, and from time to time the storyteller comes to a familiar song or refrain and everyone joins in.

Soon after I had arrived in Ladakh, I was washing some clothes in a stream. Just as I was plunging a dirty dress into the water, a little girl, no more than seven years old, came by from a village upstream. "You shouldn't put your clothes in that water," she said shyly. "People down there have to drink it." She pointed to a village at least a mile farther downstream. "You can use that one over there; that's just for irrigation."

This was one of many lessons in how the Ladakhis manage to prosper in such a difficult environment. It was also a lesson on the meaning of the word "frugality." In the West frugality conjures up images of old aunts and padlocked pantries.

But the frugality you find in Ladakh, which is fundamental to the people's prosperity, is something quite different. Using limited resources in a careful way has nothing to do with miserliness; this is frugality in its original meaning of fruitfulness: getting more out of little. Where we would consider something completely worn out, exhausted of all possible worth, and would throw it away, Ladakhis will find some further use for it. Nothing whatever is just discarded. What cannot be eaten can be fed to the animals; what cannot be used as fuel can fertilize the land.

Sonam's grandmother, Abi-le, did not throw away the barley after making chang from it. She had already poured water over the boiled and fermented grain to make four separate brews. Instead of discarding the grain, she spread it on a yak-hair blanket to dry so it could later be ground for eating. She molded the crushed remains of apricot kernels, a dark brown paste from which oil had already been carefully squeezed, into the form of a small cup; later, when it had hardened, she would use the cup to turn her spindles. She even saved the dishwater, with its tiny bits of food, to provide a little extra nourishment for the animals.

Ladakhis patch their homespun robes until they can be patched no more. When winter demands that they wear two or three, one on top of the other, they put the best one on the inside to protect it for special occasions. When no amount of stitching can sustain a worn-out robe, it is packed with mud into a weak part of an irrigation channel to help prevent leakage.

The soil in the stables is dug up to be used as fertilizer, thus recycling animal urine. Dung is collected not only from the stables and pens, but also from the pastures. Even human night soil is not wasted. Each house has a composting latrine consisting of a small room with a hole in the floor built above a vertical chute, usually one floor high. Earth and ash from the kitchen stove are added, thus aiding chemical decomposition, producing better fertilizer, and eliminating smells. Once a year the latrine is emptied at ground level and the contents are used on the fields.

In such ways Ladakhis traditionally recycle everything. There is literally no waste. With only scarce resources at their disposal, farmers have managed to attain almost complete self-reliance, dependent on the outside world only for salt, tea, and a few metals for cooking utensils and tools.

Frugality is not the only key to Ladakhi prosperity. An intimate understanding of the local environment is also crucial. This location-specific knowledge takes many forms. Villagers, for example, are highly skilled in farming at fourteen thousand feet. They know how the soil varies from field to field, are attuned to the subtle microclimates within their village, and know the characteristics of numerous strains of barley. Virtually all the plants, shrubs, and bushes that grow wild, either around the edges of irrigated land or in the mountains—what we would call weeds—are gathered and serve some useful purpose. *Burtse* is used for fuel and animal fodder; yagdzas, for the roofs of houses; the thorny *tsermang,* for building fences to keep animals out of fields and gardens; *demok,* as a red dye. Others are used for medicine, food, incense, and basket weaving.

Virtually every Ladakhi knows how to build a house, but the techniques vary depending on local conditions. Soil, for example, is slightly different in each place: in one village large mud bricks are made, in another village smaller ones are made, while in a third village straw may be needed in the mix. Centuries of local knowledge are even stored in the genetic makeup of local breeds of animals: the hooves of donkeys in villages with stony terrain, for example, are tougher than those from villages with sandy terrain. In these and countless other ways, Ladakhi knowledge of local resources emphasizes the *local*.

This close connection between Ladakhis and their environment is reflected in the Buddhist worldview, which emphasizes the interconnectedness of all life. Ladakhis are keenly aware that they depend for their survival upon the water from the mountains, the soil in the fields, the grasses at the phu. Individuals are also aware of the ways in which they depend on family and community, and how these in turn depend on the individual. In Ladakh's human-scale communities, people know that helping others is in their own best interest.

With each day and new experience in Ladakh, I gained a deeper understanding of what self-reliance means. Concepts like "sustainability" and "ecology" had meant little to me when I first arrived. With the years, I not only came to respect the Ladakhis' successful adaptation to nature, but was also forced to reassess the Western industrial societies in which I had been raised. Economic and technological development—"progress"—has reached an advanced stage in the West. Wherever we look, we can see its inexorable logic at work: replacing people with machines, local interdependence with global markets, country lanes with superhighways, and corner shops with supermarkets.

Through the process known as "development"—and more recently "free trade"—this industrial model is being spread around the globe, reducing the diversity of the world to a single monoculture. It is assumed that needs are everywhere the same, that everyone needs to eat the same food, live in the same type of house, wear the same clothes. Children from diverse cultures crowd into classrooms to learn the same Western-based curriculum. The same cement buildings, the same toys, the same films and television programs find their way to the most remote corners of the world. Across the planet, "Baywatch" beams into people's homes, pinstripe suites are *de rigueur,* and every child's ideal is either blonde, blue-eyed Barbie or gun-toting Rambo.

Sadly, this process has already begun to unravel the rich tapestry of Ladakhi culture, and with it the wisdom on which the culture was based. No Western agricultural textbook will ever contain even a small fraction of the accumulated knowledge of centuries that every Ladakhi child learns from daily experience. In Ladakh and around the world, Western science and technology are erasing other ways of knowing and doing, ways that are adapted to specific places and that have proved themselves over time. These are steps toward ecological ruin on a planetary scale.

Perhaps the most important lesson from Ladakh has to do with happiness. It is a lesson I was slow to learn. Only after many years of peeling away layers of pre-conceptions did I begin to see the smiles and laughter of the Ladakhis for what they really were: a genuine and unfettered appreciation of life itself. In Ladakh I have known a people who regard peace of mind and *joie de vivre* as their birthright. I have seen that community and a close relationship to the land can enrich human life beyond all comparison with material wealth or technological sophistication.

The story of Ladakh can help us to see that another way is possible.

defending small farms, small towns, and good work

LYNN R. MILLER

ON Valentine's Day I took my wife, Kristi, to a nice restaurant in a small city forty miles away. It was to be a romantic treat, but it didn't turn out quite as planned.

The restaurant was sold out and we were asked to sit at a small table with a couple we had never met before. The couple made it plain they did not appreciate this turn of events. Kristi and I tried to present ourselves as harmless and perhaps even just a little interesting.

I do not want to stoop to the level of cheap journalism, so I take a chance that little pieces of conversation will impart something of a complete picture without detailing the folks involved. I am not wanting to paint a picture of this couple, but I found their perspective so genuinely haunting and illuminative that I want to share pieces of it. I should add that I'm certain all conversation at that table was disjointed because we were like four people—two couples—stuck in an elevator for three hours (yes, three hours!) overhearing every word spoken in confidence between couples and forcing ourselves to share little bits of what we hoped were unrevealing pieces of ourselves. With each bit of information we struggled to find something in common. There was a lot of squirming and looking around the restaurant.

When he revealed he was an attorney, she said, "Oh great, now they'll hate us."

When I revealed we did our fieldwork with horses, there was an odd silence, knitting of brows, and glances from one to the other broken by, "You mean you cut down trees with them?!"

"Not exactly, we pull farm implements: plows, drills, spreaders—we put up hay with them and occasionally skid logs as well."

He responded, "I thought using them for logging was all that was left. You mean you actually farm with them?"

"Yes."

Silence—long silence—awkward silence.

I decided not to talk about the fact that we also edited and published a magazine entitled *Small Farmer's Journal, featuring Practical Horsefarming.*

Later, perhaps as an offering to indicate empathy with our situation, the woman said, "I inherited a farm, forty thousand acres of rice, in northern California. Tried to make it work but it was a male-dominated world, a small-town world. I got rid of it. I couldn't get out of there fast enough. You know how small towns are, and this was the worst because all the people there were small farmers. Desperate people. That whole community was only fifteen hundred people, but they had serious problems with suicide and alcohol, abusive behavior and drugs.

It was horrible. Maybe it was the hypocrisy that bothered me the most. Or maybe it was all those chemicals. You can't farm without the poisons, and the growing cancer statistics in that area scared me so I took my daughter and left."

Again silence. The kind of silence that seems to scream out, "Why did I say all of that!?!!" and "Why did she tell us that?!"

When we spoke to one another again it was because he had artfully found, he thought, a subject that was safe—bird hunting.

While he spoke I wondered why I didn't want to respond to her diatribe on small farms and small towns. But I didn't. I'm glad I didn't.

When I found myself listening to him again, both women left the table as he offered his summation: "Whether we're farmers or lawyers, none of us gets to spend enough time doing what we truly want to. Don't you think? That's why it's so important to me to get out with my gun and my dog. It doesn't really matter if I shoot anything."

I couldn't stop it. It rose out of me and I couldn't stop it.

"That's unfortunate," I said. Why did I say that? "I enjoy my work, I can't imagine doing it well if I didn't. Not for an entire lifetime. Sure there might be some unpleasantness to parts of the work, but that's part of the weave."

"You enjoy ranchwork?" he asked honestly.

"Yes, very much so, but that's not all that I do. I have a publishing business, I do a little writing, I paint pictures."

He looked incredulous. "You can't have enough time to do justice to all that? I have one line of work and I'm always busy."

"I'm always busy, too. And I like to think that the mix is important."

"Yes, but—like the painting—that's not really work now, is it?"

"None of it's work if you mean by 'work' that I must dislike it. I enjoy it all to an equal degree. I am spending my time, all of it, as I choose."

He had a disbelieving smile.

The women returned.

Silence—odd, protracted silence.

We call it Singing Horse Ranch. If you point in our direction and ask the locals, "what's out there?" likely you'll get the answer, "Nothing; rocks, junipers, snakes, nobody lives out there." And if you respond by asking, "Don't the Millers live out there?" you might hear "Oh sure, but that's just one family and they farm with horses."

I've come to understand the logic that would have a single unusual family constitute "nobody."

But what happens out here just might be worth a note.

From the beginning of *Small Farmer's Journal,* we've treated our farming and ranching ventures as adjuncts to the publication of our books and the journal. To presume to offer an advocacy of animal-powered, family-centered natural farming without the vitality of a working background would be silly and short-lived because the readership for such ideas cries out for credibility. Those who feel a natural calling to be new farmers want information based on an understanding born of experience. We have incorporated processes of inquiry into almost every aspect of our farm and ranch work for eighteen years, as an effort to answer to that need for credible information.

Should you drive in to our ranch today you might see a small sign, in the shadow of the juniper, a little to the right of the gate. It reads:

SINGING HORSE RANCH PRESERVATION RESEARCH SFJ

Preservation because we work consciously to save and strengthen the natural biodiversity of our fragile ranch.

Preservation because we work to prove the value and suitability of what some may refer to as relic technologies and methods, but what we've come to view as good sound options that fit.

Preservation because we work to save and strengthen our working family and the independence of this ranch.

Preservation because we work to design systems that allow beneficial interplay between indigenous wildlife (flora and fauna) and agrarian pursuits, so that the lines between ranch environs and the surrounding desert or forest become blurred.

And preservation because we refuse to accept the popular notions of what can be grown, accomplished, valued, understood, and marketed. Instead, we enjoy reaching well back into the agrarian heritage of this and other similar regions and rekindling old assumptions and worthwhile hazards to be preserved. And the way we preserve them is to plant them right here. Because to preserve any good idea, or hunch, you have to do the same as you do with the best preservation methods for seeds—you have to plant them and grow them and regather the seeds and then restart the cycle over again.

And finally we are always taking delight in those clear indications and measures of both our importance and our insignificance.

The result is a distinctly unimposing human presence in a breathtaking landscape of great vitality and peacefulness.

Workhorses provide the power source for the ranch. We raise them. It's been this way for over twenty years. The rewards to us, both intangible and tangible, are and have always been beyond measure. We can't imagine it being any other way.

And for all of that time we've never employed or applied any chemical toxins in our farming—be they synthetic fertilizers, pesticides, herbicides, or fungicides. We have instead employed tactics of timing, cropping, manure and compost applications, and intensive grazing. We have never measured our production levels against those of other farmers, and never will. Our production levels steadily increase, but far more important to us is the obvious increase in microbial activity in the soil, in humus content in the soil, in water retention capacities of the soil, and in natural fertility gains of the soil. More simply put: most important to us is the evidence of an increase in overall farm health. And our chief inputs consist of labor, scrutiny, and care—all of which benefit us as well.

Our ranch, at twenty-six hundred to three thousand feet elevation, is in a region of thin, sandy soils rich in minerals. Sparse-looking dryland bunch grasses provide tremendous grazing nutrition. Our ranch encompasses irrigated hay ground, improved dryland, and rough natural timbered grazing. It is located in the center of a mule deer winter range that is said to contain seven thousand deer. A fabulous assortment of birds, including hawks and eagles, abound—with numbers increasing every season. The four-legged predators are there as well, but we hardly ever see the cougars. We are excited by obvious successes in our long-range plan to prove that a viable family ranch or farm can enjoy a beneficial coexistence with wildlife. In a ranch meeting with the director of Oregon Fish and Wildlife and one of his biologists, he conjectured that the obvious relaxed comfort and subsequent proximity of wildlife could be due in part to what he termed our low-impact approach. He said that great lumbering tractors scare off wildlife, whereas work horses do not. We certainly have witnessed this in dramatic ways in our everyday work.

Our choice of this place came of certain important personal circumstances and considerations. But only one lesser factor fits into this discussion. That is the fact that everything about our ranch is considered marginal by mainstream agricultural standards. Soils, proximity to markets, growing season, buildings, proximity to urban services, elevation, and so on and so on. For these reasons and more, it fits perfectly into our belief that opportunities abound for the new small farmers we so desperately need if they would but love the work and see each small piece of success for its full worth.

Or from another side of the coin: the best opportunities to begin farming have less to do with the specifics of the individual farm and more to do with the character and values the farm family brings to the challenge. This fact is not something ordinarily spoken of as intrinsically important to farm research. But it is. Preferring to refer to IT as "applicable inquiry into whole agrarian systems" rather than "research," we believe—from experience—that any look at singular elements (whether magnesium or Tuesday's rainfall) is a damaging step backward if the goal is improved understanding. You have to have a healthy respect and overview of the whole farm enterprise, and that most definitely includes the people involved every bit as much as the germination factor of the seed.

So if you're a scientist in the purest sense, you won't find pure research at our ranch. But you will find unusual pieces of equipment or adaptations of equipment being used in the field in order to determine their true efficiency. You will see healthy young fruit trees grown in conditions that are contrary to the best establishment advice. You might witness the documentation of various effective workhorse training techniques for illustrative as well as comparative reasons. You may stumble across efforts to monitor the ways that living acids unlock hidden soil resources. You will find what on the surface appear to be primitive forage preserving and handling systems but which, when fully understood, reveal themselves to be wonderfully efficient. You might be astute enough to pick up on the fact that unusual designs, partnerships, and values are at work in gardening efforts. And you'll doubtless see that, rich as we may be in ideas and intentions, the poverty of our time restrictions does limit us.

Even so, with every passing season a new level of ease comes to different tasks and allows us the opportunity to add a new dimension to our inquiries. We look forward to the day in the not-so-distant future when we will be adding the facilities for a painting studio, a soil laboratory, a darkroom, a fully integrated barn system, a ceramics studio, and a compost "oven barn." The mixture of facilities might sound odd to you, but it harkens back to that point about the family's being such an important aspect of the whole system and how we must love our work. For us these things are most easily felt in our great appreciation of the creative process. Each of us enjoys a variety of artistic pursuits that directly and indirectly affect our work on the ranch. Kristi's beautiful natural "framing" eye and photographic skills serve us with the journal and the ranch documentation, but this "thing" is no less important to her and her fullness of character. My brother Tony puts much of his great religious fervor into sculptures he does in his little cabin, but he is no less intense in his determination to find the perfect shape for our haystacks. So our menu for ranch projects includes the means to expand on those things we know to enlarge our love of the work.

I hope I haven't painted too pretty a picture of our ranch. Visitors here are often struck by the peace and physical beauty of the landscape. The facilities, by contrast (or perhaps as counterpoint), are crude and seem always in transition. Still, I'd like to think that of the human presence here, three things are felt. One: great expectations. Two: a healthy attitude of allowance rather than determination. And three: a whole lot of humility. They serve us well—expectations, allowance, and humility. They allow little or no distinction between the work we do, the lives we live, and those things we love most. They blend together and make us a real part of our place.

We are, all of us, so often accused of being teary-eyed romantics, out of touch with the real world. And it is so easy to discount the charge because our worlds and priorities and triumphs (tempered as they are by understood and mysterious failures) are real to us.

Yet the accusation that we are out of touch comes to us across a bridge. And that bridge crosses a chasm which divides humanity. I used to believe in the simple notion that we farmers were on one side and nonfarmers were on the other, and that there was free passage over the bridge for whoever wanted to pass. I believed that a very long time ago. With my publication experience I modified my belief to show rural people on one side and nonrural people on the other, with the bridge representing a rite of passage won through experience.

Now I'm wondering if we aren't talking about something quite different and perhaps beyond verbal description. I know we're divided, but by what—differences in values or differences in perceptions or differences in experience? I have a gut feeling for who's on this side, but I can't come up with a description that is inclusive enough. I have a feeling for who's on the other side, but here, too the words fail me. I know I am where I want to be and that there's room over here for everybody, but I no longer feel qualified to even suggest that those on the other side are less than us. In fact, I don't much care for the notion of sides because it sets a tone and category to our responses; they become defensive or offensive rather than constructive. I want so much to respond to that lady's charge against small towns and small farmers. But I shouldn't—so I will.

Because a town is small does not make it good or bad. The people, their histories in that place, their values, their accomplishments, their dreams mixed together, account for the goodness or badness of that small town.

Because a farm is small does not make it good or bad. The people, the family who shepherds that farm—it is they who make it good or less than good. It cannot be bad, this small farm, because it is not capable of malevolence. Only the people are.

I know how small towns can be. They can be wonderful repositories for the intertwining lives of good people offering strength and collective forms and pieces of identity to all who are fortunate enough to be a part.

Small towns and small farms do not breed desperation, abuse, suicide, and neglect, but neither are they immune from them. We, all of us, have come to believe that they offer more opportunity to reverse the conditions of collective human misery which cause these problems. But opportunity is just a swinging door. Until we use it, perhaps it isn't a passage. We, each of us, can contribute by using the opportunity our small town represents to make it a better piece of humanity.

You can farm, and farm well, without chemical toxins. And agricultural production can increase with the better farming that results. Those who argue otherwise are often either in a position to profit from the argument or are justifiably frightened of large-scale change. But it doesn't alter the fact that it's true.

Farming on a small scale and employing the mixed practices which allow for good healthful, clean production results in stronger, happier small towns. When forty thousand acres are divided between forty or fifty or a hundred or more *independent* family farms producing a wide variety of products (and services), the bloom will return to the rose that is that local small town. How many families does it take to support a small church, a small school, a small hardware store, a feed store, a fuel depot?

The romance of who and what we are as small farmers is delicious. But no more so than the reality, and our value to the future of small places.

addicted to work

LINDA M. HASSELSTROM

I ONCE KNEW AN EDUCATED LADY, BANDED BY

PHI BETA KAPPA, WHO TOLD ME THAT SHE HAD NEVER

HEARD OR SEEN THE GEESE THAT TWICE A YEAR PROCLAIM

THE REVOLVING SEASONS TO HER WELL-INSULATED ROOF.

IS EDUCATION POSSIBLY A PROCESS OF TRADING

AWARENESS FOR THINGS OF LESSER WORTH?

THE GOOSE WHO TRADES HIS IS SOON

A PILE OF FEATHERS.

—Aldo Leopold, *A Sand County Almanac,* 1949

VIRTUALLY all of my friends have at one time or another suggested that I get away from the ranch, give up the physical labor it requires, and pursue some respectable occupation such as teaching. Why, they ask, should I waste my education and strain my muscles pitching hay to cows? Neighboring ranchers say, "Isn't it too bad you wasted all that time in college when you were just going to come back here and work anyway?" Neither group understands why laughter is the only answer I can manage.

In our admirable desire to educate ourselves, we have begun to believe that education saves us from physical labor. Many ranchers still urge their children to get college educations, "so you won't have to work as hard as I did." People who try to buy the country place of their dreams discover that they can't afford it; expensive land is often accessible only to big, destructive corporations. Ironically, by the time the ranchers' educated kids—lawyers, doctors, engineers—can afford land, they want a vacation cabin. Agriculture can't provide them with enough money to satisfy an appetite for electronic gadgets and bigger cars; feeding a habit of instant gratification, they live in towns where they can earn more. Losing their taste for labor on the land, they lose appreciation for its intangible rewards and the wisdom arising from ties to the earth.

Country folks want to buy everything town folks buy. Instead of taking pride in a different lifestyle and a unique culture, we've embraced cravings that force us to depend on urban markets and urban machinery. Rancher Ann Charter, quoted in Stan Steiner's informative *The Ranchers,* says, "When the ranchers have to live up to their city neighbors and have all the conveniences they are not going to make it. Life on a ranch has been urbanized; it is no longer a rural way of life. The rancher, he is plugged into the electricity from the city" (Steiner 1980, 97).

I occasionally teach college classes part-time, but only because I enjoy teaching; I know easier ways to make money legally. My preferred lifestyle, living and writing on the ranch, requires my constant vigilance. I could write happily for eight hours a day if someone would occasionally bring me a sandwich. I've taught a good deal, but full-time teaching requires so much of my creative energy that I find writing difficult. Cold-eyed teenage students tell me they plan to be computer programmers or stockbrokers because "that's where the money is." At eighteen, they see their goal as making money quickly so they can retire—and then "enjoy life." If I suggest that work should be something one loves, in case we don't live long enough to enjoy deferred pleasures, they look at me with pity.

Writing while living on a ranch allows me to blend physical exercise with mental, and permits me some variety in choosing what to do each day. The drawback is that sometimes the ranch work takes twelve hours out of my day, and I'm too tired or sore to write. If my primary goal in life were to make money, I probably would not live in South Dakota at all, let alone on a ranch. I'd have accepted that offer from a slick New York magazine. Money isn't my goal, an attitude often judged downright dim-witted.

My students at an engineering college were skeptical when I insisted they should be able to communicate clearly—not only out loud, but on paper. They judged success by income; many of them would be making thirty thousand dollars a year the minute they graduated. Consequently, they had little respect for advice from someone making less than an eighth of that for teaching two classes in freshman English. If I were smart, their eyes and their tongues said, I'd be doing something that paid more. Because these embryo engineers were interested in technical subjects, they expected to do poorly in English, and they did—until they took my class. They assumed that I would be unable to understand even simple chemistry problems, because my master's degree is in English. Their minds neatly classified the world:

> Technical knowledge = intellect and piles of cash
> Liberal arts = stupidity and poverty

The two types of knowledge, according to their thinking, could not coexist in the same individual.

"Education, I fear, is learning to see one thing by going blind to another," said Aldo Leopold (1970, 168). While writing this essay, I went out into a cold, wet wind and stacked green wood for twenty minutes. When I came back to the computer, my ears were freezing, my back hurt, my blood was racing, my heart pounding, and I was delighted to return to struggling with phrases on paper. When words temporarily defeat me, I can check the cows, or carry wood inside, or pile rocks around my trees. I'm often tired, but never bored. When I'm confronted with a job I detest, six other jobs I prefer can delay it another day.

The variety of work keeps me from becoming blind in the sense I believe

Leopold meant, my vision narrowed until I can see only words, or only physical labor. I believe that for a human being to see, literally or figuratively, he or she must look both near and far off; in the same way, labor should be both physical and mental in order to keep all circuits healthy.

It's popular, and in some cases correct, to call any obsessive behavior "addiction" and view it as a disease to be treated, to be recovered from. We now list work among possible addictions, and our leisure reading is filled with articles advising workaholics to relax. By those standards, since I am not happy when I'm not writing regularly, I am addicted to writing. Agriculture is also a 24-hour-a-day, 365-day-a-year job. I have seen solemn articles suggesting that ranchers and farmers are all workaholics, Type A personalities who don't know how to relax and have fun. If I am to believe what I read, I am addicted both to writing and to ranch work, and in dire need of treatment. There's truth in that accusation.

Yet we *expect* men and women to devote all day, each day of the year, to loving their families; we don't call that addiction. Christian churches expect all of us to live religion full-time; we don't call the doctor to help nuns and priests recover from a "religious addiction."

Country people generally realize that our families are not divisible from our land; our beliefs about both family and land grow out of everyday practices, rather than theory. Some of us never get around to marrying and raising children because we substitute land for family. Those who have families seem to love them and the land as if they were the same—and they are. The crustiest, most conservative, most antienvironment ranchers will say, with an oddly gentle note, "I *love* this country." Others say, "If you take care of the land, it will take care of you." Or, "We don't really own this land; we're just taking care of it for the next generation."

During summer's dry heat, I have heard ranchers say, "I ain't had no rain on me since May; there ain't enough grass on me to feed a bird." Referring to their land in the most intimate terms possible, ranchers mourn, "If I don't get rain on me pretty soon, I'm going to blow away."

I know plenty of ranchers who insist they could make more money by selling the ranch and depositing the cash to earn interest. But most of them also say, "I'll quit when they carry me off the place feet first." All ranchers know one whose wife persuaded him to retire and move to town. "You know," they say, shaking their heads, "he only lived six months. He quit working and it killed him." They never talk about whether he enjoyed his life that six months; they know he didn't, if he wasn't working.

Rancher Ellen Cotton told author Steiner: "This place is nothing. It is so small. And I'm a small rancher. But it symbolizes something to me, something I would die for. Money just isn't the thing in my life. That's not why I ranch. No rancher is in ranching just for the money; if he was he'd be in another business. If you wanted to make money on this place you'd have to be a hard-nosed person. And we'd have no room for anything else, the dollar sign would be your God" (Steiner

1980, 227). Dozens of ranchers might echo her words; probably they'd just nod and look away to hide tears in their eyes.

A joke that has made the rounds in cattle country for years made it to the *Congressional Record* in 1989. "What would you do," the city slicker asked the farmer, "if you had a million dollars?" The farmer replied, "I guess I'd just farm until it was all gone" (*Congressional Record—Senate* May 4, 1989, S4932). When a farm couple from the tiny town of Dallas, South Dakota, bought a lottery ticket worth twelve and a half million dollars in a Lotto America jackpot in the spring of 1991, the wife said, "We've wanted to buy a farm and raise our kids on it." Her husband spoke of buying some pigs and livestock (*Rapid City Journal* April 10, 1991). And Elmer Kelton, a writer of the true West, said in *The Good Old Boys,* "A man could starve to death in a year on a hundred and sixty acres. On four sections it took longer" (Kelton 1978, 24).

Once when I visited my beekeeping neighbors, talk turned to their recent trip to Germany. Bill is a quiet man who thinks and listens before he arrives at an opinion, and feels no need to force everyone else to share it. But his enthusiasm was obvious as he showed me his souvenir, an intricately constructed carrying case with everything needed to start and transport a colony of bees. The contraption was fitted with special bee-sized doors for admitting a lot of bees in a hurry. The beekeeper could create a queen by the delicate manipulation of royal jelly and a tiny imperial suite. Minute mesh-covered openings let the colony breathe without escaping. A carved depression enabled the bees to feed on sugar water, and a wee fence kept them from drowning. The whole device was only slightly larger than a roll of toilet paper, and about the same weight, but it was a marvel of engineering. Bill didn't buy it because he needed it—he moves his bee colonies by truck—but because he admired the workmanship. Later he showed me part of an old hand-made beehive, explaining the construction, much superior to that of modern hives. From plans he'd found in an old beekeeping book, he wants to build one; he doesn't need that, either, but he wants to show visitors how the old boxes were made.

Only two things about bees really interest me. First, I love honey. Second, when a swarm settles in a tree over our corrals, I want to know where Bill is so he can come and capture them. All the same, I was enthralled by the conversation. Like many ranchers of forty or older, Bill was raised to do everything as well as possible, and believes any work done with pride is enjoyable. He loved talking about his work, so I loved hearing him. His kind is a vanishing species in an America that used to teem with pride in all its labors and found enjoyment in work.

I have been speaking of work in general, work as an attitude of mine as well as an exercise of body. I also think not working, that is, avoiding physical labor, is literally killing a lot of us. We buy expensive exercise clothing and equipment to eliminate the side effects of being so well educated that we never use a muscle. But artificial exercise can't replace real labor or its satisfactions. Older ranchers were raised to believe no one deserved more of the world's goods than they could make or grow with their own hands and sweat; honest hard work guaranteed respect and survival. Surviving old-timers live under a government pretending to function even though it's a trillion dollars in debt. My neighbors supported the Gulf War, but were uneasy about the speed with which it pushed the savings and loans scandal off the front pages. They don't believe a person or a country can long perform under huge debts; they cling to their old-fashioned values, expecting the whole shaky mess to tumble down. "Somebody's gonna pay," they predict.

We country people are directly responsible for our own lives in ways most people aren't. If I collapsed from the affects of freezing on a city street, someone might call an ambulance. But when I go outside alone at thirty below zero to feed cattle, one mistake could kill me. If someone is breaking into my house, dialing 911 will get me a telephone charge—and a connection to a police dispatcher twenty-five miles away who will explain that I'm outside the police jurisdiction. The local sheriff is thirty-five miles away on a winding road. I must deal with the burglar alone. Country people learn self-reliance as a necessity, and sometimes overdo it. I was so busy being a stoic child when I cracked my wrist in a horse accident, for example, that my parents didn't take me to a doctor for three days. They were not neglectful; they simply didn't realize that I thought gritting my teeth on the pain would master it. An eighty-year-old rancher who has run his ranch, hired men, built a house and barns, and paid all his debts, has turned self-reliance into success. But he won't be recognized as Businessman of the Year.

My second husband's son lived in a small Minnesota town until he graduated from high school. His responsibilities there were simple: he had to get out of bed in the morning, get dressed, go to school, study, maybe take out the garbage or baby sit, go to his job as a stock boy in a grocery store. His parents expected him to stay sober and get acceptable grades; his school expected him to learn from books how to be a responsible citizen and to believe in the high morality of politicians, even though the news rang with examples of their corruption.

Instead, he got low grades and misbehaved; he felt unimportant and frustrated. His mother complained that he lost his jacket, couldn't remember where he put his books or his English paper. I didn't approve of his confusion or its results, but I think I understand it. Except for the baby sitting, none of his jobs was important. He knew the world was full of problems; he was bursting with youthful energy and confidence, but he couldn't believe anything he did would improve his world.

When he came to the ranch, if he forgot to feed his horse, she didn't eat. If he neglected to fix the fence, the cows got out and several people and horses had to work hard for a day in the hot sun getting them back. All of us freely explained what he'd done wrong. If he didn't turn the water on the garden, the sun fried the food we were planning to eat this winter. If he lighted a fire and forgot to watch it, he might start a prairie blaze that would burn the winter grass of a dozen ranches. After a few days, he stopped whining when we got up early; he'd work beside us, grinning, and wouldn't quit until we did. What he did, and didn't do, *mattered*.

As real concern for the earth increases worldwide, some folks take a shortcut to the natural look; fashion designers showcase clothes inspired by workers' coveralls. But lumberjack pants and plaid shirts are no substitute for old-fashioned traits.

Ranch families used to be large. Kids raised chickens and sold eggs for cash in lieu of allowances, and contributed to the family support; they were important to the whole family's survival. Now, along with their mothers and fathers, they get jobs in town, and their parents buy them a car; the well-defined connection between work and its rewards becomes indistinct. Living in the country is becoming a luxury, not a way of life.

The comparison can be pushed back into history. Before ranchers occupied this land, it was held by animals and Indian tribes, all of whom resisted the explorers and trappers who ventured here. If those men misjudged the swiftness of a river, they drowned; if they weren't fair in their dealings with the Native Americans, they risked death. What they did, and didn't do, mattered. They were not all good men, and a little later they weren't all good women; but the survivors were all tough. The stupid ones didn't pass on their genes. Only after our ancestors learned how to live here, removing the most ferocious challenges, did the land become available to less stalwart settlers.

The jury is still out on whether our easier lives are better for our mental and physical health. Among people who study such things, the suspicion is growing that we made a serious error some time back. Researchers on the origin of man believe that physically we are almost identical to the people who lived in Europe, Africa, and Asia thirty thousand years ago: "Our culture has evolved so far and so fast that there would seem to be no connection between us, but physical evolution is a much slower business. Despite all our electronics and jet aircraft, symphonic music and deconstructionism, we are they" (Wiley 1988, 23–28).

If we are physically the same people that our ancestors were, we may have a clue to why many of us are a lot sicker. If the human body evolved over hundreds of thousands of years to fit a lifestyle that no longer exists, that lifestyle would still be appropriate to us.

What are we losing, physically, by eliminating the work our bodies evolved to do? Anthropologists suggest that for a hundred thousand generations we were hunters and gatherers, while we have been agriculturalists for only five hundred generations, industrialized for a mere ten, and computerized for only one. They believe that the contradiction between our long yesterdays and our brief today is the cause of the chronic diseases that cause 75 percent of the deaths in industrial societies. The Paleolithic diet probably consisted of red meat with a lower fat content than feedlot beef, plenty of wild fruits and vegetables, and little fat, salt, or sugar, making our average ancestor as strong as today's professional athlete.

Each day, early humans faced challenges that kept their muscles strong and their brains active. Admittedly their life expectancy was shorter than ours, but that in turn benefited the species: anyone who couldn't outrun or outsmart a mastodon was removed from the gene pool. Physicians once saw degenerative diseases such as diabetes, obesity, and lung disease as natural by-products of aging; now they suspect that they are really "diseases of civilization," consequences of our less active lives rather than the inevitable result of human biology (Eaton et al. 1988).

In ranching, each day requires new skills, and most weeks involve life-and-death decisions. My mother was singing the chorus of a Kenny Rogers song one day: "You gotta know when to hold 'em, know when to fold 'em, know when to walk away, know when to stay." My father chuckled. "That sounds like it's about ranching." Although ranchers are often pictured as humble, stolid sons and daughters of the soil, they are secret adventurers; they don't like doing the same thing every day, and they don't respond well to orders. In another era some might have been riverboat gamblers. Every purchase of land or equipment, every new bull brought into the herd, is speculation. A rancher buying winter feed is betting it will last as long as the bad weather. Turning his cattle out to summer pasture ten miles from home is a wager that rain will help the grass grow until the calves are ready for market.

Some of us regard work and play as completely separate activities; the former is the unpleasant thing one does for money to do the latter in style. But, as Wendell Berry has observed, "farmers do not *go* to work; a good farmer is *at* work even when at rest" (Berry 1987, 124).

Even today, when farming requires the economic skills of an investment banker to survive and the scientific knowledge of a chemical engineer to keep from poisoning oneself, some people regard "dumb farmers" as a single word, or think anyone who *enjoys* physical labor must be too dumb to get an education or understand its worth. Moreover, urban folks may be unable to distinguish between the very different occupations and attitudes of ranchers and farmers.

In either case, a farmer or rancher *lives* at work, where everything valued is in close touch with everything else. Trying to hurry one job to rush to something more profitable or productive means losing careful comprehension; rushing a bull can be fatal. Our jobs are part of a process; there is often little gap between work and play. Berry, examining the contrasts between industry and agriculture, says the two can be hostile to each other:

> The economy of industry is, typically, an extractive economy: It takes, makes, uses, and discards; it progresses, that is, from exhaustion to pollution. Agriculture, on the other hand, rightly belongs to a replenishing economy, which takes, makes, uses and *returns*. It involves the return to the source, not just of fertility or of so-called wastes, but also of care and affection. Otherwise, the topsoil is used exactly as a minable fuel and is destroyed in use. Thus, in agriculture, the methods of the factory give us the life expectancy of the factory—

long enough for us, perhaps, but not long enough for our children and grand-children. (Berry 1987, 124)

A similar confusion infects those who consider writing as just another job. People ask why I write essays about ranching and the environment, when the "real money" is in popular fiction. If I answer that I don't like most popular fiction and have no idea how to write it, my interrogator has an answer: "Well, read a bunch of it; it's not hard to figure out."

If I answer that I don't write just for money, I'm considered deranged. Kind friends have suggested schemes to make ranch work easier and faster so I could sit at my computer all day long churning out best-selling books. When I wail about my need to work outside, they stare in disbelief.

The same mentality affects business planners who say we "can't afford" to do agricultural labor by hand. Can't afford to leave hay on steep hills or along fences for wildlife habitat; we need those wide spaces for big machinery to plow those hills, so tear out the fences. Business advisers who think along these lines would explain to ranchers—slowly, so we could grasp it—that we can't afford to keep a cow that didn't calve this year, even though her last four calves were profitable and she'll no doubt calve next year. Sell her, they'd say. No vacation for a cow. Yet when their companies don't make a profit and the shareholders don't get dividends, the bosses get a raise; after all, the company is an ongoing business requiring steady management, and competent managers don't come cheap.

According to industrial thinking, we can't afford to farm without big ma-chinery, can't afford the hand labor that supported one-family farms and ranches. Education means not having to work with your hands. Labor-saving devices to save us from doing work by hand may require fuel bought outside our region, but we don't consider that a detriment. If it's more efficient, it's progress. For recre-ation, though, we may plant flowers in window boxes, displaying the symbolic dirt under our fingernails. In our leisure time, we may prowl antique shops for sym-bols of hand labor, including pottery, furniture, rugs.

My neighbor Margaret and I both liked antiques. Once she asked if I'd ever seen an antique wastebasket. After the silence on the telephone lines had lasted quite a while, she said softly, "Our ancestors never threw anything away; they didn't have anything to waste."

One afternoon I watched artists from several New Mexico pueblos seated on a porch in Santa Fe, bargaining with tourists eager for their pottery and jewelry. The Indians leaned against an adobe wall bearing hand prints from women who patted the mud into place and whitewashed it. These artists, technically at work, smiled and enjoyed themselves; they relaxed in the warm sun, nibbling piñon nuts and exchanging low-voiced comments the tourists couldn't understand.

The vacationing tourists were edgy and uncertain; they argued with their spouses about how much they should haggle. They disagreed shrilly over which pot would look best on that shelf above the fireplace. As soon as an artist agreed, they snatched out their wallets to pay and left, looking haggard, clutching their prizes. The Indians packed up slowly at day's end to go back to their mesa where, in an unhurried way centuries old, they would make more jewelry and pots for sale.

Our national concern over lack of physical fitness has made dieting and weight machines huge industries. Yet the nation has thousands of idle workers walking the streets job hunting. Farmers and ranchers are unable to hire help; they can't compete with the wages paid by big industry. The farmers are forced to buy machines, providing employment for the workers who build them but requiring more cash. Farms and ranches go broke when the kids move to town, because a farmer can't afford to hire labor or can't find anyone who knows how to do agricultural work. We're all familiar with the scenario, because it's been the immediate cause of many farmers losing their land. Couldn't those problems be combined?

Why not offer unemployed people farm work that would improve their bodies and keep their children a long way from crack? With a little guidance they might support themselves—or at least feed their families—by gardening or raising pigs. Such a program could cost no more than one B-1 bomber or a couple of missiles, and might actually get people off welfare permanently. A trained pool of agricultural workers might save the family farm, might inhibit the pollution caused by agricultural chemicals and machines.

Would Washington economists snicker at my naive plan? I've done no cost projections, hired no economists. Perhaps they'll take my simple idea and run it through a couple of think tanks and a couple of million-dollar federal studies. The theorists might add machinery and a few experts, or require the new farmers to use chemicals, so big corporations could benefit. They would write a hundred-page document, siphoning more profit from rural areas into city pockets. Can we afford that kind of expertise?

For years we've operated on the slogan "bigger is better" and made profit our criterion for success. Now agricultural labor pollutes our water and soil; newspapers tell us so daily. Country people who love the land are suddenly its worst enemies.

Production and profit move from the country to the city, where the majority of voters live. Country dwellers are few, with less representation in government, so we have to be noisier.

Nevertheless, time is on the side of the hard-working country dweller. Armed with the strengthening effects of fresh air and exercise, and saved from the mental problems created by urban stress and overcrowding, country people who regularly do physical labor are healthier and saner than anyone in the city. We'll outlive and outsmart the critics.

Frequently, when two ancient ranchers meet, their thoughts stray to the days of horse-and-buggy transportation, when a lively pair of horses might take the bits in their teeth and run away with the wagon. The conversation goes like this:

"How are you?"

"If I felt any better I'd have a runaway."

Folks like that can wait out a lot of social upheaval before they change their behavior.

conserving communities

WENDELL BERRY

IN October of 1993, the *New York Times* announced that the United States Census Bureau would "no longer count the number of Americans who live on farms." In explaining the decision, the *Times* provided some figures as troubling as they were unsurprising. Between 1910 and 1920, we had 32 million farmers living on farms—about a third of our population. By 1950, this population had declined, but our farm population was still 23 million. By 1991, the number was only 4.6 million, less than 2 percent of the national population. That is, our farm population had declined by an average of almost half a million people a year for forty-one years. Also, by 1991, 32 percent of our farm managers and 86 percent of our farmworkers did *not* live on the land they farmed.

These figures describe a catastrophe that is now virtually complete. They announce that we no longer have an agricultural class that is, or that can require itself to be, recognized by the government; we no longer have a "farm vote" that is going to be of much concern to politicians. American farmers, who over the years have wondered whether or not they counted, may now put their minds at rest: they do not count. They have become statistically insignificant.

We must not fail to appreciate that this statistical insignificance of farmers is the successful outcome of a national purpose and a national program. It is the result of great effort and of principles rigorously applied. It has been achieved with the help of expensive advice from university and government experts, by the tireless agitation and exertion of the agribusiness corporations, and by the renowned advantages of competition—of our farmers among themselves and with farmers of other countries. As a result, millions of country people have been liberated from farming, landownership, self-employment, and other idiocies of rural life.

But what has happened to our agricultural communities is not exceptional any more than it is accidental. This is simply the way a large, exploitive, absentee economy works. For example, here is a *New York Times* News Service report on "rape-and-run" logging in Montana:

> Throughout the 1980s, the Champion International Corp. went on a tree-cutting binge in Montana, leveling entire forests at a rate that had not been seen since the cut-and-run logging days of the last century.
>
> Now the hangover has arrived. After liquidating much of its valuable timber in the Big Sky country, Champion is quitting Montana, leaving behind hundreds of unemployed mill workers, towns staggered by despair and more than 1,000 square miles of heavily logged land.

The article goes on to speak of the revival of "a century-old complaint about large, distant corporations exploiting Montana for its natural resources and then leaving after the land is exhausted." And it quotes a Champion spokesman, Tucker Hill, who said: "We are very sympathetic to those people and very sad. But I don't think you can hold a company's feet to the fire for everything they did over the last twenty years."

If you doubt that exhaustion is the calculated result of such economic enterprise, you might consider the example of the mountain counties of eastern Kentucky from which, over the last three-quarters of a century, enormous wealth has been extracted by the coal companies, leaving the land wrecked and the people poor.

The same kind of thing is now happening in banking. In the county next to mine an independent local bank was recently taken over by a large out-of-state bank. Suddenly some of the local farmers and small-business people, who had been borrowing money from that bank for twenty years and whose credit records were good, were refused credit because they did not meet the requirements of a computer in a distant city. Old and once-valued customers now find that they are known by category rather than character. The directors and officers of the large bank clearly have reduced their economic thinking to one very simple question: "Would we rather make one big loan or many small ones?" Or to put it only a little differently: "Would we rather support one larger enterprise or many small ones?" And they have chosen the large over the small.

This economic prejudice against the small has, of course, done immense damage for a long time to small or family-sized businesses in city and country alike. But this prejudice has often overlapped with an industrial prejudice against anything rural and against the land itself, and this prejudice has resulted in damages that are not only extensive but also long-lasting or permanent.

As we all know, we have much to answer for in our use of this continent from the beginning, but in the last half-century we have added to our desecrations of nature a deliberate destruction of our rural communities. The statistics I cited at the beginning are incontrovertible evidence of this. But so is the condition of our farms and forests and rural towns. If you have eyes to see, you can see that there is a limit beyond which machines and chemicals cannot replace people; there is a limit beyond which mechanical or economic efficiency cannot replace care.

I am talking here about the common experience, the common fate, of rural communities in our country for a long time. It has also been, and it will increasingly be, the common fate of rural communities in other countries. The message is plain enough, and we have ignored it for too long: the great, centralized economic entities of our time do not come into rural places in order to improve them by "creating jobs." They come to take as much of value as they can take, as cheaply and as quickly as they can take it. They are interested in "job creation" only so long as the jobs can be done more cheaply by humans than by machines. They are not interested in the good health—economic or natural or human—of any place on this earth. And if you should undertake to appeal or complain to one of these great corporations on behalf of your community, you would discover something most remarkable: you would find that these organizations are organized expressly for the evasion of responsibility. They are structures in which, as my brother says, "the buck never stops." The buck is processed up the hierarchy until finally it is passed to "the shareholders," who characteristically are too widely dispersed, too poorly informed, and too unconcerned to be responsible for anything. The ideal of the modern corporation is to be (in terms of its own advantage) anywhere and (in terms of local accountability) nowhere. The message to country people, in other words, is this: Don't expect favors from your enemies.

And that message has a corollary that is just as plain and just as much ignored: The governmental and educational institutions from which rural people should by right have received help have not helped. Rather than striving to preserve the rural communities and economies and an adequate rural population, these institutions have consistently aided, abetted, and justified the destruction of every part of rural life. They have eagerly served the superstition that all technological innovation is good. They have said repeatedly that the failure of farm families, rural businesses, and rural communities is merely the result of progress and efficiency and is good for everybody.

We are now pretty obviously facing the possibility of a world that the supranational corporations, and the governments and educational systems that serve them, will control entirely for their own enrichment—and, incidentally and inescapably, for the impoverishment of all the rest of us. This will be a world in which the cultures that preserve nature and rural life will simply be disallowed. It will be, as our experience already suggests, a postagricultural world. But as we now begin to see, you cannot have a postagricultural world that is not also postdemocratic, postreligious, postnatural—in other words, it will be posthuman, contrary to the best that we have meant by "humanity."

In their dealings with the countryside and its people, the promotors of the so-called global economy are following a set of principles that can be stated as follows. They believe that a farm or a forest is or ought to be the same as a factory; that care is only minimally necessary in the use of the land; that affection is not necessary at all; that for all practical purposes a machine is as good as a human; that the industrial standards of production, efficiency, and profitability are the only standards that are necessary; that the topsoil is lifeless and inert; that soil biology is safely replaceable by soil chemistry; that the nature or ecology of any given place is irrelevant to the use of it; that there is no value in human community or neighborhood; and that technological innovation will produce only benign results.

These people see nothing odd or difficult about unlimited economic growth or unlimited consumption in a limited world. They believe that knowledge is property and is power, and that it ought to be. They believe that education is job training. They think that the summit of human achievement is a high-paying job that involves no work. Their public boast is that they are making a society in which everybody will be a "winner"—but their private aim has been to reduce radically the number of people who, by the measure of our historical ideals, might be thought successful: the independent, the self-employed, the owners of small businesses or small usable properties, those who work at home.

The argument for joining the new international trade agreements has been that there is going to be a one-world economy, and we must participate or be left behind—though, obviously, the existence of a one-world economy depends on the willingness of all the world to join. The theory is that under the rule of international, supposedly free trade, products will naturally flow from the places where they can be best produced to the places where they are most needed. This theory assumes the long-term safety and sustainability of massive international transport, for which there are no guarantees, just as there are no guarantees that products will be produced in the best way or to the advantage of the workers who produce them or that they will reach or can be afforded by the people who need them.

There are other unanswered questions about the global economy, two of which are paramount: How can any nation or region justify the destruction of a local productive capacity for the sake of foreign trade? and How can people who have demonstrated their inability to run national economies without inflation, usury, unemployment, and ecological devastation now claim that they can do a better job in running a global economy? American agriculture has demonstrated by its own ruination that you cannot solve economic problems just by increasing scale and, moreover, that increasing scale is almost certain to cause other problems—ecological, social, and cultural.

We can't go on too much longer, maybe, without considering the likelihood that we humans are not intelligent enough to work on the scale to which we have been tempted by our technological abilities. Some such recognition is undoubtedly implicit in American conservatives' long-standing objection to a big central government. And so it has been odd to see many of these same conservatives pushing for the establishment of a supranational economy that would inevitably function as a government far bigger and more centralized than any dreamed of before. Long experience has made it clear—as we might say to the liberals—that to be free we must limit the size of government and we must have some sort of home rule. But it is just as clear—as we might say to the conservatives—that it is foolish to complain about big government if we do not do everything we can to support strong local communities and strong community economies.

But in helping us to confront, understand, and oppose the principles of the global economy, the old political alignments have become virtually useless. Communists and capitalists are alike in their contempt for country people, country life, and country places. They have exploited the countryside with equal greed and disregard. They are alike even in their plea that it is right to damage the present in order to make "a better future."

The dialogue of Democrats and Republicans or of liberals and conservatives is likewise useless to us. Neither party is interested in farmers or in farming or in the good care of the land or in the quality of food. Nor are they interested in taking the best care of our forests. The leaders of these parties are equally subservient to the supranational corporations. Of this the North American Free Trade Agreement and the new revisions to the General Agreement on Tariffs and Trade are proof.

Moreover, the old opposition of country and city, which was never useful, is now more useless than ever. It is, in fact, damaging to everybody involved, as is the opposition of producers and consumers. These are not differences but divisions that ought not to exist because they are to a considerable extent artificial. The so-called urban economy had been just as hard on urban communities as it has been on rural ones.

All these conventional affiliations are now meaningless, useful only to those in a position to profit from public bewilderment. A new political scheme of opposed parties, however, is beginning to take form. This is essentially a two-party system, and it divides over the fundamental issue of community. One of these parties holds that community has no value; the other holds that it does. One is the party of the global economy; the other I would call simply the party of local community. The global party is large, though not populous, immensely powerful and wealthy, self-aware, purposeful, and tightly organized. The community party is only now becoming aware of itself; it is widely scattered, highly diverse, small though potentially numerous, weak though latently powerful, and poor though by no means without resources.

We know pretty well the makeup of the party of the global economy, but who are the members of the party of local community? They are people who take a generous and neighborly view of self-preservation; they do not believe that they can survive and flourish by the rule of dog eat dog; they do not believe that they can succeed by defeating or destroying or selling or using up everything but themselves. They doubt that good solutions can be produced by violence. They want to preserve the precious things of nature and of human culture and pass them on to their children. They want the world's fields and forests to be productive; they do not want them to be destroyed for the sake of production. They know you cannot be a democrat (small *d*) or a conservationist and at the same time a proponent of the supranational corporate economy. They believe—they know from their experience—that the neighborhood, the local community, is the proper place and frame of reference for responsible work. They see that no commonwealth or community of interest can be defined by greed. They know that things connect—that farming, for example, is connected to nature, and food to farming, and health to food—and they want to preserve the connections. They know that a healthy local community cannot be replaced by a market or an entertainment industry or an information highway. They know that contrary to all the unmeaning and unmeant political talk about "job creation," work ought not to be merely a bone thrown to the otherwise unemployed. They know that work ought to be necessary; it ought to be good; it ought to be satisfying and dignifying to the people who do it, and genuinely useful and pleasing to the people for whom it is done.

The party of local community, then, is a real party with a real platform and an agenda of real and doable work. And it has, we might add, a respectable history in the hundreds of efforts, over several decades, to preserve local nature or local health or to sell local products to local consumers. Now such efforts appear to be coming into their own, attracting interest and energy in a way they have not done before. People are seeing more clearly all the time the connections between conservation and economics. They are seeing that a community's health is largely determined by the way it makes its living.

The natural membership of the community party consists of small farmers, ranchers, and market gardeners, worried consumers, owners and employees of small shops, stores, community banks, and other small businesses, self-employed people, religious people, and conservationists. The aims of this party really are only two: the preservation of ecological diversity and integrity, and the renewal, on sound cultural and ecological principles, of local economies and local communities.

So now we must ask how a sustainable local community (which is to say a sustainable local economy) might function. I am going to suggest a set of rules that I think such a community would have to follow. And I hasten to say that I do not consider these rules to be predictions; I am not interested in foretelling the future. If these rules have any validity, it is because they apply now.

If the members of a local community want their community to cohere, to flourish, and to last, these are some things they would do:

1. Always ask of any proposed change or innovation: What will this do to our community? How will this affect our common wealth?
2. Always include local nature—the land, the water, the air, the native creatures—within the membership of the community.
3. Always ask how local needs might be supplied from local sources, including the mutual help of neighbors.
4. Always supply local needs *first*. (And only then think of exporting, first to nearby cities and then to others.)
5. Understand the unsoundness of the industrial doctrine of "labor saving" if that implies poor work, unemployment, or any kind of pollution or contamination.
6. Develop properly scaled value-adding industries for local products to ensure that the community does not become merely a colony of the national or global economy.
7. Develop small-scale industries and businesses to support the local farm and/or forest economy.
8. Strive to produce as much of the community's own energy as possible.
9. Strive to increase earnings (in whatever form) within the community and decrease expenditures outside the community.
10. Make sure that money paid into the local economy circulates within the community for as long as possible before it is paid out.

11. Make the community able to invest in itself by maintaining its properties, keeping itself clean (without dirtying some other place), caring for its old people, teaching its children.

12. See that the old and the young take care of one another. The young must learn from the old, not necessarily and not always in school. There must be no institutionalized "child care" and "homes for the aged." The community knows and remembers itself by the association of old and young.

13. Account for costs now conventionally hidden or "externalized." Whenever possible, these costs must be debited against monetary income.

14. Look into the possible uses of local currency, community-funded loan programs, systems of barter, and the like.

15. Always be aware of the economic value of neighborly acts. In our time the costs of living are greatly increased by the loss of neighborhood, leaving people to face their calamities alone.

16. As a rural community, always be acquainted with, and complexly connected with, community-minded people in nearby towns and cities.

17. Formulate an economy that will always be more cooperative than competitive, for a sustainable rural economy is dependent on urban consumers loyal to local products.

These rules are derived from Western political and religious traditions, from the promptings of ecologists and certain agriculturists, and from common sense. They may seem radical, but only because the modern national and global economies have been formed in almost perfect disregard of community and ecological interests. A community economy is not an economy in which well-placed persons can make a "killing." It is not a killer economy. It is an economy whose aim is generosity and a well-distributed and safeguarded abundance. If it seems unusual to hope and work for such an economy, then we must remember that a willingness to put the community ahead of profit is hardly unprecedented among community businesspeople and local banks.

How might we begin to build a decentralized system of durable local economies? Gradually, I hope. We have had enough of violent or sudden changes imposed by predatory interests outside our communities. In many places, the obvious way to begin the work I am talking about is with the development of a local food economy. Such a start is attractive because it does not have to be big or costly, it requires nobody's permission, and it can ultimately involve everybody. It does not require us to beg for mercy from our exploiters or to look for help where consistently we have failed to find it. By "local food economy" I mean simply an economy in which local consumers buy as much of their food as possible from local producers and in which local producers produce as much as they can for the local market.

Several conditions now favor the growth of local food economies. On the one hand, the costs associated with our present highly centralized food system are going to increase. Growers in the Central Valley of California, for example, can no longer depend on an unlimited supply of cheap water for irrigation. Transportation costs can only go up. Biotechnology, variety patenting, and other agribusiness innovations are intended not to help farmers or consumers but to extend and prolong corporate control of the food economy; they will increase the cost of food, both economically and ecologically.

On the other hand, consumers are increasingly worried about the quality and purity of their food, and so they would like to buy from responsible growers close to home. They would like to know where their food comes from and how it is produced. They are increasingly aware that the larger and more centralized the food economy becomes, the more vulnerable it will be to natural or economic catastrophe, to political or military disruption, and to bad agricultural practice.

For all these reasons, and others, we need urgently to develop local food economies wherever they are possible. Local food economies would improve the quality of food. They would increase consumer influence over production; consumers would become participatory members in their own food economy. They would help to ensure a sustainable, dependable supply of food. By reducing some of the costs associated with long supply lines and large corporate suppliers (such as packaging, transportation, and advertising), they would reduce the cost of food at the same time that they would increase income to growers. They would tend to improve farming practices and increase employment in agriculture. They would tend to reduce the size of farms and increase the number of owners.

Of course, no food economy can be, or ought to be, *only* local. But the orientation of agriculture to local needs, local possibilities, and local limits is indispensable to the health of both land and people, and undoubtedly to the health of democratic liberties as well.

For many of the same reasons, we need also to develop local forest economies, of which the aim would be the survival and enduring good health of both our forests and their dependent local communities. We need to preserve the native diversity of our forests as we use them. As in agriculture, we need local, small-scale, nonpolluting industries (sawmills, woodworking shops, and so on) to add value to local forest products, as well as local supporting industries for the local forest economy.

Just as support for sustainable agriculture should come most logically from consumers who consciously wish to keep eating, so support for sustainable forestry might logically come from loggers, mill workers, and other employees of the forest economy who consciously wish to keep working. But *many* people have a direct interest in the good use of our forests: farmers and ranchers with woodlots, all who depend on the good health of forested watersheds, the makers of wood products, conservationists, and others.

What we have before us, if we want our communities to survive, is the building of an adversary economy, a system of local or community economies within, and to protect against, the would-be global economy. To do this, we must somehow learn to reverse the flow of the siphon that has for so long been drawing resources, money, talent, and people out of our countryside with very little if any return, and often with a return only of pollution, impoverishment, and ruin. We must figure out new ways to fund, at affordable rates, the development of healthy local economies. We must find ways to suggest economically—for finally no other suggestion will be effective—that the work, the talents, and the interest of our young people are needed at home.

Our whole society has much to gain from the development of local land-based economies. They would carry us far toward the ecological and cultural ideal of local adaptation. They would encourage the formation of adequate local cultures (and this would be authentic multiculturalism). They would introduce into agriculture and forestry a sort of spontaneous and natural quality control, for neither consumers nor workers would want to see the local economy destroy itself by abusing or exhausting its sources. And they would complete at last the task of gaining freedom from colonial economics, begun by our ancestors more than two hundred years ago.

does community have a value?—a reply

CARL D. ESBJORNSON

DURING the great flood of 1993, a woman who lived in one of the threatened Missouri towns along the Mississippi River was asked why she insisted that she would not leave this town once the waters receded. She replied that such a flood happened only once every fifty years and, more important, solidified friendships, requiring the whole community to pitch in and help build a levee strong enough to hold back the flood. She wanted to stay because, in saving itself, her community exemplified the ethic of mutual help and cooperation. I suspect that the flood proved to her the need for solid communities, and that the community is the basic social unit of human life, ensuring our survival not only in an emergency but in daily life. She knows now that she cannot live in a better place.

I cannot be sure that, prior to the flood, she had much reason to feel that way. I suspect something else—that, up to that time, her town was like so many others, made up of individuals pursuing their own careers, accumulating material possessions, and going their own way. Her town never had to really *be* a community until that flood came along and demanded of them a true network of interdependent members, each of them important, indispensable to the whole.

"Does community have a value?" This question figures in the title of one of Wendell Berry's essays on the subject, and what he has to say confirms the importance of the values my wife, Rilla, and I hold, our beliefs and practices relative to the value of community, and how these sustain us. These values include sharing among friends and neighbors, mutual help, cooperation, and consolation—not for want of self-reliance, but because self-reliance is best served in the context of neighborly support and concern. Without the values that make for true community, it is difficult to come home or to make a home. Berry asserts that this sense of community needs to be rooted in an actual place, in the long-term relationship of people to that place. The members of that community must be aware of its history and must make a commitment to the place itself as something beloved, not unlike the commitment in marriage. Such a commitment enables them to ride out the imperfections and limitations of the place where they live.

My own experience of growing up on Valley View Road in St. Peter, Minnesota, confirms that the place-based community that Berry talks about has a value. My parents lived much of their adult life on Valley View Road with the same neighbors, most of them (including my father) college professors and their spouses, who were devoted to the college, Gustavus Adolphus, as a beloved place and gave their lives to it.

Many children lived in that neighborhood when I was a boy, and I had all the playmates I needed. The mothers always looked out for us, in small ways, helping to raise us. "It takes a village to raise a child." The familiar African saying certainly applied to my upbringing. My own mother and father had difficulty teaching me the value and dignity of the little daily household tasks, but not Bea Martinson. When I went over to the Martinsons' to play with their boys, Bea would put me and them to work washing the dishes before we could play. For one who hated chores, I loved washing the Martinson dishes because I was doing it in the company of good friends. I even began purposely going over to the Martinsons' right after supper and after we had loaded our dishwasher so that I could wash the dishes with them. My mother was astonished. I had learned, however, through a kind of neighborhood communal experience, to see the importance of doing even menial tasks. I don't think my mother or father failed so much as the neighborhood succeeded in teaching me.

Over several years three families, the Johnsons, the Martinsons, and mine, pooled their resources to purchase a lawn mower, which we kept in the Martinson garage. I would trudge over there in the heat and humidity of a July afternoon, pulling the lawn mower out of the garage, rolling it across the street, and mowing our quarter-acre, hating this chore but also feeling a certain pride in sharing communal property and doing the necessary work of adding a neatly cut lawn to the appearance of the neighborhood.

I gained lasting friendships as well. Several of my playmates became close friends and confidants as we grew into our teen and college years. To this day I retain some of these friendships: by some strange coincidence, Peter Martinson and I have both ended up in Bozeman, Montana. Even though the two of us have changed, we know each other so intimately that it seems as though we instantaneously pick up conversations we left years ago. Recently we talked about learning the value of community from growing up on Valley View Road, and we agreed that our lives had been enriched by the sense of community we experienced during our upbringing. For Peter and me the superficial differences acquired in our adult years seem to matter little.

Some of my most pleasant memories are of the sociability, the conversation, the laughter, and the good cheer of neighborhood get-togethers. Our entire neighborhood often went on picnics and had potlucks. Once we even went camping together, in Flandrau State Park along the Cottonwood River near New Ulm, Minnesota. A huge thunderstorm flooded the Martinsons' tent during the night, and the following morning Vic Gustafson, an outfitter, veteran of many canoe trips to the Boundary Waters, flipped pancakes for all of us to eat.

Evenings, my parents often hosted neighborhood get-togethers on our screened-in back porch. On warm, breezy summer nights I would fall asleep to the sounds of lively conversation, story telling, Chet Johnson's wry humor and deadpan voice, and uproarious laughter—with Betty Gustafson's ringing laugh rising above the rest and out into the night, mingling with the sound of crickets. The hilarity would increase as the evening progressed, sometimes keeping me awake. I know now that they were getting buzzed on coffee, for alcohol was never served.

Still, while growing up I was sometimes bored and restless with St. Peter, especially as a teenager, impatient with small-town ways and narrow-mindedness. But I loved our neighborhood on Valley View Road and would never have consented to my parents' moving away. Like any other place, this was not an ideal place, but it was a good place, and the source of many of my convictions about "sense of place."

Good, because our neighborhood and community shared sorrow as well as joy. On April 3, 1990, my mother died from breast cancer that had metastasized to her brain. When I returned home for the funeral, I learned something more about the value of the community where I grew up, the value of love and family in the context of community; for her life and death is also the story of a long-term relationship with a place and its people.

My mother spent her last days in bed in her own room, looking out the window facing east to where the sun rose over the Minnesota River Valley and St. Peter. My father had taken her out of the hospital so she could die at home, in the house where she had lived for thirty years, where she and my father had made a morning ritual of watching the sunrise, saying morning prayers, and then reading aloud to each other. The last book they were reading, but never finished, was Wes Jackson's *Altars of Unhewn Stone.*

On the flight home for the funeral I reflected on how the significance of my mother's life was defined by the long-term friendship and love she enjoyed in her marriage, extending outward to the long-term friendships and love she experienced as a result of being able to stay in St. Peter and be a part of that community for the last forty years of her life. Her life was meaningful in relation to its context.

Accordingly, my mother's funeral was a celebration as well as an occasion for grief. The uproarious laughter at her funeral was appropriate, almost as if we were reliving those summer evening coffee parties on the back porch. For it came out of the stories told about her by the pastor during the service and by friends during the luncheon following the service—testimony to a life and the history of a place. Her living person, her love of life, sense of humor, warmth of friendship, and dedication to the church were real presences at the funeral, preserved in those stories. And one hymn we sang, "For All the Saints," selected by my sister Louise, thundered in the vast echo chamber of the First Lutheran Church sanctuary, a hymn celebrating the great community of faith to which my mother devoted her life. Most significant of all, my mother faced death with the serene conviction that her life had been worthwhile. She feared dying, and in her last months withdrew; but I sensed she was as prepared to die as one could be, because she had lived well. Her life had been pleasing to her, and thus complete.

My father did not grieve alone. He did not need a support group or a therapist. He was surrounded by people who were his friends, who cared about him. Friends and neighbors kept dropping by with food, coming around for visits, or issuing invitations to dinner. They still do—after four years. And he still has them over for dinner parties, playing the host and chief cook as my mother did when she was alive, some of the food coming out of his own garden. In between comes grief, loneliness. Or the peaceful morning meditations that he continues without her. She is still present, a presence held in place, in memory. The friendship and love that defined their marriage were nurtured in the larger context of Valley View Road, Gustavus Adolphus College, and St. Peter. Now, the quality of my dad's life is sustained in her absence by community; for he stays active, in various ways serving the life of the college and the community that has been so intimate a part of his life for so long.

Rilla and I have admired the kind of stability and deeply rooted sense of neighborhood and community that my parents experienced in their town. We have hoped for that kind of life. But we live in a different time. My father virtually walked into his job at Gustavus Adolphus in 1950 and taught there for the next thirty-five years. Some of his contemporaries had a choice of five or more academic job offers. When I applied for academic jobs, I competed with three hundred to five hundred applicants per opening. This scarcity of tenure-track jobs has kept us on the move, from one temporary job to another—migrant workers, we've called ourselves in a spirit of grim humor. I roamed from one-year stints teaching literature and writing at Oklahoma State University and the University of South Dakota, then settling in for four years at Michigan State University before budget and program cuts and internal politics ended my job there. In the 1990s universities, like corporations, are not adding jobs, they are eliminating them—"downsizing." Most of my generation, and perhaps younger generations as well, cannot expect to live very long in any one place, and some of us can expect to change careers up to five times.

Many in my generation simply roll with it, but my memories of a settled community life cause me to resist these current trends angrily and to see them as a grave social injustice. Even so, during our wanderings Rilla and I have found that the transient experience of community has a value. In Stillwater, Oklahoma, Velina, a young woman two houses down, befriended Rilla and helped us when Rebekka was born; Bill and Elizabeth, fellow University of Iowa graduates who taught in the English Department, provided us more friendship, and their son, Edward, played with our daughter Rachel every weekend; we basked in the warm welcome that we felt at Salem Lutheran Church, where we sang in the choir and played on the church softball team. In Vermillion, South Dakota, we found a community that was cool to newcomers. But Rilla chatted over the fence with Marge, our next-door neighbor, some sixty years old and a devout Catholic. Marge still writes to us, missing us and our children.

In Michigan we found a rich community life. We found it because we went about living there as if that were the place we were going to call home for the rest of our lives, even though my job security there was shaky. We lived in a pleasant working-class neighborhood in Lansing. Rilla went for walks every evening with

Lisa, a younger neighbor woman, whose husband had been laid off from General Motors and took a job driving a delivery truck for the Coca-Cola Company. Many a summer evening was spent chatting with Bill and Nell, an elderly retired couple, on their front porch. Bill and Nell often lent us tools. Rilla would help them with yard work and we looked out for one another. We found satisfaction in much else: hiking in the woods, inviting friends for dinner, hosting free-spirited potlucks. Every summer Rilla and I canned tomatoes and applesauce with Ann, a colleague of mine at Michigan State University. Hot, miserable, sweaty work, but joyful and companionable, one of the happiest times all year. We volunteered for the food bank and the rotating shelter for homeless women and children. We shopped the local farmers' market or bought directly from local growers, chatting with them while leisurely selecting produce, a sociable and relaxing contrast to the crowds, the hurry, the cold impersonality of supermarkets.

Our experience in Michigan proved that much can be said for the *effort* to live well in a place. All these—friendships, marriage, sense of place—carried us through the uncertainty of my job situation at Michigan State. Friendship, especially. For two weeks, while Rilla was away in Seattle because her sister's baby had died at birth, two friends, Celeste and Aspen, took care of our children during the day so that I could tend to my teaching duties. When grief was near, they helped.

When it became clear that my job at the university would end, and with the academic job market only getting worse, I began to think about a career change—in particular, an alternative career that would bring me closer to working for community and sustainable agriculture. Rilla and I engaged in long, late-night discussions about where we wanted to live and what we wanted to do with the rest of our lives. Rilla argued for the priority of place and community over the ambitions of career. I found these talks energizing. We came up with the notion of making "place" our vocation and talked about moving to a place with a quality of life that would enable us to find sustaining work, form long-term friendships, put in a garden every year, grow old, and die happy.

Rilla and I continued our late-night conversations until finally it was settled: we would move to St. Peter. Why not? These were my roots, remembered for the most part fondly, with deep affection, with the memory of my mother foremost in my imagination. My father urged us to move in with him until we could get situated and establish ourselves.

Returning to my old home made sense as far as we could see. But when we did return, we could not find employment. Unsettled, jobless, we were outsiders, strangers in a familiar land. Many people kept their distance. One young woman, Nancy, took an interest in Rilla and the fiber arts business she had begun in Michigan. She hired Rilla to teach a community education course in fiber arts for children, which was a success. But for the most part we felt isolated.

An April return trip to Michigan tellingly revealed just how much we had lost, for there we felt the renewed warmth, the spontaneous joy of those lovely friendships that had been sustained, even from afar, across the great gap of our loneliness and sense of loss. Our friends welcomed us back with lively conversation, potlucks—get-togethers that felt like the happiest of family reunions.

In the end, St. Peter could not hold us. Perhaps the people there knew more than we did, knew that we would leave, that we could not stay, even though we tried. We had explored the idea of community-sponsored agriculture, of starting our own market garden based on the community-sponsored agriculture model, the first one in southern Minnesota; but that required capital to begin, capital we did not have. We never found the sustaining work we had hoped would be there when we first came. Indeed, we were shocked when we first arrived in St. Peter to discover that many couples had to hold two, three, even four jobs, to make ends meet. During our last three months there, Rilla held a temporary, low-paying job with the St. Peter Greenhouse, the only work either of us could find, and work Rilla happened to love. I floated résumés. One floated to Montana State University. When the offer came, I accepted immediately. I was back to teaching literature and writing.

So we moved to Bozeman, Montana. Surrounded by spectacular mountain ranges, vast wilderness areas, and blue-ribbon trout streams, Bozeman is considered one of America's most desirable places to live. And people are following their desires—in droves. It is not just the mountain vistas, though. People are also moving to Bozeman seeking the ideal community life that has eluded them in places like Los Angeles, in some cases risking their careers and entire savings. Some come without jobs or prospects, with only their life savings, taking a long-shot gamble that they can establish themselves. Most often they fail, for opportunities are limited and the local economy cannot absorb such a huge influx. Consequently, Bozeman has a staggering rate of small-business failures, many of which are experienced by relative newcomers who came dreaming of "the good life." Only independently wealthy people, "modem cowboys" who work out of their homes and a lucky few others, are able to stay. Even some of these end up leaving. Eighty percent of the people who lived in Bozeman ten years ago are now gone.

This transience is divisive, in many respects undermining true community. The long-time residents bitterly resent the newcomers, partly because the influx has driven the price of homes beyond what many of the locals can afford and partly because the changes are too rapid, disrupting the stability, familiarity, and continuity of life in the Bozeman they once knew.

Nonetheless, the people of Bozeman, newcomers and old-timers alike, are dedicated to making the town livable and attractive, to supporting fine public schools and the arts. In short, they are community spirited. Because of the transience, this community spiritedness does not have much chance to deepen, over the long term, into the particular love of place, strong friendships, or neighborly affections that characterized my boyhood experience on Valley View Road. People have surprisingly few friends; many do not even know their neighbors. Yet what the newcomers to Bozeman desire and value most is good friends, good neighbors, and a good place to raise their children. Community does have a value and people are willing to pay a high price to find it, even to the point of risking their savings and careers, wrong-headed as that may be.

The irony does not escape me: we moved to St. Peter for the same reasons so many people migrate to Bozeman, in search of the ideal community. Our decision was based on a resistance to career motives and economic expediency in favor of cultural and spiritual considerations, in favor of a philosophy of life that gave priority to a sense of place and community. But an economy such as the one we found in St. Peter, which requires couples to work two or three jobs, makes the real work of community difficult, especially when couples barely have time for each other or for children, let alone for friends. St. Peter, where I had gone to school on the value of community while growing up, like many contemporary American small towns, today has fewer independent businesses, more low-wage jobs, less local economic self-sufficiency, and it serves as a bedroom community for some with higher-paying jobs in larger towns and cities.

Because my self-conscious decision to return did not result in community or permanence, I began to think that it might be as false to assume automatically that a hometown is a place to return to as it is to assume that a hometown is a place to leave, even though Wendell Berry points out that leaving rather than returning home is a prevailing—and unhealthy—tendency in American life. I wondered if the times demanded that we bring our sense of community with us wherever we go instead of expecting to settle and find it in any one place in particular. For Rilla and I have found that transience need not be wholly destructive of community, that community comes through a kind of grace that we readily accept as a gift and give in return, rather than as something we can have on demand. It comes out of the graciousness of others, out of bighearted, open generosity, and perhaps a free-spiritedness and love that come with spontaneous outbursts of laughter and good, clean fun, or tipping a few beers. It even comes when you least expect it. Whether or not any of us are rooted in a place, we live in a condition of impermanence (for that is the actual human and ecological condition, if the truth be known); yet community is still possible, even in transience, if we accept it as graciously as it is given. During our long odyssey Rilla and I have found friends, who became like family, who exemplified the practice of community or neighborhood in the most unexpected hours, in the midst of the our most wrenching impermanence. We have not forgotten that we spent four years in Michigan surrounded by caring neighbors, went to the local farmers' markets, went berry picking and apple picking, and drank Michigan wine in good cheer with the best friends we ever had.

Thus I reply to Wendell Berry—but not to prove him wrong. That is not the point. For he *is* right, because he asks the right questions, rather than necessarily having all the right answers; because he gives us something of substance and value to chew on; and because he has shown in his own life what can be done. Berry is also right in that, even though we have had a rich community life in transience, I value much more the bedrock stability of my upbringing and what I learned from it about living well in right relationship to others and to particular places. Out of *that* experience I received the neighborly values that have enabled me to find a semblance of community while leading a transient life.

Living in place over the long term, as my father has, with the same friends and neighbors, strengthens social ties and affections and through the gradual building of trust promotes tolerance, generosity, and a spirit of cooperation. Significant human relationships begin tentatively, warily even, and need time to grow and mature. Transience only stunts the growth of such relationships, sometimes preventing them from even taking root.

But sustainable local economies will be needed if we want truly settled communities. Our current way of life, oriented toward the global economy, is tending the other way, resulting in more bedroom communities, more commuter marriages, and ever-greater social mobility, including the ever-stronger expectation that even more people will change careers several times in their lives. The rapid outflow of capital to distant corporations and centers of commerce and finance in the current economy weakens local economies, for money flows out of rather than circulates within the local economy. People go where the jobs are, which are not long in any one place. The consequent social mobility loosens community and, along with that, social ties and affections.

Does this mean that transient community is the most we can hope for as the future of American society? Not necessarily. I have found that the desire for settled community is hidden in secret places (such as in a flooded Mississippi River town in Missouri), out of reach of the Internet and the global economy, and is like a tiny, dormant seed packed with a powerful yearning that may well outlast the depredations of our current age. Given a chance, this seed may yet bloom, like the proverbial chestnut seedling in Wendell Berry's essay "Discipline and Hope," growing into something strong and durable, its knotted roots ensuring a local habitation held in place for a long time. Yes, community has a value that may be one of the greatest of all human values, our hope and our help for years to come.

part two   COMMUNITY FOUNDATIONS

IF KNOWLEDGE AND THE THING KNOWN ARE ONE

SO THAT TO KNOW A MAN IS TO BE

THAT MAN, TO KNOW A PLACE IS TO BE

THAT PLACE, AND IT SEEMS TO COME TO THAT;

AND IF TO KNOW ONE MAN IS TO KNOW ALL

AND IF ONE'S SENSE OF A SINGLE SPOT

IS WHAT ONE KNOWS OF THE UNIVERSE,

THEN KNOWLEDGE IS THE ONLY LIFE,

THE ONLY SUN OF THE ONLY DAY,

THE ONLY ACCESS TO TRUE EASE,

THE DEEP COMFORT OF THE WORLD AND FATE.

—Wallace Stevens, "The Sail of Ulysses," 1957

matfield green

WES JACKSON

I am writing in what is left of Matfield Green, a Kansas town of some fifty people situated in a country of a few more than three thousand in an area with thirty-three inches of annual precipitation. It is typical of countless towns throughout the Midwest and Great Plains. People have left, people are leaving, buildings are falling down, buildings are burning down. Fourteen of the houses here that do still have people have only one person, usually a widow or widower. I purchased seven rundown houses in town for less than four thousand dollars. Four friends and I purchased, for five thousand dollars, the beautiful brick elementary school that was built in 1938. It has ten thousand square feet, including a stage and gymnasium. The Land Institute has purchased the high school gymnasium (four thousand dollars) and twelve acres south of town (for six thousand). A friend and I have purchased thirty-eight acres north of town from the Santa Fe Railroad for three hundred thirty dollars an acre. On this property are a bunkhouse, some large corrals to handle cattle, and about twenty-five acres of never-plowed tallgrass prairie.

South of town is an abandoned natural gas booster station with its numerous buildings and facilities. Situated on eighty acres, it was part of the first long-distance pipelines that delivered natural gas from the large Hugoton field near Amarillo to Kansas City. A neighbor in his late seventies told me that in about 1929 his father had helped dig the basement, using a team of horses and a scoop (contemporary sunlight used to leverage extraction of anciently stored energy). Owned by a major pipeline company, the booster station stands as a silent monument to the extractive economy, foreshadowing what is to come. A small area has been contaminated with PCBs. Think of the possible practicality and symbolism if this facility, formerly devoted to transporting the high energy demanded by an extractive economy while at the same time dumping a major environmental pollutant, could be taken over by a community and converted to a facility that would sponsor such renewable technologies as photovoltaic panels or wind machines.

Imagine this human community as an ecosystem, as a locus or primary object of study. We know that public policy, allegedly implemented in the public interest, is partly responsible for the demise of this community. The question then becomes, How can this human community, like a natural ecosystem community, be protected from that abstraction called the public? How can both kinds of communities be built back and also protected?

The effort begins, I think, with the sort of inventory and accounting that ecologists have done for natural ecosystems, a kind of accounting seldom if ever performed for human-dominated ecosystems. How do we start thinking about what is involved in setting up the books for ecological community accounting that will feature humans? I emphasize accounting because our goal is renewability, sustainability.

About 85 percent of the county in which this small town is situated is never-plowed native prairie. Over the millennia it has featured recycling and has run on sunlight just as a forest or a marsh does. Though the prairie is fenced and is now called pasture and grass, aside from the wilderness areas of our country it is about as close to an original relationship as we will find in any human-managed system. Even though the people left in town seem to have a profound affection for the place and for one another, they are as susceptible to the world as anyone else—to shopping mall living, to secular materialism in general.

Nevertheless, I have imagined this as a place that could grow bison for meat, as a place where photovoltaic panels could be assembled at the old booster station, where the school could become a gathering place that would be a partial answer to the mall, a place that might attract a few retired people, including professor types, who could bring their pensions, their libraries, and their social security checks to help support themselves and take on the task of setting up the books for ecological community accounting. Essentially all academic disciplines would be an asset in such an effort, but only if confronted with a broad spectrum of ecological necessities in the face of small-town reality. Much of what must be done will be in conflict with human desires, if not human needs.

Let us allow our imaginations to wander. What if bison (or even cattle) could be slaughtered in the little towns on a small scale and become the answer to the massive industrialized Iowa Beef Packers plant at Emporia, a plant to which some area residents drive fifty miles and more in order to earn modest wages and risk carpal tunnel syndrome. What if the manufacture of photovoltaic panels could happen before the eyes of the children of the workers? What if the processing of livestock could take place with those children present? What if those children were allowed to exercise their strong urge to help—to work? What, finally, if shopping malls and Little League were to become less interesting than playing "make-believe" with all ages?

One of our principal tasks as educators is to expand the imagination about our possibilities. When I walk through the abandoned school with its leaky gym roof and see the solid structure of a beautiful 1938 building, with stage curtains rotting away and paint peeling off the walls, where one blackboard after another has been carried away as though the building were a slate mine, I am forced to think that the demise of this school has resulted in part from a failure of imagination, but more from the tyranny of disregard by something we call the economy.

I am in that town at this moment, typing in a house that in its history of some seventy-five years has been abandoned more times than anyone can recall. First it was home to a family in a now-abandoned oil field a few miles southeast of here. Then it was hauled intact on a wagon into town in the 1930s, set on a native stone foundation which, when I bought it recently, was crumbling and falling away. Three ceilings supported as much as three inches of dirt, much of it from back in the Dust Bowl era. The expanding side walls had traveled so far off the floor joist in the middle that the ceiling was suspended. They had to be pulled back onto the floor joist and held permanently with large screws and plates. Three major holes in the roof had allowed serious water damage to flooring and studs. An opossum had died under the bathtub long enough ago that only its bones were displayed, lying at rest in an arc over the equivalent of half a bale of hay. Two of my seven houses, one empty for nearly twenty years and the other for fifteen, had been walked away from with their refrigerators full. Who knows when the electric meters were pulled—probably a month or two after the houses were vacated and the bill hadn't been paid. To view the contents—eggs and ham, Miracle Whip and pickles, mustard and catsup, milk, cheese, and whatnot—was more like viewing an archaeological find than a repulsive mess.

Where I sit today at my typewriter in that oil field house that relatives and friends have helped remodel, I can see an abandoned lumberyard across the street next to the abandoned hardware store. Out another window, but from the same chair, is the back of the old creamery that now stores junk (on its way to becoming antiques?). With Clara Jo's retirement, the half-time post office across the street is threatened with closure. From a different window, but the same seat, I can see the bank, which closed in 1929 and paid off ten cents on the dollar. (My nephew recently bought it for five hundred dollars.) I can see the bank now only because I can look across the vacant lot where the cafe stood before the natural gas booster station shut down. If my front door were open, given the angle at which I sit, I would be looking right at the Hitchin' Post, the only business left—a bar that accommodates local residents and the cowhands who pull up with their pickups and horse trailers and some of the finest saddle mounts anywhere. These horses will quiver and stomp while waiting patiently as their riders stop for lunch or after work to indulge in beer, nuts, and microwave sandwiches and to shoot pool. (The Hitchin' Post lacks running water, so no dishes can be washed. The outhouse is out back.) Around the corner is an abandoned service station. There were once four! Across the street is the former barbershop.

I know that this town and the surrounding farms and ranches did not sponsor perfect people. I keep finding whiskey bottles in old outhouses and garages, stashed between inner and outer walls here and there, the local version of a drug culture. I hear the familiar stories of infidelities fifty years back—the overalls on the clothesline hung upside down, the flowerpot one day on the left side of the step, the next day on the right—signals to lovers even at the height of the Great Depression, when austerity should have tightened the family unit and maybe did. There were the shootings, the failures of justice, the story of the father of a young married woman who shot and killed his son-in-law for hitting his daughter and how charges were never filed. Third-generation bitterness is common. The human drama goes on. This place still doesn't have a lifestyle, never had a lifestyle, but rather livelihoods with ordinary human foibles. Nevertheless, the graveyard contains the remains of both the cuckolder and the cuckoldee, the shooter and the shot, the drunk and the sober.

This story can be repeated thousands of times across our land, and no telling will deviate even 10 percent. I am not sure what should be done here by way of community development. I do believe, however, that community development can begin with putting roofs on buildings that are leaking, and scabbing in two-by-fours at the bottom of studs that have rotted out around their anchoring nails. I doubt, on the other hand, that a sustainable society can start with a program sent down from Washington or from a Rural Sociology Department in some land-grant university, or for that matter as a celebration of Columbus Day.

Locals and most rural sociologists alike believe the answer lies in jobs, *any* jobs so long as they don't pollute too much. Though I am in sympathy with every urgent impulse toward human welfare, rural America—America!—does *not* need jobs that depend on the extractive economy. We need a way to arrest consumerism. We need a different form of accounting so that both sufficiency and efficiency have *standing* in our minds.

The poets and scientists who counseled that we consult nature would have understood, I think, that we might begin by looking at that old prairie, by re-membering who we are as mammals, as primates, as humanoids, as animals strug-gling to become human by controlling the destructive and unlovely side of our animal nature even as we set out to change parts of our still-unlovely human mind. The mindscape of the future must have some memory of the ecological arrange-ments that shaped us and of the social structures that served us well. So many sur-prises await us, even in the next quarter-century. My worry is that our context then will be so remote from the ways we survived through the ages that our or-ganizing paradigm will become chaos theory rather than ecology.

At work on my houses in Matfield Green, I've had great fun tearing off the porches and cleaning up the yards. But it has been sad as well, going through the abandoned belongings of families who lived out their lives in this beautiful, well-watered, fertile setting. In an upstairs bedroom I came across a dusty but beauti-ful blue padded box labeled "Old Programs—New Century Club." Most of the programs from 1923 to 1964 were there. Each listed the officers, the club flower (sweet pea), the club colors (pink and white), and the club motto ("just be glad"). The programs for each year were gathered under one cover and nearly always ded-icated to some local woman who was special in one way or another.

Each month the women were to comment on such subjects as canning, jokes, memory gems, a magazine article, guest poems, flower culture, misused words, birds, and so on. The May 1936 program was a debate: "Resolved that movies are detrimental to the young generation." The August 1936 program was dedicated to coping with the heat. Roll call was "Hot Weather Drinks"; next came "Sug-gestions for Hot Weather Lunches"; a Mrs. Rogler offered "Ways of Keeping Cool."

The June roll call in 1929 was "The Disease I Fear Most." That was eleven years after the great flu epidemic. Children were still dying in those days of diphtheria, whooping cough, scarlet fever, pneumonia. On August 20, the roll call question was "What do you consider the most essential to good citizenship?" In September that year it was "Birds of Our Country." The program was on the mourning dove.

What became of it all?

From 1923 to 1930, the program covers were beautiful, done at a print shop. From 1930 until 1937, the effects of the Depression were apparent; programs were either typed or mimeographed and had no cover. The programs for two years are missing. In 1940, the covers reappeared, this time typed on construction paper. The print-shop printing never came back.

The last program in the box dates from 1964. I don't know the last year Mrs. Florence Johnson attended the club. I do know that Mrs. Johnson and her husband, Turk, celebrated their fiftieth wedding anniversary, for in the same box are some beautiful white fiftieth anniversary napkins, with golden bells and the names "Florence" and "Turk" between the years "1920" and "1970." A neighbor told me that Mrs. Johnson died in 1981. The high school had closed in 1967. The lumberyard and hardware store closed about the same time, but no one knows for sure when. The last gas station went after that.

Back to those programs. The motto never changed. The sweet pea kept its standing. So did the pink and white club colors. The club collect that follows persisted month after month, year after year:

A Collect for Club Women

Keep us, O God, from pettiness; Let us be large in thought, in word, in deed.

Let us be done with fault-finding and leave off self-seeking.

May we put away all pretense and meet each other face to face, without self-pity and without prejudice.

May we never be hasty in judgment and always generous.

Let us take time for all things; make us grow calm, serene, gentle.

Teach us to put in to action our better impulses; straightforward and unafraid.

Grant that we may realize it is the little things that create differences; that in the big things of life we are as one.

And may we strive to touch and to know the great common woman's heart of us all, and oh, Lord God, let us not forget to be kind.

—Mary Stewart

By modern standards these people were poor. There was a kind of naivete among these relatively unschooled women. Some of their poetry was not good. Some of their ideas about the way the world works seem silly. Some of their club programs don't sound very interesting. Some sound tedious. But their monthly agendas were filled with decency, with efforts to learn about everything from birds to our government, and with coping with their problems, the weather, diseases. Here is the irony: they were living up to a far broader spectrum of their potential than most of us do today!

I am not suggesting that we go back to 1923 or even to 1964. But I will say that those people in that particular generation, in places like Matfield Green, were farther along in the necessary journey to becoming native to their places, even as they were losing ground, than we are.

Why was their way of life so vulnerable to the industrial economy? What can we do to protect such attempts to be good and decent, to live out modest lives responsibly? I don't know. This is the discussion we need to have, for it is particularly problematic. Even most intellectuals who have come out of places such as Matfield Green have not felt that their early lives prepared them adequately for the "official" culture.

Let me quote from two writers. The first is Paul Gruchow, who grew up on a farm in southern Minnesota:

> I was born at mid-century. My parents, who were poor and rural, had never amounted to anything, and never would, and never expected to. They were rather glad for the inconsequence of their lives. They got up with the sun and retired with it. Their routines were dictated by the seasons. In summer they tended; in fall they harvested; in winter they repaired; in spring they planted. It had always been so; so it would always be.
>
> The farmstead we occupied was on a hilltop overlooking a marshy river bottom that stretched from horizon to horizon. It was half a mile from any road and an eternity from any connection with the rest of the culture. There were no books there; there was no music; there was no television; for a long time, no telephone. Only on the rarest of occasions—a time or two a year— was there a social visitor other than the pastor. There was no conversation in that house. (Gruchow 1991, 20)

Similarly, Wallace Stegner, the great historian and novelist, confesses to his feeling of inadequacy in coming from a small prairie town in the Cypress Hills of Saskatchewan. In *Wolf Willow* he writes:

> Once, in a self-pitying frame of mind, I was comparing my background with that of an English novelist friend. Where he had been brought up in London, taken from the age of four onward to the Tate and the National Gallery, sent traveling on the Continent in every school holiday, taught French and German and Italian, given access to bookstores, libraries, and British Museums, made familiar from infancy on with the conversation of the eloquent and the great, I had grown up in this dung-heeled sagebrush town on the disappearing edge of nowhere, utterly without painting, without sculpture, without architecture, almost without music or theater, without conversation or languages or travel or stimulating instruction, without libraries or museums or

bookstores, almost without books. I was charged with getting in a single life-time, from scratch, what some people inherit as naturally as they breath air.

How, I asked this Englishman, could anyone from so deprived a back-ground ever catch up? How was one expected to compete, as a cultivated man, with people like himself? He looked at me and said dryly, "Perhaps you got something else in place of all that."

He meant, I suppose, that there are certain advantages to growing up a sensuous little savage, and to tell the truth I am not sure I would trade my childhood of freedom and the outdoors and the senses for a childhood of be-ing led by the hand past all the Turners in the National Gallery. And also, he may have meant that anyone starting from deprivation is spared getting bored. You may not get a good start, but you may get up a considerable head of steam.

Countless writers and artists have been vulnerable to the so-called official cul-ture, as vulnerable as the people of Matfield Green. Stegner goes on to say:

> I am reminded of Willa Cather, that bright girl from Nebraska, memorizing long passages from the *Aeneid* and spurning the dust of Red Cloud and Lin-coln with her culture-bound feet. She tried, and her education encouraged her, to be a good European. Nevertheless she was a first-rate novelist only when she dealt with what she knew from Red Cloud and the things she had "in place of all that." Nebraska was what she was born to write; the rest of it was got up. Eventually, when education had won and nurture had conquered nature and she had recognized Red Cloud as a vulgar little hold, she embraced the foreign tradition totally and ended by being neither quite a good Amer-ican nor quite a true European nor quite a whole artist. (Stegner 1962, 24–25)

It seems that we still blunt our sensitivities about our local places by the likes of learning long passages from the *Aeneid* while wanting to shake from us the dust of Red Cloud or Matfield Green. The extractive economy cares for neither Vir-gil nor Mary Stewart. It lures just about all of us to its shopping centers on the edges of major cities. And yet, for us, the *Aenid* is as essential to becoming native to the Matfield Greens as the spear was to the paleolithic Asians who walked here across the Bering land bridge of the Pleistocene.

Our task is to build cultural fortresses to protect our emerging nativeness. They must be strong enough to hold at bay the powers of consumerism, the powers of greed and envy and pride. One of the most effective ways for this to come about would be for our universities to assume the awesome responsibility for both vali-dating and educating those who want to be homecomers—not that they neces-sarily want to go home, but rather to go someplace and dig in and begin the long search and experiment to become native.

It will be a struggle, but a worthy one. The homecomer will not learn Virgil to adorn his or her talk to show off, but will study Virgil for insight, for utility, as well as for pleasure.

We can then hope for a resurrection like that of Mrs. Florence Johnson and her women friends, who took their collect seriously. Unless we can validate and promote the sort of cultural information in the making that the New Century Club featured, we are doomed. An entire club program devoted to coping with the heat of August is becoming native to a place. That club was more than a support group; it was cultural information in the making, keyed to place. The alternative, one might suggest, is mere air-conditioning—not only yielding greenhouse gases but contributing to global warming and the ozone hole as well, and, if driven by nuclear power, to future Chernobyls.

Becoming native to this place means that the creatures we bring with us—our domesticated creatures—must become native too. Long ago they were removed from the original relationships they had with their ecosystems and pressed into our service. Our interdependency has become so complete that, if proprietorship is the subject, we must acknowledge that in some respects they own us. We humans honor knowledge of where we came from, counting that as baseline information, essential to our journey toward nativeness. Similarly, we must acknowledge that our domesticated creatures are descendants of wild things that were shaped in an ecological context *not* of our making when we found them. The fence we built to keep their relatively tame and curious wild ancestors out of our Early Neolithic gardens eventually became the barbed wire that would contain them.

At the moment of first containment, those fences must have enlarged our idea of property and property lines. When we brought that notion of property lines with us to this distant and magnificent continent, it was a short step to the invisible grid that in turn created the tens of thousands of hard and alien lines that dominate our thoughts today. Those lines will probably be with us forever. But we can soften them. We'll have to, for the hardness of those lines is proportional to our sense of the extent to which we own what we use. Our becoming native will depend on our emerging consciousness of how we are to use the gifts of the creation. We must think in terms of different relationships. Perhaps we *will* come to think of the chicken as fundamentally a jungle fowl. The hog will once again be regarded as a descendant of a roaming and rooting forest animal. Bovines will be seen as savanna grazers.

An extractive economic system to a large degree is a derivative of our perceptions and values. But it also controls our behavior. We have to loosen its hard grip on us, finger by finger. I am hopeful that a new economic system can emerge from the homecomer's effort—as a derivative of right livelihood rather than of purposeful design. It will result from our becoming better ecological accountants at the community level. If we must as a future necessity recycle essentially all materials and run on sunlight, then our future will depend on accounting as the most important and interesting discipline. Because accountants are students of boundaries, we are talking about educating a generation of students who will know how to set up the books for their ecological community accounting, to use three-dimensional spreadsheets.

Still, classroom work alone won't do. These students will need a lifetime of field experience besides, and the sacrifices they must make, by our modern standards, will be huge. They won't be regarded as heroic, at least not in the short run. Nevertheless, that will be their real work. Despite the daily decency of the women in the Matfield Greens, decency could not stand up against the economic imperialism that swiftly and ruthlessly plowed them and their communities under.

The agenda of our homecoming majors is already beyond comprehensive vision. They will have to be prepared to think about such problems as balances between efficiency and sufficiency. This will require informed judgment across our entire ecological mosaic. These graduates in homecoming will be unable to hide in bureaucratic niches within the major program initiatives of public policy that big government likes to sponsor. Those grand solutions are inherently antinative because they are unable to vary across the mosaic of our ecosystems, from the cold deserts of eastern Washington to the deciduous forests of the East, with the Nebraska prairie in between. The need is for each community to be coherent. Knowing this, we must offer our homecomers the most rigorous curriculum and the best possible faculty, the most demanding faculty of all time.

dwelling: making peace with space and place

DEBORAH TALL

TO say we dwell somewhere implies permanence, or at least continuity. But at root "dwell" means to pause, to linger or delay. We dwell on a subject, but eventually give it up. So what does it mean to dwell somewhere? How long do we have to stay? J. B. Jackson takes on the question, but speaks of habits rather than years, of a place becoming customary. Habits are acquired, they form over time. With disuse they are forgotten. To dwell in a place rather than simply exist in it seems to hinge on allowing such adaptive habits to form, an act of accommodation (Jackson 1984, 91).

It used to be easier. A home and its land were once widely understood as belonging to a family forever. Even today, most people in the world are born and die within a radius of a few miles. But 20 to 30 percent of Americans move each year, and the average American moves fourteen times over a lifetime. Permanent residence is at odds with our notion of property—property as commodity, as route to profit, rather than something attained to keep. The American dream requires that you own your home, but Americans rarely stay in a house longer than five years. To change not just your home or town, but the region of the country you live in, is understood as a way to change your life, and we aim to do that often. Numerous milestones—college, marriage, birth of children, a new job, divorce, retirement—almost require a change of location (Zelinsky 1973, 56). In fact, to stay in one place for life is often interpreted as being unambitious, unadventurous—a negation of American values. Moving up in the world means moving on.

The easy replacement of home ignores its emotional charge for us, ignores how important familiarity is in the constitution of home. Frequent dislocation, or the sudden destruction of a known environment, can be fundamentally deranging. It means the loss of personal landmarks—which embody the past—and the disintegration of a communal pattern of identity. People relocated from condemned slums, for instance, often suffer terribly no matter how much more "attractive" the new housing provided. Home is where we know—and are known—through accumulated experience.

When an entire place or landscape is destroyed, the sense of betrayal and disorientation is acute. Harvey Cox's shattering story of a Holocaust survivor from the Czech village of Lidice illustrates such loss in the extreme:

> The Germans had arbitrarily picked this hamlet to be the example of what would happen to other villages. . . . They came into the town, shot all the men over twelve, then shipped the wives to one concentration camp and the children to another. They burned the village completely, destroyed all the trees and foliage and plowed up the ground. Significantly they demanded that on

all maps of Czechoslovakia the town of Lidice must be erased. The woman survivor confessed to me that despite the loss of her husband and the extended separation from her children, the most shocking blow of all was to return to the crest of the hill overlooking Lidice at the end of the war—and to find nothing there, not even ruins. (Cox 1987, 422–423)

The poetry of John Clare evokes a similar sense of violation, in his case as a result of the Enclosure Act, which in the late eighteenth and early nineteenth centuries vigorously transformed the common open-field system of rural England into private holdings in the name of efficiency. Instead of the long strips and winding trails of the old communal arrangement, small square fields and straight connecting roads were rapidly imposed on the land, virtually erasing its prior boundaries and landmarks. Even streams were diverted to fit the plan. The landscape was reconfigured on a blank map; what people had lived in for generations became unrecognizable.

Inevitably, such a rapid transformation of landscape had profound personal and social consequences. Previously, a parish had been circular in conception, its village at the center of a ring of three or four large shared fields around which crops and cattle were rotated. That was *Landschaft,* from which the word "landscape" derives, and it meant more than just a way to organize space. It stood for an ideal of habitation, of people's obligations to one another and the land. A community had to cooperate and follow traditional customs in order to survive. In the common-field system, for example, harvesting of crops had to occur at the same time so that everyone's cattle could then safely be let in to graze the stubble. The entire field, of course, had to be sown with the same crop, at the same time; there was no place for personal idiosyncrasy or procrastination in such a world (Stilgoe 1982, 12–13). Observes John Barrell, "This obligatory submission to the ancient and customary was no doubt part of what made open-field parishes—thus turned in upon themselves—so mysterious to the improver, and so closed to the traveller; and the effect of enclosure was of course to destroy the sense of place which the old topography expressed, as it destroyed the topography itself" (Barrell 1972, 95–96). After enclosure, the communal sense of place and identity was divided into numerous fenced and hedged private loyalties; a parish became little more than an intersection of roads on the way to the next parish.

John Clare and others like him who had rarely been outside their own parishes were caught in a moment of violent physical and social transformation. Removed from Helpston, where his family had farmed for generations, Clare suffered catastrophically from the loss of familiars and the location of his memories; he left an eloquent record of his pain.

Ive left mine own old home of homes
Green fields and every pleasant place
The summer like a stranger comes
I pause and hardly know her face

The disorientation of removal for Clare was such that even the dependable sun "seems to lose its way / Nor knows the quarter it is in." Outside Helpston "the very wild flowers seemed to forget me"—as if it had been the known landscape that confirmed his existence.

Unable to write about his love of nature in general terms, Clare lost, with his displacement, the crucial particulars that gave his voice a body. Over the next few years, his connection to the external world increasingly slipped. He spent the last twenty-seven years of his life in an asylum writing such lines as "I am—yet what I am, none cares or knows."

When Clare's publisher visited Helpston, he was perplexed by Clare's devotion to it, his mourning of its alteration; it looked so boring a place to a Londoner. It comes as a shock, too, to discover that the strange land to which Clare was exiled was but three miles from home (Barrell 1972; Lucas 1988, 83–97).

All over Europe, from the Renaissance on, the landscape was increasingly divided as in England. A side effect was the prizing of "shapeliness" in the land, regarding the landscape as a work of art. Landschaft had become *landschap* in the hands of Dutch and Italian painters. Landscape painting reflected the growing visual preference for a landscape composed of balanced parts, while at the same time it helped to disseminate that as an ideal. Some claim people only learned to "see" landscapes by learning to appreciate landscape painting. At its most extreme, says Samuel Monk, "Nature was scarcely seen at all, for the lover of the picturesque was bent upon discovering not the world as it is, but the world as it might have been had the Creator been an Italian artist of the seventeenth century" (Monk 1965, 195). Our view is still controlled to some extent by that aesthetic norm— highway planners provide as with scenic overlooks that command us to admire the land from a carefully contrived viewpoint.

Though enclosure was largely economic and agricultural in motive, it had aesthetic implications, and it made social distinctions more visible too—between rich and poor, between places for work and places for leisure. It was in this landscape that the great English gardens were created—by, as Raymond Williams puts it, "a self-conscious observer [who] was very specifically the self-conscious owner" of a pleasing stretch of land (Williams 1973, 124). Private property now provided both topographic and social place; one's place was no longer communally defined.

The notion of place in which one owns and cares for a plot of land still exerts enormous influence on contemporary Americans. The extent and condition of our property, and our choice of style in dwelling, create a powerful emblem of our identity and status.

At the same time, though, we are awash in a landscape of mobility that eschews connections to particular plots, has no need or desire for great distinction between places, and is essentially utilitarian about the land, often lacking environmental conscience. Place has come to mean proximity to highways, shopping, and year-round recreation, rather than natural situation or indigenous character. In some ways, that has been liberating. In the hierarchy of landowners, admission to place is hard won and restricted; in the landscape of mobility, new communities—be they townhouse tracts or trailer parks—can crop up on the spot and rapidly assimilate new members (Jackson 1984, 152–156). Yet we remain caught between nostalgia for place in its traditional sense and cool detachment, between a sense of responsibility for the land and the freedom of indifference. We've been told we live in a global village, which sounds a little like a Landschaft; but in truth, the technologically shrunken world has left us without much of a foothold.

Numerous modern writers have applauded the condition of "perpetual exile" as ethically healthy, a necessary severance from the sentimentalities of nationalism, for example (Quinby 1991, 147–148). Others, though, prominently Simone Weil, have argued strongly for attachment: "To be rooted is perhaps the most important and least recognized need of the human soul. . . . A human being has roots by virtue of his real, active, and natural participation in the life of a community, which preserves in living shape certain particular treasures of the past and certain particular expectations for the future" (Weil 1952, 43).

Given how often I have moved, my community is widely scattered. I have close friends all over the world; none of them know each other. We have only our own brief intensities of common experience to bind us, our telephone calls and letters. Friendship is tethered to loss, dependent on mental reconstruction instead of daily enactment. Sometimes I feel stranded at the center of a fragmented orb, my life divided into a series of experiences and places that can never be brought together—except in the solitude of memory. My family too is deposited all over the continent. Crucial junctures in our lives take place in hospital hallways or over bad coffee in airports.

In many ways, though, our upbringings prepare us for this essential solitude. The privacy of the typical American home molds us in an image of separateness, turns us of necessity inward. Nowhere else in the world has isolation been such a common pattern of settlement as in America, especially historically in rural America. As settlers moved out onto the rectangular grids the country was carved into, their farmhouses were almost invariably set toward the middle of the plot, very rarely clustered at the corners near adjoining blocks of land so as to provide proximity to other families. In Quebec, by contrast, farm plots were made long and narrow so that houses could be set side by side along a road. Congress, debating the Land Ordinance Act, briefly worried about the lack of any central focus in the grids. Congressmen from New England believed the lack of a central meeting-house would lead the settlers into sin. But no gathering of towns or villages was conceived of in the grand design; each family went it alone. The itinerant merchant materialized, and the mobile library; social life atrophied. These settlers were people who had come primarily from urban centers in Europe. Their survival in such extreme solitude became an anticommunal American ideal (Stilgoe 1982, 104; Zelinsky 1973, 47–49).

Individualism and mobility are at the core of American identity. I am admittedly the observer and writer I am in part because of the freedom I have had to wander. Mobility is, for many of us, essential to personal and economic development. "Mobility is always the weapon of the underdog," says Cox (1966, 45). Yi-Fu Tuan too reminds us that rootlessness goes hand in hand with American ideals we tend to admire—social mobility and optimism about the future: "To be tied to place is also to be bound to one's station in life, with little hope of betterment. Space symbolizes hope; place, achievement and stability" (Tuan 1974, 8). A fixed place can obviously be seen as a trap, home to drudgery and hopelessness. "Roots are ruts," complains a rising young executive (Packard 1972, 1). "To be rooted is the property of vegetables," scoffs the geographer David Sopher (1979, 137). To Sopher's mind, the prevailing "domicentric" bias in our thinking has turned "rootless" into the stigmatizing image of the shifty vagabond and made all wandering peoples suspicious—Gypsies, tinkers, the Wandering Jew. When people are seen as lacking loyalty to a place, lacking perhaps even the ability to be loyal to places, it is easy to persecute them, to view them as threatening to communal stability. The privileged and unadventurous may rightly fear that mobility threatens established traditions, and so they exaggerate the healthy attachment to place into rigid exclusivity and sentimentality. For the underprivileged or disaffected, though, mobility may represent a lifesaving escape, the eluding of oppressive inherited values and the stranglehold of tradition. For a phase of one's life, at the very least, it is a great relief to be free of the influences and expectations that a home place holds, just as one often needs to escape the clutches of one's family in order to mature. Place requires "encounters and obligations," points out James Houston; it means accepting certain limitations. Space, on the other hand, is "the arena of freedom" (Houston 1978, 226).

As a national ideal carried to an extreme, though, mobility has created the circumstances for widespread fragmentation and damage—to people, communities, and the land. The avoidance of ties to a place, which take years to build, removes constraints, allows us to be indifferent to our towns and cities, to ignore their human and environmental plights, to say *but this isn't mine*. To cling to the right of mobility with all the freedoms it bestows is ultimately to contribute to destruction.

In other traditions, a balance between wandering and staying is aspired to, the understanding that a full life involves both venturing out and returning. In the allegorical world of mythical and religious journeys, the greatest challenge of the journey is to return home, to share the lessons of one's experience, to incorporate the journey into its place of origin. While remaining in a single place can indeed be imprisoning, wandering compulsively makes one a noncitizen. There is a delicate dialectic to play out. "Before any choice," says the French geographer Eric Dardel, "there is this place which we have not chosen, where the very foundation of our earthly existence and human condition establishes itself. We can change places, move, but this is still to look for a place, for this we need as a base to set down Being and to realise our possibilities—a *here* from which the world discloses itself, a *there* to which we can go" (Dardel 1976, 41). Or, as the poet Richard Hugo jokes: "If you are in Chicago you can go to Rome. If you ain't no place you can't go nowhere" (Hugo 1979, 7).

I come from a people in diaspora who only lightly touch the place on earth they happen to be living. My grandparents fled the pogroms of Russia and the poverty of Eastern Europe, lost the coherence of their villages, but reestablished it, to some extent, in the immigrant streets of New York. Then their children, my parents, fled the city for an American-dream suburban life, severed from the intimate communities of their childhood. None of the many homes my parents made for me and my sister resembled what they had come from. Their goal was to get as far as possible from that life, with its poverty and ghetto narrowness. Suburbia may have offered a new form of community to them, but it was more truthfully a series of stepping-stones to status. To me, the streets outside our increasingly pricey homes looked exactly the same—mass produced and bare, something for us to buy into, move on from.

Housing developments still grieve me. Ubiquitous and interchangeable, they are also such an ominously forced form of neighborhood: house colors legislated to a single shade, or choice of similar three, landscaping controlled by the neighborhood association. Even the street names have in recent years been reduced, strangled into intimacy. Moving beyond earlier schemes based on a theme (trees, racetracks), newer developments often choose a single name and cram together, say, a Windsor Court with a Windsor Mews, a Windsor Drive, Road, Avenue, Lane, and Place. A friend tells me how, visiting his mother, having forgotten which Windsor she was living on and all the houses an identical rosy beige, he drove around desperately in her car, pressing the garage-door opener, waiting to see which door would open in welcome.

No wonder we return from these visits "home" dispirited. The developments many of our parents retire into have no connection to childhood for us. Even if our families remain in our hometown, the place is often so drastically altered that our landmarks are as completely obliterated as John Clare's. We are left disoriented, unable to find our way to old haunts. Most of the fields and woods are probably gone anyway, and to see a building or a business in American suburbia that has survived intact a twenty-year or thirty-year lapse is a rarity. It's a tissue-paper world, ripping before our eyes, even more temporary than we are.

Because we've been left so little to rely on, we're forced into self-protective amnesia. If our places change so radically, so quickly, what do the lives we lived in them mean? The rhythm of change and persistence, the balance of past and present, has been warped. We ourselves have been thrown out.

Maybe my persistent yearning for a full-fledged home derives more from my Jewish background than I have allowed. Most American Jews come from irretrievably lost places. We remain half-at-home here, alert enough to pack in a hurry if need be, the ghost of the Holocaust too close for comfort. To not belong, to imagine constantly an elsewhere, becomes a chronic unease. It does not compel, or perhaps even allow, loyalty to one's present place, the making of a solid home. That is the resistance I am trying to overcome. When the landscapes in which we find ourselves are not diffused with *our* meanings, *our* history or community, it is not easy to attach ourselves to them. It cannot be a natural connection, but must be a forged one. It is easier to turn inward from a strange land than to attempt to bridge the gap.

Historically, the physical life of Jews in diaspora, in ghettos, was cramped and oppressive, often literally cut off from the cultures that surrounded and ruled them. In compensation, think some, the temporal dimension of Jews' lives—their history—gained disproportionate importance. "Their spatial existence was always a tenuous and painful reminder of their isolation from the surrounding world," says the critic Stephen Kern, "and was far less important to them than their existence in time. Thus the Wandering Jew is at home only in time" (Kern 1983, 51). Cultural identity had to be internalized, kept abstract, free of attachment to its physical setting. Yiddish is said to be the only folk language in the world that has no base in nature; its vocabulary is bereft of plants and animals, almost the entire natural world (Samuel 1978, 228).

Jews have perhaps had a complicated, ambivalent relation to nature from the start. Though natural symbols survive in ritual, Judaism is the religion that by and large defused the tradition of sacred place. It is the religion that imaginatively placed divinity *outside* nature, the religion in which God, instead of existing *as* nature, used the forces of nature as punishment (plagues of locusts, floods). Cox finds it revealing that the Hebrew concept of God "arose in the social context of a nomadic, essentially homeless people" (Cox 1966, 47). The pagan gods the early Jews set out to overthrow were the numerous place-defined, local nature deities. For Jews, holy places were not crucial because their single God was a spirit who could be worshiped anywhere. "Anywhere" meant that the where of one's life faded in significance. Identity depended on human community and common belief, not on shared location.

That tendency toward placelessness helped define the thinking and writing of numerous twentieth-century artists and intellectuals who remain highly influential. Proust is an interesting literary example, a writer for whom the meaning of places depends entirely on their personal associations. "The places that we have known belong now only to the little world of space on which we map them for our own convenience. None of them was ever more than a thin slice held between the contiguous impressions that composed our life at that time; remembrance for a particular form is but regret for a particular moment, and houses, roads, avenues, are as fugitive, alas, as the years" (Proust 1976, 144).

His plaint is close to my own on occasion, close to the fact of quickly vanishing landscapes. But for Proust, the implications are more extreme. Says Kern: "If there is a single illusion that Proust most wanted to dispel it is that life takes place primarily in space. The spaces in which we live close about us and disappear like the waters of the sea after a ship passes through. To look for the essence of life in space is like trying to look for the path of a ship in the water: it only exists as a memory of the flow of its uninterrupted movement in time. The places where we happen to be are ephemeral and fortuitous settings for our life in time, and to try to recapture them is impossible" (Kern 1983, 50). Places are ephemeral when they are treated as dispensable, when we are not embraced by their traditions or when the traditions have drained away. Even for the exiled modernist James Joyce, Dublin is what solidly persists when chronological time breaks down in his work and fantasy takes over. Place is the concrete, time the fluid. For most of us in this century, it is the reverse. "Most individuals feel almost naked without their wrist-watches," notes Wilbur Zelinsky, "but how many carry compasses, maps, or field glasses . . . ?" (Zelinsky 1973, 55). We continuously, unconsciously, transform space into time, say a city is four hours away rather than two hundred miles.

E. V. Walter, a sociologist specializing in the study of place, points to Freud as another figure whose temperamental affiliation with time rather than space has had a crucial influence on our thinking. "Freud moved theory of the mind away from grounded experience and helped to build the couch as a vehicle abstracting patient from place. Despite his own existential recognition of the inner need that yearns for place, Freud's psychology never integrated personal identity with the sense of belonging, and the real power of places" (Walter 1988, 97).

Tellingly, Walter points out, Freud even rejects the rich spatial metaphor he invents in *Civilization and Its Discontents* to explain the mind. There Freud asks us to imagine the city of Rome with its archaeological past entirely visible alongside the present, relics from previous periods occupying the same space as contemporary buildings. But just as we construct such a Rome in our minds, Freud abruptly dismisses the notion—because it is physically impossible. The Rome Freud suggests, though, where Renaissance palaces, ancient walls, temples, and modern office buildings would vie for our attention, is exactly the kind of place the willing visitor creates with tourist manuals and an open mind. In Rome, more than in most other places, it is possible to experience a vivid sense of the continuity of human generations in a place. Rome is an ideal metaphor, in truth, for the landscape of fantasy and memory.

Freud uses archaeological metaphors freely elsewhere in his writings, describing the "unearthing" of his patients' pasts and the "relics" of their experiences, yet he allies the cacophonous mental experience of places with hysteria. The mnemonic symbols of cities, for instance—monuments and memorials—are seen as comparable to irrepressible memories of traumatic experience: "Every hysteric and neurotic behaves like a Londoner who might pause in deep melancholy before the memorial of Queen Eleanor's funeral, instead of going about his business, or who might shed tears before the monument that recalls the ashes of the metropolis, although it has long since risen again in far greater brilliance. Hysterical patients suffer from reminiscences." Instead of recognizing that the symbols and memories of a place are the way people can integrate themselves with a culture, Freud regards them as a curable disease. "It seems almost as if he were advocating an indifference to one's environment," says the historian Joseph Rykwert (Walter 1988, 108).

Given this stance, Freudian psychology perhaps helped intensify our separation from place. Harold Searles laments that the entire nonhuman environment is virtually ignored by Freud and his successors because of their intense focus on the human personality and human relationships—"as though the human race were alone in the universe, pursuing individual and collective destinies in a homogenized matrix of nothingness, a background devoid of form, color and substance" (Searles 1960, 3).

This is our inherited thinking, an essential severance from place true for many of us, not just those historically in diaspora. We have been taught to live consciously in time rather than in place, with our lives divided into well-defined passages. Without the continuity of place, our sense of time is exaggerated, becomes all omnipresent drama. Wendell Berry, too, wishes psychotherapy were more attentive to restoring our connection to places. "The lost identity would find itself by recognizing physical landmarks, by connecting itself responsibly to practical circumstances; it would learn to stay put in the body to which it belongs and in the place to which preference or history or accident has brought it" (Berry 1977, 111). But that is not, typically, how nowadays we "find" ourselves.

We almost cannot, when the stage sets on which we play out our lives are struck with each act. We are left with only the plot. The where of our immediate past is often unrecognizable, our further past unlocatable. Many of us are unable to trace back our ancestry beyond a generation or two. Even if we can, we have little idea, often, of *what* we've come from, what places and experiences have, unbeknown to us, filtered into our personalities, helped shape our values and temperaments.

A weak sense of the past encourages a weak sense of place. When people are attached to their forebears, they want to remain close to where they lived, continue their traditions, tend their graves, embody their hopes. Many may remain where they were born out of habit or spiritual duty, but the staying itself is conducive to life because the lived-in land then becomes an extension of the self, the family, the group; to endanger the land is to wound one's collective body.

Lacking that connection, as most of us do, how do we come to feel loyal to a place and choose to dwell there? What makes a location *feel* like a place at all? In my own life, transplanted to upstate New York, I have been hunting down stories, discovering what is legible and instructive in my landscape. In thirteen years here, I have found festering wounds beneath fine scenery, but I have found as well a palimpsest of lives by which I might patch together a sense of connection, a poultice for my own placelessness. My place's traditions are not my own; I have had to adopt them. But having a sense of place may, by now, require a continual act of imagination.

coming in to the foodshed

JACK KLOPPENBURG, JR.,

JOHN HENDRICKSON,

AND G. W. STEVENSON

FOR virtually everyone in the North and for many in the South, to eat is to participate in a truly global food system. In any supermarket here in Madison, Wisconsin, we can find tomatoes from Mexico, grapes from Chile, lettuce from California, apples from New Zealand. And, in what we take to be an indicator of a developing slippage between the terms "sustainable" and "organic," we can even buy organic blackberries from Guatemala (which may be organically produced, but in all likelihood are not sustainably produced if sustainable is understood to encompass more than on-farm production practices and any reasonable element of social justice). We cannot, however, count on finding Wisconsin-grown tomatoes, grapes, lettuce, strawberries, or apples in any supermarket in Madison, even when those crops are in season locally.

That food in the United States travels an average of thirteen hundred miles and changes hands half a dozen times before it is consumed (*The Packer* 1992) is deeply problematic. What is eaten by the great majority of North Americans comes from a global everywhere, yet from nowhere they know in particular. The distance from which their food comes represents their separation from the knowledge of how and by whom what they consume is produced, processed, and transported. If the production, processing, and transport of what they eat is destructive of the land and of human community—as it very often is—how can they understand the implications of their own participation in the global food system when those processes are located elsewhere and so are obscured from them? How can they act responsibly and effectively for change if they do not understand how the food system works and their own role within it?

Recognizing the ecological and social destructiveness of the globally based food system, a variety of analysts have suggested an alternative founded on respect for the integrity of specific sociogeographic places (Berry 1992; Crouch 1993; Dahlberg 1993; Friedmann 1993; Gussow 1993; Herrin and Gussow 1989; Kneen 1989). Counterposed to the global food system in such analyses are self-reliant locally or regionally based food systems comprising diversified farms that use sustainable practices to supply fresher, more nutritious foodstuffs to small-scale processors and consumers to whom producers are linked by the bonds of community as well as economy. The landscape is understood as part of that community, and human activity is shaped to conform to knowledge and experience of what the natural characteristics of that place do or do not permit.

We find this vision of people living well and responsibly with one another and with the land on which they are placed to be deeply appealing. In our effort to work toward realization of that vision, we have found the notion of the foodshed to be particularly useful in helping us to analyze the existing food system, to imagine the shapes an alternative might take, and to guide our actions. It is our purpose in this essay to elaborate and extend that concept and to share out initial understandings of its utility.

The term "foodshed" was coined as early as 1929 (Hedden 1929), but we were introduced to it by an encounter with the article "Urban Foodsheds," written by Arthur Getz (1991). The idea of a foodshed immediately triggered a wide range of unexpected insights and evocative associations. The intrinsic appeal the term had and continues to have for us derives in part from its relation to the rich and well-established concept of the watershed. How better to grasp the shape and the unity of something as complex as a food system than to graphically imagine the flow of food into a particular place? Moreover, the replacement of "water" with "food" does something very important: it connects the cultural ("food") to the natural ("shed"). The term "foodshed" thus becomes a unifying and organizing metaphor for conceptual development that starts from a premise of the unity of place and people, of nature and society.

The most attractive attribute of the idea of the foodshed is that it provides a bridge from thinking to doing, from theory to action. Thinking in terms of foodsheds implies development of what we might call foodshed analysis, the posing of particular kinds of questions and the gathering of particular types of information or data. And foodshed analysis ought in turn to foster change. Not only can its results be used to educate, but we believe that the foodshed—no less than Gary Snyder's watershed—is a place for organizing. In this unstable postmodern world, the foodshed can be one vehicle through which we reassemble our fragmented identities, reestablish community, and become native not only to a place but to each other.

In expanding on these points we will depart from Getz's usage in one significant way. Getz defines the foodshed as "the area that is defined by a structure of supply" and notes that "our most rudimentary map of a foodshed might cover the globe" (Getz 1991, 26). We want to establish an analytic and normative distinction between the global food system that exists now and the multiplicity of local foodsheds that we hope will characterize the future. Since we give the term "foodshed" this normative meaning, "global foodshed" is for us an oxymoron. Within the existing food system there already exist alternative and oppositionalist elements that could be the building blocks for developing foodsheds: food policy councils, community-supported agriculture, farmers' markets, sustainable farmers, alternative consumers. We will use the term "foodshed" to refer to the elements and properties of that preferred, emergent alternative.

A Foodshed in a Moral Economy

Where are we now? We are embedded in a global food system structured around a market economy that is geared to the proliferation of commodities and the destruction of the local. We are faced with transnational agribusinesses whose desire to extend and consolidate their global reach implies the homogenization of our food, our communities, and our landscapes. We live in a world in which we are ever more distant from one another and from the land, so we are increasingly less responsible to one another and to the land. Where do we go from here? How can we come home again?

There can be no definitive blueprint for the construction of some preferred future. Accordingly, we offer the foodshed not as a manifesto but as a conceptual vocabulary, not as a doctrine but as a set of principles. Below we set out five principles that seem particularly important to us. We do not claim that these are either exhaustive or particularly original. We have drawn inspiration and insight from a wide variety of people whom we consider to be engaged—whether they know it or not—in foodshed work. We invite others to join in that work.

MORAL ECONOMY A foodshed will be embedded in a moral economy that envelops and conditions market forces. The global food system operates according to allegedly "natural" rules of efficiency, utility maximization, competitiveness, and calculated self-interest. The historical extension of market relations has deeply eroded the obligations of mutuality, reciprocity, and equity that ought to characterize all elements of human interaction. Food production today is organized largely with the objective of producing a profit rather than with the purpose of feeding people. But human society has been and should remain more than a marketplace. E. P. Thompson (1966, 203) describes a "moral economy" as exchange "justified in relation to social or moral sanctions, as opposed to the operation of free market forces." Wendell Berry (1993, 14) points to similar ethical precepts when he writes of the need for "social and ecological standards" to guide us toward the aims of human freedom, pleasure, and longevity. The term "moral economy" resonates for us and we use it here as a provisional shorthand phrase for the re-embedding of food production primarily within human needs rather than within the economist's narrow "effective demand" (demand backed by ability to pay).

Adopting the perspective of the moral economy challenges us to view food as more than a commodity to be exchanged through a set of impersonal market relationships or a bundle of nutrients required to keep our bodies functioning. It permits us to see the centrality of food to human life as a powerful template around which to build nonmarket or extramarket relationships among persons, social groups, and institutions who have been distanced from one another. The production and consumption of food could be the basis for the reinvigoration of familial, community, and civic culture. We are all too well aware of the difficulty that will be involved in realizing this most fundamental principle of the foodshed. Nevertheless, we are encouraged by such innovations as Community-Supported Agriculture (CSA)—"partnerships of mutual commitment" between farmers and consumers (Van En and Roth 1993). In CSA we have a concrete example of economic exchanges conditioned by pleasure, friendship, aesthetics, affection, loyalty, justice, and reciprocity in addition to the factors of cost (not price) and quality.

THE COMMENSAL COMMUNITY Community-Supported Agriculture also serves as an illustration of our expectation that the moral economy of a foodshed will be shaped and expressed principally through communities. In *The Left Hand of Darkness* novelist Ursula Le Guin (1969) imagines a society whose basic social unit is the Commensal Hearth. The word "commensal" (from the Latin *mensa*, table) refers to those who eat together, and the word "commensalism" is used in ecology to designate a relationship between two kinds of organisms in which one obtains food from the other without damaging it. We imagine foodsheds as commensal communities that encompass sustainable relationships both between people (those who eat together) and between people and the land (obtaining food without damage).

In human terms, building the commensal community means establishment or recovery of social linkages beyond atomistic market relations through the production, exchange, processing, and consumption of food. Such social construction will occur among producers, between producers and consumers, and among consumers. Witness the recent proliferation of small-scale cooperative and collective production and marketing strategies implemented by farmers to meet growing consumer interest in organic, locally grown, nonindustrial food. Other examples of such nonmarket cooperation from the upper Midwest include the mutual assistance commitments made within associations of small-scale producers of specialty cheeses, and the information and technology exchange that occurs through networks of farmers experimenting with the rotational grazing of dairy animals as an alternative to conventional, capital-intensive, confinement milk production systems (Hassanein and Kloppenburg 1994). With respect to new relationships between producers and consumers, emerging cooperative linkages between fresh vegetable growers and neighborhood restaurants and consumer coops parallel the birth of CSA and the revitalization of farmers' markets (Hendrickson 1994; Waters 1990). Among consumers themselves, buying clubs, community gardens, and changing patterns of food purchase reflect growing concern with the social, economic, ethical, environmental, health, and cultural implications of how they eat.

While concrete precursors of what could conceivably become commensal communities are now visible, commitment to a moral economy requires that we work to make those communities as inclusive as possible. The sustainable agriculture movement has so far tended to be "farm-centric" (Allen and Sachs 1991, 587) and has not yet seriously engaged issues of race, class, and gender even within— much less outside—rural areas. Hunger in the city is indeed an agricultural issue (Ashman et al. 1993; Clancy 1993). The commensal community should confront and address the need not just for equitable access to food but also for broader participation in decisionmaking by marginalized or disempowered groups. That progress is possible is evidenced by the activities of the Hartford Food System, which has made a priority of linking farmers directly to low-income consumers (Winne 1994) and by initiatives to foster the acceptance of food stamps at farmers' markets. The "food policy councils" now being created in a variety of U.S. and Canadian cities are indicators of the plausibility of addressing foodshed issues by relating food affairs to other fundamental community dimensions such as economic development and nutrition and public health (Dahlberg 1993; Toronto Food Policy Council 1993).

Finally, the standards of a commensal community require respect and affection for the land and for other species. It is through food that humanity's most intimate and essential connections to the earth and to other creatures are expressed and consummated. In the commensal community, production, processing, distribution, consumption, and waste disposal will be organized so as to protect and, where necessary, to regenerate the natural resource base. Responsible stewardship will involve sustainable cropping and humane livestock practices, reduced use of nonrenewable energy sources, and a commitment to recycling and reuse.

SELF-PROTECTION, SECESSION, AND SUCCESSION The dominant dynamics of the global food system actively erode both moral economy and community. We agree with those who believe that this destructiveness is an inherent property of that system, and that what is needed is fundamental transformation rather than simple reform (see, for example, Allen and Sachs 1991; Berry 1993; Friedmann 1993; Orr 1992). Still, given the current dominance of the existing world food economy, people working toward foodshed objectives will need to carve out insulated spaces in which to maintain or create alternatives that will eventually bring substantive change. In opposition to the extension of the market system, there have always been examples of what Friedmann (1993, 218) calls "movement(s) of self-protection." From the Luddites of nineteenth-century Britain to the Zapatistas of contemporary Chiapas, we have seen continuous refusal to submit without contest to the dictates of the globalizing food system. At the margins of consumer society and in the interstices between McDonald's and Monsanto and Philip Morris are all manner of alternative producers and eaters— Amish, vegetarians, rotational graziers, seed savers, food coop members, perennial polyculturists, bioregionalists, home gardeners, biodynamicists—who are producing and reproducing a rich set of alternative agrofood possibilities.

What these diverse people and groups share is that their activities and commitments involve various degrees of disengagement from the existing food system and especially from the narrow commodity and market relations on which it is based. We follow Berry (1993, 17–18) and Orr (1992, 73) in our conviction that a fundamental principle of the foodshed is the need for "secession." This principle is based on a strategic preference for withdrawing from and/or creating alternatives to the dominant system rather than challenging it directly. Certainly, in many circumstances direct opposition to elements of the global food economy is appropriate and necessary (the situation in Chiapas, or the current manipulation of the Green Bay Cheese Exchange by food corporations such as Kraft and Pizza

Hut). A primary strategy of the secession principle is "slowly hollowing out" (Orr 1992, 73) the structures of the global food system by reorganizing our own social and productive capacities. This is essentially what grazier groups are engaged in as they rediscover their own indigenous capacity for producing the knowledge they need to be "grass farmers," and as they withdraw from the agribusiness firms and agricultural scientists who have been doing their thinking for them (Hassanein and Kloppenburg 1994).

A second and corollary point is that of "succession," or the conscious and incremental transfer of resources and human commitments from old food-associated relationships and forms to new ones. Neither people nor institutions are generally willing or prepared to embrace radical change. The succession principle finds expression in a strategy of "slowly moving over" from the food system to the foodshed. Food presents people with hundreds of small opportunities to take increasingly important steps away from the global market economy and toward the moral economy. An example is the consumer who decides not to purchase milk produced using recombinant bovine growth hormone (rBGH). While the motivation for that initial, simple step may be narrowly based on personal health considerations, the potential is there for making further connections. Once the link between rBGH and Monsanto is made, the consumer may become aware of the corporate/chemical/food link more generally, and begin moving a progressively higher percentage of the household food budget into purchases from alternative food sources. Similarly, restaurants or schools may be encouraged to purchase more of their food supplies from local producer cooperatives as these foodshed alternatives generate capacity.

PROXIMITY (LOCALITY AND REGIONALITY) We see certain key spatial components to the secession and succession dynamics as characterizing the foodshed. If mitigation of the deleterious effects of distancing is the central challenge posed by the operation of the global food system, then greater attention to proximity—to that which is relatively near—should be an appropriate response. But apart from the principle of relative proximity, it is not clear precisely where the revised boundaries ought to be drawn. The limits of a foodshed will be a function of the shapes of multiple sets of boundaries; that is, of the aggregated boundaries of the climatic features, plant communities, soil types, ethnicities, cultural traditions, culinary patterns, and the like, of which foodsheds are composed. Hence we identify proximity rather than locality or regionality per se as a fundamental principle of the foodshed. Though their precise boundaries will rarely be sharply defined, we insist that foodsheds are socially, economically, ethically, and physically embedded in particular places.

We do not, however, imagine foodsheds as isolated, parochial entities. While they might be—in Marge Piercy's (1976) term—as "ownfed" as possible, we see them as self-reliant rather than self-sufficient. Self-reliance implies the reduction of dependence on other places but does not deny the desirability or necessity of external trade relationships (Friedmann 1993, 228; Gussow 1993, 14). For too long, however, trade in the global food economy has meant farmers selling low-value commodities to distant markets and processors and the subsequent reimportation of finished food products at high prices. In the foodshed, efforts would be made to increase the level of local and intraregional food production, processing, and distribution and so to retain economic value and jobs. Since economic concentration is a prime engine of distancing, secessionist and successionist alternatives ought to be built around small and midsized enterprises (dairies, cheese factories, smithies, greenhouses, canneries, restaurants, specialty markets) capable of responding affirmatively to the opportunities and responsibilities of the emergent commensal community.

The self-reliance associated with proximity is closely linked to both social and environmental sustainability. A community that depends on its human neighbors, neighboring lands, and native species to supply the majority of its needs must ensure that the social and natural resources it utilizes to fulfill those needs remain healthy. A consequence of proximate self-reliance is that social welfare, soil and water conservation, and energy efficiency become issues of immediate practical concern. For example, it is difficult for most city dwellers to be concerned about preserving farmland unless the destruction of farmland directly affects their food supply, or unless they know and care for the paving over of the land. Awareness of and affection for one's place can forestall the ethical distancing so characteristic of the global food system. In the foodshed, collective responsibility for stewardship of people and of the land becomes a necessity rather than an optional virtue.

NATURE AS MEASURE We understand the foodshed to be a socio-geographic space—human activity embedded in the natural integument of a particular place. That human activity is necessarily constrained in various ways by the characteristics of the place in question. Ignoring those natural constraints or over-riding them with technology is one of the besetting sins of the global food system, the ecological destructiveness of which is now unambiguously apparent even to its apologists. In the foodshed, natural conditions would be taken not as an obstacle to be overcome but as a measure of limits to be respected.

While restraints on human activity will indeed often be required, to interpret natural parameters in terms of "deficiency" rather than "capacity" is to fail to transcend the conventional industrial mindset. Nature may be understood not just as a set of limits but as an exemplar of the possible, as an almanac of potential models for human conduct and action (Jackson 1980; Orr 1992, 33; Quinn 1993). For example, from the perspective of the foodshed, one answer to Berry's (1987, 146) query, "What will nature help us do here?" points toward the development of regional palates based on "moving diets" of locally and seasonally available food. Who knows what lessons nature may offer us should we free ourselves to see its "capacity"? These opportunities are by no means obvious. They must be discovered in intimate, extended conversation with the land. By acting with respect and affection for the natural world, we may begin to produce and eat in harmony with and within the rhythms and patterns of the places in which we live.

Toward Foodshed Analysis

Ironically, much foodshed analysis will necessarily involve examination and explication of the structure and dynamics of the existing global food system. That food system exists and is a powerful and dominating structure indeed. Secession—even for so solitary a group as the Amish—can now be only partial and contingent. Emergent elements of what might become foodsheds are presently embedded in and often constrained by the rules, interests, and operations of regional and global actors and institutions.

Aldo Leopold (1970, 137) suggested that we need to learn to "think like a mountain"; that is, to think ecologically, to engage the hidden and unlooked-for connections among the elements of a system or between different levels of a system. Until and unless we know where we are in the larger social and political ecology of the global food system, we may not be able to move effectively toward realization of a foodshed locally. We do not necessarily have to accept the demands of the global food system, but we must understand and realistically address the constraints it imposes if we are to identify the space it permits for secessionist activities or simple self-protection.

Foodshed analysis will not eschew engagement with issues at the national or even the global level. It will ask that this extralocal investigation serve the objective of framing the prospects for successfully implementing concrete initiatives or changes within a particular sociogeographic place. Foodshed analysis will involve investigation of the existing food system in order to inform strategic decisions regarding opportunities for self-protection and secession. Such analysis should include the identification, celebration, and study of existing and emergent alternatives to the food system. Ultimately foodshed work should seek to link such elements in a system of mutual support and integration, with the objective of fostering emergence of a truly alternative system: the foodshed. While as a general rule it is advisable to think and act as proximately as we can, we must recognize that the appropriate and necessary locus of both thought and action in the foodshed may sometimes be regional, national, or even global.

Concretely, what would foodshed analysis entail? In simplest terms, it means answering Getz's basic question, "Where is our food coming from and how is it getting to us?" For us, a substantial part of the appeal of the term "foodshed" has to do with the graphic imagery it evokes: streams of foodstuffs running into a particular locality, their flow mediated by the features of both natural and social geography. Measuring the flow and direction of these tributaries and documenting the many quantitative and qualitative transformations that food undergoes as it moves through time and space toward consumption is the central methodological task of foodshed analysis.

What unit of analysis is appropriate for such study; what, after all, are the boundaries of a foodshed? What kinds of data or information ought to be collected? Answers to these questions will vary as a function of who is engaging in the analysis and what their objectives and resources are. The foodshed is not a determinate thing; foodshed analysis will be similarly variable. It may involve collection of data on local exports of corn or the capacity of the local landfill, on the distribution of edible plant species or the patterns of human hunger, on the organization of harvest festivals or the composition of the county board, on the content of school lunch menus or the forage preferences of diary cows.

Foodshed analysis will not be constructed to conform to some predetermined theoretical and methodological framework, but will be constituted by the concrete activities of those who seek to learn about the food system in order to change it. Many such projects have been completed or are under way at a variety of levels. The Cornucopia Project, organized by Rodale Press in Pennsylvania in the 1980s, chose states as its unit of analysis and emphasized collection of aggregate state-level data suited to the project's objective of raising the general public's awareness of the vulnerabilities of the national food system through state-specific reports and publicity (Rodale 1982; Rural Wisconsin Cornucopia Task Force 1982). Also at the state level, several studies by nutritionists have been undertaken in order to explore the parameters and implications for human health of sustainable, regional diets (Hamm 1993; Herrin and Gussow 1989).

Using cities as their sociogeographic framework, a variety of "food policy councils" have been created to address issues of sustainability and equity in the food system (Dahlberg 1993; Hartford Food System 1991; Toronto Food Policy Council 1993). The students and staff at several colleges have taken their own institutions as the basic unit of analysis and explored the rationale and mechanisms for getting commitments from their colleges to buy local food (Bakko and Woodwell 1992; Valen 1992). Local food projects at Hendrix College in Arkansas and Saint Olaf and Carleton colleges in Minnesota were successful in reorienting food purchasing patterns to more proximate sources. The degree of resolution characteristic of the lens of foodshed analysis can become very fine grained indeed. One of the most impressive and revealing analyses we have encountered is a self-study of a personal foodshed—"from gut to ground" (Peterson 1994)—that explores individual consumption and its implications for personal responsibility in the global food system.

An example of foodshed analysis that focuses on the urban poor is an initiative undertaken under the auspices of the Southern California Interfaith Hunger Coalition (IHC). The IHC's report, "Seeds of Change: Strategies for Food Security for the Inner City," is an ambitious and finely realized effort to take an "integrated, whole-systems approach" to assessing the need and prospects for reforming the existing food system in a specific and delimited place (Ashman et al. 1993, v). The IHC document is also of interest because the research and analysis for the report was undertaken largely by students and faculty from the University of California at Los Angeles. Much criticism has been directed toward universities (especially toward the land-grant colleges) for their subservience to industrial interests and their failure to orient knowledge production to local or regional needs.

"Seeds of Change" is striking evidence that academics can work effectively with advocacy groups oriented to transformation of the food system.

Although few of those whose efforts we have described think of what they do as "foodshed analysis," we feel they are moving in directions similar to ours. To the extent that these diverse projects and undertakings are complementary, they constitute a rich set of conceptual and methodological resources for thinking about and assessing the nature and structure of the global food system in which we are now embedded, and for helping us to consider how and where we can realistically expect to make changes.

RADICAL REFORMISM

It is apparent to increasing numbers of people that fundamental changes are needed in the global food system. Of course, we see that the question of food is simply a specific case of the general failure of late capitalism, or postindustrialism, or postmodernism, or whatever you wish to call this period of intense commodification and of accelerating distancing from one another and from the earth. We could equally well be calling for fundamental changes in the global health system, the global industrial system, the global political system, the global monetary system, or the global labor system. Ultimately, what sustainability requires of us is change in global society as a whole. We need the recovery and reconstitution of community generally, not simply in relation to food. Although we may strive to think like mountains, we must act as human beings. To start the global task to which we are called, we need a specific place to begin, a specific place to stand, a specific place to initiate the small, reformist changes that we can only hope may some day become radically transformative.

We start with food. Given the centrality of food in our lives and its capacity to connect us materially and spiritually to one another and to the earth, we believe that it is an appropriate place to begin. We offer the term "foodshed" to encompass the physical, biological, social, and intellectual components of the multidimensional space in which we live and eat. We understand the foodshed as a framework for both thought and action. If our use of the term has any virtue, perhaps it is to help people see the relatedness of apparently disparate elements, and to perceive the complementarity of different but parallel initiatives for change. We also think it useful to make a semantic distinction between where we are now and where we wish to be in the future. Thinking and acting in terms of the foodshed is an indication of our commitment to work not simply to reform the food system but to transcend that system entirely. And while a system can be anywhere, the foodshed is a continuous reminder that we are standing in a specific place; not anywhere, but here.

We need to keep place firmly in our minds and beneath our feet as we talk and walk our way toward a transformed future. Because the path is long and because we must build it as we go—the foodshed offers a project, not a blueprint—

our actions will be "slow small adjustments in response to questions asked by a particular place" (Berry 1990, 121). We share Orr's (1992, 1) hope for "a rejuvenation of civic culture and the rise of an ecologically literate and ecologically competent citizenry who understand global issues, but who also know how to live well in their places." If we are to become native to our places, the foodshed is one way of envisioning that beloved country.

"placed" between promise and command

WALTER BRUEGGEMANN

THE land as Israel's place is understood primarily as a gift from God. Thus the very first words uttered in Genesis by God to this "family of Israel" are those spoken to Father Abraham: "Go from your country and your kindred and your father's house to the land that I will show you" (Gen. 12:1). It is decisive for Israel's understanding of itself and of its place that narrative memory begins with the speech of God, which suggests that there is a transcendent element in Israel's origin and destiny. The speech takes the form of a promise, a promise that persists throughout the life of Israel and in the face of every circumstance.

The reception of the land promise has effectiveness, however, only within the ongoing relationship between giver and receiver. This promise is one of the major affirmations of the Bible concerning place: the matrix of having a place is intimately linked to having a right relationship with the promise-maker.

The high theological claim of promise does not override the Bible's readiness to be realistic about the land. When the people of Israel arrived, there were already other, non-Israelite folk there who regarded the land as their own and who did not easily accept Israel's religious claim of a land grant from God. Thus already in Genesis 12:6, just verses after the defining promise above, we are told, "At that time, there were Canaanites in the land." The presence of others in the land is a primary fact of Israel's life.

Since all of these peoples went by the name of "Canaanite," and since their presence was a great vexation to Israel, we may reflect on the significance of this presence. There is a rough scholarly consensus that the term "Canaanite" is not an ethnic term when it is used in Israel's land traditions, and even the formulary "seven nations" (Deut. 7:1, Jud. 3:1–5) is not used with any precision. Rather, the term "Canaanite" is a pejorative code word used to refer to modes of public power and social relationships that are exploitative and oppressive (Lemcke 1991). In Israel's frame of reference, "Canaanite" means anticovenantal or, we may say, antineighborly. The Canaanites are the "other" to Israel, seen to constitute a threat (putting Israel's place at risk) or a seduction (persuading Israel to abandon its covenantal vision of the land). While this antithetical mode of social organization signaled by the term "Canaanite" does not justify all the violence present in Israel's land tradition, it does help us understand why Israel concluded that Canaanite systems of land management must be eliminated if the land of promise was to be a land of neighborliness.

Given the presence of previous owners claiming to be the continuing owners of the land, Israel had very limited options. First, it could assume an adversarial relation with those occupants, as reflected in Judges 1:28, 30, 33, 34, 2:3. Second, Israel had the option of peaceful coexistence, as reflected in Judges 1:29, 32.

Thus in ancient Israel the wondrous theological claim of God's promise and gift is held in acute tension with the practical reality of displacement and usurpation. The biblical text suggests that ancient Israel was not unmindful of or at ease about this open and unresolved question.

The land of promise to which Israel came was organized in Canaanite ways. That is not to say that the Canaanites were evil, but only that the land was organized in the conventional ways of the world, so that society consisted in "big ones" and "little ones," in "haves" and "have-nots." While the land may have been organized into urban dwellers and agrarian peasants (or seminomads), the urban power structure had all the power and regularly confiscated the produce of the agrarian peasants for its own benefit.

While some observers might consider this quite normal, the Israelites fresh from the covenant-making of Mount Sinai and the social vision of Moses considered these so-called normal practices to be untenable, even if well established and conventionally accepted as legitimate. Indeed, it is this Sinai-Moses tradition of covenant and commandment that propels biblical faith and that endlessly champions "a more excellent way" (I Cor. 13) in the neighborhood. Thus even in the face of entrenched power relations, visionary voices in Israel relentlessly insisted upon that more excellent way in social relationships.

The book of Deuteronomy, which purports to be the teaching of Moses, stands as the covenantal alternative to Canaanite modes of production and ownership. It holds passionately to the strong conviction that the land of Canaan is transformable and open to change.

Two themes persist in the long address of Moses in Deuteronomy. First, Moses perceives that the Canaanite modes of social order are so effective and attractive that they constitute a threat to Israel. There is a chance that Israel will be so attracted to Canaanite ways of arranging power (exploitatively) that it will forget that the land is a gift demanding faith, and that the land is an arena for the practice of neighborly convenanting. That is, Israel may abandon its very reason for existence and simply disappear into the conventional economics of the land. Moses pauses so long in order to warn, caution, and admonish Israel that it should not be talked out of its peculiar vision of what its place should look like.

There is a second reason why Moses pauses so long at the Jordan River. Not only did Moses view the Canaanite-shaped land of promise as a threat and a seduction that jeopardized Israel's vision of social reality, but the long-talking Moses of Deuteronomy also believed that this land of promise, distorted by exploitative social relationships, could be transformed. That is, the people of Israel, powered and energized by an intentional vision, could indeed change their place and make it livable and life giving. This remarkable faith claim has been decisive for Western culture. The place is not fated; it can be brought to an alternative destiny by the intentionality of the new vision-driven inhabitants. The land as a social reality, that is, not simply as a one-dimensional piece of real estate, takes on a different quality, depending on the attitude, conduct, and policies of its inhabitants.

Places depend on the kind of people who inhabit them and take on the character of the occupants.

The particular strategy of Moses concerning the transformation of the land is to insist that the vision of covenantal social relationships, whereby the strong and the weak, the haves and the have-nots, share a common destiny, be enacted by obedience to covenantal commands. Israel's sense of place requires that the place be "managed," not by convenience or by conventional common sense or by the enactment of vested interest, but by commands that call for quite deliberate covenantal behavior. It is the commands that link together large visionary possibility and local, daily practice. Or, in the parlance of Moses, the "will of God" is linked to the claims of neighborliness. This remarkable conviction holds together affirmations that we tend to split apart. Who would have thought that the "God of gods and Lord of lords" would have to fend off bribes or would provide food and clothing for the needy? Who would imagine that it is the vision of God that issues in the social imperative about caring for needy strangers? Moses insists that how the neighborhood is ordered is related to Israel's largest vision of reality, that is, its vision of God.

Moses, however, does not settle for such a general rhetorical appeal. That appeal is followed and detailed by concrete commands, rules for conduct in Israel's new place.

1. *Deuteronomy 15:1–11* (see Hamilton 1992). Every society has creditors and debtors, so social relationships have an inescapable economic component, a dimension of social reality that makes for easy exploitation. In that ancient society, those who could not pay their debts eventually ended up as indentured workers, as debt-slaves working only to pay off mortgages. They were what we might now call a permanent underclass. Moses proposes that this indentured status is not to be permanent in Israel, because Israel anticipates a different quality of social place. The command requires that the indebted person only be kept in a position of dependence, coercion, and humiliation for a period of six years. After that the debt, if it cannot be paid, is to be canceled. Economic relations are understood as a subset of the social fabric which has larger purposes that preempt and override economic claims. Thus debt is not an ultimate determinant of social relations, for in fact the command undermines the viability of any conventional economics.

The commandment, however, does not simply entail forgiveness of a debt. It provides that the indentured worker, when released with debts canceled, shall not be sent destitute back into the economy. Rather, the creditor shall not be "hardhearted or tight-fisted" toward a needy neighbor (v. 7). The creditor is required to "willingly lend" (v. 8) or "give liberally and ungrudgingly" (v. 10). Thus the command concerns the capacity of the indebted to reenter the economy with dignity, self-respect, and viability, through neighborly care.

Moreover, while the command is famous (through the reference made to it by Jesus in Mark 14:7) in its statement that "there will never cease to be some in need in the earth," the command envisions that one day there will "be no one in need among you." This command anticipates not simply modest acts of charity and compassion, but a major transformation of economics whereby poverty is eradicated in a community that handles its wealth in genuinely neighborly ways. The radicality of this core provision can hardly be overstated. Indeed, the healthy transformation of Israel's place requires a break with both a conventional market economy and a state economy. Moses anticipates an economy of neighbors, a practice that holds for Israel not only in a simple face-to-face economy, but in every attempt to establish viable community.

2. *Deuteronomy 17:14–20.* Moses in Deuteronomy is also about the daring business of devising and authorizing social institutions and practices as new social need arises. New social reality requires new modes of power and administration. Chief among these is the institution of monarchy. The monarchy as a form of centralized power, unknown in early "egalitarian" Israel, represented what some viewed as a major distortion of Israel's common life.

Given the inescapable emergence of centralized power in the form of kingship, Moses concedes nothing in this command to conventional forms of exploitative centralized power. Monarchy is accepted by Moses, but the conventional substance of kingship is roundly refused. The peculiar form of royal power envisioned by Moses is a practice of power that does not override neighborliness. The proposed king must not multiply for himself silver and gold (that is, have inordinate wealth), horses or chariots (armaments), or wives (political alliances arranged through marriage). Social power in Israel is to avoid all the distortions of neighborliness that are routine in Canaanite society.

Moses claims the existence of an important alternative to such exploitative conventions. Instead of personal aggrandizement, the king is to spend his days of power reading the torah and pondering the distinctive memory and identity of Israel. The king is to reflect endlessly on his true place in an ongoing community of obedience, liberation, and covenant. Moses clearly believes and insists that Israel's public, structured, institutional life can be made congenial to and supportive of equitable social relations.

What Moses requires for the institution of monarchy is also required for other necessary social institutions, such as judges (17:8–13), prophets (18:9–22), priests (18:1–8), and cities of refuge (19:1–13) (see Lohfink 1982). Israel is free to appropriate conventional social practices, but in each case must recharacterize and revise these practices in ways appropriate to its own social passion and social vision.

3. *Deuteronomy 19:14.* This terse command on "boundary markers" provides none of the rhetorical appeal or flourish of the other commands we have considered. Nonetheless, it is equally crucial for Israel's covenantal notion of place. It recognizes that each member of the community must have a safe, unthreatened place (property) that will be respected and guaranteed by the acknowledgment of all the other neighbors. It further recognizes that the maintenance of neighborly relations does not depend on the capacity to defend forcibly one's personal place,

but on the coherence of the community that recognizes and accepts the legitimacy of the place of the other.

It is evident that this simple command has importance and force in more complex social relations as well. Specifically, Proverbs 23:10–11 sees that the ancient land marker that is endangered is the land marker of an orphan, a vulnerable person who in a patriarchal society has lost the male advocate who will defend that right. The mention of orphan, one socially vulnerable, suggests that even the simple command of Deuteronomy 19:14 is concerned with the threat of excessive power whereby the strong can preempt the legitimate interests of the weak. Thus, the moving of boundary markers may not concern the simple act of moving a post. It may be the much more complex and sophisticated action of smart lawyers and foreclosing banks, and in more public matters the exercise of the right of eminent domain, which gives the strong legal ways to seize land for their own purposes. The rural prophet Micah (2:2) warns against land operators who

> covet fields, and seize them;
> houses, and take them away;
> they oppress household and house,
> people and their inheritance.

The tale of Naboth's vineyard (I Kings 21) is an example of eminent domain whereby a vulnerable citizen is denied his patrimony by the operation of a royal theory of land.

Accordingly, the command of 19:14 concerns not only land management, but the ways in which economic activity is situated outside social relations that must be honored, even if they curb the free activity of market forces. Israel's simplicity of expression must not beguile us, so that we do not notice the demanding social vision that operates within such a seemingly uncomplicated statement.

4. *Deuteronomy 20:19–20, 22:6–7.* These two laws appear to be quite incidental to the teaching of Moses and have not been much noticed. The former has for the most part, been considered only in terms of an understanding of war, and the second has been studied virtually not at all. As a result of recent ecological awareness, however, in these two laws we are able to see an inchoate, but nonetheless important concern for the ecology of the land.

Deuteronomy 20:19–20 occurs at the conclusion of a long chapter of provisions about the waging of war. As everyone knows, war devastates the natural environment where it is conducted. In part, this is because of the actual work of combat. But it is also because of utilizing natural resources as material for combat. In the ancient world, a major military tactic was siege (see, for instance, II Sam. 12:26–31), for which great timber was required. Because the passions of war seem to override every other social concern, the timbers for siege are taken, regardless of the cost.

In such a context the command of Moses is remarkable. The utilization of timber for siege weapons is permitted, but with an important limitation. Israel is permitted to take only trees that "do not produce food," in other words, not fruit trees. In a rather indirect way, this text recalls the lyrical affirmation of fruitfulness in the creation narrative of Genesis 1:11, 29. The creation is intended for fruitfulness, the production of life. And that fruitfulness intended for the creation is the irreducible first reality of all social relations. The maintenance of fruitfulness that can work and fulfill its proper function is the first human obligation. Nothing must interfere—not state necessity, not the passions of war, not hate or revenge, not the love of violence or rapacious greed. A purpose larger than human conflict sets a limit on the range of human conflict, and the legitimate appetite of human control and expansion.

In a less dramatic way, 22:6–7 sounds a similar affirmation. This command presents a more domestic scene, a walk in the woods. Upon finding a bird's nest with eggs in it and the mother bird with the eggs, one may be tempted to seize both the eggs and the mother bird—to get food, or simply out of curiosity. Moses sorts out matters very carefully. The eggs may be taken, but not the mother bird. She is the agent of fruitfulness, and an Israelite may not disrupt the food chain on which everyone depends. Israel knows that rapacious acts such as killing a mother bird will disrupt the earth's work of fruitfulness, and in principle will make the earth inhospitable and finally unlivable.

These commands intend to curb the Canaanite temptation to self-sufficiency and self-aggrandizement, whereby one is free to do whatever one wants to do. These commands insist that all social acts in Israel (economic transactions, institution building, respect for neighbor, and respect for earth) situate would-be autonomous acts in a matrix of relations that concern neighborliness, which is situated in the very fabric of creation. Every act has a moral shape to it that cannot be violated without severe harm and long-range destructive consequences. Moses insists that the most minute daily act be understood in terms of its inescapable, long-term moral shape.

Because the land is both promised to Israel and occupied by others; because the land is both a threat to faith and a possible arena of transformation; because the land is saturated with large, public ethical issues, Israel understands that its life in the land is a vulnerable enterprise, freighted with danger and possibility.

On the one hand, Israel is promised that it can indeed keep the land, if it attends to the neighborly dimension of social reality in the land. Israel's rhetoric is filled with buoyant expectations, anticipating long life in the land through many generations. The commands that make life in the land possible are not burdensome, but simply the normal and inescapable markings of viable community life. Thus it is promised that "you may live long on the land God has given you" (Deut. 5:33; see also 8:1, 11:9, 21, 16:20, 25:15). All of these assurances and possibilities are set within the context of command. Attachment to this God-given place, which is safe, fruitful, and productive (blessed), is indeed conditional. Israel, in the book of Deuteronomy and more generally in its rhetoric of commitment, resolves to keep the conditions and accept the land on the terms of covenant (see also Ex.

24:3, 7, Josh. 24:21, 24–25). The condition is neighborliness, which is the only way to keep a place.

On the other hand, Israel in its most candid reflection knows that it can lose the land. And it will if it disregards the commands, if it acts as though it were autonomous and self-sufficient, free to use the land for its own greedy purposes. The promise of God to give the land does not hold for land that is held in foolish ways, without regard to neighborliness.

Thus Israel is warned that "you will surely perish from off the land" (Deut. 4:26, see also 8:19–20, 11:17, 28:20, 22). The notion of perishing is carefully nuanced. Israel will disappear through long-term natural processes. These may include drought (Deut. 11:17) or a host of pathologies (28:20–22). Or perishing may mean that the Israelite vision of neighborliness is forfeited, and by its greedy lack of caring the Israelites vanish into the landscape of Canaanite exploitation. Then it will be as though the exodus of liberation never happened, and Israel will find itself again brutally enmeshed in old patterns of oppressiveness and despair.

Israel's sense of place involves a deep either/or about the command that guarantees the promise. We should be clear, however, that the command is not an imposition of legalism, as though Moses (or God) were cranky or coercive. Rather, the command is Israel's distinctive way in which to speak about the irreducible reality that healthy place requires healthy social relationships. This conditionality cannot be circumvented by power, knowledge, or wealth, for it is intrinsic to the land process itself. The neighbor is the irreducible condition of healthy, peaceable, productive place.

We may cite two poignant articulations of this uncompromising either/or. In Deuteronomy 8:17–20 Moses draws a sharp contrast between remembering and forgetting. Remembering (v. 18) concerns the palpable awareness that God gives power to get wealth, and that power and wealth are covenantal operations. Forgetting (v. 19) is the scuttling of the awareness of God, the disregard of covenanting, and the perverted imagination of self-sufficiency that "my power and the might of my hand have gotten me this wealth" (v. 17). This deception of autonomy will lead to placelessness (v. 20).

Deuteronomy 30:15–20 presents the same issue of promise and command as a choice of life and death, which concerns the embrace of the commands of neighboring. The language is intensely theological; it concerns a choice of gods. That choice is not intellectual, however, or theoretical or cognitive. It is a concrete practical matter. Israel chooses Yahweh (or another god) not by theological verbiage, but by the way that god treats indentured servants, by the way it orders centralized power, by the way it respects boundary markers, and by the way it treats fruit trees and mother birds.

One need not be a militant theological type to see that Israel's sense of place is not outmoded or obsolete for our own time. The issues that confronted Moses in Deuteronomy are the same issues that confront a complex postindustrial, urban society. Either the neighbor is honored, respected, and cared for in terms of social policy and social practice, or deep human losses and pathologies arise that threaten us all. As Moses understood so well, there is no escape from this either/or, not by might, not by wealth, not by technological sophistication.

As ancient Israel tells its story, the community chooses death. It found the condition of neighborliness too demanding and too inconvenient. The classic account of Israel's life under the monarchy—in Joshua, Judges, I and II Samuel, I and II Kings—is a narrative interpretation of the way in which disregard of command led to exile, displacement, and disarray (see I Kings 9:4–7).

The telling of this tale in the Hebrew Bible and the Old Testament ends in exile, as though death and losing the land have fully prevailed over life and keeping the land. Alongside that descriptive account, however, is a visionary alternative. It took the courageous prophets and daring poets of Israel to move past the terrible either/or of Deuteronomy 30:15–20 and I Kings 9:4–7 and suggest there was a way for this community other than the death of antineighborliness, which it had chosen.

No voicing of this alternative is more eloquent than Ezekiel 37:1–14. The prophet must employ a daring and radical image in order to speak about a return to the land and a new possibility for life in the land. Such extreme articulation is required because such a possibility moves against the experienced reality of land loss. Israel could hardly believe the restoration to the land was possible; therefore the prophet must use images that violate all the weary conventions of Israel's despair. Ezekiel speaks about resurrection: "I open your graves and bring you up from your graves, O my people" (v. 13). It is obvious, however, that this speech about resurrection is for the prophet a metaphor. Verse 14 explicates the metaphor: "I will place you on your own soil; then you shall know that I, the Lord, have spoken and will act, says the Lord."

Israel will begin again, on the very piece of land long ago promised. What makes this second choice possible after the first choice has been forfeited is that "I will put my spirit within you" (v. 14). It is the spirit-wind-power of God that blows in and through old deathly choices, that permits Israel yet again to redecide for its life in its place. It is this redeciding that is required for a place, even if old deathly choices are still an option and a temptation.

Moses invited Israel to stand firm in its peculiar and distinctive notion of place. Between the free gift and promise and the condition of command, Israel knows that its place is at the same time its very own and not its own. It cannot scuttle the moral reality of place, cannot scuttle the God who promises and commands, cannot scuttle the neighbor who looms large just across the boundary.

Israel is peculiar in its sense of place. It offers itself persistently as a way whereby others can learn something decisive and inescapable about being in the right place. To be well placed means to listen and to care. Not listening and not caring constitute a terrible alternative for Israel, and for the rest of us.

other selves

JOHN A. LIVINGSTON

A sense of community is most simply put as an awareness of simultaneous *belonging* to both a society and a place. And also an awareness of self-identity *as* that society or place. There are as many kinds of societies and places as there are kinds of living beings, and probably just as many kinds of awarenesses; but at the most fundamental level any sense of belonging can rest only on a sense of self. Our search for a renewed sense of community will depend ultimately on a concept of self very different from that with which we have been indoctrinated. The distorted versions of both with which we have lived so long and so unquestioningly have cost nature dearly. They have cost us also. Healthier apprehensions of either community or self will not need to be invented, however. They will need merely to be retrieved. They have been here all along—in our own living nature, our animalness.

Still, the retrieval of those ancient apprehensions will encounter massive obstacles. It seems that we cannot or will not think of either communities or societies beyond the human realm. We persist in this mindset despite our knowledge of eco "systems" (abstract models of natural communities) and of animal and (yes) plant social behavior.

It seems that even though we know better, we feel more comfortable—perhaps more secure—in restricting community membership and social relations to the human phenomenon, and in effectively denying their presence in life forms that are not human. More important, any idea that community awareness or social niceties or—perish the thought—a sense of self could reside in nonhuman beings and actually cross individual and even species barriers is, for a catalog of reasons, at once bizarre and unsettling.

One of the reasons may be that if we were to concede the capacity for interspecies sociality and community awareness to selves who are not human, we would at the same time have to relinquish treasured notions of our singular, most-favored status in both evolutionary and ecospheric schemes of things. Even more difficult might be the abandonment of "objectivity," which is a means of receiving and understanding the world by firmly positioning ourselves outside, above, and beyond it—by separating us and it.

The concept of "self" is another expression of dualism. It dichotomizes the world by requiring the additional concept of "other"—or, if you prefer, subject and object. The twin notions are mutually reinforcing. They are analogous if not identical to the conceptual human-and-nature dichotomy, which, as so many have pointed out, lies at or very close to the core rootstock of human alienation from the ecosphere. Both are part of the greater cultural tradition in which we labor, part of the belief system that provides and sustains our ideologies.

Human-centered ideologies allow (indeed require) us to undertake all the familiar rationalizing that goes into the poignant task of demonstrating human emancipation from our own biological reality. Few exercises in rationalization have involved quite so much intellectual pretzel bending as has the task of demonstrating absolute human uniqueness. Our obsession with this is revealing. It is not enough that every individual, and every species, is a unique, one-time-only event. Fanatical human chauvinism demands more. All species are unique, we may acknowledge, but one species is *uniquely* unique. The claim reveals a good deal more than bruised English usage.

Thanks to studies in ethology and behavioral ecology, the religion of human uniqueness has sustained a series of notable setbacks in our lifetime. We have had to abandon a substantial list of "unique attributes": tool using and tool making, language, tradition and culture, abstraction, teaching and learning, cooperating and strategizing, and others less inflammatory, such as caring and compassion. There is not a lot left. But the ultimate fallback position, the central jewel in the human imperial crown, had always been our self-awareness. Then along came little Washoe.

Washoe, a chimpanzee, became famous as the first nonhuman being to learn the hand-sign language of the deaf and mute, a mode of communication seen by Allen and Beatrice Gardner, who raised Washoe, as more useful to a chimpanzee (because of its anatomy) than vocal signals (Gardner and Gardner 1969). (She was followed by a series of chimpanzees, gorillas, and orangutans who learned signing and some of whom taught it to their own offspring and the children of others. One orangutan taught signing to a human child.) Washoe dropped her historic bombshell one day while she was looking into a mirror. She was asked "Who is that?" She signed back, "Me, Washoe." Washoe was "self-aware."

The problem of self-awareness (or rather, the problem of our unrepentant claim, in spite of Washoe and many others, that beings who are not human do not have it) raises a number of issues. It strikes me that the role of self in nonhuman beings is profoundly different from its role in human cultures, most especially in the Western tradition. It seems to me that in our culture there is inordinate emphasis on the *individual* self, and that individual self inordinately emphasized is at the expense of other modes of self that it is possible to see in other beings. Such beings are not the slaves of ideology.

Naturalists have difficulty with this cultural preoccupation with the individual. In full awareness of an individual animal's sensibilities, its role as a vector of genetic material, and its many contributory activities within the natural multispecies community, naturalists perceive in the demeanor of a wild animal less a self-interested single entity, more a manifestation of *being*. It may be that loners, such as bears and tigers, are more evocative in this respect than more sociable species. But even these are not usually seen as mere self-serving individuals; they are seen as revelations of bearness, of tigerness, of wildness.

In highly gregarious animals such as flocking birds, the individual is lost not only to our sight but also to our awareness. Take an aggregation of sandpipers—dunlins, for example—foraging on an exposed tidal mudflat. Their coloring being what it is, even a large number of birds can easily go almost unnoticed—until they take flight. Then, flashing pale wing stripes en masse usually reveal that very many more birds were on the ground than we had thought. But that is the least of the dunlins' disclosures.

As we watch the little birds in the air, invariably we marvel at their speed and their extraordinary maneuverability. Always, too, we stare astonished at the marvelous synchrony of their movements. All change direction together. Rarely, it seems, is an individual out of phase with the others. No matter how often we have seen it, invariably we ask ourselves how in the world a flock of these mites contrives to twist and turn and rise and fall in such near-perfect unison. The operative word here is "how." Steadfast in subservience to our individualistic metaphysics, we ask *how the instructions are communicated*. How does each and every single bird know what it is supposed to do? By what means are the necessary commands (the political assumption of a "leader" is ineradicable) transmitted and received? And how can the individual bird act on them so swiftly?

Perhaps, if only in the interest of intellectual honesty and humility, it is time for us to acknowledge that we do not know what it is that determines the synchronous movements of a flock of shorebirds. We might just *consider* the possibility that this phenomenon is not mechanically based at all. Perhaps it is an aspect of being that arises from what we call consciousness.

But not from self-consciousness or self-awareness as we commonly know it. Our usual understanding of those terms is limited to the individual. It is difficult to imagine the instantaneous directional shifts of a flock of dunlins having been accomplished by dozens or hundreds of individuals, each moving independently, after having received, processed, interpreted, and acted in accordance with some mysterious "signal." That would be too much. Instead, I suggest that there is at play here some form of awareness that is shared across the entire group. The flock may be seen as having one consciousness. The individual bird (at least in the flocking season) would lose its individual identity in that of the group. For a time at least, it would *be* the group.

This speculation is supported by anyone who has ever watched a school of fish—not from above, but on their own plane and at close range. The flashing angles, turns, slants, starts, and stops are too swift, too fine-tuned, indeed too erratic, to be executed by the synchronized separate decisions of hundreds of individuals. I have marveled at this display many times, among many species of fishes, and have felt that the school is not a mere aggregation of individuals but a superorganism. It is composed of discrete physical parts, to be sure, but its behavior flows from one awareness, one consciousness, one self. In a psychological sense at least, the individual *is* the group. Flocking shorebirds and schooling fishes are manifestations of group consciousness.

There are species that gather together specifically for breeding purposes, and disperse thereafter. This is the way of many seabirds. It has been suggested that, at least in some species, successful reproduction in a given season may depend on the presence of a minimum density of breeding birds on site. When that critical mass is reached, a wave of sexual excitement moves through the colony, and the season's business commences. If for some reason the population of the colony falls below that level, the birds who remain may fail to come into full breeding condition. It is as though the colony itself were the reproductive unit, not the individual pair. The colony as a whole has its own physiological cycle, requiring a "trigger" to move it (the colony) into a reproductive mode. Like a flock of shorebirds or a school of fish, a seabird rookery may be understood as itself an entity, one qualitatively different from a mere aggregation of participating individuals.

It is a little more difficult, but no less valid, for us to perceive at least a temporary group identity in other forms of coalescence, such as those of the social insects, or the winter hibernacula of some snakes, or large bat roosts. Families of primates, of wolves, of hunting dogs, of lions, of whales, and of elephants, all behave as though, at least most of the time, the group is of "one mind" about conducting its daily affairs. Loose cannons among their members are unusual. Such groups retain their cohesiveness under most circumstances. Individuals make minor forays beyond the shifting core but are rarely out of touch. One way and another, the sundry parts of the greater whole keep in contact, as though maintaining the correct frequency to receive the behavioral consensus from moment to moment. A group consciousness prevails.

What of those whose way it is to be loners? Take bears, for example. Bears are not truly solitary, of course; adult females are usually accompanied by their most recent offspring. Males tend to forage alone, except when there is a feast of such auspiciousness as to draw them together—a salmon run, a beached whale, or, sadly, perhaps a garbage dump. Even though the animals do not ordinarily feed at such close quarters with one another, the richness of the bounty seems to offset any potential for quarrelsomeness. Usually such events are peaceable.

Even though bears forage so widely under normal circumstances, they appear to have some uncanny way of knowing where other bears are in the general area. Paul Shepard and Barry Sanders (1985, 8) have put it nicely in their *Sacred Paw:*

> If socialization is defined by living in packs or year-round mate association, then bears are solitary. But perhaps the net of bear sociality is cast so wide that primate observers like men, with their poorer senses of smell and hearing, cannot appreciate its subtlety and scale. If bears have in their heads a constantly revised map of the locations of other individual bears, should we not then consider them as truly socially oriented?

Both whales and elephants appear to be able to keep in touch over considerable distances by means of sound, using frequencies at or beyond the upper and lower limits of human hearing. Must we see these scattered solo bears, whales, and elephants as merely roaming individuals, or can we not accept them as constituting strands or knots in Shepard and Sanders' net of sociality, and by extension an unusually wide-cast but still coherent entity?

This possibility brings us toward Neil Evernden's evocative metaphor of "fields of self" (Evernden 1985, 35–54). The image of a field or a net of barren-ground grizzly beardom on the arctic tundra renders unnecessary and somewhat wrongheaded the attempt to force-fit the grizzly into a preconceived category of sociality. Individual bears are not so tightly coordinated in their movements as individual sandpipers, to be sure, but the difference may be one of degree, not of kind.

In suggesting the existence of a group self, a group self-awareness, and a group self-consciousness, I am downgrading the role of "other" in the social life of wild, whole beings. I am suggesting that the everyday consciousness of such beings, rather than being narrowly focused by each individual self, may receive the world as though through a wide-angle viewfinder that is shared by the collective. This is not to say that the widely postulated role of "other" is done away with at this level, because it may be seen, if we simply *must* see it, in, say, two howler monkey groups or two prides of lions roaring in concert. (This action is much more likely to be conventional sounding off to an audience that is temporarily more extended than usual. Both roar whether or not neighbors are around.)

What is being suggested here is that individual self-consciousness has come to be held in such untouchable esteem within our cultural ideology that we have largely forgotten or ignored the likelihood that it is no more than the most basic, radical, and fundamental form of self-awareness. And it may be not only the most basic form, but in an evolutionary sense also the oldest and most primitive, to use a word much favored by the human chauvinists. I would suggest that this most elementary form of consciousness underlies more enriched and mature forms in much the same way as the ancient so-called reptilian brain is said to underlie more recently developed cortical material. If we must speak in progressive terms, as is the custom in evolutionary biology, then we could see a consciousness of group-as-self as something of a development.

We *need* not see it that way, however. Individual self-consciousness serves an indispensable function for the newborn, for example. The newborn, as a sentient being, must presumably have some reference point for all that follows, and no doubt individual self is just that. But that isolated individuality is soon subordinated to the greater reality, which is that of the immediate family. Gradually the infant's self-centeredness metamorphoses into the consciousness of the group—or at the very least, of the parent at hand. Over time the infant ceases to see itself as the nucleus of the universe and begins to perceive itself as participating in a family-centered universe. Where the process moves from there depends entirely on the biology of the species in question. For bears, it is a loose arrangement; for primates, something tighter; for yellow jackets, something tighter still. For many species the influence of this form of consciousness waxes and wanes with the seasons.

We now arrive at a plateau that is a good deal more challenging. Beyond the consciousness of self-as-group could be posited a consciousness of self-as-community. Perhaps the word "self" need no longer be used here. As we have seen, the role of "other" already diminished as we entered the envelope of the group consciousness. At the level of the community, "other" is bereft of whatever abstract meaning or utility it may have had. In the functioning multispecies community, all participants are subjects; objective perception is no longer required (and indeed would inhibit apprehension of the world). There need be no other; the community is a whole unto itself.

This viewpoint will be seen by some as problematical, because when we set aside the concept of individual self we are at the same time abandoning the usual concept of "interest." In conventional thought, interest, like "other," is a necessary corollary of self. The economic bias of (unrelentingly competition-oriented) modern wildlife biology, for example, would have considerable difficulty in finding anything but self-interest in the behavior of individuals, species, groups of species, associations, and communities. For competitive striving is the basis of the economic model on which most contemporary ecologic (and evolutionary) interpretations rest.

Now, it is just as difficult for reductionist, number-crunching modern science to prove that nature is a free market economy as it is for me to prove that it is a compliant and cooperative community of socially interacting self-awarenesses. If, however, wildlife ecology were to award self-*identity* to populations and groups of species, it might be more persuasive in its attribution of self-interest to wild nature, and the implied function of the invisible hand in the natural marketplace. It seems that respectable life sciences are unable or unwilling to accommodate the concept of organisms' subjective interest in their personal well-being. Self-interest may be acknowledged (but only grudgingly) to the extent that it can be measured within a competitively constructed calculus.

It would seem undeniable, however, that the community that is a prairie pond or a mangrove island or an alpine meadow or a beech-maple-hemlock stand has an interest in the continuance of that association. If the individual has a consciousness of its self-interest, as it certainly does, and if that consciousness is extended to include the group, as it appears to be, then surely it is a very short (perhaps inevitable) step to individual awareness of self-as-multispecies community, with that awareness shared by all participants.

If all of the individual beings in a community share that total, greater consciousness, it is not unlikely that they may see individuals of their own and of coparticipating species not as "others" but as simultaneous coexistences or coexpressions of that place, perhaps as extensions of themselves.

When a fox draws a bead on a meadow vole, or a green-backed heron lines up a leopard frog, is the "intentionality" involved any whit different from that of a skunk digging white grubs or a tadpole nibbling algae? The dust-boiling, crunching, thumping impact of a lioness striking down a hartebeest is identical in kind, identical as a phenomenon, to the quick sharp selection of an inchworm by an oriole. Neither requires the objectification of "other." Every species eats; eater and eaten are equal coparticipants. Each *is* the community.

A coyote chases and catches a cottontail. This simple and discrete event involved two individuals. One attempted to obtain, and did so. One attempted to escape, and did not. In the course of the brief chase, both were propelled by self-aware motivations. Over those few seconds, the only consciousness in either mind, I should think, was that of simple, individual self. Group and community consciousnesses were set aside. But only momentarily. For one participant, self-awareness is no more. For the other, her immediate task accomplished, group consciousness returns with a rush; she trots denward with supper for her puppies. Later, in the evening, coyote singing will celebrate community being. Rabbits will hear, shrug, and go about their own participation.

As interpreted here, individual self, group self, and community self in living beings should not be construed as mutually exclusive, nor indeed (except in the specific case of the newborn) as either sequential or hierarchical. It is more likely that all three forms of consciousness are present and available in all wild beings at all times, and that a particular mode may be called on for temporary emphasis according to the exigency, opportunity, or requirement of the moment or the season.

It would poorly avail the coyote to go hunting in the individually self-conscious configuration. She would find little; community self would seem to be indicated for that purpose. When she spots the rabbit, she shifts down to the lowest individual self-other range only for as long as absolutely necessary to catch it—a matter of seconds. With her group and community self-awareness suspended, even for so brief a time, she is exquisitely vulnerable to those who at least occasionally prey on coyotes. Usually she gets away with her shift.

The coyote gets away with it because she knows her place. But her place is much more than the overturned stump at the forest edge under which her offspring wait. It is more than the rich floodplain meadow she systematically quarters for mice. It is even more than her intricate, filigreed web of pathways through the cornfields and the woodlots, along the ditches, under the crest of the hill, and around the pond. Her place is also the invisible sign of members of her extended family, and of other coyote acquaintances. It is the sign of foxes, and of weasels, and of cottontails. The calls of the red-tailed hawk overhead, the redwings in the marsh and the cicadas in the basswoods, the whisper of the trembling aspens and her own lightly bobbing shadow all identify not only her place, but her total essence, her very being. The coyote *is* her place; that place, her community, is a society of hundreds of kinds of plants and animals interacting together. And she knows it.

She was born with that knowledge. Awareness of self as individual, self as (same-species) group, self as (many-species) community inheres in all of us animals. The major differences in this respect between ourselves and the healthily integrated bears, monkeys, and coyotes is that our cherished individualism, celebrated at the expense of other (shared) selves, has left us stalled at an immature stage of social development. They remain whole. They know in their bones and viscera that they belong. We are taught that we do not.

Yet that teaching remains wholly in our heads. Our bones and viscera are intact, and *they* know better. They retain the ancient awareness of social as well as biological kinship with all that lives. Cruelly, our cultural and ideological inheritance, in its insistence on a qualitative separation between nature and human affairs, has deprived us of ready access to the multispecies, community sense of self. Our chauvinistic self-centeredness dictates that, as Raymond Rogers has put it, "all meaning is socially created by humans and that humans brought nothing with them from their previous relationships with nature" (Rogers 1994, 98).

Living is about interacting with one's living surround. Without constant, unceasing interplay with lives around us, like the prisoner in solitary confinement we are merely enduring. We may have been persuaded that the only living surround we need is the human community, but the condition of humankind today, to say nothing of the condition of nature, suggests otherwise.

It is possible for the individual human being to retrieve the natural awareness of belonging to something infinitely broader and richer than the narrow enclosure of our belief systems, to rediscover (it was there all the time) a self that freely and joyfully identifies with myriad nonhuman existences. That much I know. I do not know whether our culture can find either the courage or the humility to acknowledge any collective, multispecies, community sense of being that transcends our own kind. Chauvinist ideology—even in mere intrahuman affairs—dies hard.

aldo leopold as hunter and communitarian

FRANKLIN A. KALINOWSKI

THERE CANNOT BE TWO PASSIONS MORE NEARLY RESEMBLING

EACH OTHER, THAN THOSE OF HUNTING AND PHILOSOPHY: WHATEVER

DISPROPORTION MAY AT FIRST SIGHT APPEAR BETWIXT THEM.

—David Hume, *A Treatise of Human Nature,* 1888

EVERY contemporary discussion of environmental ethics that aims to be complete must include an analysis of Aldo Leopold's concept of a "land ethic." More than anything else, it is the land ethic that has contributed to making *A Sand County Almanac* a classic in modern environmental philosophy (Leopold 1970; further references to the *Almanac* in this chapter are cited by page number only). As this essay will try to demonstrate, Leopold's land ethic is part of a larger web of relationships that has as its center the idea of community. By focusing on Leopold's notion of community, we can better understand how his discussion of ethics, esthetics, and learning fit together. Furthermore, our understanding of Leopold becomes deeper and richer when we recognize that it is the idea of community that also attaches his philosophical analysis of ethics and esthetics to his personal observations on land, territory (what Leopold calls home range), and his passionate dedication to hunting as the activity best suited to link humans to their natural surroundings.

As someone whose house is decorated with guns, decoys, and the stuffed heads of animals overlooking bookshelves crowded with classics in political and ecological philosophy, I have shared experiences with Leopold that could lead me to an appreciation of the origins of his thought that may not be obvious to the non-hunter, and that Leopold himself may not have made explicit. As someone who has felt the anguish and anger of having boyhood duck marshes drained to make room for chemical plants, dunes adjacent to favorite surf-fishing sites bulldozed flat for seaside condominiums, and cherished deer woods leveled for housing projects, I know both the love that attaches a hunter to the land and the pain that comes when that community is despoiled. In this essay I try to follow Leopold in giving a philosophical exegisis of the idea of community, while not losing contact with the rootage in the land that acts as our emotional impetus.

THE IDEA OF COMMUNITY: ETHICS, ESTHETICS, AND EXPERIENCE

Aldo Leopold's concept of community is both inclusive and placed. It moves the discussion beyond the usual bounds that limit communities to only human members, and it fixes communities by making them rooted to a specific location. Similarly, there are two elements in Leopold's definition of community: one is fluid and the other is anchored. The concept is, therefore, both flexible and firm. Our response to membership in the community may change and expand, but the idea is not completely relativistic. Only those entities that have a certain relationship to a particular place are entitled to inclusion in the community.

The objective or fixed portion of the definition consists in the claim that a community comprises a collection of interdependent parts. For Leopold, the fact of interdependence, once recognized by humans, must lead us to expand our prior homocentric notion of community to include other members of the biotic system; but human interdependence with the biotic system exists whether or not humans recognize and respond to it. We humans, through ignorance or insensitivity, can refuse to be good *citizens* of our ecological communities, but we cannot alter the fact of our *membership*. The flexible, expandable component of Leopold's definition is found in the recognition and response that humans make to their communal membership. To be good *citizens* of our ecological communities requires three things: there must be an ethic founded in our instinctive moral sentiments, an esthetic that connects and sensitizes us to our surroundings, and experience to teach us to expand our environmental awareness while remaining rooted to the primitive origins of our social conscience. When this ethic, esthetic, and experience become coupled to the empirically verifiable fact of interdependence, the individual human has the qualifications for ecological citizenship. Final inclusion in the biotic community comes when persons become emotionally rooted to a place they can call their own.

When discussing ethics, Leopold used language that depicts emotions, feelings, or passions. The reader is told of his affection for a marsh; ethical relationships are said to presuppose love, respect, and admiration; and the basis of an ecological conscience is made to rest on "something we can see, feel, understand, love, or otherwise have faith in" (251). He argues that ethics cannot rest exclusively on reason or education, since these lead at best to "enlightened self-interest." According to Leopold, then, the foundation of ethics lies in the notion of an ethical conscience rooted in human passions. Whether he was aware of it or not, this view puts Aldo Leopold firmly within a historical tradition of some repute known as the "moral sense" school or the "theory of moral sentiments" (Callicott 1987, 190).

All moral sense theorists see morality as based on emotions or passions, and there is general concurrence within this school that these passions exist in the individual at birth. That is to say, morals are to be considered in some sense "instinctual." To make a morally correct choice is to select a course of action that excites pleasant feelings—a sense of satisfaction or "approbation"—within the moral conscience. Immoral acts generate the emotions of pain, guilt, or dissatisfaction, and are therefore usually avoided by ethically normal individuals. According to this school of thought, ethics involve a way of life that heightens our instinctively based moral sentiments. Ethics involve feeling the pleasure and pain of moral choices.

The place of esthetics in this scenario becomes clear if we accept a definition that was once offered to me: an esthetic experience is the opposite of an anesthetic experience. Viewed in this light, to be ethically anesthetized is to be made insensitive to both pain and pleasure, while being "esthetized" (to coin a word) indicates the process of increasing our level of emotional reaction. The esthetic experience is one that elevates our perceptual acuity. While objects that are usually viewed as "pretty" may serve this esthetizing function, Leopold unambiguously states that this is only the beginning of a process that "expands through successive stages of the beautiful to values as yet uncaptured by language" (102). The ethical experience and the esthetic experience are in many ways the same. Both are linkages to basic emotions. The boundaries of these passions can be expanded when training, education, and reason lead us to feel esthetic moral sentiments toward entities previously excluded from our consideration. This, for Leopold, is the relevance of an expanding ethical community. The ethical community is the range of entities toward which the individual feels an esthetic, moral relationship. Hence, ethics, esthetics, and community are simply three strands in an ever-expanding web of moral and emotional relationships in which humans become not only more ethical but more alert and alive. The potentially positive role of education and moral improvement consists in this expansion of the community.

With the development of civilization comes the associated increase in our understanding of ecological processes and the potential enlargement of our ethical and esthetic perception. "Ecological science has wrought a change in the mental eye," asserts Leopold. Comparing the potential of our twentieth-century sensitivity to the nineteenth-century perspective of Daniel Boone, Leopold says, "The incredible intricacies of the plant and animal community—the intrinsic beauty of the organism called America . . . —were as invisible and incomprehensible to Daniel Boone as they are today to Babbitt." Leopold then affirms the ethical value of this scientific training: "The only true development in American recreational resources is the development of the perceptive faculty in Americans" (291).

But Aldo Leopold was no unrestrained advocate of progress and civilization. Within Leopold's philosophy exist both a progressive and a primitive element. There are many contemptuous references in his work to the individual who is "supercivilized," a "shallow-minded modern," a Babbitt, or a "mechanized man, oblivious of floras, [and] proud of his progress" (227, 279, 291, 50). For Leopold, civilization has both positive and negative effects. On the one hand, it holds forth the possibility of expanding our sense of community by allowing us to see and, more important, to *feel,* the web of connections that unites the elements of ecosystems. On the other hand, the artifacts of civilization—the gadgets, specialized occupations, and massive institutions of industrialized society—threaten to disconnect us from the primal and atavistic origins of our ethical sentience. And for Leopold, when we become disconnected we become desensitized. Leopold fears that our species is becoming *too* civilized as the world is made increasingly "artificial." "Your true modern is separated from the land by many middlemen, and by innumerable physical gadgets. He has no vital relation to it. . . . Synthetic substitutes for wood, leather, wool, and other natural land products suit him better than the originals. In short, land is something he has 'outgrown'" (261–262). The function of the "conservation esthetic," therefore, is to preserve and expand the link between the environmental conduct of humans and their moral sense, rooted deep in the human conscience. The key to expanding our environmental ethics is the enlargement of our moral sense beyond humans, beyond even other sentient creatures, to include the entire biotic community—or, as he puts it, "the land." In order fully to realize Leopold's concept of citizenship in an ecological community, the sensitized individual must have an active engagement with a particular place.

A SENSE OF PLACE: LAND, PROPERTY, AND TERRITORY

There can be no doubt about Leopold's unwavering attachment to hunting and the venatic arts. From fondly recalled days of grouse hunting, to tales of his first duck kill, to stories of goose hunts in Mexico, to missed shots at deer with his homemade bow, the pages of his *Almanac* are replete with passages affirming Leopold's love of the hunt. Hunting is more than simply a "sport" or a hobby for him (indeed, with the exception of bow making, hunting is never mentioned during his discussion of hobbies); rather, it is an activity that deeply impressed itself onto his consciousness and became an integral part of how he viewed nature and wildlife. Most significant for our present discussion, hunting, for Leopold, is the model for how an ecologically sensitive person becomes linked to a particular portion of the biotic community.

In order to appreciate fully the role of hunting in Leopold's idea of community, the absolutely central role of land in his ecological philosophy must be emphasized. For Leopold, land is the basis of all food chains and the most fundamental element in "The Land Pyramid" (251, 258). It is the component upon which all else rests. At the same time, we need to recognize that the concept of land must be taken in its largest, most comprehensive sense. For Leopold, to view land merely as "soil" or as "property" is to engage in a dangerously false, myopic reductionism. Physical and philosophical subtleties here need to be appreciated. Biologically, "land" consists of "soil" *plus* the plants and animals connected with it, *plus* the energy flows that hold the web of relationships together. This diversity becomes an essential defining characteristic of land and leads Leopold repeatedly to assert that "land is not merely soil" (253, 255). Similarly, to look at land from a legalistic or economic point of view and to see only "property" is also to overlook qualities that Leopold holds essential as the basis for an ethical relationship. That is to say, if land is simply property, then a land *ethic* is (by definition) impossible. Bemoaning the current state of the human-to-land association, Leopold says: "There is as yet no ethic dealing with man's relationship to land and to the animals and plants which grow upon it. Land, like Odysseus' slave-girls, is still property. The land-relation is still strictly economic" (238). Something in the economic or property perspective on land shuts off the possibility of developing an ethic toward land. Leopold suggests the means for opening up that possibility: "It is inconceivable to me that an ethical relation to land can exist without love, respect, and admiration for land, and a high regard for its value. By value, I of course mean something far broader than mere economic value; I mean value in the philosophical sense" (261). We see again the emotional component of Leopold's ethical philosophy, this time directed toward the concept of land.

Another point that needs emphasis regarding Leopold's idea of land is his rejection of the position that the debate can be resolved into a discussion of "private" versus "public" property. The ecologically ethical community has nothing to do with philosophical conflicts between capitalism and socialism. Shifting the focus from an individual sense of ethical propriety to bureaucratic management of public property "contains no device for preventing good private land from becoming poor public land" (201). Leopold would, no doubt, concur with John Rodman's observation that, "as the human/nature relationship comes more into view, we begin to suspect that property *per se*, . . . whether private or public, may be an outer and visible sign of an alienated mode of existence" (Rodman 1977, 108). In all of these statements, Leopold is groping for some concept that will adequately capture the essence of the relationship between humans and land that is implied in the idea of being an active citizen of a biotic community.

To view land merely as "soil" is to overlook the myriad relationships that link various chemical and biological processes, and to view land simply as "property" seems also to miss some essential points. The questions are, What points are missed in these views, What alternative to "property" exists, and What is the intellectual source of this alternative? I think the concept of "territory" comes close to what Leopold is suggesting, and that Leopold's reliance on it stems from his experiences as a hunter.

What is there about viewing land as territory that distinguishes it from perceiving land as property? One difference is the fact that "territory" signifies a connection to the land that is emotional, personal, and extralegal. It implies a closeness and an intimacy that is the product of experience, history, and time, not the result of deeds, law, or other artifacts of a rational system. If one has the money, he or she can immediately own property; but the acquisition of territory, according to Leopold, takes "much living in and with" the land and the esthetic sensitivity gained only when you "live here for a long time" (180, 158).

Of course, it is entirely possible for a specific plot of earth to be *both* property and territory. The two ideas are not mutually exclusive, but neither are they the same. Leopold clearly felt a passionate sense of place with respect to the land and the "shack" that he owned in Sauk County. One can convert one's property into territory (hunting it year after year is one way to accomplish this), but it is also possible for someone to own land and never make it "their place." Conversely,

Leopold was far on his way toward developing the notion of land contained in the land ethic long before that day in May of 1935 when he became a legally recognized landowner.

A second differentiating characteristic between territory and land is the fact that territory cannot be bought or sold. In that sense, the possession of territory is inalienable. Territory, a sense of place, or "rootage," is not something easily acquired. Perhaps more significant, it is not something easily lost. Leopold makes the connection in reference to his first grouse kill. Years after the event he states, "I could draw a map today of each clump of bunchberry and each blue aster that adorned the mossy spot where he lay, my first partridge on the wing" (129). For ethical hunters, the kill produces something akin to a consecration. Good deer hunters, for instance, can locate with precision the exact spot where they made each of their kills. The death and the blood form a union between the hunter and the place that is emotional and extrarational. To talk of law, deeds, and money with regard to such a place is to trivialize and demean what occurred there. The language we use to describe the bond between the event and the spot is language that draws on the experience of the sacred. For that reason, severing the link is a feat no county clerk can accomplish. These first two reflections point to the legal and economic differences between territory and property.

A closer review of Leopold's work reveals some intriguing possibilities for extending the concept of territory in ways that the notion of property does not admit. For example, the concept of territory, unlike the idea of property, is not species specific. Only humans can own property, but many different animals can occupy a given piece of land, and their territorial claims can be and often are overlapping. In "Home Range," "Great Possessions," "Smoky Gold," "The Deer Swath," and elsewhere, Leopold displays the hunter's recognition that bedding areas, feeding sites, trails, rubs, and scrapes are all "signs" that others besides himself have territorial claims to the land. The act of hunting particularly emphasizes this point, since one of the primary goals of the hunter is to discover who else "possesses" his hunting grounds.

The concept of territory, therefore, moves us beyond individualistic and anthropocentric views of land, presenting novel possibilities for human and nonhuman relations. It needs to be recognized that when human animals drain wetlands, develop countryside, or destroy wilderness, they are ravaging land that belongs to someone else. Minimally, consideration and respect for the territory of others seems to be in order. And if territory rather than property is the appropriate category for ecological thought, then the historical, legal, and philosophical connection between "rights" and "property" that is so ingrained in Western thought leads one to wonder if current talk about animal rights does not simply perpetuate the mental habits that are the source of our current malaise. Perhaps a shift from viewing land as property to viewing it as territory may lead to the kind of interspecies relations that Leopold envisioned. We humans will probably always have some notion of legal ownership (private or public) and in that sense we may never move "beyond property" as John Rodman has hopefully suggested. What we can do is come to a realization that the philosophic faith in property and rights is eco-logically shallow and incomplete.

One final distinction between property and territory seems to follow from what has been said thus far. During his elaboration of the land ethic, in the sec-tion titled "Land Health and the A–B Cleavage," Leopold contrasts "man the con-queror *versus* man the biotic citizen . . . land the slave and servant *versus* land the collective organism" (260–261). If one accepts the previous discussion regarding territory, then it follows that the roles of conqueror and slave are philosophically and legally prohibited. A human or animal may *defend* its territory, but there is nei-ther the desire nor the ability to "develop" it. The desire is absent because the hunter (or deer, or squirrel) is quite content with the land's *present* use. It is "its place" to live, breed, eat, and be eaten. Of course, developing land that one does not own is both legally forbidden and economically foolish. Some interaction, im-pact, and management of land is unavoidable, but the final consequence of this discussion of territory seems to be that the human self-image of *Homo economicus* or *Homo faber* destroys both the land itself and the inner sensitivity that is neces-sary for producing this "biotic citizen."

The idea of territory is scattered throughout *A Sand County Almanac*. It is im-plicit in the entire book and comes near the surface at various points. We glimpse it in the wonderful opening paragraphs of "Great Possessions," when Leopold ridicules the county clerk, a "sleepy fellow" who naively believes that the author's "worldly domain" can be adequately measured by books, deeds, maps, and acres. "At daybreak," Leopold insists, "I am the sole owner of all the acres I can walk over" (44). It is there when Leopold discusses "Home Range," ponders the size of his "universe" as compared to that of other animals, and wonders, "Who is the more thoroughly acquainted with the world in which he lives?" At the end of this section the author reflects on human ignorance and animal "ownership." "Science knows little of home range: how big it is at various seasons, what food and cover it must include, when and how it is defended against trespass, and whether own-ership is an individual, family, or group affair" (84–86).

The concept of territory (as opposed to property) can also be found in the sections titled "Smoky Gold" and "Red Lanterns," where Leopold exhibits inti-mate familiarity with the flora and fauna of one of his favorite hunting spots. He reveals his delight in having an "undiscovered place" that other hunters pass by, leaving "the rest of us in peace. By 'us' I mean the birds, the stream, the dog, and myself." These sections are interesting for their combined use of the personified and the possessive. Leopold signals his attachment to the area by assigning human qualities to the stream, which is "a lazy one," winding through the alders "as if he would rather stay here than reach the river," and by calling the trees "my tama-racks," indicating an exclusivity in his relationship to this piece of land. (The hunt-ing spot being described, it should be mentioned, is located in Adams County, Wisconsin; the property that the Leopolds owned is in Sauk County.) "Smoky

Gold" and "Red Lanterns" link the act of hunting and a passionate attachment to a specific piece of land, but that land is territory, not property.

The foreword to *A Sand County Almanac* that Leopold wrote in 1947 spells out the goal of his work. "These essays are one man's striving to live by and with, rather than on, the American land. I do not imply that this philosophy of land was always clear to me. It is rather the end result of a life-journey." Leopold then describes the event that began his journey and that demonstrates for us the connection between land, territory, and hunting. "My first doubt about man in the role of conqueror arose while I was still in college. I came home one Christmas to find that land promoters, with the help of the Corps of Engineers, had dyked and drained my boyhood hunting grounds on the Mississippi River bottoms." How important was hunting in framing the worldview of Aldo Leopold? "Perhaps no one but a hunter can understand how intense an affection a boy can feel for a piece of marsh" (Callicott 1987, 282).

There is anger in Leopold's voice as he relates how his territory was defiled. The passions that the concept of territory summon forth can be not only those of attachment and love, but also those of moral outrage. Toward the end of the book, in the combative exhortation directed toward "Defenders of Wilderness," we find his call for activism. "A militant minority of wilderness-minded citizens must be on watch throughout the nation and vigilantly available for action." Those who are willing to defend wilderness are juxtaposed to "the shallow-minded modern who has lost his rootage in the land" (279). This appeal to a "rootage in the land," the phrase from which this volume draws its title, nicely summarizes Leopold's connection between the moral sense of an ethical community and a passionate, aggressive attachment to a territorial place. Leopold recognizes that resisting the spread of environmental destruction will almost certainly require individuals to defend land that is not "theirs" in the legal sense of property. Indeed, there is every reason to believe that protecting the environment will often entail defending the land *against* the actions of the people who *do* own it. This resistance and defense must call forth a devotion to the land that is essentially territorial. It requires moving beyond interactions with the land that are economic and individualistic to a relationship with a place built on the ethical obligations that one member of a community has toward another.

Something about the act of hunting increases the intensity of our passions and the acuity of our perceptions. The hunter is there not as an observer of the "other" but as a participant in an ecological community that includes prey and predator. There is a risk or possibility of failure and there are the "drums in the temples" produced by the realization of impending death (Mitchell 1980, 241). The hunter knows that almost any factor or event—the direction of the wind, the presence of a certain plant, a hoof impression in soft moss, the flushing of a distant bird, or the barely audible snapping of a dry twig—can prove to be of immense significance. In the words of Ortega y Gasset, the hunter is "The Alert Man" (Ortega 1972, 149). For Aldo Leopold, the hunter is filled with "keen delight"; outdoor recreation is "essentially primitive, atavistic"; "the trophy-hunter is the caveman reborn"; and "the true hunter is merely a non-creative artist" (204, 216, 294, 230). The hunter is engaged in an activity that is inherently "savage." For those, like Leopold, who come from a theory of moral sentiments and feel that humans must preserve the ethical wilderness within themselves, the hunter is the person least attached to the gadgets and comforts that separate and desensitize contemporary humanity. Hunting is the most uncivilized thing a modern person can do. "The deer hunter habitually watches the next bend; the duck hunter watches the sky-line; the bird hunter watches the dog; the non-hunter does not watch" (224). It is this capacity to excite perceptual sensitivity that makes hunting the ultimate esthetic and ethical experience. It is the emotional link between the hunter and his territory that acts as the example of an alternative form of relationship between humans and the land.

CONCLUSION

Aldo Leopold would have been the last person to claim that hunting must inevitably or automatically lead to a territorial connection with the land and an expansion of our sense of ethical community. He was as aware as anyone of the existence of insensitive, unethical, "slob" hunters. Hunters can become as ecologically anesthetized by the artifacts of civilization and progress as nonhunters. When this occurs, both the person and the activity are degraded. "Voluntary adherence to an ethical code elevates the self-respect of the sportsman, but it should not be forgotten that voluntary disregard of the code degenerates and depraves him." Such hunting in the absence of a self-directing moral code "is not only without social value, but constitutes training for ethical depravity elsewhere" (212, 213).

As sure as Leopold was of the existence of a moral line demarcating ethical and unethical hunting, he could not locate it and its cause with precision. Clearly, he had little sympathy for those hunters who go afield "draped . . . with an infinity of contraptions." Civilized hunters—a model that Leopold personified—are civilized because of their intellectual acumen, not as the result of modern inventions that distance them from the ascetic origins of their activity. It was when hunting threatened to become "modern" that it incurred Leopold's censure. It was when hunters forgot the essentially esthetic reason why they were in the woods that they invited Leopold's disdain.

These qualifications do not detract from the immense significance that hunting played in the life and philosophy of Aldo Leopold. Devoid of its hunting tales, the passionate attachment to fondly remembered hunting grounds, and the intensely sentient moral and esthetic theory derived from ducks, grouse, and wolves killed, *A Sand County Almanac* would not be the same book. Reason, intellect, and education are never disparaged in Leopold's work; but throughout, we learn that ecological perception and sensitivity also contain an instinctive, irrational, emotional component. The "biotic citizen" who "cannot live without wild things" is not a self-interested logician but a whole, passionate human being. Healing our environmental wounds requires that we move beyond viewing nature as merely a collection of entities "out there," belonging to someone else, that we picture as more or less "scenic." It means the rejection of passive notions of individual values where being "moral" comes to mean little more than intellectually distancing ourselves from the consequences of our behavior. For Leopold, ethical citizenship necessitated accepting the duties and responsibilities of active, participatory membership in a larger community of interdependent parts. In a contemporary society all too fascinated with the material pleasures of civilization and all too unsympathetic with the rich heritage of its hunting past, it is a process of "building receptivity into the still unlovely human mind" (295).

aldo leopold and the values of the native

GREGORY COOPER

BECOMING native to this place, to borrow Wes Jackson's useful phrase, is a matter of recognizing dual citizenship. It involves the realization that one lives in the midst of a human *and* an ecological community, and the successful native manages to integrate into both. This essay explores the following question: What kinds of values would we expect the successful native to embody? In the process, I propose to take Aldo Leopold as my exemplary native. There are several reasons for choosing Leopold. He was the first to explicitly advocate recognition of this dual citizenship. Furthermore, he remains today, despite fifty years of concerted effort to advance the debate, one of the clearest voices among the cacophony calling for an elevation of environmental consciousness. Again, Leopold realized that the most crucial, and in many ways the most problematic, environmental issues involve local land-use decisions among the private sector—decisionmaking "on the back forty," as he liked to call it. This emphasis on the local scene is important for our purposes because, as Jackson's phrase emphasizes, the native becomes native to *this* place, to a specific and concrete mix of human and ecological circumstances. Finally, Leopold had an uncanny knack for settling in, for distilling patterns in land-use practices and their relations to the ecological fundamentals of a landscape, whether the wild American Southwest or the dairy country of southern Wisconsin.

Let us begin, then, with the human community. What kinds of value commitments might integration into the human community involve? We see at once that this is a huge question, and that to a significant degree it is synonymous with one that philosophers have pursued for millennia: What is the nature of the ethical life? Not surprisingly, Leopold, a forester and wildlife biologist by trade, is of little help here. Instead, we must turn to the philosophical tradition. Broadly speaking, philosophers have given us two kinds of answers. Modern moral theory, beginning, say, with Kant, has tried to offer a thin and relatively content-free characterization of the ethical life: it is whatever life one chooses to lead, provided that it does not venture outside the bounds of the morally permissible, that is, provided it does not transgress on the ethical lives of others. In contrast, virtue ethics, which traces back to Plato and Aristotle, offers a thicker, more substantive characterization of the ethical life: it is the virtuous life—and the virtues, on this view, can be positively described.

The differences between these views for the life of the native are significant. Modern moral theory is relatively silent about the kinds of communitarian involvements required. There is no special reason, at least no moral reason, to be attentive to the projects and aspirations of one's neighbors; from the standpoint of modern moral theory, the ethical native could as well be a hermit. Community is much more important for virtue ethics. The virtuous character values friendship, camaraderie, and a sense of identification with the lives of neighbors. Of course, each of these ethical conceptions has its own strengths and weaknesses. Modern moral theory, by virtue of its pursuit of relatively thin constraints on the ethical life, stands a better chance of grounding its prescriptions in the dictates of rationality alone. But it pays the price of being largely silent on what might be taken to be the fundamental question for ethics: How should one live? Virtue ethics has a great deal to say about this question, but it can do so only by making quite substantive, and some would say controversial, assumptions about human nature.

I have no intention here of joining the debate between these two conceptions. Instead, I want to focus on the ecological side of becoming native to this place. I mention the philosophical project for two reasons: first, to underscore the fact that the values of the native, by virtue of becoming native to a *human* community, will include ethical values as they have traditionally been understood in philosophy, and second, because the most prominent efforts at uncovering the ecological values of the native have themselves been modeled after the more traditional ethical inquiries—and the above contrast between thick and thin theories has been reproduced in this literature as well. I will use this thick-versus-thin framework to give a broad overview of the kinds of projects which, if successful, would enable us to say something concrete about the evaluative life of the ecological native.

In his *Sand County Almanac,* Leopold was the first to call for recognition of the fact that we are "plain members and citizens of the biotic community". He was also the first to call for a land ethic that would reflect these newly expanded communitarian horizons. What is the nature of this new kind of community? Who are its members and what are the bonds that unite them? Most important, what is this new ethic, this "new thing under the sun," that Leopold is calling for? It looks as though there is another distinctively philosophical project here; moreover, a project for moral theory. Morality is the glue that binds human communities. What new kind of moral glue is required by a land ethic? Philosophers have taken up the challenge with characteristic zeal, and the result has been a wide range of proposals for redefining our ethical relations with nature. Some of these approaches have little direct connection to Leopold as an intellectual ancestor, others are self-conscious attempts to explicate his views, but at a fundamental level they share a common strategy—to extend patterns of moral thought familiar from the human case to the citizens of the new biotic community, and sometimes beyond.

The thinnest extensionist projects simply rework a bit the more traditional criteria for membership in the moral community. Thus, Tom Regan (1983) develops a Kantian rights-based approach that includes (at least) most other mammals by (1) arguing that the traditional criterion for moral standing, rationality, will not work, and (2) substituting other cognitive criteria such as the capacity to experience emotions and to have a sense of the future. Peter Singer (1992) extends utilitarianism to all manner of sentient creatures by pointing out that the capacity to suffer is by no means restricted to humans. The thickest extensionist projects typically involve some kind of ecological holism. Laura Westra (1994) is a good example. She invokes a kind of Aristotelean teleology at the level of the ecosystem—a kind of ecosystem flourishing. This in turn determines the virtuous path for ecosystem development in much the same way that human flourishing grounds the virtuous human life for Aristotle. In between these extremes are views such as Paul Taylor's (1986) biocentric individualism. Roughly, Taylor identifies an Aristotelean principle of flourishing for all organisms (he calls each a teleological center of life) and on that basis generates a rights-based stance that grants moral standing to each and every citizen in the biotic community—though not, as in Westra's case, to the community itself.

As with anthropocentric morality, there are strengths and weaknesses in each approach, and the seemingly interminable discussion of the relative merits of the various candidates has turned environmental ethics into something of a cottage industry. Again, I will steer clear of that debate as much as possible. I want, simply, to ask: Does any of this help us to better understand what it might mean, from an ecological standpoint, to become native to this place? Can any of these philosophical theories help us identify the land-use decisions of the genuine native? If an environmental philosophy is to be worth cultivating, it must do more than stand up to the harsh climate of intellectual criticism, it must also bear fruit; it must guide deed as well as thought. It is time to descend from these lofty abstractions and ponder, for a moment, some earthy examples, cases where the wisdom of the native is challenged and the question of what to do on the back forty can be raised in a quite specific manner.

Suppose, for example, that our native has a small dairy farm in northern Wisconsin, and that a black bear has decided that her best option for putting on enough fat to carry her through winter hibernation and the birth of cubs is to dine each night in our farmer's cornfield—with the (quite realistic) result being that the expected yield from the cornfield will be cut by, say, 40 percent. What would the genuine native do? Hunt and kill the bear himself? Arrange to have some local bear hunters hunt his land? Suffer through the crop damage and hope to collect sufficient compensation from the state to replace the missing feed? (I am supposing, as is typically the case in Wisconsin these days, that trapping and relocation is not a viable option.)

As another case, consider the introduction of exotics. Would the genuine native release, for example, the nonnative ring-necked pheasant on the farm, perhaps with the goal of developing a huntable population, or maybe just to make the landscape a more interesting place? Or suppose the farm pond is choked by milfoil (itself a pesky exotic). Would the genuine native consent to the introduction of imported grass carp to consume the unwanted vegetation? (Releasing fertile grass carp is probably illegal, but in North Carolina, at any rate, the use of sterilized grass carp has become a rather common response to milfoil outbreaks.)

Or consider agricultural practices in general. Would the genuine native abandon the traditional practice of monoculture agriculture? What about the use of commercial fertilizers? Agricultural chemicals? And if the answers to these questions are not clear-cut, can we say what further kinds of considerations would clarify the issue? Here are two specific, and actual, cases to ponder. For some years now Aldo Leopold's daughter, Nina Leopold Bradley, has been continuing the reestablishment of native prairie communities that Leopold himself began some sixty years ago. She has targeted the roadside ditches in the area around the famous "shack" in central Wisconsin. Before planting the native species, she first sprays the ditches with a systemic herbicide such as Roundup to kill the existing vegetation cover; if one didn't do something to set back the existing vegetation, the native plants would never become established. A related case, and one that I know firsthand, involves the management of waterfowl production areas (sites purchased by the federal government, typically with duck stamp dollars, and set aside as duck nesting habitat). The Wisconsin Department of Natural Resources manages a number of WPAs for the federal government, using the following overall management strategy. The ultimate goal is to establish dense stands of native grasses (primarily switchgrass) that can serve as dense nesting cover for upland nesting ducks such as mallard and teal. To achieve this goal, the uplands surrounding the ponds are burned in the spring. After burning, when the new grass is about six inches high, the uplands are sprayed with a herbicide. (Again, a systemic poison such as Roundup is the chemical of choice; however, when I was involved, we used the contact poison paraquat because, though less effective, it was cheaper.) After the herbicide is applied, or sometimes just before, the uplands are seeded with switchgrass. If all goes well (the exception, not the rule), dense and practically monocultural stands of switchgrass results. The question, then, is what would the genuine native think of such land-use practices?

As a final kind of case, suppose the back forty is a woodlot. What kinds of forestry practices would the genuine native employ? Would there be no cutting? Would there be a sequence of cutting and planting designed to take the woods back to some prior state, say to its condition in pre-European North America? Would the native use established timber stand improvement (TSI) practices so as to maximize yield in board feet? Would there be any clear-cutting? Again, definitive judgments here may require further details, so I will relate an actual case. I have a friend, call him the Colonel, who owns a farm in the Piedmont of North Carolina. The farm is mostly wooded, and the woods are mostly glorious stands of mature hardwoods, primarily oaks. One day the Colonel had a timber sale. He clear-cut about half his total woods and planted the resulting rubble in pines. His reasons were primarily economic; the hardwoods were in fact mature, and pines make a better replacement crop because they grow quicker and the market for southern hardwood is poor. It is also true, however, that the pine plantations will increase the diversity of habitat types on the farm. The question: Is the Colonel's decision to clear-cut the oaks and plant pines the kind of decision we might expect from the genuine native?

Can the philosophical theories, which are supposed to articulate a new ethical relationship with the natural world, an *environmental* ethic, guide the kind of back-forty decisionmaking illustrated by these examples? I doubt it. In the remainder of this chapter I will outline the reasons for my pessimism and sketch what I see as a more promising direction for future inquiry.

Begin with the thinnest conceptions of this new ethic, with attempts to extend modern moral theory to certain nonhuman animals. Such views have had difficulty with line drawing—with making principled decisions about which kinds of animals gain admission into the community of moral patients and which animals are left out. If one sets this problem aside, however, the animal liberationist views have one central virtue over thicker conceptions of environmental ethics: they imply concrete imperatives for specific situations. Take the case of the cornfield-raiding bear. On any animal liberationist view, the bear would be included among those beings with moral standing. Although the bear would be, in this sense, a moral patient, she is clearly not a moral agent; it would be unreasonable to expect her to act in accordance with a moral code. In fact, the bear occupies a position in the moral framework similar to that of a severely retarded human being. Suppose that, instead of the bear, a morally incompetent human had escaped from a nearby mental hospital, taken up residence in our farmer's woods, and was engaged in destruction of the cornfield. For the animal liberationist, executing the bear for its cornfield excursions would be no different, from a moral standpoint, than executing the human. And the same clear-cut prohibition would apply if the damage were being done by a less glamorous species, such as deer, raccoon, or squirrel, provided they have passed the threshold of moral patiency.

So the local implications of the animal liberationist approach are relatively straightforward. But there are two problems. First, as we have seen, modern moral theory in the domain of human relations can be criticized on the ground that the implications are too few and far between—it never really gets around to addressing the fundamental question of how one should live. A similar point holds for those views that extend modern moral theory to certain nonhumans: the implications are too few and far between—the theory never directly addresses the question of how to live on the land. Thus, animal liberationism has little or nothing to say about the other cases raised above. In fairness to those who press these views, it must be acknowledged that they typically make no pretense of giving such advice; they are not talking about how to live on the land except insofar as that life impinges on the lives of other moral patients. We could leave the matter at that, using the animal liberationist for a partial account of the ecological values of the native and turning to thicker conceptions of environmental ethics for the rest, were it not for the second problem.

The second problem is this: where the implications of animal liberationism for the life of the ecological native *are* clear, they are also, it appears, implausible. As a number of writers have pointed out (Callicott 1980; Sagoff 1995), there is considerable tension between the imperatives of animal liberation and the imperatives of an ecological view of the land. In particular, animal liberationists are compelled, by their own ethical principles, to take a dim view of predation when the prey happen to be moral patients. This clearly applies to predation by humans who, being moral agents, are in a position to know better. But it also applies, apparently, to nonhuman predators. Although the nonhuman predators are not morally culpable (they are not, after all, moral agents), the death of moral patients as a result of nonhuman predation is still a moral evil. If we can prevent it without inflicting a similarly serious transgression against the predator, then we ought to do so. If we can slow the predation of moose on Isle Royal by feeding the wolves pellets of soy protein, then we ought to do so. But predation is an essential, perhaps *the* essential, ecological interaction. If the values of the ecological native are to be driven by a newly perceived membership in the *ecological* community, and if Leopold is to be our exemplary native, then animal liberationism fails as even a partial articulation of these values.

The thickest versions of extensionism, those that promote moral obligations to ecosystems themselves, have pretty much the opposite problem. Whereas the back-forty imperatives of the animal liberationist are clear, if unhelpful, the back-forty imperatives of the ecosystem holist are virtually impossible to determine. The holist typically posits some notion of ecosystem integrity or fitness that is supposed to be key in determining right actions—one ought to do whatever maximizes, or least threatens, this integrity or fitness (see, for example, Rolston 1987 and Westra 1994). But just what this integrity or ecosystem fitness is remains a mystery. Would our pond ecosystem be better off, in terms of this teleological characteristic, with just one exotic (the milfoil) or with two (the grass carp eating the milfoil)? Would our WPA uplands have more integrity or fitness if we burned and sprayed and tried to establish monocultural stands of native switchgrass, or would it be better if we simply fenced out the cattle (and the people) and let nature take its course? Has the Colonel compromised the integrity or fitness of his woodlots by clear-cutting his oaks and planting pine? If so, why? Would TSI have been less of an affront? As far as I can determine, the answers to these questions are not forthcoming on the duties to ecosystems approach, because it has not identified the ecological characteristics in terms of which such answers could be determined. The most we are typically told is that integrity or fitness is something that ecosystems acquire in the fullness of evolutionary time and in the absence of anthropogenic influence. This yields a kind of generic imperative: always act so as to minimize human influence. But such a principle will be of little help in back-forty decisionmaking, where the question is how to live on the land, not how to isolate one's life from it.

Finally, we come to the intermediate approaches, such as Taylor's biocentric individualism. Not surprisingly, these approaches inherit both kinds of problems. The clear duties are there. All organisms, even the tiniest of microbes, are moral patients; thus their interests must be considered in any decisionmaking situation. Unfortunately, the clear duties are there with a vengeance. They come streaming in from all quarters, issuing ultimately in a kind of cognitive gridlock from which one's overall duty is simply incalculable. Consider the Colonel's two woodlots. Since it is doubtful, on this view, whether his desire to turn a buck would ever justify the massive destruction of life that even a little selective cutting would bring about, allow me to change the example slightly. Suppose, to modify one of Taylor's favorite examples, that the Colonel wants to donate one of the woodlots as the site for a new children's hospital. To build the hospital, one of the two sites will have to be cleared, which will result in the death of billions of organisms. Thus, in and of itself, the clearing of the site constitutes a moral evil. The Colonel must decide which of the two clearing operations constitutes the lesser evil, and that means, on Taylor's view, counting organisms—*all* of the organisms. He is faced with compiling, in effect, the mother of all environmental impact statements. Even if we set aside other problems (such as the intuition that the sheer number of organisms—from microbes to moose—is not the relevant issue for the ecological native), the biocentric individualist has swamped our cognitive resources to the point where only a kind of moral paralysis can result. There is little prospect for articulating the ecological values of the native from this direction.

This brief turn through philosophical attempts to extend anthropocentric ethics to the land hardly constitutes an argument that no such effort will succeed. I do hope it motivates the idea that it might be useful to look in other directions, and that is what I propose to do in the remainder of this chapter. Rather than making Leopold's land ethic, or some alternative ethics of nature, philosophically respectable by grounding it in established patterns of moral thought, perhaps it is time to look directly at the kinds of environmental values the ecological native might plausibly espouse. Here we can use Leopold as a guide. His ecological native cares about stability, integrity, and beauty, and we can ask, What would it mean for the ecological native to pursue these values on the back forty?

Consider, first, what appears to be the most tractable of the three values—stability. This is clearly an ecological notion and a substantial ecological literature on the topic exists. Unfortunately, ecologists apply the concept of stability to a number of different phenomena, including individual populations, assemblages of populations (that is, biological communities), forms of community organization such as trophic structure, and ecosystems. Furthermore, stability is used in different ways in these different circumstances. Finally, there is controversy over the causal relationships between these various senses of stability and other ecological characteristics, the most famous being the tedious debate over the relationship between stability and diversity. The upshot is that no single, straightforward notion of stability can be co-opted to articulate the values of the native. Perhaps there is a family resemblance among these various conceptions that is rooted in the idea of constancy, and on that basis one can articulate a provisional principle of constancy to guide land-use decisions. Slobodkin (1979, 80) formulates such a principle as follows: "Constancy of environmental variables generally represents, if not a good position, at least a non-deteriorating one. Any failure of constancy in the absence of strong evidence to the contrary must be considered as a danger sign."

One might object that change, in both ecological and evolutionary time, is part of the very nature of biological phenomena. The proposed principle, by valuing the status quo, is running against the very nature of nature. The proper response to such a worry is already hinted at in Slobodkin's remarks: the principle formulates a *ceteris paribus* value that is subject to being overridden by other kinds of evaluative considerations.

The second element of the land ethic, integrity, is even more troublesome. We have already seen how failure to identify ecosystem integrity with specific ecosystem characteristics leads to problems. How are we to recognize integrity when we have it, or more important, identify those situations where we are losing it? We can solve the problem by taking a clue from Leopold. His usual formulation of the land ethic is in terms of stability, integrity, and beauty, but he sometimes substitutes "productivity" for "integrity" (Leopold 1970, 199). Productivity (more precisely, primary productivity) is a recognizable ecosystem characteristic—essentially it is the capacity of the land to turn solar radiation into biomass. We can use it to formulate another provisional decision principle: other things being equal, act so as to enhance the productivity of the land. It is crucial that this principle be given a *ceteris paribus* formulation as well. Increased productivity is not always a good thing: the milfoil outbreak in our pond example probably increased the primary productivity of the pond.

The third component of the land ethic, beauty, is in a different category from the first two. It is less susceptible to a purely biological rendition. Nor is the established philosophical field of aesthetics of much help; it has a long tradition of focusing on the aesthetics of human artifacts rather than on the aesthetics of nature. We can make some headway, however, by turning once again to Leopold. He speaks frequently of a "refined taste in natural objects," and it is evident that, for him, the single most important factor in developing this aesthetic sense is an understanding of the natural processes that have shaped, and continue to shape, the land. One of the major goals of Leopold's undergraduate course in wildlife ecology was to foster this refined taste. Here is how he explained it to his students:

> If the individual has a warm personal understanding of the land, he will perceive of his own accord that it is something more than a breadbasket. He will see land as a community of which he is only a member, albeit now the dominant one. He will see the beauty, as well as the utility, of the whole, and know the two cannot be separated. We love (and make intelligent use of) what we have learned to understand.
>
> Hence this course. I am trying to teach you that this alphabet of "natural objects" (soils and rivers, birds and beasts) spells out a story, which he who runs may read—if he knows how. Once you learn to read the land, I have no fear of what you will do to it, or with it. And I know many pleasant things it will do to you. (Leopold 1991, 337)

Thus the native learns to read the story of the land, the story that constitutes this place. In the process, she comes to value, in this aesthetic sense, the characters of the story. We can use this idea to formulate our third provisional principle: other things being equal, the richness of ecological interaction and coevolutionary relationship in the community should be preserved, with special consideration given to rareness. This principle has the immediate corollary that the components of these biological relationships (primarily the individual species) and contexts that permit their continued existence (the relevant parts of the communities) should be preserved as well.

These principles are just a beginning. Still, a number of things can be said on their behalf. Since they simply attempt to render Leopold's formulation of the land ethic more explicit, they remain within the spirit of his environmental philosophy. Furthermore, they leave traditional morality in place to do what it does best, speak to the interactions among people. Finally, they allow us to make some headway in understanding what it might mean to, as Gary Snyder puts it, "live well on the land." To illustrate this relevance to back-forty decisionmaking, I will close with a brief look back at our examples.

Let us begin with the Colonel. The timber harvest is certainly a short-term disruption of the constancy of environmental variables. But it is likely not a long-term violation of the stability principle. The southern yellow pine forest toward which the harvested portion of the farm is now headed is itself well represented throughout the region. So although it is probably not the natural climax community for this site, it does represent a stable and natural alternative. It is also likely that the faster-growing pines will enhance the overall productivity of the farm. Furthermore, since the farm will now manifest two regionally common forest types—the oak-dominated deciduous woods and the southern yellow pine forest—with their associated flora and fauna, the overall biodiversity, hence the aesthetic value according to the third principle, will be enhanced. Here a caveat about aesthetics must be noted. The principle above is only part of what is involved in a "refined taste in natural objects." Leopold, for example, confesses a special love for white pine, which he tried unsuccessfully to analyze. Something similar may be at work on the Colonel's farm. From the standpoint of this "gut-level" aesthetic judgment, one might find the hardwoods superior to the pine forest—especially if the pine forest has the look of a plantation. (To avoid this look, the Leopold family often threw a handful of rocks while planting pine; a tree would be planted where each rock landed.)

With regard to the switchgrass and native prairie example, the crucial question concerns the long-term and otherwise hidden effects of the chemicals. The chemicals in the examples are supposed to break down rapidly on contact with the soil. If that is not the case, if there are long-term adverse effects, they will likely be manifest in dramatic population declines for certain species and/or reductions in productivity, and the first two principles will apply. This is an empirical issue that I will not explore, but it should be noted that uncertainty can never be totally eliminated, and the potential aesthetic gain from reestablished native grassland communities might be worth a certain degree of risk (though the pursuit of monocultural switchgrass stands is too narrowmindedly focused on the production of ducks). I should also mention that the relationship between these Leopoldian principles and the currently popular concept of sustainability is an important direction for future research, which will be especially relevant to the agricultural examples.

The introduction of exotics is always, prima facie, a violation of the aesthetics principle, and it is risky with respect to the other two principles as well. But there are exceptions. While our native would surely be reluctant to break new ground in the introduction of exotics, when a nonnative species has shown itself capable of integrating nicely into new surroundings (as with the pheasant in ecosystems of the Midwest and Great Plains), I can see no problem with releasing them on the back forty. The case of the grass carp raises, once again, a crucial empirical question: How reliable are the sterilization procedures? Two wrongs do not make a right, but if the sterilization is reliable, the introduction of the fish could bring an element of stability to the pond. If, on the other hand, fertile fish are released and they or their offspring manage to get into surrounding watersheds, it could be more disastrous than the introduction of the European carp.

Finally, we come to the bear. Nothing about the three principles speaks directly to the hunting issue. Of course, hunting may be used as a form of population control in the service of goals indicated by one or more of the principles, but the genuine native might find other ways to achieve such population control. The specific question about the black bear in the cornfield depends a great deal on context, on the larger place within which the farm is situated. If bear populations are regionally stable, then the principles offer no obstacle to killing the bear. Still, it may well turn out that the native is willing to pay the price for sharing her farm with such distinguished company—this, once again, is a matter of the particular shape "a refined taste in natural objects" might take.

Let us take stock. The genuine native recognizes that this place, this home, is simultaneously a human and an ecological community; this is the insight that traces back to Leopold. We expect that this realization will issue in a certain kind of life on the land, a kind of life we would like to encourage. This essay is about what such a life would look like—specifically, about the kinds of values that would guide it and give it shape. I have made three fundamental points. First, we should not forget that dual citizenship means membership in both a human and an ecological community, and that the former involves moral implications in the old-fashioned anthropocentric sense. This fact, together with an increased appreciation of the extent to which practices on the back forty have an impact on one's neighbors, should already give substantial shape to the normative life of the native. At present only the broad outlines of this shape are discernible. This is because the environmental ethicists, who might be expected to flesh it out, have been after bigger game. Exploring how our relationships with other humans constrain the ways to "live well on the land" has been largely forsaken in terms of the more ambitious task of extending morality into the nonhuman realm.

From the standpoint of understanding the values embodied in the life of the genuine native, we are left doubly in the dark. Not only does the human side of becoming native to this place remain mostly unexplored, but—and this is my second fundamental point—there are serious grounds for skepticism about the utility of moral extensionism in clarifying the ecological side as well. The discussion of the four types of cases suggests that, when it comes to specific practices on the back forty, the various versions of extensionism give either counterintuitive advice or no advice at all. Hence my third fundamental point: it is time to look elsewhere, and I believe Leopold is a good place to start. If we can resist the temptation to shoehorn what he says into the form of some recognizable philosophical theory, I believe we will find that he says a great deal that is relevant to our original question. The principles of stability, integrity, and beauty set out above, though provisional and tentative, represent a beginning down this road.

biological explanations
and environmental expectations
KRISTIN SHRADER-FRECHETTE

AT night I don't count sheep. Instead, soybeans and alfalfa, tobacco and potatoes row my mind, unbroken mile after mile beside the two-lane country road in Kentucky where I grew up. No one I knew on that winding, rolling, long lane of farmers ever had a fence—except to pen horses or cattle. Not the Hebels, not the Bischoffs, not the Sullivans, not the Maguires. Few fences existed in that geometry of my childhood. Years and miles and babies later, I had my own home in California. It never felt like home, perhaps because every row of broccoli or avocados or oranges or grapes was broken. Even neighborhoods, tiny little quarter-acre plots, were broken by fences. I came to dislike that geometry of my adulthood. "Something there is that doesn't love a wall, that wants it down" (Frost 1967, 34).

Biology, however, taught me that theoretical fences could be good. They could mark the boundaries of biotic communities. They could draw the outer limits of biological units of interdependence. If we knew the boundaries, we would know the biotic communities and therefore what interactions we ought to preserve and protect. Seeing the unseen fences surrounding scrub communities or wetlands communities could enable us to protect them, tell us when and where we ought not to interfere. Indeed, a whole field of biology, community ecology, has as its premise the centrality of the biotic community.

Even though biological science and preservation practice require theoretical fences to circumscribe biotic communities, our biological knowledge unfortunately does not match our environmental need. There is no clear biological notion of "biotic community" to justify many of our conservation decisions. No easily theorized fences mark off community units. In this essay I review the conceptual and scientific obstacles to developing an unambiguous community concept and show how to proceed, in the absence of this community concept, to provide foundations and boundaries—fences—for environmental preservation and definition of the communities we need to protect.

Why has community ecology—so far—been unable to arrive at a general theory having adequate power to explain and predict the structure and behavior of biotic communities? One reason is that ecologists have defined and used two of the concepts most basic to community ecology—"community," and "stability" or "balance"—in ambiguous and often inconsistent ways. Pimm, for example, lists five different ways in which ecologists think about the stability concept: in terms of (1) variables returning to initial equilibrium, (2) how fast they return following a perturbation, (3) the time a variable has a particular value, (4) the degree to which a variable is changed following a perturbation, and (5) the variance of population densities over time (Pimm 1984, 321–326). Not only are these five meanings partially inconsistent, but they do not all assume same-state variable or parameters. Moreover, despite the fact that we are able to trace some of the ways in which the community and stability concepts appear to have changed over time, historical and philosophical analysis reveals no definitive meaning for these two central terms (McCoy and Shrader-Frechette 1992, 84–99; Shrader-Frechette and McCoy 1993, ch. 2). Building a general theory of community ecology on such ambiguous, inconsistent, or unclear terms is like building a skyscraper on sand. Or, as one *Science* author put it several decades ago, "It is highly improbable that a group of individuals who cannot agree on what constitutes a community can agree to get together for international cooperative research on communities" (McIntosh 1985, 216). Much foundational work remains to be done.

Of course, complete agreement on the meaning of key terms and concepts is not essential for all communication in science. As Hull points out, "weasel words" are important to scientists because they "buy time" while researchers develop their theories and positions (Hull 1988, 6–7, 513). Although conceptual vagueness and disagreement have not destroyed the heuristic power of community ecology, conceptual difficulties have often prevented the formulation and evaluation of general scientific laws and theories about biotic communities, laws and theories that are useful for solving specific environmental problems.

Without general laws and theories to predict the structure and behavior of biotic communities and to tell us why and how they become degraded, ecologists are often divided on what holds them together and how to protect them. Because they do not know what, if anything, precisely organizes biotic communities (for instance, predation or competition), ecologists have not developed an accepted, general theory of community ecology that is capable of providing the specific predictions often needed for environmental problem solving about biotic communities. As a result, the biologist Robert Henry Peters (1991), the environmental philosopher Mark Sagoff (1985), and others have warned that community ecology is of limited importance in helping to solve practical problems of environmental decisionmaking and managing biotic communities. Indeed, there may never be a confirmed general theory of community ecology despite the heuristic power of a number of candidate theories (Shrader-Frechette and McCoy 1993). As one ecologist put it, "the search for general theories languishes" (Murray 1986, 146). This search is in trouble, in part for the reason that Schoener (1972) recognized more than two decades ago; community ecology has a "constipating accumulation of untested models, most of which are untestable."

The most prominent of the ecological theories claiming to give a general scientific account of biotic communities, island biogeography, is still beset with controversy (Strong 1979; Simberloff 1986b; Shrader-Frechette 1990). Numerous scientific disputes occur over, for example, the size and shape of nature reserves to preserve biotic communities. Disagreement likewise is widespread concerning the scope of tropical deforestation caused by various practices. In such crucial problems of conservation, island biogeography offers few straightforward answers. Consequently, scientific theories give us little help in practical conservation decisionmaking. One reason is that island biogeographical theory has rarely been tested (Margules, Higgs, and Rafe 1982, 117; Zimmerman and Bierregaard 1986, 134). It is dependent primarily on ornithological data (Zimmerman and Bierregaard 1986, 135); on correlations rather than causal explanations (ibid., 135–143); on assumptions about homogeneous habitats (Margules, Higgs, and Rafe 1982, 117); and on unsubstantiated turnover rates and extinction rates (Boecklen and Simberloff 1987, 248–249, 257). Also, factors other than those dominant in island biogeography (for example, maximum breeding habitat) often have been shown to be superior predictors of species number (ibid., 272; Margules, Higgs, and Rafe 1982, 120; Zimmerman and Bierregaard 1986, 136ff.; Shrader-Frechette and McCoy 1993). Such conceptual, theoretical, and evaluative problems with community ecology's preeminent general theory (island biogeography) suggest that developing a precise, quantitative, and explanatory ecological science is not yet possible. As a result, contemporary community ecology is unable to play any significant role in grounding environmental policy (Sagoff 1985; Peters 1991).

Despite the difficulties with ecological concepts and theories about biotic communities, community ecology can make several unique contributions to environmental policy. For one thing, it can often give precise answers to precise questions based on detailed natural-history knowledge. Ecology can also give specific answers to practical environmental questions posed in individual case studies, even though it provides no general theoretical account of biotic communities.

As a recent committee of the National Academy of Sciences (NAS) realized, most success in environmental problem solving occurs in conservation cases that involve only one or two species, perhaps because ecological generalizations are most fully developed for relatively simple systems. This is one reason that ecological management of game and fish populations through regulation of hunting and fishing can often be successful (Orians et al. 1986, 8). Applying this insight, we conclude that ecology might be most helpful when it does not try to predict complex community interactions among many species but instead attempts to predict what will happen for only one or two taxa in a particular case. Such predictions are often successful, thanks to natural history, in spite of the fact that general ecological theory regarding communities is weak. The success occurs in part because, despite the problems with general ecological theory, numerous lower-level theories in ecology provide reliable predictions. Application of lower-level theory about the evolution of cooperative breeding, for example, has provided many successes in managing red-cockaded woodpeckers (Walters 1991, 518). Such examples suggest that the practical and predictive successes might derive from a source other than general theory about communities. In the case of the red-cockaded woodpecker, successful management and predictions appear to have come from natural-history information, for example, about the presence of cavities in trees that serve as habitat (ibid., 506ff.). If the case studies used in the NAS committee report are representative, then some of the most successful ecological applications arise when (and because) scientists have a great deal of knowledge about the natural history of the specific organisms investigated in a particular case study (Orians et al. 1986, 13).

The vampire-bat case study is an excellent example of the value of specific natural-history information when ecologists are interested in practical problem solving (ibid., 28). The goal was to find a control agent that affected only the "pest" species of concern, the vampire bat. The specific information that was useful in finding and using a control, diphenadione, included the facts that the bats are much more susceptible than cattle to the action of anticoagulants; that they roost extremely close to one another; that they groom one another; that their rate of reproduction is low; that they do not migrate; and that they forage only in the absence of moonlight (Mitchell 1986, 151–164). Using this natural-history information, ecologists provided policy both to control the bats and to avoid disrupting other ecological processes.

Of course, giving practical, scientific advice about particular cases such as the vampire bat or the cockaded woodpecker does not resolve all controversy about ecological methods and about how they might inform conservation policy, especially if those methods can give us little help in defining biotic communities. A host of normative, ethical, and economic questions arise whenever one attempts to apply scientific conclusions to real-world conservation problems. Perhaps more than other disciplines, community ecology is beset with the difficulty of developing explanations and theories about different cases, no two of which are similar in all relevant respects. Because of the dissimilarity, the search for a scientific account of community structures and interactions is problematic.

Given the difficulty of finding similar cases in community ecology, environmentalists face an acute problem of scientific inadequacy. If the NAS committee is correct, however, natural history can aid the development of case studies applicable to conservation and preservation. (1) It can give ecologists a measure of practical control over the environment. (2) It can allow us to make rough generalizations, for example, about a taxon's susceptibility to anticoagulants, even though exceptions can be treated neither systematically nor according to a general concept of biotic community. (3) It can show us how to use descriptions of a particular ecological case in order to study different, but partially similar cases. For example, natural-history knowledge of cave-dwelling bats suggests that because the organisms groomed themselves immediately after returning to the cave, subjecting some of them to a lethal anticoagulant would eventually affect the population. Without a general theory of community interactions, natural-history understanding of the bats solved the problem.

There is at least one scientific, *theoretical* task that community ecology may not be able to accomplish, namely, uncovering general theories and exceptionless empirical laws to describe and explain biotic communities. Natural history, however, can help us accomplish the *practical* task of providing rough generalizations and a measure of needed protection over parts of our environment. Similarly, although science cannot tell us precisely how to protect biotic communities, our traditional political theory can tell us, in part, why we should do so. If the classic political theory of John Locke and Thomas Jefferson is correct, we ought to protect the land because the land and all its goods are part of an "original" community "produced by the spontaneous hand of Nature." Because we humans have not created the land or its biotic communities, we have no right to destroy it or use it beyond what we need. As Locke points out, God gave the land to us "in common" (Locke 1960, II, pars. 25–26; Caldwell and Shrader-Frechette 1993, 72; Shrader-Frechette 1993).

Locke also claims that because the value of land is not derived completely (or even primarily) from human labor, the community—past, present, future—retains the strongest right to control land (Locke 1960, II, par. 6; Caldwell and Shrader-Frechette 1993, 73). According to this community "law," Locke argues that we have the right to use the land or biotic communities only if there is "as much and as good" left for future people (Locke 1960, II, par. 27; Caldwell and Shrader-Frechette 1993, 76–78). If we destroy biotic communities, obviously there can never be as much and as good for other persons. Therefore, if we follow the classical Lockean philosophy according to which this country was founded, we ought never to destroy or degrade biotic communities in ways that do not leave as much and as good for others. Indeed, it is arguable that, if we follow accurately the traditions on which our nation is based, there can be no property rights as such—only "use" rights—in natural resources such as land (Caldwell and Shrader-Frechette 1993; Shrader-Frechette 1993).

If political theory tells us that we must leave as much and as good of the biotic commons for others, and if ethical theory reveals that we have no right to degrade something over which we have no full property rights, then we do not need ecological science to tell us that we ought to protect biotic communities. Indeed, we may need scientific laws about them only to the degree that we have ignored our traditional Lockean ethics. We may need the power afforded by scientific predictions about communities only to the degree that we have not abandoned our power to the original community to whom all natural goods have been given. We may need science to protect the land only because we have cut ourselves off from it, only because we now live rootless, separate from our Lockean community and from the biotic community given to us as a commons. Or, to return to our original metaphor, we may need science to protect our biotic communities only because we have built fences between us and the original community about which Locke spoke. We may need science to protect the land only because our fences have destroyed the neighborliness we ought to feel as recipients of such a bountiful commons.

In part because it is a young science, community ecology has been unable to give us precise, predictive theories and laws that enable us to protect biotic communities as fully as we would like. Ecological science has no defect, however, if it must sacrifice universality for utility and practicality, or if it must sacrifice generality for precision in environmental knowledge. Conservation and preservation practice, likewise, has no defect if it must forgo a general, predictive, scientific account of "biotic community" and must instead rely on natural history, on case studies, on political theory, and on ethics to tell us which biotic communities are valuable and how we ought to preserve them. Forced to confront the inadequacies of science for protecting communities, we must evaluate the adequacy of our values for doing so. Our values tie us to the earth. As Warwick Fox (1984, 334–335) expressed it: "The lesson of ecology is that we do share one another's fate . . . since we all share the fate of the earth. . . . We ought to care as deeply and as compassionately as possible about that fate—not because it affects us but because it is us."

barn raising

DANIEL KEMMIS

I N many instances when public undertakings or community initiatives are blocked, a latent public consensus exists that would be more satisfying to most of the participants than what finally emerges. But in fact this consensus rarely sees the light of day. To put it differently, in most of these cases there is more common ground, and higher common ground, than the people involved ever succeed in discovering. Our prevailing way of doing things blocks us. Our failure to realize is twofold: we do not recognize the common ground (a failure to realize its existence), and we do not make it a reality (a failure to realize its potential). As a result, our communities are left poorer than they need to be.

What is it that could block us from recognizing common ground? To a certain extent it is a problem of language—of how we speak publicly. Robert Bellah and his coauthors identified this major problem in their stimulating examination of American public life, *Habits of the Heart*. In preparation for writing the book, the five authors interviewed more than two hundred Americans from various walks of life, attempting to discover how these people thought about or became involved in public life. Of all the themes that emerged, the one that most consistently caught the attention of the authors was the way people used language that portrayed them as being more isolated, more cut off from the world, than their stories showed them in fact to be. When they talked about what they valued, for example, they would consistently speak as if they had chosen those values entirely on their own, or as if they could choose others at a moment's notice, whereas their stories made it clear that the values were deeply rooted in their backgrounds, their associations, the way they lived. Or they would speak of themselves as being motivated by purely selfish considerations, when it was perfectly obvious that in their family or professional lives they were deeply committed to the common good and derived substantial satisfaction from improving the lives of other people.

If these findings are even partially true, they would have far-reaching implications for the way we do public business. My own experience in public life persuades me that the findings are quite accurate, and that we live with their implications all the time. The most costly of those implications involves our difficulty in articulating, staking out, and building on common ground. Our story is really very much like that of the blind men and the elephant. Unable to come to a mutual articulation of what we are touching, we are chronically unable to benefit from its existence. To the extent that our language of individualism keeps us from naming and building on what we have in common, we are impoverished not only in language, but in many other ways as well.

I had a sense of this impoverishment one night while I sat in the chambers of the Missoula City Council and listened to testimony on a draft revision of the county's comprehensive land-use plan. Rural residents spoke passionately of their property rights and of their undying opposition to the urban arrogance that would presume to limit those rights in any way. City dwellers who supported the plan spoke just as passionately of the quality of life that was so important to them and of the need they felt for regulations to protect that quality of life against the developments that threatened it. What I did not hear was any sense of how these people's fates were interwoven, how the good life each wanted depended upon the others being secure in a different but equally good life. It seemed to me likely that if one were to ask most of the people from outside Missoula why they lived where they did, and if they could be persuaded to speak honestly, they would talk not only about living on some particular piece of land in the country but also about living within driving distance of a city such as Missoula. That city, in other words, is part of the place where they had chosen to live—not an accidental, but an integral, part. And the same would be true of the Missoulians: part of the quality of their lives depends on their being surrounded by rural land and rural living. They have a stake in that rural life; they have a stake in its being a good life.

I heard, that evening, almost no expression of their mutual stake in the shape of one another's lives. In this sense, then, it is certainly true that, when people testify at a public hearing, "their lives sound more isolated and arbitrary than . . . they actually are" (Bellah et al. 1985, 21). People in this situation do not speak of what they have in common, or of how the common good might be guarded and enhanced. What they speak of is how a proposed initiative (in this case the land-use plan) either enhances or threatens their individual rights. They speak in terms of the ideologies most conducive to their particular rights, and they leave the decisionmakers to choose between those opposing ideologies. Whichever side the decisionmakers opt for, the losing parties will either appeal to a higher decisionmaker or begin building political coalitions to reverse the dangerous trend they see in this and similar decisions. But no matter how successful their coalition building, they will never be strong enough to ensure the adoption of their own initiatives. What they will ensure is the effort to build a majority coalition on the other side. So in most localities on most issues, the political pendulum is pushed back and forth endlessly; but the higher public good, which everyone feels must be present, never emerges.

In the example of the comprehensive plan, that higher public good can be spoken of, both figuratively and literally, as "common ground." If we try to imagine the kind of thinking that would lead people, in that situation, to work for the "higher common good," we see them acknowledging to one another that they all want to live well on a certain, very specific part of the earth. If the hearing on the comprehensive plan had been a genuine "public hearing," the people from the country would have been able to hear how deeply the city residents are attached to this place, how they consistently pass up higher-paying work elsewhere just to be in this place, how they want their children to be able to have the benefits of open space, of small-town neighborliness, which mean so much to them. And they would have heard their rural neighbors speak of how important it was to them that their children have the experience of raising animals, of chopping wood—some of those simple subsistence practices that Jefferson found so important as a source of civic virtue. If people could actually hear the ways in which their neighbors' lives and hopes are rooted in this particular part of the earth that they all call home, they might begin to figure out how to go about living well together here. But the oscillation between unrestrained individualism and stifling bureaucracy never seems to come to rest on that question.

This "missing middle" that our public policy seems never to find is in fact the *res,* the "public thing" of the "republic." It is that higher common ground which we share, yet cannot find and therefore cannot occupy. When the authors of *Habits of the Heart* describe people who "sound more isolated and arbitrary than . . . they actually are," they are describing people for whom the gathering force of the "public thing" has been removed. This, they say, is what happens when people rely, as they usually do (as they nearly always do "in public"), on their "first language of individualism." Yet these authors also found that in most cases the same people have some access to what they call second languages: "If the language of the self-reliant individual is the first language of American moral life, the languages of tradition and commitment in communities of memory are 'second languages' that most Americans know as well, and which they use when the language of the radically separate self does not seem adequate" (Bellah et al. 1985, 154).

It is well to take a deep breath in turning from this one way of speaking to the other. It takes a while to get acclimated to an entirely new linguistic (and moral) landscape. Tradition, commitment, memory—these are not familiar landmarks in the procedural republic. We are prone to doubt that the same set of people can actually use both of these languages or occupy both of these landscapes. Is it really possible that people who can be what have been called unencumbered selves at a public hearing can be something quite different in another setting? In fact, it *is* possible and indeed quite common. The people at the comprehensive plan hearing were certainly relying there on their "first language of individualism"—and as a result, there was precious little public hearing going on. But there is reason to believe that those same people have access to "second languages" of "tradition and commitment" that might enable them to do a better job of seeing and articulating what they have in common.

For a start, we might refer to language of that sort in the preamble to Montana's constitution. It seems likely that people on both sides of the land-use hearing would feel very much the same emotional response to the words, "We the people of Montana, grateful to God for the quiet beauty of our state, the grandeur of its mountains, the vastness of its rolling plains . . ." Here is common language, describing a relationship of diverse individuals to common ground. The language is not that of individual rights, but of shared gratitude, echoing humility and hope. Such language is a start toward the articulation of common ground; but standing by itself, it can readily be dismissed as mere sentimentality.

We move a step farther in the right direction by remembering Wallace Stegner's call on the people of the West (the "native home of hope") to create a "society to match its scenery" (Stegner 1969, 37–38). Stegner's argument is that this can only be done by relying on some language and culture other than that of "rugged individualism." In calling for a renewal of the culture of cooperation, he invokes the barn-building culture of the not-yet-forgotten days of the frontier. He thus calls to mind precisely a "language of tradition and commitment" that Westerners as a "community of memory" can still recall.

By the time I was eight or nine years old, the wind that blew almost ceaselessly across the high plains of eastern Montana had taken its toll on our barn. We planned to tear down the old one and from its remnants build a new barn in the swale of a dry creek bank, high enough to avoid the torrents that roared through every year or two. It never would have occurred to us, in the early 1950s, to tackle this massive daylong job without calling on the neighbors for assistance.

Since my brother and I were too young to be of much help to the builders, we spent most of the day among the box elders on the creek bottom. That day stands clear in my mind, not so much for the image of the new barn rising out of the old, but for the fact that our neighbor, Albert Volbrecht, brought his children along. We didn't exactly play with Albert's children; we listened to them tell dirty stories that would have made our mother, Lilly, frying chicken up in the house, cry with rage. What fascinated me was the fact that the little Volbrecht girl was the one in the family with the best stock of stories. Her younger brothers revered her, at least on that score, for her prowess.

Although my mother did not know the exact wording of the stories the Volbrecht girl was entertaining us with, she did know the kind of language the child used in other circumstances and she heartily disapproved. She would have done anything in her power to deny my brother and me that part of our education. But there was nothing she could do about it. The Volbrechts had to be at the barn raising, just as they had to be there when we branded calves. They were neighbors, and that was that. Albert's presence loomed large on the scene no matter what the situation. His hat was the biggest in the corral, his voice the loudest, his language the foulest, his intake of beer the most prodigious. His influence was pervasive. I saw my father drink a can of beer once after the last calf was branded. I was astonished to see him do such a thing, and so was my mother. The blame for my father's indiscretion came to rest on Albert. Like his children, Albert was too fond of off-color stories for my mother's taste. The simplest event became colorful, wild, when Albert retold it. My mother accused him of being unable to open his mouth without storying. And Albert, for his part, delighted in watching my mother squirm at his bawdy jokes.

In another time and place, Albert and Lilly would have had nothing to do with each other. But on those Montana plains, life was still harsh enough that they had no choice. Avoiding people you did not like was not an option. Everyone was needed by everyone else in one capacity or another. If Albert and Lilly could have snubbed each other, our barn might not have been built, and neither our calves nor Albert's branded. Lilly and Albert didn't like each other much better at the end of the barn raising than at the beginning. Yet that day, and many others like it, taught them something important. They learned a certain tolerance for another slant on the world, another way of going at things that needed doing. They found in themselves an unsuspected capacity to accept each other. This acceptance, I believe, broadened them beyond the boundaries of their own likes and dislikes and made these personal idiosyncrasies seem less important. In addition, they learned that they could count on each other. If Albert said he would be there with a "farm hand" attachment on his tractor to lift the roof into place, he would be there with the farm hand. If Lilly said she would fry the chicken, she would do it whether she was in the mood that morning or not. And because Albert and Lilly and the rest of our neighbors were able to count on one another, they experienced the satisfaction of accomplishing a big, tough job by working together.

The point here is not nostalgia. We could not re-create the world of the frontier even if we thought we wanted to. Still, there is something to be learned form the subtle but persistent process by which frontier families learned the politics of cooperation. They learned it the way almost anything worthwhile is learned—by practice. Republican theorists have always understood that citizens do not become capable of democratic self-determination by accident. As Bellah points out, republicans from Montesquieu to Jefferson recognized that the character required for participation in face-to-face self-government can only be instilled through repeated experiences of a very specific kind. For these democratic republicans, "the virtuous citizen was one who understood that personal welfare is dependent on the general welfare and could be expected to act accordingly. Forming such character requires the context of practices in which the coincidence of personal concern and the common welfare can be *experienced*" (Bellah et al. 1985, 254, emphasis added). From childhood, Albert and Lilly and all of their neighbors were schooled in those experiences. Because of that practical education, they could overcome many of their differences; they could recognize their need for one another and act accordingly. By contrast, the people at the comprehensive plan hearing had gone to a very different school, and they too acted accordingly. Their differences seemed insurmountable to them, and they seemed to see little of their mutual need for one another. The political education that created this pessimism and isolation is exemplified by another brief story.

A group of citizens in a Western town recently began making plans to initiate a major annual art and music festival. During the first summer they wanted to hold a small one-day preview event, both to raise awareness within the community about the larger festival idea and to raise money for the next year's festival. They settled on the idea of an old-fashioned box social, where people would be asked to bring picnic lunches, which would then be auctioned. The idea gathered momentum quickly and seemed nearly certain of success until someone pointed out the possibility of a lawsuit. What if someone got sick from one of the lunches and filed suit? With that question the box social was laid to rest.

How could it be that my parents and their neighbors could have box socials but we cannot? I have tried to imagine Albert suing us because my mother's fried chicken laid him up or because he got hurt in our corral. It is truly unimaginable. He no more had that option than we had the choice of not inviting him to help with the barn because we disapproved of the way he or his kids told stories. Most of us now do have those options, and as a society we pursue them with a vengeance. We have as little as possible to do with those whose "lifestyles" make us uncomfortable. If we are injured by one of "them" (or even by one of "us"), we will not lightly shrink from a lawsuit. Short of that, we readily and regularly oppose one another at public hearings, avidly pursuing our own interests and protecting our own rights with no sense of responsibility to hear or respond to the legitimate interests of those on the "other side" or to discover common ground. More and more often, the result is deadlock—and then frustration and withdrawal from all things public. Whereas the politics of cooperation gave people a robust sense of their capacity to get big, tough jobs done together, we increasingly come to the gloomy conclusion that "anybody can wreck anything," so there is no reason to try anything. We have been practiced in the politics of alienation, separation, and blocked initiatives rather than in what Bellah calls practices of commitment, which might "give us the strength to get up and do what needs to be done" (*A Prairie Home Companion*).

Yet one of the lessons of *Habits of the Heart* is that even those who testified on the Missoula comprehensive plan do have some experience with the second languages and practices of commitment. They do not have *enough* of that experience to change the way they behave at a public hearing, and that is a growing problem for our society. But they do have snatches of such experience, and it is there that the possibility of reform must be sought.

The practices of commitment have two basic ingredients, which in combination give these practices the potential for revitalizing public life. The two ingredients are (1) a central concern with value, with standards of excellence, with what is good; and (2) a rigorous objectivity. What these practices promise (and what, in fact, nothing else can provide) is the kind of experience that enables us to identify and build on common ground. The common ground we need to find is like a high, hidden valley that we know is there but that seems always to remain beyond our reach. This hidden valley may be called common ground because it is a place of shared values. The values are shared because they are objective; they are, in fact, public values. Their being objective is what makes this common ground valuable, but it is also what keeps it hidden from us. It is valuable because the reclaiming of a vital, effective form of public life can only happen if we can learn to say words like "value" in the same breath with words like "public" or "objective."

This valley of common ground remains hidden because we inhabit a world in which values are always private, always subjective. Always, that is, except when we are engaged in practices of any sort. What barn building and violin playing, softball and steer raising, have fundamentally in common is that they deal with questions of value, with what is good or excellent (a well-built barn, a well-executed double play), but they do so in an explicitly social setting, wherein purely subjective or individualistic inclinations are flatly irrelevant, if not counterproductive.

"Every practice," according to Alasdair MacIntyre, "requires a certain kind of relationship between those who participate in it. What that relationship instills, over time, is precisely the "civic virtues"—those habits that would be necessary if people were ever to relate to one another in a truly public way. MacIntyre describes how even our homeliest practices gradually instill these civic virtues: "We have to learn to recognize what is due to whom; we have to be prepared to take whatever self-endangering risks are demanded along the way; and we have to listen carefully to what we are told about our own inadequacies and to reply with the same carefulness for the facts. In other words we have to accept as necessary components of any practice with internal goods and standards of excellence the virtues of justice, courage and honesty" (MacIntyre 1984, 191).

Strangely enough, in what we call the public realm, all of these virtues that might in fact enable us to be public are suddenly overshadowed. The "second language of commitment," which so many public-hearing contestants speak in their softball leagues or their parent-teacher meetings, becomes suddenly silent when these people think they are in a public setting. In that setting they speak their "first language of individualism," with consequences all too familiar. The person who grew up knowing that she could not arbitrarily decide what constitutes a prize-winning steer or a good time to bunt now accepts as utterly natural the idea that what she considers a good community is "her value" and what her opponent considers a good community is "his value." What this does to the tone of public discourse is predictable: "From our rival conclusions we can argue back to our rival premises, but when we do arrive at our premises argument ceases and the invocation of one premise against another becomes a matter of pure assertion and counter-assertion. Hence perhaps the slightly shrill tone of so much moral debate" (ibid., 8).

At the root of this difficulty, MacIntyre discovers the same feature that struck the authors of *Habits of the Heart* so forcibly: the feeling on the part of most people that, in the end, their positions (and certainly the positions of their opponents) are a result not of reason, but of individual inclination.

If we possess no unassailable criteria, no set of compelling reasons by means of which we may convince our opponents, it follows that in the process of making up our own minds we can have made no appeal to such criteria or such reasons. If I lack any good reasons to invoke against you, it must seem that I lack any good reasons. Hence it seems that underlying my own position there must be some non-rational decision to adopt that position. Corresponding to the interminability of public argument there is at least the appearance of a disquieting private arbitrariness. It is a small wonder if we become defensive and therefore shrill. (ibid.)

If it is true that people attain civic virtues through practices, and if it is true that many people gain such education outside the public arena, the obvious question is, What can be done to establish practices that would teach people to act and speak in public in a truly public way? That question has no simple answer. But one part of the answer may emerge from understanding how important to practices is the concrete, the specific, the tangible. It is precisely that element of concreteness which gives to practices their capacity to present values as something objective, and therefore as something public.

The barn was as real, as objective, as anything could be; but it only acquired its urgency within the context of the broader and even more compelling objectivity of the land and the weather to which it was a response. However Albert and Lilly may have differed in some of their personal values, they differed not at all in their experience of winter on the high plains. For both of them the prairie winter was cold and deadly, and it absolutely required a good barn.

Strangely enough, that objective requirement of a good barn meant that they were not free to treat their values as purely subjective. In some things, to be sure, they could afford to be subjective. Albert could value beer and salty language in a way that Lilly never would. Still, when it came to values such as reliability, perseverance, or even a certain level of conviviality, they found themselves dealing in something much more objective than we generally think of values as being. In fact, those people could no more do without those values than they could do without their barns, simply because they could not get the barns built without the values. The shaping of their values was as much a communal response to their place as was the building of their barns.

The kinds of values that might form the basis for a genuinely public life, then, arise from a context that is concrete in at least two ways. It is concrete in the actual things or events—the barns, the barn dances—that the practices of cooperation produce. It is also concrete in the specific places within which those practices and that cooperation take place. Clearly, the practices that shaped the behavior and the character of frontier families did not appear out of thin air; they grew out of the one trait those people had most fundamentally in common: the effort to survive in hard country. And when the effort to survive comes to rely on shared and repeated practices such as barn raising, survival itself is transformed; it becomes inhabitation. To in*habit* a place is to dwell there in a practiced way, in a way that relies on certain regular, trusted *habits* of behavior.

No real public life is possible except among people who are engaged in the project of inhabiting a place. If there are no habituated patterns of work, play, grieving, and celebration designed to enable people to live well in a place, then those people will have at best a limited capacity for being public with one another.

Conversely, where such inhabitory practices are being nurtured, the foundation for public life is also being created or maintained. This thesis suggests a fairly intimate connection between two potent strains of contemporary American thought. One is the revival of interest in civic republicanism. The other appears frequently under the title "bioregionalism." What is of particular interest in this context is the tendency of bioregionalists to identify their work by the word rein-habitation. In a talk with that title, Gary Snyder evokes the connection between "coming into the country" and the habituated ways that make it possible to stay there: "Countless local ecosystem habitation styles emerged. People developed specific ways to be in each of those niches: plant knowledge, boats, dogs, traps, nets, fishing—the smaller animals, and smaller tools" (Snyder 1977, 59). These habitation styles carried with them precisely the element of objectivity that Mac-Intyre emphasizes. Habitation, in other words, implies right and wrong ways of doing things. "Doing things right means living as though your grandchildren would also be alive, in this land, carrying on the work we're doing right now, with deepening delight" (ibid., 65).

It is in what Bellah calls communities of memory that these "second languages and practices of commitment" have been most carefully preserved. Accordingly, it has seemed appropriate to recall how cooperation could once have been such an important part of our culture. Of course, there comes a time for turning from what was to what may be. If public life needs to be revitalized, if its renewal depends on more conscious and more confident ways of drawing on the capacity of practices to make values objective and public, if those practices acquire that power from the efforts of unlike people to live well in specific places, then we need to think about specific places and the real people who now live in them, and try to imagine ways in which their efforts to live there might become more practiced, more inhabitory, and therefore more public.

community and the virtue of necessity

WILLIAM VITEK

REASONABLE BEINGS ARE ALONE GRANTED THE POWER OF A WILLING
CONFORMITY WITH CIRCUMSTANCE; THE BARE CONFORMITY BY ITSELF
STERN NECESSITY EXACTS FROM EVERY CREATED THING.

—Marcus Aurelius, *Meditations*

IT'S midday in late August. Looking out my office window I sense the telltale signs of autumn: lighter shades of green, a sun that no longer crests the highest maple, an absence of haze, restless animals, empty nests. My body too anticipates the changes in ways I feel but do not fully comprehend. But these observations take willful effort. My eyes are drawn back to the flashing computer cursor, impatient as a tapping foot. The computer's little fan hums, as do the fluorescent lights. A logging truck downshifts, cars maneuver for their lined spaces in the parking lot. The phone rings.

I stop what I am doing and feel my pulse. Its rhythm matches the sway of distant trees. My breathing slows. I hear briefly not the wind, but the sound of leaves touching in the wind. It's not unlike a sound I have heard before, in a doctor's office with a contraption pressed to my wife's stomach, amplifying the steady heartbeat of one of our children. The phone rings.

This daily struggle for my attention reflects an ongoing transformation toward an ecological ethos. It represents one of the most difficult challenges of the decade and the coming century because it requires from each of us a fundamental realignment of our views of happiness and success, of our relation to the natural world, and of our everyday perceptions, habits, customs, and practices. The process will be made more difficult in proportion to how deep in us go the roots of the current ethos, and I maintain that for most of us they go pretty deep.

While we might vigorously reject the scientific assumptions of Francis Bacon and René Descartes, our daily lives are filled with the products of modern science and technology: automobiles, computers, airplanes, smoke alarms, asthma medicine, the wind generator, energy-efficient lighting, even the flush toilet and the screened window. The tenets of John Locke's labor theory of property ignore the ethical and ecological values of the land, but most of us have ownership over some property and believe that our decisions concerning it are prudent ones. Although we may be critical of the philosophy of individualism, with its emphasis on self-interest and rights, few of us would give up the freedoms that came with the Enlightenment: the freedom to reject traditional beliefs that oppress women and minorities, the freedom to choose our own way, to express our sexual preferences, and to say what we think. We still speak of the sun as rising and setting; rarely do we feel the earth's rotation, our own movement, into the morning light. Indeed, the roots of our present ethos are legitimately deep, well nourished, and healthy.

One aspect of the shift to an ecological ethos is the rediscovery of community. As this collection attests, there is a growing literature that answers Aldo Leopold's call to become members—plain citizens—of a wider, more inclusive and placed community. If we are interested in reinhabiting communities and in discovering our communitarian selves, we must start by asking such basic questions as, What are communities? How do they cohere and undergo change? Why do they move in and out of existence?

At least part of what holds a community together is some notion of necessity. Something outside us—or perhaps our own natural limitations, or a decision to limit ourselves—constrains us to a place, to a community, to helping our neighbors, and in turn to being helped by them. This necessity often begins as something that is against our will, but given the right circumstances necessity turns from a constraining condition to an enabling condition. When successful, necessity leads inevitably to virtue for the individual and well-being for the community. It is a transformation made possible by choice, diligence, and practice.

To speak of necessity as a virtue invites charges of fascism, intolerance, and oppression; and rightly so, when considering the checkered history of community life. As I shall describe below, the reinhabitation of community requires a new concept of necessity, one that accepts and embraces the necessity of our naturalness and our natural limitations, and one that requires personal assent. Human communities will form in an ecological ethos only when their members submit to the external necessities of the natural world, to their natural existence, and to the internal constraints of their personal choices to be still, to stay put, to get on with the work of the local community, and to rejoice in its memories and traditions, and even in its pettiness and provincialisms. I confess that I am not optimistic. Very little in either our present ethos or our primitive past gives us much encouragement or advice on how to proceed.

The Scottish philosopher David Hume said it best: "In humans alone, this unnatural conjunction of infirmity, and of necessity may be observed in its greatest perfection" (Hume 1983, 485). It seems that human beings, because of our limitations and necessities, seek out one another and engage in cooperative behavior. With time and the right conditions, practices and customs arise that celebrate this heretofore instrumental gathering. Stories are told, memories are formed and revered, a community is defined. Still, stories and memories alone will not do. What keeps a community together is the inability of its members to leave, either because of the dangers that lie outside the community—a forbidding desert or an enemy clan, for example—or the ties that lie within the community—traditions, laws, fear of being cast out, rejected, or destroyed. These laws and traditions, like songs and memories, function as constraints and arise out of the necessity of being together.

The idea that necessity and constraint can form communities and enable virtue is not difficult to demonstrate. Our infirmity and necessity show themselves most visibly in our birth and infancy. Our creation is a social act, our suckling the first social experience outside the womb, the family the first and most primal community. Nearly all traditional, labor-intensive activities occur in groups: the hunt, the harvest, the barn raising. And what traditional community is not held together by external necessities or the public and enforced commitments to a god, a leader, or an ideology?

We can find examples in contemporary society as well. Many of us had music lessons of one sort or another as children, and we remember them with varying degrees of pain and pleasure. Our competence rarely exceeded our expectations, so we had to submit to hours of tedious practice. When our interest waned, parents and teachers would supply external constraints, mixing reward with punishment, stories of success with ultimatums. If we stuck with it (and few of us did), there came a point when the diligence and practice paid off. We reached a high level of competence, perhaps even virtuosity. We became musical. Only then did we understand the necessity of hard work, thank and honor our taskmasters, and submit ourselves to the discipline of musicianship. Success was shared both by the individual musicians and by the community of people who helped develop their musical talents.

There is also the necessity of work that must be done. Not long ago my house needed painting, and I was not in a financial position to pay someone to do it. It was a job born of necessity, and there were plenty of days when I felt exceedingly constrained. I did not freely choose to paint my house, nor would I choose to do it again. But having submitted to the practice and discipline of painting a house, I was free to do a great deal of thinking, not only about ladders and paints, but about philosophical ideas as well. I also confronted my fears of home repair and learned a thing or two about carpenter ants, scaffolding, and the art of scraping. There was community building too. I freely borrowed neighbors' tools and ladders, sought their advice, enjoyed their praise and encouragement. It would be an exaggeration to claim any virtuosity from this experience, but I did acquire a bit of knowledge and at least some wisdom about home ownership.

Similarly, the moral life provides us with enabling constraints and plenty of opportunity for virtue. Our daily lives, for example, are filled with promises, both mundane and sacred. Promising is an inherently social act born of a necessity that requires us to commit ourselves with mere words to a future only vaguely seen. The promises we make and remake in a lifetime of marriage constrain us in many ways, but likewise make possible strong family ties and the pleasures that come from them. One thinks of Odysseus and Penelope, an ancient couple who would not stay separated despite many hardships, temptations, and threats. Their restraint and diligence made possible a virtuous reunion.

Closer to home I am reminded of a farmer in my county—now deceased— who at age seventy-five was stricken with an illness that kept him from the evening milking for the first time in seventy years. He cried when he told me this. Whom had he let down? Few of us can appreciate the constraints placed on dairy farmers, but just think what seventy years of twice-daily milkings can do for your sense of place, your character, and your community.

David Kline, a contributor to this volume and an Amish farmer living in Fredericksburg, Ohio, shared a similar story about his father. Although he lived to the age of eighty-seven, his father never saw the Redwoods, the Sierras, the Great Plains, or even the Mississippi River. "He was too busy," David said, "helping his neighbors and enjoying the creation around him." Another member of the Fredericksburg Amish community, when interviewed about the car accident that had killed five of their children as they walked along a country road, said this: "We could take it a lot easier if he—the driver—would feel sorry. It's a little harder to forgive since he doesn't seem upset. But we have to forgive him. And we will." The clarity of these words reflect the depth of this man's discipleship and practice in the Amish community.

The connection between the rural life and religious discipline is likewise brought out by Kathleen Norris:

> Gradually the novice discovers that a forced observation of little things can also lead to simple pleasures. A young monk once told me he'd been delighted to find that the worn black wool of the habit he'd been given was excellent for sliding down banisters. He demonstrated, and for a moment became an angel: without feet, all irrepressible joy.
>
> It's when the novices move toward survival, embracing the deprivations of monastic life as a personal, inner necessity, that they begin to feel truly free. They also begin to understand the depths of joy, and how little it has to do with what the world calls happiness. Like the farmer or rancher who willingly takes on economic hardship, remaining in Dakota out of love for the land, these monks can grow to a profound understanding of fast and feast. One makes sense only in terms of the other, and both may be seen in terms of play. Like country folk everywhere, monks develop an ability to party simply but well. "No one celebrates like we do," says Benedictine Joan Chittister in a recent commentary on the *Rule* (Norris 1993, 214)

Daniel Kemmis recalls a memory in his essay "Barn Raising" (in this volume) about living on the Montana Plains in the 1950s when a barn raising required neighbors, and neighbors meant the likes of Albert Volbrecht and his family, none of whom were particularly blessed with social graces, especially Albert. They were the sort of people from whom Kemmis' mother Lilly would have preferred to remain distant. Kemmis writes:

> In another time and place, Albert and Lilly would have had nothing to do with each other. But on those Montana plains, life was still harsh enough that they had no choice. Avoiding people you did not like was not an option. Everyone was needed by everyone else in one capacity or another. If Albert and

Lilly could have snubbed each other, our barn might not have been built, and neither our calves nor Albert's branded. Lilly and Albert didn't like each other much better at the end of the barn raising than at the beginning. Yet that day, and many others like it, taught them something important. They learned a certain tolerance for another slant on the world, another way of going at things that needed doing. They found in themselves an unsuspected capacity to accept each other. This acceptance, I believe, broadened them beyond the boundaries of their own likes and dislikes and made these personal idiosyncrasies seem less important. In addition, they learned that they could count on each other. If Albert said he would be there with a "farm hand" attachment on his tractor to lift the roof into place, he would be there with the farm hand. If Lilly said she would fry the chicken, she would do it whether she was in the mood that morning or not. And because Albert and Lilly and the rest of our neighbors were able to count on one another, they experienced the satisfaction of accomplishing a big, tough job by working together.

These examples are meant to demonstrate how necessity holds us together; how, through diligence, discipline, and practice, we are enabled to practice virtue and achieve well-being. They indicate clearly how the necessity of rootedness brings forth the fruit of community.

It is here that my liberal friends object to my "romanticized" view of the world. Where I see virtue, they see vice, corruption, oppression, inequalities, and hierarchies. Where I see diligence, they see drudgery. Where I see the commitment and fidelity of Penelope and Odysseus, they see the treachery and deceit of Clytemestra and Aegisthus. Both the Baconian-Cartesian scientific paradigm and Lockean individualism, they tell me, sought to free us from various sorts of necessity. Bacon and Descartes sought to control nature so as to make our lives better, longer, more productive, and happier. Locke and others wanted to overthrow the tyrannies of monarchies, religious oppression, and abusive traditions. These scholars shared a fundamental belief that humans can think for themselves and are free, within limits, to act on their own choices. The Enlightenment sought to free us from necessity of every kind, and it was not all bad.

There is a sense in which my friends are correct. Who among us would choose a life where half our offspring died before their first birthday, or where we were destined by caste or tradition to live a life we did not choose? The advances and victories of the Enlightenment were hard won, and in both cases—scientific and political—are rightly described as revolutions. Surely we must go forward in the re-creation of communities and traditions, taking with us three centuries of social gains and scientific discoveries.

To my mind, the Enlightenment got it half right. We are better off without traditions and hierarchies that oppress our freedoms and choices, and that force us to act against our will. The half it did not get right has to do with our control of nature, and the sense that we are above nature. If my assessment is correct, our task of building communities becomes doubly hard; and here let me sketch an alternative concept of necessity that is more appropriate to our present and future community building. It has two parts.

We must first accept and embrace the necessities of our naturalness. We are natural beings whose bodies must be worked, whose minds must be challenged, whose skin must be touched, whose hearts must be loved. Our voices must speak promises and sing lullabies, our feet must run marathons, follow the plow, and dance into the night. But we are mortal beings too, constrained and enabled by the advice Aldo Leopold observes in the natural endowment of all living things: "suck hard, live fast, and die often" (Leopold 1970, 114).

We are also beings in a place; on the earth, of course, but more importantly in the soils, climates, geographies, customs, and stories of the Pacific Northwest, the Rockies, the Kansas plains, the Maryland shore, the Mohawk Valley, the Great Salt Lake, the Adirondacks, and even the streets of Brooklyn, Baltimore, Kansas City, Miami, and Los Angeles. The necessities of our naturalness and our nativeness must be embraced wholeheartedly if community life is to return.

Yet this is not enough: we can always say no to these necessities and deny them a little longer. We can run to the mall, watch TV, take a trip to Disneyland, move every three years, tighten the skin on our faces, enlarge or reduce our breasts, chins, buttocks, and bellies, replace defective body parts, or have ourselves frozen. Thankfully, we can no longer count on institutional hierarchies to keep us in line. We are, as Sartre says, "condemned to be free," and so we must both accept our constraints and choose our necessities. We must embrace our mortality and submit ourselves to a place, to a community discipline. We must remain in a place long enough—and put up with its constraints and limitations, as well as the critical remarks of friends and colleagues—to discover the goods of a community of people and a home territory. Though we choose the necessity of staying in one place, in one community, we must imagine that this necessity comes from another source—from the landscape itself, from previous or future generations, from our neighbors—lest we too easily give up and move on.

Described in more philosophical terms, accepting our naturalness and our nativeness is an ontological or metaphysical necessity because it is an empirically testable state of the universe. Our hopes for a spiritual afterlife somewhere off the planet have not been shown to be an accurate predictor of reality. Our backyard compost heaps and garden soils are far more informative in these regards: black, cool, fertile, and yes—in their death and corruption—very much alive. Our human communities too offer us in memories, in testaments to our positive influences, and in our contributions to the gene pool, a longevity beyond our conscious earthly life. While the longevity found in the rebirth of the soil and in our community's collective memory may not be what we have come to expect, if that is all there is, then it can be enough. Accepting our mortality frees us to focus on the details and practices of this life, this landscape, this community of people. With acceptance comes diligence and attention to the repetitions and rhythms of daily life: from the dishes, the diapers, and food preparation; to births, marriages, and funerals; to the changes of season and the passing of another year. We see these moments and events as the living cycles they are, and celebrate our inclusion. We're at the dance; we know we're at the dance; and we're dancing.

Choosing to become a member of a placed community, on the other hand, is a moral necessity that we ought to choose but are free to reject. This moral necessity springs from the goods, and the good, that can be achieved for oneself as well as by practicing virtue in a community setting. Of course, this conception of the good represents only one choice among many rival philosophical and religious accounts of happiness, and there is no telling in advance how our individual lives will turn out because of our adherence to one system or another. Still, we can use past and present successes, stories, and role models to fire our own commitments and routines until they become learned, practiced, and virtuous. Moral necessity is a personal choice of, and adherence to, one form of life over another. Committing oneself to a community, to a place, and to a common good is that kind of choice.

Although they can be conceived of as separate, the moral and metaphysical notions of necessity are linked. The more fully we accept our metaphysical necessities, the easier it becomes to choose the constraints of community.

In his essay "An Amish Perspective" (this volume), David Kline describes the discovery of an arrowhead in a field he was harrowing. David's family has been working this land since 1918, so his roots already go deep, but the arrowhead prompted him to consider his Paleolithic relations. It forced his roots deeper into a landscape that now holds his father, his neighbor's children, and thousands of years of fertility, respect, toil, and disappointment. The arrowhead objectifies his metaphysical limitations and strengthens his commitment to the soil that holds it, to the family and friends who work that soil, and to the flora and fauna living there.

I retell Kline's story as a bridge to my own experience and struggles with necessity. My home territory is the Racquette River watershed in northern New York's St. Lawrence Valley. This river valley landscape is both wild and productive, and its people are hardworking, connected to the land, and filled with community spirit. I moved here in 1987 to my first teaching job—what I thought would be a temporary stop, the first on a professional climb to success. Since that time I have increasingly come to see this place as home, a place to work hard and well, to care for a piece of land, and to help and enjoy my neighbors.

I too have an arrowhead. It was given me by Jeremy Hibbert, one of my students, during a recent graduation ceremony at my university. Jeremy belongs to the local community and his family has roots in the land. Like Kline, he found it while plowing the soil, and for eight years he carried it in his wallet for good luck. Giving me this arrowhead—which I now carry in my wallet, and for similar reasons—was a noble gesture. It symbolized the gift exchange that connects teachers and students, newcomers and natives, the industrial age with our hunter-gatherer past.

I trembled a bit when I received this gift, because I realized that assenting to the necessity of community may require more than I am willing to give. My worldview and its discourse have been shaped by a Cartesian grammar and a Lockean vocabulary. I have not yet fully let go of my centeredness in the universe or my feelings of control and superiority. I am likewise torn between the desire for a professional reputation and the desire to stay at home helping my neighbors, building fences instead of professional networks, gathering sap instead of lines on my curriculum vita. Terry Tempest Williams suggests that the most radical act we can commit is to stay at home, yet I often travel long distances at my university's expense (and in service to its reputation and mine) to share her message. I live this paradox still too fearful to choose, to commit to a side. I know the new words and can speak them clearly, and I wholeheartedly embrace the new concepts. But I am a novice and I bumble along.

I recently sat on the bank of the Racquette River as it raged with the spring thaw while my children, Elizabeth and Andrew, played along the stony shoreline. I asked myself what it would take to muster the courage to become native to this place. This newly found sense of rootage in the land is both a satisfying and a terrifying experience because it requires us to stand firm and to stay put, to be moved by rivers ever downward and not by job offers that tempt us upward on ladders of our own making, where all we can do is fall like the natural objects we are. Commitment to community requires us to feel the necessity of a place, and to care deeply about the land and its people. As yet few words, and even fewer role models, come to its defense. In the midst of novices I can at least be thankful that rivers are patient teachers.

There are obvious paradoxes in choosing necessity, in traveling thousands of miles to tell people to stay at home, in becoming native, and in being enabled by submitting to constraints. Farmers and ranchers are no strangers to similar paradoxes: the land is cared for and plowed, animals protected and slaughtered, children loved and worked. These paradoxes sometimes stretch the limits of human comprehension, yet we should evaluate and judge them not in terms of the words or arguments that fail to spring to their defense, but rather in terms of the land's fertility and the strength of family ties. Measured in this way, the paradoxes nearly vanish. So too do the distinctions between humans and nature, soil and terrain, crops and flora, livestock and fauna, farmer and naturalist.

It is not enough for each of us to attend to our work. We must become attentive to our naturalness and our nativeness. It is not enough to improve our individual lives. Each of us must commit to improving our communities. Like the wandering Odysseus, we need roots to hold us down and make us well. On his ship Odysseus needed to be tied to the mast, but at home in Ithaca his center was firmly rooted in the living tree and generous soil that anchored his bed, and hence his marriage, his family, his community, and his island landscape. It was, after all, for the routines of family and place that Odysseus rejected the offer of immortality.

We too must begin the trip back home, giving up our own illusions of a world of infinite resources and a life ever after, and making peace with the land and its rhythms. We must open our senses to the direction of the wind, a change in temperature, shades of blue in the western sky, homeward geese, seasonal scents, and soil ready for seed. We must feel the motion of our moving planet and see the ground beneath our feet for what it is. Necessity, prosperity, and fertility are linked in communities, and are limited by the harsh and glorious cycles of the living, moving from leaf to flesh to stone. Virtuosity, and the well-being it engenders, are the social offspring of these natural cycles. They are there for the taking if we are willing to endure the labor.

defining normative community

JOHN B. COBB, JR.

COMMUNITY is one of those many good things that we recognize chiefly in their absence. When people feel that no one cares about them, they mourn the loss of community. When they see society falling apart, they recognize the need for community.

Thomas Hobbes depicts a communityless world in which individuals seek only their own benefit. He wrongly supposes that this describes the "state of nature," the state from which we were saved by a contract with one another designed to create order. Of course, a society brought into being as Hobbes describes would be far removed from community.

Adam Smith knew that sympathy is a powerful force that binds people together. He knew that strong community feeling plays a positive role in economic relationships. But he did not develop this point. Instead, he emphasized that individuals sell as high as possible and buy as cheaply as possible. This rational individualism became the basis for market economics.

Although not all political theory followed Hobbes and not all economic theory followed Smith, our dominant political and economic theories have, like theirs, ignored community. Even though practice has assumed community, theory has had its effects, and community has declined. Society has become more like what theory depicted.

The greatest value of individualism is personal freedom. People who break their ties to traditional community are free to live where they want, do what they want, create their own norms and values. A closely related gain is the ability to objectify and criticize. While immersed in a tribal or rural community, one cannot criticize its ways of thinking. To be able to view those beliefs alongside others is to become a free thinker. Also, minorities have gained rights against majorities; and individuals, against society. Part of the social contract has become the defense of the human rights of all people against those communities that would abuse them.

With so many forces working against traditional community, and with the real gains that came with the individualism that replaced it, strong reasons are needed if we are to support efforts to renew community. These reasons exist, globally and locally. Indeed, the political, economic, and educational systems that undercut community themselves presupposed it and cannot function without it.

The nation-state that derived its ideology from individualism in fact derived its stability and power from the communities of which it was composed. The idea of a state that relates directly to each individual within it is unrealistic, most closely approximated in totalitarianism. But in fact no totalitarian government can dispense with intermediate levels, many of which must have some character of community.

The economic system of individualism aims at eliminating from the marketplace all motives except individual profit. Economic theory shows that unchecked competition leads to the efficient allocation of resources and the rapid improvement of technology. The result is an increase in total production and consumption. This individualistic system works brilliantly in achieving precisely the goals it has announced.

In the process, it systematically destroys communities. Its application to U.S. agriculture has depopulated the countryside, and its application to industry has led to abandonment of many older sites in search of others where labor is cheaper and environmental standards lower. In the "developing" world, people are forced out of their traditional villages in order to constitute a labor force for colonial and neocolonial masters.

On the other hand, successful production requires workers who are honest, diligent, and loyal to their employers. These virtues are not learned in the marketplace. They must be learned in exactly those communities that are undermined by the economic system.

The educational system that prepares people to succeed in the market economy also presupposes community. In recent decades the United States has spent more and more money on an educational system that continues to decline. Hardworking teachers complain of lack of parental support. Yet parental support is largely a function of a healthy community. The educational system has not transmitted community values or taught youth the value of traditional community. It has, in other words, contributed to the decline of that community apart from which it itself inevitably declines.

At a personal level, the kind of freedom that individualism allows loses its value. Freedom from traditional community values can lead to loss of all sense of importance. Freedom to do what one wants ceases to be significant when one does not want anything very much. Consumerism expresses not freedom, but slavery to purely material values. Freedom from responsibility for others is equally a loss of the assurance that others are ready to be supportive.

What emerges when community is fully destroyed is not real individualism. True individuality depends on community. Although community can stifle many yearnings of the individuals it nurtures, the very emergence of those yearnings comes about only within the context of community. It is not the case that true individuality and true community are mutually exclusive. On the contrary, they constitute a polarity in which neither attains its fulfillment apart from the other.

It is time now to ask more directly what constitutes community. I do this in two ways. First, I describe what constitutes community without regard to whether community is desirable or what groups it should comprise. Then I ask what makes for a healthy community.

The previous discussion presupposes, without articulating, elements of what constitutes community. Within a community there is mutual responsibility. Those for whom one has no responsibility are outside one's community. Furthermore, the organization of the community expresses this mutual responsibility. The members cannot individually fulfill all of their mutual responsibilities, but collectively there is some effort to do so.

A state may or may not be a community. It may not accept any responsibility for some of its members. The Nazi state took considerable responsibility for those German members who accepted Nazism; it took no positive responsibility for most of the minorities within its borders and even undertook to eliminate some. A similar situation can develop in former colonies whose boundaries pay no attention to existing tribal communities. If one tribe gains political control of the state, it may assume little or no responsibility for members of other tribes, using the machinery of state instead for the aggrandizement of the victorious tribe. That tribe may then constitute a community (at least by the criterion now under consideration), but the state does not.

The United States is becoming more of a community in some respects and less in others. We have been forced to realize that for centuries the dominant European peoples took no positive responsibility for nonwhites. Major gains have been made in extending to ethnic minorities the rights of citizenship and assuming a positive responsibility for their well-being. Yet our acceptance of responsibility for economic failures has diminished. We tolerate a level of homelessness and exclusion from economic opportunity that would have been unthinkable a few decades ago. In general, our willingness to pay taxes in order to meet the basic needs of other Americans has declined markedly.

There are nongeographical groups that meet this requirement of community. Many Jews, for example, accept responsibility for other Jews, wherever they may be. This strong sense of mutual responsibility has been important in the support of Zionism and the state of Israel. It is built into the self-understanding of that state.

It is somewhat meaningful to speak of the scientific community in this respect. Although the mutual responsibility there is not as strong, when a scientist is arrested in one country for political reasons, often scientists elsewhere take particular pains to assist. They also accept responsibility for policing the work of fellow scientists so as to maintain the standards of the guild.

A second mark of community is its role in defining the identity of its members. To those for whom the United States functions as a community in this way, American identity is important and is manifest in the way one describes oneself. Normally those for whom being American functions as a major element of identity feel great loyalty to the United States. Often they resent criticism of the nation, especially of its international policies. But critics of these policies may also have a strong identity as Americans. They select just these policies to criticize because it is painful to them that the state, citizenship in which provides much of their identity, acts in ways they cannot support.

For most citizens of the United States the nation does function as a community in this sense. For some, their states or regions also function in this way. Especially in the former Confederate States, being a "Southerner" is often an important part of the residents' identity. Being a Kansan or a New Yorker can also be significant. However, easy mobility has reduced the power of the state as a source of identity for most Americans. The role of states as communities has, in this respect at least, declined. Smaller political units usually function even less effectively as communities.

Not all communities, considered as givers of personal identity, are geographical. The nongeographical groups identified as accepting mutual responsibility within the group are also sources of identity. For some people, being a Jew or a scientist may be the most important identity. Indeed, where it expresses itself in a strong sense of mutual responsibility, this identity must be quite important. On the other hand, identification with a group may not lead to responsibility for all other members of the group. For example, many for whom a Christian identity is quite strong do not, as a result, undertake to care for all other Christians in a distinctive way. Their Christian identity may express itself instead in seeking to meet the needs of those who are in trouble regardless of whether they are Christian or not.

Partly because of the vast size and multiple divisions within Christianity, if identity expresses itself in mutual responsibility, it usually does so in terms of a subgroup. In the Roman Catholic context, a religious order might be involved; in the Protestant context, a denomination. More often it is a matter of one's own parish or local congregation.

The breakdown of traditional communities has made self-identification in nongeographical ways increasingly important. Multiple types of self-identification play major roles in different aspects of an individual's life. One may identify with one's hometown or alma mater in regard to athletic competition, while identifying with one's firm or profession in the economic world. For other purposes one may identify with a group that holds to the same political ideology within and across national boundaries. For still other purposes ethnic identity may be primary. In this sense, most of us, especially in the United States, are members of a variety of communities.

A third notion involved in community has not yet been made sufficiently explicit. To be a member of a community is to participate in its life, and to some degree in its decisions. A family in which the wife and children are simply told what to do by the husband-father is not a community in this respect. Still, equality is not required. A very hierarchical family can still be a community as long as the members make distinct contributions to the whole and consent to the authoritarian structure.

Similarly, a tribe may function as a community whether it is relatively egalitarian or highly hierarchical in its structure, as long as hierarchy does not mean a concentration of totalitarian power at the top. In other words, community requires basic consent of the governed to the way in which decisions are made; it does not require equal participation in those decisions.

Just as community does not require equal participation in governance by all, so formal equality does not guarantee community. In the United States a large portion of the electorate does not exercise its political rights because it judges that the system that determines their lives will not be affected by the outcome of the election. In short, massive and increasing alienation from the political process has accompanied a systematic legal extension of the franchise. Judged by this measure, community is declining.

The same issue arises with respect to nongeographical groups. Here alienation normally expresses itself in simply leaving the group. A Jew who ceases to support the general policies of international Jewry and is alienated from the way these policies are formed can largely opt out of this identity in a way that is much more difficult for the citizen of a nation.

When community as participation in the national life declines, other forms of community are likely to take over. For many of the most alienated, these new forms of community are parasitic on the national identity. The various mafias are examples. Youth gangs also function in this way.

Other less extreme expressions, such as the various caucuses, are found within both geographical and nongeographical communities. These do not reflect complete alienation from the larger community. But their members tend to take the existence of the larger community for granted and to identify themselves primarily with the group represented by the caucus. Thus African-Americans may take the existence of a denomination or a political unit for granted, while organizing to demand justice from it. Other ethnic groups and also women may adopt such stances. These too may be parasitic on the larger community in the sense that their purpose is to redistribute its resources regardless of the effect on the larger community. On the other hand, they may be seeking to compel the larger community to fulfill its own goals more responsibly and thus understand their caucus work as responsible participation in the larger community.

Our description of community implies norms in the sense that a particular group or society may be more or less of a community. The more responsibility the members take for one another, whether expressed directly or indirectly, the more of a community it will be. The more strongly people identify themselves by their membership, the more the community functions as a community. And the more members perceive themselves as full participants in the life and decisionmaking of the group, the more truly it is a community.

We should recognize that it is not always desirable that every group function strongly as a community. Indeed, if the nation-state constitutes a strong community, this fact reduces the possibility for other groups, geographical or not, to be communities. The focus of community on the nation-state from the mid-seventeenth century to the mid-twentieth century was the cause of destructive national rivalries and wars. It also led to extensive assaults on other loci of identification and participation, culminating in totalitarianism.

The more natural focus of community on ethnic groupings is equally problematic. Where ethnicity and the boundaries of the state correspond, we have another version of the same problem. Where they diverge, ethnic groups struggle for power or autonomy. Because in many nation-states ethnic identities are quite diverse, the splintering effect can lead to chaos.

One proposed solution is the transfer of strong community to larger levels— to the continent or the whole of humanity. Much can be said for this approach. But the alienation that is already felt at the level of the nation-state is likely to increase. The remoteness of government from the citizen, already detrimental to participation in the United States, would be exacerbated.

The opposite solution is to emphasize local communities at the expense of larger ones. Here participation can be increased. Yet there are severe limitations to this proposal as well. First, so many of the decisions that determine the life of local groups cannot be made at that level; the weakening of community at higher levels simply transfers power from community to other forces such as the market and its chief transnational players. Second, when local groupings have unchecked power, they often rule some of the residents of the region out of the community. The rights so painfully won for minorities are unlikely to survive long when unchecked power is transferred to localities. Of course, the assumption here, based on historical experience, is that many local societies will not function as "communities" for all their residents.

A third option is to aim to weaken all communities. This can be in the name of individualism. It can also be in opposition to concentration of community feeling at any one level. We should learn to identify ourselves at many geographical levels, each of which involves some participation and mutual responsibility and gives us some portion of our identity, but none of which dominates the others. We should also gain much of our identity through participation in a variety of non-geographical groupings. This direction reduces the risk of fanatical conflict between communities, and it can restrict the ability of any level to deny the basic rights of its citizens.

Despite the merits of this approach, it provides too little self-identification for most people. We need primary identities. These can be multiple to some extent, but not drastically so. Also, the kind of participation that is possible at local levels is not possible at larger ones. These considerations lead me to a somewhat different formulation.

First, an essential norm for desirable community is self-transcendence. That is, a healthy community must itself call for responsibility to others beyond its own membership. It must call for cooperation with other communities. It must relativize itself as an inadequate object of ultimate loyalty.

Second, given this self-relativization, in the primary community members should have some personal acquaintance with one another, and some of the mutual responsibility should be exercised directly. Instead of distributing loyalty over many levels of community as in the third proposal above, the larger groupings should function as communities of communities.

"Community" has been defined in terms of the grouping of individuals—but the meaning can be extended without much difficulty to the grouping of communities. A community of local communities would be a grouping of communities that took responsibility for one another, that provided an important part of the self-identification of the local communities (and thus of their members), and that made its decisions in ways in which all of the member communities participated.

The local community would make those decisions that can be made locally. The community of communities would make those decisions that can only be made at the larger geographical level. Also, it would restrict the freedom of local communities in at least two ways.

It would prevent local communities from degenerating into expressions of the power of the majority over the minority. In other words, local communities would grant sufficient power to the community of communities to make sure that some minimum of human rights, including the right of participation in governance, was preserved throughout the larger community. It would also prevent each local community from damaging the environment of its neighbors or harming them in other ways. Each would gain from the assurance that its neighbors were restricted in this way.

These communities of communities would still function in rather small geographical areas, perhaps counties as the political map of the United States is now drawn. They would need in their turn to enter into community with other communities of communities, so that a state might be the appropriate level to think of a community of communities of communities. I will not pursue this to the national and international level. It is simply a way of thinking of political life as structured from below upward, rather than from the nation-state both upward and downward, as at present.

Given the self-transcending nature of the local community, that is, its commitment to serve not only its own members but also the larger good, there is no danger of its becoming too strong. Its strengthening along the three lines I have suggested is at the same time a strengthening of its commitment to be a valued member of larger communities. As the larger communities recede from accessibility, the sense of participation of the individual within them inevitably declines; but because important issues are also decided locally, the result is not alienation from the political process as a whole.

One difference between the working out of this model and the third one above is that members of a local community would not vote directly for representatives to make decisions for the communities of communities. They would select persons known to them to take part with representatives of other local communities in making those decisions that are made at the next level. They would leave to that group of persons, who would come to know one another personally, the selection of representatives to the larger levels. Personal knowledge would operate in this selection process at every level, so that packaging candidates for television sound bites would decline in importance.

My point is not that in this or any other way corruption of the political process can be avoided. Still, a nonalienating process can reduce it and provide channels for correcting it as it arises. The New England town meetings have been less subject to corruption than nationally organized political parties.

The amount of significant power that can be exercised at the local level depends largely on the nature of the economy. If we continue on the road to a globally centralized economy, then this proposal for community-oriented reconstruction of the political process can be of minimal value. If we move instead toward a decentralized economy in which relatively small regions are relatively self-sufficient, then the political power exercised in such regions will be significant.

Alongside a political structure organized from the bottom up, there should be many communities that are not geographical but religious, scientific, and cultural. To live in a small local community in no way needs to cut one off from ties to persons with similar interests around the world. The fact that the primary community is geographical (as long as the community is a self-transcending one) should not discourage membership in multiple communities.

The present functioning of the United Nations also suggests that these nongovernmental organizations can play a meaningful role at many levels of community of communities. Of course, such structures can be distorting. Nevertheless, private groups crossing political lines can bring badly needed information and commitment to issues of human rights, the environment, economic development, and social justice. To hear from these groups and be guided by them, when their members represent nongeographical constituencies, can be an enrichment of community governance rather than a distortion.

The model of community and communities of communities gives little guidance in terms of application to difficult cases, such as towns or villages or neighborhoods of substantial ethnic diversity. In such places the functioning communities are often defined principally by ethnicity.

One may respond to this situation in two valid ways. One is to integrate the separate communities into one geographical one, where common concerns and identities outweigh those that are ethnic or separatist. In some places this can work and should be done; in others, forcing diverse ethnic groups into political units drawn on geographical lines will be counterproductive. The town meeting will be at best a place of conflict between the two groups, one in which full, free discussion of the merits of a proposal or of a representative will not take place. The real discussions will occur in caucuses internal to the ethnic groups.

In cases of this sort, the local ethnic groups should be recognized as the unit communities. They are more likely to function in a self-transcendent way when they are able to manage their own affairs and elect their own representatives to the community of communities where larger concerns are dealt with. Since it is very important that the unit communities function strongly as communities of mutual responsibility, identity, and participation, trying to work against the natural connections of ethnicity will usually prove counterproductive.

The objection that people must get to know one another across ethnic lines is valid. But these contacts should not be competitive and threatening. People who have control over their own lives are much freer to be open in friendship to others than are those who are struggling for autonomy.

This whole vision of a world renewed on the basis of community presupposes the reinvigoration of local face-to-face communities, exactly those communities from which so many moderns have fled. I have acknowledged that there were reasons for that flight, but I believe that such communities can be renewed without parochialism and tyranny. In any case, the inevitable collapse of societies that destroy their community base means that risks must be taken for its restoration.

Although local communities can exist in urban neighborhoods and can be brought into being in suburbs, one cannot expect these to provide the primary basis for political and social reorganization. An adequate community must have a quasi-communitarian relation to the land, which can be achieved far more successfully in a rural location. Also, the possibility of achieving a significant measure of economic self-sufficiency is greater in a rural than in an urban context.

The relation to the land can be quasi-communitarian in that some of the defining elements of community can apply. The land can be part of what gives a person identity. Human beings can take significant responsibility for the land. They can recognize a community of interest with the other creatures who inhabit the land. But they cannot expect these other creatures to adopt a conscious concern for them or to participate with them in political processes. The closest we could come would be to appoint members of the human community to represent the interests of other creatures in the political assembly.

While the renewal of community in urban neighborhoods is urgent, the deepest challenge is to create new rural communities that move toward relative self-sufficiency through a nonexploitative relation to the land. These might develop in a variety of ways. One is idealistic experimentation. A second approach could follow from policies of land redistribution resulting from the rising price of fossil fuels and the need for more labor on the land. A third could come from the growing frustration with urban living and the renewed longing for closer contact with the land. A fourth could stem directly from the environmental movement.

Thus, forces are at work that may lead to a renewal of rural life in this country. They are more likely to do so as this renewal is understood as a part of an urgently needed economic, political, social, and environmental redirection of the national life. We need images of what rural community can be that counter the hostility still directed against it. Whatever contribution Matfield Green can make to this process (see Wes Jackson's essay in this volume) should be respected, appreciated, and honored.

Community, like everything worthwhile in history, is ambiguous. There have never been ideal communities and there never will be. But without communities, however imperfect, society can only decay. The restoration of local communities, especially rural communities of human scale, is essential to national renewal.

in search of community

PHILIP SELZNICK

MANY writers (and readers) are troubled by the fact that the idea of "community" is so elusive. There appears to be no consensus as to its central meaning. Much the same may be said, of course, regarding many other key concepts in social science and philosophy, including "morality," "justice," "the political," "law," "culture," and "rationality." In each case a working definition may serve the purposes of a particular argument or inquiry. Nevertheless, each term has rich connotations to which appeal may be made when some new line of inquiry is pursued. This process needs some discipline, but to try to stop it altogether would be futile and self-defeating.

A useful discipline is adherence to the rule that definitions in social theory should be weak, inclusive, and relatively noncontroversial. It is in the formulation of theories, not definitions, that we properly argue about the dynamics and kinds of law, authority, socialization, or community. Hypotheses regarding rudimentary or elaborated states belong to the realm of theory. They should not depend for credibility on how a key term is defined. The point is not to eliminate controversy but to transfer it to a more appropriate place, where empirical investigation is relevant and helpful.

An appropriately weak, inclusive, and neutral definition of community is the following: *A group is a community to the extent that it encompasses a broad range of activities and interests, and to the extent that participation implicates whole persons rather than segmental interests or activities.* Thus understood, community can be treated as a variable aspect of group experience. Groups can be more or less full-blown communities; and they can approximate community in different ways.

It is not slipshod to speak of the European Community, the Catholic community, the university community, or the law school community, or of the police as an occupational community. The main point is that a framework of shared beliefs, interests, and commitments unites a set of *varied* groups and activities. Some are central, others peripheral, but all are connected by bonds that establish a common faith or fate, a personal identity, a sense of belonging, and a supportive structure of activities and relationships. The more pathways there are for participation in diverse ways and touching multiple interests—for example, worshipping in Catholic churches, attending Catholic schools, contributing to Catholic charities, reading the Catholic press—the richer is the experience of community. Thus community is a comprehensive framework within which a common, multifaceted life may be lived.

Sociologists have often said that community necessarily presumes locality (see Schnore 1973). Most "community studies" focus on particular villages, towns, or neighborhoods, where (more or less) complete rounds of life can be observed.

This approach makes sense, as a practical matter, because common residence is a congenial condition—perhaps the most congenial condition—for forming and sustaining community life. However, communities can be formed in other ways as well, for example on the basis of concerted activity and shared belief. In the interests of coherent theory, we should avoid confusing a congenial *condition,* or a highly probably *correlate,* with an essential or defining feature.

Treating community as a variable attribute of group life allows for the possibility that special-purpose institutions may become communities, or at least quasi-communities. This form of community occurs most readily when purpose is not too rigidly or narrowly conceived, when leeway is allowed for controversy over ends and means, and when participation is a significant part of a person's life within the organization. Thus community is more likely to develop in military or police organizations, which encourage a shared lifestyle, than in, say, marginal business firms where employment is sporadic, personnel turnover is high, training is unimportant, and work is highly routine and specialized. In other words, the emergence of community depends on the opportunity for, and the impulse toward, comprehensive interaction, commitment, and responsibility. These are variable outcomes; they require congenial conditions; but they are not necessarily peripheral or unimportant, even within special-purpose organizations.

This argument leaves intact the analytical distinction between community and special-purpose organization. The "pure" organization is an instrument for mobilizing human energies in disciplined, goal-directed ways. A community has generic functions but no special purpose. This contrast is one of the hardiest and most useful in sociological theory. Therefore it is surprising to read that "unlike all other terms of social organization (state, nation, and society, etc.) it [community] seems never . . . to be given any positive opposing or distinguishing term" (Williams 1976, 66). The difference is often blurred in social reality, and we frequently want to move organizations *in the direction* of community; but the distinction remains a useful starting point for description and diagnosis.

ELEMENTS OF COMMUNITY

It has been said that "community" is a word that "seems never to be used unfavourably" (ibid.). That is surely an exaggeration, for the experience of community has many detractors who emphasize its potential for oppression. Nevertheless, the generally favorable usage is easy to understand when we remember that community—like culture, friendship, socialization, family life—has prima facie moral and social benefits. Typically communities provide settings within which people grow and flourish, and within which subgroups are nourished and protected. This process establishes a presumption of moral worth. The presumption is rebuttable if a given community is too thin or attenuated to provide an effective framework for common life; too rigid and stultifying to serve the needs of personal and institutional development; too insular or self-destructive in its dealings with other communities; or is otherwise inadequate from the standpoint of critical morality. The same logic applies to our appreciation of family, friendship, law, and culture.

Thus understood, a normative theory of community is at once critical and affirmative—affirmative in that it explores, identifies, and embraces the positive contributions of community to human flourishing; critical in that it asks of a particular community how far, in what ways, and with what effects it deviates from a standard. The standard may allow for moral plurality, that is, for different but roughly equal renderings of the good community, but it should have enough bite to distinguish the better from the worse, the genuine from the spurious.

Community is not a unidimensional idea. On the contrary, an adequate theory must take into account the varied sources of community and the multiple values at stake. These constitute a complex set of interacting variables. The following are the most important.

HISTORICITY The bonds of community are strongest when they are fashioned from strands of shared history and culture. They are weak and precarious when they must depend on very general interests or abstract ideas. Furthermore, the character of a community largely reflects the particularities of custom, language, and institutional life; a heritage of significant events and crises; and historically determined attributes such as size, geography, and demography.

Historicity has prima facie moral worth. Rootedness and belonging make for individual well-being as well as commitment to others; and a sense of history is needed for sound collective judgment of means and ends. Communities, like persons, can do better, and be better, if they understand their own possibilities and limits. To reach that understanding, however, brute particularity must be transcended. The quest is for principles latent in the community's culture and history. Once formulated, such principles become resources for internal dialogue. They are instruments of reflective morality, that is, they are authoritative standpoints from which to criticize and change specific beliefs, norms, and practices. At the same time, the principles express a distinctive ethos and a special experience.

IDENTITY A shared history and fate tends to produce a sense of community, manifested in loyalty, piety, and identity. Every effort to create a community fosters such feelings and perceptions. A formed identity is the natural product of socialization, which is carried out not only in families but in most other institutions as well. When socialization is effective, it is always accompanied by some identification of self and other, self and locality, self and association. The outcomes are highly variable, however. The mere fact that an identity-forming process is at work does not tell us how effective it is; nor does it say what kind of self—conformist or independent, supine or resourceful—is being produced.

Of all the elements of community, the moral worth of a formed identity is the most problematic. (Here is one reason to avoid the common error of equating a *sense* of community with community itself.) Fixed identities—local, religious, ethnic—are likely to generate demands for self-affirmation, which all too often lead to insularity and withdrawal. This parochialism is a chief source of virulent antagonisms. Hence the formation of identities can be destructive of community. The gains in security and self-esteem must be balanced against the loss of more comprehensive, more inclusive, more integrative attitudes.

MUTUALITY Community begins with, and is largely supported by, the experience of interdependence and reciprocity. These very practical conditions account for the voluntary and rational components of community. If people and groups do not need one another, if nothing is to be gained from reciprocity and cooperation, community is not likely to emerge or endure. For this necessary condition to be sufficient, however, mutuality cannot be too narrowly focused. It must go beyond impersonal exchange, beyond coordination for limited goals. To be effective in forming community, mutuality must implicate persons and groups as *unities* and not only in respect to segmental activities or roles. In the context of community, mutuality contemplates continuing relationships and high stakes.

PLURALITY According to the pluralist and corporatist doctrines of Tocqueville, Lamennais, Gierke, and others, a community draws much of its vitality from "intermediate associations," such as families, churches, and membership groups of many kinds. They are havens of protection and vehicles of meaningful, person-centered participation. Through significant membership in such groups the individual's relation to the larger community can be extended and enriched. A community is impoverished when people are stripped of their group attachments and left naked before an impersonal or central authority. And the group structure of society generates countervailing forces to moderate the influence of any single power bloc.

Thus understood, plurality is a normative idea. It does not refer to *any* dispersal of power and commitment, *any* proliferation of interests, groups, and authorities. A healthy differentiation of institutions, and of personal, family, ethnic, locality, and occupational groups, depends on the capacity of each to preserve its own well-being—within a framework of legitimacy and without fracturing or fragmenting the social order.

AUTONOMY Although pluralism has great merit, it also has a cardinal weakness: it is the assumption that individual well-being is effectively guaranteed by group autonomy and integrity. Pluralists have rightly emphasized that individuals need nurture and support, and group protection against external domination. But "subsidiary" groups can be oppressive, often more so than the state. Therefore pluralist theory must be modified as necessary to protect freedom in association as well as freedom of association.

A concern for personal autonomy does not settle what freedoms are appropriate in the context at hand; nor does it assume that autonomy is equivalent to unconditional opportunity and choice. It does assume that the worth of community is measured by the contribution it makes to the flourishing of unique and responsible persons. As an attribute of selfhood, and of self-affirmation, autonomy requires commitment as well as choice.

PARTICIPATION It is elementary that personal autonomy can only be achieved in and through social participation. This postulate does not preclude physical isolation. People who choose to live alone, or prisoners in isolation, depend for mental health on prior socialization and on participation in a socially constructed symbolic world.

But what kind of participation? Some kinds encourage rationality and self-determination; others undermine them. Some are egalitarian, others demand a spirit of subordination. The most rudimentary (and important) forms of communal participation have to do with the basic continuities of life: procreation, child rearing, work, kinship, friendship. Participation in broader religious or political contexts builds on those continuities and tends to be distorted if they are weakened or absent. The mass mobilization of detached individuals is not a paradigm of communal participation. The lesson is that participation reflects and sustains community insofar as it entails multiple memberships and diverse commitments. The more compartmented, specialized, or singleminded the activity, the more limited is its contribution to the life of a community.

INTEGRATION All of the elements noted above require supportive institutions, norms, beliefs, and practices. These must exhibit enough coherence to sustain the foundations of a common life. Hence we see the emergence of distinctively integrative political, legal, and cultural institutions. The quality of community depends, to a large extent, on the character of these institutions. How we perceive and construct the political and cultural order—as a tight system of integration and subordination, or as a framework within which plurality and autonomy may flourish—becomes a central concern.

A fully realized community will have a rich and *balanced* mixture of these elements. To have a community, or to strive for community, none can be completely sacrificed. We cannot ignore the givenness of received custom and decisive events, but the appeal to historicity must respect the other values, insofar as they are affected. Similarly, the claims of plurality and autonomy must be balanced against those of mutuality and participation. In this normative theory, the moral quality of a community is measured by its ability to defend all the principal values at stake, to hold them in tension as necessary, and to encourage their refinement and elaboration.

It does not follow that any state of affairs less than a fully realized community is necessarily deficient from a moral point of view—any more than we would say that the morally best person is necessarily the best integrated or fully rounded. Different types of community—religious, political, occupational, institutional, international—will have different mixes of the main elements. A religious community may well give greater weight to historicity and mutuality than, say, an enterprise-based community. And religious communities may differ among themselves in the weight they give to various forms and sources of fellowship. There is always room for debate about the kind of community a group should be.

THE LIMITS OF GEMEINSCHAFT

Our understanding of community owes much to—and is distorted by—the well-known polarities of *Gemeinschaft* and *Gesellschaft*. Building on the work of Gierke, Maine, Marx, and other nineteenth-century historians and social theorists, Ferdinand Tönnies (1855–1936) hit on a striking way of characterizing the evolution of modern society (see Tönnies 1887). He did not trace that evolution. His book is analytical rather than historical, a study of social types, not of sequences. Nevertheless, the work has a major place among efforts to understand the transition from a kin-based world of organic unity to an exchange-based world of artificial association.

The German word *Gemeinschaft* connotes moral unity, rootedness, intimacy, and kinship. Although usually translated as "community," it really refers to a *kind* of community, one that fully realizes values of historicity and mutuality—and does so even at considerable cost to personal mobility and autonomy.

In gemeinschaft, social practices and institutions are infused with intrinsic worth. Beliefs and institutions are "affirmed," not chosen or designed; they are valued for themselves, not for extraneous ends. As a result, people "remain essentially united in spite of all separating factors, whereas in the Gesellschaft they are essentially separated in spite of all uniting factors" (Tönnies 1963, 65). The gemeinschaft model closely fits what is often called a folk or traditional society, as well as an idealized feudal order.

Gemeinschaft brings to mind a society warmed by intimacy and united by brotherhood. The imagery is seductive. There is a near-irresistible temptation to treat what was offered by Tönnies as an analytical device—an ideal type—as if it were the full embodiment of a moral vision. But there is more to community than intimacy and brotherhood, just as there is more to family life than love and sharing. Gemeinschaft does not encompass the full range of variables that constitute community or that affect its quality.

The limits of gemeinschaft may be seen if we consider the difference between commune and community. An account of the hippie communes of the 1960s put it this way:

> Typically, communes were made up fairly uniformly of young people who identified with the hip subculture of drugs, rock and voluntary poverty. . . . By contrast, the community embraced a greater diversity of people, not just the hip and the young. Where communes left finances, work and decision to the fickle will of group consciousness, communities leaned more heavily on definite structures: work systems, treasurers, and corporations. Many were united around a single craft or art. . . . The physical, as well as emotional, distance was greater in a community than in a commune. Traditionally, a com-

munity was made up of separate houses rather than a large common dwelling. (Houriet 1971, 205–206)

The commune is a quest for communion rather than community. Communion is a psychic unity, whereas community embraces a range of activities and associations. Because it is narrowly based on psychic unity, the commune is an inherently unstable social form. If more stability is desired, the commune must become a community.

The lesson is that communities are characterized by structural differentiation as well as by shared consciousness. A natural community—even a highly organic community—cannot be completely homogeneous. As a framework for common life it must develop some division of labor, some system of authority, some proliferation of roles, groups, and institutions. These structures are sustained by ongoing, interdependent activities, not by symbolic experience alone. The basic fact is that participation in communities is mediated by participation in families, localities, personal networks, and institutions. This core participation preserves the integrity and rationality of the participants. We do not think of participation in communities as irrational or self-destructive. On the contrary, without community rationality is often precarious and may be undone.

Thus the demands of community are not necessarily opposed to rational judgment and personal autonomy. On the contrary, a radical abridgment of these values signals the distortion or destruction of community. Community is a framework within which ordinary social life can go forward. Normal life is lived concretely, in the light of practical needs and circumstances. A community cannot flourish if it does not foster and support the skills people need, including common sense in personal relationships. The rationality of basic skills is preserved even in highly integrated communities, including the preliterate communities studied by anthropologists.

Nor will a community prosper if it tries to be completely homogeneous in thought and action. This was understood by Aristotle, who in his *Politics* criticized Plato for assuming "that it is best for the whole state to be as unified as possible" (McKeon 1941, 1261a). In Aristotle's theory, the political community is the arena within which a common life is carried on and perfected. But perfection must take account of social reality, which includes the need for diversity, that is, for differentiated groups, roles, occupations, and functions. As a corollary, Aristotle wrote, "the principle of reciprocity . . . is the salvation of states." It may be said, indeed, that the integration of communities depends at least as much on interdependence—Durkheim's "organic solidarity"—as it does on symbolic cohesion or "mechanical solidarity" (see Durkheim 1893).

Why this unity in diversity? Why is it correct to say, for example, that "*a certain degree of separateness of the parts* is necessary if the whole is to be considered a community"? (Feinberg 1988, 104; emphasis added). The answer lies in what it means to share a common life. A common life is not a fused life, for in that case there would be no need for regulation or governance, no need to take account of individual differences, no need for adjustment, reciprocity, or cooperation. The tacit assumption is that people and groups participate in any community, large or small, as individuated and self-regarding entities. They are independent as well as interdependent.

Thus the distinctive function of community is the reconciliation of partial and general perspectives. A community must recognize the legitimacy of egoism as a basic aspect of humanity and therefore as a necessary starting point for group life. If egoism did not persist, there would be no need for community; if it had no moral and social worth, we might try to rid ourselves of it by repressive measures or by attempts to fashion a wholly altruistic self. But that is not the mission of community. Its true function is to regulate, discipline, and especially to channel self-regarding conduct, thereby binding it, so far as possible, to comprehensive interests and ideals.

What we prize in community is not unity of any sort, at any cost, but unity that preserves the integrity of persons, groups, and institutions. Thus understood, community is profoundly *federalist* in spirit and structure. It is a unity of unities. That principle has been implicit, and very often explicit, in much that has been said about morality and community (see Etzoni 1988, Ch. 1; Rawls 1971, 520 ff.).

This line of argument suggests that it is as wrong to make a fetish of solidarity as it is to glorify unfettered choice or unconditional independence. Each is, in its own way, corrosive of community. The first, in reaching for total integration, turns community in to a parody of itself. The second offers an ethos too thin to sustain more than a minimal moral order. A genuinely communitarian doctrine— one rooted in the experience of common life—resists both extremes. It seeks theories and strategies that promise stable accommodation and conjoint fulfillment of all the values entailed by the ideal of community.

One such strategy looks to institutions as the primary agencies and most reliable safeguards of community. Institutions embody values and enhance integration, but they do so in ways that resist homogeneity and sustain differentiation. Strong communities are *institution centered*. Their cohesion and moral competence derive from the strength and integrity of families, schools, parties, government agencies, voluntary associations, and law. Where there is respect for institutions in all spheres of life, values of solidarity, duty, and restraint are vindicated. At the same time, a variety of perspectives, reflecting the variety of institutions, is appropriate and legitimate.

A focus on institutions turns attention away from the psychic cohesion so often associated with the idea of community. Instead of seeing community in the emergence of like-minded, undifferentiated individuals, we see it in a network of distinct but interdependent institutions. This perspective does not eliminate the need for attention to core values, but the latter are likely to be strong, and effectively implemented, if they are built into the premises and govern the operation of major institutions.

Here we can detect echoes of conservative doctrine, which treats institutions, not individuals, as constitutive of community. This is an important if partial truth. It need not follow that institutions must be unresponsive or that, in their operation, only the status quo is protected. When the integrity of universities is respected, so too are academic freedom and the possibility of dangerous thoughts. Although the rule of law carries an inescapable message of restraint, it also enlarges horizons and secures new rights. The conservative insight need not prejudge whether a particular institution merits survival, renewal, expansion, or replacement.

part three   **BECOMING NATIVE**

A PLACE IS NOT A PLACE UNTIL PEOPLE HAVE BEEN BORN IN IT, HAVE

GROWN UP IN IT, LIVED IN IT, KNOWN IT, DIED IN IT—HAVE BOTH

EXPERIENCED AND SHAPED IT, AS INDIVIDUALS, FAMILIES,

NEIGHBORHOODS, AND COMMUNITIES, OVER MORE THAN ONE GENERATION.

SOME ARE BORN IN THEIR PLACE, SOME FIND IT, SOME REALIZE AFTER

LONG SEARCHING THAT THE PLACE THEY LEFT IS THE ONE THEY HAVE

BEEN SEARCHING FOR. BUT WHATEVER THEIR RELATION TO IT, IT IS MADE

A PLACE ONLY BY SLOW ACCRUAL, LIKE A CORAL REEF.

—Wallace Stegner, *Where the Bluebird Sings to the Lemonade Springs,* 1992

redeeming the land

RICHARD CARTWRIGHT AUSTIN

IT is now fifteen years since 1995, when the Reverend Anne Stem, pastor of two small Lutheran churches in rural Redemption County, fashioned the plan during winter evening conversations with Wally Boggs, who taught agronomy at Central College, and Father John McKay, who chaired the economics department at Mercy College. They decided to buy the whole county, or as much as was for sale, and redistribute lands, homes, and workplaces to people willing to covenant for a just society that respected the earth. They would show America an alternative to the harsh exploitation and rapid depopulation of landscapes that prevailed elsewhere. They believed the plan could double the county's population in twenty-five years and create a vital, self-sufficient community with a diverse culture that would inspire people elsewhere to work for similar changes.

Stem could see that the Lutheran community had been in steady decline for forty years. Her two congregations were both aging, and although a lot of land was currently on the market, only a few young men and women considered buying a farm or taking up another trade in the community. Dr. Boggs saw his agronomy classes dwindle year by year as Central College, a Presbyterian liberal arts school that had once made an important contribution to regional culture, turned to students from the East who had been refused by their first-choice colleges. Father John was disappointed that Mercy College, principally a technical school, had little impact on the community beyond providing the training that helped young people move away. The Catholic population had dwindled to less than half of what it had been when he was ordained in this diocese; indeed, the future of the college was now under official review.

Because Redemption County was somewhat hilly and thus less suited to farm consolidation than other counties in the region, the credit crisis had not struck here as swiftly. Nevertheless, for a decade farm credit banks and insurance companies had been foreclosing larger farms. More recently, the county office of the Farmers' Home Administration had begun a broad foreclosure campaign against smaller farmers who had dropped behind on mortgage payments. Passage of the North American Free Trade Agreement and an expanded GATT treaty on world trade had made it clear that the Clinton administration would continue Republican policies of reducing agricultural trade restrictions and farm protections, thereby opening world markets for the benefit of large producers. Redemption County would probably compete poorly, but even if farms were consolidated further and devoted to export commodities, the result would be continued declines in population, economic vitality, and local culture, coupled with intensified abuse of the land.

The new plan required a great deal of money, for initially the Covenant Community Trust, as it was called, needed to raise the capital for land reform without access to governmental tax receipts. The three leaders enlisted the participation of several Christian denominations; then two large philanthropic foundations that supported agricultural policy research agreed to provide major funding if large tracts of land and other properties could be assembled. Another breakthrough came when the president of an insurance company took a personal interest in the project. He arranged a land swap among several banks and insurers who together held about a fifth of the county's property in foreclosures, so that substantial acreage could be optioned to the trust.

Meanwhile, the organizers led intense and often heated discussions across Redemption County. The plan offered immediate relief to farmers who were overwhelmed by debt, and promised economic growth for which the county had longed, but the proposal was unconventional and unfamiliar and would encourage an influx of people of uncertain race and background. After many local church congregations voted to support the plan and welcome new people, and the trustees of both colleges agreed to direct their educational programs to the effort, the county Board of Supervisors also resolved to cooperate.

These were the goals of the Covenant Community, as it came to be called:

To make land and shelter available to those who need them at a price they can afford

To modify traditional property rights on these lands in the interest of environmental integrity

To provide training in new farming techniques and other necessary trades

To establish networks of neighborhood support and economic discipline based on voluntary commitment rather than collective ownership or the pressure of debt

To give preferential incentives for trade and exchange within the community in order to build a county economy with some self-sufficiency and a culture with some resiliency

To inspire the spread of such values in American society

The pages that follow explain how these goals were pursued.

The Covenant Community Trust not only serves as the instrument to redistribute lands and free them from debt, it also retains a legal interest on behalf of the land itself and the biotic community upon it. When the trust deeds lands to individuals or families, it retains 50 percent ownership of the land—although not of buildings or other improvements—as trustee for the nonhuman community on the tract. Each participating landholder prepares an annual conservation and production plan for review by the trust, and trust representatives periodically inspect landholdings. In cooperation with the colleges, the trust provides training for prospective landholders as well as continuing education and field support in ecology, conservation, forestry, animal health, and other disciplines. Where reclamation and restoration of a healthy ecosystem are particularly difficult, the trust may provide financial assistance to the landholder. Under agreement with each participating landholder, the trust receives 10 percent of all agricultural sales destined for shipment outside the county. After five years' residence, landholders may sell their homes, lands, and other facilities, or portions of them, and may purchase additional lands, but the trust's legal interest in the natural vitality of these lands continues.

That first parcel of lands offered to the trust by the insurance company included farmland of varying quality scattered throughout the county, plus several town and village properties. The trust decided to purchase those lands and other properties, regardless of their quality, that could form the basis for four potential rural neighborhoods, plus properties in Central City near one college or the other. Land was evaluated for its reclamation requirements and productive potential, then was subdivided into small farms that families might tend with simple machinery. Many of these included an existing house either on the land or in a nearby village, some of which stood in need of substantial repair. Other homes and buildings acquired by the trust were designated for mechanics, tradespeople, and professionals who might contribute to the neighborhood culture and economy.

When established county residents who were threatened with foreclosure asked for assistance, the trust attempted to purchase their farms at a fair price regardless of location, assuring the owners that after retraining they might return to their former homestead. In the case of a few large farms, however, the trust insisted before purchase that it be allowed to subdivide portions for other homesteaders. When local people who had previously lost their farms asked to join the Covenant Community, they were given preference; a few were even reestablished on the land they had once tilled.

The trust advertised, both locally and in national journals, that rural homesteads were available to those who were ready to commit to an experimental community. All participants were required to spend a year in residence at Central College for orientation and training, then work a five-year apprenticeship on the land before they received title to their property. Those with means paid for their training, land, and home as they were able, while others received training and homestead without cost. When the popular media picked up the news, applications flooded in. This enabled the Covenant Community, from the beginning, to select diverse and promising participants.

Even local residents who wished to participate were required to let their farms lie fallow for a year and to move with their families into the college housing. This requirement was resented at first, but it quickly proved a saving grace for the program. Men and women, many of them middle-aged, halted patterns of work that had become inflexible and began to think more seriously about their lives and their environment. The opportunity for locals and newcomers to get acquainted on campus was indispensable preparation for the cooperation they would need in the neighborhood communities to be developed. Participants shared a core curriculum on homesteading techniques, environmental science, community relations, practical economics, and biblical covenant ethics. They also chose among specialized courses in such practical fields as carpentry, ironwork, engine repair, forestry, plant genetics, animal husbandry, and intensive gardening, as well as liberal arts studies in religion, literature, the arts, and political science. Some participants arrived with specialized training and experience, and a few were able to study longer than a year before taking up their homestead. All learned that regular, continuing education would be important to their covenant commitment. By the end of each year a few had dropped out and a few more needed to be screened out, but usually three-quarters or more were ready to affirm the covenant and take up their homesteads.

Affirming the covenant requires commitment in three areas: ecological responsibility, economic discipline, and sabbath observance. Members must promise to respect the integrity of the land and the living community upon it, including both wild and domesticated animals and the natural systems that support life. They affirm that the well-being of the Covenant Community depends on a healthy environment, and they pledge efforts to improve the quality of their land. This commitment to ecological welfare is institutionalized in landholding partnerships with the Covenant Community Trust, which acts as a trustee for natural life.

Economic discipline takes three specific forms. First, members pledge to use the technologies approved by their neighborhood covenant council in return for neighborly assistance. This promise is the heart of the matter. Homesteading and subsistence living require a great deal of cooperation, yet neighbors can help each other efficiently only if their productive endeavors complement each other and, more particularly, if their technologies are compatible. The amazing efficiency of Amish neighborly assistance, for example, depends on rigorous technological discipline so that one farmer may substitute his equipment for that of another and practice common skills with confidence. Forty men can erect a barn in a day because the design and building techniques do not vary from one barn to another or one year to the next. In the covenant neighborhoods, however, the intention is not to build a traditionalist society like that of the Amish but rather to found innovative communities. The efficiency of neighborly assistance is therefore somewhat less. Nevertheless, neighbors must harmonize their technologies if they are to be useful to one another.

Of the four original neighborhood communities, one decided to farm with horses rather than tractors although, unlike the Amish, they use electric power for many chores and some farmers own a car or pickup truck. Farmers can support one another with compatible equipment, while the community includes a mechanic, an electrician, and a blacksmith. Over the years another neighborhood group has collectively acquired a fine tractor and a full range of tillage and harvesting equipment, housed in an old garage in their village. One member works full time to maintain this equipment, while another operates it on the community farms. In one community nearly half the families needed new homes and agreed on a standard design so that materials could be prepared or purchased at lower cost and cooperative work could proceed more efficiently.

Neighborhood covenant groups meet every Sunday evening to plan cooperative activities for the week. While members are free to undertake novel projects on their own, the covenant standard is that when neighbors expect help from one another they are to agree on common technologies and procedures so that the assistance may be given efficiently, even in emergency situations.

The second element of economic discipline is a common wage scale. Barter and neighborly helpfulness are encouraged, to reduce the need for cash income to pay wages, and this procedure contributes to the stability of each homestead. Nevertheless, on occasion wages must be paid, and there are services for which salaries are required. The Covenant Community recognizes that a variety of vocations are needed in a healthy society—whether farming, medicine, teaching, carpentry, art, or preaching—and that those who practice *any* useful vocation are entitled to comparable dignity. Therefore it determined to make all professional wages the same. When one covenant member provides a skilled service to another in return for a wage, that wage is fifteen dollars an hour. Unskilled and apprentice labor is paid at the rate of five dollars an hour. People are free to work outside the community without wage restrictions. However, now that Mercy and Central colleges are fully within the covenant community, professors, secretaries, and maintenance personnel all receive fifteen dollars an hour. Doctors and nurses at the new Covenant Clinic are paid the same. There has been no shortage of applicants for these positions up to now, for many people feel that the quality of life here provides an added reward.

The third aspect of economic discipline is *scrip,* a nominal paper currency that circulates among community members. A member must accept this paper currency, printed by the community, for one-fourth of the value of financial transactions with another member, and may accept it for more. This discipline is designed to stimulate trade within the community and reduce the temptation to seek bargains from outside suppliers. If a quarter of my college teaching salary comes in scrip, I am sure to spend that portion within the community. If my neighbor who farms with horses and takes care of his land can sell me corn for four dollars a bushel, three dollars in cash and one in scrip, I will not be tempted to buy agribusiness corn at three-fifty in cash. As the community grows, the scrip system provides an incentive for the development of new crops, services, products, and businesses in the area.

Established merchants in Redemption County were irate when the covenant community introduced scrip, for they were sure it would deprive them of a share in the promised growth of local trade. When a few tried accepting scrip, however, they found they could use it in partial payment for products and services from covenant members who were willing to take scrip even though not obligated to do so in this instance. Merchants became more resourceful in buying from the local community as well as in marketing to it. As the Covenant Community has expanded, most county merchants have come to accept scrip for some portion of payment because it brings them trade. Business is growing.

The third covenant commitment, sabbath observance, is not designed to compel religious worship but rather to limit power and greed. Most participants in the covenant are religious, but it is not a specifically Christian community and there are no religious requirements for membership. The sabbath pledge is a promise to rest every seventh day and allow others that same rest, to refrain from long-term debt, and to forgive one's debtors. Homesteaders pledge not to turn their difficult work into perpetual drudgery nor to impose drudgery on family members, draft animals, or the land itself.

This pledge builds community, for neighbors need confidence that on one day each week they will not be needed for production assistance; societies need collective rhythms of relaxation so that cultural and recreational events may be scheduled. Since the Covenant Community defines its sabbath from sundown on Saturday to sundown on Sunday, hardly a Saturday evening passes without a community supper, dance, musicale, play, or some other social activity, while sandlot baseball thrives on Sunday afternoons. Even if you are poor and tired—indeed, especially then!—you need recreation.

This pledge embraces "sabbatical" disciplines as well, including the biblical ethics that inhibit long-term debt. The most important part of the whole scheme may be placing people on the land without debt and then giving them incentives not to borrow. Debt ties families to the money economy and forces farmers to specialize in those crops that will satisfy their creditors rather than meet their own needs and the needs of their neighbors. Debt erodes personal freedom and damages the social fabric of a face-to-face community. Therefore Covenant Community members must promise not to mortgage their land or otherwise borrow money—even from institutions outside the community—for terms longer than six years, and must pledge that every seventh year they will remain debt free. The community acknowledges that brief borrowings may be necessary, but long-term debt forces people into drudgery and threatens the homestead. Likewise, all covenanters must forgive debts to other members that run to the seventh year, for a community cannot flourish when some people hold others to perpetual debt.

The biblical injunction to let the land lie fallow every seventh year is given a more imaginative, less literal application. The Covenant Community Trust tries to ensure that the biotic life and fertility of agricultural land are sustained and, if possible, improved. In addition, the trust insists that one-seventh of every farm be permanently maintained in a predominantly wild condition with appropriate habitat for birds and other wildlife. This acreage can include forests from which wood is harvested occasionally, streambanks and bogs where native plants are allowed to flourish, and even wild fencerows.

Sabbatical also embraces the covenant members themselves. While nobody is forced to leave their farm or their job every seventh year, and no funds are available for subsidized sabbaticals, the community nevertheless encourages people to take a break from vocational routines every seventh year. If some have the means to travel, their neighbors will watch the homestead, care for their livestock, or temporarily rent their fields. Other people trade jobs on sabbatical, so farmers and craftspeople may help teach at one of the colleges while faculty get practical experience in the field. Some spend the year working outside the community. A growing number spend part of their sabbatical on tour, interpreting the Redemption County experience to people in other parts of the country. The Covenant Community encourages sabbatical because those who work hard need both rest and new experiences if they are to continue growing as healthy and productive persons.

Life was hard for many homesteaders during the first years. The work was unfamiliar, housing was often inadequate, money was scarce, even food was occasionally in short supply. Many people could not afford a car or a truck. Although the covenant community, anticipating this problem, provided a van network from the very beginning, some found it galling to be so dependent. A few desperately searched for jobs that would provide quick cash. Most individuals, however, learned through experience what they had been told during their orientation year: neighborly support during hard times was more valuable than a marginal, uncertain job.

At the beginning, the challenge to each covenant neighborhood was compounded by problems of deciding on technologies and economic disciplines, and by the unfamiliarity of cooperative work to get big jobs done. To remodel a house or build a barn, one could not ask a banker for a mortgage, but instead had to ask neighbors for their time and talents. Each covenant neighborhood included a variety of people, and not all were poor. Fortunately some had resources that were helpful to others, but this very fact created tensions. Those who felt desperate resented having to turn to those who seemed more secure, whereas families with resources resented the nagging feeling that they should give more help to neighbors in difficulty with whom they worked nearly every day. It took time to learn the great variety of services and skills, including friendship and insight, that could be exchanged among neighbors, and to discover that a family who required a lot of help at first was indeed likely to return help later on.

Some of the most valuable assistance came from neighbors who were not members of the Covenant Community. They knew the land and the region, and while covenant farmers might wish to improve on local practices, some of them had to learn the rudiments of farming. So a neighbor who could give advice was appreciated. Some old-timers had rusty, horse-drawn equipment behind their barns that could be rehabilitated and put to work. Others sang the old songs and played the tunes that soon became popular at the Saturday night musicales.

Many new families on the land, however, differ from those that old-timers remember. Some homes are filled with children, but many families have just one or two, and some households include no children at all. Some housemates are friends and companions rather than families in the traditional sense. Quite a few retired couples among the newcomers appreciate the community life and, supported by pensions, work at reclamation more than production. African-American families have taken up farming here despite the harrowing tales of hardship they heard from their grandparents. Other families who had been migrant workers appear resilient to hard work, but some need special help to broaden their education and resolve traumas from the past. Some of the Vietnamese, Mexican, and Latin American immigrants bring distinctive cultural knowledge and skills to the community.

The traditional pattern of father in the fields and mother in the kitchen is no longer prevalent. Many women who do not choose to work on the farm find jobs elsewhere, so each covenant village includes a day-care center. The village restaurant is a popular social focus, for many families do not eat all three daily meals at home. Several restaurant managers have become sophisticated in obtaining neighborhood produce and other services in return for discount meals, so that cash-short families can be accommodated. A reservation is needed to eat at one village restaurant on a Friday night, for that is when the best cooks in the area take turns preparing special menus.

In many families one or more members work outside the Covenant Community. Some teach in the public schools or work in the county hospital. Others provide sophisticated services to corporations or universities from their home computer terminals. The Covenant Community encourages interaction with the larger society, for isolation is not one of its goals. Indeed, now that the community is being noticed, accommodating visitors and tourists has become a significant business. Frequent conferences are housed at Central College, and every summer visiting young people live on farms to participate in work and study that provide the farm family with assistance while expanding appreciation for the covenant experiment.

Nevertheless, the community tries to provide for its own needs so that the number of expensive "imports" from conventional suppliers may be reduced. Small canneries have opened in two villages to help homesteaders prepare food for themselves and items they may sell. One village set up a sawmill, added a planing mill, and is now building furniture that is admired locally. Mercy College has developed an advanced shop for the reconditioning of old farm equipment, and plans are under way to manufacture certain hard-to-obtain items for the small farmer. Last year the Covenant Community opened a sewing factory in Central City that is making work clothes under the "Back to Earth" label; these are favored in the community and it is hoped that visitors will like them as well. Another covenant member owns a car rental garage, to supply those who have only occasional need for a vehicle.

As the Covenant Community matures, relations with the surrounding society become more complex. A waiting list of applicants for homesteads in the county is maintained, but now that the Covenant Community Trust has interest in nearly a third of the farmland, additional land is more difficult—and more expensive—to obtain. Some who have the means purchase land for themselves and then deed an interest to the trust so that they may join the covenant. However, the community is becoming concerned that since it lacks political power—including the right to tax and the right to condemn land—opportunities for the poor are shrinking as land prices rise.

Other problems are stimulating interest in political activity. At first the additional children from new families were a boon to the local schools, filling underutilized classrooms and attracting more state aid. Now additional classrooms are needed, and many covenant parents are dissatisfied with the quality of instruction. Two covenant members have already been elected to the school board, but finding acceptable sources of fresh revenue will not be easy. Since most covenant members live on modest cash incomes, they share the general distaste for property taxes. One member has announced her candidacy for the state legislature, in hope of effecting a law that would allow the county to expand the state income tax or sales tax as a more acceptable means to raise revenue for local use. She also advocates a statewide land reform program that would use tax funds to condemn land and thereby make new homesteads available. Covenant Community members are learning that they must develop their political influence and encourage others to undertake reforms as well.

Every year a few resign from the Covenant Community. Some move away, but others remain on their farms and even continue some of the practices learned in the covenant. A few members have been expelled for blatant violation of covenant standards, and one neighborhood was nearly destroyed by controversy. The Community Land Trust, by policy, will not repurchase property that it has already encumbered, for it prefers to extend environmental protection to new tracts, but the market for such land remains strong.

The rapid development of culture in Redemption County rests on three pillars. The first is the religious commitment that undergirds social and environmental efforts. People need deep resolve to persevere when the way is hard, and they need extra strength to remain helpful when neighborhood relationships are taxing. Since these individuals did not organize as a religious sect, but instead institutionalized their efforts at the environmental and social levels, religious commitment can help the covenant people to remain flexible in these areas. "When our faith is involved, but not at stake," Anne Stem observes, "we are more likely to criticize our social and environmental behavior."

The second pillar is education. Every adult in the Covenant Community participates in at least one class each week except during the harvest months. Education encourages people to reflect on their experience. Through classes one person's discoveries can be shared with others and appraised by the group. Continuing education also provides an opportunity to explore interests that have no apparent connection to daily work. In this community a poor farmer may become a philosopher and may even have an opportunity to teach.

The third pillar is rest and recreation, enjoyment and expression, through arts, worship, music, sports, food, and sensuous alertness to natural beauty. This community is not dour but lively and the time taken for rest and recreation is used to the full. This community is the flowering of a culture.

The landscapes of Redemption County are becoming more beautiful. Many of the larger fields are now divided with fencerows, hedges, trees, ponds, and bogs that enrich the view. More birds and frogs are heard, and more rabbits and squirrels are seen. Many older, smaller fields that had been weedy and eroded have become lush and neat. New timber stands are growing. Tired old farmhouses have been remodeled, and gardens thrive beside them. The landscape is dotted with new homesteads where people can be seen at work. Horses, cattle, hogs, and sheep abound, as well as chickens, geese, and turkeys. The countryside smells fresh and looks alive.

Even those who had been most fearful of the Covenant Community enjoy Sunday drives on the country roads more than they once did. "Many of us have fallen in love again with the land we are tending and the place where we live," Anne Stem concludes. "We want to care for the life here because it is so beautiful."

creating social capital

CORNELIA BUTLER FLORA

AND JAN L. FLORA

INCREASINGLY in postindustrial North America, households choose where they live based on preference for place. A substantial number are choosing to move from urban areas to more bucolic, peaceful locations. That choice is often based on attraction to the physical aspects—scenery, amenities, recreational possibilities—as well as the infrastructure necessary to commute physically or electronically.

Local culture, including social networks, contributes to community attraction and a sense of place. These social networks are many faceted and embedded in one another. Your dentist is also your tenor in choir and fellow bowling-league member, whose spouse serves with yours on the town council and whose daughter dates your son.

The influx of upper-middle-class households often causes problems in the proposed destinations. The affluence of the in-migrants drives up property values. These people almost always move from areas of higher real estate values, which (coupled with the necessity of paying capital gains on the profit made from selling a home) gives them both the capital to spend above local market value and the motivation to use it for housing. Further, as they acquire lakefront or other attractive property, they tend to privatize and limit access to environmental areas that were once public and open to access (Spain 1993). Thus, their attraction to the physical place decreases their insertion into the social space of community.

The social distance between newcomer and old-timer often increases as newcomers note that although the pace of life is preferable to that of their previous urban existence, rural life has certain inconveniences. On a winter morning, the roads are not plowed early enough for them to commute to work on time. The schools do not offer foreign languages. The public library is only open from ten till four on three weekdays. The charming farm next door spreads manure from its picturesque cows on the fields—which smells. So they go to their local elected officials to protest, as they learned to do in city life. They lodge their complaint in the urban manner—specific, to the point—and imply that the official is personally responsible for obvious inefficiency in the system.

Social distance between newcomer and old-timer can increase when economic development comes up. For the old-timers, a major problem is a fixed income and increasing expenses. They seek to attract industry to decrease their property taxes, which constitute a higher proportion of the income of old-timers than of newcomers. They look with favor on fast food establishments and Wal-Marts. These retail facilities offer low-cost, good-value products—and treat their customers with uniform respect. The newcomers are appalled that the environmental capital would be threatened and the picturesque nature of Main Street would be sullied by a Hardee's. With organizing skills gained from their middle-class professional training, they do their best to stop these intrusions into their personal visions of place.

In the case of Floyd, Virginia, a Hardee's was built after a bitter battle pitting the "come-here"s versus the "been-here"s. The newcomers began with an antagonistic stance of "we don't want it here, period"—a stance that could serve as a negotiation point in an area where networks are not so embedded. Instead of becoming the basis for compromise, here that stance fueled conflict, bringing forth deep hostilities of the old-timers to the newcomers so busy watching cholesterol that they had little time for neighbors. Because of their domination of the county commission, the old-timers won and Hardee's was built, with some deference to local architecture. In an effort to heal the breach, the grand opening was made the occasion for a local bluegrass music festival—valued by all residents in Floyd. Healing takes time and effort.

Newcomers often become involved in more diversified activities for economic development and are frequently the leaders in such efforts. We have found that very often the staff of economic development corporations and chambers of commerce in rural areas are newcomer women, intent on making the community a better place in which to live, according to their experience in urban or suburban areas. The response of the old-timers is generally, "If things were so good in San Jose, why don't you go back there?" (The other common response to a new idea is, "We tried that twenty years ago and it didn't work.")

In all these cases, the actions of newcomers increase conflict within the community by focusing on the environmental capital of locality and ignoring the importance of social capital. And old-timers, by not recognizing the importance of social capital, do not see the newcomers as an important resource for the community and fail to integrate them into it.

Reciprocity and mutual trust are the components of community social capital. Putnam (1993b, 35–36) describes social capital as "features of social organization, such as networks, norms, and trust, that facilitate coordination and cooperation for mutual benefit. Social capital enhances the benefits of investment in physical and human capital." (Environmental capital encompasses the quantity and quality of water, soil, forests, biodiversity, and scenery. Physical capital includes physical infrastructure, tools, and financial capital. Human capital is individual skills, experience, training, and education. Capital of all kinds, as conceived here, is an input or intermediate output that contributes to individuals' or communities' wealth, income, or quality of life.)

For many newcomers to rural communities, individual efforts to "become native" create the embedded networks that can contribute to their quality of life—and make their survival strategies easier. *Affluent* in-migrants, however, can easily ignore social capital, as they are able to substitute financial capital, paying for goods and services—including police protection and security systems—that social capital otherwise offers. The patterns of interaction they bring from suburban society, where there is even greater separation of where people work, live, shop, socialize, and are educated, make it seem normal to individualize leisure (bowling as individuals, not in a league) rather than engage in the kinds of activity that build reciprocal relationships of trust and interdependence.

Social capital has a number of configurations. Each variation has different implications for community and how newcomers can become native to place. Social capital can be horizontal, hierarchical, or nonexistent. Horizontal social capital implies egalitarian forms of reciprocity. Each member of the community is expected to give, and gains status and pleasure from doing so. On other occasions, each is expected to receive as well. Each person in the community is seen as capable of providing something of value to any other member of the community. Contributions to collective projects, from parades to the volunteer fire department and Girl Scouts, are defined as "gifts" to all.

Both old-timers and newcomers can work to create opportunities for all residents in a locality to contribute and where all contributions are valued. For new comers, it is important to establish that they do not think they are better then the old-timers because of higher levels of income or education or more urban experience. And for old-timers it is important to make newcomers native to place by forgiving them for not having a great-grandfather born in the community and thereby acknowledging that one can be linked to place by more than kin ties.

Hierarchical social capital also builds on norms of reciprocity and mutual trust, but those networks are vertical rather than horizontal. Traditional patron-client relationships, typical of urban gangs, are created (Portes and Sensenbrenner 1993). Those at the bottom of the hierarchy—who obviously are beholden to the few at the top—are the majority of the population in such communities. The receivers of favors owe incredible loyalty to their "patron" when the time comes to vote for public office. As a result, horizontal networks, particularly those outside the sphere of influence of the patron, are actively discouraged. Dependency is created and mistrust of outsiders is generated. This type of social capital is prevalent in persistent poverty communities (Duncan 1992).

Often communities with hierarchical social capital have a history of dependence on a single industry, owing to features of the environment such as mineral deposits for mining or potential sources of power, which located textile mills near rivers. Outsiders are attracted because these communities are often located in scenic areas. Newcomers, who are not dependent on the local patron for their livelihood, represent to the old elite the potential of alternative power and influence. So the local patrons often work hard to either (1) co-opt newcomers to make them allies who understand why "these people just can't be trusted to do anything for themselves" or (2) isolate newcomers and make life extremely uncomfortable in ways that range from "forgetting" garbage pickup to outright vandalism. The newcomers often feel most comfortable keeping apart from the community entirely or going along with the existing power structure. There are important exceptions, where alliances have been formed with those at the bottom of the hierarchy, and through hard work—and considerable risk—new forms of more horizontal social capital have been created.

Absence of social capital is characterized by extreme isolation of residents from one another. In these communities there is little trust, and, as a result, little interaction. Such communities tend to have frequent population turnover and high levels of conflict. Some are bedroom communities. When predominantly middle-class and upper-class communities lack social capital, they are able to substitute physical capital: private guards, fenced neighborhoods, and elaborate security systems. Poorer communities often sustain high levels of crime and delinquency.

Newcomers can create physical barriers that substitute for social capital. There are no existing local organizations to join or local bosses to confront. Affluent newcomers can often manage fairly well in such settings, as they can isolate themselves physically and have the experiential knowledge to reach the county and state officials if they have a problem they cannot solve individually. However, if they have children and are forced to confront the low levels of social capital and the resultant poor schools, they often resort to home schooling or boarding school. Their functional needs are met, but in a place-neutral way.

When new migrants enter a community, unless they have previous ties, they personally have low levels of community-based social capital. That, in turn, reduces community social capital unless positive action is taken to build trust and reciprocal relationships. Our research suggests that the best way to do that is to concentrate on building *social infrastructure.* By understanding how social infrastructure builds social capital, both newcomers and old-timers can use social construction to strengthen the community by the diversity represented by newcomers, rather than weakening it through creation of isolated groups and individuals.

Despite the multiplier effects of social capital, conventionally it has received little attention in the community development literature or in practice. One reason is that it is extremely hard to measure because of its necessarily high level of abstraction; it "inheres in the structure of relations between actors and among actors" (Coleman 1988; S98).

Coleman has identified social structure that facilitates social capital on the individual level. He found that social network closure (seeing the same people in more than one setting—in the case of his study, at church functions, at school functions, and as parents of your children's friends) was critical for children and families. At the community level we have identified some basic social structures within a community—entrepreneurial social infrastructure—which can be seen as contributing to the development of community-level social capital: (1) symbolic diversity, (2) widespread resource mobilization, and (3) diversity of networks.

Symbols are the source of meaning for humans. Meaning is not intrinsic in an object but is socially determined through interaction. Different human groups have different sets of shared symbols. Indeed, the same object may have very different meanings for two different groups. The meaning given to the object in turn determines how one acts toward it. Symbolic diversity within a community means that while symbolic meanings for objects and interactions may differ, there is appreciation among community members of the different meaning sets. Symbolic diversity brings a recognition of differences, but the differences are not hierarchical. "Different than" does not mean "better than."

Where there is symbolic diversity, people within the community can disagree and still respect one another. There is *acceptance of controversy.* Because differences of opinion are accepted as valid, problems are raised early and alternative solutions are discussed. Members of the community are able to separate problems ("We need better medical care") from specific solutions. For instance, if the problem is defined as the need for better medical care rather than the need for more doctors, community members will recognize the possibility of more than one solution ("We need a doctor"). People feel comfortable suggesting alternative solutions without being accused of contributing to the problem. The emphasis shifts from argument about whether there is a problem to discussion of alternative solutions to a more broadly defined problem. Thus, an individual can argue for one solution, and at a later time support an alternative solution. The person's identity is not conflated with her or his position on a particular issue. Communities that view newcomers as a resource rather than a threat accept their participation in controversial questions. Newcomers in turn accept local "etiquette" regarding how issues are addressed.

Because controversy is accepted and issues are raised early, politics are *depersonalized.* Community members do not avoid taking a public position. Stands on issues are not viewed as moral imperatives. Because problems can be addressed early, one's stand on an issue is not equated with one's moral worth. Risk of character assassination, and destruction of one's job or ruination of one's social life, are lessened for those who take on public charges. The much-discussed burnout of volunteer public officials, often related to the volume of abuse they face from their constituents, is thus less. Newcomers and old-timers avoid labeling one another with derogatory names such as "flatlander" or "stick-in-the-mud."

High levels of symbolic diversity generate a *focus on process,* rather than on ends only. Instead of the sports analogy for community development (where there is an obvious beginning and end, written rules, a neat system of scoring, clearly demarcated opposing teams, and a definitive final outcome) such communities are more likely to evoke a parenting analogy: while there may be a distinct beginning, there is no steady march to the goalposts, no ending gun when losers and winners are recognized. Process collectively recognizes celebrations and concerns. Communities that focus on process tend to have many local celebrations, but also mechanisms of showing concern for those with problems. Problems are something that happen to good people, not a sign of moral weakness.

Symbolic diversity results in a *broad definition of community and permeable bound-*

aries. Such communities find it easy to become part of multicommunity and regional efforts, not by giving up community identity, but by expanding it.

The ability of a community to mobilize resources is critical for social capital to develop and is a vital part of community-level social infrastructure. *Resources are defined broadly,* allowing a wide range of community members to contribute. For example, elderly community members may not have large quantities of cash, but they have important knowledge of community history. The experience of newcomers in addressing community issues in other locations is recognized as an asset, not a liability.

There is also *relative equality of access to resources* within a community. For example, it is assumed that every child should have the opportunity for a good education. High school dropouts are viewed as a community-level problem, not the fulfilling of one's social destiny based on parental social status. A wide variety of resources, from swimming pools to golf courses to schools, are open to all, rather than being reserved for elite social groups. Public ownership is the most common way of ensuring broad access. If newcomers form their own organizations or social clubs, that immediately creates the appearance of unequal access.

To enhance equality of access, resource mobilization includes a willingness to *invest collectively.* Communities invest in themselves through school bonds, public recreation programs, community festivals or other fundraising events, and volunteer fire departments and emergency squads. Newcomers who participate in these activities contribute to community social capital formation. The expectation is that all will contribute in some way, and mechanisms are in place to facilitate such participation. If newcomers are wealthy or retired homeowners *and* oppose school or industrial revenue bond issues, the willingness of others to invest collectively in the community will be strongly affected in a negative way.

Finally, there is *individual investment* of private resources. Banks in these communities have high loan-to-deposit ratios, choosing to invest locally rather than in safe but distant government securities. Local entrepreneurs can obtain both equity capital and debt capital. And local people put individual dollars into local community development corporations and enterprises, frequently assuming that there will be no payback or that the payback will be in the distant future. Newcomers build social capital when they volunteer time and contribute money to community projects.

Networks are a crucial part of social capital, and one of their critical features is *diversity.* While internally homogeneous groups are often the basis for diversity within the community, there must also be formal and informal community networks that include individuals of diverse characteristics: young and old, men and women, various racial and ethnic groups, different social classes, and (often most difficult) newcomers and old-timers.

Networks that contribute to sustainable community development *link horizontally* to other communities. We refer to this as *lateral learning* (Flora and Flora, 1993). Communities that develop this kind of networking often take a diverse group of people to a community that has done something they want to emulate. They visit together, ask lots of questions, come back determined to adapt the idea—and do it even better.

Vertical networks to regional, state, or national centers link a large number of community individuals and groups to resources and markets beyond community limits. Where there is a single gatekeeper between the community and the outside, no matter how well connected that person is, the concentration of power in a single individual contributes to hierarchical, not horizontal, social capital. Newcomers are likely to have a different set of vertical linkages; including them will expand the community's vertical linkages.

Finally, community networks are *inclusive.* They are participatory, not representational. It is understood that adding more people to the table can mean a larger community pie, not a pie that has to be cut into more pieces. Adding diverse groups to the leadership networks develops community social capital, and newcomers are among those diverse groups.

Building social capital and social infrastructure provides an important avenue for becoming native to place. By identifying local strengths—points of agreement about use and enhancement of physical capital or environmental capital—social capital can be increased. Frequently, community development efforts must be initiated in areas that are not related to economic development.

Samuel and Andrea Jefferson (not their real names) moved to southwest Virginia from the Ivy League community where they had been activists. They chose the location because of its beauty and the economic and social decline the area had experienced since it was cut over. They wanted to live, as they put it, "where they could make a difference." There was little local industry, some farming, and a lot of poverty. They brought with them some financial capital and a determination to invest it to improve the community.

They bought a farm and began learning how to farm. Despite their personal distaste for smoking and its consequences, they used the tobacco allotment that came with the farm and worked with a neighbor to learn the rich tradition and agronomic practices surrounding tobacco production. They joined a local church. Andrea became a reporter for a local newspaper, while Samuel concentrated on farming and building a bed-and-breakfast on a beautiful hill on their property. They hoped to get it started, then sell it to a local couple to run as a part of tourism development for the area. Samuel became a leader of chamber of commerce programs aimed at economic development, and their young children entered the public schools.

Each of these activities brought frustration. Other newcomers, attracted by the low housing prices, were entering the area, which made for discipline problems in the schools and on the school bus. The Jeffersons could not find a local couple able to manage the bed-and-breakfast, much less interested in taking on the financial responsibility of owning it. And there was considerable resistance by portions of the community to the newly instituted economic development efforts. Samuel and Andrea, despite persistent attempts to build social capital, were still viewed by many as meddling outsiders, probably ready to leave at any moment.

Exhausted and discouraged, Samuel turned his efforts to the children and their school. Local history was an area of interest, so he organized an oral history project involving in-depth interviews with many old-timers by the schoolchildren and an ever-increasing number of parents. A project for a community historical center and living farm emerged—with enthusiasm from all sides. It seemed a natural part of who they were, allowing all to see each other positively. While many had viewed Samuel's efforts at economic development as self-interested, the work on local history was defined as "community work." Samuel admitted he had dropped out of economic development. Yet levels of community social capital were increasing. New community networks were formed. People were able to discuss alternative ways of carrying out the project, engaging in controversy, not conflict, because they had to figure out together the best way to proceed in order to meet their agreed-upon goal. Even the poorest members of the community could contribute to revealing and celebrating the local history, the elderly by telling their stories, the young people and the newcomers by listening appreciatively and recording them. Symbolic diversity and resource mobilization continually increased. And the Jefferson family, including the children, who although born there were viewed as the progeny of outsiders, all became more native to their chosen place.

Becoming native to place implies contributing to that place as well as receiving strength and renewal from it. New migrants, particularly those with college education and professional pasts, understand the need to contribute to the physical capital of a place, through giving money to local causes and paying property taxes. Such new migrants often are vitally concerned about the need to preserve and enhance environmental capital. Sometimes, particularly if they have school-age children, they are concerned about human capital creation and work hard to improve the schools.

Because it has lacked a name, social capital is frequently neglected by those who move into an area by choice. The actions they take to enhance the other kinds of capital tend to result in the destruction of social capital, as those who *are* native to that place perceive the newcomers as pushy, elitist, and constantly complaining. Another set of new migrants isolate themselves—and their various forms of capital—from the community of place, not recognizing the vital role of social capital in maintaining and enhancing the very resources that attracted them to the place initially. For both groups of newcomers, the charm of the place declines. Return migration to the cities occurs, or another move to a place that will "feel" more comfortable.

In contrast, those newcomers who set out to create social capital *first*—who participate in local activities, who help organize actions to celebrate place, both culturally and environmentally—find themselves becoming native to place. It feels right. Their neighbors know and appreciate them—and they know it, because they know and appreciate their neighbors. Social capital is a resource that is not depleted through use. While it cannot be appropriated by an individual, it can contribute to everyone's quality of life.

re-ruralizing education

DAVID W. ORR

IT AIN'T WHAT WE DON'T KNOW THAT GIVES US TROUBLE,

IT'S WHAT WE KNOW THAT AIN'T RIGHT.

—Will Rogers

AT the top of my list of the things that we know that "ain't right" I would place the belief that we are now an urban species, and that by and large this is a good thing or at least one that cannot be changed. For 99 percent of our evolutionary career, however, *Homo sapiens* lived in small bands and tribes in places that would today be considered wilderness. For most of the remaining 1 percent we were either rural or lived in small hamlets and towns surrounded by countryside. From an evolutionary perspective, the vast megalopolitan areas of the twentieth century are a sudden aberration. Urban ideologists presume that our rural origins are unimportant and go on to assume that (1) an affluent and democratic culture does not require a stable and prosperous rural foundation; (2) we are smart enough to provision megalopolitan areas with food, water, energy, materials, public safety, transport, employment, entertainment, and dispose of their wastes, and do all of these things in perpetuity; (3) cities, in contrast to everything else on earth, have no maximum size beyond which they decay or collapse; (4) urban and suburban life can satisfy our deepest needs; and (5) we will never change our minds. Urban boosterism masks a wager of sorts that our evolutionary past is of no consequence, that our bets do not need to be hedged, and, as biologist Robert Sinsheimer once put it, that nature does not set traps for unwary species.

On each count I dissent. I do not believe that a democratic culture can remain healthy for long without rural vitality. Human smartness always competes against human cussedness, stupidity, and shortsightedness. There are certainly limits to scale that apply to cities and everything else. Anyone caught in the weekend rush to escape the metropolis knows that urban life does not begin to satisfy all of our deepest needs. Will we ever change our minds? Ask the nearest pollster about human fickleness. And does nature set traps for unwary species? It would be wise for members of an upstart, hyperactive species with a large brain to ponder the possibility.

Before going further, however, I must bow to the numbers that show unequivocally that humans continue to herd themselves into metropolitan regions. The United States, for example, is overwhelmingly urban and suburban and becoming even more so. In 1950, almost half of Americans still lived in rural areas. By 1990, however, the number was less than one in four (22.9 percent), and only 1.9 percent of Americans lived on farms (Johnson 1990). Within a few years the world average will be 50 percent and that too, we are told, will continue to rise until the vast majority of people will be city folk.

What is it about these numbers that "ain't right"? What long-term forces could possibly stop or even reverse the trend toward urbanization? You can make your own list, but mine includes such items as: (1) the end of the era in which we can burn fossil fuels cheaply and ignore their ecological costs—and it is cheap fossil energy that allows us to provision large urban populations (Smil 1991, 298–316); (2) the vulnerability of concentrated populations to new diseases such as AIDS and ebola and the return of old ones such as tuberculosis in more virulent form (Chivian et al. 1993; McMichael 1993; Preston 1992); (3) the decline of ecological resilience worldwide (for instance, species loss, desertification, deforestation, soil erosion, climate change, increased ultraviolet radiation), which will reduce the surpluses that provide cities with food, materials, water, and waste cycling; (4) the unmanageability of all cities beyond some scale; and, not least; (5) the preferences of a persistent majority of people who say that they would rather live in small towns or rural areas were it economically feasible to do so.

In other words, the shift in the balance between urban and rural will result from cumulative, long-term changes in the big numbers that have to do with energy, ecology, carrying capacity, viruses and microbes, limits to our ability to organize complex things, as well as the preferences of a large percentage of the population. These factors, however, will not force people to return to rural areas, certainly not in a way that solves either rural or urban problems. Dozens of overcrowded, poverty-ridden, disease-infested cities offer testimony to the power of human inertia. Even if people want to leave, they may find themselves trapped. The costs of relocation are beyond the means of many. Jobs in rural areas are often hard to find. Returning to the farm is not likely for people who have forgotten how to farm and whose family members no longer live on farms. Moreover, rural life will continue to be disparaged by all the image makers, media moguls, and spin doctors who prey on dependent and gullible people.

If these factors are not enough, it is becoming harder to find the country. All too often what one finds instead is the ruin that has accompanied the colonization and exploitation of once-rural places: dumps, rural slums, freeways, theme parks, second-home developments, mobile-home "parks," resorts catering to rich urbanites, and uncontrolled sprawl. It is easier to buy rural real estate than it is to discover anything resembling true country.

Nevertheless, in the face of epic changes looming ahead, it is difficult to avoid the conclusion that "long before 2030 the trend toward ever larger cities and an increasing ratio of urban-to-rural dwellers is likely to have reversed" (Brown et al. 1990, 188). The question, I think, is not whether the urban tide will ebb, but when, how rapidly, and whether by foresight or happenstance. In other words, the choice is whether those returning to rural areas in the century ahead do so, in the main, willingly and expectantly as "homecomers" with the appropriate knowledge, attitudes, and skills or arrive as ecological refugees driven by necessity or perhaps desperation. If large numbers of people reinhabit rural areas as ecological refugees, the results will be awful in every way. Carried out with foresight, re-ruralization will still not be a return to a mythical agrarian past, although there are traditions that will need to be dusted off and put to use again. If it is done right, the re-ruralization of the next century will require a combination of invention, rediscovery, and ecological imagination.

What does the prospect of re-ruralization have to do with education? Whether it occurs destructively or constructively will be determined in large part by what people returning to rural areas know, what they expect, and what they can do. For all the fashionable talk about cultural diversity, schools, colleges, and universities have been agents of fossil-energy-powered urban homogenization. There is *one* curriculum, the urban curriculum, which, as Wes Jackson notes, prepares the young for "upward mobility" (Jackson 1994, 3). We educate the young, from country and city alike, to be urban with urban appetites, skills, minds, dependencies, and expectations. As a result, today's high school or college graduate is unprepared for any but an urban existence in a world that is rapidly losing the kind of cultural information and practical know-how necessary to make a post-fossil-fuel world prosperous. If the human future will be as much (or more) rural as urban, what will the young need to know in order to build prosperous rural communities in the century ahead?

For one thing, they will need to know how to do more than they are now being taught to do. In order to provision themselves sustainably, they will need to know how to meet a large portion of the essential food needs of a community from local farms and gardens. To make the transition to a post-fossil-fuel world they must know how to generate a large portion of their energy needs from renewable resources as well as how to sequester carbon in trees, plants, and soils. To build resilient economies, they must understand how to add value to local products, how to substitute local goods and services for imports, and how to increase the economic multiplier effect of money spent in the community and control investment capital. They will need to be able to purify waste water without chemicals, eliminate toxic wastes, and restore degraded environments. And they will need to know how to raise children who recognize the value of good work and become competent citizens and good neighbors (Platt et al. 1994).

Yet a considerable number of the practical skills necessary to a post-fossil-fuel world are being lost. David Kline, an Old Order Amishman from Holmes County, Ohio (and a contributor to this volume), for instance, describes his father as a man of many skills: farmer, husbandman, thresherman, sawyer, orchardist, mechanic, carpenter, blacksmith, and plumber (Kline 1994, 6). Outside the Amish community these are no longer common skills. The more serious loss is the decline of the qualities of mind that permit a wide range of skills to flourish. A mind that knows how to do many things well has a complexity, agility, and resilience unknown to the specialist (what Nietzsche called an inverted cripple, that is, one with a single overdeveloped faculty instead of an impaired one). It is a mind capable of shifting from one material to another, from one set of tools to another, and from mechanics to biology to animal husbandry all in the same day. It is a mind with the wherewithal to design, build, repair, grow, heal, form, tinker, orchestrate, improvise, neighbor (the verb), and tell good stories—a mind with range and stretch to it.

Among the practical things the young will need to know about, agriculture is by far the most important. For a world destined to be at least as much rural as urban, agriculture will become more, not less, important for a large number of people. To build a sustainable agriculture in the post-fossil-fuel world will take the kind of individual who farms with nature rather than against it. That kind of farming requires detailed knowledge of how nature works in a particular place, the kind of knowledge that comes only from patient and alert observation. Writing about the location of fruit trees in the landscape, for example, the farmer and writer Gene Logsdon suggests growing fruit trees along the forest edge. This is where nature puts fruit trees—where the trees get the sun they need, as well as frost protection. Grazing animals feast on surplus fruit, and insect predation here is rarely as prevalent in orchards (Logsdon 1994, 136). This is useful knowledge. It is the kind of knowledge that promotes Aldo Leopold's "integrity, stability, and beauty" in working landscapes, with a bit of cash on the side. It is the kind of knowledge that comes from affection for a particular place, the necessity to earn a living from it, and the understanding that biological diversity enhances that living in the fullest sense of the word. It was not generated as a research project to get tenure, but as an act of pleasure and stewardship. It is the kind of knowledge, moreover, that one needs in order to create ecologically complex working landscapes that underlie development that is both sustainable and sustaining. In fact, there is no other realistic basis for "sustainable development" as the world's population rises from five and a half billion to twelve billion in the twenty-first century.

Beyond practical know-how, the young will need much more ecological imagination than they now exercise. Landscapes shaped by cheap fossil energy will have to be made over in the century to come. Ecological imagination is necessary to re-envision rural landscapes that preserve wildness, support biological diversity, harness sun and wind, store carbon, and create zones for hunting and gathering. That will be a landscape with wildlife corridors, forests, wilderness areas, small farms, technologically advanced wind machines, restored land, and competent people. To create such landscapes, however, America's youth will need new and ecologically solvent metaphors to describe what they first must dream.

Finally, because rural communities sometimes have been closed, intolerant, and poor, the young will need to know how to remodel rural institutions and in some cases, create new ones that work better. To do so, they will require a great deal of political savvy and social inventiveness. Often rural communities failed, and continue to fail, because they lost control of banks, capital, and land to absentee corporate owners who cared nothing for rural places or people. The corporate stranglehold on rural economic life drains capital from rural economies, leaving behind little except dependency and ruin. There is no escaping the fact that this is a political problem that can be solved only by determined citizen action that demands corporate accountability and creates community control of local resources and economies. But rural communities that are more inclusive, democratic, and economically self-reliant must be imagined before they can be created. For this we need models and working examples that stretch people's social imagination of what is possible and fires their moral energy to do what must be done.

What would it mean for schools, colleges, and universities to respond to the challenge of re-ruralization? What would it mean to prepare young people, in Gary Snyder's words, "to find their place and dig in"? I offer five suggestions.

First, it would require reestablishing strong local schools, once the keystone institution in rural communities. Beginning in the early years of the twentieth century, many small rural schools were consolidated into large, "modern" schools in order to promote efficiency and improve education. On both counts the educational results of consolidation were far less than professional educators had confidently predicted. When students from the two kinds of schools were tested, "the differences in scores of the two groups were not as large as they had expected. . . . In some subjects there was no difference at all . . . in others the pupils in the one-room schools actually did better than those in the [consolidated] schools" (Fuller 1982, 241). The statistical comparisons of rural and urban schools used to justify consolidation were biased so that "positive characteristics were overlooked and negative ones highlighted" (Matthews 1982, 1629). The characteristics of rural schools that were overlooked included all those qualities that could not be easily measured: "The slower pace; the less pressured environment; the spirit of cooperation; the opportunities for leadership development; the less formal interactions among students, staff and parents" (Matthews 1982, 1631).

In fact, small rural schools often produced fine results precisely because they were small, intimate, and informal, and did not have lots of distractions. Moreover, small rural schools involved the community in ways that the larger, consolidated schools could not, by fostering "a close relationship between parents and policy makers, a reflection of the values of the immediate culture, a valuing of that culture, and a type of preparation that enabled students to remain in the culture. *The modern terms for these attributes are 'citizen participation,' 'community control,' and 'serving the community' "*(Matthews 1982, 1629; emphasis added).

Whatever their shortcomings, small schools held many rural communities together and were training grounds for the kind of community-scale democracy necessary to rebuild and maintain rural communities. By removing control of the schools from the community, consolidation and standardization undermined democracy and community alike and contributed to the urban in-migration.

It is instructive to note that the new wave in public education is smaller schools precisely because they do a better job of educating and containing costs. Urban school systems in Philadelphia, New York, Chicago, and dozens of other cities are dismantling large schools and creating smaller ones with four hundred or fewer students—for reasons that are remarkably similar to those of the "ignorant" farmers who decades ago opposed the closing of their rural schools (Chira 1993).

Second, education that equips people to "become native to a place," as Wes Jackson puts it, will require a curriculum shaped in part by the particularities of location, bioregion, and culture. The modern curriculum has been shaped largely by the contrary belief that knowledge could be standardized and mass produced regardless of differences in regional ecology and culture. Accordingly, school consolidation went hand in hand with the effort to make the curriculum of rural schools like that of urban schools (Conant 1959). One result was to destroy the self-confidence of rural people and make young people ashamed of their circumstances, family, and places. Such education demeaned the knowledge of place and region that once enabled people to live largely within their ecological means. By destroying "location-specific" education, schools trained children, in Helena Norberg-Hodge's words, "to become specialists in a technological, rather than an ecological, society . . . to forget traditional skills and, worse, to look down on them" (Norberg-Hodge 1991, 111). Re-ruralization, in contrast, will require a curriculum that honors tradition, locality, rootedness, ecological competence, and the attributes that hold people and land together in harmony.

Third, re-ruralization will require the adoption of a more liberal liberal arts education, one that includes food, agriculture, land, water, energy, shelter design, wildlife, and forests. We are not now headed in that direction. Agriculture, for example, has all but disappeared from the liberal arts curriculum. It has been consigned to land-grant institutions, where at the graduate level it is dealt with as a series of highly technical specializations rather than as a liberal art with technical aspects. The result is that we are becoming a food-dumb society, fed by technicians and ignorant of the most basic facts about what we eat (including how unhealthy much of the industrial diet is), with what consequences, and at what true cost to ourselves and others. These are fit subjects for liberal inquiry and, unless approached with great pedagogical dullness, are not inherently any more "vocational" than, say, poetry or chemistry. Such subjects are worthy of admission into the liberal arts curriculum because they are central to life and to the human prospect.

Furthermore, the liberal arts curriculum ought to include the analytical abilities and practical skills that the young will need in order to think clearly about systems, context, patterns, and ecology. In coming decades they will need to know how to restore ecosystems and watersheds damaged in the industrial era, how to design farms that fit the ecology of place, how to run civilization on sunlight, how to design products that are both useful and long-lived, how to eliminate toxics and waste, how to maximize materials and energy efficiency. To teach these things, the curriculum must change so that what today is taught intermittently at the margin becomes central. The long separation of disciplines must be ended, along with the artificial and debilitating distinction between the theoretical and the practical.

As one example of what educational institutions might do to foster both liberal learning and practical skill, Michael Hamm of Rutgers University has organized an urban gardening program for children, adolescents, and older citizens of

New Brunswick, New Jersey. Hamm's project is intended to convey knowledge about gardening, composting, agriculture, nutrition, ecology, and direct marketing while helping an inner-city community take control of a significant part of its food supply. In its first year of operation (1993) the community harvested more than five thousand pounds of fresh vegetables, fruits, and herbs, of which a thousand pounds were donated to area soup kitchens and senior centers. Hamm has plans to extend the program to other New Jersey cities including Perth Amboy and Newark. His is the kind of imaginative outreach that colleges and universities ought to sponsor, encourage, and develop.

Fourth, educational institutions must be brought into the effort to rebuild rural communities and re-ruralize urban areas. The three thousand colleges and universities in the United States have a combined buying power of some $114 billion, and with it the potential to exert a great deal of leverage in the development of sustainable local and regional economies. Agriculture (not agribusiness) would be given a large economic boost if a number of these institutions purchased locally grown food from farms operated sustainably. In return they would raise the quality of the food they serve, thereby improving the health of their students, lowering expenditures by reducing the costs of transporting food long distances, strengthening the local economy, and improving their ethical posture by reducing their complicity in a food system that is neither just nor sustainable. Similarly, with $73.9 billion in endowment funds, colleges and universities have a significant investment leverage that could be used in ways that improve rather than degrade the world their graduates will inherit (Celis 1993).

Fifth, the education necessary for re-ruralization must become a bigger and broader effort that captures the public imagination in a way formal education seldom does. The writer and agriculturist Louis Bromfield, no particular friend of higher education, had something like this in mind nearly a half-century ago when he said that there was a "missing element in our education" (Bromfield 1950, 258–59). He proposed the creation of "pilot farms" in every region of the country along with smaller centers of "information and education." He envisioned, in other words, an alternative education and research network, independent of both government and educational institutions.

To some extent Bromfield's ideas have come into existence, but without the national foundation he proposed. There are now some hundred fifty nonprofit organizations located in nearly every state promoting sustainable agriculture, all engaged in some combination of education, research, and public outreach. As a result of these efforts the sustainable agricultural movement is gaining considerable momentum. And the outlines of sustainable rural communities are beginning to emerge in experiments with community-supported farms that sell directly to nonfarm members, rural development banks, rural land trusts, and local currency systems (Jacobs 1994; see also essays by Jack Kittredge and Susan Witt and Robert Swann, this volume).

If we and our children are to return to rural areas in the twenty-first century not as refugees, but as homecomers, is all of this enough? I do not think so. What is missing is a cultural revolution through which we discover (or rediscover) a larger concept of land and ourselves. Sustainable agriculture or sustainable forestry, narrowly conceived, have to do with provisioning human needs—but with greater care for the long-term. We are not likely to have the stamina to do the utilitarian things necessary for the long haul if that effort is not resonant with what is deepest in us, including our evolutionary hardwiring (Kellert and Wilson 1993; Wilson 1983). We do not live by bread alone. A merely utilitarian landscape cannot sustain the part of us that needs wildness, spirit, mystery, delight, beauty, celebration, and attachment to place. Any effort to re-ruralize that does not come out of a broad vision of humans in the landscape will sooner or later fail because it will not hold our loyalty and affections for long.

How such a cultural revolution will come about I do not know. It is possible, however, to describe some of the changes that we must make. For one thing, attachment to the land and development of the ecological imagination necessary to see it clearly must begin early in the mind and experience of children (Nabhan and Trimble 1994). It is therefore imperative that we preserve the small wild places where children's ecological imagination can take root and grow. It is also imperative that their early experiences of nature be good ones and that these be encouraged and validated by attentive, loving adults.

Second, our legal and economic relations with the land must come to have the qualities of a covenant. The "central learning" in the covenant relationship between Yahweh and the Israelites, according to the Old Testament scholar Walter Brueggemann, is the paradox that "grasping for home leads to homelessness" (Brueggemann 1977). By trying to own and control land, in other words, we end by destroying both the land and ourselves. We are inescapably only trustees of the land in a fiduciary relationship to generations unborn. The only choice we are given is how we exercise that role whether with wisdom and foresight or otherwise (Brown 1994; see also Walter Brueggemann's essay, this volume).

Third, we need to reweave the threads of wildness, wilderness, biological diversity, agriculture, rivers, forests, roads, human settlements, and economy into a new view of the landscape. We need visions that stretch our notions of ecological possibility. One such vision, "the wildlands project," is proposed by Dave Foreman, John Davis, David Johns, Reed Noss, and Michael Soule (Foreman et al. 1992). We also need to stretch our notions of how to feed ourselves. In more ecologically diverse and resilient landscapes it would be possible, for example, to supplement agriculture by designating common areas for hunting and gathering, as proposed by Paul Shepard (1973). As an example, publicly owned forests along the banks of the Oka River south of Moscow historically have been used by local people for gardens and as places to harvest wild foods. On almost any weekend dozens or hundreds of people carry baskets into the forests or fish the Oka River. I know of no good reason why similar zones could not be established elsewhere, particularly in urban areas. Aside from their usefulness, they would add grace to the landscape and resilience to the human societies that depend on it.

No enlargement of our sense of the landscape is possible without a deeper ecological perspective about ourselves. We are reflections of our places. Locality is etched on our minds in more ways than we can know. We are eddies in one watershed or another. We are, as Stan Rowe puts it, "deep air mammals." We are parts of larger parts, pieces in a larger ensemble. We are, as Gary Snyder says, shot through with wildness beyond our imagining. *Homo sapiens* not only lives in the landscape but also inhabits a larger historical and evolutionary topography. We are time-travelers journeying between a starting point hidden in the mists of history and destinations yet unknown. It is the particular conceit of the modern mind to believe that our destiny is no less than the total control of our destiny—a scam conjured up in air-conditioned boardrooms high above the streets of New York, Chicago, Los Angeles, Tokyo, London, Singapore. That world, with its megacities, centralized economy and instantly mobile electronic capital, biotech food factories, billionaires, and homeless on the streets, cannot be made sustainable. Nor do I believe for a minute that were such a world possible it could sustain what is deepest and best in humankind. Our true destiny is at once more sober yet far more grand. It is a world built from the bottom up by competent citizens living in solid communities, engaged in and by their places.

a public philosophy for civic culture

WILLIAM M. SULLIVAN

LIKE all other peoples, Americans today find themselves perplexed by startling developments in their society and in their lives. These changes emanate from a vortex of global technological, economic, and political transitions. "Globalization" is a term often applied to the increasing scale of exchange across and through national and cultural boundaries. This accelerating flow of information, goods, services, and people is rapidly changing not only the structures of government and power, but the patterns of work and everyday life, even the very face of the earth itself, with unprecedented speed. The end of the relative geopolitical stability imposed by nearly half a century of cold war has suddenly revealed a world seething with myriad reactions to the realization that all societies are now caught up in an encompassing, but rarely desired, interdependency.

The most disconcerting, and perhaps most revolutionary, development has been the weakening of the capacity of national states to control the economic destinies of their peoples. An inchoate awareness of this disturbing loss of control has begun to affect political stability in all the developed countries, plunging long-dominant political constellations into disarray while turning electorates fearful and surly. Behind these events lies the destabilizing movement of the emerging global economy toward near-anarchy, pitting nations and often segments of nations against one another in an economic competition for which no one quite knows the rules.

As national governments lose their power to control the economic events on which their success depends, one trend seems clear. The disruptive dynamics of the new global currents are making some people and places, even within the same national society, winners while others lose economic viability—with all the attendant social costs of decline. The new economy, that is, does not distribute its rewards in the way the midcentury economy did. It favors privileged city-regions spread primarily through the prosperous nations, which can bring together high concentrations of technical skill and social organization.

This development gives special importance to recent work in the social sciences that has sought to analyze the sources of economic and social viability of some of the most conspicuously successful regions. A landmark study of Italian regional governments by Robert Putnam and his colleagues has underscored the key ingredient of economic and social viability in the contemporary context. Successful modern regions, it turns out, are civic societies. They are able to balance competitive enterprise with a cooperative spirit, making it possible to combine a high standard of living with strong levels of trust and loyalty among citizens toward their government and toward one another (Putnam 1993).

In civic societies, the customs that govern everyday life sanction engagement by citizens in public issues, a concern for fellow citizens, and a willingness to tolerate differences while working toward common objectives. These norms are grounded in a dense pattern of organizations and associations that at once sponsor individual enterprise and sustain cooperation. Putnam calls these practices a civic culture. By contrast, he discovered that in regions where the civic culture is weak or nonexistent, citizens tend to think and act exclusively in their private interest, often living in mutual suspicion and fear. Such uncivic places are also significantly poorer in material terms than the civic regions. For any given locality in Putnam's study, civic culture turns out to be the only significant predictor of economic success. "The social capital embodied in norms and networks of civic engagement," argues Putnam, "seems to be a precondition for economic development, as well as for effective government. Development economists take note: civics matters!" (Putnam 1993a, 35–42, 57).

If this analysis is correct, then even as technological change drives a dizzying process of ever-tighter interconnection, it is less the hardware than the "soft stuff" of communication, culture, morality, and religion that is revealed as the chief source of social power as well as of morality. Just as policy analysts have come to recognize that economic strength is the prerequisite for military security, the strength of a society's civic culture may be the most important resource for its growth and prosperity. Learning how civic cultures develop and how they can be nourished thus becomes a matter of practical as well as theoretical importance. In this connection a society's public philosophy, or shared framework of public discussion and deliberation, also becomes a key resource. By providing the metaphors and understandings through which individuals and groups make sense of their situation and respond to it, a public philosophy can help or hinder the crucial process of civic development.

LIBERAL VERSUS CIVIC PUBLIC PHILOSOPHY

American political culture has been dominated by the outlook of a philosophic liberalism. As a public philosophy, liberalism has portrayed civil society as ideally a sphere of contractual arrangements among autonomous individuals seeking their own ends. Government serves as a protective carapace, an instrument to stabilize property relations derived from the play of the market or a mechanism by which to advance the emancipation of individuals. In the twentieth century, American politics has tended to oscillate between these two conceptions of the role of government, "conservatives" favoring the former view and "liberals" the latter. In both, the public realm is instrumentalized.

The public realm, however, includes not only government but also associational life, those aspects of civil society in which individuals consider common concerns and interests. Since the public philosophy of liberalism rarely sees this realm as a context for the realization of positive goods, its functioning commands little dignity or value in itself and has been largely neglected in American political discourse. Yet it is precisely in the myriad aspects of associational life that civic culture is formed. A strengthened civic culture will require a public philosophy that attends to those institutions and processes by which citizens form and sustain a genuine public realm. And the public realm is precisely the focus of the civic republican tradition of public philosophy.

Consider the idea of citizenship itself. The civic republican conception of citizenship has been a singularly long-lived and, in purely pragmatic terms, amazingly resilient ideal. Citizenship as a symbol has generated a coherent understanding of the good life and the human place in the world. And like all genuinely emblematic symbols, that of the citizen in the commonwealth has remained powerful in part because of its compactness and evocative qualities. It has at times of civic renewal in modern society evoked new possibilities for living, calling on idealized images of the self-governing city republics of antiquity or renaissance Europe, or the revolutionary republics of the United States and France. Debated, contested, modified by theory and experience, the notion of the citizen reaches today's world from varied channels, still providing vital stimulus to action.

Even on cursory inspection, the classical notions of citizenship strikingly sum up a vision of life that is also a moral ideal. The tradition of republican citizenship stretching from antiquity to the American Revolution links power and authority within the state to the deliberative activities of citizens rooted in the social, economic, psychological, and religious spheres. By contrast, philosophic liberalism has conceived citizenship far more abstractly. The mechanisms of governance, the delineation of the institutions of the state as contrasted with those of civil society, the contractual relationship of citizens with the state, the ideas of authority and legitimacy, all float in a kind of Cartesian ether. Setting the republican and liberal views side by side, the troubling sense that there have been large losses as well as gains creeps upon us unavoidably. The principal loss in the liberal vision is identifiable immediacy. It is the loss of a conception of the relationship among the political, social, economic, psychological, and religious dimensions of individual identity and citizenship as a way of life.

The contemporary starting point for developing a fuller conception of citizenship than the abstract liberal view must be the recovery of a sense of civic life as a form of self-development. The kind of self-development with which the theorists of the civic life have been concerned is in many ways the antithesis of the connotations of self-development as nearly narcissistic concentration on one's inner life and welfare. Rather, citizenship has traditionally been conceived as a way of life that changes the person who enters into it. The process is essentially a collective experience.

Indeed, the notion of *citizen* is unintelligible apart from that of commonwealth, and both terms derive their sense from the idea that we are by nature political beings. Self-fulfillment, like working out a personal identity and orientation in the world, ranks heavily on taking part in a communal enterprise. This shared process is the civic life. Its root is involvement with others: other generations, other sorts of persons, whose differences are significant because they contribute to the whole on which our particular sense of self depends. Thus mutual interdependence is the foundational notion of citizenship. The basic psychological dynamic of the participants in this interdependent way of life is an imperative to respond and to care.

From the viewpoint of liberal public philosophy, such a civic vision represents a distinct overvaluing of the social, and particularly the political. For philosophical liberals, whatever their loss from finding public life only an impersonal mechanism of individual and group assets and debits, gain a richer private life free of state or majority tyranny. Indeed, mutual dependency and care do sound more like private than public values, as liberalism makes that division. But—if we put aside Alexis de Tocqueville's revelations of the coercive effects of public conformity—it is evident than no constitutional democracy actually operates without drawing on large reserves of civic bonds, a culture of trust and connectedness that liberal public philosophy does not take into account.

In contemporary polities, however, the cultivation of the fuller sense of citizenship goes on largely in the associational life of civil society. The difficulty is that, cut off from public scrutiny and discussion, the responses of individuals and groups to economic and social changes are likely to become defensive and self-serving. Public discussion of the interdependence of individuals and groups is basic to the civic vision because it enlightens and challenges disparate parties about their actual relationships and possible responsibility for them. The citizen comes to know who he or she is by understanding the web of social relationships. This realization is not only cognitive; it requires experience, finding one's way, and thus coming to know, in practice, who one is.

At the same time, it is important to see that the civic tradition does not necessarily absolutize or romanticize participation in public life. The dangers of misguided, fanatical, and irresponsible political involvement have been well documented. Some of the most eloquent warnings of those dangers, such as Tocqueville's, have come from theorists of citizenship who understood the positive contributions of modern liberal notions of liberty, as well as the limitations of those notions as guides to civic life. The point, rather, is that the notion of involved concern within an interdependent community provides the standard for a collective enterprise in moral self-transformation in which moderation and restraint can be learned as part of a larger effort to pursue justice and the common welfare. The civic ideal is thus alluring and disquieting, at once fragile and morally inspiring in the responsibility it demands.

THE AIMS AND TENSIONS OF CIVIC CULTURE

The language of civic republicanism addresses the human aspiration toward a life of responsible inclusion within a community of mutual concern. With its concern for justice and participation, the civic tradition also speaks to the public value of exploring and developing those personal qualities that point beyond competitive success and economic well-being. It does this not by abstracting from social inequalities and economic needs, but by addressing them as human, moral realities.

In the imagination of the great speakers of this tradition, such as Martin Luther King, Jr., social and economic relationships are translated into the moral and personal meaning they have for members of a polity. Poverty and unemployment, for example, cease to be unfortunate side effects of capitalist economic growth, to be neglected benignly or tidied up managerially. They appear in their full reality as institutionalized denials of dignity and social membership, glaring failures of public responsibility. As such, these issues emerge as painful spurs to challenge and change the shares of power and the institutions of collective coordination, even when these are identified as transnational in scope and direction. The logic of King's republican understanding of politics led him to broaden the civil rights struggle to confront institutional arrangements that perpetuate poverty. Just before his assassination, he was advocating a coalition that would join opposition to the war in Indochina and military-industrial priorities to a broad struggle for economic and social democracy.

The potency of the civic vision lies in philosophical and pedagogical commitments. These entail the realization that the personal quest for a worthwhile life is bound up with the reality of interdependence and so with power. Large-scale social processes cannot remain merely technical issues left to the market or the bureaucracy, but must be understood as part of the texture of personal living—just as personal life is woven into the patterns of collective organization.

Thus the fundamental language and symbols of the American civic tradition link private and public, personal and collective responsibilities in synoptic form. American patriotism is not a nationalism based on immemorial ties of blood and soil; neither is it a kind of large-scale commercial contract among self-interested seekers of advantage. As observers from Tocqueville on have reported, the underlying conception that animates patriotism in America is moral, even religious: the notion of civic covenant. Unlike the liberal idea of contract, which emphasizes mutual obligations within clearly defined limits, a civic covenant is a bond of fundamental trust founded on common commitment to a moral understanding.

Covenantal morality means that, as citizens, we make an unlimited promise to show care and concern for the just organization of our common life. It is the commitment to such a trust that is summed up in the mutual pledge of loyalty which concludes the Declaration of Independence. Within the civic perspective, the business of politics at its highest is to fulfill those covenantal promises within the changing flow of events. In practice, which is rarely politics at its highest, this civic understanding provides the sense of conscience and idealism against which the institutions and conduct of our collective life must be judged.

At the heart of civic public philosophy is the notion that the chief end of politics is the pursuit of the common good. However, that term is today a vexed one, signifying to some an unjustified collective coercion of individuals and to others a largely vacuous appeal to noble sentiments. To take either position is to fail to understand that the conception of the common good, with its long history in the civic tradition, is part of a language that articulates a way of living. In any practical context, language functions as more than the purely descriptive vehicle that is the ideal of analytical science. A political philosophy is always more than a neutral description. It is also—what is more important—a proposal and a vision. Political philosophies propose to evoke an experience of a kind of life. Indeed, it has been a distinguishing peculiarity of philosophic liberalism that political language should be shorn of its evocative dimensions. Yet all traditions of thought, all forms of life that have been consciously cultivated over long periods of time, are rich with highly charged, compact phrases and gestures that serve to evoke a whole scheme of meaning.

If we are willing to grant to the civic tradition the possibility that its language points to a way of life that is meaningful on its own terms, then our imagination can rise to a new practical demand. The common good expresses that demand by describing a possibility: the idea of a civic life. To understand this possibility requires at first, in Wittgenstein's phrase, coming "to feel our way around" in its characteristic language. Such an adventure may enable us to see in a fresh way the contemporary problems of globalization and its impact on specific places and people. For the language of the civic republican tradition provides an understanding and an evaluation of the social conditions on which it depends. The chief of these conditions is an interpretation of psychological and moral development.

How, then, is a civic life possible? How can we conceive of individual fulfillment as realized through mutual commitment to a common good? The answer the civic tradition has given is clear: civic life is possible because human nature is naturally disposed, given suitable education and effort, to find important fulfillment in what the tradition calls a life of virtue. Civic virtue is the excellence of character proper to a citizen. Compared to the liberal emphasis on liberty as freedom from external constraint, the civic conception emphasizes the substantive or positive dimension of freedom understood as the capacity to attain one's proper good, where "goodness" describes full enjoyment of those capacities which characterize a flourishing human life.

As Alasdair MacIntyre has reminded us, various societies have upheld differing hierarchies of virtue. The idea of civic virtue need not force us to affirm that it is the best of all possible human dispositions, only that for social beings such as we are, living well requires a shared life, which is possible only when the members of a community trust and respect one another. To participate in such a shared life is to show concern for and reciprocity with one's fellows. Such participation is at the same time beneficial to the individual by activating his or her social capacities, finding a common good by sharing an admirable and worthwhile form of life.

This classical notion of freedom as virtue is quite different from the modern liberal notion that depicts individuals struggling against constriction. The concept of civic virtue focuses on the carrying out of social roles as the essential means through which individuals can recognize their capacities and work to achieve excellence. From the Promethean standpoint of modern culture, it is easy to mistake this ideal for mere static completion or passivity. In fact, it is neither static nor passive. Rather, the categories of civic discourse propose a way of seeing life that is different from modern utilitarianism's calculus of subjective satisfactions.

The ideas of civic virtue and the common good suggest that life is worth living not because it provides opportunities for sensation and pleasure, but because it affords the purely human satisfaction of recognizing oneself as a significant part of an ongoing way of life that is good in itself because of its resonances of meaning and beauty. Curiously, that indispensable tool of the utilitarian market culture, modern advertising, has long grasped this point profoundly, if narrowly. What is most advertising but the rhetorical association of a commodity, such as a car or a cigarette, with a symbol of a commonly desired way of life or admired ideal of character: the Beautiful People or, *de gustibus*, the Cowboy?

The task of civic intelligence is to clarify these inchoate appeals, to find and to weave a harmony among the various threads of significance embodied in family life, in the various skills and professions, in religious and artistic traditions. In its most general formulation, the notion of civic virtue as freedom is captured in the idea of human dignity. Medieval natural law theorists brought Christian theological commitments to bear on the Greek and Roman notions of a common humanity developed by the Stoics in their statement that the fundamental natural end or purpose of political life is to provide justice, and hence moral dignity, for all.

TOWARD A RENEWAL OF CIVIC PUBLIC PHILOSOPHY

Classical political philosophy formulated the life of civic virtue as one standing in opposition or at least in contrast to the orientation toward self-interested gain characteristic of marketing behavior. The aim at private satisfaction, which classical theorists labeled economic, is concerned with wants that are in principle limitless. Civic virtue, on the other hand, shares with the other moral virtues a fuller integration of the powers of the self. This integration was conceived as at once the goal and the effect of participation in civic life.

Virtue, the *arete* (excellence) of the Greek theorists describes the disposition of a person whose conduct is guided by a shared, consciously held value or principle rather than by private, unexamined needs and desires. This kind of excellence, moreover, is a personal ideal as well as a collective one, in that it describes a personality sufficiently integrated both to live up to commitments and to cooperate with others to achieve common values. In traditional ethical language, such an integration of the personality is described as courage, the ability to sum oneself up in word and action, in temperance and self-control, an ordering of the person so that the higher values consciously affirmed can predominate over merely private impulses and desires.

For civic thinkers, the achievement of maturity or virtue consists in a genuine transformation of motives, not simply in their recombination. This change takes place only through a certain kind of educative social interaction. Civic moral education is, then, natural in that it fulfills some of humanity's distinctive need to be at once reflective and yet independent members of a community. This peculiarly human form of life, however, requires active artifice for its continuation. We must take care to nurture ourselves and our environment, including our progeny and one another. And that task is possible only through the development and maintenance of a full moral education in a civic community that includes political culture.

It is complex task, ever more so as the interconnection among places and peoples grows more intricate. A civic culture is necessarily defined by two poles: it aims at a universal sympathy, an ideal enunciated by the Stoics and given expression in Christian teaching; yet civic culture is grounded and always learned in particular circumstances, certain historically rooted places and communities. This tension between specific settings and the goal of a universal community reflects in another form the root polarities between individual autonomy and mutual care. It also poses the formidable cognitive problem of how to conceive the relationship of practical politics and political theory.

For the classical tradition, as for the Christian Middle Ages, civic life was considered to draw its ultimate referents from the realm of *theoria,* or disinterested contemplation of the universal principles of the nature of God. The higher reaches of human nature were achieved not so much outside human society as in the qualitatively higher realm of philosophical sagehood, the egoless mirroring of the cosmos. Theoretical knowledge, in this classical sense, set limits to the claims of the political by providing a conception of the human place in nature, situating the shifting events of politics within a universal perspective that showed the finitude of political endeavor. While this ancient sense of theory has been supplanted by the irreversible revolution ushered in by modern science, something of the moral tone of respect for nature and an awareness of human limits seems forced on us by the threat to the natural environment posed by economic and technological development.

In this perspective, the great liberating aspect of the civic tradition for our present circumstances is its challenge to the idea of inevitable economic and technological progress, which today rules most thinking about the future of global society. Here the mutual dependence of all societies and groups is more intricately woven than in any previous epoch, yet it is denied not only by technological triumphalism but by the equally myopic celebration of the unlimited potential of the free market. Economic advancement, creative destruction fueled by ever-new techniques and tempered by an eye cast toward playing fairly—in a word, progress—must work inscrutably toward a better tomorrow. That is the dream turned nightmare from which we must sooner rather than later awake. A fuller development of a civic understanding of the global condition could help to rouse us from this dangerous dogmatic slumber.

In America the civic vision has a number of variants, with many roots. This is appropriate in a diverse society that must learn to integrate increasing variety. Yet the central notions of the citizen and the commonwealth—the moral imperatives to live according to the principles of justice and mutual support grounded in civil covenant—are held in common. It is the sharing of these ideals, rather than blood, soil, or economic growth alone, that holds out hope for a just community that embodies the sense of dignity in a nation worthy of the respect of all. This goal, too, is fitting, for the quality of political fellowship is determined by what is shared.

land: challenge and opportunity

SUSAN WITT AND ROBERT SWANN

WE ABUSE THE LAND BECAUSE WE REGARD IT AS A COMMODITY

BELONGING TO US. WHEN WE SEE LAND AS A COMMUNITY TO WHICH

WE BELONG, WE MAY BEGIN TO USE IT WITH LOVE AND RESPECT.

—Aldo Leopold, *A Sand County Almanac,* 1949

ALDO Leopold presented a bold challenge to environmentalists: if we are to foster a culture of love and respect for land, then land can no longer be an item to
buy and sell on the market. Leopold was describing not just a new land ethic but
a transformation of our relationship with land in fact and deed. Nothing short of
a fundamental change in the economic treatment of land can affect the attitude
toward land rooted in the American psyche. Nothing short of a radical overhaul-
ing of an established system of land ownership will achieve the results Aldo
Leopold envisioned.

Is Leopold's statement the banner of a broad new environmental initiative, or
does it represent the utopian musings of an eccentric? How much do we dare to
achieve?

Many problems of our age demand brave new solutions. The rapid breakdown
of existing systems calls for courage, flexibility, vision, and steadfast determination. No family is left untouched by the tragic consequences of an unhealthy environment, by increasing violence on the streets, by the unfair distribution of resources, or by the alienation that comes from the absence of community.
Fortunately, there is growing recognition of a shared responsibility for these conditions and a willingness to share risk in order to achieve shared results.

Over the last ten years the environmental movement has learned that it is
not enough to say no to the developer of the site down the street without saying
yes to some other form of appropriate economic livelihood for our neighbors.
Our conscience can no longer be eased by an aggressive campaign to recycle
the vast amount of waste from the consumable goods that come into our homes
or by other well-intentioned but reactive measures. A change to more energy-
efficient light bulbs makes only a small dent in the nation's excessive use of nonrenewable energy. The protection of one piece of land by means of conservation
restrictions raises the price of adjoining lands and makes them more prone to in-
appropriate development. A ban on sales of ivory fails to prevent mutilation of the
elephant.

It is time for action of a broad and populist nature informed by common cause
and common consent, action that is bold and affirmative, action that reflects a new
understanding of our responsibilities to the earth and to one another. Future generations deserve nothing less. We must and can meet Aldo Leopold's challenge.

Centralized planning for use of state-owned land has proved to be a great failure, as has the unregulated exchange of land on the open market. How shall we create a new system of land allocation and use that is fair to all and ecologically sound? What might such a system look like?

The economist Ralph Borsodi, in his 1968 book *The Seventeen Problems of Man and Society,* distinguishes between what can be legally owned, and thus traded, and what belongs in the realm of "trusteeship," to use Mahatma Gandhi's term. Whatever an individual creates as a result of labor applied to land—the harvest from a garden, the home built of wood from the forest, the sweater knitted from spun wool—is private property and may rightfully be traded as a commodity. However, the land itself and its resources, which are earth-given and of limited supply, should be held in trusteeship and their use allocated on a limited basis for present and future generations. When an individual is allowed private ownership of such a limited resource, that individual has an unfair economic advantage. The scarcity of arable land and a growing demand for it result in an increase in the value of the land through no effort on the part of the landowner. The potential for speculative gain inherent in the present system of private land ownership places tremendous pressure on the landowner to maximize the dollar value of the land by developing it. Zoning regulations and conservation restrictions are limited and increasingly costly methods for ending our tradition of land exploitation.

A further result of the ability to commoditize land is that wealth generated by a community will flow first into land—from which high gains are anticipated—rather than into new small businesses. The local economy stagnates when a community's capital is tied up in land. Credit for the small-business owner tightens. The region loses its diversity of enterprises, which is the basis of a more sustainable economy and a more environmentally responsible business sector. When a region *unties* its capital from the land, it creates new investment capital. That capital in turn can activate the imaginative and entrepreneurial skills of the community, generating new local businesses that will produce goods and services once imported from other regions. New investment capital can both facilitate increased regional production and steel regional economies against fluctuations in the broader economy.

During the height of the spending spree of the 1980s, in the E. F. Schumacher Society's region of the Berkshire Hills of Massachusetts a weekend pastime of area residents was to put a For Sale sign in the front yard and offer the property at a highly inflated price to see it there were any takers. The possibility of "hitting the jackpot" is seductive to many—it is a gambling game with the land at stake. The ever-present possibility of selling land at a big gain and then leaving the area erodes the commitment to community and place that is the last safeguard of our shared inheritance: the rivers, lakes, fields, forests, and wild lands.

The community land trust (CLT) concept as developed by Schumacher Society president Robert Swann offers a practical way to take land off the market and place it in a system of trusteeship on a region-by-region basis. Swann was inspired by Ralph Borsodi and by Borsodi's work with J. P. Narayan and Vinoba Bhave, both disciples of Gandhi. Vinoba walked from village to village in rural India in the 1950s and 1960s, gathering people together and asking those with more land than they needed to give a portion to their poorer sisters and brothers. The initiative was known as the *boodan,* or land gift movement, and many of India's leaders participated in these walks.

Some of the new landowners, however, became discouraged. Without tools to work the land and seeds to plant it, without an affordable credit system available to purchase these necessities, the land was useless to them. They soon sold their deeds back to the large landowners and left for the cities. Seeing this, Vinoba altered the boodan system to a *gramdan,* or village gift system. All donated land was held by the village itself. The village then leased the land to those capable of working it. The lease expired if the land was unused. The gramdan movement inspired a series of regional village land trusts that anticipated community land trusts in the United States.

The first CLT in this country allowed African-American farmers in the rural South to gain access to farmland and to work it with security. Swann worked with Slater King, a cousin of Martin Luther King, Jr., to establish New Communities in Albany, Georgia. They relied on the legal documents of the Jewish National Fund in structuring the organization. The JNF began to acquire land in Israel at the turn of this century and now holds 95 percent of the land in Israel. It has a long and established legal history of leasing land to individuals, to cooperatives, and to intentional communities such as kibbutzim. Swann and a group from Albany traveled to Israel in the 1960s to study the results of this leaseholding method. They decided on a model that included individual leaseholds for homesteads and cooperative leases for farmland. The group then purchased a five-thousand-acre farm in rural Georgia, developed a plan for the land, and leased it to a group of African-American farmers. The legal documents have been tested and refined since the 1960s, and hundreds of community land trusts are now operational, with many others in the planning stage. The perseverance and foresight of that team in Georgia, motivated by the right of African-American farmers to farm land securely and affordably, initiated the CLT movement in this country.

A community land trust is a not-for-profit organization with membership open to any resident of the geographical region or bioregion where it is located. Its purpose is to create a democratic institution to hold land and to retain the use-value of the land for the benefit of the community. The *effect* of a CLT is to provide affordable access to land for housing, farming, small businesses, and civic projects. This effect can be achieved when a significant portion of the land in an area is held by a CLT.

Some CLTs are set up as tax-exempt charitable organizations for the purpose of building housing for the poor, but this structure limits their activities to that single issue, and maintaining tax-exempt status takes precedence over achieving the CLT's purpose of broad-based land reform. We do not recommend seeking tax-exempt status, but instead urge the creation of a community land trust organization that can own and manage land for a multiplicity of uses within a region.

A CLT acquires land by gift or purchase and then develops a land-use plan for the parcel, identifying which lands should remain forever wild and which should support low-impact development. A community land trust fosters healthy ecosystems and an appropriate social use of the land. The planners solicit input from residents of the region to determine the best uses of the land—as recreational space, wildlife preserve, managed woodlots for a local industry, secure farmlands for the region, affordable housing, or affordable office space. The land trust then leases sites for the purposes agreed on. The lease, which runs for ninety-nine years, is inheritable and renewable on the original terms. The leaseholder owns the buildings and any agricultural improvements on the land but not the land itself. Upon resale, leaseholders are restricted to selling their buildings and improvements at current replacement cost, excluding the land's market value from the transfer.

The resale restriction ensures that the land will never again be capitalized and will provide affordable access to land for future generations. The land-use plans ensure that the resource base is maintained and enriched, not depleted. Thus, the community land trust lease is a tool for meeting social and ecological objectives.

The CLT as a regional landholding organization is an innovative concept compared to conventional patterns of landholding in the United States, but its roots go back to the tradition of the early settlers in New England, who brought the practice of the "commons" with them from England. The CLT is not merely a method of holding land in common; it is a way for the community to hold land for the "common good." This means holding land not only to protect it from overdevelopment but also to guarantee that the best land is preserved as farmland and that ecologically sensitive areas are not destroyed in the rush to develop.

The CLT offers farmland as well as house sites and commercial sites via a long-term lease. The leaseholder pays the CLT a monthly rental for the land, and the trust in return is responsible for tax and mortgage payments on the land. Properly managed and financed, the income from the land lease is sufficient to create a fund for the purchase of additional land. Typically, the land-use plan in the lease will limit the number of structures per site and specify farming practices that renew the soil. The leaseholders become owners of any buildings and improvements they make on the land, but they are not permitted to sell or sublet the land itself, which remains permanently owned by the trust.

The community land trust is a democratic institution, with the potential to hold most of the land in a region. The leasehold method provides both security and equity for leaseholders by encouraging their long-term investment and helping them to establish deep roots in the community. Members of the CLT provide not only for themselves but for the community as a whole.

Land held by a CLT is not necessarily contiguous or limited in the total acreage held. The Woodland Community Land Trust organized by Marie Cirillo in Clairfield, Tennessee, holds more than a thousand acres of land in several noncontiguous parcels. It is a vehicle for residents of the region to regain control of and access to lands that have been stripped of their best resources by corporate owners and then abandoned. Small timber-based businesses, camping, ginseng growing, and housing are current uses of land that once excluded local people.

The CLT recognizes that human beings are a part of the ecological reality of a region and that in order to reach ecologically sound goals, we must also support economically sound objectives. The CLT approach to land-use planning requires a compatible and sustainable mix of conservation, recreation, housing, farming, and regional small-scale industries. Thus tracts of land will be used in such a way that the houses do not intrude, or intrude only minimally, on farmland and forest. Because the community land trust is the owner of all lots on a tract of land, it can cluster housing, build shared driveways, and designate common-use areas, thereby limiting the amount of land needed per household. Individuals lease a house site, not a house lot.

We will give as an example the community land trust with which we have the most direct experience. In the town of South Egremont, Massachusetts, where we live on CLT land, local zoning calls for two acres of land per house, with 150 feet of road frontage. Such zoning encourages the breakup of farms and forest because driveways run across open space to each house. The Community Land Trust in the Southern Berkshires, as it is known, holds a 9.7-acre tract with four house lots located under Jug End Mountain. The houses are clustered so as to intrude as little as possible on the surrounding orchard. Each household leases a half-acre house site rather than a 2.4-acre lot. Because the CLT has title to all four lots, it can lease parts of each one to create a house site, as long as the house itself falls within the lot lines. This permits site-specific planning and makes the lease a more refined planning tool than zoning. Our own house is on lot B, our shared driveway on lot A, and our garden on lot C. The majority of the 9.7 acres has been left intact as an orchard.

The CLT leases the orchard separately to Bernard Kirchner, a local farmer, who cares for and harvests the apple trees, first planted on the leasehold by his grandfather. His lease is unaffected by any future change of ownership of the homes. The security of the lease provides him with the incentive to plan for the long-term health of the soil and trees and thus to farm sustainably. Bernard has also planted perennial stock—raspberry plants, asparagus plants, and young apple, pear, and cherry trees. Should he need to move from the site, he can sell his improvements (fencing, apple trees, and other fruit stock) but not the land itself. With equity in the site he is encouraged to invest for the future and to remain a member of the community.

The Community Land Trust in the Southern Berkshires paid the market rate for this land in 1980. Over the years, lease fees collected on the house sites paid off the mortgage. Housing, the most intensive use of the land, carried the burden of financing it. The CLT was therefore able to keep the cost of Bernard's lease very low—he makes his payments in cider apples—securing an affordable source of food production for the region.

The Community Land Trust in the Southern Berkshires also holds title to twenty-one acres in Great Barrington known as Forest Row. This site includes preserved land, a common recreational area, woodland, and eighteen units of housing clustered on five acres. The land-use plan and housing designs were developed in collaboration with the future homeowners. Even with careful planning and unit-owner participation, the CLT was unable to keep purchase prices as low as it would have liked because of the high cost of construction.

The problem was tackled by the Fund for Affordable Housing, a separately organized charitable entity. As a tax-exempt organization, the fund can accept donations to subsidize construction costs. It has built two homes at Forest Row for sale to low-income families.

The Fund for Affordable Housing also administers a second-mortgage loan fund financed with investments from Berkshire residents and vacation homeowners. The loan pool provides low-cost second mortgages to unit owners at Forest Row, thus lowering monthly mortgage payments. Eighty percent of the original loans have been repaid, and some early borrowers are now lenders to the fund.

As a volunteer organization modeled after Habitat for Humanity, the fund organizes community assistance for the construction of the homes it builds. Community members who are well versed in the particulars of housing development are chosen for the board: architects, builders, and bankers, who volunteer their professional skills. Once the housing is built, the fund does not have the staff to manage resale restrictions (which keep the units affordable for future generations) or to oversee land-use provisions, so affordability and land-use standards are maintained by working cooperatively with the CLT.

This association between the Fund for Affordable Housing and the Community Land Trust in the Southern Berkshires represents an ideal form of cooperation between a charitable organization and a nonprofit CLT. The partnership provides affordable access to land and affordable home ownership for year-round residents who otherwise would not be able to live in this high-priced vacation-home region.

Another example of cooperation between landholding organizations is the work of the Great Barrington Land Conservancy (which has tax-exempt status as a conservation group) and the Community Land Trust in the Southern Berkshires. The office building known as Riverbank House, located on Great Barrington's Main Street and owned by the CLT, has been the home of many small nonprofit groups. When the CLT bought Riverbank House, the steep riverbank behind the building was littered with debris from years of neglect and from a fire in the building nextdoor. Rachel Fletcher, a CLT member led the board of directors in cleaning up the riverbank, resulting in a cleaner lot and greater community attention to the Housatonic River and its environs.

Rachel next conceived the idea of a Housatonic Riverwalk to parallel Main Street, and the town has shared her dream. More than one thousand volunteers have helped in cleanups and trail-building along the river. The work of the volunteers, combined with the actual costs of building materials, created improvements to the properties valued at an estimated hundred thousand dollars. These improvements, though desirable, could not have been justified economically by the commercial use of the properties; however, the partnership between the charitably organized Great Barrington Land Conservancy and the nonprofit CLT helped facilitate this popular project.

The Great Barrington Land Conservancy now holds a ninety-nine-year lease along the trail. Tax-deductible donations for materials to build stairs down the steepest part of the bank went to the conservancy as lessee of the site. The long-term lease is a lien on the properties and protects the community's investment of money and time for the benefit of future generations. Other property owners will be asked to sign similar leases in exchange for a cleanup of their banks.

Recently the Community Land Trust in the Southern Berkshires joined with members of several local *conservation* land trusts to establish a fund to purchase tracts of farmland. The land will be leased back to farmers at a reasonable cost, thus reducing the overall indebtedness on the farms. The buildings and equipment will still be owned by the farmers and may be sold at replacement value to future lease-holders. The lease agreement is a tool to protect present and future affordability of the land for farmers and ensures that conservation measures are incorporated into agricultural practices. The land fund provides a method for consumers to support a continued local agricultural base in their community.

Another application of the community land trust concept was initiated by Winona LaDuke of the White Earth Land Recovery Project in Northern Minnesota. She is using the CLT as a vehicle to regather tribal lands of the Anishinabeg people, also known as Chippewas and Ojibways, lands lost to private absentee landlords and to county, state, and federal governments. Through gifts and purchases White Earth has already reclaimed significant tracts of cultural lands, including maple-sugar groves and a raspberry farm, which provide employment for tribal members who process and sell the products.

The community land trust is a flexible civic tool for holding land on a democratic basis for the common good while facilitating private ownership of structures and improvements. Unfortunately, the accumulation of land in CLTs has been very gradual. It is true that each new piece of land in a CLT has its own story of hope and good work and that each piece serves to remind the general public that land is "a community to which we belong." But there is no broad movement to decommoditize land. Environmentalism is the new religion of our age, but it is only a Sunday morning religion. We discuss Aldo Leopold at dinner parties and clean up riverbanks on weekends but still reserve the right to sell to the highest bidder the land we own and care for. We have yet to fully imagine and embrace a culture in which land use is allocated by social and environmental contract rather than by checkbook. The community land trust is a proven tool for change. When will we dare to use it?

An opportunity arose to apply the community land trust concept on a regional basis when E. F. Schumacher Society staff was asked to work with Buryat farmers at Lake Baikal. The Olkhon raion (region) on the west bank of Lake Baikal in Siberia is a geologically unique region of sixty-five hundred square miles. It is home to ninety-five hundred ethnic Buryats, who are the indigenous people of the lake region. Shepherds today as they have been for generations, the Buryats are caught up in the wholesale changes sweeping the former Soviet Union. They remain a close community tied to the land, yet they know they must establish an independent economic system to provide an adequate livelihood for their communities without endangering the extraordinary ecosystem of Lake Baikal, which they hold sacred.

The people of Olkhon have identified a number of possible small businesses for their region: production of traditional medicines; manufacture of traditional clothes, rugs, and cloth woven from the wool of their sheep; and a small cannery for preserving locally grown foods. Investment in these new enterprises is complicated by the question of land ownership. Under Soviet law all of the land of Olkhon—and all buildings and farms—belonged to the state. Investors need security of ownership if they are to invest, yet if the land is privately allocated to permit business investments, it can easily be sold to interests outside Olkhon, its resources can be exploited, and the local community will lose the important land base that is its strength and the foundation of its culture.

In order to preserve traditional patterns of land use in the raion and to foster a healthy economy based on sustainable yields, the E. F. Schumacher Society has established the Olkhon Center for Sustainable Agriculture. The center is working with farmers and officials of the Olkhon raion to establish an Olkhon community land trust to hold all the productive lands in the region. This CLT will formalize an ecologically sustainable land-use plan, already developed by local officials in collaboration with American consultants, for the Olkhon raion; provide generational land-use rights for residents of the raion, reflecting historical and current family land-use patterns and securing cultural continuity; provide for private ownership of buildings and other improvements for the residents of the region so that investment in homes, farms, businesses, and public infrastructure is facilitated; arrange an efficient means to transfer equity in improvements without capitalizing land values in the process, so that ownership of homes and businesses remains affordable to residents of the raion and so that year-round residents are given priority in purchasing improvements for sale; and establish a locally controlled and democratically structured system for management of land allocations and for oversight of lease terms.

Once in place at Olkhon, the community land trust can become a model land tenure system for other regions of the watershed. The ecological significance of this extraordinary lake (Baikal holds one-fifth of the earth's fresh water), the still-strong roots of the Buryats in their traditional culture, and the important model that the Olkhon Community Land Trust can provide for the fair distribution of land lend importance and urgency to this work. Even more significant is the fact that a project such as this one at Lake Baikal can help our Western minds imagine what it would be like if all the land in a region were freed from debt and freed form trading to the highest bidder: in short, freed to be the "community to which we belong."

E. F. Schumacher, author of *Small Is Beautiful: Economics as if People Mattered,* suggested that the best strategy for action is simply to begin: "Perhaps we cannot raise the winds. But each of us can put up the sail, so that when the wind comes we can catch it." We believe that a community land trust is just such a sail. A local CLT is, by its very existence, a means for educating the public on issues of land tenure; it can "catch" and hold land as it is freed for the community. With the forming of community land trusts around the country, a movement is growing that can lead us into a new cultural relationship with the land. We need only dare to raise the sail.

A handbook of legal documents for establishing a community land trust may be ordered from the E. F. Schumacher Society, 140 Jug End Road, Great Barrington, MA 01230; (413)528-1737, E-mail EFSSociety@aol.com.

community-supported agriculture:
rediscovering community

JACK KITTREDGE

COMMUNITY'S NOT A SENTIMENT. IT HAS TO DO WITH NECESSITY—WITH PEOPLE NEEDING EACH OTHER. IF YOU ALLOW THE LARGER INDUSTRIAL SYSTEM TO REMOVE THE PATTERN OF NEEDS THAT IS THE FORCE HOLDING PEOPLE TOGETHER, THEN YOU LOSE THE COMMUNITY.

—Wendell Berry, *Safe Food News,* 1994

MANY Americans would accept without challenge the statement that, in general, modern time-saving conveniences have led to less work, more leisure, and greater happiness. They would be surprised to hear E. F. Schumacher's contrary assertion that the more value people place on time in a culture, the less they are able to relax and enjoy it, the more they need to fill it up with "productive" activity. But studies seem to support Schumacher's view. Today's average employed American works 163 more hours per year than he or she did twenty-five years ago. Witold Rybczynski of McGill University, looking at a longer time frame, has found that we work longer hours than we did before the industrial revolution. Religious festivals, saints' days, and the like reduced the medieval workyear to well below the modern level of 2,000-plus hours.

Nor do measures of "happiness" support the myth of modern progress. Despite a 45 percent increase in U.S. per capita consumption over the last twenty years, our quality of life (as measured by Fordham University's Index of Social Health) has dropped 51 percent. Surveys by the University of Chicago find that, despite near-doublings in real Gross National Product and personal per capita consumption spending, no more people report being "very happy" now than did in 1957. In fact, people in the same social stratum report the same happiness level in such diverse societies as those of the United States, Israel, Brazil, and India. To the extent that happiness is connected at all with material wealth, it correlates with one's status relative to others, not any objective level of "things." Of those Americans earning less than fifteen thousand dollars a year, 5 percent say they have achieved the American dream. Of those earning more than fifty thousand, 6 percent say they have done it.

What studies do support is that happiness is not closely linked to consumption, but rather to contentment with family life, especially marriage, followed by satisfaction with work, leisure to develop talents, and friendships. By these standards, quality of life has actually declined somewhat over the last generation. Visits with neighbors and friends, family conversations, and time spent at family meals have all decreased since midcentury. Parents spend 40 percent less time with their children now than in 1965. We have increased our TV viewing time by 39 percent since 1960 and now spend an (incredible) average of one year of our lives watching commercials.

These statistics suggesting that we work longer hours and commune less with others during leisure are reflective of a historical process that some feel has been at work since medieval times. The rise of nation-states and the victory of industrial over artisan-based production have stripped away many of the connections that average people had to place and to one another. The strong central role of the church in community life is gone. Local, more personal government has been supplanted by national authority. By and large, we no longer produce our own necessities of life: food, clothing, shelter. Entire specialist industries have arisen to provide services once received through the extended family: child care, health care, entertainment. Gradually the individual is being peeled away from the fundamental connecting integuments of church, village, family, craft, and place. To the extent that they exist any longer, they are temporary and attenuated. Today we commonly have multiple professions and serial families. We move every few years. We are offered wealth instead of honor; poverty has taken the place of disgrace. The only "belonging" that has grown stronger in our lives is as national citizens.

But allegiance to the nation-state is thin stuff for daily satisfaction and, as we have seen, the accumulation of things does not bring happiness. Many of us crave stronger and richer human connections. As the old forms of belonging pass from our lives, we begin to recognize how valuable they were. An alternative, holistic viewpoint is emerging, which takes inspiration from life's vast intertwined networks. It is finding adherents in fields such as natural science, healing, and artificial intelligence. So, too, a number of alternative institutions are emerging that relocalize power and oblige their members one to another. Food cooperatives, barter clubs, home schooling groups, land trusts, and other organizations are efforts to take more control over providing our basic needs in association with others. One bright new addition to this list in Community-Supported Agriculture (CSA) projects.

The CSAs are joint ventures between consumers and farmers to produce food. In most cases the consumers put up money early in the season to become "shareholders" in that season's harvest, and the farmers provide the skills to raise the food. In more consumer-initiated models, a community group will rent or acquire land, set a budget, and hire the farmers. Other farm-initiated models begin when a farmer decides to start a CSA and seeks members as an alternative to current marketing arrangements. Some CSAs are church sponsored, some are committed to serving a particular disadvantaged population, and others are oriented around dietary preferences.

Most CSAs raise fresh vegetables as their primary product. Many add herbs, cut flowers, and small fruits to their product mix. A smaller number provide eggs, tree fruit, dairy products, and meat or poultry. Some also offer breads, jams, vinegars, and other farm-processed foods. Determining factors are the way the farm is set up and what the farmers are skilled at raising.

Commonly, a CSA will have one or more "distribution days" each week. Early that morning crops are picked and brought in out of the sun. They are cooled and sometimes sorted into individual bags or boxes to be picked up by the shareholder later in the day. Other models leave the produce to be sorted by the members when they come to pick it up. Some remote CSAs include delivery; sorted and bagged orders are brought to a pickup spot close to consumers, or even right to their homes.

The central idea of CSAs is traceable to roots in Japan and Switzerland. In Japan's postwar boom, land became expensive and difficult to maintain in agriculture. By 1965 the problem was so advanced that an organization known as the Seikatsu Club formed for the purpose of protecting land by keeping it in productive farming. Loosely translated, *seikatsu* means "food with the farmer's face on it." Largely organized by mothers and wives as the traditional household food buyers, local groups function by pooling the purchasing power of many families (fifteen hundred is a typical number) and setting up or cooperatively supporting specific local farming operations. The Swiss CSA beginnings were in Baden, outside Zurich, where a farmstand owner sought a more formal commitment from his clientele. In 1980 the customers formed a group called *Tomnibur* (Jerusalem artichoke) for the purpose of supporting this produce operation. The idea was brought to the United States after a few years and the movement has spread rapidly. In 1993 more than four hundred CSAs were in operation in this country.

While community-supported agriculture is gaining adherents across the country, the idea seems most popular in the northeastern states, perhaps because the hilly terrain favors small farming operations and high population densities make direct marketing feasible.

In northern New Jersey much of what was recently farmland is now glass and steel corporate research complexes, conference centers, or upscale retail strips. But the Stony Brook Millstone Watershed Association maintains miles of hiking trails and a small nature center in Pennington. It also has about nine acres of cropland, a greenhouse, a barn, a farmhouse, and some farm equipment that it leases to Jim Kinsel, who operates the Watershed Farm CSA.

Kinsel has 220 subscribers at $360 per share. He grows a wide variety of mixed vegetables for a season that starts late in May and runs twenty-four weeks until mid-November. Subscribers come once a week on their pickup day to bag and take home their share of the produce. Weekday distribution starts at one in the afternoon, which allows a reasonable pace for harvesting, but many Saturday people want to pick up early and get on with their weekend plans. So Saturday's distribution starts at ten, forcing Jim to pick a lot of produce Friday night and store it in the cooler.

There is no work requirement at the Watershed CSA, but a core group of shareholders has evolved that handles all the incoming checks and keeps the books, enabling Kinsel to concentrate on farming. He estimates that about 80 percent of his subscribers renew the next year—which may be a result of the farm's close ties to the Watershed Association. "People sometimes make a recreational outing of coming to the Watershed. They like the appearance of the farm, the atmosphere, the connection with the Watershed—so they feel they're not only supporting the farm but also open land. It all contributes," Kinsel says.

Skip Paul operates Wishing Stone Farm in Little Compton, Rhode Island. He decided to open a small CSA in 1992. At first he brought the CSA vegetables to his farmstand and tried to do the distribution there. Then he decided to let shareholders pick up right from the farmstand displays. He gives them a list of four or five items that they must take—the general harvest of that period—but then they can take as much or as little other produce as they want, to make up their own box.

The farm has attracted twenty shareholders at $295 each. Paul is intentionally keeping it small until the problems are ironed out, after which he hopes to go to seventy-five or eighty shares. He is not sure there is that much demand, however: "The CSA looks promising but there is a lot of recidivism. It's hard to tell why people join the first time around, so it's hard to find the right mixture to keep them happy. I was surprised to find that when we had a bumper crop people wouldn't take advantage of it. They didn't want to deal with processing or freezing the extra. Our lives have gotten so busy and complex we're all geared toward convenience now."

Matt and Scout Proft raise vegetables in one of Vermont's Green Mountain valleys, but on the hillside they raise poultry. "People can join a mixed poultry CSA, a chicken CSA, or a vegetable CSA," Scout explains. "With the chicken and poultry ones, we let people know when the birds are going to be done and they can pick them up fresh or we'll freeze them and people can pick up when they want. That way we can accommodate tourists who are here only for a season."

The Profts have about thirty members in their poultry CSA. Members pay in May—$120 for mixed poultry—and they receive three broiler chickens totaling twelve pounds, a turkey for Thanksgiving, two pounds of turkey sausage, a brace of pheasants, and a smoked turkey breast. The chicken CSA costs $74, and people get nine broilers or about thirty-five pounds of chicken. Like farmers in any CSA, the Profts find it wonderful to get the money up front. Paying for thousands of birds and their feed until slaughter is a major financial burden, and the community support that early financing represents lets them get bank credit so they can buy needed processing and freezing equipment.

Agriculture in the United States has been fundamentally changing over the last fifty years. Once, in the nineteenth century, we were a nation of farmers. Even as late as 1935, there were almost 7 million farms in this country. It has never been an easy way to make a living, however, and after World War II many farmers were attracted away from the land to jobs in industrial production. In 1991, only 2.1 million farms were left.

As farmers drifted away, neighbors bought up their property. Concentration in farmland has proceeded to such an extent that today over half of gross national farm production is generated from only 4 percent of our farms. These megaoperations dominate the market, whereas the 2 million and more small and medium farms net an average of less than three thousand dollars per year.

Such modest returns have driven more and more farmers out of trying to compete in commodity production with large, specialized corporate farms. Instead, they have sought product mixes and niche markets that allow higher value sales. Part of that strategy has been direct sales to consumers at farm stands, farmers' markets, and pick-your-own operations. While this has paid off for most small farmers, the strategy is not without problems. It is risky in that it requires producing a diversity of crops without prearranged buyers, costly because it involves investment of substantial capital that is not recovered until after harvest, and time-consuming since allocation of substantial effort to marketing conflicts with time spent in the field during the growing season.

All of these problems are neatly avoided under a CSA arrangement. Members buy shares before the season begins, thus the crops are sold even before they are planted. No effort is wasted, because every bit of produce grown will go home with a consumer. Marketing efforts are shifted to the winter months, when most farmers have fewer conflicts. Finally, since the funds are provided at the beginning of the season, farmers need not borrow for seed, equipment, fuel, labor, and the other expenses of a long growing season.

Food consumption patterns in America have been changing over the last generation. Concern about risks associated with fat and cholesterol has led to a reduction in consumption of red meat, eggs, and dairy products. Animal-rights feelings and awareness of the environmental costs and inefficiencies involved in raising grain for feed have swollen the number of vegetarians and vegans among us. Diseases, allergies, and chemical sensitivities have convinced many that fresh, unprocessed, organic produce represents the most healthy alternative available to food buyers today.

Although nothing about the CSA structure legislates that the food grown be organic, the entire thrust of the movement yields that result. Consumers who go to so much trouble to seek out local fresh vegetables do not want them raised with toxic chemicals. They are close enough to the farm to see or hear about farm practices and to evaluate farm management.

The most immediate benefit to consumers of joining a CSA is the guarantee of regular, fresh, organic produce throughout the growing season. No more getting to the farmers' market late and finding that what you want is sold out. No more limited selection at the natural-food store. Short of having your own garden, joining a CSA is the best way to assure your family's nutrition.

A secondary benefit is learning about new foods. Many consumers who first come to a CSA are woefully ignorant of the hundreds of varieties of fruits and vegetables that can be raised in their part of the world. The conventional food system in this country is oriented to producing a few of the most popular fruits and vegetables, and then only the varieties that are suitable for long periods of storage, that stand up to rough conditions of picking, packing, and shipping, and that look most colorful and appealing on the store shelf.

None of these requirements pertain to the harvest and distribution of produce in a CSA, so growers are free to raise crops that have been selected solely for their delicious taste and high nutritional content. Hundreds of heirloom varieties of standard and unusual crops still exist. While they may not ship or store well, they have been passed along by generations of gardeners and small farmers simply because they taste so good when eaten fresh. Discovering them has been a treat reserved until now for only the most sophisticated gardeners.

Not just the members and growers are affected by CSAs. The surrounding community benefits whenever local purchases keep money circulating close to home. Most CSAs sponsor occasional farm tours to let children in school and day-care groups learn about farm animals and soil and plant care. They also reduce the waste stream associated with our food system. The produce goes from harvest to table packaged only in reusable bags or cartons, eliminating the cans, bottles, foil envelopes, aluminum or styrofoam trays, and glossy packaging, all of which serve only to clog the local landfill.

Perhaps most important to nearby residents, however, is the fact that CSAs are a way to keep land in farming. In many parts of the country the local farmer is simply disappearing. The rewards are not adequate to keep young people coming into the profession. Net real farm income is 10 percent less than it was in 1940. Farm households dependent on farming for all their income earned $18,800 in 1991. The average U.S. farmer is now almost sixty years of age. In some cases CSAs are the only reasonable way to farm; retail prices, customer appreciation, and early payment are significant inducements to stay in this marginal business. The number of functioning CSAs and organic farms is actually increasing, even as overall farm numbers decline.

Many Americans place a high value on living in areas where open land is preserved—whether by farming, recreation, or scenic use. With development pressures increasing competition for the remaining open land, farm enterprises that can retain such land and keep it from being developed need to be encouraged. But open land is not only preferred by many for aesthetic reasons, it also helps local communities stay financially stable. A recent study of land-use patterns and local town budgets in Virginia, Connecticut, and New York compared the revenues from residential, commercial/industrial, and farm/forest property taxes to the costs of serving those users (such costs as public works, education, police, and fire). Whereas residential taxpayers required $1.36 in services for every dollar they paid in taxes, farmers cost only 21¢ per tax dollar paid.

On a broader basis than simply growing food, CSAs and other local farming operations provide solutions to several of our tougher modern problems. Anyone involved in the escalating waste crisis knows how difficult it is to find ways to dispose of all the trash our culture produces. Incineration pollutes the air and land-fills are filling up. At the same time, studies show that we are using our topsoil ten times faster than it is renewing itself. What is topsoil but stabilized, decayed waste? Properly composted, all of our food waste, some industrial processing waste, and all of our paper and wood waste can be turned into clean, productive topsoil at decentralized farm sites throughout the country.

Most people support the view that even "retarded" people, who once were kept at home and given menial tasks, need useful work and should be given as much responsibility as they can handle. In our fast-paced, automated service econ-omy, not many low-skilled, low-stress jobs remain. Where can such people be given safe, productive, pleasant employment? Although properly managing a farm is one of the more complex enterprises a person today can attempt, plenty of the jobs on a farm are simple and relatively pleasant—and need doing. Feeding ani-mals, weeding crops, fixing fences, and a dozen other chores are regular, time-con-suming, and vital jobs, but are easily learned and do not produce much stress.

A number of teachers in inner-city schools, desperate for ways to reconnect with their students' minds, have turned to agriculture as a teaching device. We all like to eat, and most young people still express wonder at the simple miracles of germination and birth that take place in the natural world. Building on these be-ginnings, teachers have started school gardens, compost piles, and small livestock-raising projects to capture their pupils' imaginations. Some have become enter-prises that earn student pocket money via the sale of produce to the cafeteria, that teach science and engineering through practical examples, and that give plenty of opportunity to learn small-business skills. Students who excel in this environment and begin to take pride in their abilities are advanced to more responsible posi-tions in local farms, gardens, and greenhouses.

Increasingly, consumers are concerned about the use of toxic chemicals in raising food. Yet over the last thirty years U.S. sales of pesticides have increased twenty-seven-fold to a current level of seven billion dollars. Antibiotics are now administered in feed to 80 percent of all poultry, 75 percent of hogs, 60 percent of beef cattle, and 75 percent of dairy cows. Ninety-two percent of the lettuce harvested in this country is grown in California and Arizona, where sixty-two dif-ferent chemicals are used on it. Groundwater pollution from at least forty-six pes-ticides has been found in twenty-five states. In Iowa and Nebraska, half the wells are contaminated; in California, twenty of the thirty-three counties report de-tectable residues.

Much of the incredible productivity of North American industrial agricul-ture has been based on using up two irreplaceable capital assets: topsoil and pe-troleum. When our ancestors settled this continent, they benefited from the largesse of thousands of years of natural soil creation, virtually undiminished by agriculture. The careless practices of our modern world have seen up to half of that soil washed or blown away, and each year every acre loses an average of 7.7 tons more. Only when the last of this prehistoric legacy is washed to sea and we are on a "level playing field" with the other continents will we appreciate the magnitude of our folly.

Perhaps the most egregious feature of modern agribusiness is its dependency on energy. Scientists estimate that primitive farming—the technology that spawned the agricultural revolution and enabled civilization to develop—required an input of one calorie of energy (mostly muscular) for every five calories of food produced. Now fertilizers, petrochemicals, mechanization of production, processing, and global transport and distribution have reversed that equation. For one modern food calorie to reach your table, between eight and ten calories (mostly petroleum) must be spent.

To the extent that CSAs offer local produce, grown without chemical input by small-scale farmers or gardeners practicing composting and cover cropping, they are providing a solution to these problems in our mass food system. As the difficulties become more obvious and more costly, such a sustainable local alternative should become still more appealing.

In addition, CSAs are suggesting ways to solve problems other than those related to agricultural productivity. Many are experimenting with ways to ease local income disparities. Some price their shares on a sliding scale so that the affluent pay more. Others set a budget, and then the members bid what they can afford for a share. If the numbers fail to balance, the budget is revised and new bids are made until committed income matches planned expenses. Many CSAs provide an opportunity for members to substitute labor for cash by working off part or all of the share price. A few CSAs give one or more shares to local food banks, which in turn distribute the produce to local families in need. At some, a "freebie" table enables those who don't like a particular item, or have too much of it, to leave it for someone who prefers that or needs more than a share provides. At other CSAs, conscious efforts to reach out to the poor include registering as a vendor with the U.S. Department of agriculture food stamp program and employing the homeless.

One strength of traditional American communities was the amount of collective work that went on. Barn building, quilting, joint harvesting, church repair—all contributed to the sense of having earned the right to "belong." Many of those functions have been transferred to the industrial, money economy now, where machines and a few skilled people perform them continually. On a CSA farm, however, sometimes nothing but many hands will suffice, and the older model of joint work is called for.

As the analyst Brewster Kneen said in 1989, many of those who buy shares in a CSA farm are "engaging in it in a way very similar to the ways 'family' members participated in the multi-generational farms of the pre-industrial age." To the extent that alternative institutions recenter our lives in small, local groups of people with whom we have mutual obligations, they can rebuild human community. CSAs, in particular, can satisfy the most fundamental human need and do so in a way that provides us with delicious enjoyment, bonds us in useful work together, and humbles us with continual consciousness of our place in the wonder of nature.

community farming in massachusetts

BRIAN DONAHUE

WESTON, Massachusetts, where I lived and farmed for most of two decades, is only twelve miles west of Boston. To the naked eye it appears to be a bedroom community inhabited by beltway professionals. Yet Weston still thinks of itself as a small, rural New England town. Weston isn't rural anymore, but it does behave like a small New England town, using the same town meeting form of democratic local self-government established three and a half centuries ago by Puritan farmers. Very few private farmers are left in Weston. After an absence of more than three hundred years, common farming has reappeared in a new form.

Nearly one-quarter of the land in Weston today is commonly owned. The same is true of several neighboring towns. This is a recent development in New England history, although it has an almost forgotten precedent. Many of the original towns settled around Massachusetts Bay in the 1630s started out with a common field system. Farmers owned small private mowing and tillage lots, and had tightly regulated rights to graze livestock and cut wood on the undivided "commons" that made up the bulk of the town's land. Over succeeding generations almost all this common land passed into private ownership, where it remained for three centuries.

Community-owned land reappeared in the decades after 1950, when many townspeople became concerned that rapid residential development was destroying the very rural character that made towns such as Weston attractive. This central dilemma of suburbanization has not been solved, but it was at least mitigated by the purchase of "conservation land" in large and small pieces throughout the town. In all (counting state-owned land), some twenty-five hundred acres in Weston are now protected open space. This is our modern commons.

Very little land in Weston is farmed anymore, although nearly all of it once was. Most of the artfully ditched and walled countryside has grown up in either trees or houses. Weston's conservation land was not acquired with the idea that it should be farmed again. Quite the opposite: it was acquired thanks to a Thoreauvian impulse that we should surround ourselves with wild places; that we should deliberately *not* use it. A few efforts were made to manage the first town forest lands back in the 1950s, but by the 1960s this approach gave way to the strictly preservationist view that we ought to just let nature take care of it, except to keep a few trails open for walking and riding.

The idea that human communities need to be embedded in larger natural communities where biological diversity flourishes around them is commendable. But is wilderness in the suburbs desirable, or even possible? By the 1970s a new idea had emerged and gained ground, which was that it might be more beneficial to actually use this land in ecologically responsible ways than to just enjoy its unkempt beauty while our resources were being extracted willy-nilly from more distant, expendable parts of the planet. This was partly a return to a "conservationist" stance, but it shared the preservationists' distrust of conventional farming and forestry and sought a more holistic alternative. A few neighboring towns generated similar movements to create nonprofit organizations that would care for common land and educate young people—what we have come to call community farming. Each town's community farm runs a bit differently, but the central idea is the same: to involve people with the land.

Most of us who got into community farming did not do it for reasons of nostalgia. We did it because we were preparing for a more decentralized, energy-scarce future, bringing our food supplies closer to home. (In the 1970s we thought this future was right around the corner.) We also did it for subversive educational reasons, to cloud the minds of suburban youths with sustainable thoughts. However, we soon discovered that agriculture has a broader appeal. The landscape for which many suburbanites were nostalgic was not wild but agrarian: small farmsteads, pastures, orchards, woodlots, stone walls, wooden bridges, millponds, villages. These features were termed rural character. We simply pointed out that to have rural character, you need rural activity: you have to go out there and actually farm the place. Unlike wilderness, the rural landscape is one of human involvement, not human withdrawal.

When we laid claim to reviving the rural character of the landscape, we also tied ourselves to its history. We weren't simply trying to invent a new ecoagrarian world, we were rescuing an older one. Most of the places where we worked bore the marks of the past; for better or worse, they had been prepared for us. In spite of dramatic changes, the land has a continuous history to which we are connected. The same is true of the human community: the acquisition and care of conservation land arises from a deep New England tradition of collective responsibility for the welfare of the place called a town. The degree to which this tradition has adapted and perpetuated itself even in what is now a transient suburb, populated largely by nonnatives, is truly remarkable—and heartening.

I don't mean to romanticize the suburb, which in most ways still epitomizes all that is wrong with Americans' relation to the land and to one another. Nor do I mean to romanticize the small New England town that preceded the suburb, although I do admire the beauty of the form. In spite of an image of convivial harmony with a diverse landscape through the turning seasons, New England small farms were not always ecologically in tune. The idea that people bear individual or collective responsibility for the place they inhabit has rarely been applied to the care of the land itself, at least until recently. Common land has been missing from New England for a long time, replaced by a tradition of private property rights that unfortunately recognizes little common interest in the way the land is used.

Still, in many New England towns, that common interest is gradually being reasserted. Small communities that have well-defined identities and that retain face-to-face, participatory democracy with the power to act for the common good remain a strong institution here. There is much to criticize in our past, but there is much to cherish and build on, as well. Community farming emerges from the best of the New England tradition of deeply rooted places. It is a model that can be adapted to many other regions, but to make it work there must be a base of land that is under local community control, in places that can think and behave like communities.

The very names of Weston's two community farms capture the evolution from ecofuturism to nostalgic appeal: Green Power Farm appeared in 1970, and Land's Sake was founded in 1980. Green Power was the brainchild of an irresistible anarchist, a Harvard graduate and one-time New Hampshire farmer and schoolteacher named Bill McElwain, who brought together a group of volunteers and began using neglected suburban farmland to grow fresh produce for the inner city. Weston embraced McElwain as its resident rural character and mentor for disaffected children: he was made project director of the newly formed Weston Youth Commission, which had been set up to address teenage alienation and prevent drug addiction. I began working with Bill in 1975, when I dropped out of nearby Brandeis University. For years I duly recorded all the kids who worked at Green Power as "potential drug abusers," although we regarded them more as potential citizen farmers of the coming ecological age.

We taught kids to cultivate fifteen acres of vegetables, and shipped the food to inner-city community development organizations for a dollar a crate. We were probably the largest grower of collard and mustard greens in all Massachusetts. We also made cider and syrup by seasonal turns in a funky sugar house that Bill and his band of suburban guerrillas built from local white pine right next to the spanking new, concrete middle school. Needless to say, kids swarmed over these enterprises, appearing through the steam to skim the scum from boiling sap during their study hall and lunch periods, and vanishing again into the hive. Although the age of ecology has not yet arrived, a few of those young people are farming to this day.

McElwain's unabashed operating philosophy was that it is easier to gain forgiveness than consent, and for a time there seemed to be no limit to what Green Power could get into. We certainly got the town's equipment into some unlikely spots. One Sunday evening, Weston selectman Harold Hestnes was surprised to receive a phone call from a New Hampshire state trooper, inquiring what a Weston dump truck with no lights was doing hauling a load of pine boxboards down the interstate. Hestnes didn't rightly know, but he could roughly guess. Harold was a typical selectman, conservative but attached to anything rural, and willing to forgive an ultraliberal character like McElwain—up to a certain point. The pine that went to the New Hampshire box mill came from one of Harold's neighbors, an eminent endocrinologist who had decided to raise sheep for equal parts nostalgia and biomedical research. I later kept sheep in that pasture myself. And I still have some of the apple boxes we made from those boards: my wife,

Faith (a Weston native and former potential drug abuser), keeps yarn in one of them. I can prove all of what I say.

Cutting pines to clear pasture for sheep, milling some of that pine into boards, nailing up crates to collect apples for cider, hauling the rest of the pine to the sugar house to pitch through the maple syrup evaporator the next spring—this was heady stuff for a young ecotopian. There were a few square miles of community land in Weston, and so far we were only working about fifteen acres. With all that land devoted to tree crops, organic farming, greenhouses, aquaculture, human waste recycling, and a few bees, we figured we could just about feed, clothe, and house the whole town. We could employ and reeducate every kid Weston could produce. It was a great vision: others were talking about local self-reliance; here we had this entire suburb to work with. We were *doing* it. Unfortunately, there was indeed a limit to what Green Power could do, and we had already reached it: by the late 1970s the tax revolution had overtaken us, town budgets were being cut, and Weston was not about to let Green Power get any bigger.

We needed a new approach. In 1980 we borrowed an idea from Codman Community Farms in neighboring Lincoln and incorporated a nonprofit organization. Our stated purposes were to manage conservation and private land in Weston in ecologically sustainable ways, to employ and educate young people, and to cover as many of our own costs as possible from sales of natural products and services. Doug Henderson, one of the cofounders, named us Land's Sake, in honor of his grandmother, a New Englander who often used that expression. Henderson is a Weston native who had a distinguished foreign service career before he returned to Weston, turned his attention to what was happening to his hometown, and swore off diplomacy forever. Bill McElwain sits on the Land's Sake board, too. Land's Sake aimed to carry on what Green Power had pioneered, but to pay its own way and control its own purse strings. Even at the local level, it was the right time to get out of government.

We signed up a few dozen charter members and went to work—I think our first project involved transplanting peonies. Probably nobody thought much would ever come of it. I was headed back to school, fascinated by the many-layered history of the land I was working on. For a few years I ran Land's Sake after hours with a rototiller, a chainsaw, and a 1963 Jeep pickup. The conservation commissioners who held the keys to the town's land were tentatively supportive, but deeply skeptical of our utilitarian urges. Yet a decade and a half later, Land's Sake has absorbed the old Green Power projects into a much larger, comprehensive town farm and forest program. Ten percent of our budget comes from membership donations, 30 percent from the town in payment for contracted services, and 60 percent from sales of natural products. We have by no means accomplished all we set out to do, but community farming in Weston is certainly thriving in its twenty-fifth year.

Community farming can involve all kinds of rustic pursuits. For us, a project was worth a try if there was suitable land for it, if we had the staff and equipment to tackle it, if it involved young people in some way, and if there was a ready market. A few of our projects will provide some idea of the scope of Land's Sake, and of the connection between what we do and the history of farming in New England: market gardening, cider pressing, maple syruping, sheep keeping, and forestry. Some pursuits worked better than others for us. If you're going to try something similar, plan to put a couple decades into just getting it going. Mainly, it takes sheer cussedness and perseverance in the face of the well-founded opinions of your neighbors, the social equivalent of the weather. I also recommend that you find more starting capital than we did.

The project that gives us a visible identity we call the Case Farm, but nearly everyone else in town simply calls it Land's Sake. We cultivate a parcel of town-owned land that was formerly part of the Arnold Arboretum's Case Estates, right in the center of Weston. The Case Farm exemplifies what Land's Sake is all about: it is beautiful, it is organic, it involves people with the land, it is worked by kids, and in good years it makes a pile of money. We have about twenty-five total acres in rotation: twenty in cash crops, and five in legume green manure. The Green Power land a few miles away now grows field crops such as potatoes, winter squash, and pumpkins; the Case land concentrates on pick-your-own vegetables, fruits, and flowers. Small, irregular fields are laid out among specimen trees from every temperate part of the planet. Between the farm stand and the street lies an acre planted with annual and perennial flowers in hundreds of small curving beds. We sell cut-your-own flowers for as little as ten cents a stem. Delirious customers stagger out of the flower garden with fragrant bouquets that typically cost about half the store price. That only means they'll visit the farm twice as often—and dead-head our flowers for us, too.

The rest of our produce is not as cheap. We grow an uncommon variety of vegetables, but our biggest money crops after flowers are strawberries and raspberries. The farm is thronged with local residents and young families from the city. They know the berries haven't been sprayed, so they don't have to worry if the children eat while they're picking, and we don't worry about it either. All that sampling and trampling has already been figured into the price of the berries. We know what we're selling. The farm is designed to encourage people to get out and enjoy the land—at the same time it's real, it isn't a put-up job or petting zoo. People walk around amazed that such a place exists just ten miles from downtown Boston.

Everyone in Weston feels as if they own the farm, which they do. Many of them have kids working there who "get dirt under their fingernails" while "learning where their food comes from," as their parents (who usually have no idea themselves) are fond of saying. In the Green Power tradition, we deliver twenty thousand to thirty thousand pounds of fresh produce every year to city homeless shelters and soup kitchens, for which the town pays us at wholesale rates. A century ago hundreds of market gardens flourished in the towns surrounding Boston. There is no reason there couldn't be hundreds of Land's Sakes on the outskirts of every city in America today. Once awakened, the market for fresh produce is virtually limitless. The keys are the protected land, the organic methods, and the children.

We press apple cider at the farm every weekend in the fall, using an antique two-barrel hand mill and press. We truck in a few bins of drops from commercial orchards and squeeze a few hundred gallons of cider. In spite of the laborious methods, we don't lose money. Of course, a good deal of the labor is provided by the customers themselves: babes in arms dangle over the hopper dropping in apples; their toddler siblings crank away with both hands, the handle sometimes lifting them right off the ground; their eager fathers carry them on around. People are thirsty for this kind of experience, and not just in museums. They help screw down the press, the cider floods out into a bee-covered tub, gets poured through a coarse filter into a tank, and we hand it to them in a jug. That's *it*? That's cider? Its the same magic as pulling a carrot out of the ground—completely astonishing in its simplicity.

Naturally, people swear it's the best cider they ever drank. I find it too sweet, because it's made from the wrong apples. We can't get anything but McIntosh, Delicious, and Cortland apples from the orchards anymore. When I first came to Weston, several new housing developments had recently gone into abandoned orchards. We used to sweep through backyards with troops of Brownies, filling our pine boxes with apples such as Baldwins, which make a wonderful, tart cider. I'm already nostalgic for the 1970s: I can't find Baldwins in any quantity anymore. We tried to grow our own cider apples. We replanted an orchard with Baldwins and Russets and other old New England varieties fine for both eating and cider, but that project failed. Apples today are a particularly difficult—almost impossible—crop to grow organically in New England. Over the centuries, many American pests have adapted themselves to these Eurasian fruit trees, and Old World pests have gradually become well established. The worst of these is the apple scab fungus. Scab utterly defeated us.

It wasn't always that way. Apples and cider have a distinguished history in New England. Apples throve in New England towns of the seventeenth and eighteenth centuries whereas barley did not do particularly well, tied up good tillage land and demanded scarce manure, and had to be harvested during the busy summer season. Apples could be grown on hillsides and picked late in the fall. Hence hard cider soon replaced beer as the daily beverage and prodigious quantities were consumed. Sour apples from ungrafted trees were perfect for cider. Because farmers set out those seedlings that grew most vigorously, in time these trees constituted a locally adapted "land race," resistant to diseases such as scab. Surface blemishes were of no consequence in the cider mill. Usually one or two trees in an orchard produced apples worth eating, and grafts of the best winter-storage apples circulated. Apples in New England were an ecological success story.

Then cider orchards practically vanished during the temperance movement of the 1830s and 1840s. In their place, commercial orchards of grafted trees sprang up in towns around Boston to meet the growing urban demand for table fruit.

Routine use of pesticides to ensure a cosmetically attractive product soon followed, bequeathing us a radically transformed orchard ecology that features new pests and more virulent strains of pathogens such as scab. These orchards flourished through the first half of the twentieth century and linger to this day, although slowly driven farther away from the city by rising land values. Today the New England apple industry has been deeply undercut by competition from the West Coast and beyond. The market has been pruned back to a few shiny varieties that ship well, and all the orchards in Weston are gone.

I miss them. Where orchards still flourish, they form a distinctive part of the landscape, covering the hills in a belt between the forests above and the fields below. There is strong demand for cider, and not enough cull apples to meet it. It seems to me that it ought to be possible to plant low-maintenance orchards with both modern scab-resistant and traditional scab-tolerant varieties to make premium cider. A few locations around New England have brought back high-quality hard cider and apple wine, too, like the Nashoba Valley Winery in nearby Bolton. I feel sure that orchards and cider deserve a prominent place in the future of New England farming, but so far Land's Sake has done little to improve these prospects. With a little research and perseverance, it could happen.

We also make maple syrup, although not as much as we used to. Once, every February, we hung fifteen hundred buckets along the roads, and for the next six weeks or so we would haul crews of middle school kids around after school, collecting sap. Back at the sugarhouse a big old Leader evaporator boiled syrup far into the night, tended by a crew of maple enthusiasts who always seemed to materialize. The climate in Weston is too mild to make fancy syrup, but nobody complained except me. We held a sugaring-off party at the end of each season and in a few hours sold nearly a thousand quarts of this coveted badge of Weston citizenship: maple syrup made by the students of the middle school.

Sugar maples are not native to Weston—in fact, *Acer saccharum* was rare throughout southeastern Massachusetts when the English arrived. It may have been partly that the climate was warm and favored white oak and pitch pine for most of the past ten thousand years; but I believe it was also because southern New England Indians set fires that severely limited the range of sugar maples and other northern hardwoods. Sugar maple only became established in Weston during the late nineteenth century, when it was planted along the roads by public-spirited citizens who wanted to make the place look more the way they thought a New England town ought to look. The same thing was going on in towns throughout the region. In some respects, the picturesque New England towns that make us nostalgic were created by our great-grandparents in an earlier wave of nostalgia. They did a nice job, I must say.

Unfortunately, much of what they did so well we have undone just as thoroughly, employing that instrument of accelerated landscape torture, the automobile. Road salt and related insults have killed most of the grand old roadside maples in Weston, and the rest are on their way out. Young trees planted to replace them do not thrive. Land's Sake is currently down to hanging just a few hundred buckets. Some of the healthiest maples we tap are in the cemetery—firmly rooted in the remains of the very people who planted them. I love to point this out to the kids as we hang buckets among the headstones: those folks are still taking better care of their trees than we are, even from the grave.

There is hope for the future of maple syruping in Weston, though. Before they died, the roadside maples spread thousands of seedlings into adjoining woods. These shade-tolerant maple saplings do well under the oaks, and having escaped from road salt and power-line crews, they flourish. As part of our forest program, we thin oaks in some places to let the maples come through. Some are now reaching tappable size. In another decade or two we will have working sugar bushes in Weston, away from the roads. That is, we will unless, like sugar maples throughout the Northeast, they decline from acid rain and smog, the automobile pursuing them even into the forest.

We acquired sheep because my wife is a spinner and weaver, and because we wanted to reclaim a few of Weston's vanishing pastures. Not that Weston was ever a sheep town. The early-nineteenth-century New England sheep boom took place up country; our area was devoted to cows. In either case, many of the stone walls for which New England is famous were created when agriculture commercialized after the Revolution and pastures swept across the glacial till uplands, which yielded the requisite stones. Weston was 80 percent to 90 percent cleared and farmed by the middle of the nineteenth century: today's woods are filled not only with walls, but with numerous stone dumps in the back corners of former hayfields. The land never tires of heaving up stones when it is disturbed, and New England farmers continue to remove them from the little land that is still cultivated.

Clearing so much upland was a bad idea, not only because it decimated forests and disrupted streamflow, but because farmers did not understand how to keep their grassland fertile and productive. The nutrient boost provided to the thin, acid soil by cutting and burning the forest only lasted for a few years of haying or a few decades of grazing at best, as the manure flowed to cornfields and the meat and milk and wool flowed to markets. Ameliorating clover grew scantily over the granite for lack of adequate lime. The pre–Civil War agricultural boom in New England required "skinning the land," and so the land grew bony. In the second half of the century New England farmers began buying cheap Western grain to feed their cows, and let their exhausted pastures relapse to huckleberries and hardhack, juniper and pine. As farmers specialized in milk and imported nutrients mined from the topsoils of the Midwest, New England's skin began to grow back.

Far too much land in Weston was cleared. Fortunately, enough of the forest was still there to reclaim it. It is good that the forest has recovered, but it would be nice to see *some* of the landscape still growing grass—I mean, other than ornamental lawns. Pastures and hayfields have all but disappeared from Weston. We kept our sheep on small pockets of grass around town, driving the forest back to the original stone walls and exposing them again. When I uncovered those walls, I really began to feel a kinship with my forebears. Grazing rotationally, using portable electric fences to subdivide pastures, liming faithfully, we about covered our out-of-pocket costs.

Our labor brought us no return except pleasure. We had the pleasure of eating and selling delicious grass-fed lamb, and of having our sheep sheared every spring by Kevin Ford and Carol Markarian, perhaps the only professional blade shearers still active in New England. Best of all, we had the pleasure of watching many of the pastures we managed slowly but steadily improve, the white clover spreading. Properly grazed, moderately stocked, with vigorous legumes and plenty of lime, pastures can be kept productive indefinitely. Nutrients that walk off as weight gain and wool are replaced by what is fixed from the air and brought up from the subsoil. As we revived long-neglected land with our sheep, I felt I was slowly grasping an essential skill that my industrious predecessors who strained those fields from the stones apparently never mastered.

New England farmers had their worst blind spot when it came to the value of their forests. It wasn't that they feared and hated the wilderness—a comfortable relationship with the woods was already well established by the end of the seventeenth century. Quite early, farmers developed a thorough understanding of the diverse growth habits and useful qualities of the trees in the surrounding forest, from the dominant species such as white oak and pitch pine, to less common trees such as black ash and white cedar. Americans relied on trees for such a wide range of uses, requiring so much intimate knowledge and skill, that the period before 1850 has been referred to as America's Wooden Age. The forest was a crucial, well-integrated component of the ecological landscape of New England towns during the colonial period. There is much in this close functional understanding that I would love to recover.

Beyond this admirable working relationship, there was certainly no full appreciation of the beauty and ecological importance of forest in the landscape that has developed in our time. To the extent that such values did exist, no effective mechanisms protected these *common* benefits of forest once all the land had been parceled out into private ownership. Even so, at the end of the colonial period substantial tree cover still remained in private woodlots, often clustered on difficult soils in upland corners where they adjoined similar tracts in the next town. Forest was only protected as long as practical necessity gave it value, and limitations in the colonial agricultural system kept cultivation from spreading over all the available land. With the nineteenth-century adoption of cultivated "English" hay (timothy and clover), the introduction of coal for fuel, and the transition to a rapidly expanding commercial economy, most of this remaining woodland was recklessly cut and cleared for hay and pasture. It was the disappearance of the economic necessity to conserve woodland for local use that allowed deforestation. In many towns such as Weston, forest was very nearly eradicated.

Forest was restored to New England by good fortune, not by ecological awakening. The extractive upland pasture and hayfield system failed to sustain itself, the economic picture changed again, and the forest returned. The densely inhabited southern New England landscape is forested today because virtually *all* resources are imported from other regions and the land is used for next to nothing. Forest exists not because it is sufficiently valued, but because the land is in transition from agriculture to suburbia. Unfortunately, forest is once again becoming too fragmented to be ecologically healthy. Roads and development are breaking it into small pieces the way agriculture did a century ago. It would be wonderful to see agriculture return to New England, but the first ecological priority is to protect our forest before we lose it again. By acquiring conservation land, we recover the means to exert community control over a fundamental common resource: the integrity of the dominant natural element in our landscape, the forest. After three hundred years, we have the opportunity to protect and manage the forest holistically, at the landscape scale of entire towns. Whatever agricultural revival New England enjoys should fit into a continuous matrix of protected forest.

The necessity to protect common forest does not mean that it must lie in a wilderness state. Some parts of it should, perhaps. But it is also necessary to restore functional intimacy with the trees, only in an ecologically responsible way. In Weston, working with the Conservation Commission, Land's Sake has been implementing a long-term management plan for about fifteen hundred acres of town forest. The goal is to protect and encourage biological diversity, to see to it that large parts of the forest form mature ecosystems but that other parts are in younger stages as well, and to harvest firewood and timber on a sustainable basis. In practice, we aim to thin periodically for firewood, and cut timber and regenerate stands on a 120-year to 140-year rotation using the shelterwood method of harvesting. This routine is a fair mimic of the natural hurricane disturbance cycle in our region.

We have been practicing this kind of forestry for more than a decade, and it has been well received by those who stroll in Weston's woods. We hold neighborhood walks to explain what we are doing before and during every cutting operation, and we do a meticulous job of low-impact logging. Young people split and stack about a hundred cords of firewood every winter; the woodpiles seasoning between the still-standing trees have great appeal. Our forest plan is the work of John Potter, who got his degree from the Yale Forestry School but who began his forest career splitting wood in a red maple swamp in Weston when he was fifteen. Split, seasoned firewood fetches $175 a cord in Weston, a return that makes good forestry economical. If the price of fossil fuel reflected its full ecological cost, sustainably harvested firewood would be a bargain.

Like the other Land's Sake projects I have sketched here, community forestry works both culturally and ecologically because it involves community members with the land in ways that lead them to take responsibility for it. Community farming puts inhabitants back in touch with the nature and history of their land, so that they may learn how to live well with it, both celebrating what has gone before and trying to do better. I certainly do not believe that all farming should be community farming. I do believe that every place needs some common land, and one community farm.

It might be objected that community farming as I have described it is suitable only for the suburbs. Land's Sake certainly has adapted to suburban conditions and has benefited from Weston's willingness to protect land even in an expensive market, and to pay us to take care of that land and to educate young people. More than anything, we have taken advantage of a strong local market for high-quality natural products, a market that we helped to create. Perhaps in a more traditional farming community, community farming would not be necessary. The fact is, large parts of this country within driving range of cities and the beltways surrounding them are relentlessly suburbanizing. An economy driven by fraudulently cheap fossil fuel has relegated truly rural areas to the ruthless extraction of one or two commodities, carried out by a handful of isolated industrial machine operators of one kind or another, too few and too disenfranchised to hold communities together. Meanwhile, on the fringes of the metropolitan areas fed by this extraction, the better-off urban refugees fan out in search of the security and serenity of the rural character they have lost, destroying it a mile a minute as they go. We need to meet this movement head on, and to make use of its economic potential. I may not know what to do about reviving the rural places that are dying, but I think I know how to handle the expanding suburbs.

The first key is to protect more land. Places such as Weston have preserved about a quarter of their land as open space, but we need to do better than that. Conservation biologists suggest that about half of any given place should be set aside to protect biodiversity in its native ecological state—forest, prairie, wetland, or whatever. To be fully protected, much of it should be commonly owned. Not all or indeed most of this land needs to be *wild* to perform this function. As far as I am concerned, it can be grazed and logged, hunted and fished, as long as its ability to maintain the ecological integrity of the landscape is not compromised. Most of the other half should be kept in ecologically sustainable forms of agriculture, privately owned but protected from development by easements. An easement amounts to a way for society to reimburse a landowner for taking care of the common benefits of open land, by reducing taxes. Perhaps less than a quarter of the land need be used for commercial and residential development. We could confine ourselves to central villages and outlying clusters on the most appropriate building land. This pattern of villages surrounded by rural neighborhoods out to about an hour's walk from the center existed once in New England, and it made sense.

The second key is taking good care of the land. A substantial part of the native half of the landscape should be managed not piecemeal, but holistically at the local community level. Ecological health is a common good that must be jealously guarded. Actual management operations—logging, for example—could perfectly well be done mainly by private contractors who meet high standards. As for agricultural land, I would be delighted to see most of it remain in the hands of private farmers—as long as they too live up to stringent limitations on soil erosion and pollution of surface and ground water, which are common goods. I do think every place should have one community farming and forestry program, to involve young people with the land and to show the way toward an ecologically responsible relationship. Here is one way the suburban fringes of America's cities *could* be reinhabited.

How the suburbs *will* grow is another matter. There is little chance that more than a tiny fraction of what I have described will soon come to pass, given the current lopsided competition for land. Suburban sprawl appears to be an unstoppable juggernaut, and it is hard to imagine political and economic mechanisms that could bring such a large amount of land under local community control, even in New England. All the momentum is toward continued abuse under the banner of unfettered private property rights. The common ecological, economic, and aesthetic benefits of the land we all ought to enjoy will remain largely unprotected, and will continue to take a terrible beating in place after place. Still, we have to do all we can with the tools we have, and we need a vision of where we should be going, if we intend to turn this tide.

All places are important. It is vital that they see themselves as places, as communities of people and land. What community farming offers is a working expression of this vision of a place at its ecological best, so that more people can see it. It offers a way for members of new suburban communities to connect with the agrarian history of the places they now inhabit, and to participate in creating an ecologically sensible future instead of another automotive wasteland. To make the vision of rooted places more widely shared in our culture, those of us who see it can create more community farms. People will only come to a useful "sense of place" when they help build places that make sense.

works cited

Allen, Patricia L., and Caroline E. Sachs. 1991. "The Social Side of Sustainability." *Science as Culture,* vol. 2, pt. 4, no. 13: 569–590.

Ammerman, Nancy T. 1991. "North American Protestant Fundamentalism." In M. E. Marty and R. S. Appleby, *Fundamentalisms Observed,* pp. 1–65. Chicago: University of Chicago Press.

Ashman, Linda, Jaime de la Vega, Marc Dohan, Andy Fisher, Rosa Hippler, and Billi Romain. 1993. *Seeds of Change: Strategies for Food Security for the Inner City.* Los Angeles: Interfaith Hunger Coalition.

Ayer, Jules Alfred. 1952. *Language, Truth, and Logic.* New York: Dover Publications.

Bakko, Eugene B., and John C. Woodwell. 1992. "The Campus and the Biosphere Initiative at Carleton and Saint Olaf Colleges." In David J. Egan and David W. Orr, eds., *The Campus and Environmental Responsibility,* ch. 9. San Francisco: Jossey-Bass Publishers.

Barbour, Ian. 1991. *Religion in an Age of Science.* San Francisco: Harper San Francisco.

Barrell, John. 1972. *The Idea of Landscape and the Sense of Place, 1730–1840: An Approach to the Poetry of John Clare.* Cambridge: Cambridge University Press.

Bellah, Robert N., Richard Madsen, William Sullivan, Ann Swidler, and Steven M. Tipton. 1985. *Habits of the Heart: Individualism and Commitment in American Life.* New York: Harper & Row.

Berry, Wendell. 1977. *The Unsettling of America: Culture and Agriculture.* New York: Avon Books.

———. 1987. *Home Economics.* San Francisco: North Point Press.

———. 1990. *What Are People For?* San Francisco: North Point Press.

———. 1992. "Conservation Is Good Work." *Amicus Journal* (Winter): 33–36.

———. 1993. *Sex, Economy, Freedom and Community.* New York: Pantheon Books.

Black, Antony. 1984. *Guilds and Civil Society in European Political Thought from the Twelfth Century to the Present.* London: Methuen.

Blouin, M., and E. Connor. 1985. "Is There a Best Shape for Nature Reserves?" *Biological Conservation* 32: 277–288.

Boecklen, W. J., and D. Simberloff. 1987. "Area-Based Extinction Models in Conservation." In D. Elliot, ed., *Dynamics of Extinction,* pp. 247–276. New York: John Wiley.

Brandon, R. 1990. *Adaptation and Environment.* Princeton: Princeton University Press.

Bromfield, Louis. 1950. *Out of the Earth.* New York: Harper.

Brown, Lester, et al., eds. 1990. *State of the World: 1990.* New York: W. W. Norton.

Brown, Peter. 1994. *Restoring the Public Trust.* Boston: Beacon Press.

Brueggemann, Walter. 1977. *The Land.* Philadelpha: Fortress Press.

Caldwell, L., and K. Shrader-Frechette. 1993. *Policy for Land: Law and Ethics.* Savage, Maryland: Rowman and Littlefield.

Callicott, J. Baird. 1980. "Animal Liberation: A Triangular Affair." *Environmental Ethics* 2: 311–328.

———, ed. 1987. *A Companion to A Sand County Almanac.* Madison: University of Wisconsin Press.

Celis, William 3d. 1993. "Universities Are Scrambling as Investment Incomes Are Declining." *New York Times,* October 20.

Chira, Susan. 1993. "Is Smaller Better?" *New York Times,* July 14.

Chivian, Eric, et al. 1993. *Critical Condition: Human Health and the Environment.* Cambridge: MIT Press.

Clancy, Katherine L. 1993. "Sustainable Agriculture and Domestic Hunger: Rethinking a Link between Production and Consumption." In Patricia Allen, ed., *Food For the Future,* ch. 11. New York: John Wiley.

Coleman, James C. 1988. "Social Capital in the Creation of Human Capital." *American Journal of Sociology* 94 (Supplement S95-S120): 95–119.

Conant, James B. 1959. *American High School Today.* New York: McGraw-Hill.

Congressional Record—Senate. 1989. May 4, p. S 4932.

Connor, E. F., and E. D. McCoy. 1979. "The Statistics and Biology of the Species-Area Relationship." *American Naturalist* 113: 791–833.

Cox, Harvey. 1966. *The Secular City.* New York: Macmillan.

———. 1987. "The Restoration of a Sense of Place: A Theological Reflection on the Visual Environment." *Ekistics* 25: 422–423.

Crouch, Marti. 1993. "Eating Our Teachers: Local Food, Local Knowledge." *Raise the Stakes* (Winter): 5–6.

Dahlberg, Kenneth. 1993. "Regenerative Food Systems: Broadening the Scope and Agenda of Sustainability." In Patricia Allen, ed., *Food for the Future,* ch. 3. New York: John Wiley.

Dardel, Eric. 1976. Quoted by E. Relph in *Place and Placelessness.* London: Pion.

Disch, Robert, ed. 1970. *The Ecological Conscience.* Englewood Cliffs, New Jersey: Prentice-Hall.

Duncan, C. M. 1992. "Persistent Poverty in Appalachia: Scarce Work and Rigid Stratification." In C. M. Duncan, ed., *Rural Poverty in America,* pp. 111–133. New York: Auburn House.

Durkheim, Emile. 1893. *The Division of Labor in Society.* Trans. George Simpson. Reprint ed., New York: Macmillan, 1933.

Earman, J. 1978. "The Universality of Laws." *Philosophy of Science* 45: 173–181.

Eaton, S. Boyd, Marjorie Shostak, and Melvin Konner. 1988. *The Paleolithic Prescription.* New York: Harper & Row.

Ellison, Ralph. 1953. *Invisible Man.* New York: Signet Books.

Etzioni, Amitai. 1988. *The Moral Dimension.* New York: Free Press.

Evernden, Neil. 1985. *The Natural Alien: Humankind and Environment.* Toronto: University of Toronto Press.

Feinberg, Joel. 1988. *Harmless Wrongdoing.* New York: Oxford University Press.

Flora, C. B., and J. Flora. 1993. "Entrepreneurial Social Infrastructure: A Necessary Ingredient." *Annals of the Academy of Social and Political Sciences* 529: 48–58.

Foreman, Dave, John Davis, David Johns, Reed Noss, and Michael Soule. 1992. "The Wildlands Project." *Wild Earth* 3.

Fox, W. 1984. "Deep Ecology: A New Philosophy of Our Time." *Ecologist* 14: 344–345.

Friedmann, Harriet. 1993. "After Midas's Feast: Alternative Food Regimes for the Future." In Patricia Allen, ed., *Food for the Future,* pp. 213–233. New York: John Wiley.

Frost, R. 1967. *The Poetry of Robert Frost.* New York: Holt, Rinehart, and Winston.

Fuller, Wayne. 1982. *The Old Country School.* Chicago: University of Chicago Press.

Gardner, R. A., and B. T. Gardner. 1969. "Teaching Sign Language to a Chimpanzee." *Science* 165: 664–672.

Getz, Arthur. 1991. "Urban Foodsheds." *Permaculture Activist* 24 (October): 26–27.

Gould, S. J. 1981. *The Mismeasure of Man.* New York: W. W. Norton.

Gruchow, Paul. 1991. "America's Farm Failure." *Small Farmer's Journal* (Summer): 20.

Gussow, Joan Dye. 1993. "But What Can I Eat in March?" *Natural Farmer* (Spring): 14–15.

Hamilton, Jefferies M. 1992. *Social Justice and Deuteronomy 15.* Atlanta: Scholars Press.

Hamm, Michael W. 1993. "The Potential for a Localized Food Supply in New Jersey." Presented at the conference on Environment, Culture, and Food Equity, Pennsylvania State University, June 3–6.

Hartford Food System. 1991. "Solutions to Hunger in Hartford: Rebuilding Our Local Food System, 1991 Action Guide." Harford: Hartford Food System.

Hassanein, Neva, and Jack Kloppenburg, Jr. 1994. "Where the Grass Grows Again: Knowledge Exchange in the Sustainable Agriculture Movement." Unpublished.

Hedden, W. P. 1929. *How Great Cities Are Fed.* Boston: D. C. Heath.

Hendrickson, John. 1994. "Community Supported Agriculture." *Direct Marketing,* no. 41 (May). Madison: University of Wisconsin—Extension.

Herrin, Marcia, and Joan Dye Gussow. 1989. "Designing a Sustainable Regional Diet." *Journal of Nutrition Education* (December): 270–275.

Hirsch, E. D., Jr. 1967. *Validity in Interpretation.* New Haven: Yale University Press.

———. 1987. *Cultural Literacy: What Every American Needs to Know.* Boston: Houghton Mifflin.

Hirsch, E. D., Jr., Joseph F. Kett, and James Trefil. 1988. *The Dictionary of Cultural Literacy.* Boston: Houghton Mifflin.

Houriet, Robert. 1971. *Getting Back Together.* New York: Coward-McCann.

Houston, James M. 1978. "The Concepts of 'Place' and 'Land' in the Judaeo-Christian Tradition." In David Ley and Marwyn S. Samuels, eds., *Humanistic Geography: Prospects and Problems.* Chicago: Maaroufa Press.

Hugo, Richard. 1979. *The Triggering Town: Lectures and Essays on Poetry and Writing.* New York: W. W. Norton.

Hull, D. 1988. *Science as a Process.* Chicago: University of Chicago Press.

Hume, David. 1888. *A Treatise of Human Nature.* Reprint ed., Oxford: Clarendon Press, 1983.

Jackson, John B. 1984. *Discovering the Vernacular Landscape.* New Haven: Yale University Press.

Jackson, Wes. 1980. *New Roots for Agriculture.* San Francisco: Friends of the Earth.

———. 1994. *Becoming Native to This Place.* Lexington: University of Kentucky Press.

Jacobs, Jane. 1994. *Systems of Survival.* New York: Vintage.

Johnson, Dirk. 1990. "Population Decline in Rural America." *New York Times,* September 11.

Kappel-Smith, Dianna. 1994. "Salt." *Orion* 13: 44–51.

Kellert, Stephen, and E. O. Wilson, eds. 1993. *The Biophilia Hypothesis.* Washington, D. C.: Island Press.

Kelton, Elmer. 1978. *The Good Old Boys.* Garden City, New York: Doubleday.

Kern, Stephen. 1983. *The Culture of Time and Space, 1880–1918.* Cambridge: Harvard University Press.

Kiester, A. 1982. "Natural Kinds, Natural History, and Ecology." In E. Saarinen, ed., *Conceptual Issues in Ecology*, pp. 345–356. Dordrecht: Reidel.

Kline, David. 1994. "A Farming Community." *Plain Magazine, 1994* (special issue: Agriculture): 5–8.

Kneen, Brewster. 1989. *From Land to Mouth: Understanding the Food System.* Toronto: NC Press.

Le Guin, Ursula K. 1969. *The Left Hand of Darkness.* New York: Ace Books.

Lemcke, Nils Peter. 1991. *The Canaanites and Their Land: The Tradition of the Canaanites.* Sheffield, England: JSOT Press.

Leopold, Aldo. 1949. *A Sand County Almanac.* Reprint ed., New York: Ballantine Books, 1970.

————. 1991. In Susan L. Flader and J. Baird Callicott, eds., *The River of the Mother of God.* Madison: University of Wisconsin Press.

Livingston, John A. 1994. *Rogue Primate: An Exploration of Human Domestication.* Toronto: Key Porter.

Locke, J. 1960. In P. Laslett, ed., *Two Treatises of Government.* Cambridge: Cambridge University Press.

Logsdon, Gene. 1994. *The Contrary Farmer.* Post Mills, Vermont: Chelsea Green.

Lohfink, Norbert. 1982. "Distribution of the Functions of Power." In *Great Themes from the Old Testament,* pp. 55–75. Edinburgh: T. & T. Clark.

Lucas, John. 1988. "Places and Dwellings: Wordsworth, Clare and the Anti-Picturesque." In Denis Cosgrove and Stephen Daniels, eds., *The Iconography of Landscape.* Cambridge: Cambridge University Press.

MacIntyre, Alasdair. 1984. *After Virtue.* Notre Dame: University of Notre Dame Press.

Margules, C., A. Higgs, and R. Rafe. 1982. "Modern Biogeographic Theory: Are There Any Lessons for Nature Reserve Design?" *Biological Conservation* 24: 115–128.

Matthews, Walter M. 1982. "Rural Education." In Harold E. Mitzel, ed., *The Encyclopedia of Educational Research,* vol. 4, pp. 1627–35. New York: Free Press.

McCoy, E. D. 1982. "The Application of Island Biogeography to Forest Tracts: Problems in Determination of Turnover Rates." *Biological Conservation* 22: 217–227.

————. 1983. "The Application of Island Biogeographic Theory to Patches of Habitat: How Much Land Is Enough?" *Biological Conservation* 25: 53–61.

McCoy, E. D., and K. S. Shrader-Frechette. 1992. "Community Ecology, Scale, and the Instability of the Stability Concept." In M. Forbes and D. Hull, eds., *Philosophy of Science Association 1992,* pp. 84–99. East Lansing, Michigan: Philosophy of Science Association.

McIntosh, R. P. 1985. *The Background of Ecology: Concept and Theory.* Cambridge: Cambridge University Press.

McKeon, Richard, ed. 1941. *The Basic Works of Aristotle.* New York: Random House.

McMichael, A. J. 1993. *Planetary Overload: Global Environmental Change and the Health of the Human Species.* New York: Cambridge University Press.

Mitchell, G. C. 1986. "Vampire Bat Control in Latin America." In G. H. Orians, et al., eds., *Ecological Knowledge and Environmental Problem Solving.* Washington, D. C.: National Academy Press.

Mitchell, John. 1980. *The Hunt.* New York: Alfred A. Knopf.

Monk, Samuel. 1965. Quoted by David Lowenthal and Hugh C. Prince in "English Landscape Tastes," *Geographical Review* 55 (no. 2): 195.

Murray, B. G., Jr. 1986. "The Structure of Theory, and the Role of Competition in Community Dynamics." *Oikos* 46: 145–158.

Nabhan, Gary, and Stephen Trimble. 1994. *The Geography of Childhood.* Boston: Beacon Press.

Norberg-Hodge, Helena. 1991. *Ancient Futures: Learning from Ladakh.* San Francisco: Sierra Club Books.

Norris, Kathleen. 1993. *Dakota: A Spiritual Geography.* New York: Houghton Mifflin.

Orians, G. H., et al. 1986. *Committee on the Applications of Ecological Theory to Environmental Problems, Ecological Knowledge and Environmental Problem Solving.* Washington, D. C.: National Academy Press.

Orr, David. 1992. *Ecological Literacy: Education and the Transition to a Postmodern World.* Albany: State University of New York Press.

Ortega y Gasset, Jose. 1972. *Meditations on Hunting.* New York: Charles Scribner's Sons.

Packard, Vance. 1972. *A Nation of Strangers.* New York: David McKay.

Packer, J. I. 1958. *Fundamentalism and the Word of God.* Grand Rapids, Michigan: Wm. B. Eerdmans.

Packer, The. 1992. "From Grower to Consumer: An Elaborate Odyssey." *The Packer* (June 13): 11.

Peters, R. H. 1991. *A Critique of Ecology.* Cambridge: Cambridge University Press.

Peterson, Richard. 1994. "From Gut to Ground: A Personal Case Study of a Foodshed." Unpublished.

Piercy, Marge. 1976. *Woman on the Edge of Time.* New York: Fawcett Crest.

Pimm, S. L. 1984. "The Complexity and Stability of Ecosystems." *Nature* 307: 321–326.

Platt, Rutherford, et al., eds. 1994. *The Ecological City.* Amherst: University of Massachusetts Press.

Portes, Alejandro, and J. Sensenbrenner. 1993. "Embeddedness and Immigration: Notes on the Social Determinants of Economic Action." *American Journal of Sociology* 98(6): 1320–50.

Preston, R. 1992. "Annals of Medicine." *New Yorker,* October 26, pp. 58–81.

Proust, Marcel. 1976. Quoted by E. Relph in *Place and Placelessness,* p. 144. London: Pion.

Putnam, Robert A. 1993a. *Making Democracy Work: Civic Traditions in Modern Italy.* Princeton: Princeton University Press.

———. 1993b. "The Prosperous Community: Social Capital and Public Life." *American Prospect* 13: 35–42.

Quinby, Lee. 1991. *Freedom, Foucault, and the Subject of America.* Boston: Northeastern University Press.

Quinn, Daniel. 1993. *Ishmael.* New York: Bantam Books.

Raab, P. V. 1980. "Equilibrium Theory and Paleoecology." *Lethia* 13: 175–181.

Rapid City Journal. 1991. April 10.

Rawls, John. 1971. *A Theory of Justice.* Cambridge: Harvard University Press.

Regan, Tom. 1983. *The Case for Animal Rights.* Berkeley: University of California Press.

Rey, J. R., and E. D. McCoy. 1979. "The Application of Island Biogeographic Theory to the Pests of Cultivated Crops." *Environmental Entomology* 8: 577–582.

Rodale, Robert. 1982. *The Cornucopia Papers.* Emmaus, Pennsylvania: Rodale Press.

Rodman, John. 1977. "The Liberation of Nature?" *Inquiry* 20: 83–131.

Rogers, Raymond A. 1994. *Nature and the Crisis of Modernity: A Critique of Contemporary Discourse on Managing the Earth*. Montreal: Black Rose Books.

Rolston, Holmes III. 1987. "Duties to Ecosystems." In Callicott 1987, pp. 246–274.

Rorty, Richard. 1982. *Consequences of Pragmatism*. Minneapolis: University of Minnesota Press.

———. 1989. *Contingency, Irony, and Solidarity*. New York: Cambridge University Press.

Rosen, D. E. 1978. "Vicariant Patterns and Historical Explanation in Biogeography." *Systematic Zoology* 27: 159–188.

Rural Wisconsin Cornucopia Task Force. 1982. *The Wisconsin Cornucopia Project: Toward a Sustainable Food and Agriculture System*. Madison: Rural Wisconsin Cornucopia Task Force.

Sagoff, Mark. 1985. "Fact and Value in Environmental Science." *Environmental Ethics* 7: 99–116.

———. 1995. "Animal Liberation and Environmental Ethics: Bad Marriage, Quick Divorce." In Sterba 1995, pp. 166–172.

Salwasser, H. 1986. "Conserving a Regional Spotted Owl Population." In G. H. Orians et al., eds., *Ecological Knowledge and Environmental Problem Solving*, pp. 227–247. Washington, D.C.: National Academy Press.

Samuel, Maurice. 1978. Quoted in Houston 1978, p. 228.

Schnore, Leo F. 1973. "Community: Theory and Research on Structure Change." In Neil J. Smelser, ed., *Sociology: An Introduction* (2nd ed.). New York: John Wiley.

Schoener, T. W. 1972. "Mathematical Ecology and Its Place among the Sciences." *Science* 178: 389–391.

Schumacher, Ernst F. 1973. *Small Is Beautiful: Economics as if People Mattered*. New York: Harper & Row.

Searles, Harold F. 1960. *The Nonhuman Environment in Normal Development and in Schizophrenia*. New York: International Universities Press.

Shepard, Paul. 1973. *The Tender Carnivore and the Sacred Game*. New York: Scribners.

Shepard, Paul, and Barry Sanders. 1985. *The Sacred Paw: The Bear in Nature, Myth, and Literature*. New York: Viking Press.

Sher, J. P., ed. 1977. *Education in Rural America*. Boulder, Colorado: Westview Press.

Shrader-Frechette, K. S. 1990. "Island Biogeography, Species-Area Curves, and Statistical Errors: Applied Biology and Scientific Rationality." In A. Fine, M. Forbes, and L. Wessels, eds., *Philosophy of Science Association 1990*, vol. 1, pp. 447–456. East Lansing, Michigan: Philosophy of Science Association.

———. 1993. "Locke and Limits on Land Ownership." *Journal of the History of Ideas* 54: 201–219.

Shrader-Frechette, K. S., and E. D. McCoy. 1990. "Theory Reduction and Explanation in Ecology." *Oikos* 58: 109–114.

———. 1992. "Statistics, Costs, and Rationality in Ecological Inference." *Trends in Evolution and Ecology* 7: 96–99.

———. 1993. *Method in Ecology: Strategies for Conservation*. Cambridge: Cambridge University Press.

Simberloff, D. 1986a. "Introduced Insects: A Biogeographic and Systematic Perspective." In H. A. Mooney and J. A. Drake, eds., *Ecology of Biological Invasions of North America and Hawaii*, pp. 3–26. New York: Springer-Verlag.

———. 1986b. "Island Biogeographic Theory and Integrated Pest Management." In M. Cogan ed., *Ecological Theory and Integrated Pest Management Practice,* pp. 19–35. New York: John Wiley.

Simberloff, D., K. L. Heck, E. D. McCoy, and E. F. Connor. 1981. "There Have Been No Statistical Tests of Cladistic Biogeographical Hypotheses." In G. Nelson and D. Rosen, eds., *Vicariance Biogeography: A Critique,* pp. 40–63. New York: Columbia University Press.

Singer, Peter. 1992. *Animal Liberation: A New Ethics for Our Treatment of Animals.* New York: Avon Books.

Slobodkin, Leonard B. 1970. "Aspects of the Future of Ecology." In Disch 1970, pp. 71–90.

Smil, Vaclav. 1991. *General Energetics.* New York: Wiley-Interscience.

Snyder, Gary. 1977. *The Old Ways.* San Francisco: City Lights Books.

Sober, E. 1981. "Revisability, A Priori Truth, and Evaluation." *Australasian Journal of Philosophy* 59: 68–85.

———. 1988. *Reconstructing the Past: Parsimony, Evolution, and Inference.* Cambridge: MIT Press.

Sopher, David E. 1979. "The Landscape of Home: Myth, Experience, Social Meaning." In D. W. Meinig, *The Interpretation of Ordinary Landscapes,* p. 137. Oxford: Oxford University Press.

Soulé, M. E., and D. Simberloff. 1986. "What Do Genetics and Ecology Tell Us about the Design of Nature Reserves?" *Biological Conservation* 35: 19–40.

Spain, Daphne. 1993. "Been-Heres versus Come-Heres: Negotiating Conflicting Community Identities." *Journal of the American Planning Association.* 59(2): 156–171.

Stegner, Wallace. 1962. *Wolfwillow.* New York: Penguin Books.

———. 1969. *The Sound of Mountain Water.* Garden City, New York: Doubleday.

Steiner, Stan. 1980. *The Ranchers: A Book of Generations.* New York: Alfred A. Knopf.

Sterba, James P., ed. 1995. *Earth Ethics.* Englewood Cliffs, New Jersey: Prentice-Hall.

Stilgoe, John. 1982. *Common Landscape of America, 1580–1845.* New Haven: Yale University Press.

Strong, D. R. 1979. "Biogeographic Dynamics of Insect-Host Plant Communities." *Annual Review of Entomology* 24: 89–119.

Taylor, Paul W. 1986. *Respect for Nature: A Theory of Environmental Ethics.* Princeton: Princeton University Press.

Thompson, E. P. 1966. *The Making of the English Working Class.* New York: Vintage Books.

Tönnies, Ferdinand. 1887. *Community and Society,* ed. C. P. Loomis. Reprint ed. New York: Harper, 1963.

Toronto Food Policy Council. 1993. *Developing a Food System Which Is Just and Environmentally Sustainable.* Toronto: Toronto Food Policy Council.

Tuan, Yi-Fu. 1974. "American Space, Chinese Place." *Harper's Magazine* (July), p. 8.

Underwood, A. J., and E. Denley. 1984. "Paradigms, Explanations, and Generalizations in Models for the Structure of Intertidal Communities on Rocky Shores." In D. R. Strong, D. Simberloff, L. G. Abele, and A. B. Thistle, eds., *Ecological Communities: Conceptual Issues and the Evidence,* pp. 151–180. Princeton: Princeton University Press.

Valen, Gary L. 1992. "Hendrix College Local Food Project." In David J. Egan and

David W. Orr, eds., *The Campus and Environmental Responsibility,* ch. 8. San Francisco: Jossey-Bass.

Van Der Steen, W., and H. Kamminga. 1991. "Laws and Natural History in Biology." *British Journal for the Philosophy of Science* 42: 445–467.

Van En, Robyn, and Cathy Roth. 1993. "Community Supported Agriculture." University of Massachusetts Cooperative Extension System, Amherst.

Wagner, Peter C. 1979. *Our Kind of People: The Ethical Dimensions of Church Growth in America.* Atlanta: John Knox Press.

Walter, E. V. 1988. *Placeways: A Theory of the Human Environment.* Chapel Hill: University of North Carolina Press.

Walters, J. R. 1991. "Application of Ecological Principles to the Management of Endangered Species: The Case of the Red-Cockaded Woodpecker." *Annual Review of Ecology and Systematics* 22: 505–523.

Waters, Alice. 1990. "The Farm-Restaurant Connection." In Robert Clark, ed., *Our Sustainable Table,* pp. 113–122. San Francisco: North Point Press.

Weil, Simone. 1952. *The Need for Roots: Prelude to a Declaration of Duties toward Mankind.* Trans. Arthur Wills. New York: G. P. Putnam's Sons. Reprint ed., New York: Harper Colophon Books, 1971.

Westra, Laura. 1994. *An Environmental Proposal for Ethics: The Principle of Integrity.* Lanham, Maryland: Rowman and Littlefield.

Whitehead, Alfred North. 1978. *Process and Reality.* Ed. D. R. Griffin and D. Sherburne. New York: Free Press.

Wiley, John P., Jr. 1988. "Phenomena, Comment, and Notes." *Smithsonian* (October), pp. 23–28.

Williams, Raymond. 1973. *The Country and the City.* New York: Oxford University Press.

———. 1976. *Keywords: A Vocabulary of Culture and Society.* New York: Oxford University Press.

Williamson, M. 1987. "Are Communities Ever Stable?" *Symposium of the British Ecological Society* 26: 353–370.

Wilson, E. O. 1983. *Biophilia.* Cambridge: Harvard University Press.

Winne, Mark. 1994. "Community Food Planning: An Idea Whose Time Has Come?" *Seedling* (Summer): 1–4, 8.

Woodwell, G. 1978. "Paradigms Lost." *Bulletin of the Ecological Society of America* 59: 136–140.

Young, Henry James. 1990. *Hope in Process: A Theology of Social Pluralism.* Minneapolis: Fortress Press.

Zelinsky, Wilbur. 1973. *The Cultural Geography of the United States.* Englewood Cliffs, New Jersey: Prentice-Hall.

Zimmerman, B., and R. Bierregaard. 1986. "Relevance of the Equilibrium Theory of Island Biogeography and Species-Area Relations to Conservation with a Case from Amazonia." *Journal of Biogeography* 13: 133–143.

contributors

RICHARD CARTWRIGHT AUSTIN, Appalachian Ministries Educational Resource Center, Abington, Virginia

WENDELL BERRY, Port Royal, Kentucky

WALTER BRUEGGEMANN, Columbia Theological Seminary, Decatur, Georgia

PAUL CUSTODIO BUBE, Department of Religion and Philosophy, Kansas Wesleyan University, Salina, Kansas

JOHN B. COBB, JR., Professor Emeritus, School of Theology, Claremont, and Co-director, Center for Process Studies, Claremont, California

GREGORY COOPER, Department of Philosophy, Duke University, Durham, North Carolina

BRIAN DONAHUE, Director of Education, The Land Institute, Salina, Kansas

DAVID EHRENFELD, Department of Biology, Cook College, Rutgers University, New Brunswick, New Jersey

CARL D. ESBJORNSON, Bozeman, Montana

CORNELIA BUTLER FLORA, Director, North Central Regional Center for Rural Development, Iowa State University, Ames, Iowa

JAN L. FLORA, Department of Sociology and Community Development Extension Specialist, Iowa State University, Ames, Iowa

LINDA M. HASSELSTROM, Cheyenne, Wyoming

JOHN HENDRICKSON, Institute for Environmental Studies, University of Wisconsin, Madison, Wisconsin

WES JACKSON, Director, The Land Institute, Salina, Kansas

FRANKLIN A. KALINOWSKI, Departments of Environmental Studies and Political Science, Warren Wilson College, Asheville, North Carolina

DANIEL KEMMIS, Mayor, Missoula, Montana

JACK KITTREDGE, Barre, Massachusetts

DAVID KLINE, Fredericksburg, Ohio

JACK KLOPPENBURG, JR., Department of Rural Sociology, University of Wisconsin, Madison, Wisconsin

JOHN A. LIVINGSTON, Professor Emeritus, Department of Environmental Studies, York University, North York, Ontario

LYNN R. MILLER, Editor, *Small Farmer's Journal, featuring Practical Horsefarming,* Singing Horse Ranch, Sisters, Oregon

HELENA NORBERG-HODGE, Founder and Director, The Ladakh Project, Berkeley, California

DAVID W. ORR, Department of Environmental Studies, Oberlin College, Oberlin, Ohio

HARRY W. PAIGE, Professor Emeritus, Center for Liberal Studies, Clarkson University, Potsdam, New York

SCOTT RUSSELL SANDERS, Department of English, Indiana University, Bloomington, Indiana

PHILIP SELZNICK, Professor Emeritus, School of Law and Department of Sociology, University of California, Berkeley, California

KRISTIN SHRADER-FRECHETTE, Program in Environmental Sciences and Policy and Department of Philosophy, University of South Florida, Tampa, Florida

G. W. STEVENSON, Center for Integrated Agricultural Systems, University of Wisconsin, Madison, Wisconsin

WILLIAM M. SULLIVAN, Department of Philosophy, La Salle University, Philadelphia, Pennsylvania

ROBERT SWANN, President, E. F. Schumacher Society, Great Barrington, Massachusetts

DEBORAH TALL, Hobart and William Smith Colleges, Geneva, New York

WILLIAM VITEK, Center for Liberal Studies, Clarkson University, Potsdam, New York

SUSAN WITT, Executive Director, E. F. Schumacher Society, Great Barrington, Massachusetts

ERIC ZENCEY, Goddard College, Plainfield, Vermont

index